CW00969534

Enigma Books

Also published by Enigma Books

A Crate of Vodka

By

Alfred Kokh and Igor Svinarenko

Translated from the Russian by
Antonina W. Bouis

Enigma Books

All rights reserved under
The International and Pan-American Copyright Conventions.
Published in the United States by

Enigma Books
New York
www.enigmabooks.com

No part of this publication may be reproduced, stored in a retrieval system, or transmitted, in any form or by any means, electronic, mechanical, photocopying, recording, or otherwise without the written permission of Enigma Books.

Copyright © 2009 by Alfred Kokh and Igor Svinarenko

Translated from the Russian by Antonina W. Bouis

First English-language edition.

ISBN 978-1-929631-89-6

Library of Congress Cataloging in Publication Available

A Crate of Vodka

Table of Contents

Foreword

A Crate of Vodka is written by one of Russia's most prominent journalists and one of its most controversial writers. Igor Svinarenko is considered a "golden pen" of journalism by his peers; his voice is honest and funny; his interests as wide-ranging as his travels; above all, Igor's point of view rarely represents the opinion of his editors. Co-author Alfred Kokh was part of the group of young reformers headed by economics minister Anatoly Chubais who were accused of receiving a bribe in the guise of a book advance, and the "writers' case" was kept in the headlines for months by the opponents of the revolutionary market reforms by Yegor Gaidar. As deputy prime minister in charge of privatization in the heady years of Boris Yeltsin, the first democratically elected president, Alfred has an insider's view of the dramatic, revolutionary period that changed the country.

The premise of *A Crate of Vodka* is that the only way to figure out what happened during the transition from Communist USSR to democratic Russia is over a meal and a bottle of vodka—a time-honored tradition when political talk had to be confined to the privacy of one's kitchen.

The two authors discuss the 20-year period from the death of Leonid Brezhnev, the General Secretary of the Communist Party, in 1982, until 2001, the 9/11 terror attacks in the United States, and the end of the world order as we knew it. Twenty years, twenty chapters, twenty bottles, a full crate of vodka.

The literary conceit involves many voices, the play of stylistic changes between the dialogue of two intentionally controversial, amusing, and "drunken" friends, and the thought-provoking essays and commentaries they add on topics that require further exploration. The format creates the illusion of light-heartedness; the content is very serious, touching on events that were crucial in the development of democratic, market-oriented Russia—the collapse of the Soviet Union, reforms, privatization, the Chechen wars, hotly contested elections.

We get a two-track look at the country's changes, through Alfred's life in academia, then politics, and finally business, and through Igor's in journalism.

Both careers followed an arc from *sovok,* the dreariness of the Soviet way of life, to openness to the world and a Western style of operation. Their coping mechanisms were similar: reading banned literature in *samizdat* (literally, self-published, that is, manuscripts typed, with carbons, and circulated), listening to jammed Western radio stations, finding friends and mentors they trusted. Neither intended to change Russia or fight the system. But they found themselves in a place and time that needed people like them, presenting challenges and opportunities to use the talents that had no application in the Soviet system.

They started in different cities and in different fields, but they met in Moscow at *Medved,* a men's magazine with good writing. Igor was the new publisher, Alfred the new co-owner. They both wrote extensively for the magazine on a broad range of topics. Alfred's insightful analysis of history and commentary on current affairs, for *Medved* and other publications, led to the idea of working on a joint project. *A Crate of Vodka* was born there and appeared in monthly installments. It was then published in book form, in four volumes, and condensed here. started out writing for a provincial paper that was run by the Communist Party, as all media were, covering harvests and happy workers. With the advent of perestroika, journalism that exposed the worst aspects of system came into the fore, and his local reports were carried in the national papers. This led to his move to Moscow. As journalists and editors learned how to avoid the grip of Party censorship, independent media began to flourish. Igor received the Journalist of the Year award from the Soros Foundation, created by American financier George Soros. The independent newspapers and television and radio stations were also turning into private businesses. After the collapse of the Soviet Union, they became powerful tools in the hands of the oligarchs. Igor quit working at *Kommersant* when it was sold to Boris Berezovsky, because he wanted to work in independent journalism.

Another powerful media baron, Vladimir Gusinsky, became Alfred's arch-enemy. Alfred had left academia to run for mayor of a small town, and then headed the pioneering privatization program for Anatoly Sobchak, mayor of St. Petersburg. He eventually followed his friend and mentor and future First Deputy Prime Minister Anatoly Chubais to Moscow and the federal government and was put in charge of privatization on the national scale. He faced many demands and made many enemies. Much has been written about the loans-for-shares auctions, but this may be the clearest picture of how they worked—and how they did not—you will ever read.

Alfred tells his side of his relationship with Gusinsky—from working together to help Yeltsin get re-elected against big risks to being persecuted in Gusinsky's media empire; he describes the rift: becoming the subject of trumped-up criminal charges instigated by Gusinsky and Berezovsky after they lost the auction for Svyazinvest telecommunications. After the charges were dropped and Kokh had returned to Russia and resumed work in the private sector, he was hired by Gazprom Media to negotiate with Gusinsky, who had failed to repay huge debts to the energy giant Gazprom; Gusinsky lost his collateral, NTV television Channel 4 and other parts of his media holdings, and the scandal rocked Russia and much of the world.

Many familiar figures appear in the course of these twenty chapters. Very often, Alfred and Igor have different takes on them. Politicians like Gorbachev, Yeltsin, Gaidar, Chubais, Nemtsov, Zhirinovsky, Chernomyrdin, and Yavlinsky; oligarchs like Fridman, Aven, and Potanin; and dissidents like Sakharov, Solzhenitsyn and Valery Abramkin are revealed in the stories told about them.

Both characters go out of their way to be politically incorrect and to goad each other (and the reader)—it is the stylistic equivalent of the freedom of the era. They speak plainly and outrageously about the events that shaped their lives and the fate of their country. Their topics include sex and Russia's faltering demographics, religion, marriage, crime, government, politics—almost every subject that ever comes up among friends. Their discourse yields an inside story of what was going on in Russia, a backstage tour of oligarch turf battles—in politics and commerce—and a look into the hearts of two people who are passionate about their country and its future.

A.W.B.

Preface to the American Edition

by

Alfred Kokh

Five years have passed since we finished our book. The more time passes the more I'm amazed by the accuracy with which we defined the window of the "liberal renaissance." Exactly twenty years passed from the death of Leonid Brezhnev to the terrorist attacks on New York on 9/11.

Leonid Brezhnev was last Soviet leader to have worked with Stalin, and George W. Bush was the first American president since Franklin D. Roosevelt to have to deal with an enemy attack on America.

The death of Brezhnev and 9/11 radically changed not only Russia and America. Those two events changed the face of the entire world. It will never be the same.

The period between those two events encapsulated my youth. From twenty-one to forty. I was so many different things in those years. Student. Graduate student. Janitor. Steeplejack. Mason. Worker in a secret laboratory. College instructor. Mayor of a city. An official responsible for privatization first in St. Petersburg and then throughout Russia. Deputy prime minister of Russia. Accused of criminal acts. Businessman. Bankrupt. Businessman again. Manager hired for a hostile takeover. TV host. Head of a failed election campaign. Journalist. Traveler. Writer. And besides all that, husband, son, and father. All that fit into twenty years. The most wonderful twenty years in everyone's life.

When I was younger, I was amazed that the elderly recalled the Brezhnev period with such delight. They said things were better then. I remember those days very well. At the time, I saw nothing good in them. The stores and people's heads were empty, and the emptiness was filled with propaganda. Not like things were later, in the late eighties and early nineties, thought I.

But I finally got it. That was their youth. And so they recall it with pleasure. As I do mine. Perhaps my youth, viewed objectively, was no better than theirs. Crime, inequality, old people dumped in the garbage. Soldiers begging in the streets. The most abject poverty next to the most outrageous wealth. How is that better than Brezhnev's imposed equality and grave-like silence?

Could I have no arguments? Was it really a question of taste and sub-jectivity? I was almost ready to agree when I suddenly realized: We were free! Free. For twenty years we were free. And no one can take that away from us. When a man spends twenty years of his youth being free, he will never again be able to play the game called "how sincerely I love the President and his policies."

We are the first generation of Russians whose youth came at a time when you could say what you thought, do what you pleased, and choose what corre-sponded with your ideas of good and evil. No one before us had that gift. No one had that experience. And that makes it even sadder that the meaningless and ruthless Russian regime has once again laid its heavy hand on our frail shoulders.

Could liberty be nothing more than fashion? The seventies saw the flourishing of totalitarianism. It only seems that the regime lightened in com-parison to Stalin's day. No, it did not; it was the people who adjusted. The most intransigent were killed and others just left. The rest, who were more obedient and easygoing, learned to live with the system and hide their objections in their fist.

I remember myself. I was thrilled to become an Oktyabrenok and Pioneer (children's Communist social organizations). I had no serious doubts about joining the Komsomol (Young Communist League) and it was only in college, in my senior year (and that was 1983), that I started to understand a few things. I started comparing what my grandmother and grandfather, my aunt and uncle, and finally, my parents had told me with what they were force-feeding us at school and college, and I discovered that they were lying to me either at college or at home.

All my family came from the countryside. Simple peasants over whom the twentieth century rolled with special force. The Civil War, collectivization and industrialization, the war and subsequent famine—they experienced it all. And they told me about it.

Now I am describing my youth in this book, the way my ancestors once told me about theirs. Comparing their tales with mine, I see yet again how lucky I was to have those twenty free years. Freedom with new force will not return to Russia soon. The majority does not want it nor understands what it is for. May the next generation at least get an idea from our book of what freedom is.

Although of course, describing freedom is as impossible as describing sweet or sour. It has to be tasted. It has to be enjoyed.

I relished that pleasure. And no one will take it away. And that is what our book is about.

Preface to the Russian Edition

The book's concept is clear from the title. We would get a bottle, sit down to drink it, and begin talking... When the bottle was empty, the topic was, by definition, exhausted: no more drinking or exchanging wise thoughts that day. One might also guess from the title that the book will have twenty chapters. In fact, the number comes not so much from the fact that there are twenty bottles in a crate of vodka, but from our idea that at the end of the twentieth century, an entire era took place in just twenty years. Before our very eyes it began, developed, showed itself in all its horrible beauty, and then with great theatricality, with cheap effects and expensive special effects, it ended. Brezhnev died in 1982 and in 2001, terrorists bombed New York and Washington. In between, in 1991, a great empire collapsed. All of that fit into our slice of time, exactly twenty years—like vodka bottles in a crate.

This is the era that will be described in brief in the course of conversation between us, two cynical and impossibly impartial authors who have seen a thing or two, been to a place or two, and were personally involved in one or two epochal events. We have infused our discussion of the era with personal commentaries, sometimes digressing far afield—engaging, in those instances when we could not stop ourselves, in such compelling topics as alcoholism, polygamy, and love of homeland.

The fact that Alfred has German ancestry and Igor's family is Ukrainian allows us to look at our country and our fellow countrymen with some objectivity. We are also not afraid of looking stupid. We both have a very high regard for a sense of humor in others and cannot but look with pity upon people who have completely gone over to a pure and healthy way of life, abandoning the search for truth and beauty in favor of the search for the perfect diet.

Alfred came up with the idea for this book, thinking that a free dialogue between two writers could be of interest to more than just themselves. But if we had been given a guarantee that this book would not please readers, we most surely would have scoffed and gone ahead meeting, drinking, and talking, and no one would have kept us from taping these conversations, transcribing and cleaning them up, and adding our commentaries.

Introduction

by

Padma Desai

From its title to its contents, *A Crate of Vodka* is nothing if not original. In turn exhilarating and mystifying, inspiring and cynical, revealing and holding back, uplifting and frustrating, it is always engaging. So much so that I have decided to join in the dialogue with my own observations about the absorbing and confounding drama that Russia has turned out to be. Of course I will keep away from vodka for fear that I might outdo Alfred Kokh (hereafter Alik) and Igor Svinarenko (hereafter Igor) in the liberal sprinkling of swearwords which I have picked up living on the Upper West Side of New York City.

I learned that Alik's family, of German origin, moved from Kazakhstan to Russia. Igor is Ukrainian. As for me, born and raised in India, I am an American. A total outsider, can I dare engage them in a conversation which fully displays their command of Russian history and their love of Russian literature and above all, their year-after-year, intimate involvement with the unfolding scene in their *rodina*? Can I match the colorful drama of their personal lives as it has interacted with the dizzying, up-and-down fortunes of their homeland in a single generation? But wait a minute. I realized that, when I first lived in the Soviet Union in 1964, Alik was three years old and Igor was seven. Doesn't that give me a head start in understanding the Soviet system and discovering Russia?

But I need to go before 1964 and establish my credentials as a determined wisp of a girl desiring to explore Russia. Growing up in a provincial town on the

Indian west coast, I discovered Dostoevsky as a teenager in my father's library. It must be around 1945. I read *Crime and Punishment* in an English rendering by Constance Garnett, a prodigious woman with "Victorian energies and Edwardian prose." I reacted to it as a love story gone miserably wrong rather than as a morality tale of sin and redemption. I resolved there and then that I must read it in Russian. Years later when I introduced Vagit Alekperov, the Lukoil CEO, to a Columbia Business School Russian group, he asked me in a private conversation if I had indeed read Dostoevsky's masterpiece in Russian. "Not yet," I remember telling him. "It is my retirement project."

So when Russians ask me "why Russia?" I almost routinely say "because of Dostoevsky." "But he is so disturbing!" I am told. To which I react saying "That is exactly why!" What is the point of venturing into a scholarly enterprise lacking in challenges!

In 1955, I went to Harvard University on an American fellowship and completed my PhD degree in Economics. But I also started learning Russian in the university's Slavic Department. I was not intimidated by the Cyrillic script, six cases, three genders and mind-boggling tenses. How could I? I had spent years in India learning Sanskrit with a different script (from that of my mother tongue), eight cases, and three genders, all imparting a complicated but mathematically precise structure and an ornate musical tapestry to the language, resembling Russian. I memorized and sang verses from the Bhagavad Gita and read the classical Sanskrit play *Shakuntalam* which had mesmerized Goethe. Goethe had read it in a German version translated from English and had missed the splendor of the original in Sanskrit. While I mastered the language, I had endless fun with page-long word formations adding a prefix or a suffix until the original root disappeared into a labyrinth. One had to be a detective in the style of Sherlock Holmes patiently and systematically discarding the additions back and forth until the prime suspect, the original root, appeared. Russian, I discovered, was similar.

Would Alik and Igor be surprised to learn that American language instruction at every level from primary school to university has to be entertaining? My absorption into the intricacies of Russian grammar at Harvard turned out to be challenging but amusing as well. The teacher said: Complete the following sentence: "No sooner had it stopped raining than…(*kak tol'ko perestal dozhd'*…)." One imaginative class fellow, naturally an American, wrote: 'The KGB knocked on the door (*KGB stuchal v dver'*)." I thought the KGB would knock on a door in the middle of a hailstorm! Einstein figured in the class lessons too. In one of his early pronouncements, he had said: "It does not matter how I dress because nobody here knows me." A few years later he was reported to have said: "It does not matter how I dress because everybody here knows me." The brain twister was the double negative in the first sentence: *nikto menya ne znaet*.

I notice that Tolstoy and Chekhov figure in the vodka-flavored dialogue of Alik and Igor in a manner which I found upsetting to my teenage absorption in these Russian masters. Of course, as Igor says, Tolstoy "...strolled through the village, screwed everyone, then wrote a bit, then plowed a bit." Ah, but what majestic, mind-blowing works deserving of eternal homage! Does Igor know that Charlie Brown, the lead character in Charles Shultz's memorable *Peanuts* cartoons, chooses to read *War and Peace* on New Year's Eve rather than join his buddies in an evening of dinner and dance? And Chekhov, says Igor again "...really did use that razor [Occam's] to cut away the flimflam." But didn't he, in the process, create genteel, enduring themes full of sad irony? One may horse around over vodka about lesser literary figures but not about my teenage literary giants from a faraway land! And how can I not be upset at the changing literary tastes of young Russians? When I ask them about their reading favorites, I am told they prefer Boris Akunin and John Grisham (the latter in translations), both steeped in murder and mayhem.

I taught at the Delhi School of Economics (from 1959 to 1968) as Associate Professor, sought every opportunity to visit the Soviet Union, and finally got it in 1964 when my elder sister Savita asked me to spend the summer with her in Odessa. Her husband Paramanand Desai was the Indian consul in the city. Indo-Soviet trade under the leadership of Nehru and Khrushchev had been flourishing. Three ships arrived in Odessa port each month with cargo of tea and dry fruit, jute material, textile apparel and shoes from India, and three Soviet ships left the port carrying machines and equipment to India. It was necessary for the Indian Government to have an official presence in Odessa for speedy handling of the trade. The only other foreign presence in the city at the time was the Cuban consulate.

The consulate, freshly painted and situated on an acacia-lined street, glowed in the gentle summer light. Its welcoming appearance however was marred by the permanent presence of a Soviet guard in a booth by the side of the entrance. No Soviet citizen was allowed to visit the consulate without prior official clearance nor could the consul and his wife visit the locals. *nel'zya!* The city looked morose and preoccupied as if it was in permanent mourning. Odessa, I was aware, was known in the Czarist days as the "Pearl of Russia" and as "Little Paris." The French and Italian cafes of its cultural heyday, which I imagined Pushkin and Tolstoy had visited during their stay, had disappeared. When Mark Twain passed through Odessa in 1869, he wrote: "We saw only America. There was not one thing to remind us that we were in Russia." On the other hand, Alik, I discovered, gets berserk talking about Odessa located in Crimea which Khrushchev had given away to Ukraine in 1957. He is ready to start an invasion.

"If we conquer the Crimea, what are they going to do to us?...It does not belong to Ukraine." Calm down, Alik!

Among regular visitors to the consulate were Indian students, who talked about their experiences in the institutes where they studied. Some turned up, towels in hand, with a view to taking a bath in the consulate. I thought that was strange until I learnt that their alternative was to stand naked in a line at the entrance of a public bathhouse, a practice they tried to circumvent by covering their midriff with a towel. Indian men observe a strict taboo against appearing naked even in private places in the company of men. *"Snimai, snimai,"* the Russians shouted asking the Indians to take off their towels at which they fled.

The students, all fluent in Russian, brought jokes which they picked up from their Russian classmates, jokes which caught the flavor of the times and the governing style of the leaders. Stalin, by all accounts, was ruthless whereas Khrushchev vacillated.

The jokes brought out the sharp contrast in the two leaders' handling of the specific situations confronting them.

In one joke, Stalin, having met with a group of visitors, discovered that his pipe was missing. He sent Beria, the KGB chief, in pursuit of the delegation. Upon returning from a fruitless search, Beria informed Stalin that he had dispatched half the group of visitors to the gallows and the remainder to the gulag. Stalin, in the meantime, had located the pipe in his desk drawer. I thought the joke caught the essence of the meaningless murders and deportations of millions of innocent victims during Stalinist purges.

By the time Khrushchev appeared, the humor had become subtle, intellectualized, and a bit mellow. My favorite joke, titled "Khrushchev's Dilemma," related to the Russian woman astronaut Valentina Tereshkova who had just returned from space in 1964. In the joke, she came back to earth pregnant and created a dilemma for Khrushchev who was still the Soviet leader. He had to either accept the Biblical doctrine of Immaculate Conception or admit that an American had traveled in space first. Over the years, I was to pick up the changing flavor of the stories as they appropriately reflected the shifting Soviet-Russian scene from Mikhail Gorbachev in the mid-1980s to Vladimir Putin in the decade beginning in 2000. I am sure Alik and Igor have an abundant stock of jokes which are missing from their dialogue.

In 1968 when I migrated to America for good and got an appointment at the Harvard Russian Research Center, I had resolved to finally emerge as a leading American scholar of the Soviet and Russian economic systems. But in order to accomplish that goal, I had to first establish an American identity. I discarded the sari and switched to pant suits but I was stuck with my brown skin and black eyes. I started traveling frequently to the Soviet Union, to Moscow and St.

Petersburg and Nizhny Novgorod and other cities as a member of American delegations but the Soviet hosts raised eyebrows when I declared that I was an American. In 1980, I was appointed Professor in the Economics Department at Columbia University followed by the award of the prestigious Gladys and Roland Harriman Professorship of Comparative Economic Systems. By that time, I was fully recognized as a leading economist-scholar of Russia.

Mikhail Gorbachev became Soviet leader in March 1985. With his appearance, my professional career as an American scholar of the Soviet scene moved into an exciting trajectory. I watched the titanic power struggle between Gorbachev and Yeltsin that unfolded in 1986, watched their reform initiatives, and wrote about them tirelessly. In the end, my assessment of their contributions has not changed to this day. Gorbachev introduced powerful winds of change. In the words of the historian Martin Malia (in an interview in my *Conversations on Russia: Reform from Yeltsin to Putin,* Oxford University Press, 2006, hereafter *Conversations*), it allowed people to expose what Solzhenitsyn called 'the Lie,' "the pretension of the system to be rational, just, egalitarian, and not coercive. ...But he did not intend to destroy the system and restore capitalism." As Alik remarks: "...Gorbachev was too weak intellectually to come up with something to counter the official line." Indeed the continuing bread lines had prompted the following joke. An exasperated customer awaiting his turn tells a fellow sufferer that he will locate Mikhail Sergeyevich and kill him. He returns after a while to the breadline and declares that the second line to dispose of the Soviet leader was even longer.

As the first step in the perestroika economic reforms, he attacked vodka consumption by Russians. In 1986, state factories, which produced vodka, were ordered to cut back output. The measure was a colossal failure. Ninety percent of the price of a vodka bottle consisted of retail tax. As production dropped, tax revenue inflows in the federal budget plummeted but illicit vodka distillation-samogon-flourished. The measure was eventually withdrawn. As a Russian friend remarked: "When Russian parents select a bridegroom for their daughter, they do not ask if he drinks but how he behaves when he is drunk." The conversation between Alik and Igor on the anti-alcohol campaign is animated and revealing. I did not know that the campaign, a "Sisyphean task," was the brain child of Raisa Maximovna who "not only did not allow her hubby to drink, she tried to make everyone else keep him company."

Alik mentions that he had climbed on a lamppost on Suvorovsky Boulevard in St. Petersburg to catch a close glimpse of Gorbachev who was visiting the city. I, on the other hand, was more fortunate. I saw him (with a Finnish colleague, Dr. Pertti Naulapaa) in the mid-nineties in his office in the Gorbachev Foundation. The meeting was hastily arranged and I had left my recording machine behind but I had brought for him my *Perestroika in Perspective: The Design and Dilemmas of Soviet Reform* (Princeton University Press, 1989). The book's jacket cover has a cartoon by Tony Auth of the *Philadelphia Inquirer* in which Gorbachev, hammer in his outstretched hand, is energetically, even joyfully dragging Yegor Ligachev, his obdurate Communist colleague toward perestroika. We settled down and I found him unusually relaxed and pleased as he showed the jacket design to his interpreter Pavel Palashchenko.

Toward the end of the meeting, I brought up the issue of two mistakes on his part. "Why didn't you work up an outline of a Union Treaty among the republics earlier in 1989 as Andrei Sakharov, the human rights activist, had suggested? Perhaps it could have saved the Union." He nodded in agreement. I was surprised that he did not bring up the contentious issue of Yeltsin's maneuverings that, he occasionally argued, had destroyed the Soviet Union. I thought my second question would arouse him sufficiently to perhaps shake his courteous demeanor.

I had often wondered why he had desisted from a frontal attack on the authoritarian role and ideology of the Communist Party of the Soviet Union. Perhaps because he feared that he might be removed from office by the Communist brass (as Khrushchev was) if he forced the pace of change. He could indeed be dismissed by them because he derived his authority from them. Perhaps the most damaging mistake of his presidency was that he did not legitimate his authority by seeking to be elected president by popular vote when he could have managed to do so in the winter of 1990. (He was elected president on March 13, 1990, by an indirect vote of the Communist Party Congress of People's Deputies.) So I asked: "Why didn't you seek to be elected president by a general election in early 1990? As late as May, public opinion polls placed you as the most popular leader ahead of Yeltsin. If you had popular support, you could have handled the Politburo, dictated the pace of restructuring the Union and perhaps held Yeltsin at bay." He agreed with that idea too. Perhaps he was in a mellow mood; perhaps he did not want to argue with a woman scholar and display his marvelous gifts of loquaciousness for which he was known around the world. The interview, I felt, lacked a vigorous back and forth exchange of views.

Whatever Gorbachev's failings, Western analysts credit him with one monumental achievement. The Cold War ended under his watch. Ronald Reagan, who was elected American president in 1980 (and was reelected for a second term in 1984), had vowed to end the "Evil Empire." And he accomplished his goal. But wasn't the Soviet Union defeated? Alik and Igor decisively think so. They go further and argue that Soviet defeat should have been acknowledged openly and explicitly by one and all. "...they covered up the defeat... The line was that 'friendship' won. And now we're like best friends (Igor). And the polite Westerners decided not to remind us that we had lost." (Alik). Indeed Alik gets carried away: "We needed to form a group with defeated Germany, defeated Japan—then our nation would have become more focused. People would have understood that they were closer to one another than they thought. Instead, they started looking for scapegoats. This one is rich, this one is poor, who stole what—bullshit. We had no sense of defeat, and that's a shame: Defeat unites people."

But here is a concrete example of the Western view of the Cold War that Alik talks about. In an interview in my *Conversations,* former U.S. Ambassador Jack Matlock gave colorful details of the joint Reagan-Gorbachev enterprise as the two presidents walked the Kremlin grounds in May 1988 followed by newspapermen. According to Matlock, one of them asked Reagan: "Is this still the Evil Empire?" He said, "No, that was another era, another time." Then someone asked, "Well, who is responsible?" And he said, "Mr. Gorbachev, of course. He is the leader of this country." One more question [to Reagan]: "Who won?" "Well, certainly, the Cold War ended on terms that had been set by the West, and specifically by the United States, and yet I think both sides won."

Clearly, the Reagan-Gorbachev overlap from 1985 to 1988 had set the stage for the end of the Cold War and for the liberation of Eastern and Central European countries, followed later by the dissolution of the Soviet Union in late 1991. But didn't these outcomes meet U.S. strategic *interests?* At the same time, didn't the liberalizing changes under Gorbachev fulfill the U.S. desire for the initiation, although halting, of liberal *values* in the Soviet Union?

What about Yeltsin? Did he also, perhaps unwittingly, fulfill American *values* and *interests* even though he was strikingly different from Gorbachev? He contested elections, four of them. And we Americans hold free elections as an abiding *value* of the American arrangements. He went further and destroyed the Communist system. That fully satisfied American *interest* as well. In a post-retirement interview (published in *Moscow News* dated October 22–28, 2003, and reprinted in my *Conversations*), Yeltsin had declared: "What was needed was a kamikaze crew that would step into the line of fire and forge ahead, however strong the general discontent might be…. I had to pick a team that would go up in flames but remain in history." A little later, he had added: The reformers' "maximalism exasperated me." Their maximalism consisted in working up a program of slashing the Russian government's budget deficit, removing subsidies from the budget to Russian consumers and producers, freeing up the prices, privatizing all the assets in a single swoop, and opening up the economy in a set of proposals that came to be known as shock therapy.

By all accounts, Russians were euphoric in the early days of the Yeltsin presidency ready to believe him when he said, according to Igor: "We have just to get through two or three years, and then happiness will be upon us." These were "naïve, trusting, beautiful times. There was never another period like it." Across the Atlantic, the destructive impact of the shock therapy on the Communist planned economy met the approval of U.S. policy makers under the Clinton years from 1992 to 1999 which coincided with the Yeltsin presidency. Referring to the "chemistry" between the two leaders, Strobe Talbott, Deputy Secretary of State in the Clinton Administration, elaborated in his *Conversations* interview: "Bill Clinton bonded with Boris Yeltsin. Big time. And he used that bond to get Yeltsin to do things that were hard for Yeltsin but important to us. That is the story of the last eight years more than any other single thing." At one point, Clinton had reportedly summed up the interaction imperative in a memorable one-liner: "We can't ever forget that Yeltsin drunk is better than most of the alternatives sober."

How have I assessed Yeltsin's contribution? His kamikaze crew of re-formers demolished the kit and caboodle of the Communist authoritarian system and the planned economy. In so doing, they planted the liberal idea in the land of Lenin and Stalin. And history changes with ideas. But I firmly believe that Yeltsin did not introduce, much less develop, the basic institutions of liberal arrangements such as a party system or fair elections or a free press or strong legal and financial institutions. These were unlikely to spring like Athena from the brow of Zeus in a country with a long history of Czarist and Communist authoritarianism. Nor did the electronic and print media of the kind known in the West multiply under Yeltsin.

And the eight years of Yeltsin's presidency (ending in December 31, 1999) were tumultuous. While pro-Yeltsin Western analysts approved of the political advances in Russia, his policies created significant economic disorder and public discontent, and raised problems of governance in Russia's vast territory.

Take the freeing of prices in early 1992. The costs of essential goods rose dramatically in a way that essentially wiped out the saving people had accumu-lated during the Soviet days of shortages. Bread lines disappeared but bread prices rose higher than wages. Alik and Igor are not in full agreement about the consequences of price liberalization. "I remember that sausages had been 3 rubles a kilo and suddenly it was ten," says Igor. Alik, an ardent free market reformer, responds: "But it was there! That's the whole point, there was sausage. No more shortages."

Again, price decontrol destabilized enterprise balance sheets. A textile factory charged higher prices for its apparel but it ended up paying even higher prices for the raw cotton. Again, with the dissolution of the Soviet Union in

December 1991, old predictable supply chains also fell apart. Factory managers also seized money making opportunities. In the old days, according to Alik, "People were ashamed to be interested in money." By contrast, the Soviet-era managerial discipline had disappeared in the new, free-wheeling, money-grabbing world of markets. In a word, enterprises across the country started making losses. As a result, managers stopped paying wages to their workers and taxes to the state budget. Just imagine! Workers did not receive wages, and the state did not receive tax payments from factories during many months from 1994 to 1997. Shortfalls in budget revenues created government defaults of wage payments to state sector employees and pensions to retirees. The pervasive withholding of wages from workers and nonpayment of pensions to retirees intensified the public's discontent. My coauthor Todd Idson and I analyzed this phenomenon in *Work without Wages: Russia's Nonpayment Crisis* (The MIT Press, 2000).

What role did asset privatization play in the Sturm und Drang of the Yeltsin era?

Alik, who played a major role in the process from start to finish, provides an impassioned, blow-by-blow account, revealing details which begin from the thirteenth vodka bottle and end with the final, twentieth one. Naturally he gets personal, almost lachrymose but feisty as well. "I had a lot of trouble writing this commentary. This is one of those cases where memories and thoughts pile up, stifling you, getting mixed up and intertwined...Naturally, I worried about seeming prejudiced. I cannot maintain my objectivity and stay above the fray on this issue. I tried very hard to be at least calm, if not objective. Well, this is what it is. Don't be too hard on me, kind reader."

The first phase of auctions of stores in Moscow began in April 1992. "We sold a lot of them. Almost all of them. People resisted at first, and then they started buying. It was very important to explain to the labor collectives the potential benefits of the sales. They took part in the auctions and won. It was fun!"

The second phase was voucher privatization which began in the fall of 1992. Yeltsin announced in an executive decree that all Russian citizens born before September 1, 1992 would be issued a voucher in the amount of 10,000 rubles each. Here is how Alik describes the conditions under which the program was launched. "No consumer demand or social equality; low interest on the part of foreign investors; more than 240,000 state enterprises, which required us to use...spontaneous privatization—that is, a mass transfer of property belonging to state enterprises into other forms of property, outside of the legislative framework. It was to solve all these problems that the voucher was invented, a magic wand for the Russian economy. Distribution of vouchers among Russian citizens began in the fall of 1992." The process was completed on July 1, 1994.

How do I assess the motivation underlying the adoption of this "magic wand?" In my understanding, voucher privatization was initially planned to start in early 1993 but was brought forward and launched at breakneck speed in October 1992. Alik justifies it in terms of a dire economic need. I believe its timing and speed were driven by political considerations. By mid 1992, inflation was beginning to get out of control because the Central Bank of Russia had begun releasing massive cash in the economy. The monetary control of the budget, which was the essential pillar of shock therapy, was overturned. The reform momentum was lost and a new front had to be opened up to resuscitate it. The public had to be brought in the act in an intimate way for the purpose. And what better way to accomplish that goal than distribute a voucher worth 10,000 rubles to each man, woman and child? It was not intended to make them instant capitalists but they thought they would become partial owners of companies in which they placed their vouchers. It was not surprising that the country wide referendum which followed in April 1993 turned out to be a resounding success in favor of the President (*da*), his policies (*da*), and against the Supreme Soviet (*nyet*). The people freely expressed their mistrust in the Communist-dominated legislature. The lawmakers should have voluntarily disbanded but they did not.

The final phase of privatization, the loans-for-shares program, had also the overriding political goal of ensuring Yeltsin's election as president in June 1996. The oligarchs provided the cash for financing the campaign (and also for partially covering the federal budget deficit) in exchange for stocks in the leading companies which were auctioned in November 1995. It was after the auctions "that the oligarch class was formed, and that guaranteed Yeltsin's reelection in 1996." What would have happened if Gennady Zyuganov, the Communist leader, were elected President of the Russian Federation? At the minimum, "he would send the bankers [Berezovsky and Gusinsky, among them] packing. Be glad you're alive, he would say." "And the Commies were sure to put [Chubais] against the wall …for the excesses of the reforms." "Berezovsky, Gusinsky, and Chubais assured Yeltsin's victory in 1996."

Alik tells a riveting story of how the auctions were arranged, who participated and who felt left out, and how Yeltsin's presidential campaign was fought. He nevertheless issues a word of caution. "But let me repeat. I'm talking as an outsider. Only three people know the inside stuff completely. The time will come when they—Chubais, Berezovsky, and Gusinsky—will tell it like it was. I think we will learn many interesting things then."

As far as I am concerned, the details are enough. Alik goes out of his way to argue that the loans-for-shares auctions were conducted with proper procedures. "We not only introduced down payments but also demanded guarantees that the participants be able to pay at least the starting price." Also, note this after-the-fact, justificatory tone:

> When the country needed money, we put big enterprises up for auction. ... there were people who paid the money (where they got it is a different question, one for the law). They took the enterprises, with their debts, losses, and shit—and brought them up to a fairly decent level. Now even the West recognizes the quality of Russian management. ... And now why are so many people [bureaucrats] who didn't want to participate in our auctions, didn't want to give us money, now busily trying to ruin those poor oligarchs.

Here is my question. How did ordinary Russians view the loans-for-shares program which followed the economic distress resulting from price decontrol and months of wage nonpayment? They viewed it as a shady policy maneuver which handed over the most valuable assets of the economy among them oil, nickel, and metallurgy, to a group of preferred oligarchs at a pittance of their true value. They believed they had built them under Soviet Communism from Stalin to Brezhnev with their blood, sweat and tears. Besides, how had the oligarchs accumulated the cash to buy the assets? Alik blithely says "it is a different question, one for the law." Really? The jokes of the period reflect the flagrant and pompous display of their ill-gotten wealth by the oligarchs. In one version, an oligarch shows off three swimming pools in his country estate to a foreign visitor. "This one is a hot water pool, the second one here is a cold water pool, and this final one, without water, is for those who do not swim."

Of course Yeltsin was elected in June 1996 but the oligarchs who secured his victory "fell at each other's throats in 1997." The remaining years of his presidency, until his surprise resignation in December 1999, were marked by political and economic disarray including the sovereign debt default of August 1998.

I believe that Yeltsin was fully aware of the massive uncertainties facing Russia. When he was asked in the interview reproduced in my *Conversations* why he selected Putin as his successor, his response was a resounding one-liner: "Because he is not a maximalist." In other words, the successor had to keep away from further market-based liberalization or from a sharp reversal of the course in the opposite direction. A maximalist tilt of either kind was a no-no. The chaotic situation needed a middle-of-the-road correction and Putin, in Yeltsin's view, was the right choice.

The consolidation of federal authority under Putin's two presidential terms ending in May 2008 proceeded further than Yeltsin had visualized. He crafted political stabilization via authoritarian means including media control, and promoted economic recovery via state control of the energy sector which provided hefty foreign exchange earnings until 2008. This twofold agenda, in my view, bears witness to Putin's belief that the Russian state has to be strong in order to fulfill Russia's national interest. The Russian oligarchs, who had captured industrial assets in the oil and mineral sectors, could flout Russian laws and act against Russia's interest. At the minimum, the presence of a state watchdog in these units was necessary in order to prevent them from doing so.

Alik and Igor take a cautious, on-the-one-hand, on-the-other-hand approach in assessing Vladimir Vladimirovich. "A non-law-abiding nation like Russia needs a strong hand… but he can't control the entourage," says Alik. Igor reflects on the contrast with life under Brezhnev: "We lived under Brezhnev and no one gave a shit. And now we have a strict and wise leader. He's getting everyone in line, including the vertical command and control structure. But this could pass, too…" Alik also talks colorfully about the temporariness of the Putin phenomenon among the young in Russia: "For them, for the youth, he's just a brand. …He thinks the people love him. But as soon as his brand gets worn out, like Rasputin vodka, it's over. He thinks he's won the love of the people. But that love is like the love for Coca-Cola." Finally Igor offers this historical continuity of the Russian tradition: "For a thousand years Russia always had one responsible leader, who cared about the fate of the people entrusted to him. … For all that we respect Vladimir Vladimirovich personally," he adds dryly.

At the same time, I sense that Alik and Igor are not quite happy about Putin's top-down governance with a vertical command structure. It lacks free elections at all levels and robust debates on issues of public concern. The "vertical" bothers me too. But I do believe Russia and Russians have changed from the time more than four decades ago when I lived in the Soviet Union. The lives of most ordinary Russians (till the emergence of the financial crisis that hit Russia in September 2008) have been far better than ever before. The steady economic growth of 6.5 to 7 percent a year in the seven years starting in 2000 had offered more Russians occupational mobility, higher earnings, and improved standard of living reflected in more housing, cars and telephones, and travel. Millions of Russians, urban, educated, and feeling European, began earning their living as citizens rather than as employees of a Communist state.

In view of these improvements, I would resolve the Putin riddle by invoking Winston Churchill. Years ago he had described the Soviet Union as a riddle wrapped in a mystery inside an enigma, adding that the key to solving it was national interest. In the long stretch of Russian history, Putin is the latest leader who has sought to carry out that agenda via a strong state. His policies sent a clear message to Russians and foreigners alike: that the Russian state, endowed with economic resurgence, political stability and widespread popularity under his presidency, will pursue Russia's national interest and its geopolitical role as defined by Russians--not as defined by the West. Naturally there was a fly in the ointment. The consolidation of political authority under Putin marked a reversal in the identification of common *values* with the West. From American policy making perspective, Putin had damaged the prospects for Russia's democratic evolution.

This brings me to my second observation. Russians, it would seem, have entered an implicit contract with their leader and agreed to surrender critical freedoms in exchange for a better life. These positive features marking the nascent appearance of a middle class are now threatened by the financial crisis which unfolded in Russia in September 2008 as in other economies around the world. Will the turmoil irreparably damage the widespread gains of the past seven years under the vertical command structure crafted by a single leader? Will it irretrievably postpone the emergence of a system of political arrangements in which informed dialogue between the rulers and the ruled replaces authoritarian governance in which policy decisions are imposed from the top? Haven't Russians debated these issues throughout their history? Will the gains of the recent past help them successfully overcome the potential for turbulence this time around? Or will these gains be lost in job losses, street protests and blood-letting? Wouldn't Alik and Igor want to sort out these alternative scenarios over another bottle of vodka?

Padma Desai is Gladys and Roland Harriman Professor of Comparative Economic Systems and Director of the Center for Transition Economies at Columbia University. Her latest book, *Conversations on Russia: Reform from Yeltsin to Putin*, a collection of her interviews with leading policymakers in Russia and America, was published by Oxford University Press in 2006.

A Crate of Vodka

1.

1982

The First Bottle

A new life began with the death of Leonid Brezhnev. The bang of the Soviet leader's coffin being dropped at his funeral was like the bang of cannon fire on the battleship Aurora in 1917.

Very few people knew that the "period of stagnation" would end with that… The authors did not know. One of them—Alfred Kokh—was sweeping the streets of Leningrad and in his free time mastering the science of economics at his institute. He used to daydream: "Twenty years from now, I'll be teaching college economics. I'll drive a Zhiguli, I'll have a little dacha, I'll vacation in Sochi and sometimes even in Varna!"

The second author, Igor Svinarenko, was a reporter for the regional newspaper in Kaluga. He wrote daring articles, trying to be as bold as he could between the lines; he followed the banned literature being circulated in samizdat, *(underground typed manuscripts), and he had girlfriends. He saw his life twenty years hence this way: "I'll publish a slender volume of essays, save money and buy a hunch-backed Zaporozhets, and even go on a package tour to Paris."*

These dreams have seemed ridiculous to the authors for a long time now: Life turned out to be much richer. But have they found happiness?

Alik, you go first. Tell me what you were doing the year L. I. Brezhnev died—so, 1982. Who were you?

I was in my fourth year of college… That fall I had started work as a night janitor. A night janitor isn't like an ordinary janitor; he only comes in when something happens during the day that can't wait until morning to be fixed. His salary is lower than the regular guy's, around 90 to 120 rubles a month. But he works less—sporadically—and always at night. It's the best job for a student. These jobs were grandfathered, passed down from older students to younger ones. I kept the job for five years, from 1982 to 1987. By then I had my PhD and was still working… What were you doing?

I had just given up my experimentation, ended my nomadic life, and decided to drop anchor. I reregistered my passport, got a divorce from my first wife, registered for the draft, got cured of gonorrhea, and picked up my diploma… I worked those two years and also moonlighted in *samizdat* and even for the administration of housing repair for the Donbass region.

Well, the moonlighting goes without saying. In 1982 I was drafted, and I couldn't moonlight anymore.

Kokh's Commentary:

I did my army service in the town of Gryazovets, in the Vologda Oblast. My unit performed financial services for the Chief Regiment. We were there for two months; we swore an oath and received an officer's rank. Since that time, I have carried with me a very persistent idea of the Soviet Army that cannot be explained in a few words. Without dwelling on my opinion of the battle-readiness of our troops—which has hardly improved since then—I will mention just two traits that discouraged me at the time and for which I can find no rational explanation to this day. First: I did not understand then, and do not understand now, why a solider is allowed to bathe only once a week. Where, in what regulations, is that written? And if it is written, then why? You get athlete's foot because the boots are all used, and stink, and you can't really wash foot wrappings (which are worn instead of socks) very well in cold water, or your removable collar lining for that matter. Not to mention the skin diseases: the rank and file suffered terribly from boils. I know the idea is to toughen them up—"hard training, easy war" and all that. Second: I have never understood why a soldier has to be poorly fed. It's not enough that the new guy gets hazed and beaten up by the men about to be discharged; but he gets starved, too. Just look: According to the charts, which we knew well in the financial department, everything looks fine. Calories, fats, carbohydrates. It could be better, but it's adequate. But the food is delivered to camp, and the officers and NCOs attack the warehouse like vultures. Everybody gets some meat, butter, grain, and so on. They all have families and children. They get it for free from the soldiers' pots. The soon-to-be-discharged quickly line up for a fry-up of potatoes and bacon. They take butter from the younger ones. So what's left for our young soldier? Undercooked liver with remnants of manure, fish skeletons, and shrapnel (sorry, I meant barley). The poor little soldier stands on guard duty, his pockets stuffed with bread. That's all he eats for the first 18 months—just bread. It would be different if the state didn't have money to feed the army. But it does, the budget allocates funds

* * *

Svinarenko's Commentary:

Thank God, I spent only a month in the army. It was after I completed the weekly military training at Moscow State University, where they taught us specialized techniques for propaganda. During a war, if one were to occur, I was supposed to persuade those serving the Bundeswehr that they would be better off surrendering to us.

The most interesting component of the military course was the one on "Interrogation of the Enemy." Our instructors shared their experience with us: If you stick the wire clips from a field telephone under the nails of the big toes of your subject, for example, and then give the handle a twirl, the poor wretch will scream in pain. But they also explained that such special measures don't elicit reliable information. If a man is afraid, he'll lie and try to tell you what you want. And if he decides to tough it out like a patriot willing to die for his country, you'll have a lot of explaining to do about why you signed out a POW and returned an enemy corpse.

The camp schedule was edifying. Sunday was bath day, and Monday we dug trenches and had rifle practice. We spent the rest of the week covered in dirt from the trenches, drawing maps and attending lectures. On Sunday we would get clean, only to get dirty again the next day for the week ahead.

We were given new uniforms, of a very old cut—circa 1943, with stand-up collars. That was when they introduced the bizarre shoulder boards, too: green flannel with raspberry braid.

We lived in tents, in the woods, and a drunken woman walked around the camp with a knapsack full of vodka bottles that she sold us. We would pour the vodka into the flasks we were required to wear on our belts. It was very handy!

* * *

Well, Igor, in 1981, I moonlighted, working on the construction of the Togliatti fertilizer plant. For two months. I remember that I made close to a thousand rubles then.

So that's when you started making money.

Hahaha. Please, don't try to turn me into a hero. Please.

Did you pay taxes?

They were withheld from my paycheck. There was no alternative.

Right. So, Brezhnev dies, and you're working as a janitor.

A *night* janitor. It's very different. So, they buried him. Why are you asking me all the questions? It's not an interview. You tell me your feelings, Igor, and I'll tell you mine.

Feelings? About Brezhnev's death? Well, I… It was as if I had known an era was coming to an end. I stopped my wanderings and took a job with a newspaper. In Kaluga. At a Komsomol (Communist Youth League) paper. In a section devoted to—ha!— the working youth, and Communist upbringings. So I was working away, and it was my turn to put the paper to bed. It was November 11, and they announced that Brezhnev—

Don't forget that they didn't have the usual concert for Militia Day on November 10. I realized then that the old guy must have kicked the bucket. I thought it was a bad sign that there was no concert.

What do you mean, a bad sign?

Funny. I felt sorry for the old guy, to tell the truth. And they dropped his coffin…

They wrote later that it hadn't been dropped, that it was a twenty-one-gun salute starting or something.

Come on, of course they dropped it; the whole country saw it, Igor. The whole world saw it. They dropped the coffin, and he almost fell out.

I had a plan for that evening: I was going to sign off on the issue at 9 p.m. and head over to the dorm at the Kaluga Pedagogical Institute to celebrate *Fasching*. It's a German holiday, like carnival. Partying, orgies. Russians get drunk and fight, but Germans drink a bit and quietly and peacefully go off to fuck girls. A different concept. *Fasching* is a kind of legalized violation of moral standards. You can get married for the night—there are even special certificates; everything is clear and official. So-and-so marries so-and-so from such-and-such hour until such-and-such, with photos of the pair of them.

Just the day before, my paper had published a letter from a German student. She wrote how wonderful everything was in Russia, how much she loved it. I wrote down her name and decided that I would go find her so we could go celebrate that magnificent holiday together.

Ah, her love for the land of the Soviets aroused you that much?

The land of the Soviets and Ukrainians.

You had sexual feelings for someone who praised our country.

I'm a German scholar. Used to be. I spent my fifth year of college in Germany—in Leipzig—studying journalism, Alik, and I had the fondest memories of German girls. They're like a separate nation, because the men are significantly worse and more boring. Sorry, I didn't mean you. And since I knew no one in town, and here was a published name, I felt as if I had a friend.

I see. In other words, you won't admit that you had an unhealthy interest in socialism? You wanted to fuck it.

No, no, she wrote about something else: how she liked the wooden houses that don't exist in Germany. You're German, and I see you have a stone house, too.

But I have a wooden one on the property as well. Way over there, see it?

That one way, way over there? That's still your property, Alik? …
So there I was, instead of going to a German party, I had to sit and wait for them to bring me articles to sign off on. In other words, I celebrated the holiday practically like a bottled brain, in the home city of the great dreamer. I sat there for a long time, because no one knew how to bury Brezhnev or how to tell the nation he had died. The head of the Komsomol regional committee asked for instruction from the Party, and they applied to the Central Committee. The response was: We don't know yet either, call back at 2 a.m. They went to look at the *Pravda* archives for 1953, since Stalin had been the last acting head of the USSR to be buried. They copied the layout outright. You know, a black frame around the entire page, and responses from the workers, who mourned and therefore would over-fulfill the Plan, and the Party would gather even more tightly around the Leninist Central Committee. It's pure idiocy and hard to believe today… Anyway, it all ended around 5 in the morning. Where could I go at that hour? The orgy would have been over by then.

So the man not only died, but he ruined your sex life, too. Here's what I was doing. I wasn't bothering anyone, I came back from school, swept the courtyard, sat around "repairing" the tea kettle, when the foreman (who was actually a fore-woman) came over with her doleful face and said, "We're going to put up the flags." In those little holes, you know? The buildings all had them, little holes in the walls to stick flags in. Not a difficult task, but it's a pain. There were tons of holes and tons of flags.

So Alik, you and the forewoman were performing an imitation of sex—sticking flags into holes.

She was just using me for my manly powers!

See, I told you.

I had to drag around the flags and the ladder, and she would run up the ladder and insert the flags.

If she had known that the future former deputy prime minister was hauling the ladder for her, she would certainly have fallen from it.

I rejected all responsibility and worked as a brute beast. I hauled the ladder and flags. She decorated our entire neighborhood on orders from the Party regional committee. I watched the television coverage of the funeral with pleasure. I liked it a lot. Not just the part where they dropped the coffin, but the whole thing. My friends and I bought a lot of beer, and we settled in to watch... The old guy would have been happy to see us.

What did you drink? Your favorite Bitburger?

Oh, no. It was Zhigulevskoe, no label, just numbers stamped on the bottle cap.

I buy it sometimes even now—it has a slightly bitter taste, one familiar from childhood. As a child, I spent every summer in Zhdanovo, in the south of Ukraine, an industrial city on the shores of the Azov Sea. My maternal grandparents lived there—Ivan Matsuyev and Vera Kovaleva. My grandfather, a proletarian and ex-army man, liked to drink. I remember how he would come home, staggering, from somebody's house, and silently put up with his wife's scolding. He was always easygoing and tactful. The morning after tying one on, he would behave impeccably, taking his time before getting down to business: "Grandma, give me a ruble, our grandson is asking for a beer." She would give it to him—what else could she do?—and we'd go off to the bar. It was a simple place: standing room at the counter, no seats. Grandfather would hand me a plate of pretzels, heavily salted, and let me sip the foam from his mug of beer. Forty years later I can still remember the slightly bitter taste of the thick foam and the piercing flavor of the salt crystals imbedded in the glazed surface of those small, stone-hard pretzels. I also remember the great sense of calm I felt with my grandfather on our beer quests. He loved me, deeply—and he was eager to share the most solemn pleasures of his life with me.

Grandfather Ivan spoke scornfully about the official line when I was around. He tried to explain things to me—but I didn't get it then, and for a long time my Party-member father won in the struggle for my affections. It was real beer, you know... It's a real beer.

You're telling me? I grew up in Zhiguli. I lived in Togliatti, Kuibyshev Oblast, between 1969 and 1978. That was a powerful experience. The auto plant was still under construction, and the city with it. Mud everywhere. People came from all over the Soviet Union for the housing: Russians, Tatars, Mordovans, Chuvashes, and Ukrainians. There was just one movie theater for the whole city. Culture, *shmulture*—there was nothing! I was the only boy in the Avtozavod district to finish grade school without any Cs. The favorite pastime was gang fights, one block against another. They fought murderously, with lengths of pipe, with bicycle chains. My folks, foolishly—that is, unthinkingly—sent me to a music school. You can imagine an adolescent wandering through that macho crowd with a little folder full of sheet music. And then my last name wasn't normal. They beat me every day—until I dropped music and signed up for martial arts instead. I studied sambo. Things grew easier. When I think back, I shudder. After graduation, half the class wound up in prison. Some are serving second or third terms. Some are buried in the cold, cold ground. God helped me get into the Leningrad Financial-Economic Institute and out of there.

And you drink Zhigulevskoe even now?

With great pleasure!

Just look, Alik: your entire future life was set out in 1982.

No, it wasn't.

First, you began earning money, as a day laborer and as a night janitor. Second, you became involved in state affairs.

And how was that?

You hung state flags out in the street. And third: You brought order to the country. First with a broom, on a single block of Leningrad.

Yes.

Did you privatize anything at the time?

No, that wasn't possible—there wasn't much privatization at the time. Ah, when I think back to our apartment on Red Cavalry Street (now Cavalier Guards Street again), next to the Smolny Institute. It was a communal apartment, damp, rats running around, the floor caving in here and there. The window opened onto an interior shaft. It was fun, living there. I had a neighbor, a boy who was studying at a technical college. He rarely went to class, and he set up his guitar to play through a massive speaker and started learning a song called "Earth through a Porthole."

He wrote it?

He was just learning it. He would start at around ten in the morning, repeating each line a hundred times, give or take. It drove my wife crazy. She would say, Come on, take a break. I'll give you something to eat.

Whose wife?

Mine.

The same one you have now?

Of course. I have only one wife.

How did that happen, Alik? Everyone has had lots of wives and you have only one.

Funny. I guess it's my one shot at originality. Gives me something to show off!

Really, showing off aside, what would you like to see happen to marriage?

In today's demographic situation—the social situation, too—I'm for polygamy.

Serial polygamy or parallel?

Hm… Parallel. I don't believe in abandoning wives. If you're really in a bad way, in the bloom of love and all that, then you should acquire the new one while keeping the one you've got. Since modern morality won't allow that, they came up with this idiotic system of replacing wives. What are you supposed to do with the old one? Throw her in the trash? You can't do that. Now, if she finds herself someone new, that's different. But if she doesn't? Some fashion this is, abandoning wives. You have to shoulder the burden to the end, until death do you part. That's what I think. Understand me?

Kokh's Commentary:

Perhaps this is not apropos, but I've been thinking about this for a while. Our great ancestors, from Russia's recent history—Peter the Great, Catherine the Great, all the Alexanders, including Stolypin—they all had a similar view of

Russia. They didn't think about political or nonpolitical methods. Or whether one was an aggressor or a non-aggressor. They thought about the country— about its people, its position vis-à-vis other countries and nations. And at first they came to an unhappy conclusion. The economy was weak, the army was weak. The geopolitical position could not be worse: on the outskirts of Europe, without access to the sea, and with the real Asia (China, India) also far away. Economically, they depended on unreliable agriculture. There were bad harvests, starvation. Seven to eight months of the year a snowbound country, then spring flooding for another two months. What to do? The fertile lands were under constant threat of attack. In some places it was Turks, in others Crimean Tatars, in still others Mongol hordes of varying size and all kinds of mountain tribes. And the Cossacks paid lip service to the tsar's authority, while in reality they enjoyed robbing and carousing. You couldn't force them to push a plow if you whipped them. And if you tried to settle the land with *muzhiks* (peasants) who knew how to work it, the Cossacks would rob them and then lure them into service in their roving gangs.

Peter I began fighting the Turks. He took the Sea of Azov with great difficulty. He had to give it back; he couldn't hold on to it. He went into Moldavia with Wallachia (the Prutsky Expedition) and was captured; his wife had to pay his ransom. The Derbent Expedition ended up being a bust. The Ottoman Empire was still strong then, too much for Russia to handle. So they started the Northern War against the Swedes. It took almost twenty years, and they won by the skin of their teeth. Sweden was weakened then, after the Thirty Years' War, and the king, Charles XII, was very young and foolish. So, Russia got access to the sea, started doing some trade. But that didn't solve the main question, what is now called "the issue of national food security." It didn't add any arable lands. And the country still needed non-freezing ports. They had to go back to fighting the Turks.

So Catherine II declared war on the Turks. It didn't go well at first, but then they got the hang of it (Potemkin, the Orlovs, Rumyantsev, Suvorov) and it moved along. Russia took all the northern lands above the Black Sea, the Kuban, they conquered the Crimea…. They began settling the regions, building ports for trade and military use. They plowed the land, gathered their first harvests. Life grew easier. It was the Golden Age of Catherine the Great. The population kept growing. And there wasn't enough land to feed them all.

They kept going. Georgia, fertile but with bad connections. Over the Caucasus Mountains with their hostile tribes. From the south, Persians and Turks again. More war. Alexander I and Nicholas I and even Alexander II all made their mark in the region. They reached Erzerum. They also had the idea of annexing the Balkans and making Constantinople the empire's capital: The

Balkan peoples were Eastern Orthodox Christian, and they would accept the Russian tsar over a sultan. But the European nations got in on the act. They wouldn't let Russia do it. England and France started a war in the Crimea and stopped our expansion. The Terek was Russian and safe, and Georgia was fine, too. But the population kept growing. We needed more land.

And so Alexander I started toward Asia. He was excited by the stories his tutor Zhukovsky had told him about Alexander the Great. The Russians took the land with fire and sword, crossing the Amu Darya and the Panj rivers, the Salang Pass, and, beyond that, Peshawar, Kabul—all held by the British crown. They stopped and looked around. Oh my, look how much they had conquered! Time to settle the lands. And the people kept multiplying. Then serfdom was abolished. People fled the villages. Some to the cities, some to the new lands. They held a new census and gasped: were the biggest country in Europe.

Alexander III and Nicholas II built lots of railroads, the better to handle Mother Russia. Then the Trans-Siberian Railroad began. Stolypin broke up the peasant communes. They began taking over southern Siberia. A population forecast was made for thirty years in the future and beyond. An honest one, not like the Soviet Gosplan. Four hundred million people in the Russian empire by 1940! In 1980, six hundred million. How about that?

"And then came the Hegemon and everything fell to ashes." Whenever people proudly claim that the Bolsheviks industrialized the country and won the war, the question must be asked: "At what cost?" The answer is simple. The price was approximately fifty million killed in the war and the camps, and a hundred fifty million who were not born as a result—in today's numbers, the equivalent of another Russia. Each of us is shadowed by a fellow countryman who was not born. Thank you, Comrade Stalin, for our happy childhood.

The present demographic situation is monstrous. The ethnic Russian population is declining. The population is aging. Soon, very soon, there will be two pensioners for every worker. This despite the fact that the life expectancy, especially of men, is only around sixty. In the not too distant future, Russia will be primarily Muslim.

Even the territory left in the Russian Federation after the collapse of the Soviet Union is too much for us. For three years in a row we've harvested more grain than we can eat. For a hundred forty million people. So there. It's time to admit a terrible thing: The country's population is incapable of servicing its territory. There are not enough us for all that space: the Center, the Urals, Siberia, the Far East, and the endless Russian North. I'm sure scholars have a formula for the relationship between the size of a country and the minimal population needed to guarantee its sovereignty. I mean, so that there is a sense that there is a state on that territory. Pensions, education (at least primary), health and welfare, police, border guards, postal service, communications. I'm not even talking about outside aggression.

Let's take stock so far. Our great ancestors conquered a country for us in which a population of three hundred to three hundred fifty million people could live in relative comfort, without crowding, productively and purposefully. That was what they were counting on. That's what they worked for. Having that goal in mind, they died believing that they had not lived in vain. And then we, and most of all our grandparents, thinking about Russia's special path, through hard labor and wars (Civil, Finnish, Afghan, Chechen…), through abortions and divorces, vodka and prisons, denunciations and camps, brought the population of Russia down to one hundred forty million—and the number of ethnic Russians even lower (no one knows if there are even eighty million ethnic Russians).

No more emotionalism. To put it simply, for three hundred years Russia's goal has been to make its territory (especially in terms of quality) match its growing population. Now the situation is reversed. We need to make population match the country's size. Let's look at all the possible sources of population growth.

Of course, we have to bring back to Russia all the people in the CIS countries who consider Russia their homeland. It looks as if that tactic has been exhausted already. Probably everyone who wanted to move here from Kazakhstan and Central Asia already has done so—and brought along some Tajiks, too. And people from the Caucasus. With a dollop of Georgians, Armenians, and Azeris. Russians don't seem to be in a hurry to leave the Baltic countries, despite all the "discrimination against the Russian-speaking population" they claim to suffer there. I don't think they will move. They're not stupid. They're practically in Europe already, while here in Russia it's back to visas, ineptness, and all the other nonsense. I doubt anything will happen in Ukraine. They might come back to work in Russia, but they won't move with their families. There's no housing or steady work. God only knows how it will end in Russia, while in "Khokhlandia" (from the Russian derogatory slang word for Ukrainian, *khokhol*) life may not be much, but at least it's settled.

Let's ask ourselves if there ever was a country that faced the problem of needing a steep increase in population to master its territory. The answer is obvious: The United States of America in the nineteenth century. After the annexation of Louisiana, Texas, and California and the pioneers moving to the Midwest, the country realized it had to settle the new lands. Natural growth of the existing population would not solve the problem in the foreseeable future.

Across the Atlantic Ocean lay overpopulated Europe, with its wars, cruel monarchs, famines, pogroms, epidemics, and all the others joys of life at that time. One potato crop failure in Ireland gave America a million citizens. Pogroms against Jews in tsarist Russia: another million. Colonists moved in droves to America, the Promised Land, with rivers of milk and banks of honey. Where they gave out land for free on a first-come, first-served basis to whoever got there first and marked it. The state realized the positive aspect of this and created an efficient bureaucratic machine for naturalizing the newcomers. Anyone who has been to the museum of immigration on Ellis Island in New York can appreciate the scope of that process. In the course of a few decades, millions of people came to America and found a new homeland there.

Of course, you will say that the Old World was rather close to America on the sociocultural plane. It was primarily Christian, and tied to the New World by an enormous number of familial and historical bonds. The flow of that population did not demand overcoming a cultural barrier between the local population and the arriving colonists.

In Russia the situation is much worse. Potential sources of new immigrants must meet two criteria: Life in their countries must be much worse than in Russia, and there must be excruciating overpopulation. Only Southern and Southeast Asia meet those criteria today. To be more precise, mainland China and India.

India is better for us, for the following reasons. First of all, Indians have a better idea of the European mode of thinking (as a result of British occupation) and speak English well, which will make the initial interactions easier. Second, Indians—judging by their behavior in other countries to which they have migrated (U.S., Great Britain, UAR, the Arab oil states)—are not aggressive, try to get a good education, and fit in.

However, there are obstacles to stimulating a flow of Indians to Russia. First of all, the climate. Indians will simply die from the cold in wintertime. They've seen nothing like it in England or Canada. Yoga is not going to help. And then, what would they do here? Russia's industrial centers already suffer from relative overpopulation, and Indians are not going to move out to the sticks, particularly Siberia or the Far East, because without the experience of surviving in our conditions and without knowing enough about our agriculture, they will not be able to assure themselves of a better life than they had back home in India.

So that leaves China. We have to face it: An influx of Chinese immigrants is inevitable. In fact, that process has been going on for a long time, and there are more than a million Chinese immigrants here already. You have to be blind not to notice.

And really, it makes perfect sense. There are fifty to seventy million Chinese people living along our far eastern border; on the other side of it, there is emptiness (we're lucky if there are a million people there). The climate isn't an issue—it's unlikely to be more moderate on the Chinese side of the Amur and Ussuri rivers than in Siberia.

Cultural gap? What do they care? Chinese chauvinism over the four millennia of Chinese ethnos and statehood is so much a part of the national mentality that they feel no need for international socializing, or even for formal contact with our government institutions. Fake marriages are no problem. From their point of view, they're just giving the stupid customs of the local aborigines their due. If that's what they want (think the Chinese), if that's the easiest way to legalize my position, and it's no skin off of my back, then let that silly girl pretend to be my wife for two days for a hundred bucks. No point in studying Russian. We need only the most rudimentary vocabulary to sell in flea markets. Anyway, Russian is a temporary phenomenon: in ten years, we Chinese will be the majority, and those barbarians will start learning Chinese.

The Chinese concept that the whole world is divided into the Celestial Kingdom and the Barbarians is comparable only to the Ancient Greeks. A culture's belief in its own exceptional, categorically superior nature can be so strong it requires no proof; it's similar to our stubborn belief in certain elements of Russian spirituality.

The aggressive Chinese expansion into the Russian Far East is, in a way, a kind of occupation. These aren't Indians, who always behave like guests. These are vital, adaptable, self-sufficient workaholics, who do not scorn any business, be it prostitution or drug trafficking or a respectable small retail trade like tailoring—or even agriculture. The omnivorous nature of the Chinese, healthy in immigrants, flourishes like a lush flower in the soil of Russian corruption, shiftlessness, and indolence.

So, I repeat, Chinese expansion is inevitable. We can't deceive ourselves into thinking that it can be checked through stricter measures of state regulation. This, I think, is how the situation is perceived in the mass consciousness: "If nothing is done, the Chinese expansion will continue at increasing rates; in the near future, they will be the absolute majority of the population in the Far East, and, further down the line, Russian sovereignty of the territory will come under question. But (that thinking goes) if we tighten border controls, limit Chinese entry into our territory, and deport those who are here illegally, we can avoid the expansion."

In my opinion, that is incorrect, and, forgive me, naïve. The migration of large masses of Chinese people into Russian territory is inevitable. Opposing it is like trying to stop a hurricane—the movement of air from a region of high pressure to a region of low pressure. (What is Chinese migration to our Far East but the flow of people from a high-density region to a low-density one?) This process cannot be stopped by any state measure, no matter how severe: All the cohorts and legions of Rome could not hold back the "great movement of people," despite their iron discipline, decimation, and other shows of empirical will and power. What can a state do in the face of laws of nature?

The wisdom of nations and the governments they appoint lies in not wasting energy or wealth in the service of old fetishes of national homogeneity. To stubbornly resist historical and biological processes that are planetary in scale is maniacal; in such an unequal battle, defeat will be as complete as it is inevitable. True wisdom lies in putting those processes to use for the nation's prosperity. Eastern wisdom says: "Yield and conquer." That is the basis of the philosophy of judo, by the way.

The alternatives, in fact, are the following: Either, through draconian measures, the state regulates and tries to stop Chinese migration, and then ends up with it in almost the same levels, but now completely illegal and basically criminal, giving rise to ethnic conflicts, hatred, and a surge of corruption among the bureaucrats who have anything to do with illegal immigrants. With our general skinhead xenophobia, this could lead to a full-on, bloody slaughter. Or, on the other hand, we maximally ease the procedure for the legalization of immigrants and focus our efforts and means on developing a speedy and efficient technology for the adaptation and naturalization of new citizens. For instance, and I'm just being delirious here, why not draft all new citizens of the right age for army service?

If the procedure for naturalization is simple and understandable, and if the immigrant can acquire now-vacant land—or work in his new country and have the opportunity to open his own business, however small—then what we will have, in rather short order, are millions of loyal and hard-working citizens. This has been demonstrated in the experience of Chinese immigration to the U.S. and other countries. And the desire for higher education among the Chinese is a commonplace by now.

* * *

Svinarenko's Commentary on Kokh's Commentary:

Chekhov wrote about the inevitability of Chinese expansion back in 1890: "You start running into the Chinese in Irkutsk, and here they are as thick as flies.... The Chinese will take the Amur from us—that's indisputable.... Everyone laughs that Russia is fussing over Bulgaria, which isn't worth a plugged kopeck, and has completely forgotten the Amur River."

Solzhenitsyn raised the issue, too, back in the days when Chinese restaurants in Moscow were considered exotic. For all that, he felt that the Chinese would take away Siberia and the Far East rather than assimilate. The example of the British settling the American prairies is useful, I think, because it supports the version that Solzhenitsyn and I share. The settlers did not assimilate with the local population, like the Comanches, but instead imposed their ideology on the New World, instilled their language, religion, and traditions. To succeed, they first carried out ethnic cleansing. Out of fairness, NATO should bomb the U.S. as much as it did Yugoslavia for its ethnic cleansing. But let's set aside issues of morality and justice. Looking at it cynically, the white immigrants built a fairly decent country on those empty, dreary prairies dotted with the occasional wigwam. It looks as if the Chinese are planning to take that route, especially since I don't think they have a choice. I've seen the wonderful new cities built in China over the last five to ten years. They're not the cardboard, ticky-tacky housing put up in Russia for Russian refugees from the former Soviet republics. ("Russian refugee" sounds oxymoronic; try to imagine American refugees or even Chinese ones). I've been to those settlements in central Russia. But the Chinese are building themselves modern megapolises with skyscrapers and transportation hubs. We're not building cities like that in Russia today. And the Russian refugees aren't going to plow with oxen in knee-deep water, or eat boiled chicken claws, or transport the harvest on freight bicycles, as the Chinese do easily. We also have to remember that, according to statistics, there are ten Chinese for every Russian. That's a much more catastrophic imbalance than nine Russian men for every ten women. For the time being, these overwhelming forces are multiplying very slowly, because of strict sanctions in China against having more than one child per family. In Russia, their numbers will multiply uncontrollably. (Not so with the Russians themselves, who are not kept by anyone from procreating—whose quasi-state religion actually calls upon them to do so. Be fruitful and multiply…. All the preconditions are there, but no….)

Continuation of Kokh's Interrupted Commentary:

These sources for an increase in population by immigration do not preclude the most important one: We need to have babies. More and more. The nation must realize that it has no choice. Either ethnic Russians start having children, or the nation will disappear as an independent ethnos in a historically brief time. It will age and die out. It will be assimilated, diluted, crossbred. It's not enough to have children. The children must be healthy and viable—people who can guarantee themselves and their own children worthy lives. Not winos and homeless bums, not layabouts and leeches, but energetic citizens, confident in their strength. Citizens who see that the quality of their life is a function of their labor.

Now let's look at the situation from another side. Here is a family. Two sexually mature adults, a man and a woman. They live and prosper. They screw and have a baby. Then they gradually get sick of each other. Starting with an innocent flirtation on the side, and then serious affairs. And now he's torn: On the one hand, a bored and boring wife; on the other, his new one and only. How didn't I notice before that this is my destiny, how could I have married that bitch, and so on. Alcohol. The inevitable break-up and divorce, with the wardrobe being sawed in half.

The old wife and child are left behind, and an attempt is made to start a new nuclear family. At first, once again, everything is fine. Summer vacations, romantic evenings. Then the same old grind, a new baby, washing machine…. Flirtation on the side. Damn it, the old prostate acting up. Viagra. She's so young and beautiful. What a bastard I am. She loves me so much. Pension. Old age. Death.

Let's sum up: Three healthy women and one man manage to create two children. And was he the only man? The three ladies probably had had other affairs. With contraception and maybe two or three abortions. Four people created two children. And one of them grows up in a broken family (juvenile hall, eternal hopelessness, misery, a mother who grew old before her time working three jobs, and hatred for the father who abandoned them). And it's all the fault of monogamy. Monogamy is a luxury for a dying nation. Especially when that nation is under threat of another energetic people unburdened by the prejudices of a custom that came from somewhere or other.

The more contemporary institution of polygamy in Islamic countries shows its effectiveness both demographically and financially. It seems to me that it does allow all three women to realize their basic destiny to become a mother—more than once. The children in such marriages are not brought up feeling hurt or damaged. They do not have the complexes found in children of broken families.

That's my reasoning. And practice is ahead of custom, with illegitimate children becoming more and more the norm. We must institutionalize the existing phenomenon. After all, polygamous patriarchal marriage is to me a more natural phenomenon than same-sex marriage with the right to adopt children. What are they going to teach them?

Naturally, the polygamous marriages must be voluntary. But give it some commonsense thought: Is it better to be left alone with a baby in your arms while your former husband—the baby's father—comes around once a month, if you're lucky, to play with the child and give the family a sweaty hundred-ruble bill? Or to be in the honorable (and fully legitimate, that is, with the right to inheritance) position of elder wife?

Of course, the suffragette ladies will start waving their hands at me and screaming about male chauvinism. Let 'em. I am convinced that the great majority of single women—both those who have been dumped by "morally unstable" husbands and those who are prevented from being with their lovers by the ball and chain of marriage—would have agreed to polygamy a long time ago if it hadn't been for our famous concern for their equality, an equality that dooms them to a lonely, impoverished, and often childless old age.

Abandoning wives is swinish behavior, in my opinion. That is, if there are children. When there are no children, it's baloney—not a marriage, just screwing with a bit of ceremony.

* * *

You were already married in 1982, Alik?

I'd been married for two years, we had our daughter! I got married at nineteen! And you were a bachelor and screwed German girls.

Why do you say screwed that way? It was a radiant and grand feeling that I kept through the years. We're still family friends. I was a bachelor at the time, temporarily; it was a break between family lives.

Svinarenko's Commentary:

It really was grand and radiant. You will laugh, but in the evenings, my German girlfriend played the violin for me. She got an A in Russian, apparently thanks to me. It's interesting: When I was in a good mood, we spoke German, and when I was in a bad mood, Russian. When we were both in a bad mood, we'd revert to our native tongues. It's funny that she was a Communist. When I tried anti-Communist agitation, she called me a fool. We would argue and sleep apart. It ended with her leaving and marrying a Communist, and now they are both out of work. She called me recently and told me that she called their fourth child Sven. "I'm touched," I said. "Really touched. I didn't expect that." "You idiot," she replied. "It's not in your honor. The baby was conceived in Sweden."

* * *

How many times have you been married, Igor?

With a license, twice. And there were several relationships that the courts would have recognized as common-law marriages.

Ah, keeping a joint household.

Yes.

How many children do you have and with how many wives?

The two children, fortunately, are with only one wife. My present one.

Well, Igor, I'm telling you that by my lights, I don't know how you see it, but you've only had one wife. And still have her. The rest? So, you slept together, so you cooked porridge together. So what? "How many times have I done that for nothing…" Remember that, in Hemingway? The portrait of Mr. Whatever-his-name-was, in Montreux.

This reminds me, Alik, did you know one of our friends took a cure at La Prairie in Montreux?

Alcoholism?

No, cirrhosis.

Oh, so that he could go on drinking.

Have you ever been there?

No.

On the ground floor of the clinic there's a regular restaurant and bar. You can drop in and drink and eat like a normal person. Or you can have gruel made with water and raw carrots, for your health. So, he's staying there, treating his liver. The guys come to visit him. He takes everyone to the bar, orders carrots and all that shit, and fat-free water. Then he invites us upstairs to see his rooms. He opens the refrigerator, takes out a bottle of vodka, cuts up some salami, and says, let's have a toast. Are you fucking crazy? You're on a diet! He replies, "Hold on, didn't I eat my porridge? I did. So now I can take a break. I'll go back down to eat porridge again for dinner." So he starts boozing. Listen, we said, you're spending so much money for this clinic—

—And he'll tell everyone how he took the cure for his liver.

—and he says, Big deal, money. I've got lots of money.

By the way, dear friend Alik. I've gotten a glimpse into the meaning of capitalism and privatization just sitting here with you. Look: We had two fish, a big one and a little one. You told me straight away that the little one was better. I started with that, figuring that I would also get a piece of the big one from you. But you've eaten the whole big fish faster than I ate the little one.

No.

I can see. Then you told me: Here, have some more, and magically pulled out another small fish from under the newspaper covering the plate. Eat this, you say. Two small ones are almost like one big one.

So Alik, after this, are you still trying to tell me that you managed Russia's privatization honestly? Well, well …

Back to my alcohol point: So, I said to him, How can you drink vodka all day with a liver like that? You're going to die; you have to stop drinking. And he says, You know, I've only got two or three years to live, in any case.

A regular Prince Hamlet, the bastard.

That was eight years ago. Back then, he said, So I'll drink for two years. and it will be over. And I said, Hold on, you're missing two nuances here.

Well, of course. What if he doesn't die?

No. First, no one can guarantee you even those two years. And second, it's not only that man is mortal—

But that he is suddenly mortal.

That's it—suddenly mortal. He goes to take a leak thinking, I'll have a pee, and then I'll do something with my life.

"But Annushka has already spilled the oil." And you slip on it and die. Bulgakov's *The Master and Margarita*: "Yes, man is mortal, but that's only half the problem. What's bad is that he is sometimes suddenly mortal, that's the trick! He cannot even say what he will be doing this evening."

You go to pee and never come back. He thought about it for a bit … and changed the subject.

Alik! Tell me something. You're so passionate about polygamy, I need to know: Have you practiced it yourself?

No. No, no. Not in my meaning of the word: A wife is someone with whom you have children.

Well then, I had a friend in 1982. He has children from three wives. That's not counting his first wife, because those children are already grown. And one day one of his girlfriends becomes pregnant. In your terminology she was not yet a wife, but a kind of fiancée. He says, Stop! I've got a wife, and I have children with her. And now here's another one pregnant. She's not too eager to have the baby, but he's deeply devout, was even church warden—

Warden, that's our level!

Anyway, he's a religious Russian Orthodox man, and he didn't want her to have an abortion.

That's right.

That's not all he decided. He decided to live without lies, as Solzhenitsyn called on Russia to do.

Oh-ho. And what is that?

Well, I fucked the girl—

So I have to tell all the other girls—

Including my wife—

Now that's stupid.

Wait, that's only the beginning. There's more.

Where is it written that you have to inform your wife? He is guilty not before his wife, but before God! And He sees everything, you don't need to report to Him.

But a father should bring up his children?

Yes, he should.

And a family must live together?

Yes.

Thus, he decided, let the new girl have the baby and we'll all live together.

Ho ho! Hee hee!

So anyway, he persuaded his wife to live without lies. They all went off to Siberia to live there.

How many people?

One woman with two children and one with the baby. And him.

And how did he use them?

How am I supposed to know?

Didn't he tell you? In what order … or did they all go to bed together?

Alik, Alik! You have nothing but sex on the mind! He was worried about something else entirely. We discussed the theological aspect of the question. He considered converting to Islam.

There was nothing else he could do.

But he said that he couldn't because he loved Christ.

Muslims also love Christ.

But not as much.

Hahaha! Who measures degrees of love? It either exists or it doesn't.

Why are you laughing again?

All right, let's be serious. Look, when you read the Bible—

They're all polygamous.

Yes. Abraham has a wife and several concubines. And the children of the concubines were considered legal. Isaac, Jacob, Joseph, and so on, all the way to Solomon, who had a fucking horde of wives and concubines. "Even though discord based on jealousy and family quarrels is possible among several wives of a single man, however *in reality* life often creates amicable relations among them, since one wife lightens the work of the other and helps create well-being for them all. The Bible tells us that wives of patriarchs brought concubines to their husbands." *Brockhaus and Efron Encyclopedia,* in the "Polygamy" article. And then: "And Solomon had 700 wives and 300 concubines." 3 Kings 11:3. And then all of sudden there's monogamy. How did that transition occur?

It's very simple. Let me explain.

I'm all ears.

Before, people lived without lies and now they all fuck each other but tell everyone that they lead monogamous lives.

Why don't you tell me how the family model switched from polygamy to monogamy? You can read and read the Holy Scripture and find nothing about monogamy.

And Christ?

Christ was unmarried.

But he wasn't a virgin.

No one knows really, Igor. The only thing he said about all that was that if you have adulterous thoughts, you've committed adultery. I quote: "You have heard that it was said, 'Do not commit adultery.' But I tell you that anyone who looks at a woman lustfully has already committed adultery with her in his heart." Matthew 5:27–28.

You mean he didn't see any difference between real and virtual sex?

A nice piece of ass walks by, and you think how good it would be to have it. And that's a sin. But if you don't think that, then your problem isn't ethical, it's medical. Because then you're either impotent or homosexual.

And he also goes on to say an important thing that a lot of people misunderstand; it deals with this contradiction. He says, basically, that there are two commandments that are the most important: Love God with all your heart and soul, and love thy neighbor as thyself. That's it, the entirety of the law and all the rules: "Thou shalt love the Lord thy God with all thy heart, and with all thy soul, and with all thy mind. This is the first and great commandment. And the second is like unto it, Thou shalt love thy neighbor as thyself. On these two commandments hang all the law and the prophets." Matthew 22:36–40.

Great plan. In other words, you fuck your wife, and you can fuck his wife, too. Love thy neighbor as thyself.

Keep it up, then you'll be fucking him, too, Igor, and masturbating. Don't blaspheme. We'll cross out what you said. No, Jesus simply thinks that if a person loves people, does good for them, then that is significantly more important than whether that person is screwing around or not…. All that was Moses' invention. Remember the old joke about Moses going up the mountain, with the Jewish people waiting below in the Sinai Desert? He's struggling, fighting up there, lightning bolts and smoke…. He comes back down and says: "I bring you the law from God. It has one hundred twenty commandments." And he starts reading them out. The Jews listen and listen, and then they say, Moses, fuck off. Go back up there and work things out with God. We don't like this. He parted the sea, did a lot of stuff, but now he's setting up so many conditions, we'd rather go back to Egypt. So there."

And they did return to Egypt, in the Six Days' War, Alik!

…So Moses want back up to argue with God. He came and said, "Jews, I have good news and bad news. The good news is that there are only ten commandments now. The bad news is that adultery is still in there."

That's a harsh joke. And then there are the Mormons. It turns out that in internal discussions they were beginning to consider giving up polygamy. People think we're queer, they said.

Well, certainly not queer! Hahaha. Do we toss this, too, or leave it in the text?

I don't know, Alik. Let me continue my story about my friend's polygamy? So they went into the *taiga*, deep in the forest.

Anyway, first one wife left him, then the other, then he moved to a former Soviet republic and had another child there. He was serious about it. Fucking, seeking the truth, loving Christ—he wanted to combine them all.

He wasn't too good with the second commandment—love thy neighbor. All his women were miserable.

But he wanted to do what was best.

And it came out as usual.

Enough! Alik, back to 1982. As for that German carnival at the Pedagogical Institute, I went there for the closing in March 1983.

You're getting into '83 already!

But I started out for the carnival in '82 and got there in '83.

We'll talk about it next time.

In Kaluga, despite the state produce program, you could buy eggs and smoked *moiva* and those packaged cheese products—which suited me fine.

Native Kaluga foods.

There were different kinds of vodka. From the *haute cuisine* point of view, it suited me.

What's *haute cuisine*?

High cooking. In French. Like *haute couture*.

Ah…

Well, according to media mogul Sergei Lisovsky, that's what is completely lacking in Moscow. The poor fellow has to drag himself to Paris or London for a decent meal. There's just nothing to eat at all in Moscow or Vienna.

He hasn't been to Berlin.

They say there's good cuisine now even in Dar-es-Salaam; the Indians brought it. But nothing in Moscow.

His partner Vladimir Zhechkov is the same way.

Come on!

He keeps saying, This is crap, there's nothing to eat. He stuffs himself, leans back, and—burping delicately—announces that there is nothing to eat. Haha! And no place to eat. In St. Petersburg, either. There's absolutely nowhere to go in St. Pete at all.

I'm really going to screw you up now, Alik: Gluttony is a mortal sin!

Where is that written? The monks wrote that. The Lord never talked about it.

To hear you talk, the Lord never said anything about anything—all he wanted was for you to drink, smoke, fuck, and deprive yourself of nothing.

He didn't say anything about smoking, that's for sure.

So you say that you can do what you want, stand on your head—

—just love people. That's all. And don't forget your God. That's it!

Fine. But let's get back to 1982.

There are some good jokes about Brezhnev. One of my favorites is when he convened the Politburo and says, "Comrades, I have to tell you terrible news: Arvid Yanovich Pelshe is getting senile." "Goodness, Leonid Ilyich, why do you say that?" "Because he is! I was walking down the hall today and I said, 'Hello, Arvid Yanovich.' And he says, 'Hello, Leonid Ilyich. Only I'm not Arvid Yanovich.' You see, he doesn't even know who he is anymore."

And there's another good one about Brezhnev. He says, "You're all pigs, totally unrefined and impolite. I'm ashamed to be in your company. Last night at Suslov's funeral, when the band struck up, I was the only one to ask a lady to dance."

Well, if we're talking about the end of the Brezhnev era…then what kind of country is this, where we had a leader like that and lived that way and yet everyone felt fine and happy.

Happy. I'm very pleased with my youth. It was my youth; it was merry, good, and profound. It was saturated. I have nothing to regret about my youth, even though it took place in the Brezhnev-Andropov-Chernenko period.

That's not what I mean, Alik. You know I'm talking about the fact that the country could be run that way. One sixth of the planet's land mass and a superpower. And everyone saying, Oh, that's fine. So maybe

this period now is only a temporary surge of will power that will fade away quickly? And we'll be back to dancing on Suslov's grave. If you start the day doing nothing, drinking beer and burping, and then suddenly you do 15 minutes of work, those minutes mean nothing. And you go back to the beer. What kind of worker are you? You're not. And it's the same thing here. We lived under Brezhnev and no one gave a shit. And now we have a strict and wise leader. He's getting everyone in line, including the vertical command and control structure. But this could pass, too, like those 15 minutes of work—and once again people will be back to drinking beer and not giving a shit. And eating those little cheeses. Different people need different things, Alik.

We've tried it all. Even *foie gras*. So what?

You and I had *foie gras* last night, what of it?

You did. I didn't.

All right, you had *jamon*. There was nothing special about eating *foie gras*, right? It's been better.

So.

So, maybe everything will return?

Shut up. As our Communist friends like to say—

People have better devils than you do friends.

You know what else they say, Igor? The Russians are unique, adding the historic phrase, "They're the only nation that is satisfied with little." The nation has very modest needs.

Yes, the needs are very low.

Whose? Yours or mine?

The Russians'.

Ah.
And what relation do you have to the Russian people?

I live among them.

My mother is Russian. So I have blood ties, too.

So, according to Jewish custom, you're Russian; otherwise, you're German, is that it?

Let's get back to 1982.

I would like to sum up the discussion on polygamy and adultery.

From what point of view?

You keep saying this is written and this is not.

We're bookish people, Igor.

And I've just come up with a very powerful argument.

Let's have it.

What was the lifespan of the people you keep quoting? Methuselah and so on.

You mean the old patriarchs? They lived hundreds of years. Abraham was 175. "And these [are] the days of the years of Abraham's life which he lived, a hundred threescore and fifteen years." Genesis 25:7.

All right, let's say it was 175 years. When did they start writing? Not at fifteen?

So.

It's what I thought. I could tell a deep and great thought was coming up on me, and here it is. How old are you now?

Forty-one.

And do you want to fuck more now than you did twenty years ago?

Less.

How much less?

[*After a pause to weigh and compare, comes the verdict with great authority*]: Ten times less.

Now imagine that your interest falls by another ten times when you're sixty-one, and by the time you start, at age 141, writing the rules of who can fuck and how many wives he can have, you don't remember about sex at all. So you're not going to say a single word about it. Then your descendants will say: We don't know anything about this, there are no instructions or limits on fucking. Alfred Kokh has given us permission to fuck whatever moves. [*This is a slight echo of the main theme, the extreme age of the leader who ran the country until 1982.*]

Agreed. The hormonal factor is present. If we go back to the New Testament, Jesus is, according to various calculations, between 22 and 27. Hormonally, in good shape. That's why he's more permissive about sex.

And maybe the Book should not be read prematurely, Alik, but at the right moment. Not at 10 or 17 but at 60.

Well, 1982 is turning out rather ingloriously. How did you imagine your life would be twenty years later? What did you think you'd be doing?

I had a very clear picture of my biography. I would go to graduate school, defend my dissertation, get a job—first as assistant, and then as senior instructor, and then assistant professor. I doubted they would let me become a full professor because of all the things my parents and I had done... So, today I would be a docent. But it would have been a good position. I would be a doctor, dissertation defended, 100 percent secure. And with a salary half that of a professor in a low-prestige college, I'd be getting five hundred a month... I'd vacation in Varna, travel to Prague and Warsaw, Riga and Tallinn. Sochi every year. And I'd have a good car.

You'd buy a Volga.

Oh, no. I wouldn't be able to afford a Volga. But something like a good Zhiguli, that I'd have. I think I'd have a dacha, half an acre. Near St. Petersburg, in a good location, in Mgla or Luga.

Maybe you would have been happier than you are now.

Well, certainly not less.

No one would attack you.

No one would attack me, but I would be dumber.

Why?

I wouldn't know the world.

What world?

The entire world!

So now you know it, Alik, and so what? A wise man learns about the world without leaving his courtyard, the ancient Chinese used to say.

That's bullshit. Last summer I went to the monastery in Saint-Michel. In Normandy, you know? It's so beautiful. And I was in a grove of sequoias in California, the biggest trees in the world. Can you understand that without seeing them? No! Or Niagara Falls? Or Capri? Naples? Or to watch the waitresses in the Neapolitan cafes casually toss leftovers into the bay and put back clean plates on your table? There's Santa Lucia for you. Or the laundry hanging across the street? Or being cut off by Vespas? How can you miss that? Or Vesuvius? Can you tell me why we're supposed to be deprived of that? To only guess that these things exist? See them only in photographs? How about seeing the *Mona Lisa* at the Louvre? Strolling on the Champs Élysées or in the Latin Quarter? Having a meal in little restaurant? Why be deprived of that?

But a large part of the Russian population is still deprived of that! Even after your privatization.

They've deprived themselves of it. The state hasn't. They haven't earned the money. All right, the state hasn't helped them make money, it's screwed them. But at least it's not forbidding them to go to Paris whenever they want.

But on the other hand, what is the main goal? To save your soul, to suffer. Suffer... so that...

Bullshit, Igor. What you are saying is bullshit. Where is that written? Tell me, where?

You are a Pharisee and a bibliophile.

I'm no Pharisee. But a bibliophile—of course. We have a book religion. The text is sufficient and independent. The text is our religion. Here is the text that is called the New Testament—and that is our religion. What is written there is holy and what is not is just made up. A monk sits around, jerking off in his room and suffering, and then announces that all the other people who believe in our Lord Jesus Christ but do not suffer as he does will not be saved. That's because he doesn't want to suffer alone. He wants everyone else to suffer. Misery loves company. Why do we need these interpreters? Let's listen to the voice of God!

But we know it only in the delivery of reporters: Matthew, John, Luke, and Mark...

At least it's firsthand reporting.

You're not telling me you don't know how reporters write? Go read a newspaper.

Remember how Bulgakov has Yeshua responding to the written list of his sins? This, this, and that. And Yeshua says, Everything written here is a lie. I never said or did any of these things. But nevertheless, we have no other way out.

Kokh's Commentary:

In *The Master and Margarita*, it is put this way:

> "You, for example, are a liar. It is written very clearly: Incited people to destroy the temple. People have testified to this.
>
> "Those good people," said the prisoner, "learned nothing and mixed up everything I said. I am beginning to fear that this confusion will continue for a very long time. And all because they do not record accurately what I say."
>
> A silence fell. Now both ailing eyes gazed heavily upon the prisoner.
>
> "I repeat, and for the last time: stop pretending to be mad, robber," Pilate said softly and in a monotone. "There is not much written about you, but it is enough to see you hanged."
>
> "No, no, Hegemon," the prisoner said, straining to convince him. "There's just one who follows me around with goat parchment, constantly writing. But I took a look once at that parchment, and I was horrified. Nothing at all of what is written there have I ever said. I begged him: for God's sake, burn your parchment! But he tore it out of my hands and ran off."

* * *

You've set yourself up in a fine way, Alik; I can do what I want, I don't owe anyone anything, nothing is written anywhere, all I have to do is love people and that's it. Terrific. Very clever!

I'm not being clever! That's the way it really is. Ha-ha-ha-ha.

All right then, how are you different from a pagan?

Listen, pal, do you want a punch in the mouth?

Where is it written that you should punch me? Where is it written that khokhols get punched in the mouth? Really....

At least the ones who accuse you of paganism. That's easy. Listen, unlike pagans, I believe in a single God. Omniscient and omnipresent.

You must admit that this doesn't require great effort on your part.

That's what you think.... It's not obvious at all. Because one wants to believe in the god of water, the god of the sea, earth, wind, and fire.

I've never wanted to, Alik.

Well, in any case, about 90 percent of people tend toward paganism. Because they believe in ghosts, superstitions, god of the hearth, crickets, table-turning, all kinds of crap! On the level of daily life, paganism appears everywhere. And secondly, I have no god but God. No one is an authority for me. I don't bow down to some idiot. I don't make sacrifices to anyone.

What do you mean by anyone? People?

And gods, because I have only one God, and, as you know, He does not require sacrifices. He sacrificed His own Son. That is the fundamental difference between Christianity and other religions. In other religions, God demands that people make sacrifices for him; in Christianity, God made the sacrifice. A fundamental inversion.

But a faith like that doesn't require great effort on your part.

God only sends trials that you can handle. He never sends tribulations that are impossible—because He has forbidden suicide. If He sends a trial that is beyond a person's strength, that person will kill himself. As for money, that's a separate discussion—for 1990.

2.

1983

The Second Bottle

The main topic of 1983 is the fact that is was the first time a Chekist—a KGB man—came to power, a rehearsal for Putin. The second main topic is drunkenness.

By that year, one of the authors, Kokh, had graduated from the institute and begun working in Leningrad, the hometown of Vladimir Vladimirovich Putin. The second author, Svinarenko, continued his work at the Kaluga Komsomol newspaper and went on a business trip to the German Democratic Republic, where Putin was at the time, working for the KGB. Now, from today's vantage point, they recall what they saw and understood back then, positioned as they were in two fundamentally important geographical locations—places to which the guarantor of the Constitution had made prolonged visits on his way to the Kremlin.

The theme of drunkenness is not accidental. It is touched upon because in 1983 the Soviet people were given a cheap vodka called "Andropovka." The electorate let out a collective sigh of relief.

So, Alik, you were in the cradle of the revolution with Putin, while I was making another trip to the GDR, where he was working. It's as if we were doing reconnaissance. As if we had known... Let's define briefly what each of us was doing then.

I had graduated from the institute. There was a long drinking spree—our whole dorm partied for a couple of months to mark our graduation. Then the bout of drinking ended, and I started graduate school. Here's the story: I was studying economic cybernetics. And the dean of the department asked me to come study there. Actually, I'm telling a white lie: I was from out of town, and I didn't have a permit to stay in Leningrad. The department had a place reserved for someone who would then be obligated to go teach at Krasnoyarsk University. And so I—

—made an arrangement with General Alexander Lebed. He was still alive then. Or with Oleg Deripaska.

No. This was 1983! What are you blabbering about, Igor? Naturally, getting a Leningrad boy to go to grad school and get a degree just to go teach at Krasnoyarsk University was hopeless.

So you went, knowing that you'd be able to avoid Krasnoyarsk?

No, actually, I didn't know… In 1983 I was a rather pure, naïve boy. Despite working as a janitor for a year. And having developed a taste for vodka even before that.

Were you a janitor like the one in *The Twelve Chairs*?

No. Even though I like the lines from the book: "The janitor's room was warm to the point of stinking. The janitor's felt boots didn't add any ozone to the air either." So. There was a lot of angst about getting into grad school, at least among the out-of-towners—

—the exiles, the state-repressed—

Yes, yes! And so I was given my chance. I was invited to apply; I passed the entrance exams and the minimal requirements for a degree candidate. I did well, in fact. I think I even got an A in English, though I still don't speak it particularly well… And then as it turned out, the day after I began my dean up and died.

I was assigned to some professor who didn't want to work with me, spent a year doing nothing. It was only in 1984 that I was assigned to a real scholar.

Listen, why did you go into science?

First, what do you mean, why? And second, you're slipping into interview mode again, sir!

Slipping, am I? Well, Alik, it's a professional deformity of the psyche. All right. As for me, I was still working at the Kaluga paper. I had met a German girl, the one I didn't reach in 1982 because of the death of one L. I. Brezhnev. And so I entered into an unlawful relationship.

Why unlawful? We discussed it in the last chapter and decided that it was a good thing.

Well then, into a lawful relationship. Alik. The important thing is: "They" tried to recruit me that year.

Oh, oh! Why you? And what I really want to know is this: Did they want you to work for them or just be a snitch?

A snitch.

And now, of course, you're going to tell us that in the end you were not recruited.

Naturally!

That's what they all say.

I refused. But I was afraid to tell them the real reason, so I tried to wriggle out of it....

The old "It's not my thing"...?

Yes. But I was too shit-scared to tell them about my political convictions, which made me totally opposed to working for the KGB.

Totally opposed? What, you were born a dissident?

Not born one, no, but around 1981 I got my hands on *Gulag Archipelago*. Once I read it, I fell under the sway of its rhetoric: the monstrousness of the Bolsheviks and all that, you remember.

Yes.

It got to me, it tore me apart. And I had fallen into bad company. My friends would say, If you join *that party* we'll not only refuse to say hello to you, we won't even sit down next to you to take a shit. But basically, it's all Solzhenitsyn's fault. Before I read him I used to think, Well, Grandpa Lenin loved little children, as all that propaganda went, what the hell, everything's fine. And I had been brought up to think that Chekists and that whole crowd were clearly decent people... And then my own grandfather was a Chekist—

Ah, your grandfather was a Chekist?

Yes, not an exile like yours... A real Chekist! First he served in the Komsomol regional committee. In those days it wasn't like now, I mean like 1983. In 1919, that career led you down a different path. You had to sleep with your pistol under your pillow... After that he worked in a food redistribution platoon, and then in special forces as a machine gunner—

you can imagine what kinds of questions were resolved with machine guns...

Executions.

Probably. Then they transferred him to Kharkov, to the provincial Cheka headquarters. They showed him the barracks and the dining hall, then took him down to the cellar. He said, What's that stink? You'll get used to it, they said. This is where we waste them. You what? Well, we bring 'em down here and shoot them in the back of the head with a Nagant revolver.

And the blood was rotting on the walls?

No, the blood just dries up. What rots is the brains. Hmm. Are we getting too enthralled by the Cheka theme? Since we have nothing against V. V. Putin, eh? At a tender age, I accepted all this; I thought, right, there's the enemy, he doesn't like us; who knows what he'll think up next, so give him a bullet in the brain. And then that Solzhenitsyn crept up on me.... But my grandfather figured it all out without Solzhenitsyn. In 1992, before he died, he said to me, holding up his dry, aged hands: "I killed so many people with these hands! I gave my whole life, my whole mind to the party, they told me you have to kill for a better life, and I killed. And now it's too late, you can't change anything. And our life, it turns out, is worse than everyone else's."

Kokh's Commentary:

Here, my brain just refuses to comprehend. When I look at our history between 1917 and 1956, I fall into a stupor. You can start to believe Lev Gumilev, with his phases and stages of development of the ethnos.

In terms of logic, I can understand (but not accept) Hitler. In fact, in order to bring the people around the *Führer*, you have to invent an external enemy—in his case, the Jews—and then involve the whole nation in bloodshed.

I can understand (but not accept) the passion of the Revolution and the Civil War. Up against the wall with all those capitalists and landowners—those lousy exploiters. I don't understand why they had to get rid of priests, professors, and cultural figures. But all right, let's say they overdid it in the heat of revolutionary zeal.

But then, but then! The Civil War is over: You've conquered everyone you wanted to conquer. Some of them you've killed, some are in prison, some have managed to leave the country. No one is keeping you from building your Utopia. But instead, what happens? Denunciations, anonymous letters, false testimony.

And frequently it's mutual. Brothers denouncing brothers, sons denouncing fathers, wives husbands and husbands wives … and so on and so forth. Pitting neighbor against neighbor or comrade against comrade becomes as easy as taking a leak. The slightest excuse is enough—his wife is beautiful, we need the room in the communal flat, a promotion at work. It might be even simpler: He punched me out when we were drunk, so I'll write an anonymous letter about him. "It is my duty to inform…. He recited Our Father in the toilet…. Sincerely, A well-wisher." And he's gone…. Disappeared somewhere. Brrrr. There he is! Wielding a hoe, nonstop. Icicles dripping from his forehead. Dystrophy…. And now he's kicked the bucket. There he is, in the second layer of corpses, sprinkled with lye. Why do they bother with lye in the permafrost?

And then things get more interesting. Comrades, this is a mistake! I'm an honest man! You're not honest, you bastard. A punch in the teeth. In the liver. The solar plexus. Prisoner Pupkin, when we read your accusation to him, remembered he had had counterrevolutionary conversations with you, and that you shared his opinion, you bastard…. And there it is. An honest confession is the crown of evidence. It lightens your conscience and lengthens your term. And off went the Stolypin train … down the rails … the railroad … where the express train speeds…. In other words, to Vorkuta and the camps.

How many people did Stalin and his henchmen kill and imprison after the Civil War? Say, a hundred thousand. Maybe two hundred. They couldn't have done more. First of all, they didn't have more enemies than that—real or imagined. Second, the human mind can't remember the names and images of more people than that. But there were millions, tens of millions of people arrested and killed. And all those millions were done in by an evil dictator. That was the creativity of the masses. That was enthusiasm and vigilance. That was denunciations and anonymous letters.

And it wasn't Stalin and Molotov and Beria shooting the Menshevik offal in the back of the head at night in the Kremlin. No, that was thousands of peasant boys, dressed in uniforms, shooting their brothers.

Millions of Russians destroyed by the words and deeds of more millions of Russians.

People often say that the Jews created the revolution. Say that were true (although it isn't). Afterward, after the revolution, it wasn't the Jews who forced people to write anonymous denunciations. That was done voluntarily, not under the whip. While of sound mind and clear memory. That was done by the God-fearing people. By the way, the Jews got it almost as bad as the Chechens and Kalmyks.

I sometimes think that some kind of self-destructive mechanism was set off in the ethnos, which then infected the entire nation like an epidemic. On TV, they'll sometimes show herds of whales that for no apparent reason start beaching themselves. Kind people come in rowboats and cutters to drag them back out to sea. And they beach themselves again, over and over.... Like the salmon that spawn and then refuse to go on living. Or a giant herd of antelope racing toward a cliff.

The way God destroyed Sodom and Gomorrah. And here, it was as if someone had commanded: "Kill one another, and destroy your nation."

If you take the population of any species of mammal and kill ten percent of the strongest sexually mature males, then take another twenty percent of the strongest sexually mature males and females and isolate them from the population and one another for their entire reproductive period—well, after that experiment (some kind of anti-eugenics), the question of what will happen to the population becomes rhetorical. In the worst case, it will die out; in the best, it will degenerate and be reduced in number.

The Russian nation did that to itself. Voluntarily. It vanquished the occupying army, but not the envy of neighbors. And yet it is written in the Good Book: "You shall not bear false witness against your neighbor.

"You shall not covet your neighbor's house. You shall not covet your neighbor's wife, nor his male or female slave, nor his ox or ass, nor anything else that belongs to him." Exodus 20:16-17

The people are punished by self-extermination for that envy of neighbors and denunciation of neighbors.

In school, we studied words called homonyms. That is, words that sound the same but have different meanings. For example, raise/raze. Sometimes it seems to me that the word *Russian* has become a homonym. It has two meanings. The first is the name for people who lived in our country before 1917. The second is the name for the Russian-speaking Europoids who live there now. They are two different peoples. With different attitudes toward each other, toward their history and their goals.

* * *

One night, Alik, my grandfather was awakened by shots in the building. He grabbed his rifle and ran toward the sounds—it could have been almost anything. He and his comrades found the room and flung open the door, and there was the Cheka commissar of the school for the province. He was sitting on the bed with the smoking gun in his hand, staring blankly at the wall. He had been shooting at it. Oh, they said, that's nothing; he gets that way sometimes. He had served in frontline units and had personally executed more than seven hundred people, after which he got a little strange, so they transferred him to teaching.

Why was he shooting, then?

Very simple. When you kill someone, that person comes to you later, as if alive. So those seven hundred people would visit the commissar. And he would shoot at them as if they were alive, until the bullets ran out. And you couldn't take away his pistol, because the circumstances they were working in were complicated. You couldn't be without your pistol—the enemy class was all around you.

Did they visit your grandfather, too?

Of course. He told me that even if you kill someone in wartime with your machine-gun—this was the Second World War, in the infantry. He had left the Cheka after the Civil War and spent the rest of his life working in the mines. He said even a German, pardon me Alik, even he will come to you.

People have forgotten all that now, Igor! I remember in the early 1990s people were so aware of that. And now they've forgotten. And they say: But at least there was industrialization as well as the camps!

Yes… Anyway, in 1983 I found all that unpleasant. Profoundly unpleasant. So I could not be friends with the KGB on any account. I tried to get away as best I could, telling them that I drink, that I'm terribly scatter-brained… All my sins are written on my face….

They'd be better off with a guy with an honest Komsomol face…

Yes. And I had read books like *"How To Behave Under Interrogation."* There were all kinds of tricks. For instance, when the Chekist turns the conversation to unpleasant things, you have to ask questions in response. They get upset right away and say: I'm asking the questions here! And then you say: Ah, so this isn't a chat, it's an interrogation! Then let's keep a record, with a written explanation of what case you're interrogating me about, in what capacity, and who's accused of what, and whether or not this is in contradiction of our Constitution and the Helsinki Accords signed by the USSR—and you just keep that up. They don't like it when you take it literally. In any case, they didn't like it then—who knows what they're like now. That rhetoric would not have impressed my grandfather at all in 1920, but in 1983, in those gentler vegetarian times, it worked.

So, what happened? Did the Chekist give up and apologize?

Naturally. Oh, sorry, he said, this is just a chat, let's chat. I had him figured out. He made an appointment to meet on the boulevard. I came a half hour early and saw him run around the building looking for the janitor—to get the key to the secret apartment. It was amusing to watch. At the appointed hour I walked up to him, having watched him from my hunting blind, so to speak. So I wasn't so scared.

And how did he try to influence you? How did he work you over?

He had some minimally compromising information on me. Someone had snitched. I suspect a certain guy—he dreamed of joining the Party, which was hard for journalists, and so he must have earned points this way, anyway someone had told them that I owned banned books. Berdyaev, Lev Shestov, some other philosophers—harmless... And so they said to me that the essay "Spirits of the Russian Revolution," written by one of the above, was anti-Soviet. How can it be anti-Soviet—there was no Soviet regime on the horizon when it was written, and the revolution in the title was the one of 1905. They said, you should have guessed. All right, I said, why can you read it while I can't? He didn't have a good answer... And then he went on: Come on, work for us and we'll forgive you. "I can't!" I said. Why not? he asked, figuring I didn't have a thing to go on. But I said, "The honor of an officer, you believe in that, don't you? Well then, you'll understand. I'm a lieutenant in the reserves (we had military training at the university), and I can't snitch on my comrades."

You said that? No shit?

I'm telling you, Alik, that's exactly what I said. I think the real thing was this: I didn't value my career very much. I quit Soviet newspapers from time to time when they got to be too disgusting. Those old types were still sitting on the regional committee—all puffed up like turkeys, trying to look smart, couldn't say a damned word. There was a lady in charge of the newspapers and propaganda there, she looked just like Goebbels! An amazing likeness—imagine that, eh? In general, there was no great joy there. And if they had kicked me off paper, fuck them, I'd just have gone to work on some construction site. Big deal! I think that's why they let up on me—they saw that I wasn't afraid of losing my job. (What kind of work was that for them? Why did officers have to do that? Why did they waste a major on me? He made three times my salary...) All right, I didn't give a shit. But if you imagine poor provincial intelligentsia, who really did become part of the Soviet life, who stood in lines for apartments and cars—when they were threatened, I imagine a lot of them cracked.

Many years later the manager of a fancy nightclub explained it to me with an illustrative example: At the club, some of the girls start offering intimate services starting from the first night, while others only dance at first. But when the virgin sees her friends making easy money through prostitution week after week, she either gives in or quits. The latter is much rarer. But you exiled Germans, I don't see any amusing stories about the Cheka from you. I won't force you to speak…

Sorry, I can't tell you anything about being recruited. I had such a constant reputation as a pissy anti-Soviet that no one ever tried to recruit me or asked me to join the party. I was very un-ambivalently on the other side of the barricades. They were more likely to look for people in my circles to snitch on me. Which, however, did not keep me from getting a job at a secret facility in 1987.

Don't skip ahead! Let's go in order. So, Andropov came to power in 1982 and got into it in 1983.

And in February 1984, he croaked. Yes…Andropovka vodka on the one hand and on the other, his crackdown on work discipline, so that people who skipped work were arrested in movie theaters. Did they do that in Kaluga?

Yes. But as a reporter, it was easy for me to avoid it.: "Are you crazy, I'm here in the beer hall lying in wait with other reporters from the *Komsomol Projector* for a story, quiet!" To me, the meaning of this particular year is that it was the first time a Chekist was in power.

Yes. That was like John the Baptist.

I wanted to say John the Baptist, but I bit my tongue. And you barked it out without thinking, Alik.

Why without thinking?

How can a Chekist be a Baptist?

You're not going to deny that V. V. Putin is the Christ of the Russian land? Or will you? Come on, Igor, just look me in the eye!

Boy, you exile types do talk crazy…

He's just like a savior.

But he has already lived too long.

How long did Christ live? Tell me, then.

From the previous chapter of our book, you must know that the exact lifespan of Christ on earth is not known, but some data indicate 33 to 37 years.

Oh, yes, that's right.

Perhaps, in comparing Putin with Christ, you want to say that it's not clear what either of them actually did for most of their lives? That it is hidden in the murky dark?

And then, suddenly, right into Jerusalem.

Let's say that... But which of us played the ass on which he rode in?

Pavel Borodin! Hahaha.

Not bad. So, we could say that the Putin era began in 1983. But not very successfully.

Why not successfully? What wasn't successful about it? Look, they gave the people Andropovka to drink at 4.70 rubles a bottle, and that raised Andropov's popularity among the people. I didn't give a shit where he was leading the country, but I'll tell you what I said back then: Look at our great fortune, we have a leader who's in his right mind! He understands what he's saying. I was so sick of Brezhnev with his mush mouth.

Remember the joke about how he would pronounce "sotsstrany" just like "sosiski-sranye"—turning Socialist nations into crappy hot-dogs! But even though Andropov enunciated, he didn't say anything useful. *Also sprach Zarathustra*. He didn't sprach for shit. Hmmm... Look, all Andropov needed to do to win popularity was produce cheap vodka. Putin had a harder time in that sense, because there was plenty of cheap vodka floating around. It's no longer the case that a man's monthly salary is enough for just ten bottles of vodka; thank the party for that. A man can put away a bottle a day.

Without damaging the family budget.

So Putin, to get people to like him, had to put the squeeze on Jewish oligarchs.

Svinarenko's Commentary:

Here's another way to compare Andropov and Putin. Both went through the procedure of elections. I voted for the former and didn't even bother going to the polls for the latter. Here's how the first went. It was either 1979 or 1980, and there were elections to the Supreme Soviet USSR or RSFSR. I was a student in Leipzig. So, one Sunday morning at 6 o'clock there was loud knocking on my door. I opened it… Men in civilian clothes who spoke Russian without an accent told me to get dressed quickly and come with them. What else could I do? I went… They brought me to a bus parked by the dorm and they loaded up all the Russian dorm residents. "So, they've taken all of us," I thought.

They took us to the Soviet Consulate. At the entrance near a bust of Lenin there was a group of Pioneers in white shirts and red ties, saluting. So these fellows in civilian dress led me to the voting urns and made sure that I cast my vote for Yu. V. Andropov without fail; he was nominated, as I recall, by the workers of the Gorky Television Factory. Maybe it was a message for Sakharov, who had been exiled to that city, a reminder of the iron hand? I voted… As for Putin, I didn't go to vote for him because there weren't any elections by then. There was an appointment. What kind of election is it when the other candidates don't have a chance? If you recall, the "election" was announced in such a way that no one had a chance to prepare for it. Besides which, thank goodness, no one dragged me out of bed so early in the morning… I should note that on the day of the national approval of Putin's appointment as president (which the press called an election), I wasn't even in the country. I was on a business trip to Santiago-de-Chile.

* * *

The people's love has grown more expensive, dear Igor. And let's not forget: Yeltsin made vodka cheap, but he didn't get the people's love…

He didn't make it cheap, it just became cheap.

But he created the conditions for it. By the way, I'm afraid that the people's love will keep on going up in price; the bar will be raised, and a couple of oligarch's heads won't be enough to buy it… That's why Yeltsin didn't get the people's love, because he didn't chop off heads.

And how can you have the people's love without that? It doesn't exist without it, alas.

That's very sad.

Eh, Alik, just who gives a fuck whether it's sad or not? It's true, and that's the way it is. Valery Abramkin, honored *zek* [prison camp inmate] of the USSR, told me that in some of the prisons he had observed real democracy at work. Everything was decided collegially, collectively. But if that goes on for too long, people get tired, and they don't like it anymore.

Then a criminal boss comes along, and they give all the power to him. People have a need for a strong hand—that's not empty talk, there's a reason it gets so much attention. Abramkin's theory is that people have a very strange but profound need for an external conscience—to let other people make the decisions, to free them from the burden of choice so that they can always lay the responsibility on someone else. If things go bad, it's not the people's fault, it wasn't their idea... But you can't attack the boss, either. This scheme creates a balance in society. Under Brezhnev, you could do whatever you wanted, stand on your head—and the people got tired of it. They wanted a strong hand! And it is always found. And given to them.

The worst thing is when you have a strong hand—

Let's not get sidetracked into a conversation between two romantic democrats.

No, no. And I have nothing against a strong hand, when it is strong. I developed a lot of my mentality in Chile. We got some training from ministers who were in the Pinochet government.

Well, it's a long story with Chile, Igor. When we get to 1991—that's when I went there—we can go into more detail. A strong hand, when it's really strong, that's harmonious; it's a dictatorship in its complete, mature form. Pinochet didn't try to pass himself off as a democrat, which he was not. He knew they needed to build a liberal economy, and he built it; he knew they needed to stifle the opposition, and he stifled it. Just as he was supposed to.

It's much worse and more dangerous for the nation as a whole, especially a non-law-abiding nation like Russia, when the strong hand is not strong. And when he knows, deep in his heart, that that's the case.

It's like the Chinese situation with the Communist Party.

Yes.

They shoot bribe-takers, and the economy is on the rise.

Svinarenko's Commentary:

About a strong hand....

The tenth anniversary of Pinochet's regime was in 1983. I wrote about it this way: "Then, in 1973, I would gladly have gone to fight in Chile for Allende against Pinochet. I would have wielded my native Kalashnikov with such profound feeling! I would have tenderly learned Spanish words like *venceremos* and *no pasaran*! I would have rushed into battle, unafraid of death, under a simple homemade red flag! I would have been excited by meetings with left-wing girls who certainly would have traveled there—still hot from 1968 in Paris! Oh, ho-ho.... It seemed beautiful, easy, and lovely to be left-wing and kill those who interfered with the establishment of justice—in whatever form suits you best. Yes.... If you're not a leftist at 20, you have no heart. If you haven't become a conservative by 30, you have no brain. How wonderful it is that sometimes God does not allow our dreams to come true!"

And further: "It pained me to think that we, unlike the Chileans, did not manage to seize power from our leftists in 1973. We had Russian Communists an extra 18 years in our country, and in half of Europe, they forced their primitive concepts on others, hated anyone who was richer or smarter, robbed people and shared the loot, sent diversionary forces and killers into decent countries, instigated Afghans and Africans to war, squashed Magyars and Czechs under tanks.... Basically, their usual foul acts. The mighty old man Pinochet spared his country the humiliations that are inevitable under a Communist regime. He overthrew the regime when he got sick and tired of it, when he couldn't stand it any more. Unlike the Eastern Europeans, who waited for permission from the kindly foreigner Gorbachev, Grandpa-General Pinochet acted like a man, and shot from the hip.

But we didn't have anyone in those years who could have brought the country in line with common sense. Who had the strength, the intelligence, and the conscience. It just didn't work out that way.

* * *

What's much worse and more dangerous for the country, especially one that is not law-abiding, like Russia, is when the strong hand is not strong. And deep in his heart, the man understands that.

Are you talking about Andropov?

No, Igor, about someone else.

Ah, there is such a man, and we all know him.

Yes, yes. And I'm sure that deep in his heart he understands that he's not a strong hand and that his entourage plays the role of the strong hand. But he can't control the entourage.

A strong hand is like a very firm handshake…the firmest possible.

There are strong people in the entourage. They may not be very smart, but they are tough… So, in order not to look foolish before the entourage, the not-strong hand starts playing at being a strong hand. And then he usually overacts the part. Like the prosecutor in Vladimir Voinovich's book who was so afraid that people would find out he was kind that he demanded the death sentence for everyone. A strong man who knows he is strong doesn't need to appear strong. Understand?

It's like the fag who makes a point of spending time with whores.

Well, that would be a latent fag. Real fags don't hide that they're fags.

That's what we're talking about—strong, firm hands and not-strong ones.

In that sense, Andropov was a balanced personality. A strong man: He shot down the Korean plane.

Svinarenko's Commentary:

The foreign media were talking—even then—about terrorists and bombs. But Chief of Staff Marshal Nikolai Ogarkov admitted right away that Soviet fighter jets had "stopped" the plane with two air-to-air missiles, and, as we remember, accused the South Korean plane of spying for the United States. No one believed that, and it reached the point that eleven Western states stopped air traffic with the Soviet Union—only for two months, though.

Interestingly, during his visit to Seoul in November 1992, President Boris Yeltsin called the actions of the Soviet military "mistaken," and expressed deep regret over the tragedy that had played out over Sakhalin. Soon after, in 1997, there were reports that a former high-ranking Japanese military intelligence agent confessed that the South Korean plane had been on an assignment from the American intelligence services; it flew over us to activate the Soviet anti-aircraft system and pinpoint the radio-location stations. The real intelligence planes couldn't do it—the system picked them out right away without revealing itself.

There was also the ship. All these equipment-failure catastrophes were happening, for no apparent reason. The specialists started blathering that this was just the beginning, but no one listened.

On June 7, 1983, TASS made this report: "From the Central Committee of the CPSU and the Council of Ministers. On June 5 on the Volga, near Ulyanovsk, the passenger ship *Alexander Suvorov* had an accident with human losses. The Central Committee and the Council of Ministers express profound sympathy to the victims' families."

This is what had happened: The ship, for some reason, attempted to pass under a low point on the bridge. The upper deck was too high: It was sheared off, along with the captain's bridge and the film auditorium, which was packed with people. To make things worse, a freight train was crossing the river just at that moment. It was hit with such force that it spilled logs and coal onto the ship.

In the end, one hundred seventy-six people died.

Then they started investigating. Since it was the cook's birthday, they decided that everyone must have been drunk. But then they dredged up the bodies of the navigator and wheelsman, and there was no alcohol in their blood. Witnesses later recalled that the navigator had been very engrossed in a mystery novel with a complicated plot. Booze had actually saved quite a few people—those who were drinking in their cabins instead of going to the movies or taking the fresh air out on deck. The press wrote about two families traveling on that ship—the wives had both passed on the vodka, only to die in the film auditorium, suffering horribly.

Since they could not find any live culprits, they gave the captain ten years. He served six, was paroled, and soon after died of cardiac arrest; they say he had taken it all to heart.

* * *

Alik! Let's pose a hypothetical question: What if Andropov had survived?

Then maybe we would have had reforms earlier. I mean economic ones. Political ones would have been doomed, of course—the same reason the Chinese are still all in uniform.

So, it was a rehearsal for Putin.

I don't know, Igor, analysts are trying to convince us that Andropov was a proponent of economic transformations—à la liberalism—but there were legends like that about Beria, too. And Khrushchev had him shot for attacking the bases of socialism.

President Ronald Reagan was hopping mad over the downed plane, but Andropov kept calm: "Reagan? Who's that? Why don't I know the name?" I think that Andropov shot down the plane not to show the Americans how tough he was, but to show us Russians. Think about it.

I will. He also wrote poetry.

Yes, maintaining the image of a liberal and enlightened person.

Kokh's Commentary:

Actually, in my opinion, there is nothing more dangerous for civil society than the intelligence agencies in power. I'm not talking specifically about the KGB or FSB, CIA, MI6, or Mossad. Just intelligence agencies per se.

For what is an agent of an intelligence agency, if he is a good one?

First of all, he has learned that he is the country's elite. And it doesn't matter whether it is the elite or not. The important point is that he thinks it is. That's what he was taught.

Second, he has been trained to conspiracy. He likes conspiracy, he believes in it, he lives it. He does not understand the need for public power. He does not believe that when a politician publicly declare his motives, they are true. He has been taught that public statements are made only to distract people, and in fact, people's real motives are as a rule constant and simple: eat, shit, copulate, and yearn for gold. He despises people.

Third, he was taught to love abstract states and abstract people. Just as concepts. For him the priority of the interests of the state over the interests of the people is obvious. Or, to put it another way: the interests of the state are the interests of the people, and the people cannot have interests that are separate from the interests of the state.

Fourth, because of the specific nature of the intelligence services, he has been trained to despise the law. There is no crime that he would not commit in the name of the interests of that abstract state. The law is for plebeians, and he is the elite. He protects the security of the state, which is populated by tiny, unreasoning creatures (the people). For the sake of the security of those people he keeps them in ignorance of his thoughts and actions and is prepared to take on terrible sins. The plebeians cannot understand that. He is a god and there is only one law for him—his superior.

From these four points it is clear that the authorities must maintain the strictest control over the agencies. The authorities must not be integrated with the intelligence agencies. Comrade Stalin in the thirty years of his rule purged the agencies three times, killing Chekists by the thousands (the Yagoda, Yezhov, and Kobulov-Merkulov waves). The FBI had a major shake-up after Hoover. I'm certain that analogous events occurred in all the secret agencies of the world.

But if the agencies are subordinate to structures that were formed by former intelligence agents, that is, by people with this mentality, then the very method of management becomes nontransparent. The agencies formulate their goals, evaluate their own work (always very highly, for some reason), and award themselves decorations (by secret decree). The state becomes an annex of the secret agencies. The authorities do not lower themselves to polemics with even a constructive opposition, and the response to any inconvenient question is: "So, you're asking why we are budgeting for inflation of 12% instead of 15%? Let us tell you that we know the real reasons for your question. You are not interested in the country's investment process. In actuality you are an adulterer and have a secret mistress. So there." Curtain. End of the debate.

Alik, let's get back to the proper events. So, I went to the German Democratic Republic, on a so-called friendship tour—our proletariat was taken there to drink with their proletariat. Well, there was a meeting, speeches from the stage, a banquet. In the morning our guys woke me up—Igor, we're going to die if you don't help us find some hair of the dog. What's the problem? There's a supermarket across the street—go get what you need, and drink it. But that's impossible, it's 7 a.m., they won't give us any now, we have to make a deal with the guys in the back... So, I went to the store with them. And it was chock full of drinks, from beer to liqueurs, and all kinds of things to snack on—and it was all almost free.

As it should be. Our government used to tell us then that it was doing us a huge favor by letting us have some vodka. They made it into the people's favorite form of entertainment, because it was hard to get.

And our proletarians said to me in that East German store, "What idiots we are, getting married in Russia, when we could be marrying German girls and living here! The vodka is cheap, there's tons of beer, the girls are easy, what more do you need?" They were prepared to sell out their homeland for a slice of salami, that's what the Communist Party had reduced them to. They suffered, they wept, they threw up—it was not easy for them to see life as it was in the GDR. We drove into a village, and they couldn't believe it was a village: It had paved roads, street lights, plumbing and sewers. It was hard for the proletariat—I don't know how it was for Putin. The KGB was very strict; we were watched to make sure we slept in our own beds—that's just an aside about the KGB in East Germany. In order to see one of the local girls, we had to go through a whole conspiratorial rigmarole.

Who did they think would be surprised if we made the Soviets look bad? You couldn't flee to the West from there—the Stasi would have found you for sure. As for the East Germans, they knew our faces very well.

It was deeper than that, Alik. On November 7, when I was studying in Leipzig, we were called in to the Soviet consulate, where they had flags, Pioneers, music—and they gave us a lecture about how all German women are whores, how we could screw them, but if we married one, that was the end, we'd be recalled to the Soviet Union and sent into the army. All this was spoken under the red banner in front of a bust of our leader.

Why couldn't you marry them?

You're asking me? How should I know? But on the whole, I can say this about the GDR: They had everything that Soviet citizens could only dream about.

Tell me, please, Igor, the standard of living of the GDR then: Was it higher or lower than today's in Russia?

I think that broadly people in the GDR lived better then than our people do today. They really had an abundance of goods, and high wages.

Well I'll give you the grub, but their threads were for shit!

They liked them. And there was a lot of Western stuff available. Jeans made in underground factories in the GDR cost 120 East German marks, but you could buy Wranglers on the black market for 160. Buy and wear 'em with no trouble. Of course, there were lines for cars, about a ten-year wait. But anyone could get an apartment. As I recall their life back then, it was nice and cozy…

Then why haven't they adjusted to Western life yet? If you were to unite Moscow with the FRG, everyone would blend in after a year, the workers and the whores…

Good question. I think because they had gone through a cold civil war. The GDR government let its people know that the Russians had conquered fascism so they were cooler than you; your fathers and grandfathers fought for Hitler, you should be ashamed of yourselves. So the government created a nation with a horrible inferiority complex. When they were drunk, the East Germans kept telling me how nobody loves them, and rightly so, what was there to love about them… I tried to console them, told them that nobody loves us khokhols, either, but we don't care. So there. The West Germans repented, started giving Jews money and apartments and traveling to kibbutzes. The West Germans seemed to have atoned for their sins of fascism. And the East Germans have not atoned for their Communism, because Communism, of course, is a wonderful thing…

So they have guilt without atonement? I can't agree with you there, Igor. Think of all the equipment we brought out of there after the war, isn't that atonement?

You capitalists measure everything by the buck…

Then, when Russian soldiers fucked German women, wasn't that their personal atonement? Expiation?

That's fucking ridiculous (sorry for the pun).

Then how come there are so many dark-haired people in Germany?

Drop it.

And there were no spiritual achievements. The East Germans had no literature, no films…

They saw everything from the West, they had FRG television. I think that Putin watched the same stuff as I did in the GDR. The same movies. Bertolucci's *1900*, Bob Fosse's *Cabaret*, Milos Forman's *One Flew Over the Cuckoo's Nest*. They all played in ordinary theaters. That expanded one's vision, naturally—things were still very somnolent in the Soviet Union. What else? Apparently, Putin bought Salamander shoes there— that was a joint enterprise between the East and West Germans. He went to beer halls, ate hot dogs and pig's feet, drank beer—

And gained a lot of weight. And he saved money—he brought back a Volga from there. What did you bring back?

Just a pair of trousers, that's all. I think Vladimir Vladimirovich drank less than I did, that's why he could buy a Volga.

He had a higher salary, too.

Probably. I got a stipend of 448.50 East German marks, which at the official exchange rate was worth 140 rubles. But there, that was enough for three pairs of brand-name jeans.

Which you sold on the black market.

No.

Look me in the eyes!

Sure. I'm looking. No, I didn't think of my jeans as currency. On my stipend I could drink 0.7 liters of brandy every day and even have some-thing to eat. By Soviet standards, that was sheer luxury. What can I say about it today? Life in the GDR was beautiful, merry, and easy. Even though they had their dissidents, and the Stasi oppressed them.

Dissidence in the GDR was expressed by climbing over the wall.

That's right. This may be the most important point: Everyone dreamed of escaping from the GDR. And Putin must not have liked sensing this. I think he felt like a prison camp guard: if you remove the barbed wire, everyone will run away, nobody likes you. … This tormented him so much, I think—and I hope I'm not overestimating him—that soon after, he created a situation where living in Russia is prestigious. They're not going to let just anyone in. And they'll even kick some out, who'll beg to come back but won't be allowed. And people will see that you have to earn the right to live in Russia. In part, it's the experience of the Wall. I remember that powerful sense of border: visible, real, palpable. When you see two rows of barbed wire with guards and German shepherds patrolling between them… And you see all this from a distance—you can't even get close to the barbed wire. I mean, Putin must have had a lot to think about when he was in the GDR during the Andropov period. He had to have thought about it.

Yes… So, you lived in the GDR and then went back to Kaluga.

All right…The topic of drinking is very important—in connection with Andropovka, with which Yuri Vladimirovich marked his ascension to the throne. Some fell for it, but some people kept on distilling their own *samogon.*

I made *samogon* myself. I started in 1983.

Do tell!

What's to tell? I did it in the kitchen, in our communal flat.

What was your recipe? I've already forgotten, even though I used to do it too. Do you remember?

Of course I do. You fill a jug with twenty liters of water, add 5 kilograms of sugar, crumble in a loaf of black bread and a stick of yeast, and after that it's a matter of taste. You can toss in a jar of fermented jam, or rinse a honey jar with boiling water and throw that in.

Did you grate potatoes? Add tomato paste?

No, no. But rotting apples—you can get them at the grocer's and run them through a meat grinder, that's good.

And then you put a hose on the neck, right?

Yes, definitely a hose. And then you start distilling. A pressure cooker—you put a tube on it, then a chemical glass pipette, you know, from a lab. I did it for a while, and then decided to make *braga* instead—why the fuck waste all that time? It was cheap and good enough: Twenty proof, sour, just the thing for student life. You can drink a lot—you can drink all day! It's called pruno in the U.S. Prisoners make it out of fruit.

It tastes like Chablis.

That depends on the additives. If it's pure bread, it smells only of bread… It must have been around that time that I discovered Havana Club. For degrees of proof per ruble, it was even better than Andropovka.

Svinarenko's Commentary:

The peak of my drinking came in 1983. I remember it very clearly, since in 1984, on the eve of the prohibition, I cut down sharply on my per capita consumption—I couldn't go on living that way. This was the first determined reduction in the series of reductions that followed. Back then I didn't distill my own; I drank official vodka and fortified wines like Kavkaz. I remember clearly, I still have that taste in my mouth, the taste of warm vodka that you drink out of a water glass and chase down with a warm piece of pink boiled sausage on a piece of crumbly black bread. Taken schematically, my life looked like the lives of a significant portion of the Soviet people: In the morning, go to work; at 11, a dose of hair of the dog; then some more work; and at 6, a trip to the store, and then onward…. Drinking until two or three in the morning. Interrupted by forays to procure more vodka, from cab drivers or restaurants—they didn't have all-night kiosks back then. The table talk was usually either discussions of books or edifying tales from the pages of life (abroad, mind you, but still rather limited in scope. That, and stories about trying to get girls into bed. It was a lot like *The Decameron*. On the whole, it was fun and educational, but I had a growing feeling that life was passing me by. Every day was the same. I could see my future: me, twenty years later, a seedy intellectual sitting on a bare mattress set over naked springs, unmatched socks all over the place, alone, the room impoverished, precious books of which I've grown tired on the shelves, no money, lots of debts, working for some dull clod or other, a view of sheds outside the window, and the stink of hake fried in margarine in the air….

And I wanted to do something grand! When you drink, though, it's not so bad. I guess that rut was exacerbated by Andropov's cheap vodka.

* * *

How much did you drink then, Alik?

Well, a friend and I could put away a bottle. I couldn't drink half a liter by myself then, it was too much for me. It still is.

A half-liter is too much for me now, but then I could manage a whole liter. It was fun! We drank a lot. My job as a rural journalist predisposed me to it. You'd drive to a kolkhoz on a jeep to write some deathless prose along the lines of: "Nevertheless, the rate of preparing feed leaves more to be desired. Per head of large horned cattle there are 13 centners of conditional feed units, whereas…." The chairman of the farm is expecting you, the table is set, the *salo* is sliced, the vodka is chilled, the lunchroom waitress has put on her make-up and pushed up her boobs. We can eat here, or if you prefer, go down to the river…

But let's get back to our sheep. As for the KGB, I've figured out why Yeltsin fired everyone. Anyone would have done the same thing in his place after a bit of thought. Well, you remember, there was renaming, re-staffing, reshaping, changing directors… In fact, it was a clean-up of the KGB. Even I tried to defend them back then: All right, get rid of the ones who pushed needles under the nails of dissidents. But some of them are chasing down spies and bandits, let them do their jobs! Yeltsin figured out faster than I did what had happened. He sat down and said: "So, I have this mighty machine, the KGB. What do I know about it personally? It's a secret police that is supposed to be protecting the state. Then how could the boys and I break up that state in Belovezh Preserve without a thing happening to us? And why did Gorbachev learn about it after the American president did?" Remember that?

Well, something like that, Igor. It may be apocryphal, but it sounds good. He may not have learned about it later than the American president, but he had even less influence over it than the American president did.

So, there were two possible versions of the story, if you wanted to explain why the KGB did nothing about Belovezh.
Version 1: The KGB didn't know what happened at Belovezh.
Version 2: They did know, but they failed to report back to Gorbachev.
The first variant is very bad—they're just spongers living off state funds and doing fuck-all. Now for the second: They knew but didn't tell…. Why? Because they were working for a regional leader (which Yeltsin was at the time)? Then tomorrow they could start working for the Chechens or the oligarchs against the Kremlin. Or were they working for the Americans? That's amusing, too. Or maybe they were waiting for the dust to settle and then join the victor? Or were they playing their own

game? All these possibilities are very bad, and each would require that the KGB be done away with. The state doesn't need a secret service like that. And so Yeltsin got rid of a useless—even harmful—structure.

Here's another version: They reported to Gorbachev, but he didn't take action. That's all. They couldn't act alone, and Gorbachev—because of his personal traits—didn't do anything.

Do you believe that Gorbachev knew, Alik? If he had known, he would have roared at them, or at least blabbed about it later… Do you actually believe that version?

Not really. He did give orders for the storming of the television center in Vilnius and for breaking up the demonstration in Tbilisi. He had guts. What would it have cost him to take those guys in Belovezh? He could just arrest them.

So then, it looks as if the KGB was just acting tough when it really didn't know anything, or how to do anything.

I agree with that completely. If you want my opinion, Igor, I support your first version. They knew nothing! They're complete… Well… All they know how to do is hassle businessmen. But they have nothing to do with the real security of the country. They can't do anything and never could, not even in Andropov's time. I think it's the same situation with the CIA and the FBI. Read some spy books—one organization is always trying to thwart the other. One annihilates the actions of the other. That's all. If they were both gone, I'd say thank the Lord.

All right. Now here's yet another version, Alik: Let's say the KGB understood that everything was about to collapse. They sat down and pondered. So, let's leave, take a temporary retreat, and let the democrats take power.

You're talking about 1991. What does that have to do with 1983?

Because 1983 was a rehearsal for the takeover by the Chekists. In 2000 they took power, but before that they gave it up in 1991. How could that have happened? They took the party gold, threw the guy who was in charge of that gold and of the Central Committee administrative affairs out the window, and all traces of the money vanished. They invested the gold in business and put Chekists or informers in charge… The plan was this: Let the democrats squabble and piss it all away, show what they're capable of—

—and then we give those Jewish businessmen our Vova Putin! Like idiots, they'll bring him to power, and then he'll destroy them.

Well, what do you think? A beautiful version, no? So, fellow citizens of Russia, are you pleased with your democrats? Not so much. So here we are with our strong hand, and you're happy now, aren't you? We are. So then, don't pull any crap we don't like… I should remember to write a thriller along these lines when I'm on vacation.

That's impossible.

Why? The Nazis ran off from the Reich, took all the gold, and hid.

But that went down differently: It was scattered, like a mosaic. They didn't come back, they didn't return to Germany ten years later, they didn't offer any kind of regime alternative to the occupation forces. Everyone stole his piece, and they're all holing up now in the jungle, each in his own villa.

Alik, are you serious? Do you really think that the KGB watched the growing arrogance of the democrats and didn't sense anything themselves, didn't prepare exit strategies? That they didn't study the Nazi experience, when they started transferring shares to other continents? That they didn't try to figure out a way to avoid the mistakes of the Nazis, who—as you say—couldn't come back? By the way, we may be underestimating their influence. I drank with some ethnic Germans in Chile whose parents had been real Nazis. And these guys are all officers and generals, not unimportant under Pinochet, and no one can actually say today that the economy of Chile wasn't built on the gold of the Reich. On its brain trust. Not a hundred percent, but some of it.

Let's assume that's true. It's all fine, except for one thing. In order to create such a project—so complex and difficult, with a large underground—you needed a brain center, you needed the leader of the project, the moral authority who sits offstage and pulls strings and makes everything work. Who is that? Who?

Listen, since Chubais is already to blame for everything, let's put him in charge of this project, too. It doesn't matter if we do it retroactively.

If he had been in charge then, they wouldn't be fucking him the way they are now. You know that, Igor.

Yeah, yeah, they're fucking him, and it's all for show—he feels great, in spite of it all. I wonder how much money he spends on all this PR that he's allegedly being fucked so violently? But somehow they can't fuck him to death. It's all a conspiracy, the kind the Chekists love.

Svinarenko's Commentary:

A word in defense of the Chekists.

Even though I am a dyed-in-the-wool anti-Soviet and Neanderthal anti-Communist who has hated the KGB for a long time, I will nevertheless approach the question soberly and impartially, as is my wont. Out of fairness, I will say that they have done a lot of good things for the country.

Since we are talking about the Cheka, let's look at one of the poetic definitions that the sell-out PR guys of the Communist Party came up with for them: knights of the Revolution. What is a revolution? How to describe it? We can use other poetic terms: a storm, the explosion of the wrath of the people, a bloody harvest, and other crap.

But let us describe the event in strong language, define the components of the Revolution, list the deeds that are integral to it. They include, without a doubt: murder, robbery, plunder—how could they not? And also terrorism ("We will respond to White terror with Red terror," and before that the romantic heroes of Soviet literature like Zhelyabov and the others, I forget their names, and Stalin, Kamo, Savinkov and others, they all were bomb-throwing killers). And—it goes without saying—banditry, organized crime, and mass riots. And also attempts on the life of a state or public figure. Also included: acts like violent seizure of power or violent retention of power, and armed rebellion. And let us not forget the gathering of evidence (using force, mockery, and torture)—an integral part of the revolutionary process!

You may be confused by the order of action—for some reason starting with murder and then terror, and only then mass riots. But it has nothing to do with me—that is the order in which the specialists decided to list these acts in our Criminal Code. The whole Revolution is in there, in a rather haphazard order. Just look:

Article 105. Murder—minimum 6 years.

Article 161. Robbery—minimum 1.

Article 162. Brigandry—minimum 3.

Article 205. Terrorism—minimum 5.

Article 209. Banditry—minimum 10.

Article 210. Organization of a criminal association (criminal organization)—minimum 7.

Article 212. Mass riots—minimum 4.

Article 277. Attempt on life of state or public figure—minimum 12.

Article 278. Violent seizure of power and violent retention of power—minimum 12.

Article 279. Armed rebellion—minimum 12.

Article 302. Forcing evidence (through violence, mockery or torture)—minimum 2.

Having committed all these acts, the participants in illegal armed formations won and took power. How can that be described in today's reality? It would be like Shamil Basayev's Chechen units destroying the federal army and the police, and taking the Kremlin, ferociously killing any officers or Russian Orthodox priests they catch on the street. This is what the rebellious Russian people did on a very broad scale, without any bin Ladens.

Should this be punished? Evidently, yes. But how? Of all those crimes, the very first one, under Article 105, is enough for execution or a life sentence. Hm….

For the sake of curiosity, try adding up the minimum sentences. You will laugh—it adds up to seventy-four years. Seventy-four years to be deprived of freedom! From 1917 until 1991….

Yes, ladies and gentlemen. Like it or not, the Revolution was but a long chain of criminal acts. Robbery, terror, and banditry. The fact that it was carried out by more than one person, by almost the entire nation, merely exacerbates the crime—the way gang members are punished more severely than individual criminals. In general, the people who were on the side of the Revolution were criminals. The punishment—deprivation of freedom—was a fair sentence for them. And not all of them were sent to the camps—far from it. The vast majority did their time in a lighter regimen: hard labor with chemicals, in settlements. They were in communal farms, kolkhozes. The labor was forced, of course. And the convicts did not get passports. But the regimen was rather free: They could live in separate housing instead of in the camps, and they could go into the city occasionally, with the permission of the camp (I mean, the kolkhoz) administration. It's well known that vodka only leads to trouble for convicts. So if there is no vodka in the camp zone, there's no problem. It was harder to manage on the farms—you can get high on fertilizer, after all.

Actually, the leniency of the punishment was unprecedented. We must be happy that our ancestors were merely sent to settle in places, that Russia was not bombed the way Yugoslavia was, even though there had been less illegality and crime there than in Russia.

So, really, what we needed was a bona fide trial, with all the formalities and procedures that would entail. But where could such a court have been found in the savage and ruined land—when even today, I fear, we still don't have such a court? The formalities were not applied, and the procedural side was dubious, to say the least; but in concept, it was correct. Vengeance followed crimes; there was punishment. Better than nothing.

And here is one more confirmation, on a more personal, emotional level. My grandfather was a Chekist, and he performed the job fully: he shed a lot of blood. But for all that, he was the nicest man. He volunteered for the front, he worked in the mines, he lived very modestly. On holidays, he could drink not even a glass, but a shot of wine. He exercised, worked in his garden, and personally tried to inculcate the habits of labor in his grandsons. He killed people because it was a Party directive, for the good of future generations. He had an excessive love of justice and a belief that it could be created by human hands. In his old age—dragging his leg, which was wounded in 1941, and using a cane—he worked for the Party Commission checking up on stores, hoping to arrest all the thieving managers. He never displayed any greed, or sadism, or love of power. I can easily picture a million young men like him, who came to work every day to their Cheka offices and worked at their jobs, using handguns, and sincerely believing that they were building a radiant future for new generations—that is, for us.

In that paradigm, Stalin was also a blind weapon of vengeance. ... Send those rebels to the kolkhoz, to the kolkhoz with them! That was even humanitarian compared with what they had done.....

Perhaps Stalin suspected this: after all, as a seminarian, he had to have read the Bible. The lesson with his son, who was imprisoned by the Germans, he also must have understood—for it is written in the Good Book: children will pay for the sins of their fathers unto the third and fourth generation. So, if one wishes, one can see a certain logic in concentration camps for the children of traitors of the Homeland.

One more argument: The peasantry as a class is not only unreliable—it rebelled against the tsar and created slaughter, and therefore could start killing, hanging, and burning Bolsheviks tomorrow—but it is economically unjustifiable. Who needs all those villages with their hovels and idiotic country *mores*? That's suitable only for Africa and impoverished Asia. We need individual farms (or we should buy grain from warm countries; we live in a zone that is risky for agriculture), and we should bankrupt the remaining peasants, so that they move to the cities and work like normal people in factories. Which is exactly what happened through the active intervention of the KGB.

I can understand that, from a human point of view. Why should we leave all those fighters, who had just killed half the population, scattered all over the country? We don't care in the name of what ideals and under what circumstances it was done; we know that these people can't be trusted. It would be like expecting loyalty and years of honest service from Chechen fighters, if they turned in their weapons tomorrow and joined kolkhozes.

3.

1984

The Third Bottle

The stagnation period had become extreme. Life stagnated. People gladly drank vodka, read vociferously, and had an animated interest in the "parallel culture" that was thriving beneath the radar.

In essence, the main characters of this book could have defined the situation this way: "I have bad news and good news. The Soviet regime will last for our lifetime, but it's so ineffectual that it won't interfere with our lives."

So, Alik, we're up to 1984. Incidentally, that's the title of a popular book by our colleague George Orwell. And, in fact, he guessed it right—1984 was the last full year of the Soviet system, because in 1985 it started going downhill. Alexander Blok had guessed it, too—"wearing the crown of thorns of the Revolution will come 1916." Well, he was just off by a year; that's acceptable.

Yes.... 1984 as the apotheosis of the stagnation period! Andropov died. In February, in the arms of his dialysis machine. Kidney failure. There was a story going around that the wife of Shchelokov (who had been a minister of the interior) asked to see him—

—and sprinkled heavy-metal salts into his tea? They make your kidneys fall out!

No salts, no tea—she shot him with a pistol, Igor! And got him right in the kidney. Andropov had put her husband away. So she got her revenge.

Are you serious about this?

No, of course not. However, Andropov, as I understand it, for all his Communist and totalitarian beliefs, was not at all stupid. I think he was sure that he would last another five years or so. Otherwise he wouldn't have taken the job. If he had known that he was doomed, he wouldn't have become General Secretary, and would have found himself a successor. But he took on the job and acted decisively—the Korean airliner, a few other things.... But then, *pow!* he was done for. I think something happened there....

He thought he would build a "vertical of power."

He thought he would, but you've seen what happened instead. Remember, in the first chapter, we talked about the fact that—

—man is suddenly mortal.

Unexpectedly, yes.... Something makes me think that something unexpected happened there, and that his term in office was abruptly—and quickly—cut off.

Back to business, Alik: What else happened in 1984?

Let's see, 1984. I started my dissertation. I went to the House of Architecture, to the very end of graduate school. My dissertation was on the development of cities, and they had very good seminars there on my topic. As you know, St. Petersburg *is* an architectural monument. The whole city, and especially its historical center. There was a debate between the progressives and the traditionalists. The main issue was this: Should you be able to build contemporary buildings in the historical center? The progressives, and I considered myself one of them, had a very interesting argument—

—that if you do nothing, change nothing, repair nothing, it will all fall apart.

Yes, of course, but that's merely a utilitarian argument. In a broader formulation, the argument was that St. Petersburg's historical center was built to be 70%. The historical center of a contemporary city is 70% office buildings. Therefore the existing structures do not correspond to the needs of a contemporary city. Residential buildings must be replaced by office buildings. That means you have to tear it everything down and build fresh. But even if you wanted to retain the old facades, didn't matter—at the time, they wouldn't allow knocking down of anything, the sense that all the historic interior components, all the supporting beams and engineering had to be retained. They wouldn't even allow the old rivets to be removed. The old apartments of those who would come from their country estates to spend the winter in town? They had only one toilet per floor because the lady and the gentleman had chamber pots brought to their bedrooms. In contemporary life, when not every renter has a roster of servants, this approach is unacceptable. One john per floor is not enough. So, that means new walls, new plumbing… Then, the wooden floors need to be changed to reinforced concrete. There were no elevators, and they were needed. Engineering, telephone wiring, Internet—all of that's too, even behind old facades. In general, wherever you look, you end up having to tear down the house and build it again.

Alik, are you trying to say that Luzhkov's idea is right—razing all of Moscow's antiquity and filling up the city with new stuff?

Of course he's right! Absolutely. He did that, and now the city is alive. Not like St. Petersburg, which is a city-museum. Eventually the museum will fall apart, and that's it. Like Venice—in another 70 years no one will be able to see it, because it will have disappeared underground. Underwater. But this is just the engineering argument for razing and rebuilding. There are architectural arguments as well. The progressives have a very interesting point: "If you, comrade traditionalists, had lived 150 years ago, when there was a completely different church on the spot of St. Isaac's, you would not have allowed it to be torn down. It was a very lovely little church, but small, and there had been another before it. You would say no, it's a historical monument. Eighteenth century, or whatever. And St. Petersburg would not have gotten St. Isaac's Cathedral. And if you traditionalists had come out to defend Nevsky Prospect, it would not have gotten Eliseyev House or the Singer book store…."

And why the hell did you chop down all the trees and drain the swamps—how could you ruin the environment to build that city in the first place!

That's it exactly! Where is the line where a city's development must stop, Igor, beyond which it can only be preserved? I don't understand that very well. If you want a city to live and have a population, that is a noble desire. But then it has to develop continually. Something must be happening in it, new buildings must go up—even those that prove to be mistakes! But if it's a city-museum, then you have to be like Venice, where most of the population lives on the mainland and comes to work in a boat, in order to give tourists rides on the canals. Only millionaires have apartments right in Venice. They spend a week smoking bamboo and then go somewhere else for the rest of the year…

Why did you take part in such an abstract discussion? You seem to be a serious, pragmatic person....

Well, it had direct bearing on my dissertation topic. I was working on the elaboration of a mathematical apparatus for tying industrial sites with concrete building locations. All those conceptual things were very important to me. What is a city, how do you distinguish a city from a village?

Hell if I know.

You see, Igor: I was working on profound and important things that were of interest to me. I still feel it's an important topic. What is the difference between Moscow and St. Petersburg? That the preservation tendency won out in St. Petersburg and the developer tendency in Moscow.

And there really aren't any other cities in Russia, are there?

I'll agree that the rest are "urban settlements." Well, maybe Samara, Nizhny Novgorod, and Kazan, all of which have historical centers, can be conditionally considered cities.

Conditionally, and prematurely. Yes, those were lofty issues you were working out, Alik! As for me, I headed the newspaper's "rural youth" section in 1984. That was a dizzying moment. My salary went up from 125 to 145 a month. So, $145—wait, not dollars! And then I also got extra fees for my writing, so it was about 200 a month.

I was making about the same. Graduate fellowship, my janitor's salary, and my family helped out. How was the food situation in Kaluga?

Fish, especially *moiva*. Processed cheese, eggs...

Right—standard provincial fare. The good grub would disappear from St. Petersburg later, but in 1984 things were still fine.

There was a sausage commuter train from Kaluga to Moscow—it took three hours, if I'm not mistaken.

Like from Geneva to Courchevel.

Or like flying from Moscow to Paris; sometimes it's three hours, sometimes three and half, depends.... Whenever I got to Moscow, the first thing I did was go to a hot dog place and eat five thin hot dogs, like it was some kind of delicacy.

My pal Victor Vekselberg worked in college at a meat factory and personally made those "milk hot dogs." Even though he's a billionaire now, to this day he likes stumping people with the question: "How many hot dogs can you make with one kilogram of meat?" So, answer the question, Igor!

Hmmm. Five.

Way wrong. Twelve! And that's according to the technology. And as long as no one is stealing the meat! Hot dogs are a meat product that is only half meat.

You mean you can eat them during Lent?

Sort of. It's like a homeopathic dose of meat.

Meanwhile, back at my newspaper, there were also office intrigues, the struggle for the department head chair…. The passions boiled over! Since I wasn't pushing myself for the job, they gave it to me—that way no one's feelings would be hurt. After that, I would be expected to join the Party and ask to be transferred from the Komsomol newspaper to a Party one…. That was a very dreary prospect, and I even considered going to graduate school, just for a change of pace. And to get away from the Party ideology, and the creeps who enforced it.

And then Andropov was replaced by Chernenko. To tell the truth, Igor, I felt sorry for the old guy—his shoulders were hunched up all the time, and he kept gasping for breath. Remember when they brought him to some election or other, and Viktor Grishin had to hold him by the elbow?

When they filmed him at the Central Kremlin Hospital, but they set the scenery to look like a real polling place in Moscow?

And remember how his breathing was so heavy?

As if he were fucking on the air. Live!

Svinarenko's Commentary:

Really, it was like a parody of a porn film. The heavy breathing, the panting, the rolling eyes. He's standing there, giving a speech, and none of us can tell for sure whether or not there's a specially trained girl pleasuring him behind the lectern. You could see it as an artistic foreshadowing of the Clinton-Lewinsky theme.

* * *

I remember, Igor, that when I had to go to Krasnoyarsk, to do some research at the local university, they already had a bust of him—local boy made good, you know—and had even started building a memorial to him. The money ran out, and they dropped it.

In 1984 they built a big memorial to Lenin on Oktyabrskaya Square. A composition with many figures. Today you can only shudder—what a waste of resources, on all kinds of nonsense! You're building a monument to a tsar now, so you have an idea of the approximate costs. Lenin on Oktyabrskaya Square! That's a lot of money! They were just throwing it away…

And all the money they threw into the military industrial complex? Thinking that they had one?

What about Africa, Alik? I asked the blacks there if they remembered blowing the money we'd given them, how we'd tried to educate them… No, they didn't remember a thing and knew nothing about Russia— they think our national language is Portuguese. The Communists took all my money and gave it to those Africans. As soon as that robbery ended, I bought a car, traveled to Paris, and got a second pair of shoes.

Just think what Havana alone cost us!

I hadn't been to Havana then, Alik. But I almost went on a tour to France and Portugal, right in 1984—that's another important event.

Aha! Go on.

It cost 650 rubles, through the Union of Journalists—they got a special rate. My personal life was rather complicated at the time, I was getting tired of all the hassles, and so I came up with a way to cut through a knot of problems: from settling my personal woes to finding work in the real mass media (as opposed to a propaganda leaflet for provincial bureaucrats). This was the plan: I would travel around Portugal like an ordinary tourist, but then in Paris I would, as they say, "choose freedom" and stay on as a permanent resident. I would apply for a job at Ekho of Liberty.

You mean Radio Liberty.

Whatever. It was time to bring some perestroika to that station! I had sketched out my ideas in preparation for the trip.

Svinarenko's Commentary:

I had a high regard in general for Radio Liberty; only the BBC was better. But I could see the station's flaws. That stealthy, dissatisfied voice, which seemed to creep up on you from around the corner, must have repulsed a lot of potential listeners of foreign broadcasts on shortwave radio. I thought I could convince them that the announcers should switch to a less disgusted tone. And stop gloating over Soviet miseries. In my opinion, they should have been trying as hard as they could to appear impartial. Because the people who were listening were those who pretty much knew everything already and agreed with their opinions. But anyone who was a bit more loyal to the regime would be frightened off by the malice. It was radio predestined for their own people—the dissident and near-dissident crowd. Just like Soviet propaganda, but in reverse.

They should have started in a roundabout way, first exposing various trifles and then moving on to fundamental issues. They should have had a program called "For Beginning Listeners" that would allow that in some ways Lenin was good, and that Russia sometimes did provide socialism with a human face.

* * *

But first I had to leave the country, Alik. Today there are people who lie and say that there was more freedom under the comrades. But every trip had to be approved by the regional committee of the Communist Party in your hometown. Even for non-Party members! A *troika*— I mean a trio—of your colleagues had to sign off on your character. The party organizer, Milenushkina, a nice lady with a sense of humor, refused to enter the ritual formula "morally stable" in my form. Her logic was that while she knew that I didn't have orgies at work, she couldn't vouch for my free time. That didn't keep me from getting all my documents. I was ready to go, I was already worrying about how I would pay back the money I borrowed for the trip. I decided to send my creditors jeans from the West—to pay them back in kind. I had started studying a little English and French, reading adaptations of books about Maigret.

Svinarenko's Commentary:

During the Soviet era, foreign languages were purposely taught in such a way that that people would never learn how to converse, or be able to listen to foreign-language radio or enemy TV, if they were able to tune it in. It was one of their big ideas, to instill in people a fear of emigrating: If I do escape, what use will I be where they don't particularly need me, especially if I don't speak the language? It was a subtle plan and executed with great scope. Millions of citizens spent years studying languages in schools and colleges, passing their exams—and could do no more than barely translate, with a dictionary, a text about class struggle. Yet languages would have been a good thing for people to know in a country with a universal draft and an assortment of probable enemies. But ideology proved stronger than considerations of military benefit.

Under the tsars, large masses of Gymnasium graduates learned languages marvelously well, even though there were no high-tech methods of instruction, and international contacts were weak. By contrast, there were thousands of all kinds of refugees, political émigrés, and foreign students living the USSR—so it would be no problem finding good teachers among the native speakers of a language. Nobody stopped them from having quality programs on radio and TV, so those who wanted to could learn. But other goals were considered more important.

* * *

But then, Alik, a friend of mine, someone who was close to the KGB, as we all knew, told me the following: I would without a doubt be officially denied permission to go to Paris. It would be the equivalent of being kicked out of school; a black mark that would keep me from traveling even to the socialist countries, which the KGB had never stopped me from before—even though I was divorced, a drinker, and unreliable. It would be better for me to withdraw my request. And I did.

So you didn't escape to the West, poor Igor. Though it wasn't a very clear attempt—real flight is when you're caught at the border wearing your shoes backwards or cow hooves on your feet—to camouflage your tracks—and you've been stockpiling hard currency for months…

With the blueprints of a secret plant, so that you'll have some money when you first get to the West.

But there was none of that, I take it? Hm, 1984 really demonstrated all the feebleness and weakness of the sovok. It was the height of incapability.

Feebleness, pallor, weakness. Just the endless reading of anti-Soviet books…

Well, yes. If we're talking about spiritual perfection, Igor, then 1984, like all the years of stagnation, brought us a lot. More books became accessible— Faulkner, Salinger, Fitzgerald, Hemingway. And what great science fiction! Lem, Asimov, Bradbury, the Strugatsky brothers, and H. G. Wells. You could read those books and lose yourself in them.

You're right about the reading. But I also remember saving up money and buying… no, not a dacha, but a sweater. And then I saved up some

more and bought a watch. Not a Rolex like yours, but a Vostok for 32 rubles. I'm touched by the memory.

Listen, the scale of demand was not the same… But the degree of emotional response to a gift was the same.

Sure, whether you traverse three seas or four or five, what the hell is the difference?

When you realize where the bar was—and it was very low—then a Vostok watch made you as happy as a Rolex. I lived on the poverty line—we've spoken about that already—but I didn't feel poor. Even the wealthiest people in those days did not live much better than I did. The gap was much smaller than it is today.

The "desk" on which I wrote my dissertation was the space between the bookshelf and the window sill: I'd placed a part of the crib against the wall. There was oilcloth covering it, my papers were spread out on it, the typewriter sat on it, the lamp lit it up…. I felt wonderful there!

Ah, Alik, after we learned that Nabokov wrote his immortal prose sitting on a bidet in the bathroom—his son, Dmitri, recounted that—what right do we have to complain about our inconveniences?

You can't follow Nabokov's example while living in a communal flat for two reasons, Igor: First of all, they don't have bidets.

Aha. "We didn't shoot because, first of all, we didn't have any shells."

But there's a second reason, and it's also weighty: The neighbors would have killed you. For hogging the bathroom all night.

How many bidets do you have at your dacha here?

Here I have two bidets. So I could take one over as a writer easily. Or use the toilet.

And how many toilets do you have now?

Let me count. … One, two, three…. Four, five six…

But you don't write on them; you work in the kitchen.

No, I have to disappoint you: I write in my study. You know, I write in the study, operate in the operating room, and eat in the dining room.

Yes, I've returned to the ideal, that primitive old-fashioned model; I'm a traditionalist in that sense. I haven't reinvented the wheel and have no desire to do so. I try to shit in the toilet, sleep in the bedroom, exercise at the gym, and swim in the pool.

Did you have a sense of the end, that final year?

I did. I did! Think back, remember that… [*Kokh coughs like an asthmatic*]… That's the end! A person can't breathe.

But we still thought the Soviet regime would last for our lifetime.

We sensed that it was changing, Igor. On Easter night, they showed "Melodies and Rhythms of the Foreign Stage" on TV to keep young people from going to church. They sensed that the young people were moving away from Communism. So, here, you creeps, watch Western San Remo, just don't go to church! And once or twice, they showed Mashina Vremeni, our Moscow rock group. They had "Records Spinning" on TV. Don't you remember? It was all happening! I didn't think about it too much, but I had a sense that the finale was sneaking up. What I thought was that I would have to be a secret dissident all my life, you know, trying not to quote the classics of Marxism-Leninism in my articles and dissertations…. Trying, at least trying, to have a clear conscience. But I did sense that the machine was running down.

And then, when it did all end, did you have the feeling that we had screwed ourselves, Alik? What was the point of all our posturing? There were people no dumber than us who had joined the Party, made money and careers, and nothing terrible happened to them. Look at Igor Malashenko—when there was one set of rules, he worked in the Central Committee, and when the rules changed, he went to work for Vladimir Gusinsky…. So simple.

Svinarenko's Commentary:

Malashenko told me—back in Moscow, sitting in Gusinsky's opulent office in the former COMECON building—he said into my tape recorder: "I won't hide it, I lived well back then, too. I had an extremely high status. A monthly salary of two hundred eight rubles! A two-room apartment in a Central Committee-owned building! In the so-called Tsar's Village—I got it through the Academy of Sciences. I was a learned secretary! I got to travel, had internships in America! Well, those were the rules then. OK, I accepted them and played by them. In that sense I am a conformist. You could call me an opportunist, or you could describe me positively as a flexible person. I need to know the rules of the game. I started out as a warrior on the ideological front. I played the game of the Cold War on the Soviet Union's side. I used all my ingenuity to beat the Americans. In discussions whose meaning can't even be explained today—what were we breaking our spears for? It was a game. That's how we play chess—I like that image; it holds for nuclear strategy as well. Although it's true that we lost the Cold War—and I regret that this fact has never been openly acknowledged. I thought that we would have to withdraw from battle; the absurdity was obvious... But, like the guy in Pantleyev's children's story, I had given my word of honor and stayed at my post. But now the rules of the game had changed. The measure of success is money? OK. I'm playing. And I think I'm doing rather well."

I can't refrain from noting the echoes between Malashenko and my co-author—I'm referring to Kokh's famous interview where he said that the Russians are all at fault since they imprisoned and executed themselves, after all the external enemies had been defeated. And in 1997 Malashenko said to me: "I'm irritated by all the talk that these bad Communists showed up and created the revolution and the regime. As if the Bolsheviks were Martians who came down in spaceships and raped our poor, good country. In fact half of our fellow countrymen were ready to arrest the other half and keep them in labor camps or kill them outright. Think how much was spent and wasted for decades! We still can't climb out of that hole."

* * *

First of all, you're veering into interview mode again, journalist Svinarenko!

Come on, look how much I've talked about myself already.

And second, I'll answer your question. You see, I never set myself the goal of being successful at any cost. It's my childish idealism, beaten into my head from way back—my parents, my late aunt, my uncles who worked in the mines My father was a Communist! And how! He was a career man. He was like Malashenko. Not that he was a Party functionary—he was a pure production man. But he went to Party conferences, eagerly. Though, really, what he wanted with the Communists I'll never know—they screwed him when he was six.

Did you say that to him?

No, in principle I understood him—those were the rules of the game. He should have asked himself that question! My mother was angrier, of course.

Years have passed. And where is Malashenko now?

In New York; not so bad, either. That's where his arc took him from the Central Committee of the CPSU. Did I ever tell you that I spoke at the Nixon Center in Washington at the height of the NTV scandal? And I said, "What is this? Explain it to me! Here I am, sitting before you: I, Kokh, who as a doctoral candidate in science worked as a janitor because I was not a Party member and therefore could not find a good job. And now who's teaching me about democracy? Central Committee functionary Malashenko and Higher KGB School instructor Yevgeny Kiselyov. And for some reason you're upset by me and not by them!" Ha, ha, ha.

And how did your conversation with the Americans end, Alik?

If you recall, after a few trips that Boris Jordan and I made to Washington, passions cooled in the capital over the stifling of freedom of speech in Russia. We explained very clearly what freedom of speech was in Gusinsky's hands, how much he charged not to attack people in his media….

And how much was it?

They say his fee was $50 million a year. They say! I don't know that for a fact. In any case, I didn't pay him a single kopeck. Maybe that's why he attacked me so vociferously in 1997. But let's get back to 1984. Why didn't I vacillate? I think it was idealism—there was nothing rational about it. I think that's it…. Or maybe no one invited me to play the game, and I didn't want to beg to be let in. Too lazy, and I was put off by the idea.

Isn't Paris worth a mass?

No, it isn't. Think about it: I had planned out a career for myself in which I could do things without stepping on my own throat too much: assistant, senior instructor, assistant professor, full professor. I wouldn't have to join the Party and I'd still be fairly well off materially. And read good books and talk with smart people. For instance, my late advisor, Professor Ovsievich. I'd go to lectures by all those wise old men, you know, Panchenko and Gumilev. Likhachev spoke sometimes. It was not a bad compromise, given the framework of that system.

I had an interesting idea then, Alik, to go back to working as a janitor or watchman, and read books—it seemed quite tempting suddenly. Drink some homemade wine, wear work clothes… Load some stuff, come home, brew up strong tea and crackers, and read and read….

And a friend might come over with a bottle.

And maybe some idealistic girl would have sex with you—then it would be very fine indeed.

It was a whole underground era.

Yuri Rost, the photojournalist, still walks around in work clothes and uses a length of rope for a belt.

Why, Igor, how do you explain that? Is that just posturing? I'm sure he makes decent money.

He doesn't make a lot at all. But that worries him even less. And there's always a friend to pour him a glass of Agdam or give him a Jeep....

Or an idealistic girl to sleep with.

Oh, yeah, there are plenty of idealistic girls in Russia!

Many men try to get rich for women. Rivalry plays an important part in that. Hey, we've come upon an important theme: the formation of the Russian intelligentsia in conditions of non-temporality. The t-shirt, books for scrap paper, asceticism that felt decadent... It was a blast! Books, conversation, vodka, smokes. Grass. Think back! It was a positive experience! By 1984 the intelligentsia—I hate that word—the young people from the underground—they had found an antidote to *sovok*.

There was an underground in Nazi Germany, too.

No, that's a bad analogy. Nazi Germany should be compared to Stalinist Russia. In one country everyone pissed boiling water over Comrade Hitler and in the other over Comrade Stalin.

The Roman Empire?

Hardly. We know their mores but not their mentality. I think the closest analogy to our stagnation period then is contemporary America. Along with the official politically-correct culture that runs around waving the red-white-and-blue, that maintains that there were black cowboys, there is an alternative culture that lives parallel to it. There people smoke marijuana, listen to different music, embrace white racism.... And they don't bother each other, they don't get involved with each other.

That's true. The press in the U.S. is always full of hysteria about political correctness and a healthy lifestyle. I was very worried about it when I went to live in Moscow, Pennsylvania. When I got there, I went straight to the bar to drink and eat. Everyone in there was drunk; the smoke was so thick you could hang an ax in it, and a lady I met for the first time in my life sat next to me and started telling me dirty jokes—and not for the raunchiness, but for the humor! So they tried to frighten us off

for nothing... I can officially assert that the alternative culture there is alive and well!

That's how it seems to me, too. During the stagnation period we had the official life, which was later destroyed by the alternative culture. And now the official line is coming back! So we will have to develop an alternative culture again. Show the young people how it's done....

And who's going to do that?

We are, Igor. The young people don't know how to do it; they grew up in a country that had neither the official line nor the underground. By "youth" I mean my daughter, for example—the older one, who's graduating from college. We have the know-how. We'll formulate it all, and they'll join us.

Do we have the strength and desire to do that?

Doesn't matter. They'll do it without us eventually, in any case. It's forming, I can sense it. Everyone has access now to powerful technical means like the Internet, which of course we didn't have. Now you can download any piece of music, any video you want, copy it to a disk, and stick it in a CD player. There's an enormous number of faxes, printers-schminters around. You can create any design you want, any television show.

So what are we going to teach them? How to make moonshine?

Yes. And make up killer jokes. And how to do fuck-all....

And how do you intend to combine business with doing fuck-all, Alik?

What does business have to do with it? You're so strange!

Ah, either you fight for ownership of Slavneft Oil or you own 20 kiosks and you're happy with life, is that it?

Well, yes. Or you simply work in the security market. No one ever sees you, you're online all day, and you have your modest income.

You have to think on the Internet...

You know, getting a PhD in science requires some thinking, too. Even more than in scientific Communism. It's a very important topic: The creation of an alternative culture that does not contradict the official one. They develop in parallel, without bothering each other. Abuladze made his film *Repentance* while Chkheidze made *Your Son, Earth: Tale of a Regional Communist Secretary*, or something. No one bothered anyone else. I remember how the theme of alternative culture sounded in 1984: a rock club appeared in St. Petersburg that united Tsoi with Akvarium—

And then it vanished, that alternative culture.

It vanished along with the official one for which it was an alternative. Now the process is being repeated. The official line presented on ORT and RTR television demands an alternative.

The alternative now seems much more cheerful than when Brezhnev was slobbering and muttering on all the channels. Today the state channels show soap operas about positive gangsters ("The Brigade") and then porn (*Eyes Wide Shut*)...

And in between these high-rating and entertaining shows, Igor, the state channel still tells us what a wonderful president we have. It may be true, probably is. But I still want to hear from Solzhenitsyn and Voinovich. From the late Astafyev. He had praised Yeltsin. At the very least, since there is no Tolstoy, from Shevchuk. That's why an alternative culture is necessary. Remember, Marx said something like this: "An idea that captures the masses becomes a material force." It's the same with an alternative culture: The more of the masses it captures and drags away from the shitcan with the official line, the more material it will become. It wasn't Gorbachev who made perestroika, that's bull. Gorbachev did a lot. Under Gorbachev, we had the biggest military budgets in the history of the Soviet Union. No one is denying him his achievements; I agree that he was the one to storm Tbilisi, Baku, and the TV tower in Vilnius—all as it should be... But Gorbachev was too weak intellectually to come up with something to counter the official line.

He enjoyed life under Chernenko. He rambled on about Lenin, the Party-schmarty.

Of course! It wasn't Gorbachev who created perestroika, Igor. It was the underground! Alternative culture! People like Grebenshchikov, Tsoi, Makarevich, Shevchuk, the Mitki—it sounds clichéd, but they overthrew the official line.

The Mitki overthrew Communism? With their bare hands? Are you telling me this as a learned economist?

Not just the Mitki. Also, oil prices fell. And that was the basis of our budget. We used to extract 600 million tons a year in the stagnation period. And now it's 350. In the good years, during the energy crisis, oil cost $40 a barrel. Those were incredible, unheard-of prices! Three times more than now. But we lived less well, of course. Because all the money went into the military-industrial complex. And then the deposits began to dry out; we used barbarous extraction methods. We got less and less, while the Arabs, Venezuela, and Mexico keep getting more, and there are platforms in the North Sea now. Also, the oil prices started going do-o-own. They began using more efficient engines in cars.... In general, the budget grew poorer... It's a long story. When we get to those years, I'll go into detail.

And how do you know all that, Alik? You were an ordinary grad student.

I learned it later, when I worked in the government. I saw all those statistics.

You looked back?

Of course. I was looking for the roots of the crisis.

So you understood—

No. I did not believe in Gorbachev's good intentions. I understood that he was trapped in a vise for completely objective reasons.

Seems like it. Otherwise he wouldn't look so worn out.

Of course. He had no alternative! He had to liberalize, in order to give progress a push. He didn't give the impression of being particularly smart.

Ah. I see. You're trying to say that in the past the communal apartment kitchen was the hotbed of underground culture. And now it's the banya at your dacha?

In my banya. At your magazine. On Boris Jordan's TV station, *[where he went after leaving NTV a week after this conversation was recorded.]* Anywhere you like!

I see you're developing a criminal romanticism about resistance to the regime.

There is no resistance! It's simply parallel development. Resistance is pointless—they'll put you away and squash you like a bug. We don't bother you, you don't bother us. That is how 1984 differed from 1983. There was an increased tension between the underground and the official line in 1983. With the death of our responsible leader, the official line retreated and allowed the underground to develop. The two cultures developed in parallel. Afterward, the alternative culture gradually turned into the mainstream and consumed the official line.

Svinarenko's Commentary:

This doesn't compute. It sounds as if it could consume the official line now! Yet Alik says they develop in parallel: we don't bother you, you don't touch us.... Well, which is it? It's a very important question. Why would they want to be consumed yet again? They're probably going to try to prevent that. What methods will they use? Censorship? Arresting a few people? Exiling them? Buying up all the most colorful people of the alternative culture? This works very well in TV. When pressure is put on a non-official channel, everyone goes on and on about how the journalists from that station will end up unemployed, seriously and for a long time, if they make the slightest attempt at resistance. A few months in the fresh air, in the cold—and those journalists rethink their lives. You can be certain that none of them will call for rallies the next time. Does that mean that an effective scenario for dealing with the alternative culture has been developed and implemented?

* * *

Kokh's Commentary:

During the stagnation years, how did you—how did any of us—form our ideas of truth and falsehood, power and the people, justice? From television? No! From books, from the music we listened to, from films, and from talking with each other.

Nevertheless. Did we watch TV? Yes. Did we watch the news? We did. Did we watch *Vremya* news? We did. Did it affect us? Not at all. I almost always watched the May Day parade. And the November Anniversary of the Revolution, too. It created a party mood; we were waiting for guests, it was fine. The propaganda effect of television at the height of the stagnation period was zero.

So, they'll scare off the talented ones. They'll buy the weak, talented ones. So what? The more monotonous TV becomes, the fewer alternatives it offers, the less it will be believed. People will watch it. Shows like *Song 2004*, *Ogonek*, soap operas, *Windows*. That's fine. You can't catch faith with ratings. It's not so much; "I watch if I believe, and I don't watch if I don't." The more accurate evaluation of the alternative approach is, "I watch, and I mock."

As the propaganda component in television increases at the expense of information, the influence on people's moods decreases. The ratings won't suffer—advertising revenues, either. But people's behavior at the polls will depend less and less on the positions put forth by TV.

The official line always smells of rotten meat! Those cultural figures who followed one another into United Russia—fantastic! You couldn't imagine better negative publicity!

The dialogue:

"I never licked the asses of the Communists!"

"Why?"

"Because I didn't like them."

"And now?"

"Now, it's different. Now I like them."

How's that? It's almost verbatim. That's how things are, brother.

* * *

What was the mainstream then turned into, Igor? Negative depictions in art, which the official state film studio, *Goskino*, churned out for ten years—shootouts and bandits. Actors in white suits made in Moscow factories drove around in used foreign cars circa 1972 pretending to be tough bandits and rich guys. Valentin Gaft played some hard-core thief. That's what the Soviet mainstream turned into, that's what they spent state funds on! In the meantime, the alternative culture just a little later created totally normal films: *Taxi Blues* and *Land of the Deaf*. That became the mainstream, winning prizes in Cannes and so on.

So, you think that 1984 is like today—

Yes, I think so. Because now the official line has become apparent and obvious again.

But can patriotism be depicted without propaganda?

Perhaps. What is Russian patriotism? Where is it reflected? Give me a literary work! *Iron Flow? The Rout? The Quiet Don?*

Hm. Maybe *The Flight* or *White Guards*? No, they're not it, either.

Then what is? Where is Russian patriotism shown with talent and beauty?

Maybe we foreigners just can't understand the Russian soul?

No, come on, Igor, let's figure it out. We were assigned so many books in school, we've read so much. Let's figure it out.

***How the Steel Was Forged?* The man doesn't need money, he's building a narrow-gauge railroad, and then his back is broken and he's held up to Pioneers as an example. Hm. How about Maresyev—the pilot's legs are amputated but he still flies and fights.**

By the way, it's a good book, *Tale About a Real Man*.

That's what I'm saying. Did you think I was joking?

The man fought against the enemy. There's nothing bad in the text except for a hysterical commissar who attacks him, asking: Are you a Soviet man?

What else? *Chapayev?*

No. Even though it's become part of the folklore.

The Young Guards?

That's cheap stuff, written to order. Why are you digging around in Socialist Realism? Let's move farther away.

Bunin. "The Village."

Well, in that case, I'd rather pick Leo Tolstoy's *"Landowner's Morning."*

Hmmm. Platonov?

Well.....

Leskov?

All homespun?

"Lefty."

A ve-e-ry patriotic work.

They study it in school.

As an exposé of the brutal tsarist regime, Igor.

But the craftsman solved the problem with the mechanical flea. He made shoes for it, but it stopped hopping. But our people were still proud. The tsar gave him some reward for it... Shalamov?

Things are pretty bad if Shalamov is our positive patriotism.

How about: *One Day in the Life of Ivan Denisovich?*

Yes, that's patriotism. No fooling. But not positive. How about *War and Peace?* It's a good work. Bolkonsky, Bezukhov, old Tsar Nicholas.

But the girl screws that scoundrel Kuragin—

While the real men are fighting to defend their homeland. ... "I was the battalion scout, and he was the headquarters clerk... yet he slept with my wife." Pure Andrei Bolkonsky.

So where's the positive then, Alik?

I'm telling you, it's still *War and Peace.* Another powerfully patriotic work, which I believe instills an astounding attitude toward the Russians, toward Russia, and Orthodoxy, is Leo Tolstoy's *The Cossacks.* Just remember Lukashka and that girl, what's-her-name, Maryana. And his *Sebastopol Tales*. Remember the stories?

Very vaguely. What about Gaidar? "The Drummer's Fate." You have your bravery and struggle, this and that … The father is released from the camps….

Will you stop it! A country in the thralls of spymania is patriotism?

All rightie. Then what else do we have that's patriotic, Alik? We've listed Platonov, that's not it.

Shukshin, for example.

Dovlatov. No, not him, he's an émigré.

But you remember how he described being an émigré. His wife went on a trip, and he got bored. He thought, fuck you, I'll get drunk without you. He did, and got depressed.

Brodsky? "Better to live in a distant province by the sea"? That's rather weak as patriotism.

The regime keeps demanding it! Give us some patriotism, why are you such non-patriots! Tolstoy wrote—as we just established—more patriotic works than anyone else, but the regime hated him. They even excommunicated him from the church. They considered him practically a revolutionary. Isn't that strange?

Alik, you compare our stagnation period with the current situation in the U.S.; do you mean that you expect everything there to collapse, too?

I think so. Everyone is sick of their political correctness. They lie to themselves, they corrupt their history, they make up stories about things that never happened to them. And they've forgotten everything! For instance, that during the Holocaust, the Americans passed some kind of law banning entry to Jews. With only a few exceptions, like Einstein and Oppenheimer. I mean, it's one thing for France, which Hitler had conquered; but Britain didn't let Jews in, either! Hitler was ready to let all of them go, he hadn't planned on killing them all at first. (Which is no justification for him.) But the people had no place to run to. The Jews were shipped off to concentration camps because the so-called civilized countries did not let them in because of paragraph 5—that line in your passport that states your nationality. There were quotas for Jews in the USSR for residence, higher educational institutions, and everything else…

So, you think they're going through this process?

Absolutely. I feel it, when I'm in New York. There is constant renewal. I don't feel rap music at all, and I don't understand why the Russian group *TaTu* was popular in the West—I know I'm not going to catch up to it. But it's the same as my parents telling me I was nuts when I listened to Led Zeppelin. And if I were to play them for my daughter, she'd say, why listen to that old stuff? That's understandable. "Lilies-of-the- valley, sweet greeting of May…."

Before I forget, since we're talking about young people, Igor. Here's what Putin doesn't understand, it seems to me. For them, for the youth, he's just a brand. Putin's been made famous like a brand! Through pure commercial advertising methods. It's like the Che Guevara poster. Young people aren't interested in his revolutionary fervor but in that combination of red, black, and the beret. So Putin for them is just an amusing stamp. "Whack them in the outhouse"—he knows his karate moves. He thinks the people love him. But as soon as his brand gets worn out, like Rasputin vodka, it's over. He thinks he's won the love of the people. But that love is like the love for Coca-Cola.

Kokh's Commentary:

A bit more about the relationship between the mass media and the regime, and the influence of that relationship on electoral behavior.

Consider Nixon and Yeltsin.

You can win an election without the support of the press. A landslide. Like Nixon did in 1972. Like Yeltsin in 1991.

The power of the mass media, and it really is a fourth estate, is not legitimate. In the day when the principles of three branches of power and of checks and balances were being formed, back in the late eighteenth century, no one—not Jefferson, not Franklin, not Washington—imagined the influence that the press would eventually have. After all, the three traditional branches of power—executive, judicial, and legislative—draw their legitimacy (or pretend to) from the will of the people. Only the fourth power does not depend on it.

And yet it has a direct and often stronger influence on the life of those people than the other three combined. What can the government, parliament, courts, and prosecutors do? In the worst case, they can jail or kill. The press can do much more. It can change consciousness.

Therefore, in my opinion, Putin is doing everything right. He is placing the press under the control of the totally legitimate executive power. The principles of classic democracy have been restored. Once again there are three branches of power, checks and balances—everything works in a clear way. There are no breakdowns in the work of the constitutional bases created by the press.

And the people, you may ask? What about the people? People will behave the way they usually do in these situations. They will treat the mass media (and television in particular, and mostly) as the government's *dazibao,* where in addition to entertainment they will hear and read the government's assessment of the government's work. "And personally, dear Leonid Ilyich Brezhnev..." If they praise Comrade Pupkin, then he's being prepared for a promotion; if they scold him, then he's doomed and will be fired. Come on, in a way even that's information.

I am not afraid, here, of repeating myself: The opinions of the mass media will have zero effect on the voting. Why are you trying so hard?

It's all clear, it's all OK. And people will go to other places, other sources for the truth, or analysis. What will come of this, God only knows. I hope it's not the knife and shiv. No one controls the alternative sources—which are impossible to control, in any case. They don't have a bold owner like Gusinsky. And they can't get a license, since there aren't any. Some freshly minted Kashpirovsky will appear and start holding "séances" in stadiums. And then the masses will pick up their hatchets. The effect of the most innocent media can be totally unpredictable. I'm certain that the Moscow authorities had not expected such a "meaningless and ruthless revolt," to use Pushkin's term, as the one that took place after the Russia-Japan game was shown on screens set up in the streets. Personally, I was in shock.

In order to control *samizdat,* the Soviet Union had to maintain a huge suppression machine with the KGB, informants, and nuthouses. Now, that is fundamentally impossible. Even if you were to imagine that it's in the plans.

Today, people's need for *samizdat* is sharply reduced, because they can find all the information they want easily in legal mass media. But as the "merger of the KGB into capitalism" limits free access to independent sources of information, and trust in the official media falls, a total *samizdat* will appear, and the effect of all that *samizdat* on the minds of our citizens, as I've said, is unpredictable—just as the results of a soccer match could not be predicted.

I will list just a few words that did not exist in the legendary days of the *samizdat* during the period of stagnation: video recorder, DVD player, CD player, satellite television, cable television, the Internet, personal computer, diskette, cellphone, Xerox, fax, printer, mini-printing press, trip abroad.... Phew, I think that's enough. If I've forgotten anything, it's even more proof that if we have total *samizdat* in our era, it will be impossible to fight, even if you sympathize with the idea. And the degree of its effect and its scope will be such that the innocent stagnation-era *samizdat* will remind us of a children's game of tag.

But what I consider most important is that this *samizdat* will not be primarily political and in opposition to the regime (although there will some of that, too) but mostly a crazy mix of stuff like Aum Shinrikyo and "all bureaucrats are fags."

That scares me. What about you?

* * *

Every leader thinks he's won the people's love, Alik.

No, I don't think that Yeltsin thought that about himself. He understood, he was conscious of that tragedy. He looked at his ratings before the 1996 elections, and he understood everything. That's when he roused himself… By the way, what was going on in the international arena in 1984?

What do you mean? Of course it was the Olympics! In Los Angeles.

That's right! I remember it well. Someone brought me a T-shirt with the logo of the Los Angeles Olympics; a good T-shirt, American, and with a tolerable price…. I was too scared to buy it—how could I wear it? How? If I went outside in it, they'd put me in cuffs right away. How can you wear that, they'd say.

There was some intrigue with those games.

Well, they didn't come to Moscow over the war in Afghanistan, so in revenge, we didn't go to them.

Did we gain anything from that?

Nothing. They did their running and jumping, and then in 1986 CNN television mogul Ted Turner and Gorbachev came up with the Good Will Games, so that the athletes could compete against each other.

So this was a last attempt to squash the United States.

A totally hopeless one, Igor. But their attempt to squash the Soviet Union in 1980 was also hopeless. Because athletes came from many different countries and walked beneath the white Olympic flag instead of their country's flag. And the U.S. teams lost the Olympic cycle. What do you expect from Reagan? He was the most orthodox of the orthodox….

He said he would break the evil empire, and he did. He took one look at our sleepy, half-dead leaders and said, I can kill these guys with one arm behind my back.

As we've already discussed, there was an unexpected event with oil.

And, believe it or not Alik, I ended up in charge of the newspaper each time a general secretary was buried. The system gradually worked itself out, we developed the order of things. Here's what I mean: With Brezhnev, I signed off on the issue at five in the morning. With Andropov at midnight. And with Chernenko, at 9 p.m., right on schedule. All the outlines were ready and waiting; it was all written. The Party had drawn even closer around the Leninist Central Committee, and so on. We had a response from an outstanding wordsmith on the death of the general secretary—by the way, how did he know that Chernenko was going to die? I didn't have a very nice moral-ethical image, and it wasn't very nice that I ended up being on duty each time one of them kicked the bucket. I walked around the editorial offices so drunk, so happy, so proud… But why are we racing ahead of ourselves? In 1984, Chernenko was still practically alive.

4.

1985

The Fourth Bottle

The Communists uproot vineyards all over the country. Even so, Kokh the drinker meets Gorbachev in Leningrad and experiences "monarchic delight."

Mikhail Sergeyevich raises his approval ratings by offering new wares on the market: "acceleration and perestroika." The provincial Party apparatchik Boris Nikolayevich Yeltsin moves to Moscow. In preparation for his struggle against the those in favor, he does some market research—and comes up with photo-op rides on trolleybuses.

But the sovok *[Soviet way of life] continues to seem eternal.*

Meditations on the nature and characteristics of the Russian uprising.

Okay Alik, let's go. First of all, in order for so-called perestroika and all that stuff to begin, Konstantin Ustinovich Chernenko had to die—personally.

That happened on March 10, 1985.

Did you feel sorry for him, as you had for the previous personae?

Yes, I did. What, am I supposed to be ashamed of that?

All right, all right… And what were you doing then?

I was in grad school. I finally had a regular supervisor. I had spent a year hanging around like shit in a sewer—I'd been assigned some semi-Party scholar who kept writing reports for the oblast committee and the city committee. And then they gave me a regular scientist from the academy—the Institute of Socioeconomic Problems. He also worked part-time at the Leningrad branch of Steklov Mathematics Institute, and he was a part-time professor at our economic institute. His name was Boris Lvovich Ovsievich. He's gone now. May he rest in peace. In order to earn his half-pay he took on two graduate students—me and Lenya Limonov. Actually, that's when I started writing my dissertation. I had wasted 1984.

Like the entire Soviet nation. But then came Gorbachev. He was appointed head of the funeral committee for Chernenko, and everyone knew that meant he was the one! The choice had been made.

I remember how he astonished everyone by his pointed way of putting a glass of milk on the lectern.

I don't remember the milk. And then, why was it necessarily milk, Alik? It could have been eau de cologne with water. Same color... An opaque white liquid. And if you suck on a lump of sugar after each sip, it's actually not bad. Of course, you burp a lot afterward. Tastes citrus-y.

Remember there were rumors that he spoke English? And that he was oh so very Western? And his woman wasn't fat like all the others, but elegant...

And she tried to turn him and everyone else off boozing and alcoholism, like every wife in Russia.

A Sisyphean task!

Everyone was a Sisyphus except Raisa Maximovna, may she rest in peace. She succeeded! She not only did not allow her hubby to drink, she tried to make everyone else keep him company.

They say he's not interested in drinking in general.

I had read that he was used to drinking red wine down south where he's from, so vodka just wasn't that important to him.

My father's from the south, too—Krasnodarsk Krai—and even in Togliatti he's trying to grow grapes, with maniacal stubbornness. The grapes don't make enough sugar, and you get very sour wine that turns completely sour very quickly.

Tell him to distill it, Alik. He'll get terrific *chacha*! So. Gorbachev starts the job, and in April he makes his first programmatic statement, at some plenum or other, I guess. He started to say something—

—something like, "we can't go on living like this."

Yes. Andropov had been a lively speaker—not half-dead like the others—but this one added a human element This is what you gab about in your kitchens, but I'm going to say it from my tribune. We need to work, stop bullshitting around, put competent people in positions.

Didn't that start later? We have to figure it out... Oh, I remembered something from my own experience. I saw the General Secretary practically as close-up as I'm seeing you now! We met in St. Pete.

Come on, more details from here on in, Alik.

So listen: In St. Petersburg there is a square called "Uprising." There used to be a monument of Alexander III there—it's now in the courtyard of the Russian Museum. A solid rider on a solid steed. Remember?

Hm. In a round, rimless hat.... It's called an *as'ka*.

And across the way there was a church. Academician Pavlov used to go to that church. Even in Soviet times, he used to go pray there every day—a Nobel laureate! Because he was so honored, he was allowed to pray. But as soon as he died, they tore down the church.

How interesting! Look, Alik, the formalities were observed: There's political correctness for you.

They didn't bother the old man. That was a manifestation of the humanity of the Soviet regime.

Exactly. And now, they just marked the sixtieth anniversary of the death of the great plant geneticist Nikolai Vavilov—and in St. Petersburg, in the very spot where he kept his samples of special heirloom grains, they are now building a residence for our dear leader and favorite supervisor.

Yes! They say the collection is worth billions of dollars.

They didn't eat it in the blockade, when everyone was starving.

And now they'll destroy it.

Better then to sell it to Armand Hammer. As is our wont.

He died a long time ago, Igor!

Oh.

Don't forget, Igor: Another notable event in 1985 was the fortieth anniversary of Victory Day. And in its honor they stuck an obelisk on top of the muffin—well, the bed—where the Alexander III statue used to stand.

Phallic.

No, it looks more like a chisel.

Which is also a phallic symbol. With elements of pornographic precision: There is a kind of phallic flattening.

Well, anyway, the obelisk is like the one in the Place de la Concorde. Not Egyptian, but also out on a monolith. So, Gorbachev came for the opening of the monument during the May holidays. He had started doing his "walkabouts" on the streets by then. And he came out at the intersection of Ligovsky and Nevsky. There was a drugstore on the corner... And I was walking by it. I had just gotten a haircut on Suvorovsky Boulevard and was walking to the institute. And I saw Gorbachev coming straight at me! So I...

Don't be a tease, Alik! What did you say to him?

Nothing. I was 10 yards away from him. It was the first time I had seen a figure of his rank and stature in person. Close up. With a little persistence I could have gotten close enough to touch him. But instead I climbed up a lamppost. And looked at him from there.

Why did you climb up a lamppost? To prove you were taller than him?

No, no! To get a better view!

And why didn't you get closer?

Well... I actually had nothing to ask him.

And now, in hindsight, imagine that you, today, are talking to him back then—what would you say?

The me of today would have even less to talk about with the him from back then. Think about it. If I tell him what will happen after 1985, he won't believe me. And today's me has no interest in listening to whatever he would have said. It's all silly. Abracadabra!

Let me tell you what I felt at that moment—we're talking about the sensations of the era, after all! I had exactly the same feelings that Petya Rostov had when he saw the Sovereign. Remember that scene in *War and Peace*?

No. Alik, but I know you're eager, again, to refresh my memory?

Kokh's Commentary (actually, Leo Tolstoy's):

And so, Leo Tolstoy, *War and Peace*, book 3, chapter 21:

> At the sovereign's luncheon, Valuyev said, glancing out the window: "The people are still hoping to see Your Majesty."
>
> Lunch was over, the tsar stood and, finishing his cookie, went out onto the balcony. The people, with Petya in the middle, rushed toward the balcony.
>
> "Angel! Father! Hurrah, Father!" shouted the people and Petya, and once again the old women and some of the weaker men, Petya among them, wept with joy. A rather large piece of the cookie in the tsar's hand broke off and fell onto the balcony rail, and from the rail to the ground. The coachman wearing a jerkin, who was nearest, rushed over and grabbed the piece of cookie. Noticing that, the tsar had the plate of cookies brought to him and started throwing them from the balcony. Petya's eyes filled with blood, the danger of being trampled in the crowd excited him even more, and he threw himself toward the cookies. He did not know why, but he had to have a cookie from the tsar's hand, and he could not give up. He rushed, knocking over an old woman who was catching a cookie. But the old woman did not consider herself vanquished, even though she was lying on the ground (she kept trying to catch them and kept missing). Petya pushed aside her hand with his knee, grabbed a cookie, and, as if afraid of being late, shouted "Hurrah!" again, his voice hoarse.
>
> The tsar left, and after that most of the people started to disperse.
>
> "I told you we should wait, and I was right," various people said happily.
>
> Happy as Petya was, he was sad that he had to go home and know that all the pleasures of that day were over....

* * *

So, Igor, our Petya Rostov experienced monarchic delight. And I did, I did, too! I, a twenty-four-year-old graduate student, experienced monarchic delight. I was under its spell for a long time. When the crowd dissipated, I went to the institute. And something like this was in my heart: *I loved the tsar.* I had seen Gorbachev, and he was talking to the people... it was a special emotion; it can't be compared to anything else. I never felt anything like it again. Even when I spoke with Yeltsin... or Putin.

I understand you. I remember it! It was like, here's our country, our homeland, and now we're going to do something—for Russia. I remember that feeling. I also remember watching TV with a friend in April 1985, drinking, and Gorbachev was on. I thought—how far is he going to go? Is he going to dismantle Communism?

Come on, that wasn't apparent in 1985. They were describing the situation as socialism with a human face…

What he was thinking we can't know, Alik; let's discuss his actions. On May 17, 1985, his historic resolution on the war on alcoholism was published.

It was a terribly destructive thing for the economy.

The budget is usually fed on vodka.

That's just the financial side! But there were other things as well: mentality, the people's attitude toward the regime, and so on. We've already talked about how well Andropov understood that—he gave them cheap vodka. While this one destroyed the vineyards. Okay, take away the vodka, but why destroy the vineyards?

And did they all turn to idiocy? To destroying vineyards?

Well, there are different kinds of decrees. The prohibiting ones, as a rule, don't work well. Just as water always finds a hole, the people always find a loophole, a way of countering it. But there are decrees that repeal existing prohibitions. Those are always executed well.

You mean, a decree repealing the war against alcoholism would have gone over well?

Yes, I remember in 1991, I think it was, when people were beginning to starve; Yeltsin issued a decree on free trade.

Yes, in December 1991, Alik. I remember how—instantly—little babushkas popped up on Tverskaya Street selling cans of sprats and jars of green peas and mayonnaise. I remember stocking up there for New Year's.

Yes, the cops stopped chasing away those babushkas and suddenly there was food aplenty. That decree was executed on a moment's notice—and it saved the country, by the way.

While the decree on alcoholism—they had to support it ideologically. Including the press. So I was forced to fight alcoholism too.

Do tell!

First of all, Alik, I laughed in the faces of my comrades. Journalists are real winos—always have been, historically.

On what basis did you laugh in your comrades' faces?

Because I, tired of my boozing ways, had voluntarily cut down on consumption already.

And which time was this? You had cut down before!

This was my second or third time. After I cut down in 1984, I reached the point where I could go three or even four days without a drink. In those days, that was extremely exotic. They were all in pain, desperate to find some booze. And I would mock them: "Suffering, eh? Serves you right, you alcoholics! We decent folk drink only on holidays, not like you!"

Svinarenko's Commentary:

Old notations. It sounds blasphemous somehow ... but you can't remove the lyrics from a song.

April 1985: "A *subbotnik* [mandatory "volunteer" labor on Saturday]. A drinking party, but a small one. Managed to prevent an extravagant one."

June 1985: "Weekend. Sitting home writing a piece. Got eleven pages so far. I'm in good shape. I have to maintain that good shape at any cost. It's good that they've put limitations on drinking."

October 1985: "I'm in good shape. Must continue in the same way. No drinking! And I'm not. For a long time now. I drink very little, and rarely."

***

We also carried out raids against boozing and alcoholism, Alik. The press was forced to do that. So I came up with a kind of raid that would at least be helpful to others: A brigade would go into a tavern, order vodka and *zakuski*. Everyone drank, except me: I would put mineral water in my shot glass (the way we did for Parfenov's TV show *Namedni*, when we drank water pretending it was vodka and contorted our faces picturesquely). Then we'd ask for the bill. It would be full of overcharging mistakes, as usual: 40 kopeks plus 40 kopeks equals 1.40 rubles, and so on. We'd check the bill and call for the manager, or whatever they were called in those days. The bar guys would yell that we were drunk and making a scene. And then I would stand up in my white suit: "Who's drunk? Me? You are mistaken. We are going to write up this inspection, and I will go to the drunk tank to have my alcohol level checked." I turned the war on alcoholism into a peaceful task—a fight for justice.

I was also distilling my own then. From bread. The vodka might have been gone, but I persisted zealously in my sin. If I could buy something, fine—if not, I'd have my own sour stuff.

Yes, Alik, there were lots of jokes: "The train stop announcement—this is the start of the line to the liquor store station. Next stop—Liquor Store."

Remember this one? The little boy asks, "Papa, now that vodka is more expensive, does that mean you'll drink less?" "No, son, you'll be eating less." You know what else is interesting? How the Party apparatchiks in the provinces reacted to all the events. A regional Party Secretary returned to Kaluga after that first Gorbachev plenum. And something unprecedented happened. For the first time in his life, the chief Kaluga Communist did not simply gather the local media bosses in order to whisper in their ears, he spoke to all the press. And not in his office—he came to the newspaper club himself. There was huge crowd, standing room only. We thought, well, it's started, he's going to say something like: "All right, we've played the fool long enough. We won't try to look important and put our idiots in office; we're going to work seriously now and find capable people. And no one will have to listen to the Voice of America anymore—now you will write about everything yourselves." But the secretary talked to us about something different: Where each delegation sat, how they'd looked at Gorbachev, what was served in the cafeteria... Perestroika made a profound impression on him.

Well, Gorbachev had just come in. The bosses with senile dementia were still strong in 1985...

Svinarenko's Commentary:

In late 1985, I was targeted again by the provincial KGB. They were harsh and aggressive—they wanted to recruit me. They had found some books I owned, as before... Disgusting, isn't it? Perestroika and a spree of democracy all around, and these guys... Why were they bothering me—weren't they ashamed? And why did they even need a client like me? It seemed stupid. They may have been given orders to conduct a final draft before retreating to the underground. And to go for the most unexpected characters, people no one would ever suspect. Like me. Then use them to carry out the KGB's orders. It's true, no one would have suspected that I was being operated by a set of strings—especially theirs!

There were only very subtle signals that something might change. But Gorbachev gave us great hope.

* * *

Was Yeltsin around then, Alik?

I don't remember. Let's look it up! [*They check the Internet.*] Aha! He was in the Moscow City Committee between 1985 and 1987.

So that's it. We didn't know it then, but they were already comparing the size of their cocks.

I don't know. That contradiction did not exist in 1985.

But Boris Nikolayevich was already eyeing the job, learning to ride the trolleys…

No, no, he started that when he was forced to retire. When he was subjected to harsh criticism at the plenum and told, "Good-bye, dear comrade." In 1985, Gorbachev was still doing a solo number.

The rest of them understood that Gorbachev had the top position in that market, and they had to get a move on and, come up with something quickly. I remember something else from 1985. Why had I reduced my alcohol consumption? It wasn't only because I was tired of it. But out of transcendental considerations, too: I wanted to go beyond my daily life and start up a serious project. And so I started writing for the big Moscow newspapers, criticizing the local authorities a bit. You can imagine the secretary of the oblast Party Committee opening *Sovetskaya Rossiya* and reading: "There's a shitload of individual defects in Kaluga Oblast." And my signature. The shock! They would call me in to the committee for a stern talking to. Some boss would ruminate out loud: "Now, look at who you are and who I am. You are a minor employee, you're even lower in the hierarchy than an instructor. For you I am tsar, God, and military leader. You are in my power. And suddenly, I pick up a Central Committee newspaper, and it's written there that I am practically shit. Now I have to write an official response to them: 'Thank you for the criticism; you are correct in pointing out that I am shit; I promise to take appropriate measures and, by the anniversary of the revolution, to become not-shit.' And that humiliates me in front of you! Is that fair? It's not playing by the rules…"

I tried to explain that it was nothing personal, and that it *was* playing by the rules, and that crooks don't care when the cops try to catch them. Then another article would be printed. They couldn't do anything to me directly, so they would sneak up from the flank—the committee brigade worked for ten days, following my tracks, and wrote 10 pages refuting my work, saying that I misinterpreted things, talked to the wrong people, maliciously did not reflect obvious successes, distorted policy, wrongly illuminated, and so on. They called me in to the bureau meeting of the Oblast Committee and said that raising the question of my Party membership was overdue. I replied that putting it that way—that I did not belong in that Party—was a great honor for me, because I had never been a member. So thanks for the high marks. "What?" they demanded. "You're the responsible secretary of the newspaper and you're not a Party member? Fine, go along. But you, secretary of the paper's Party organization, you please stay. We have a separate issue to discuss with you."

Well, then, what else did we have in 1985, Alik?

Nothing much. And what was going on in the international arena? Reagan—nothing else.

Nothing. What about your personal life?

Well, I was married. Already. My daughter was five… What is there in my personal life to discuss—my life with my wife?

Where did you travel?

Every summer, like a bullet, I fired off to my father's place on the Volga and spent the entire summer there. We were building a house for him. The brick house turned out so big that he was accused of violating Party ethics and was practically kicked out of the Party—he was chewed out, fired from his job. He eventually found some other work. How did it happen? Father bought a house; we even tried living in it at first, but it was impossible—the house had no foundation and the lower beams had rotted… We lived just one summer in the old house and then razed it. It was a beautiful place! You could see the Volga, the ships…..

Couldn't you live in the old house while you built the new one?

There wasn't room on the lot for two!

Ah, you were following the Gorbachev **plan, Alik: We're going to do all this rebuilding, this perestroika, so it's with a human face… and then it turns out that you have to knock everything down. Well, well… We chose that path on a grand scale—for the entire country. It wasn't the best path.**

Svinarenko's Commentary:

In those years I traveled around the country for work—I would take vacation time from my Kaluga newspaper and head out. The Kaluga bosses were very unhappy with me. The editor of the paper kept trying to show them how hard he was trying with me. For example, he wouldn't give me time off, not for any reason. What if I wrote another piece for a big paper, with another slam? I figured out the perfect trick: I began giving blood. For every pint of blood, the donor is supposed to get two days off from work—by law. So, in the morning you go to the transfusion station; they stick this huge needle in your vein, and you pretend to pump an invisible wrist expander to make the blood flow better. Then you go to the office with a note: Give me two days off! And the editor— this is the kind of person he was—would give them to me right away. "I don't need today! I'll work today!" I would say. "No," he replied. "By law, I have the right to make you take one of your days off right away. So here it is. That leaves you with just one more." I bought my freedom with blood, literally. And he poured that blood onto the ground. He was a Party member, and working on his career. He considered himself not just decent, but principled. I can still remember the wise smile he was attempting to perfect. He must have seen it in some film about a Party secretary. Actors smile like that in films on proletarian themes—you know, the wise old laborer…. Today, when the craft of journalism is in decline in Russia—dwindled down to almost nothing, just PR—it's very, very strange to remember that.

* * *

There are different paths. The Czechs took one, we took another, China took a third. You have those three scenarios, Igor.

Our path leads nowhere.

Why do you say that? I don't think so.

You don't?

No.

But things started wanly, and they're going wanly.

What happened, happened. I think that Gorbachev wasn't a particularly well-meaning person, but he wasn't ill-intentioned, either. The problem was that he wanted the wolves to be sated and the sheep left whole—and that just isn't possible.

There, you see? That's what I meant. It's not one or the other. But, Alik, you mean to say it could have been worse?

Yes! The senility would have gotten worse, the economic situation would have worsened for objective reasons, and the screws would have been tightened more and more…The stagnation would have been completely indolent, absolutely terrible. I don't rule out the possibility of revolts. It's only an illusion to think that there is a nation of 150,000,000 [*it was almost 300,000,000 then*] and that the entire range of its opinions is represented by political parties, from the Communist Party to Union of Right Forces. Back in 1985 they didn't have this division yet; there were only right-wingers and left-wingers and in mirror image, at that. I am certain that reality is not that way at all. Every person has a bit of God and a bit of the Devil inside. I think the divine in man is a thin membrane wrapped around the devil sitting inside.

You think things are that bad?

Yes. It's not yin and yang.

Just a membrane?

Yes. Just a thin membrane. A film of civilization, the ability to live in communal residences, to build a sort of social world… But if you let the devil out, it's very hard to drive him back in. Very! They let him out during the Civil War, and then it required those horrible mass repressions to chase him back inside. You wrote about it.

Who am I! Custine wrote about it, about Russian revolts.

Svinarenko's Commentary:

From the notes of the celebrated Marquis de Custine about Russia (1839).

Recently, in a remote village, there was a fire; the peasants, who had long suffered from the cruelties of the landowner, took advantage of the confusion, which they may have created, and grabbed their enemy and impaled him, and then roasted him alive in the fire's flames; they considered themselves not guilty of this crime, for they could swear that the evil landowner had wanted to burn down their houses, and they were simply defending themselves. Most often in such cases the emperor has the entire village sent to Siberia.

Here's another account:

Peter interrogates under torture those criminals (the *streltsy*) himself; then, following the example of Ivan the Terrible, he becomes their judge and executioner; he forces the boyars who retained their loyalty to him to chop off the heads of the disloyal boyars he condemned to death. From the height of his throne, he watches the executions unflinchingly; moreover, he feasts as he watches, combining his own pleasure with the suffering of others. Intoxicated by wine and blood, holding a chalice in one hand and an ax in the other, he personally chops off twenty heads from *streltsy* in an hour, and, proud of his terrible mastery, greets each death with a new glass. The following year, in response either to the revolt of the tsar's *janissaries* or to the harsh reprisals, new rebellions arose deep in the provinces. Peter's faithful servants brought eighty *streltsy* in chains from Azov to Moscow, and once against the tsar personally chopped off their heads, and his boyars were forced to hold them by the hair during the executions. (*The History of Russia and Peter the Great*, by Monsieur le Comte de Seguir. Paris: Boudouin, 1829.)

Why do these foreigners interest us? Their cool gaze. Our observers immediately want to justify us, lighten things up; they bring up the concept of the God-bearing nation inappropriately, blame the environment, the climate, whatever. I see a fundamentally important aspect of the Russian mind in this: Once it sees a problem, it feverishly seeks a cause and justification. It finds satisfaction in finding it. In itself, this is not terrible, the first reaction being not to correct or solve a problem but to approach it from a philosophical angle. What's terrible is that after finding the answer to an abstract question, the Russian is completely satisfied. He feels he has done his duty—and loses interest in the topic. The question remains unresolved. But people are happy, both with the situation and with themselves. For example: all these stories about revolts. Russian thinkers—both serious ones and kitchen-table ones—reduce their concept of revolt to the ethnos's ancient need for freedom and justice. And then the topic is closed

Pushkin used two adjectives to describe a Russian revolt: *meaningless* and *ruthless*. It should be noted that he had never seen any other revolt, not having been allowed to travel abroad. And the Russian revolt he did see was a rather weak one—when the Decembrists took their stand. He didn't see the real one, the Pugachev rebellion—he was born too late—and he judged it the way you and I talk about the events of October 1917, and subsequent ones. But for two hundred years, now, people have remembered and quoted his beautiful phrase about Russian revolts. Even though the French revolution was cruel, too…. But it had meaning! A less progressive form of rule was changed to a more subtle one, and production relations were changed with a subsequent rise in productivity. Russian revolts are different: Get your fill of looting and murder, and then establish order and get back to work, making up lost time and rebuilding. Apparently, the main difference between revolt and revolution is that revolts do not increase the production of labor. It's like a football riot—a useless waste of time and money. You end up in the same place where you started.

* * *

Kokh's Commentary:

Oh, Igor! A fine one you found to quote, Astolphe de Custine. He didn't even spend a full year in Russia. His memoirs are a mix of rumors, anecdotes, and tenth-hand facts. Let me give you real historians. For a warm-up, the peasant revolts in Ukraine in 1648:

> The peasants, armed with whatever was at hand, formed round-up mobs and acted as they wanted, answering to no one. They called themselves Cossacks, too; but often Khmelnitsky did not even know of their existence. Whenever a mob appeared in a locality, the peasants joined it, and rushed into the house of their *pan* (Polish master). Then everyone perished: the old, the young, the servants, if they were not Orthodox; the property was looted and divided up among the members. The popular vengeance was even more horrible against Jews…. And almost in one fell swoop nearly the entire Jewish population of Ukraine vanished. (I am quoting V. I. Yakovenko's *Bogdan Khmelnitsky. His Life and Public Activity*, 1902.)

And how could we overlook Stepan Timofeyevich Razin? The peasant revolt under his direction, Astrakhan, 1670:

> The Cossacks celebrated their successes noisily and merrily in Astrakhan. They caroused and drank daily. Stenka Razin was constantly drunk, and in that state decided the fate of people who had committed some misdemeanor and were to be judged by him: He would order one drowned, another beheaded, a third maimed, and a fourth, on a whim, released. (I'm quoting from D. I. Ilovaisky, *The Father of Peter the Great*, 1894.)

Or maybe we should look at a 20th-century revolt? N. Kryshevsky describes the behavior of sailors in Crimea in 1918 this way in *Archives of the Russian Revolution*, vol. 13, pp. 107–108) "In the morning, all the arrested officers (forty-six, total) were lined up on board transport, with their hands tied, and one of the soldiers kicked them into the sea, where they drowned. This vicious event was seen from shore, where their relatives, children, and wives watched…. They all wept, screamed, and pleaded, but the sailors only laughed. Among the officers was my comrade, Colonel Seslavin, whose family was also on the shore pleading with the sailors to spare him.

The worst death was that of Staff Captain Novatsky…. Already heavily wounded, he was brought back to consciousness, tied up, and thrown into the boiler of the transport *Rumynia*."

The Whites, naturally, were also no slouches. They also burned the red-bellies in boilers and carved stars on their backs. In response, the Reds cut uniform stripes on the legs of Cossacks. The viciousness on both sides reached Pugachev levels. No, *mores* are not getting any gentler.

But perhaps the end of the 20th century will hearten us with a wave of charity and kinder behavior? Let's look at G. N. Troshev's *My War. The Chechen Diaries of the Trench General*: "There is much to be said about the beatings, sadistic torture, public executions, and other 'delights' of being held by Chechens—but nothing will surprise the reader anymore. But chopping off heads and taking

scalps of live soldiers, crucified bodies in building windows—the federal troops
had never seen anything like that before they got to Grozny."

Simple Russian boys did their bit, too. It is not known for sure whether
Budanov raped Elza Kungaeva before choking her to death (but, then, it's not
clear why both were naked when the soldiers summoned by Budanov came in).
In any case, the court did not establish that. But the court did establish without a
doubt that the dead girl was raped by the soldiers who had been ordered to bury
her, and they even stuffed a shovel handle into her vagina. That is not a scalp
from a living person, but the face of viciousness is easily seen here, too.

The absence of moral progress over the last five centuries is just as obvious
as the presence of technical progress. Thus, the danger of even the most
Christian people turning into a herd of crazed beasts is just as relevant today as it
was back then.

* * *

What about Leo Tolstoy? He wrote about the God-fearing people in Tula
Province who caught horse thieves and burned them alive, without waiting for
the police.

Are you saying that a revolt had been possible in 1985, Alik?

I'm not talking about 1985 per se, but just about that period in general—and
that direction was one of the possibilities then. Think what would have
happened! It only takes one transgression, and once the crowd gets its first taste
of blood… Then you can't stop it. Only with bullets, only with executions.
Shouting, "People, stop and think!" won't do it.

It seems to me, Igor, that we can formulate the conditions under which
revolts occur. I don't want to refer back to Lenin—

Why not? Go ahead, the hell with it.

—but he wrote that revolutionary situations occur when there are objective
and subjective preconditions. The objective ones are [*here both authors quote the
classic in unison*] "an increase higher than usual of the needs and misery of the
masses." This precondition was there, especially in 1988 and 1989. Higher than
usual! There is a subtle point with the subjective preconditions. "The leaders
can't, and the people won't"—that's painfully obvious. The popular desire for
revolt, like everything else animal and subconscious that lives in us, is a desire for
violence. Flinging glasses of mineral water at each other in the Duma, arguing in
the press, fighting with your wife, a game of paint ball, sex, political fighting—
they are all a kind of ersatz revolt. The potential for aggression that is in all of us
must find an outlet. That holds for the potential for aggression of an entire

nation, as well; it too must be sublimated into something and given an outlet. Otherwise, there will be a revolt.

Kokh's Commentary:

In my memory, Russia was on the brink of a revolt two times. The first was in 1991, when the coup happened. The second was in 1993, the firing upon the White House (the Russian Parliament). Both times, people died. The first time, three died accidentally. The second time it was about 140, and not at all accidentally.

However, mass rebellions were avoided. Let me note right away that such a result of a serious confrontation was almost a first in Russian history. Why?

In my opinion, willingly or not, the authorities managed to redirect popular aggression into a relatively peaceful streambed. The people were given a surrogate of revolt—a legal political fight. Every evening on television and in the other media people saw officials, politicians, and elected leaders smear one another with filth and insult one another horribly. Accuse one another of every deadly sin. They screwed. Fought. Got drunk like pigs. A great number of absolutely free media offered the people access to the politicians of their choice. From Stalinist Communists to liberal anarchists. From Black Hundreds statists to militant Russophobes. On Sundays there were rallies for every taste and preference. A series of referenda and elections. Put Yeltsin's gang on trial. And so on.

And it worked. There was no rebellion. Vicious cruelty was sublimated into a virtual shoot-out. An imitation rebellion was a good vaccine against a real rebellion.

Our tsars, including Lenin and Stalin (and actually Khrushchev, too, with his Novocherkassk), were prepared to confront the elemental aggression of the people with an organized machine of state terror that was even crueler. They were prepared to drown any attempt at revolt in a sea of human blood. And they did it more than once.

Is today's regime ready for manifestations of insubordination?

Once oil prices fall and need and misery rise above usual levels, what will happen? The mechanism for sublimating aggression has been dismantled. Will we shoot? The "fake fight" in the Duma does not reflect even 10 percent of the spectrum of popular opinion.

An imitation revolt can stop a real one. An imitation revolt is real, open, and legal political struggle, not an imitation of political struggle—like when you have to go to the Kremlin for permission to criticize the Kremlin. Imitation imitations are secondary products, they don't work.

Please do not consider this commentary a call to revolt. It's just that I am afraid.

* * *

Then, Igor, tell me why the regime lost power in 1917? The objective preconditions had matured, that's true. But the important thing is that the regime did not give the people a way to sublimate their aggression into something else.

Hello! What about the war with the Germans?

No one wanted that war! No one wanted to fight—people didn't know what they were fighting for. No one was attacking us; we were the ones attacking…

To get the straits! There was a reason!

Go explain to an illiterate peasant about those straits. Now when the Nazis attacked us in 1941, everything was easy to understand. Who was right, who was wrong, did Stalin want to attack first or not—we're only getting around to that now. But back then, it was clear. And even so, think of all the people who gave themselves up. The situation was propagandized to look like the enemy attacked and we were innocent as lambs. And it worked. But when no one was attacking, when we attacked over some shitty Serbs?

They're like our brothers.

Are they brothers of the Tatars? Or the indigenous peoples of the Caucasus? The wild divisions fell by the hundreds—and the Serbs were not brother Slavs to them. What about the German generals who were in the tsar's headquarters and commanded our troops, and taught them how to fight the Germans? Boris Jordan's grandfather was a general staff colonel and fought in World War I against the Germans, yet he was a Baltic German—how were the Serbs his brothers?

Svinarenko's Commentary:

During the last Balkan crisis, I got accredited with the NATO headquarters in Skopje, before the start of land operations in Kosovo.

I wrote then: "Without a doubt, the people who are the closest and dearest brothers of the Serbs are the Macedonians. And are they all as one? I wouldn't say so. For example, it's night in the middle of the Macedonian capital, Skopje. People are leaving the discos. I'm musing over the draft-age boys who are walking out into the dark with their girlfriends—not to go be partisans against NATO, but to enjoy the pacific delights of love. And at the same time, making their way across the Hungarian border to help their Serbian brothers, whom they've never seen in their lives, come the hungry Russian volunteers, who have a change of underwear and five dollars for pocket expenses.

"NATO has no conscience!" fumes a Macedonian I stop in the street. "This is wrong! How dare they!? NATO even brings vegetables and water by plane from across the ocean for their soldiers! They enrich their farmers, but to be fair they should be buying food from Macedonian peasants! They're undermining our economy!"

I try to sympathize, but I'm not very convincing—just a minute ago this man had been demanding from Russia, in my person, that we bring over our *Zenith* SS-300 missiles. "Our economy is feverish because of them!" he continued. "The good whores used to cost $40, and NATO drove the prices up to $150. Plus the whores expect baksheesh—you know, jewelry, gold…."

"Well, that's a kind of investment—that is, a positive factor for the economy, isn't it?"

"Hah! Positive. Since the bombing of Belgrade they're not letting those poor bastards into town! So that important sphere of service is dying!"

"So?"

"So, let lots of Russian volunteers come! They get paid well, don't they?… What, they're unpaid? You must be kidding. That doesn't happen…."

The policeman at the exit from the refugee camp tugs my T-shirt that says "Moscow" and—gazing loyally at me—says what I've grown used to hearing in recent days: "NATO no gut. Roosia no help? What is problem?"

I stop and decide that the time has come to come clean with them and explain things to them:

"How much do you earn? Five hundred marks? And you own your house? And you have a car? Good. Your Russian colleagues have lived in trailers in the steppes ever since they were kicked out of Europe. Their salary is lower than yours, and it's never even paid. We have a terrible climate, and there's Chechnya, and the president has been hospitalized for years (it was Yeltsin then); the Communists are giving us grief. It's sickening! And now you want me to start a world war. A fine time you've picked for that!"

I spoke harshly, as a big brother. He listened in silence, and so did his pals. After a while they took out a half dozen Easter eggs, left over from the holiday, apparently offered as humanitarian aid for our poor officers."

* * *

Let's consider, Alik: Wasn't the Soviet Union a terrorist state? The USSR suppressed the Czechs and the Hungarians, sent arms to Africa, supported the partisans in Mozambique and Angola who attacked the

UAR, and trained diversionaries in our military schools—Kurds, Palestinians, and so forth....

Go take a look at West Point and all the foreigners being trained there.

So what?

Nothing. I think it's a universal practice. Especially for the superpowers. They love some Bokassa for a while, and then they discover that he eats children.

Now, don't exaggerate. He only ate adults!

You know, Alik, I really like the terminology: "an increase higher than usual of the needs and misery of the masses." That means that there's a good, normal level of need and misery.

Yes. I'll give you an example: the black community in Los Angeles. It lives in its usual need and standard misery. And then two cops beat up a black-assed guy—

You mean a black-assed African-American.

Yes. They beat him up, and that started something huge! Worse than all the riots in the black ghettoes of Detroit and the cities in the South.

That wasn't about need and misery, it was about an unjust trial, Alik, and the blacks were outraged.

Did you see the videotape? No? Oh boy. It began with the video. Look, in Moscow the people from the Caucasus are the blacks. Let's say you're from the Caucasus. You know very well what the Moscow cops are like and how to behave around them and so on. And then, you, an Azerbaijani, get drunk and run into three cops in a patrol car and start yelling at them: "Hey, you shitty faggots!" They say, "Watch it, buddy!" And you yell, "I shit on you!"

Who taped it?

Someone from a nearby building.

What a difference. Our prosecutor general poses with naked whores for the video camera while their cops attack blacks on camera. Different mentalities, what can I say?

And now, imagine that there's the trial of the cops. They say, oh, he interfered with police activity, and so we showed him. The court says, "You were behaving antisocially, pal, and they just tried to get you to be orderly, and you beat your head against the road yourself so as to incriminate the cops…" And here the lawyer shows the video—take a look at that, please.

And then what happened?

Then the police were put in prison, of course. But riots broke out in the black ghetto.

Why riot? The cops were put away.

They were put away only after the riots, Igor. The riots began when the video was shown on TV. What is there to be said? I'm a white man and I wouldn't risk jerking around the police in New York. Especially if I were drunk—it would end badly. I wouldn't risk jerking the cops around in Moscow. I wouldn't start. Drunk. At night. Alone.

We used to think back then that people were better and more honest, that they were industrious, that they could limit themselves, give up certain things for the greater good…

My generation went into the army when the Afghan war began; if people were kicked out of college, they were sent there. By 1985 they were coming back. We'd sit and drink and they would tell us about the war…

Well, the Afghan vets didn't set the tone for the time. On the whole, people were naïve and trusting; they didn't expect they would do the events in Baku or Sumgait—everything was fine, everyone was nice and sweet.

And Gorbachev thought "My people love me."

And the proletariat was proud of allegedly being the most progressive class. They thought being a worker was not simply dragging around metal and getting drunk, but also creating the history of the modern world. They sincerely thought, here I am, a laborer, I'm the best—and who are you?

An intellectual in glasses.

People really thought that, Alik! Workers got respect and honor, apartments and sanatoriums for vacations… And when the proletarians were stripped of the illusion that they were at the forefront, it was a terrible psychological blow. Suddenly, there was no one lower than the proletarians in society.

Well, the peasants, maybe.

Peasants are at least fed, drunk, and full of tobacco, to quote Pushkin. The proletarians have nothing. And just yesterday they thought they were so cool. After the proletarians, the poets and writers lost status. People used to listen to them, jaws dropping. No more. People expected the truth from TV, from the leader personally—and yet they were grown-up people. That year even people like us—forget about us, people like you—had selfless feelings and thought about the common good. How long did that naïve time last?

Until around 1989.

The Congress of People's Deputies, that's right, Alik. And then there was another surge in 1991 with the coup attempt.

With that second surge I went into government. I was elected mayor in 1990, and then so on. The decline was in 1987–1988.

All the authorities kept saying, we just have to get through two or three years, and then happiness will be upon us. Gorby used to say that, right?

No, only Boris Nikolayevich. He used to say, I'll lie down on the tracks… Shock therapy.

Naïve, trusting, beautiful times. There was never another period like it.

So how can we define the usual level of need and misery? When your salary is enough to buy food?

I don't know how to define it, Igor. Back in 1983-1984 I lived on the brink of poverty. Rats running around, the neighbor in our communal flat drunk, barely making ends meet. But we didn't consider ourselves impoverished. Our threshold of need and misery was lower than usual! If I lived that way now, I'd consider myself impoverished. But not back then. I made 200 rubles a month and my wife made 130, and that was fine.

An important point: In those days there was a comparatively low interest in money. You agree, don't you?

People were ashamed to be interested in money. Although I wasn't. Many of my friends were black marketeers, so I started developing a tolerant attitude back then. But people who are ten or fifteen years older than me couldn't even imagine such a thing.

Take me: "Me sell things on the black market? Never!"

I made a few attempts. Even though it was dangerous…

We all worked unloading freight. But I don't understand the Moscow ideology very well. Some oligarchs told me that they had been Communists and at the same time they worked unloading trucks at the Beriozka dollar store. They were boys from elite Moscow families. We didn't have that in St. Petersburg.

Svinarenko's Commentary:

I didn't have any money, either. Not just no interest in it. No one had forced me to major in journalism, I could have gone to college in Donetsk and become a store manager, or a dentist, for example. With my school medal they would have taken me into trade school or medical school without admissions tests. What kept me from choosing the easy path to quick riches? Who knows? But the strangest thing is this: I don't regret not becoming a rich dentist specializing in prosthetics. Or, for example, an oil magnate. When people say that money doesn't buy happiness, it always sounds rather unconvincing. But when I was young I thought—and still do today—that if you win, you can take the money or you can take something else. Naturally, with money you can buy many pleasant things and services. But I've seen people who got nothing but major trouble from money, and some even had shortened lives—among people very close to me. There was one time in 1993 when I came incredibly close to drowning in the ocean near Australia—I was caught in a riptide. I managed to get to shore with the last of my strength, and fell onto the sand panting like a whipped horse. I truly could have drowned, while some poor, miserable wretch would have lived for another fifty years, never leaving his crummy Ivanovsk Oblast, having no money for expensive vacations.

* * *

So, the interest in money, Alik—

—Was on the level of satisfying minimal needs.

What was that? Protracted childhood?

Who the hell knows? No one was preparing us for capitalism. It appeared on its own.

Could you live poorly now? Or would you say, kill me instead?

What would be the point of this experiment? I don't understand it. What's this great need to live a poor life? I don't feel the need. And then…Prince Menshikov, for instance, was one of the richest men in Russia—

He stole everything in St. Petersburg.

What difference does that make?

What do you mean, what difference?

He built everything first, and then he stole it. But it doesn't matter.

You make me laugh, Alik. How can it not matter?

All right, all right, he was probably a thief. And then he was exiled to Berezov. They say he felt fine there. Chopped wood, took steam baths in his banya. Of course, he had no money.

Hmmm... Berezovsky was exiled to London, and Menshikov to Berezov.

I'm telling you about him to show you what kind of people were forced to live in exile, poorly, and still managed fine.

A friend told me that if things revert to a Soviet regime, he'll stay in Russia anyway. He's ready to trade in his BMW for a Moskvich, driving and belching smoke, because he's spent time in the West and realized that it bores him and he didn't want to live there.

In that sense, Igor, I'm not afraid of poverty. I just feel sorry for my children. I crawled out of shit, and I can crawl back in. I wouldn't be ashamed to wear a cheap quilted work jacket.

What about the children? Why are you sorry for them?

They were born into a good life, and they're not equipped for any other.

Maybe you should prepare them for that life, as well?

What for?

Take Bunin: He was a nobleman, and he mowed grass, hung out with the peasants, ate gruel with them.

I see. Nevertheless, when he was faced with a choice, he hightailed it to France. For some reason, he didn't want to keep on mowing with the people. While Tsvetaeva, who was from that same crowd, ended up hanging herself in Elabuga.

Bunin managed to survive when the peasants came to burn down his place in 1917. He went out onto the veranda, just in case, for a clear conscience, not expecting it to work, and shouted at the peasants—something like "Get out of here, you swine!" Out of old memories of the way things were, they left, burnt by the sun.

Svinarenko's Commentary:

From Bunin's *Accursed Days*:

How unbridled the village grew last summer, how terrifying it was to live in Vasilyevskoe! And suddenly came the rumor: Kornilov had introduced the death penalty. And almost all of July, Vasilyevskoe was as quiet as quiet can be. But in May and June it was scary to walk down the street; every night you would see the red lights of a fire on the black horizon. They set fire to our barn at dawn once, and then all the villagers came and shouted that we had set it ourselves in order to burn down the village. At noon the same day, the neighbor's cattle yard went up in flames, and they came from all over the village again and wanted to throw me into the fire, shouting that I had set it, and I was saved only by the fury that set me cursing and attacking the screaming mob.

* * *

Bunin understood and immediately split—first to Moscow and then, via Odessa, to Paris. Nevertheless, Alik, don't you think you should give your children a different experience—not just being rich, but also a simple life?

Like what? Go mowing with them? Where?

Like American millionaires who send their children to work as waiters for the summer. Do you know about that?

I've read about it, but I've never seen it.

I have. In America, not here, of course.

You're lucky.

5.

1986

The Fifth Bottle

*P*erestroika was growing stronger. Acceleration was increasing. Glasnost was off the charts: even the Chernobyl catastrophe was revealed after only a few weeks. But the "friendship between the peoples" was still getting heavy PR, even after the "events" in Alma-Ata, where the Kazakhs beat up Russians.

The event of the year was Sakharov's return to Moscow... It may have been the tipping point: the father of the hydrogen bomb, and also the country's main dissident, was set free and offered up to the legal press. This was it: complete permissiveness! What's white, what's black, who's a friend, who's an enemy—how could you tell anymore? That's how great kingdoms perish. Sic!

First, Alik, talk a little about your life at that time.

I continued writing my dissertation.

You seem to have spent a lot of time writing it. How many chapters is it that you have to keep talking about it?

I used all the time allotted—three years. From 1983 until spring of 1986. And I defended it sometime in February, 1989.

And what discoveries did you make in your dissertation? For science, for the country?

You don't have to make any discoveries for your doctorate.

Come on!

It's enough to demonstrate innovation.

You mean any clod can sit down and write his dissertation and defend it?

Sure, if there is something new in it.

It's enough to write something that no one has written before you? We reporters do that every day.

You're right. In that sense, we're all doctoral candidates. But let's not exaggerate. Writing a dissertation isn't all that easy.

What's the minimum for a PhD in Scientific Communism?

Well, let's take that as an example. You have to pass philosophy—

Marxist-Leninist.

No, all philosophy.

Yeah, right, all of it.

I swear. As I recall, we studied Aristotle and Mach and Occam's razor—

Tell us about the razor.

It's the principle of economy, but for thinking. Roughly: If there are several ways of demonstrating a postulate, the truest one will be the simplest one. Why explain in a convoluted way, if you can explain it simply? There was this fellow Occam, and he basically said you have to cut away all the excess.

Leo Tolstoy obviously was writing before Occam.

Well, he was a count; he stayed at his estate and worked… Scribbled.

Ah, first he strolled through the village, screwed everyone, then wrote a bit, then plowed a bit. Not a bad set-up!

I really don't like this image you've chosen for yourself: You look like an idiot.

Why an idiot? It's well known that he had half the serfs in Yasnaya Polyana. That the people there all look like him. Haven't you ever heard this?

I heard it mentioned once or twice. But, he wasn't the only one, Igor.

And his wife really let him have it.

Yes.

Tolstoy was rebuked for starting to advocate a healthy way of life—that is, not healthy but quite the contrary—abstinence! After he had screwed several dozens of thousands of women.

He said: You are living incorrectly, copulating without end, eating meat. You should eat carrots and think about eternity. They replied: Grandpa, when we're seventy like you are, we will also eat carrots and stop copulating! He says: No, you should start right now, while you still want to do it. They replied again: Old man, that's not fair—give us a chance to catch up with you. And we'll kill some people in war... If you had started abstaining at the age of twenty, we might listen to you now...

Listen, we've talked about this already.

Well, it's an eternal theme.

As eternal as it is banal. Even Ilf and Petrov discuss it in *The Twelve Chairs*—that Tolstoy ate meat when he was writing *War and Peace.*

Kokh's Commentary:

I. Ilf and E. Petrov. *The Twelve Chairs*, chapter 19: "Respect Mattresses, Citizens."

> Liza cried.
> "Leo Tolstoy," said Kolya in a trembling voice, "didn't eat meat, either."
> "Ye-e-s," Liza replied, hiccupping with tears. "The count ate asparagus."
> "Asparagus isn't meat."
> "But when he was writing *War and Peace* he ate meat. He did, he did, he did! And when he was writing *Anna Karenina* he gobbled, gobbled, gobbled, too!"
> "Shut up!"
> "Gobbled! Gobbled! Gobbled!"
> "And did he gobble when he wrote 'The Kreutzer Sonata'?" Kolya asked acidly.
> "'The Kreutzer Sonata' is short. I'd like to see him try writing *War and Peace* on vegetable cutlets!"

* * *

You mean to say that you are not interested in eternal themes, Alik, because you do not intend to live forever?

That's in Ilf and Petrov, too: "I don't need an eternal needle or the Primus stove, because I do not intend to live forever."

So, to sum up, Tolstoy wrote without the help of Occam's razor. Chekhov, though—who screwed around no less than the count—cut out every superfluous word. But he didn't go on about it too much.

What do you mean, didn't go on about it? What about in his letters?

Except in the letters, then. But he didn't take it upon himself to teach people; he felt that *that* was personal and private.

Tolstoy didn't go on about his passion, either. On the contrary, he shouted from every rooftop, "Stop doing that, stop fooling around!"

But Chekhov really did use that razor to cut away the flimflam, Alik. Unlike some. So, where did we stop? Ah, I remember. So, you got your degree. But I didn't. I wonder why? What was I missing? Probably scholarship seemed dull to me, compared to the reporter's life. And I lacked the perseverance for the dispassionate examination of facts.

You can't say I'm particularly persevering. If you like what you're doing, you don't notice the time fly. For example, yesterday I was editing our fourth chapter and I didn't notice two hours go by at all. I can't say that I had the same drive when I was writing the dissertation, though there were a few moments like that... When you have the drive, when you like what you're doing, then the word "perseverance" doesn't apply. And especially if you're being paid for doing what you would do anyway... Now if you're a young man and you want to have sex all the time, and you have sex, are you being persevering? Or if you keep at the boozing, because you like boozing...You go on a bender, you drink for one day, two days, three—what a persevering fellow, eh? And then you stop drinking because you're tired.

Some say that humans are incapable of doing what they don't want to do, Alik. It's easier to kill them. When someone says he's doing it for the homeland, the children, or his wife, he's just lying in order to appear altruistic. And make himself look good. And get something in exchange.

I had an interesting thought. They say Russians are a lazy people, and they say the British are industrious. Please note, Igor, that I've intentionally avoided mentioning the Germans.

Or Ukrainians.

Yes. So, if you interpret industriousness as the ability to force yourself to do what you don't like... Then think how miserable the English must be! They keep working on things that they don't like.

What kind of things did they have to do? Big deal! Horsewhip Hindus on their plantations, sail around in ships…

Drop it, already. Ships! What about in the mills? During the Industrial Revolution?

The alternative was starving to death.

Exactly. But that's an industrious nation. In Russia, when you're faced with starvation, you revolt! Heads fly! Round the clock! *Because people like it.*

The point is that the British, like other Europeans, were placed in situations where you either work or starve. There was a third option in Russia—the most pleasant one. You talk about rebellions: When people rebelled in England, the police came right away and hanged everyone.

The police came and hanged everyone here, too.

But here you could run off to the Don River. It's an enormous country. A long stretch of poorly guarded borders, expansive territory, Cossacks everywhere from Khortitsa and the Don to Ussuri—that's what created this kind of mentality: if you don't like something, kill the master and run away.

In Europe everything is divided up, the territory is already mastered, every cop knows all the thieves in his precinct… Like in the French crime novels, where the commissionaire sits in his office and thinks: "So who committed the theft? Jean is behind bars, Roger is dead; that means it must be Michel." He goes to Michel's place, knowing his address and that of his girlfriend, and Michel gives up right away because he knows he's got nowhere to run…

So here's my idea: The European mentality, which is so unlike ours, formed that way because people had no place to go.

I don't agree, Igor. How about jumping on a ship and becoming a pirate? Essentially, it's just like the Cossacks.

In Russia, with the diffuse regime and lack of roads, a man could travel by way of forests and back roads from any point in the country to the Cossacks. To the Don or the Ussuri. But in Europe there are all those cordons and cops.

I don't agree, Igor.

OK. So we have two versions, yours and mine. You think that it was possible to cut and run in Europe the way it was here, and I think that you can't run away there.

There is always room for adventure in life. Why couldn't you—from any European city—just go to the port and sign up with the pirates?

You think there are pirates just hanging around the ports, and no one is arresting them?

They were sitting around in the taverns hiring people, disguised as innocent sailors. Haven't you read any books?

Speaking of books and writing, you had almost finished writing your dissertation. You were headed down a well-marked road, and everything was clear to you.

No. I had problems getting a job. I wasn't registered to live in Leningrad; my residence permit was for the "Leningrad region." No one would hire me. Even with my degree, I continued working as a janitor. Well, formally, I didn't have the degree yet, but I had finished all the courses and was waiting for the inevitable defense—my turn was coming.

Your rights were trampled.

No they weren't. I was very happy. By the way, after I defended my dissertation and went to work at the institute, my parents stopped helping me financially—that was it, I had finished school, I was independent. So we were worse off than when I was a janitor.

In 1986, Alik, I was still working for the newspaper in Kaluga, but I wrote for the big papers, too—*Sobesednik, Komsomolskaya Pravda, Sovetskaya Rossiia*. That was considered very cool in those days. They weren't like today's papers, but real ones, high quality, big-time—sort of like *Kommersant* in the early 1990s.

Why had they noticed you? There were lots of provincial journalists. Did they appreciate your witty pen? Had you captured the spirit of perestroika?

When perestroika started, the Central Committee demanded that the national papers publish striking material. Where can you get striking materials? Naturally, on the spot, locally. Send us information on all the local problems. And people said, sure, we'll report on that—and that was it for us.

And you didn't care?

Well. It's entertaining, all these powerful emotions.

It's just like now—you can't criticize the Kremlin, but since we're on the path to democracy, then you have to criticize somebody. Let's pick on the local little tsars. And who knows the situation better than the local journalists? Then let's take the most talented of them, like Svinarenko—

Well, for example?

You can criticize everything except the president; he's like Caesar's wife, above suspicion. But the governors are fair game. And ministers. That's why everyone's going on about how bad they are. In that sense we have made progress.

Yes. In the past we could criticize only janitors, like you, Alik, and now we criticize ministers. With impunity, by the way. The Komsomol newspapers were allowed to do more even then—letting off steam, all that... There was a logic to it all: Don't touch the foundations. One of the top managers of today's media journalism—a big democrat, naturally— used to pace around his office, tearing out his hair. Why did I bring him that article, how could I endanger him that way? How was I endangering him, I'd ask—it's not printed, we're the only two people to have read it. He'd scream no, it's a trap, a provocation—what if they find out the kind of people he's been harboring?

This is the article he axed: A certain fellow in Tula—by the way, also a PhD in economics—founded a so-called worker's club, where he gathered proletarians in the evenings and went over production issues with them. The Party attacked him right away—expelled him—and he was left out there swinging in the breeze. I wrote an article that asked why they were bothering the man: Let him work with the proletarians and tell them whatever he wants, they won't understand anyway. It's funny to remember now, but they used the morality clause on him: He'd gotten a divorce and then remarried. Which, as a Party member, he was not allowed to do.

Why not? Are Communists Catholic or something?

Yes they are. Moreover, fuck them. What are you bugging me for? Did I write the CPSU bylaws or something?

I'm against divorce too, Igor, but I want to understand them... They had rejected marriage.

Yes, that was Alexandra Kollontai fooling around with sailors and Lenin with his mistress, Inessa Armand, and so forth.

The Communists really were nuts about family issues. But I want to understand the reasons, Igor. Can you explain it to me?

I can!

Go on.

Hmmm. According to the Communist version, a man must get used to the idea that he belongs completely to the Party. That it rules him completely. When he divorces, he puts his emotions and instincts above party discipline.

I don't understand.

What don't you understand? The bosses tell him not to get a divorce, and the bastard does it anyway.

I don't understand what business it is of theirs!

If you divorce your wife, the momentum might lead you to say: "The hell with you, too!" They lose control of you.

Hmmm.

I think that was the idea. It's like when you come to a monastery and take vows: Sit there, and be quiet. It's obedience school: They tell you something, and you go do it. And don't question things that are not up to you. For example, if the family dies off tomorrow, it will be announced to you from the stage of the Communist Party Congress.

I still don't understand.

Why are you making me responsible for the CPSU? I don't give a shit about it!

But as an engineer of human souls you must understand why the Communists loved the institution of marriage. The very one that was destroyed in the end by socialism.

What do you mean, destroyed? And why that institution?

Because it led to the personalizing of some property. To the instinct of personal property. To the defense of one's own children, rather than all children. The family destroyed Communism. Why didn't the peasants want to march their bulls off to the communal farms? Because they had families, that's why.

It could have happened for another reason, too. When a Russian man divorces his wife and starts living alone, he immediately quits shaving,

starts drinking vodka in the morning, messes everything up, stops going to work—the usual story.

So they had a utilitarian approach?

Quite possibly!

"Since we Communists can't deal with the drunkenness of Russians, let their wives deal with it." Like that?

Exactly! Haven't you ever noticed, Alik: A married man is always clean and decent looking, but once he gets a divorce, he turns into a pig… The local drunks start gathering at his place, the furniture all gets sold, there's bottles getting tossed out the window, people screwing in the corner on an old coat… The place turns into a refuge for bums and crooks.

No more showing up at work.

Right. And then a Party member is no longer distinguishable from a street bum.

Then what can be said of non-members?

It's the end for them, too. A Russian man is like a child. First his mother takes care of him, gives him candy and makes him go to school. Then the wife picks up the baton and takes on this noble and thankless task… God forbid a man is left without a mistress—in the sense of "master"—it's all over for him then. He's uncared for. Statistics show us that the married man lives longer and is healthier than the bachelor. Why? Because his wife doesn't let him drink or go out whoring too much. She tries to rein him in. Like the Party.

Which became the bastion of petty bourgeois principles.

There aren't any others, let's be frank.

Well, there are grand bourgeois principles. But nothing beyond that, I agree.

As for that missionary of economics, the one in Tula, the joke is that he quickly realized the divorce was a mistake and married the same woman again. He tried to persuade them that morally, he should be pure in the Party's eyes. Even during his temporary divorce, he didn't sleep with anyone else; he spent his time littering the brains of the proletariat with economics. They told him, essentially you're right—but formally, you

got a divorce and then got married again. **They considered his one wife to be two separate women.**

So the seditious part was that he had been divorced temporarily? What didn't they like about the article?

The editor explained it to me. It's just one step, he said, from a worker's club to independent unions; and from them just half a step to an attack on Article 6 of the Constitution.

On the leading and directing role of the Communist Party?

Yes. All the "rebellion" was getting through the Komsomol press, but here I felt I had hit a barrier: No touching below the waist. You can't touch the ass. You can fondle the breasts, but no ass. That was the limit of legal criticism, Alik. Don't touch the girl's ass—understand?

Yes.

That's how it went. Small hassles with the Kaluga bureaucrats. And a stormy personal life. I wasn't married then. Adventures, arguments, it was all very wearying. You're married, you don't remember what it's like to be on the market... You were married even then, so there's nothing you can tell about your personal life.

Right, I can't. Do you know that in the ancient world there were two kinds of states, theocratic and secular? You know how the theocratic ones were organized? The owner of the state and of the people was God. People obeyed the teaching and were governed by priests and military leaders. The secular one, of course, was headed by a completely secular emperor, who governed by totally secular means. Then they began adding that he was a god or a semi-god.

Like a half-breed.

Yes. So, in terms of the management system, our regime is a secular state. At its head is the emperor, whose person is not subject to criticism. Everything else can be criticized, within reason. That leads to a positive atmosphere. But Communism—that was a theocratic state. You can criticize Comrade Brezhnev as much as you like, but remember that as a person he's a piece of shit, he is merely the conduit for God's will and the holy teaching. When he opens his mouth, he's not speaking personally—he's not some flesh and blood man from Dneprodzerzhinsk—and when you criticize him, you are attacking the foundation, our religion. Comrade Brezhnev is nothing; he is conduit and priest. He is an oracle! He has received the message, and he passes it on.

A vestal of sorts.

Exactly, Sybillae. That's why Communism in the Russian version was a theocratic state. Thoroughly religious! And that's why it would not accept the figures of any other religion. Because they were competing in the same arena.

Let me tell you something, Alik. Try asking the following of a contemporary Russian priest: "Why do you have to pray standing up in Russian Orthodox churches, while other religions let you sit while you pray? Even the Orthodox in the Balkans sit during the service." He will probably reply that people come to church not for pleasure but to perform an act of self-denial. Where else have we heard about exploits! Where have we seen that asceticism, the burning eyes, the demand for self-denial... That's why Bolshevism went over so well in Russia.

Yes, we were trained to perform exploits...

Even the terminology is the same. The Bolsheviks really did work in that field. Mortification of the flesh... Why eat sausage? Have some carrots, and shut up. That is, the Bolsheviks exploited the centuries-old habits of the people. By the way, you say that the Bolsheviks protected the family. They were the ones who banned abortions, back in 1936. Comrade Stalin did it. He wanted to strengthen, if not the family, then morality.

They hammered the idea of right and wrong into his head back in the seminary.

Right... Have we forgotten anything about 1986? Wait—Chernobyl! It happened right before the May 1 holiday, in late April. It wasn't announced until after all the May holidays were over.

Only because the foreign radio stations began reporting on it almost on the next day, Igor. The clouds of radiation traveled.

I was fishing from the first to the third of May that year—on the Reseta River. It's in the south of Kaluga Oblast. On the border with Bryansk Oblast.

Not Bryansk!

Yes, Bryansk! Ha! Which was later declared a danger zone. Our fishing trip consisted of spending all day floating in rubber boats in very slow water, barely noticeable, casting our fly rods. We'd catch a pike here, an okun there... All day long in the fresh air! All that radiation! All that radioactive dust falling on us! That's how we boated through the danger

zone... Kolya Nizov, our chief fisherman and organizer, he was on the river every weekend and day off. He died in his prime—something about his blood, and he wasn't even fifty. It's no joke, boating in the Chernobyl region.

In 1987, when I started working in a closed institute, there was a radiological safety department, which must have been for submarines, since the institute belonged to the ministry of shipbuilding. Whenever you walked past it—

You couldn't get it up.

No, worse. Every day there would be a new obituary and photo... In the line of duty... Doctoral student.... They sent entire labs full of them to Chernobyl to set up radiological protection—and they all died.

When Kolya was dying, he said, Bury my fishing sneakers at the river. What do you think? We did it. [*After the Russian nuclear explosion, another member of our fishing party died of cancer, the journalist Igor Babichev. And then I ended up in treatment, too. ...*]

Here's another one, Igor: I had a friend when I was young, whose father was an avid mushroom hunter. He kept bringing mushrooms back from southern Belorussia. That was the fallout zone! She said, "Oh, that's just nonsense! Why don't you believe every word in the papers while you're at it? Don't pay any attention! Everyone in Belorussia eats them." A year later, her father died... of cancer.

Another fisherman from our group, Grisha, was a teacher, and he always brought kids from the school down to the river. There were foxholes and blinds, spent shells, all that stuff leftover from the war... So he took kids there for patriotic studies—and to get some fishing and swimming in, too. The kids must have swallowed a lot of Chernobyl there, too. Our leaders are always whining about how the West is so wary of Russia. But we hadn't told them about our explosion! Or that a cloud was headed their way. What can you expect from people like that? How can you trust them? Basically, it was a nuclear terrorist attack on them.

No, it's deeper than that. They thought: It's bad enough that they didn't tell us, but they didn't even tell their own people! They had studied the Soviet Union pretty well by then, and they understood why the West had not been informed— that was normal, they expected it. We weren't supposed to tell them, they were the enemy. But not to tell your own people... That's what stunned the West.

"They're ready to fuck over their people just to stay in power! There's no hope for us at all," they thought.

And they chased the kids out for the May Day parade. Instead of saying: Kids, stay home, breathe through cheesecloth. Adults, drink as much alcohol as you can to dissolve the radionuclides.

Even better would have been: get out of here—go as far away as you can. But they didn't say that. Because for them, the people were no longer people. They treated people like work stations, like machines.

But not everyone! There's a very important exception—this just killed me during those years, Alik. They kept it pretty quiet, but they did a remarkable thing: Usually, if a Party member wanted out of whatever hellhole they'd put him in, they would torture him viciously, berate him for fleeing the front lines, and so on. And they'd threaten him: they wouldn't let him go, they could expel him from the Party, so good bye career—that sort of thing. But they made a decision about the regions affected by the catastrophe: Communists could be taken off the work rolls without any discussion. Or any guilt trips. What was that about? An attempt to save the cadres? Or plain old cynicism—you know, let the ordinary people die, but save the Party members? Or were they regressing from the new kind of Party back to the old model? In general they had always felt that the idea was more important than the actual people—

What idea? If the people all die off, who would carry out the idea?

Let me tell you this, Alik. Didn't the film *Go and See* come out that year?

Elem Klimov's film? I thought it was pretty weak—it's a horror show, nothing more. *Ivan's Childhood* was more powerful, and it didn't spill its guts all over you.

That's not the point—whatever you watch now, it all seems weak, even *1900*, which everyone was flipping for then. I'm talking about something else, how the Party hacks worked me over for my review of the film.

What did you write?

There's a scene where the partisans capture some Nazis and decide to have them shot. A German officer says: We hate you, and even if you shoot us, we will still win, and you're stupid and wrong. So I wrote: Look, the guy is ready to die for an idea. That's a positive trait. But here's the

problem: What if the idea is pure shit? Maybe it's not worth dying for, then? I was called into the Party offices. They said, See, we knew that your little exposés would lead to no good; you've reached the point of making apologies for fascism; you find positive traits in Nazis.... I replied, What are talking about? And they replied, We're no fools, we know which "idea" you had in mind—what other idea is there?...

You should have said, "You've given yourselves away!"

Exactly. It was hilarious. My editor-in-chief was sitting there, and he was attacking me too. And I said, You, of all people, should keep quiet. He furrowed his brow even more. I had anticipated the agenda of this meeting and had come prepared: I took out the page that he had signed off on—my article, with his signature on it. That meant: OK to print. This was the guy who wouldn't let me take time off after donating blood.

So the West has reason to be upset with us, friend Alik. Russians keep wanting other people to trust them, but they don't trust themselves. It's not very nice. As for Chernobyl, I'll tell you—that was Chubais's department. That was his company, United Energy Systems (RAO UES)!

No, no, no! Nuclear reactors have nothing to do with Chubais, that's Rosenergoatom.

You're always defending Chubais for whatever comes up. I remembered something else thinking about energy. Have you been to the restaurant Uzbekistan recently?

About two weeks ago. I like *chebureki*.

Did you notice an item on the menu called "light bulb shashlyk"?

No.

How could you miss it? Light bulbs means balls.

What kind of balls—rubber?

Bull balls! Bull! I immediately thought about "Ilyich light bulbs." That's about electricity and energy.

Fine. The eternally living Ilyich and his balls on a spit....I prefer *luliakebabs*, they're particularly good in Brighton Beach.

I like going there. Pelmeni, vodka, Plexiglas counters in the shops.

Have you noticed that there are no supermarkets there?

It's easier to steal in supermarkets.

Probably.

So, we're clear on Chernobyl... It was the last nail in the coffin of Communism.

It was a colossal financial loss, too, Igor. Huge amounts of money were spent to eliminate at least some of the consequences. If they hadn't done what they did, it would have been even worse. Think of all the people who were killed! They had said that thirty million people would die in the end. It was also a mortal blow to the Soviet Union in terms of trust in the regime. The people began to understand the scale of the catastrophe and the scale of the treachery. And they people said, Sorry, no thanks...

Stalin, after Hitler tricked him, came out a month later and said, "Brothers and sisters, save me!" But Gorbachev didn't come out and say, "Save me!"

And they didn't.

Svinarenko's Commentary:

I'm going to quote Grachev, who was the General Secretary's press secretary then:

The true scale of the tragedy was not realized by the country's leaders until a few days later. Also, this was the first—and therefore an especially terrible—sign, a bad omen. A symbol of disaster that would overshadow perestroika forever. The system blew up—like a complicated mine in the hands of an inexperienced sapper.

... Chernobyl turned into a tough test of the promises of perestroika, and in particular of the most demanding one—the promise of glasnost.

The worried silence of the Politburo, trying to figure out the true size of the tragedy; the requisite attempts of the local Ukrainian authorities to downplay its scale in order "not to upset Moscow"; the fear of the agencies responsible for the construction and management of the reactor—all these essentially minor concerns, the worries of confused people who didn't understand what had happened, together formed a knot of bureaucratic interests and intrigues. To cut it would have required a desperately needed display of political will.

Gorbachev was silent for fourteen days. And even though on the level of practical steps the authorities' reaction was appropriate to the tragedy, neither the country nor the outside world has full clarity about what really happened. Of course, due to the global nature of the catastrophe, it was obvious from day one that it could not be covered up, but apparently Gorbachev had to overcome a purely psychological barrier to admit it. The same barrier that Yuri Andropov could not (of course, he was hovering between life and death then) overcome when the Soviet air force shot down the South Korean passenger plane. When he finally appeared on television with an address to the nation and gave a frank account of what had happened, Gorbachev made an important discovery for himself: "A full confession" not only softened the consequences of the blow that had been struck to the political and moral authority of perestroika, but it freed his hands for decisive action in an extreme situation.

… Having bared his soul, he emphatically assured the members of the Politburo: "We are acting under the supervision of our people and of the entire world. So let's not try to hide anything. Tell them openly what happened; people expect that from us here and abroad." … No longer on the subject of Chernobyl, when he responded at a Politburo meeting to Chebrikov—who was against the publication of Vasil Bykov's novella "Sign of Disaster," having vigilantly found in it an "undermining of collectivization"—Gorbachev fumed, "Yes, there will be excesses. Everything will be washed away by the flow that will form. There will be foam, and rubbish, but it is a sign of spring, of renewal, part of the democratization process. The flywheel has to be spun. Don't be afraid. The important thing is that the people are reacting, lifting up their heads. Hitting them on their heads, commanding again—that would be a betrayal of democracy.

* * *

It was a rehearsal for the collapse of the Soviet Union, Alik. A dress rehearsal.

Yes, the first run-through. Academicians shot themselves, if you remember. Alexandrov, president of the Academy of Sciences, quit… Afterward came the awards for the uninvolved and punishment for the innocent.

How much money do you think they stole during the clean-up, Alik? Tell me, as a learned economist.

I don't understand the mechanism for stealing money in the Soviet Union. How could you steal seriously in those day? Officials didn't have offshore accounts. Somebody could swipe enough for a dacha or a new model Zhiguli… It fell off the truck…

There was also a Congress of the CPSU. You might remember.

Really, a Congress?

How pleasant that it can all be forgotten: congresses and other crap like that… Goodbye, Satan! Yes, there was another congress. And then the secretary of the Kaluga committee came back from it and called all the journalists in again.

Ah, yes, the 28th Congress. Communists for Democracy, etc, etc.

I don't remember… So, the secretary returned. We were waiting to see what he would say. And he said they'd been told that criticism was needed, but it had to be constructive. In other words, nothing changed.

They're impossible to change! Gorbachev, even if he had wanted to change things, would never have succeeded. Ever! Those local bosses could never be forced to work differently! They only respond to money. Former first secretaries, the ones who are governors now—did you see how many of them went the commercial route? For the money! They were being told to close down the Party distributors, give up their cars, and run for election…You get elected as chairman of the council, and then we'll appoint you First Secretary. That really was how they were expected to behave. Their response was, What the fuck do I want to do that for? I stepped over people, betrayed my comrades, reported to the KGB—and for what? So that my family and I could shop in closed stores and eat good ham and sausages—

That are bad for your health.

Yes. And drink good "embassy" vodka. Get rabbit fur coats without waiting in line. And you, you bastard, you want me to run for election. To be elected by those same comrades I sold out. You can't change the rules of the game that way. And they could have added: Please note, Comrade Gorbachev, that you yourself aren't prepared to ask for the people's vote. You want specially selected deputies to elect you at a congress—no general elections for you!

Gorbachev violated an important principle of negotiations. When you want to take something away from someone—

—offer him something in return.

Gorbachev didn't offer them anything. That was his weakness as a businessman.

The Communists always suffered from the lack of a balanced position. They would say, Give it up first and then (maybe, if you're still alive) we can talk… If you don't give it up, then you certainly won't stay alive. Comrade Stalin, he didn't fool around with those Party cadres.

In other words, there were only prohibitions: drinking, whoring, divorcing, having a nice dacha—all were banned. And now they weren't even allowed to go to the special Party stores… So what was it all for? What could they do?

I can answer that: You could have a state-owned dacha as long as you held your post, Igor. And you could screw your cook, as long as you were her boss.

But when you stopped being the boss, the pretty cook would just say *ciao*. As long as you were a big boss, you could travel abroad—even, miracle of miracles, to capitalist countries. So you *have* to hold on to your job for as long as your heart is still beating. And do whatever they tell you, without discussion. Because without that job, you're just a piece of you-know-what. If you lose the job, you can have a dacha that's only 6 *sotki*. Without heat or a bathhouse—you're not a director of some industrial base!

I remember the reason they limited dachas to 6 sotki: Allegedly, they figured that a piece of land that size, in our climate, was too small for a family to grow enough food to start to feel independent—and tell the state to go to hell.

That's not true! A family can manage on that, Igor. Some Russian dacha owners manage to get a harvest on 6 sotki that would be the envy of Dutch, French, or German farmers! Potatoes, vegetables, berries…

There were some Soviet statistics indicating that so-called personal plots produced a third of the potatoes and half of all the meat in the country. I remember that well, as an agrarian journalist. So… Officials were given all kinds of pleasant things—not to keep, but sort of to rent. That was popular under the Soviets—skis, televisions, tents, furniture—all on loan. The big shots got dachas and cars.

Leasing.

That's becoming a popular business, judging from the ads. It even makes sense—you just rent a dacha and you don't have to worry about repairs and all that… What books were you reading then?

In 1986? I was re-reading Herzen's *My Past and Thoughts*. An interesting book!

Hm… The last time I picked it up was in 1981, when Poland was dealing with the forming of the Solidarity union.

It was in that book—official literature, recommended reading!—that I saw criticism of Marx, for example.

I don't remember. What did it say, that he lied about everything?

It was the first time I was exposed to the idea that the instigating force behind all revolutions is envy. Herzen wrote that in the book.

No wonder he was exiled to London. Like Berezovsky. Who is sort of the successor to *The Bell*.

Please, Igor, I beg you. The man who almost died to get the current regime into power suddenly flares up with such hatred for it, and starts saying, Oh no, oh no, beware!

He used to steal cars. They've charged him with that.

Who knows what happened… The law enforcement agencies have had varying attitudes toward Berezovsky. You remember how the Aeroflot case was dropped for lack of any charges against him. And then it reappeared. What's that about? Did he steal alone, or with someone else? And if it was with someone else, they're still in charge of the company, aren't they? My feelings for Berezovsky are complex, but let's be objective—it just doesn't happen that way.

He's a fun guy, right?

Right.

No one's ever amused the Russian public the way he has, Alik! He's got scope. Back in 1986 there was also a lot of material on UFOs. Allegedly the U.S. had been preserving a flying saucer that crashed in 1947—with the corpses of aliens in it…

I remember that. Then it turned out that the Russians had invented flying saucers long ago, and they exist. Somewhere in Saratov. Like shoeing a flea, even though it died.

But still flies. What do you think about space aliens?

I was never particularly interested in the topic. I've never thought about it. What is the point of thinking about it?

Well, to shift the blame on them for something or other—the murder of Listyev or Sobchak.

Are you sure that Sobchak was murdered? That he didn't die of natural causes?

See, you didn't say: "What are you going on about, how could anyone have killed him!" You are merely asking a specific question, whether I'm sure. He died at such a convenient time…

But in his own bed.

Yes. So did Stalin, practically. I like the version where the guards were afraid to go into Stalin's room, the doctors were afraid to treat him, the

Politburo was afraid he'd survive, and TASS was afraid to announce the great leader had kicked the bucket.

Cheyne-Stokes respiration. Stalin had that before his death, that was reported.

All right. And Chumak doesn't interest you either, Alik?

No, he doesn't. But the fact that Chumak interested so many people in Russia? That interests me.

A man who used to organize Chumak's concerts—

That's a fine word for his performances.

Anyway, he booked stadiums for him. Chumak would be onstage, but the crew would already be drinking. During intermission, they'd tell him to join in, but he'd say, I can't, I still have the second half of the show to do, the people are waiting. They would throw out advice, what to say to the audience. Chumak came out onstage once and said into the mike: "And now, before we start the second half, twenty minutes of healing silence."

Ha!.

Kokh's Commentary:

By the way, Mavrodi and all those other pyramid schemes started with these concerts. Hustle city. If it were up to me, I would give intelligence tests to all the people who went to see Kashpirovksy and Chumak, who bought shares of MMM and all those other Khoper-Invests. I'd have them certified as feebleminded and take away their right to vote.

I'm certain that the list of those people would correspond ninety-nine percent with the list of people who vote for Zhirinovsky and the Communists. They truly are subnormal.

Like that Vlastilina. She tricked thousands of people. They caught her and put her away. She served her time and got out. Now listen closely: She went back to Podolsk, opened another office just like the last one, another hustle, and thousands more people rushed to her with their bank books.

It's over. She can't be put away again. All those people who go to her have to be put into mental institutions, urgently. Why not? They might set a fire tomorrow. Or kill someone. They're not responsible for their actions, obviously. They'll just say again, as they did the first time: What was the government thinking about? Why did it let her trick us again? Didn't it know we were fools?

* * *

Let me finish about Chumak, Alik. And then he went to drink with the rest of the crew. Just think how many people in the audience were cured in those twenty minutes from their chronic diseases—or gave up drinking, stopped cheating on their wives... or their wives stopped cheating on them. I mean, the majority of the population is not adults, they're on the level of African-Americans or village girls who go to fortune-tellers—people who need simple constructs, who need myths. How can you explain contemporary economics to them? It's a waste of time. You have to give them Chumak, who will heal them. You have to give them Berezovsky—there, he did the stealing, and everyone else is Russian and honest. You have to give them Yeltsin—a real *muzhik*, he drinks first thing in the morning and he's free the rest of the day. He sang and he danced—he's pleased with himself, and fuck everyone else. Simple constructs. But you eggheads, you need more complex constructs—with Cheyne-Stokes and dissertations and going off to visit Harvard—showing off, in other words. Do you have the feeling that the country consists of two different nations? As the classic once said, every national culture has at least two national cultures? Or maybe even three, but certainly two. Chumak, that's ours: It's the eternal dream of the Russian people. Why burn down estates when the master goes and rejects everything himself, and travels on the trolleybus the way the early Yeltsin did? Do you understand what I'm talking about?

I like that about the two cultures.

At that point, Alik, how did you see the future of the country?

Well, as a man who believed whole-heartedly in perestroika—

Are you joking here?

Of course not. It's the pure truth. I thought, at last... We are as one, the Commies will realize how much damage they have done to their people... And we don't need to hang them from the lampposts, they're ready to change. They will start perestroika with themselves! I thought, everything is OK now.

So, you believed that things would work out and everything would be fine?

Yes, that's it. That's what I thought. And, really, things did work out, more or less.

And now you're reaping the fruits of your discernment.

Yes, but I also pray God that we don't break off into a revolt. Because Russian rebellions, as we know, are meaningless and ruthless. I see the revolt theme gives you no rest.

It does not. I was turning from the Ring Road onto Kutuzovsky Prospect one day, and there was a big traffic jam. For no apparent reason. But when a cop started running around nervously, it was clear that they were clearing the way for Putin. Some people get upset by this, but I'm fine with a certain level of security. I understand that the Chechens would love to get him. And I thought in horror, what if they do? What would happen to the country then? God forbid!

According to the Constitution, his place would be taken by Prime Minister Kasyanov. By the way, they recently showed a woman who gave birth in a traffic jam while Putin was traveling through town. Her husband helped with the delivery, while a doctor gave him instructions over the phone.

Even in America, Alik, presidents are killed!

So what? Did anything change as a result? They even killed Lincoln—and so what? Did the North change its attitude toward slavery? Or the South? Or after Kennedy's death, did America wake up and get tough with Cuba? Overthrow Castro? What happened? Nothing... Whereas when Alexander II was killed, things got worse. Including for the people who killed him. Or maybe things got better, too? There was incredible economic growth under Alexander III. The "policy for small business" and all that. And there were no wars.

By the way, about Alexander II and sovereigns in general: For a thousand years Russia always had one responsible leader, who cared about the fate of the people entrusted to him... For all that we respect Vladimir Vladimirovich Putin personally, we must admit that the poor nation had one sole father. And no one tried harder to liberate it.

And no one hurt the nation more than the revolutionaries in The People's Will—who tried so hard for that will.

Don't forget, Alik, you have to put "will" in quotes. Like *"Pravda."*

Speaking of will, there were the Good Will Games.

Yes—and by the way, it's all true. They deported bums and prostitutes from the city and put salami in the stores. It was so clean in Moscow for the games.

How did they determine who was a prostitute?

The police precincts at all the hotels had lists. So the prostitutes who didn't work hard enough for the KGB, didn't inform enough, were sent out of the city—temporarily. At journalism school, there was a girl who worked as a whore (a successful combination of the two oldest professions, haha). She used to wear a one-piece camisole that clung to her naked body—it had a seam running right along the … um, the axis of the organism. Once, she tried to bribe a professor because she couldn't pass the exams, and he shouted that he didn't want her whore money. He must have worked for the KGB as well, since he knew who did what.

Was she attractive?

Today, she'd get $300–$400. I remember that CNN first appeared broadcasting those games. And then it was everywhere: in Iraq, at our coup, at the shooting on the White House…. We thought we'd make up for the Olympics, and that would be it. No one suspected that we'd be fostering CNN.

Back to the assassination of tsars. How do you think this country should be run, Igor?

We should call in some Varangians, I guess, like the Slavs did in the tenth century, to rule us. In a thousand years only one leader of the highest rank—I'm still on about Alexander II—showed concern for his people. And he ended up badly… But it's not even the fact he was assassinated that bothers me—that's his own problem. My problem is that he was an exception. For the other 980 years, the country was run by people who acted like strangers. They cared about everything but the well-being of their subjects. They all had the same rhetoric as Communist leader Zyuganov: Yes, we screwed up the last 70 years, leading the country who knows where, and we lived worse than anyone else, and gave power to whomever; but now, give us another chance at power and this time we won't screw it up… We could say that state sovereignty for Russians never led to anything good. That is, sovereignty is good only as an exception, when you have an Alexander II. But if you don't, then who should be in charge? Some mythical Varangians?

Well, the Varangians didn't expect to have to run a country like this…

Let's consider, Alik, just what kind of administrative alternative can we offer Russia? Russia is always run by seeming foreigners, who take the money and run, caring not at all about those peasants and proletarians…. Eh?

Oy! Well, needs must, Igor is expecting a response….

Kokh's Commentary:

Arguments on power in the third week of Lent, with double pneumonia and pleurisy (eight days without smokes, and my rear end like a sieve from antibiotic shots…)

First Argument (Confucian)

Confucius. *The Analects*. Book 12, chapter 7.

1. Tsze-kung asked about government. The Master said, "The requisites of government are that there be sufficiency of food, sufficiency of military equipment, and the confidence of the people in their ruler."

2. Tsze-kung said, "If it cannot be helped, and one of these must be dispensed with, which of the three should be forgone first?" "The military equipment," said the Master.

3. Tsze-kung again asked, "If it cannot be helped, and one of the remaining two must be dispensed with, which of them should be forgone?" The Master answered, "Part with the food. From of old, death has been the lot of all men; but if the people have no faith in their rulers, there is no standing for the state."

Obviously, we've already parted with food and military equipment. But the phenomenal level of people's faith in the current regime, which cannot be explained either by its adepts or its foes, is fully in the stream of Confucian thought. In that sense, today's regime is acting properly. The path to the heart of the people does not pass through the stomach, no matter what Marx and Engels may have shouted. The people's love is elusive and fragile. And it often turns into intense hatred. The reverse rarely happens. That has been tested experimentally. You know that.

Book 8.

Chung-kung, being chief minister to the Head of the Chi family, asked about government. The Master said, "Go before the people with your example, and be laborious in their affairs." "How shall I know the men of virtue and talent, so that I may raise them to office?" He was answered, "Raise to office those whom you know. As to those whom you do not know, will others neglect them?"

This is understandable and technological. Elevate your friends and comrades. Don't berate them too much for bribery and corruption. And everything will be okey-dokey.

And in conclusion:

Book 17. Chapter 18.

The Master said, "I hate the manner in which purple takes away the luster of vermilion. I hate the way in which the songs of Chang confound the music of the Ya. I hate those who with their sharp mouths overthrow kingdoms and families."

No commentary needed here. It's all clear. And sad.

Second Argument (Ancient)

Plato. *The Republic.* "On Justice As Benefiting the Strongest."

Each type of government enacts laws that are in its own interest: democracy, democratic laws; a tyranny, tyrannical laws, and so on. And in enacting these laws, they make it quite plain that what is "right" for their subjects is what is in the interest of themselves, the rulers, and if anyone deviates from this he is punished as a lawbreaker and "wrongdoer."

There it is—the reasoning power of the giants of antiquity! "In enacting these laws, they proclaim them just." You could even say, "proclaim them to be justice."

Just the other day, the State Duma passed a law on automobile civic responsibility. All car owners are required to insure their cars.

Ha! All, but not all. Rather, almost all. Everyone except the state. That is, if you get hit by a state car, you'll get paid … *zip!* Even if your car is insured. Because your insurance company won't get any money from the state. So! Go, tricolor license plates! And that's called justice. So sit quietly and don't make trouble, citizen car owners.

Actually, this is unconstitutional and is pure discrimination based on type of property. By the way, state officials did not pay taxes only in the Middle Ages. By more recent times, not to mention modern times, they were made equal with all other citizens. By making itself exempt from automobile responsibility, the state has leapt back into the Middle Ages! Even the British queen pays taxes today, not to mention insurance fees with private insurance companies. Discrimination on any level is savagery. So I congratulate our elected officials. They must have forgotten that they were elected by the people and not by chief of staff Surkov.

Aristotle: *Politics.* Book Five

VII. 9. But above all, every state should be so administered and so regulated by law that its magistrates cannot possibly make money. In oligarchies, special precautions should be used against this evil.

20. But of all the things which I have mentioned, that which most contributes to the permanence of constitutions is the adaptation of education to the form of government, and yet in our own day this principle is universally neglected. The best laws, though sanctioned by every citizen of the state, will be of no avail unless the young are trained by habit and education in the spirit of the constitution—if the

laws are democratic, then democratically; or oligarchically, if the laws are oligarchic. For there may be a want of self-discipline in states as well as in individuals."

Well, we understand that stealing when you are in an official position is wrong. It's amusing that this was understood long ago (2,500 years ago), but there is no antidote yet.

What's interesting is this: It turns out that, according to Aristotle, there are various kinds of virtue and justice. One for democracy, another for oligarchy, and still another for tyranny. And they are all different virtues and justices.

Let us imagine a virtuous man from a tyrannical state. What is he like?

He loves the tyrant. Just adores him.

He gladly gives his last coin for any of the tyrant's projects, and in general identifies the tyrant with the state. For him, the interests of the tyrant are the interests of the state.

He hates opportunists, all kinds of discussions, and opposition.

He does not believe in private life. Private life, in his opinion, is the lot of failures.

Serving the state—the power, as it is put today—is the goal of real men.

By the way, despite popular opinion, he is no ascetic. He enjoys earthly goods, believing they are his due in exchange for his love and loyalty.

Now, let us imagine such a man in a high state position in a democracy. Would he, as Aristotle says, sympathize with the state structure? Unlikely. He would think that under democracy everything is faked. The deputies fake their shouting, the bosses fake their criticism, you have to fake being honest.

Aristotle was Alexander the Great's teacher. The young man was the son of King Philip and, therefore, was brought up in the tyrannical spirit. And he was to conquer Persia—that is, a country that got the tyrannical mentality in its mother's milk. Guess what state structure Aristotle suggested Alexander institute in the territories he conquered? Right, tyranny. How did you guess? Now, in our best of all democracies, a significant part of state positions are held by people of a very tyrannical nature. They call themselves "statists." Will they be able to keep from sliding into the swamp of tyranny? It's very doubtful, although I say, Please, God, prevent it.

The flag is democratic, the emblems are monarchic, and the anthem is tyrannical. As the author of both texts to the anthem said, "It's a mishmash." In other words, a complete violation of Aristotelian principles. What will come of this? We have to re-invent the bicycle again.

And in conclusion of this argument:

Third Argument (Christian)

Epistle to the Romans from St. Paul. Chapter 13:1–7

1 Let every soul be subject unto the higher powers. For there is no power but of God: the powers that be are ordained of God.

2 Whosoever therefore resisteth the power, resisteth the ordinance of God: and they that resist shall receive to themselves damnation.

3 For rulers are not a terror to good works, but to the evil. Wilt thou then not be afraid of the power? Do that which is good, and thou shalt have praise of the same.

4 For he is the minister of God to thee for good. But if thou do that which is evil, be afraid; for he beareth not the sword in vain: for he is the minister of God, a revenger to execute wrath upon him that doeth evil.

5 Wherefore ye must needs be subject, not only for wrath, but also for conscience' sake.

6 For this cause pay ye tribute also: for they are God's ministers, attending continually upon this very thing.

7 Render therefore to all their dues: tribute to whom tribute is due; custom to whom custom; fear to whom fear; honor to whom honor.

My concept of Christian virtue does not coincide with Apostle Paul here. And here are our hierarchy who bleat: "All rulers are from God.... There is no ruler who is not from God."

With conversion to Christianity, all monarchs, even the best of them, started training their people in humility according to Paul's epistle to the Romans. Here is a characteristic excerpt from Alexander II's Manifesto of 19 February 1861 (on the abolition of serfdom):

But general common sense has not wavered in the conviction that by natural reasoning a person freely using the benefits of society mutually must serve the benefit of society by fulfilling certain obligations, and by Christian law every soul must be subject unto higher powers (Romans 13:1) and render all their dues, especially to those to whom is due tribute, custom, fear, and honor (7); that the rights legally acquired by landowners cannot be taken away from them with a decent reward or voluntary concession; that it would be objectionable to all justice to use landowners' land and not bear responsibility for it....

But there were other instances. When, calling on God, they overturned the existing regime, temporarily "forgetting" the epistle to the Romans. Here, for example, is the Declaration of Independence of July 4, 1776, signed unanimously by all thirteen United States of America:

We, therefore, the Representatives of the United States of America, in General Congress, Assembled, appealing to the Supreme Judge of the world for the rectitude of our intentions, do, in the Name, and by Authority of the good People of these Colonies, solemnly publish and declare, That these united Colonies are, and of Right ought to be, Free and Independent States, that they are Absolved from all Allegiance to the British Crown, and that all political connection between them and the State of Great Britain, is and ought to be totally dissolved; and that as Free and Independent States, they have full Power to levy War, conclude Peace, contract Alliances, establish Commerce, and to do all other Acts and Things which Independent States may of right do. — And for the support of this Declaration, with a firm reliance on the protection of Divine Providence, we mutually pledge to each other our Lives, our Fortunes, and our sacred Honor.

It's hard to call the founding fathers godless. And naturally, they knew about Paul's epistle. Then where is truth? What is to be done?

St. Paul, sensing that the consequence of bringing Christianity to the pagans would be the cruel repression (primarily by Romans) of members of the new faith, tried to soften the blow, saying, in effect, "We'll pay our taxes, we recognize that your authority comes from God, please, don't beat us!" That is why this passage appears only in the epistle to the Romans. There is nothing like it elsewhere.

He may have bought some time this way. Therefore, when the persecution did begin, the community was stronger, the faith was systematized and was capable not only of bearing the blows of the pagans but of becoming the state religion of Great Rome.

And what about Christ? What did he say about secular power, how did he teach us to treat it?

He didn't say anything. He didn't want to lie, nor did he know how to lie, while telling the truth…. You know how that always ends up. Strictly speaking, even without any programmatic statements by Christ regarding the authorities, the authorities quickly figured out what was what was going on and crucified him.

It is here that Gennady Zyuganov would enroll Christ in the Communist Party. But no deal, Comrade Zyuganov. Christ was no Communist. He was an anarchist. And like any anarchist, an idealist.

Much closer to Christ, and at the same time more realistic, is Martin Luther (*On Secular Authority: How Far Should It Be Obeyed?*):

Luther explains that not all baptized are Christian.

> For the world and the masses are and always will be un-Christian, although they are all baptized and are nominally Christian. Christians, however, are few and far between, as the saying goes. Therefore, it is out of the question that there should be a common Christian government over the whole world, nay even over one land or company of people, since the wicked always outnumber the good.

And while Luther recognized the sad need for secular authority as the lesser evil, nevertheless he did not idealize secular authority in the least (ibid, Part two: *How Far Should [Secular Authority] Be Obeyed?*)

> You must know that, from the beginning of the world, a wise prince is a rare
> bird, indeed; still more so, a pious prince. They are usually the greatest fools or the
> worst knaves on earth.

Thus, not all authority is from God. For instance, one that serves its own interests comes from the Devil. And really, if a ruler wants to obey God's intentions for secular authority to defend and save the good and punish the bad, but also wants to use his power to become rich, then he is serving two masters simultaneously. Yet it is written that "No man can serve two masters: for either he will hate the one, and love the other; or else he will hold to the one, and despise the other. Ye cannot serve God and mammon." (Matthew 6:24)

How they all agree, these wise men. Once again, we hear about demagogues and big talkers. And now we have the Pharisees added to them. Almost as a synonym.

Fourth Argument (Synthetic)

Friedrich Nietzsche, *Human, All Too Human (A Book for Free Spirits)*. Section 8: "A Look at the State"

> 460. The great man of the masses. It is easy to give the recipe for what the
> masses call a great man. By all means, supply them with something that they find
> very pleasant, or, first, put the idea into their heads that this or that would be very
> pleasant, and then give it to them. But on no account immediately: Let it rather be
> won with great exertion, or let it seem so. The masses must have the impression that
> a mighty, indeed invincible, strength of will is present; at least it must seem to be
> there. Everyone admires a strong will, because no one has it, and everyone tells
> himself that, if he had it, there would be no more limits for him and his egoism.
>
> 449. The apparent weather-makers of politics. Just as people secretly assume
> that a man who knows something about the weather and can predict it a day in
> advance actually makes the weather, so even educated and learned men, calling on
> superstitious belief, attribute all the important changes and conjunctures that
> occurred during the government of great statesmen to them, as their own work,
> when it is only too clear that they knew something about it sooner than the others
> and made their calculations accordingly; thus they, too, are taken as weather-
> makers—and this belief is not the least tool of their power.

Today's authorities, shamelessly attributing to their dubious achievements the good weather that has settled temporarily over the territory that it rules by chance, are trying to demonstrate their will-power to the public.

In fact, having mastered the principle of "divide and conquer," our current ruler has broken the powers that be into several warring parties, and now, by the very logic of that breakup, has forced them to eye one another closely and jealously to prevent any successes.

Truly, the wordmongers, demagogues, Pharisees, and supermen will destroy us.

Doing what you think is necessary without expecting gratitude is the alternative strategy the current regime can't make up its mind to adopt.

That is, of course, if it thinks it necessary to do anything.

I'm very sorry, but I can't make my lips form the phrase "strengthening the vertical of power," that is, expanding the state apparat and finding cushy jobs for your friends.

* * *

Think about this, Alik. There was unrest in Alma-Ata. The Kazakhs beat up on Russians. That's the way it is with southern republics—the Americans had a revolt in Los Angeles, we had one in Kazakhstan. Your native German lands, by the way.... Just a little black humor. You're going to laugh, but I had said to my friends who lived there—they had moved from Russia for work reasons—"Drop everything and come back to Russia!" They laughed at me and told me I didn't understand a thing. One of them even bought some land, started growing something, and it was all taken away from him—because the land was Kazakh and he was just a Russian. I don't know how I knew all this ahead of time. A rare instance of my predicting the course of social development.

Svinarenko's Commentary:

In connection with those "events," I will quote my text about Russians—Russian-speaking refugees—who moved from Alma-Ata to Lipetsk Oblast. The refugees recalled 1986 this way:

> They (the Kazakhs) walked through the city with green banners shouting at the soldiers: "Vanka, why did you come here?" If you were on the bus, the Kazakhs would say right in your ear: "We'll show the Russians!" The city became alien almost overnight. I realized that it was turning into a foreign place, and I tried to get my husband to leave. By the way, exiled Chechens lived right next to us in Kazakhstan, and I never thought that I would be following their destiny.

> They shut down the Russian-language school at our state farm, so we had to move to Alma-Ata. Things were normal there—everything in Russian, and the school was calm. We had to live in a dormitory, but I was next in line for an apartment. But then they got rid of the line.... The Koreans and Germans moved back to their homelands, and we did too.

And here is the account of a refugee who had been a police sergeant in that former life. He decided to move in 1986: "Remember what was going on in Alma-Ata then? Riots! They burned cars, broke up concrete slabs in the square and threw the pieces, shot howitzers at the government house. It went on for three days! We couldn't handle it with just our billy clubs. They brought in laborers from the factories, and they dealt with them...."

* * *

Oh, don't forget that the *Nakhimov* sank that year. What a scandal, Alik! It was the picture of the beautiful life, elite vacationing. Not a Mediterranean cruise, but still... My parents once took a cruise on it. One of my friends, Yura, graduated from the trade institute and got a job on the *Nakhimov*—in the restaurant, as deputy director. He spent some time sailing on it. He told me about the good times onboard ship—the full package, in every form. And his cognac supply. So. Not long before the catastrophe, my friend transferred to work on land.

Svinarenko's Commentary:

Here is the official report: "On August 31, 1986, as it was leaving Novorossiisk Bay, the *Admiral Nakhimov* (built in 1925) collided with a bulk carrier, the *Petr Vasev*, and sank in 7–8 minutes. The death toll was 423 of the people on board, plus two divers later."

The most interesting thing about the ship is that it was a war trophy. It used to be called the *Berlin*. The first time it sank under its maiden name was back in 1945—it was torpedoed by a submarine. The second time the *Berlin* sank was in 1947, right after it was raised from the ocean floor.

Curiously, the ship was deemed unsafe for carrying passengers... But the Black Sea shipping department decided to take it out for a last cruise before scrapping it. They sent it out with a thousand passengers on board—why, no one knew then or knows now. But its last cruise really was its last...

* * *

There was another ship that sank that year too, Alik. The story is very typical of the period. It's about democracy, really—as it was understood by Soviet people in those days. Subordinates who discover a problem are supposed to report it and act according to instruction. Instead, they showed local initiative. Thanks to that particularly manifestation of democratization, a very complex, expensive, and dangerous piece of equipment—a submarine with nuclear missiles—sank. This time, fortunately, the crew was saved with very minor losses.

Svinarenko's Commentary:

The situation developed along classic lines. While still on shore, they discovered that the lid on the missile tube was broken. But they didn't bother to repair it. Naturally, during the voyage, water leaked into the tube. Officer Petrachkov, the one responsible for this, did not report the accident but instead unplugged the sensors. The submarine went out and soon— unbeknownst to the commander—filled up with water. With the officers we sometimes have, who needs saboteurs or terrorists! To keep the ship from sinking completely, Petrachkov decided to blow out the tube with compressed air—and did. They blew so hard that the defective lid was blown off completely. To make matters worse, they also damaged the missile itself—which wasn't an ordinary missile, but had a nuclear warhead (there were sixteen such missiles on board). Fuel started leaking from the missile. Leaking and leaking... and the commander still was not informed! They must have thought it would work all work out... The only thing that Petrachkov did report to the commander was that the sensors (which he had unplugged) were not working. They decided to surface, to test them. As they were rising, there was an explosion in the tube—what else could be expected from a mix of rocket fuel and compressed air?... As the rest of the submarine was decompressed, the fire spread. Despite all the efforts of Petrachkov, the vessel did not sink right away. It burned and took on water for three more days. It was impossible to save it. But the important thing was done: They stopped the nuclear reactor. Seaman Preminin did that, at the cost of his life. (He was posthumously awarded the Gold Star.) The personnel left the vessel. It sank, "with practically no damage," at a depth of five and half kilometers. As usual in these cases, there was a story that the explosion was caused by a collision of the K-219 with an America APL Augusta underwater, but that's a rather feeble hypothesis.

* * *

Now, Alik, let's see what else was there that year? The resolution on reversing the course of northern rivers. There was so much written about it then! Yet, what was it? The debates on the subject resumed—it was either the path to happiness or the embezzlement of Russia. They released Sakharov from exile. That was a barometer, of course. We used to listen to the foreign radio stations for news of him and suddenly there he was in the Soviet papers, which could write about him freely. That's when it became clear that so-called perestroika was really advanced... Ideas were floating around that all those Party hacks would be kicked out and the dissidents brought in—they were all over the place then. The longer someone had served time for the truth, the higher his position in office would be. And then they would get together, quickly pass all the correct and beautiful laws, and we would go forward to the radiant future! It was hard to remember then that the public needs one thing and eggheads need another, and they have nothing in common.

Svinarenko's Commentary:

Sakharov was sent into exile in 1980. They cleaned Moscow of bums and prostitutes for the Olympics, and, while they were at it, got rid of the out-of-favor academician as well. Engaged observers called this "a desperate act of the Brezhnev regime."

It would be hard to envy the Soviet bureaucrats who were supposed to solve the Sakharov issue. Really, what could be done about him? First they thought they could shame him. A Statement from the Scientists of FIAN, the Lebedev Physics Institute at the Academy of Sciences, was organized. They slapped together a text and got several hundred signatures under it. It was full of marvelous sentences like: "A. D. Sakharov, despite numerous warnings from the administration and work colleagues … acted in a way that harmed the détente of international tensions. In his August 21 statement to foreign correspondents in Moscow, he appealed to the capitalist world to pressure the Soviet Union to change the existing norms of life in our country, and called on capitalist countries to agree to a policy of disarmament only if the USSR would allow interference in its domestic affairs. His remarks were an impetus to yet another anti-Soviet campaign in the reactionary Western press, which struck a blow against the détente in the international situation. We decisively condemn such actions by Academician A. D. Sakharov. We wholly and fully approve the program for peace passed by the Twenty-Fourth Congress of the CPSU and the practical steps taken by the Central Committee CPSU and the Soviet government to implement it. The scientists and all workers of the Physics Institute hope that Academician A. D. Sakharov will heed criticism, think about the negative consequences of his statements, return to active scientific work, and stop activity that is unworthy of a Soviet scientist." Delightful lines!

Sakharov composed a reply that the Party committee promised to publish. Here is a quote from it: "I maintain that the solution to problems of world significance—peace, environment, standard of living, freedom, the very preservation of humanity and humanness—is possible only via the path of a profoundly equable process of convergence of the capitalist and socialist systems. I also maintain that a truly fruitful détente is impossible without the creation of conditions of mutual trust, openness, glasnost, and democratic control in both converging systems.

"I consider such open expression of opinion in this highly important international question my moral duty, just as are open statements in defense of freedom of conscience, national equality, rights of political prisoners, and inmates in psychiatric hospital prisons. I call for immediate political amnesty and a democratic solution to the problems of freedom of leaving the USSR. I have appealed to the U.S. Congress in an open letter on the last issue.

"My position meets with understanding and approval from the widest circles in almost the entire world. Only in our country, unfortunately, has there been a campaign of 'condemnation,' which with its traits of disinformation and petty quibbles definitely does not promote the growth of the country's prestige. This campaign truly has harmed détente. In my opinion, this campaign is shameful."

This in deep-dark 1973! Madness! It's impossible to believe that this was written by the father of our Soviet hydrogen bomb! "Something's happened to his head, the Yids have bewildered him, sent Elena Bonner to ensnare him." That's a quote from a KGB USSR officer. In general, the country did not mature enough to see this text published until 1991. It's not surprising that they tried to neutralize Sakharov.

And then came June 1986. A certain professor named Durr—a German, that's a greeting to you, Alik—wrote a letter to Gorbachev.

Here's the gist: "I do not know the direct causes of his [Sakharov's] forced residence in Gorky, but I must stress that many citizens of the FRG, and especially those who sincerely support détente between military blocs, are very worried by the unresolved 'Sakharov affair.'"

No more than a month went by—and you will laugh, but in July the embassy passed along a response to the professor. Verbal, but very powerful. They told him about a "positive reaction to the letter on the part of M. S. Gorbachev" and even about a "possible positive decision."

And then, in December 1986, Sakharov returned to Moscow....

And remember how people awaited Solzhenitsyn's return then! What a powerful potential of delight and awe was hidden in that! The titans of thoughts, the fathers of Russian democracy, would gather in Moscow, and then such bliss would unfold that the rest of the world would envy us. But Solzhenitsyn did not come. No, he didn't say: "Bug off, what do you need me for? You're still going to lie, steal, loaf, drink, betray, kowtow to the West, be videotaped in saunas, go crazy over money, and promote Mavrodi for president...." He didn't say that. He didn't come to us for the longest time for plausible reasons; allegedly, he had to finish the books he had begun; he spared us. But then, of course, he couldn't resist, and like every decent person, he came. And so, really, do the Russians really need him?

I have the impression that Solzhenitsyn knew what would happen ahead of time, just as he knew that Communism would collapse. Then what does he know today about us and about the country that we will understand only after another gap of time?

* * *

Kokh's Commentary:

Sakharov. A funny, awkward old man. Yet he wasn't old at all at that time—64. He did not look good. He was all sick. The hunger strikes, the hassles, and so on. He was force-fed nourishing broth through a tube. In order to strengthen democracy.

He turned out to be no orator. He stammered and uttered banalities. He threw pearls before…you know what. His social theories were an absolute calque of rather shopworn Western theories of convergence. They were born in the 1960s, when the West shat its pants over the Soviet success in space and the sweep of the so-called national liberation movements.

Galbraith, Rostow and other loafers created the theory as a reaction of the leftist professors to the strengthening of the Communist bloc. The main thesis of that theory was capitulationist—the *sovok* was eternal; therefore, we have to find a ways to coexist with it. Hence the "socialism with a human face" and the vile "Roy Medvedivism."

By the time Sakharov appeared as an active political figure—that is, in the 1970s—those ideas were beginning to stink, and in the 1980s, under the blows of the neoconservatives, they were buried deep and were beyond decomposing.

In that regard Sakharov was an inveterate *shestidesiatnik,* a relic from the 1960s. As was Gorbachev, come to think of it.

By the way, there is a piquant little episode involving Gorbachev and Sakharov.

WORKING NOTES OF A POLITBURO MEETING, AUGUST 29, 1985

> Chebrikov. According to specialists, if Sakharov is given a lab, he might continue work in the field of military research. Sakharov's behavior is formed under Bonner's influence.
>
> Gorbachev. That's how Zionism works!

Veteran of World War II, a lieutenant of the medical corps, wounded, Elena Georgievna Bonner, an agent of world Zionism! A thought worthy of the author of perestroika and new thinking. The hell with him. We're not talking about that now.

We're talking about Sakharov. Yes, his views, which even for those days were banal and quotidian. We were reading books that were more striking by then. Solzhenitsyn, for example.

But still, Sakharov had touched me. He plucked a string in my cynical soul. How?

I'll try to explain. From today's lofty vantage point, it is easier to do. First of all, because I've become smarter myself. Secondly, because I've read his memoirs, and many things that back then I only sensed intuitively I am beginning to understand.

The First Touch

First of all, a modesty of incredible scale. And a modesty that was not only personal but a modesty on the emotional level. He seemed to be embarrassed by his feelings. He was afraid to show people his emotions. He felt that it would not interest the public. This is how he describes his first love.

> ...To check my determinations I gave a number of dubious samples to the chemistry laboratory. Some of the samples were entrusted to Klava. Either out of carelessness or a failure in the draft hood, she got hydrogen sulfide poisoning, This incident served as one of the impetuses to our coming together in the winter of 1942–43. (D. Sakharov. *Memoirs.* Chapter 4. *At the Factory During the War Years.*)

That's it. What do you think? This is the description of an event that determined his family life for many years. This woman gave him three children, whom he loved dearly.

Do you think that he, a twenty-year-old youth, was not buffeted by passions? You're wrong. Of course he was. It's just that he felt it indecent to show people his feelings. Unseemly. People are not interested, and you're pushing your emotions on them. People will read that only out of politeness.

Or here's how he describes his acceptance into graduate school:

> In late December 1944, I got a notice to go to Moscow to FIAN, to see the famous theoretical physicist Igor Yevgenyevich Tamm and take entrance exams for graduate work. The notice was sent to me after my father had appealed to Igor Yevgenyevich with a corresponding request (I sent my work to both at the same time). He had known father since the 1930s and treated him with great respect and trust.

Here's how an ordinary person would describe this event. He would have written the truth. That is, I sent Tamm my works. Tamm read them, fell down, and urgently invited me to graduate school, despite the fact that the war was on and I was needed at the defense plant with my invention of equipment to test the quality of shells.

But a man of pathological modesty like Sakharov could not write that. Physically. He just couldn't. He probably thought, how could I possibly write that Tamm liked my work? People will think that I am boasting about being talented and smart. Better to write that I got into graduate school through patronage. The reader will berate me, will say that Sakharov is like everyone else, but at least no one will say that I'm a braggart suffering from delusions of grandeur. Saying bad things about oneself is correct, but telling the truth—that is, calling oneself a great scientist—is immodest and wrong. Wrong to the point of convulsions. Just wrong, and that's all.

A third episode. When Sakharov was included in a group working on defense topics.

"As for my candidacy, I heard that allegedly Academician S. I. Vavilov, director of FIAN, said: "Sakharov has very poor living conditions. He must be included in this group; then we can help him out.""

Would a normal person tell this story? That he was included in a privileged group through connections in order to help him solve his housing problems? A normal person—no. Sakharov—yes.

Beria, who knew of his talent and his work, personally requested his inclusion in defense research. Beria. Personally. Himself. Requested (!). Understand? You understand, but he finds it immodest to mention. Better to humiliate myself and say that it was done through pull. How do you like this little Jesus? Truly his kingdom is not of this world.

When I was a student in St. Petersburg, I often encountered similar behavior among the old professors. My scientific supervisor was of a comparable type. He tried to lose himself, vanish, remain unseen in any room. He gave up his seat even to students. He bowed to everyone, like a Chinese bobble head doll. I can't tell you how modest he was. It was only after a year's work with him that I learned he was the equal of Leonid Kantorovich (who won a Nobel Prize). It's an entire ethic that is lost now. It was defined very succinctly by the late Academician Panchenko, our Petersburg guru: You must live unnoticed.

The Second Touch

Secondly, the scale of Sakharov's spiritual rebirth. God hasn't granted me the talent to describe it. It's for the greats to do.

> Creator of the most horrible weapon of the twentieth century, thrice Hero of Socialist Labor, like general secretaries of the Communist Party, and meeting with them, an intimate of that narrow circle where "not allowed" does not exist for any need—this man, like Tolstoy's Prince Nekhludov, woke up one morning and sensed that all that luxury in which he was being drowned was just ashes and his soul sought truth and it was hard to justify the work he was doing.
>
> Here we discover the main trait of this man: Transparent trustfulness that comes from his own purity. As a child who does not understand the sign "Epidemic Zone," thus defenselessly did Sakharov wend his way from the sated, smug, and happy caste to the insulted and humiliated. Who but a child could do that? On the

way out he left on the doorstep the "extra money," which was paid to him by the state "for nothing"—150,000 in Khrushchev's new money, 1.5 million in Stalin's rubles. (A. I. Solzhenitsyn, *The Oak and the Calf*, 3rd addition. December 1973).

The scale of the moral leap is astonishing, especially in view of our own clearly understood inability to do something similar.

Where did it come from? There was this man. A quiet technologist. Sated, successful. Honors and respect…

And then suddenly, bam! I cannot keep silent! And he lays out the whole truth. Right in their fat mugs. Not caring what happens. Here, eat this. And I don't need the change, and I don't need my coat!

The Third Touch

Third, he astonished me with his incredible calm. Completely defenseless. Physically weak. Unaccustomed to a hard life. All hassled, with rolling Rs and a stutter. But absolutely firm. No arguments or threats worked. Nothing.

Apparently his scholarly brain perceived political compromise with the *sovok* as an intellectual fiasco. As scientific cowardice. Really, if the solution is found— that is, the *sovok* is hit—then why pretend it is not so? Didn't you, Lavrenti Pavlovich Beria, teach us that if we see that a scientific direction is leading to a dead end, we must immediately report that so as not to waste the people's money? This is exactly the same case!

Yes, my dear old professors. Absolutely willing to compromise in quotidian things, unnoticed and companionable, they were fanatically unbending when it came to their work. Their work was the search for the truth. That was their understanding of science. You could never achieve anything with them based on compromise. You could only prove something if you had your arguments in hand. If you could prove, you had them. They would follow you anywhere. My prof even fixed the style of my dissertation. He said that if he was my supervisor, then the text should be interesting to read, otherwise he would not sign off on it.

Sakharov was like that. Once he understood that socialism was not the future of humanity but its calamity, having tested his hypothesis a thousand times, he came to the conclusion that it was true. That was it; it would be easier to kill him than to make him change his mind. I know that you can't come to terms with or scare off people like that. The KGB people used themselves as a measure for everyone; that's why they tried their enema nozzles on him.

Instead of a Conclusion

Sakharov died in time. If he were alive today, they would be badgering him even more than before. He would be a kind of moral inversion of today's spiritual mainstream.

The old man was modest and morally powerful and he had a Spartan stoicism. That contrasts so strongly with the hero of our times: show-off, conformist, brown-noser.

But as for saying something new in social science, there wasn't that. Probably, he was stronger in physics.

* * *

Alik! Why are we going on about lofty things? Where's the prose of life? Why is there so little about money?

I'll explain everything about money to you in later chapters. I might even tell you how I made my first million. And how I spent it. Perfect conversation over vodka.

6.

1987

The Sixth Bottle

*P*erestroika was still consuming the public. Kokh was still attracted to a scholarly career. Svinarenko was boring people with his news reports from agricultural campaigns. The young German pilot Mathias Rust was establishing the tradition of foreigners making guest appearances on Red Square.

During the emptying of the sixth bottle, the decision was made to exchange Kaliningrad for the Crimea, and a way to combat crime was discovered. Also, the riddle of why Russia was divided into exactly seven federal okrugs was solved. And finally, the point of the obscene Russian form of slang, mat, was clarified.

Come now, Alik, talk first about what your life was like in 1987.

I was 26 years old then. I had defended my dissertation by that time... And I was working in a closed scientific research institute, giving it my all. We were involved in economics there, nothing secret or confidential. We were working on very specific things: Here's a steel plate and you have to build a ship out of it. Weld a trough. How can you position the pattern pieces on the plate so that you waste as little of it as possible?

And if you had not economized, fewer submarines would have been built, and there would be fewer of them to get rid of. We'd be saving money on dismantling rusting ships.

No, there would be just as many ships—only we would have used more steel. Defense is now financed according to the "remaining balance" principle. It was different back then…

Hold on, hold on… What's the story here? You say that defense operates on the remaining balance principle… Culture and retirement, and education, and all the rest—that's all based on the remaining balance principle, too. What isn't based on this principle? Anything?

Go on and take a look at what principle is used to finance the administration of presidential affairs. Is it the remaining balance principle? Take a look at the state apparatus and at the Duma, too. Are you kidding? This is how it is now: The public sphere has been handed over to the local level now—let local self-government deal with it. And health care, too. As for culture—that's on a self-supporting basis. It's foolish to finance it: The state will get blamed for using it as propaganda… When all is said and done, only one real debit item is left in the budget, and that's our own support. And that's why we honestly admit what it is we're doing—financing ourselves. That's the kind of logic our present authorities use.

Svinarenko's Commentary:

Well, obviously, that's human nature for you! You have to accept it and live with it somehow, the way the disabled resign themselves to their handicaps. Of course, it's more pleasant to think that we're really so wonderful and unselfish, and that we're all ready and willing to fight for an idea and to be as concerned about what's not ours as we are about what is ours. But that's not the case. History and actual fact demonstrate that it isn't possible to change people. Now the Bolsheviks attempted to inculcate a lack of selfishness. They educated people, cultivated them; they tried diligently, they made strict demands on them—and what a huge number of bad students they sent out into the world! And nothing was accomplished anyway. Man is, in any case, a thief and a petty shopkeeper, but if you make him angry—if you try to take something away from him—not only will he steal, he'll murder, too. So this self-financing apparently, is inevitable; you just have to dress it up with some niceties. The way closed retail distributors in Moscow used to hide beneath the guise of institutional dining halls. And the Kaluga retailer was located out of town entirely, away from pedestrian traffic—although, oddly enough, it was located right on the road leading to the Kiev Highway, which people used to travel to Moscow.

And our capitalists do need to be reined in somehow, you see; they've eclipsed the Party apparatchiks when it comes to personal immodesty. Of course, it's all, like, honest: The guy's paid his taxes and can, like, grow fat with a clear conscience. But if something happens, it's not the tax collector who's going to come and burn him down and hang him from a lamppost, it's someone who's poor and unhappy with his lot. And it would be all right if someone who owns gold toilet bowls got hanged and if that could be the end of it! But of course they'd impose some kind of war communism on everybody else, too, and there wouldn't be any soap again, and we'd all have to line up for vodka...

Now how do thinking people behave? Here's an example: Lucky Luciano, the famous Mafia mobster, loved luxury, and he was in everyone's face—that's why he couldn't stay out of prison. Whereas Meyer Lansky, the chief bookkeeper of the very same Mafia, wore worn-out shoes and used public transportation. But then, he lived in peace and never spent a day in the slammer. And he had a lot more money than Luciano did. Incidentally, there's even an opinion that the Italian was chairman in name only, and that Lansky was the real Don. It's worth noting that this Lansky's birth name was Sukhovlyansky, and that his parents were Russian citizens... Maybe all of our troubles arise from the fact that people like Lansky left Russia in their time, and that the merchants who frequented the "Yar" and threw their paper money into the fireplace stayed behind—and in the end, it was they who drove the country to revolution and ruin...

* * *

Kokh's Commentary:

A conversation about the ineffectiveness of the government in general and law enforcement agencies in particular—Igor's discourse on Meyer Lansky and Lucky Luciano (we'll include Al Capone and Bugsy Siegel here, too, as well as my impressions about a trip to Naples, that is, to the Naples suburb of Castellamare, Al Capone's hometown, and to Palermo, and the village of Corleone 50 miles away)—compelled me to write this commentary, a dilettante's discourse on fighting crime.

How, indeed, do you actually fight crime? There are the budgetary constraints. There are already more people employed by the Interior Ministry (including domestic troops) than there are people employed by the army. This creates the impression that our government fears its own people more than it fears foreign aggression. And if you add the penitentiary system to this and the system of court officers who are now formally subordinate to the Ministry of Justice, it's an altogether depressing picture.

It's obvious that the police in its present form is not very effective at fighting crime. Often the officers themselves become the weapons of "commercial raids" and criminal infighting. There are accounts that in many cities the RUOP—the Regional Crime-Fighting Administration—is itself a front for criminals and that this false identity is forced on merchants. Let's face it: these are not always (to put it mildly) fabrications.

Increasing the number of Interior Ministry employees won't solve this problem. I don't have the statistics, but I think that if you add up the total number of police officers, FBI agents, and National Guardsmen in the U.S., it's unlikely that their indicators per capita would be that much higher than ours. It seems to me that the problems of fighting crime and protecting social order can be solved using considerably fewer people. Then the wages of people who fight crime would rise, of course, assuming the present level of financing is kept constant.

Why is fighting crime in Russia so ineffective?

In my view, there are two reasons.

The first is that people settled in our cities haphazardly, every which way. I go to the U.S. often and live there for extended periods, mainly in New York and Chicago. People there live in socially and ethnically homogeneous neighborhoods. There's a Chinese neighborhood, an Italian one, a Russian one, and so on. There are neighborhoods for the poor and for the middle class, and there are places where the rich live. I can't imagine a yuppie from Wall Street taking a stroll around Harlem or the South Bronx; or the opposite, a black thug wandering along Fifth or Park Avenue anywhere from the East 30's to the 80's. And if a yuppie should suddenly wander off into such an alien neighborhood, he wouldn't be surprised if he were robbed. The first thing that the policeman taking his statement would do is ask: "What the hell were you doing there? Blame yourself! You've got no case here—next time you'll be smarter. So give me your statement and then stop wasting my time." And the thug on Fifth Avenue is going to have to be a good little boy. He won't bother anyone, he'll just keep repeating "Sorry, sorry!" over and over. Otherwise a policeman will pick him up and take him to the station. And there it'll take until the wee hours of the morning to sort out who stepped on whose toes.

A well-known New York joke: A man in Odessa calls his aunt in Brighton Beach, "So how are things in America?" Answer: "I don't know. We don't go there." This is a good illustration of the ethnic and territorial stratification of America's population within the confines of a giant megalopolis.

It's a lot simpler to maintain law and order and fight crime within the framework of this kind of territorial organization of a population. The police know beforehand where the hotbeds of crime are and which neighborhoods they don't need to worry about. They also know where people (often the same kind of thugs) will deal with the "violators of agreements." I've been in neighborhoods in Tokyo where there is no police presence at all. I'm not joking, I'm serious. The Yakuza is responsible for law and order there by arrangement with the police. It's almost official. Police statistics in the Chinese neighborhoods of American cities record almost no criminal activity—because none is reported! Crime victims there don't go to the police—they sort things out themselves.

It would be appropriate to remember Alexander Herzen here, who marveled at the organization of police work in England. He described this scene: Two drunken residents are beating each another bloody near a drinking establishment in London. A policeman is standing nearby and yawning. Herzen asks him, "Why aren't you intervening?" The answer stuns him: "Neither of them is calling for help. When they call me, I'll be there in a flash… And I'll separate them in an instant. In the meantime, it's considered their private business. If they needed me, they would have called me long ago. After all, they can see me standing here." Herzen says, "In my country, the policeman would have pulled them apart long ago, arrested them, and taken them to the station. He would have locked both of them up. And his superiors would have praised him for a job well done." But with such an understanding of law and order you need considerably more police officers in Russia than in England. What's more, in Moscow you can be robbed of every stitch of your clothing right on Tverskaya Street. It's impossible to imagine anything that happening in downtown Manhattan.

Whether or not the kind of territorial distribution of residents that exists in America is good, it does make the work of the police much easier. We had a similar situation in Russia before the revolution. But everything got mixed up in the last hundred years—so many wars, construction projects, deportations, and camps. An academician sharing the same prison plank bed as a criminal. A Latvian SS man cutting timber in a brigade with a Comintern Jew.

People settled in towns in the Soviet era in a crazy, helter-skelter way. Not where they wanted to live, but wherever they got the authorization to go. Every day people travel from one end of an enormous city to the other. A city with a system of housing people like this needs a mass transit infrastructure that is unprecedented in history. And, lastly, the number of police officers that such a city needs in order to maintain law and order is incomparable. No government has enough money for such a police force. This is how corruption arises, links with organized crime, etc. Incidentally, let me remind you that Al Capone was not sent to prison by the police, with whom he was on friendly terms, but by tax agents—what's more, they were federal agents from Washington, not local ones.

The housing market will stay active for about another twenty years, then everyone will have his own place. Things will ease up. The daily migration of the population within cities will decrease. People will begin to recognize locals on the streets. Strangers will become more obvious. It will get easier for the police. When a crime has a reliable chance of being committed within only a third of a city's territory, it's much simpler to prevent it. It'll be possible to make do with fewer police officers.

The second reason, in my view, is that people have stopped trusting the police. They're afraid of the police. As the proverb says, "Better that your daughter is a prostitute than your son a cop." Think about football—English fans fight with Turkish fans. Liverpool fans fight with Juventus supporters. Only Russian fans (for no matter which team) fight with the police. Both sides prepare for the fight ahead of time. They make up chants. The police are on edge; they're ready to fight at the slightest provocation.

Our people don't want to be witnesses. As soon as they see a crime, they vanish instantly. They don't report anything to the police. They don't want to cooperate with them. They don't believe in their sincere attempts to find the criminals. Ordinary folks serving as jurors acquit hardened criminals. There's a silent war going on between the people and the police.

So the heart of the matter isn't financing. That would be enormous enough in and of itself, by our standards. But there must also be a social contract between the people and the authorities. Otherwise people will rather seek protection from some homegrown Vito Corleone than from the government. "Oh, Don Vito, you were my father's friend, do me the honor, be the godfather of my firstborn son." Maybe Vito ought to join the police force?

* * *

So, Igor, we've established that everything in our country is financed on the remaining balance principle—except for the government apparatus. Everything operates on this principle, while the bureaucrats are scooping money from the treasury with full ladles. The renovations being they're doing at the ministries these days! Even oligarchs don't have offices like this. The Ministry of Transport is all marble; the Ministry of Finance is mahogany. In short, we're being ripped off like there's no tomorrow.

When you walk into a ministry, you see a well-fed and well-heeled bureau-crat—as they say, the entire country has fed and shod him... They have dachas and cars... Bureaucrats in our time didn't live they way they do now.

Well, except the Party ones.

No, I'm talking about my time, when there weren't any more Party members; when it was me, Chubais, Boris Nemtsov. ... Pavel Borodin, for instance, didn't even give me a dacha.

And I suppose, you didn't have a lounge, did you?

We did. But compared to today's lounges—it was a piece of shit. And the way they harassed me over $100,000, the fee for a book! Nowadays even the heads of sub-sections laugh at this figure. But that's not the point. Here's what I'm getting at. Nobody can complain about what's not financed on the remaining balance principle. Our bureaucrats look splendid; they have wonderful offices and first-rate living conditions, and their children are all studying in Switzerland. End of story—this is what the government has decided to pay attention to, so it's all good.

Listen, which accounting column do they use to get their children to Switzerland, Alik? How is this officially recorded?

A person signs something, and boom—his kid's in Switzerland. So why is socialism worse than capitalism? I'll show you why with this one case. Defense in the USSR was not financed on the remaining balance principle by any means; for example, not even in the year in question, 1987. There were transportation systems, communications systems, and all kinds of rockets with varying ranges. But a young guy—that little shit, Mathias Rust—flew through all of it! And no one could do a thing! No interceptors, no rockets, no sonar of any kind helped... And what if we now suddenly started financing defense on something other than the remaining balance principle? I don't think any Rust-type character would be able to get through. Because of capitalism! Now that we've started financing bureaucrats on the remaining balance principle, they're fine. And the military will be, too. And what was it like during Soviet times? The country held its pants up with hemp rope, there was nothing to eat, and enormous sums were spent on defense... Oil, gas, everything went to defense. But this defense didn't defend a fucking thing! Incidentally, complaints are made about the government apparatus, how they ostensibly don't govern. But that's exactly why we pay them money—so that they don't govern! Because our economy is capitalist and liberal. And our bureaucrat does a great job at his function of not governing. And as soon as he's short of money, he says, "All right, I'm going to start doing some governing now!" And bribes start coming to him instantly, and he signs everything....

But this amounts to pennies at the national level. How much do they steal, these bureaucrats?

I think that the amounts are large.

Yes... I do love our government apparatus. Now, Alik, there was a chart published about five years ago in some newspaper. And a map showing offices. The entire structure of the RSFSR was in its old familiar places. Except for Gosplan. And what happened to the buildings that the

old Soviet establishments occupied—COMECON, and the Warsaw
Pact—not to mention the CPSU and the Komosomol buildings? Are they
sitting there, vacant? Or were they given to orphans or to the committee of
soldiers' mothers? Or to children's clubs? No sir! Bureaucrats from the
Russian organizations moved in, and as Academician Fyodorov aptly put
it, they're multiplying like bedbugs.

And they need more room, Igor! Even though the branch ministries, which
formed the backbone of the government, were liquidated—and they contained
the most bureaucrats!

And so, nothing can be done about this shameful phenomenon...

Svinarenko's Commentary:

I just came across a most curious bureaucratic document—dated, in fact,
1987. I would have given a lot to get my hands on it then. But I would have
thumbed through it—and then what? Added one more tune to the same old
opera: The communists are scumbags, etc.

However, back to the point. This 192-page publication, published in
paperback, duly numbered and stamped SECRET, was called "A List of
Information Banned from Open Publication." Moscow, 1987. The byline was
"The Chief Administration of the Council of Ministers of the USSR for the
Protection of Government Secrets in Print (Glavlit USSR)." You're going to
laugh, but an example of what was not permitted in print was "reference to the
low political and moral condition of the personnel of the Armed Forces of the
USSR, including negative relations between military service personnel..." That
is, the thieves, sadists and murderers in the Soviet Army were classified!

* * *

As far as I can see, Igor, we've only been increasing the number of
bureaucrats these past years. All these authorized representatives in the
districts... You know, they're just personnel departments that never existed
before, they were created from scratch.

**Indeed. And it's all being carried out according to Zbigniew
Brzezinski's plan! The Americans, in fact, conceived a plan for bringing
down the USSR a long time ago—this was the first stage, Alik. And the
second stage was to divide Russia into exactly seven parts. But the
Americans didn't have terms like federal *okrugs* and vertically-integrated
power.**

Why not get rid of the governors? And the provinces? Both were retained! Right now institutes and archives are moving out of Petersburg, and the usual federal presences of one sort or another are moving in to take their places. That means that institutes aren't worthy, and that state institutions are. And they've dreamed up *okrug* courts and *okrug* offices of the Public Prosecutor that didn't exist before… So our country is divided into seven military *okrugs*—and that's fine. Since the provinces don't have their own subdistricts, let there be seven subjects of the Federation!

Do you remember when a comrade of ours guessed why there were exactly seven *okrugs*?

Of course I do! So that each of the G7 nations had its own federal *okrug* to supervise! Now how was it that we divided it up? England got the northwest; France got the central region (because Muscovites travel to Paris and to the Riviera); the south went to Italy—warmth, and all that. The Volga Region… Who's responsible for that?

The Germans, Alik, will be responsible for the region along the Volga. I have to remind you?

Hmm… How could I have forgotten… Next. The Urals went to the U.S., Siberia to Canada. The Far East to—whom else but Japan?

So the Russians are incapable of governing Russia themselves?

That's the conclusion that follows from your commentaries to the previous chapter, not from mine.

Ah… So that's how you're talking now. So in your view, Russians govern Russia splendidly!

I didn't say that. I didn't touch on the subject at all, Igor, and I wasn't about to evaluate how well the Russians govern their own country.

Yeah, sure, you'll do this later in your famous interview on Radio Liberty.

Perhaps. But I didn't do it in 1987. If you'd like, if you insist, I'll give you an evaluation: Not brilliantly! They don't govern brilliantly!

But let's return to 1987. So, you're working…

Right. I was earning 170 rubles a month, if you factor in the upcoming raise I was to get when I received my doctoral degree. Our department, by the way, was named Resource Regulation and Conservation.

Not bad—sounds brave and patriotic. Not just pushing a shovel
around, but saving resources for your homeland. Not like my department,
Communist Education. Yes... I turned 30 then, in 1987. I remember
getting very serious about this round figure. It was approaching, looming;
it confused me... The nearer my birthday came, the gloomier I got, and I
got to thinking about life. Well, naturally I had a drunken bash. We drank
until early morning... And evidently the feeling of solemnity and of the
fatefulness of that moment was picked up by my guests. And I remember
that two of them were standing in the nook...

Why are you saying "nook"? The word is "corner"!

I know that. It's a kind of deliberate vernacular. It sounds cozier. On
the whole, the Russian language sounds rather insipid and vague to me.
Compared to some other languages.

I don't know other languages well enough. But I have to say that I don't feel
at all constrained by having to express all my emotions in Russian. I can express
whatever I please in this language!

I can also express quite a lot. Because it's my primary language. But I
see its flaws and half-baked nature. For example, there is an unforgivably
large number of inadequate verbs. And there's nothing to justify this.

What do mean by "inadequate"? For example?

Well, for example, you can't say, I'll victor. In general, there are a lot
of verbs which don't hold up. Lie-lay, put-place, like that. The list of
exceptions is wearying—besides of its being, I repeat, absolutely
unjustified. Then there's the taboo lexicon, which has its place in
primitive-communal systems, but not in civilized societies! Anglo-Saxons
use the word "fuck" in literature and in films, but we're not allowed to—
it's taboo. And what a great word it is!

Svinarenko's Commentary:

From the Brockhaus and Efron Encyclopedia

Taboo is a term borrowed from the religious-ritual institutions of Polynesia and
which is now accepted...to designate a system of particular religious prohibitions...

...Taboo constitutes a web of rules which encompasses all the details of life,
and which deprives a society of the possibility of unfettered evolution. The
psychology that created the taboo...has been a principal cause of the stagnation of
many ancient civilizations.

Have you noticed the epithet that is bestowed upon a society where taboos are currently the convention? Primitive! And there's nothing insulting about it. After all, we did indeed live under communism for a great many years. The similarity between that system and a tribal-clan system bothered me in early childhood, and I interrogated adults about why calling them certain names was forbidden. They said it was not permitted, if only because we had Party committees and missiles—unlike, as we used to like to say, Upper Volta.

About Russian Mat, a Millennia of Talking Dirty and its Relation to the Vagueness of our Mother Russian Language:

B.A. Uspensky, the famous mat scholar, offers the following: "Thus, mat, according to this set of received ideas (which are reflected both in literary texts and in linguistic facts) is *"pes'ya bran'*,*"* or dog swearing; it is, so to speak, the language of dogs—or, to be more exact, their linguistic behavior (that is, strictly speaking, the barking of dogs), which expresses its corresponding content. In other words, when dogs bark, they are in essence quarreling using expletives in their own language; mat expletives are, if you like, the barks of dogs translated into human language.

The typological closeness between various cultures of thieves—French, English, and Russian—even with all their national idiosyncrasies (such as sharply differing attitudes toward, say, homosexuality, in French and Russian criminal "subcultures"), has long attracted the attention of researchers.

Vladimir Zhelvis, Ph.D. (whose dissertation was on mat), made this important point: "As far back as the Battle of Waterloo, when English troops encircled a group of proud and brave Frenchmen, a duke said to them, 'Soldiers, you proved your courage, and we don't want to kill such glorious warriors. You can go.' The Frenchmen said, "Merde"—and the duke was so infuriated by this mortal insult that he ordered the insolent fellows to be executed by cannon. Two hundred years passed, and then the nation's president François Mitterrand used this same word, "merde," to bid farewell to students graduating from the university. In contemporary French the word means something akin to "break a leg."

Obscene language in our country is not stagnating; in spite of everything, it too is evolving.

A. Gorokhovsky points out that "mat remains obscene language only insofar as its effect remains offensive. There's a trend happening in contemporary Russia where expressions like 'Motherfucker,' 'Fuck you,' and 'Suck me' are being reduced to the status of introductory or parasitic words; no one takes them literally any longer, and to a large degree it's just the mere fact of referring to formerly disgraced words that elicits negative reactions."

In other words, everything is moving in the direction of all taboo vocabulary gradually disappearing from the Russian language.

* * *

So what actually happened at your birthday bash, Igor?

There was this one moment. So, this guy is standing in the corner. other guy walks up to him with his hands behind his back and says, "Close your eyes! I'm going to show you a magic trick now." So the first guy closes his eyes. And then the magician gets out a cutting board, places it on top of the guinea pig's head and, swinging with all his might, splits the board in half with a kitchen cleaver. People are stunned. The guy on whose head the board was busted cries all night and then goes and has a subcutaneous anti-substance abuse ampoule inserted. The one who performed the trick goes to the bathroom to screw somebody, and hangs himself some time later. Life was tough in those days...

So all in all, I turned thirty. I called all my girlfriends to a meeting and announced that they were fired: "Thanks to all of you—you're all free because I'm not planning to marry any of you." They replied, "Nobody's forcing you to get married anyway, what's the problem!" "No," I said, "it's not your problem, it's mine. Since I'm not planning to marry you, what do I need you for?" That's all there was to it. Then I also got myself fired. I said, that's enough already. I decided to work on serious subjects, not provincial journalism.

Now wait, so when did you finally get married?

In 1988.

And so, you got married right after you fired everyone. It was that simple.

Well... Incidentally, Alik, cooperatives also started up in 1987.

Yeah, you could already make the big bucks.

And I remember that I went over to *Sobesednik* to submit a news item and met Vladimir Yakovlev there. He had already left the paper and was putting together the Fakt cooperative just then. And so we're both standing in the editorial cafeteria, and everybody is ordering soup and their second course, and he says, "Now then, why don't you give me a full tumbler of black caviar and a pack of Marlboros!" Wow! And he says to me, "Would you like me to lend you at a ten-ruble note, and you can return it when you have the money?!" I took it. And why not?

Svinarenko's Commentary:

Then, three years later, I came to the old *Kommersant* and met Yakovlev in the hallway. I had thirty rubles in my pocket—my entire fortune at that time. I pulled out a 10-ruble note and was about to return my debt, but he just burst out laughing and wouldn't take it.

* * *

I thought then, Alik: What a turn life has taken! Look, people are making bucks... Making almost seven hundred rubles a month. And right at the same moment, Yakovlev says, "Now why don't you come work in my cooperative, and you'll make seven hundred rubles (obviously this sum was on the tip of everyone's tongue)." That is to say, that glass of caviar wasn't just something he bought, it was part of his strategy as a headhunter. I got depressed because this question shifted from the purely theoretical, superficial level into the realm of reality... And I turned him down!

So what was he producing in that cooperative?

Nothing. He was selling information about cooperatives! So, I realized I didn't really want to be involved in business. Moving cash around, from one pocket to another... He says, "Come on over, we'll create a first-rate newspaper! Well, not right away, in a little while..." And he starts to describe an imaginary ideal newspaper—roughly speaking, the future old *Kommersant* which was already forming in his head. I listened to him and said, "When it comes time for the paper, give me a shout right away, and I won't make you wait for me." Well, as we know, that's pretty much what happened.

Do you remember what holiday it was the day Mathias Rust flew in? It was May 28, Border Guards' Day!

You're kidding!

It's true. The border was sealed off!

If he had landed somewhere else, not on Red Square, they would have kept it quiet. But it was impossible to keep quiet.

People thought it was a film shoot, a joke... So you think that under socialism, the military just squandered all that dough, and that was it—that's why even the most basic Air Defense System didn't work...

That's what I think.

Now there was some talk that they spotted Rust, that they tracked him, but then simply decided not to shoot him down.

Yeah, right—and that's why he landed in Red Square… Five years earlier they shot down a Korean Boeing; there were more than two hundred people on it and they didn't even blink! And here, all of a sudden, son of a bitch, they were overwhelmed by humanism. They were asleep at the switch, Igor! One hundred per cent!

In 1987, there was also a train that blew up near Ufa, remember? There was a leak from the main gas line. The gas collected in a low spot. A train was passing by it, someone tossed a cigarette butt out the window, and there was an explosion. Hundreds of people died.

We were being given signs that everything was shutting down.

I'm not an advocate of reading into things, Igor, but it was obvious that everything was going down the tubes… The Soviet Union stank to high hell… It was already beginning to shift from being a great power to being the laughing-stock of the world. And the state workers, whose functions include being proud of a great nation—they don't even see it now. It took a long time for the *sovok* to expire, so we have to talk about it from year to year, in every chapter. If it had only dropped dead in one day, like Czechoslovakia! Everything would have become clear immediately: Havel is the president, and you, communists, sit tight, if you don't want to get smacked in the face, and go get jobs as metal workers. Here's a vacancy, by the way, that just opened up—Dubcek had, in fact, worked as a metal worker for twenty years after the Prague spring, before he was appointed Chairman of the Parliament. And our place would have still been dying if those fools hadn't cooked up the 1991 coup that finished off the Soviet Union!

Evidently, ending it quickly was impossible, Alik. After all, even we took it seriously. We snickered, to be sure, but we didn't go to demonstrations.

What do you mean? I went to some rallies.

Do you remember, the dissidents came out onto Red Square…

I'm talking about something else. There were analysts in the Central Committee of the CPSU—Boris Fyodorov, Igor Malashenko… They spoke English fluently… And Yevgeny Primakov was at the Institute of Economics…

They could have come up with something! And they call themselves analysts… I begrudge them the money! During the five years that they were expiring, those Commies—the amount of money they borrowed from the West and tossed to the winds! We haven't been able to pay off their debts to this day. And if they had immediately said that it was all over, and that they were out of here—then it all would have ended with less blood being spilled. Well, in that same year, 1987, they could have handed the whole business over and gone back to their homes, and found jobs as metal workers! Do you know how much money we could have saved?! If these… along with the deceased Valentin Pavlov, as their chief, hadn't run up these debts?! If Gaidar had arrived five years earlier?! Then they wouldn't have destroyed the budgetary system, inflation would not have spiraled out of control, and we wouldn't have had the confiscation reform that wiped out people's savings…

They still would have stolen the dough, Alik!

Oh come off it! As if the kind of bucks they blew had never been stolen in Russia before! As if billions aren't being stolen now!

Remember the Russian shuttle?

Yes. Ten billion to launch an unmanned shuttle—for what?

It was a response to the Americans!

Then ask me, a taxpayer: Do I agree to respond to the Americans in this way—by sending it up once and leaving it there?

Making an impression is more important than money!

That's when you're spending money that doesn't belong to you. To me money is more important than making an impression.

Now, Alik, you say, "If Yegor Gaidar had appeared in 1987…" But he couldn't. He was engrossed in something else then. On the contrary, he started working at just that moment, in 1987, at *Pravda* and at the *Kommunist* magazine.

Yes, since he was a Communist. But if we had adopted normal laws in our country, riding the democratic wave right after the coup, as all the Eastern European countries did—and specifically, the law banning members of outlawed political parties from certain professions—then Gaidar, Chubais, Shakhrai, and Boris Fyodorov wouldn't have been able to work in the government. Because they were Communists!

If Gaidar went to work at *Pravda*, then he thought it would be for a long time. Otherwise, why the hell get involved with it? To disgrace himself? Obviously he wasn't going for just a year or two, he was serious… Now after the war in Germany, even though there was a ban on them, many Nazis nonetheless continued to work for the government.

Well, over there, Gehlen—who was Canaris' deputy, deputy head of Wehrmacht intelligence—worked in intelligence, and then in the FBI after the war. And it was all right.

What does that prove? That there aren't enough normal cadres anywhere or at any time. They are only two to three per cent of the actively working population. Of course, people like this were Party members when the Nazis and Communists were in power. Or underground producers. Well, if you outlaw them—then what, do you hire their infamous, second-rate cohorts for key positions?

As for "underground producers," who made and sold what people wanted on the black market, there are different kinds of protest. For example, Sakharov and Solzhenitsyn protested openly. But there were others—underground producers, breaking down the system from the other side They created the foundations of private ownership relationships; they'd show up in Sochi with bucks in their pockets and wind up with babes on their arms.

Nice play on words—"bucks and babes."

Babes are, formally, Komsomol gals; they go to school, but they have a different, a non-communist, system of values: a fast Volga model 24, the Dagomys resort, restaurants, the beach, champagne in a bucket… Get it? Who was breaking the regime down more: underground producers by the hundreds and thousands, or Sakharov and Solzhenitsyn, who numbered in the single digits? And then there were the many thousands of dealers who were also breaking it down…I'm not talking about directors of shopping warehouses—they epitomized the very face of socialism. But the black marketeers dealing in foreign goods and currency and underground producers—that was capitalism!

To listen to you, Alik, in this sketch, the dissidents turn out to be jerks?

No!

But they weren't making the big bucks, were they?! They weren't building capitalism!

But they were defending other things—democracy, not capitalism. They were defending non-communist values, while the director of a center, the head of a housing office, and the secretary of a regional committee defended socialist ones! So the hard-currency speculators stood for the values of a free democratic society. They're also included in the two-to-three percent! But the second half of this two percent of the active and enterprising population for some reason doesn't want to govern itself... And allows itself to be governed by the half that are communists, people who have never pounded in a single nail. They have never earned money; they've lived off the budget all their lives!

In general, the science of psychology teaches us that the informal leader in any collective isn't the smartest person by a long shot, but often the opposite—intellectually below average.

Svinarenko's Commentary:

V. Foks. *"Introduction to Criminology"*

Very often the level of intellectual development of leaders is below average for a given group. A person with a higher level of intellectual development is more sensitive to significant factors in the environment and takes many different aspects into account in making a decision. A less intellectually developed but practical person can make a decision based on a small number of factors and without exhausting all the available information. Thus he provides the other members of the group, who may be more nervous or anxious—and this is especially important— with a feeling of security and stability. In providing emotional stability, the leader tries to surround himself with people on whom he can rely and who need his leadership. Apparently this is the case in political groups, but also other cliques, gangs too.

* * *

But, listen Igor: the leader doesn't have to be better; he has to be adequate. I'll give you a simple explanation.

I gave you a scientific one, and you're giving me a correct one?!

What do you mean! I'll also give you a scientific one.

But you're not a psychologist.

You're right, I'm not a psychologist, I'm a cyberneticist. And we know that cybernetics is the science of management. Psychology is just a particular instance of cybernetics. As any science, on second thought, is an individual case of cybernetics. Cybernetics studies informational systems, my dear comrade...

There, there, I see that you're a specialist in the mass media— meaning you studied information systems back at the Institute, ha-ha-ha!

So I'm saying to you now, Igor: Everything's very simple. The governing system has to interact with every element of the governed system. In any case, that's the desired parameter. And if you're talking about a human collective, then if a person is very smart, here's why it isn't good: The distance between him and the dumbest person is so great that contact between them becomes impossible. That's why the person whose intellectual distance from each separate element is not too great becomes the leader... Then he establishes contact with the largest possible number of the elements of the system. Let's imagine a collective in the form of a pie that is ten centimeters thick. Let's say that manageability is lost when the distance between the leader and the elements is greater than five centimeters. If the leader is very smart, if he's at the very top, then he is in contact with the first five centimeters, but going down the pie he begins to lose contact. If the leader has a mediocre intellect, then he's in the middle of the pie—it's five centimeters up or down from there. He reaches everyone, and that's why he governs effectively.

At one time, you know, they did used to say: "Accessible to all."

Now, Chernomyrdin, who was a folksy and intuitive person, said the same thing: that to govern a country, you have to know how to talk to the workers in the smoking lounge. Just try and send an academician to the smoking lounge! Not only does he not smoke, but he also doesn't understand the point of *mat*— so he won't be able to govern this collective.

Yes... And it's the same scene with the dissidents. Take Czecho-slovakia—compact and thoroughly dissident. Havel could talk to an enormous number of people. No problem. Whereas our dissidents found understanding only among their own kind, within the circles of dissidents and near-dissidents. What about the soldiers, the proletarians, the collective farm workers? They need a steady feeding trough instead of political freedoms. So a dissident can't govern Russia.

Well, I'm not so sure about that, Igor... If a dissident is smart, he could...

If he could, then he would be governing.

I just remembered something about China. Who was Deng Xiaoping? A typical dissident. Mao sent him to the camps. When he left the camps, he went into hiding. Then came Hua Guofeng, then the Gang of Four, then boom! Deng became the general secretary. And he said, "Mao and communism are the only things that are true, but we're going to take the specific character of the Chinese into account." I draw your attention to this—he's a dissident.

He's a special case.

Now there you go again... Are you and I men of science or not, Igor? There are no exceptions in science. Science isn't like the Russian language, you know... If you can cite a contradictory example, then the hypothesis is incorrect. I even have more than one example: Dissidents give orders both in Czechoslovakia and in China. And why couldn't they in our country? Well, maybe it's because our dissidents are kind of lousy? Now I look at Sergei Adamovich Kovalyov, and I see clearly that he shouldn't govern the country.

Right, do you remember: He was walking along a street, and he was pulled into a shell game, and they took all his dough? He even went and got some more, and they won it, too. So he went to complain to the police.

That's it. A good man, honest. But I wouldn't trust him to manage himself. I don't even need him as a counselor. I've got my own rich life experience. I know without him who the Chechens are—I lived in Kazakhstan. Why should he tell me how freedom-loving they are! And that they're, like, honest...

In his great dictionary, Dal says about Germans, about you, Alik, the exiled ones: "Germans are like willow branches: No matter where you stick them, they take root!" And then I remember hearing the announcement that Brodsky had received the Nobel Prize on the Voice of America and the BBC.

I remember. But I didn't read him in 1987. Even though I was pleased: He was a native of Petersburg, one of us, a parasite. I love that atmosphere depicted so well by Sergei Dovlatov. That's the St. Petersburg I knew.

Was Petersburg worse than Moscow or not?

I didn't know Moscow. Moscow began for me in 1993. I think that, in any case, it wasn't worse. But the avant-garde was clearly more powerful in Petersburg than in Moscow. Brodsky... He probably hung out at the same underground apartments that I did. With some effort, you could probably find that we had mutual acquaintances.

You and Brodsky do have a mutual acquaintance—Kaplan.

Ah, Roman at the Russian Samovar in New York... Of course.

Brodsky... Who else was writing about Petersburg then? Andrei Bitov, Vassily Aksyonov... I happened to start reading them, the paragons, recently; I thought, well, now for some aesthetic pleasure—but none came. Somehow it just wasn't... It wasn't right...

Well, a man writes when he's got a hard-on. The hormonal effect is very important here, Igor. If it's up—you write, if it isn't—that's it. Your legs, head, memory may be what they were before, but the result is crap.

A man is basically a chemical robot. He consists of 90 percent water in which various chemicals are dissolved. You add some vodka, and it's a command to the robot to change his behavior and the direction he's moving.

Right, you pour a glass into him and he'll start up dancing right away, Igor.

The Children of the Arbat **came out then.**

Did you read it?

No.

I didn't, either. Why did everyone make such a fuss over Anatoli Rybakov?

I don't know. For all my love of dissidents, I couldn't read it.

It's not clear why *The Children of the Arbat* was hyped so much. *The Gulag Archipelago* and Varlam Shalamov's work were more than enough to understand everything.

There was also the discussion of what to do with Kaliningrad.

Why not give it away?

Well, just let it be.

What for?

Say you've got this television. Do you give it away or just let it stand there?

No, not a television for an example. Let's make it a piece of land, and I'm living on it. And across the road, somewhere off in the distance, I own another piece that I'll never get around to working. What's more, there are some roads over there, and a gas station nearby. And this guy comes and says to me, "Let me take your piece and add it to mine, and I'll build a barn there." And it's more expensive for me to maintain my piece than it's worth! As for Kaliningrad, I don't understand at all why we took it. Why did we add Eastern Prussia in 1945? Who needs it?

To have it!

If they wanted to add something, Igor, why didn't they add all of Poland? The Allies didn't allow it? The world has been operating according to the principle of economic, not territorial, expansion for a long time. Tiny Japan controls half the world. While Brazil and Russia can't control themselves. And so what? I don't understand what "let it be" means! There are people living there, it has the highest number of people with AIDS and drug addicts, the lowest standard of living of all the regions in Russia…

In Kaliningrad?!

Yes, yes! There's never been any industry there, just military bases. And now the Baltic Fleet is a thing of the past. There was a port there that connected through the Baltic republics to metropolitan areas. The port isn't functioning now. We used to have a port system before: Klaipeda, Riga, Ventspils, Tallinn and Vyborg. And now Petersburg is the only one left. And so they're building new ports—Vyborg and Primorsk. Why not return it? I'm ready to agree to any kind of logic, just lay it out to me… But the reason can't be that it'll come in handy someday, like Gogol's miserly Plyushkin saving string.

I don't understand a damn thing in your reasoning. I don't want to just give it back. Let's trade it for something!

Let's! This is the kind of conversation I understand. It's easy to talk to Westerners this way: We give them something, and they take it with pleasure. But they don't want to give anything in exchange. We should tell them this: We'll take something that belongs to someone else in exchange for something that doesn't belong to you. Your job is simply not to notice that we're ripping it off. They'll agree to deals like this with pleasure. For example, let them not notice how we take Crimea away from the *khokhols*. Ukraine will convene the UN Security Council about the Crimea, and there they'll say, the hell with you, the situation with the Crimea is altogether incomprehensible, it was taken from the Turks, etc.

Go on…

Now that'll be a conversation! That'll be something new! It'll be interesting when Rogozin declares this.

Can't we take Crimea first, and maybe give Kaliningrad back later?

No, that's not the way to work with them. You have to do it simultaneously. Besides, you don't even have to send troops there; we have troops there already!

Clever.

Yes. Tell them that we've been thinking for a long time and have decided that Crimea is Russian. As for you, *khokhols*: Sorry! You can be indignant but the commandant's offices were long ago given the instructions to deport all the representatives of the Ukrainian government across Perekop. And we're going to swear-in all the military... The residents of the Crimea will be happy! We'll immediately put aside money in the budget for the construction of a bridge across the Kerchensky strait. And I'll buy a little land there. I'll build a little house, I'll send my children there...for the whole summer... And you can have Konigsberg—but with our citizens. It's all the same to us whether you unify it with Germany or with Poland... But bear in mind that our Russian people— citizens of the European Union—will be there. And the funniest thing will be if these Russians bolt back from Kaliningrad to Russia, if they don't want to live in Europe. And we'll then resettle them in the Crimea! Hah-ha-ha! Drug addicts don't give a fuck where they shoot up. ...

Svinarenko's Commentary:

Aha, I finally understand how Russian business works! On the basis of this small example. Evidently this is our all-purpose principle: Two people exchange a third party's property—and they both win. The third party, to whom it belongs, loses. The most striking manifestation of this principle is the oil business. Bureaucrats give away oil that doesn't belong to them to so-called businessmen. And the latter, with this oil that doesn't belong to them, pay the bureaucrats with money that doesn't, for all intents and purposes, belong to them. That is, the parties exchange valuables and, at the same time, get rich.

* * *

Think about it, Igor. If we had supported Bush in the war with Iraq, we would have said, "How much longer can we put up with Kuchma's mockery against his own people? Why, he's just a pure unadulterated dictator; he bumped off a journalist with a Georgian name. And the wiretaps that the FBI deciphered show that he's an amoral character. That's why we're starting a war for the liberation of the Ukrainian people. And the Crimea is Russian—it's ours!"

You're rejoicing as if we had already taken the Crimea back, Alik. Clever, by the way. That's how it works with you Germans: You take

Konigsberg from Russia and the Crimea from us *khokhol*s, and at the same time, you're taking it to build yourself a dacha. Not a bad arrangement! Giving away what doesn't belong to you and taking all the best for yourself! So that's how our Russian (or your German) business gets developed!

Igor, you should thank me, a half-breed, for not taking the Crimea and uniting it with Germany as was the plan back in the day—they wanted to build a national sanatorium of the Third Reich! And your droning on about holding onto Kaliningrad is stupid and unoriginal! So then, don't give it up. And everyone there will die out, and whoever doesn't, will leave... Because it's impossible to live there...

7.

1988

The Seventh Bottle

Life began more and more to resemble life today. The myth of friendship between the peoples of the USSR collapsed: Slavic gangsters in Moscow declared war on their Azerbaijani and Chechen colleagues, while the republics wanted to just up and break away altogether—Estonia even proclaimed independence. As for the former fraternal republics of Armenia and Azerbaijan, they began a real war.

The authorities admitted to another problem: Thirty-eight actual drug addicts came to light in Moscow. Soviet organized crime responded enthusiastically to the "Law on Cooperatives," and nearly 600 cases of racketeering were recorded.

Kokh and his comrades Chubais and Gaidar were preparing to head up the organization of a new economy. Svinarenko was exposing the unadulterated truth in the newspapers. Well, to put it crudely, he was doing a PR job on the truth. Unpaid.

Oh, Alik! I just remembered! Nina Andreyeva distinguished herself in 1988 with her letter denouncing perestroika.

Now, did anybody really care about her?

What are you saying? There was a panic! Everyone thought that was the end of the thaw!

This Andreyeva's reasoning was hackneyed. It didn't hold up; it was pathetic. Maybe you, at the newspapers, experienced panic. But me, I didn't panic at all... I didn't think that it was important.

At the newspapers, we thought it was. We were tracking all the sedition... Nina Andreyeva's piece coming out in print was an issue of fundamental importance for me. What was next? If it was all over—then I was out of there. I'd quit the paper and return to construction work.

It was a tempest in a teapot. I was sure she'd get a rebuke.

Alik, you're trying to talk about Nina Andreyeva from the point of view of the present. As if anyone was worried about her line of reasoning at the time.

I repeat: I had no reaction to it then. Maybe my serenity is exactly what I'm surprised about in retrospect.

Svinarenko's Commentary:

Andreyeva stirred up a sensation. All across the country! Her letter was deemed worthy of an investigation by the Politburo! Moreover, there weren't any other items on their agenda. Their meeting lasted neither more nor less than two whole working days, with breaks for lunch. They decided to send a commission to the editorial office of *Sovetskaya Rossiya* to clarify the circumstances. As soon as the commission arrived, it seized the original letters (to determine if they were fake) and banned publications that supported Andreyeva.

Yuri Karyakin wrote about it in *Ogonyok* magazine—at that time everyone listened to him with their mouths agape.

> ... Andrei Nuikin warned that a counter-attack is being prepared, and he turned out to be right: Nina Andreyeva's letter appeared... I'm convinced that the entire chronology of events outlined in her manifesto, in all their dramatic and comic detail, will come to pass. How was the choice to publish it made? With what strategy in mind? How many local newspapers carried it? How many copies were made of it? How many favorable discussions of it were organized? According to whose instructions? How was local initiative stirred up? By whom? Why wasn't there a single word against it in the press—except, it seems to me, for *Moskovskiye Novosti* and *Tambovskaya Pravda*? How was it that one individual's (presumably private) opinion—an opinion opposed to the Party's and the government's entire policy for renewal—was able virtually to dominate the press, unquestioningly and indivisibly for those three weeks (twenty-four days to be exact)? Why was it virtually imposed —through the press or in other ways—on the entire party, the entire population, and the entire country? How did it square with the slogan, "More democracy, more

socialism"? With glasnost? With the Party's regulations and its program? And how is it in accord with the state Constitution? Who was this Nina Andreyeva, of the suddenly unprecedented, incomprehensible omnipotence? And if it wasn't her own opinion, then whose was it? And if it belonged not to an individual but to a platform, then whose, specifically? And why would its real authors hide behind a poor chemist? And, finally: If this was possible, then wasn't something worse possible?

As you can see, some people got very frightened then. As we are wont to do, we immediately thought of the worst-case scenario, and there was depression, and the so-called intelligentsia began packing crackers for the road to prison... And also rejoicing: "Well, thank God, everything fell through, so now everything's going to be bad, just as we predicted!"

It wasn't just *Ogonyok*! Even *Pravda* became alarmed: An anonymous article (they say that A. N. Yakovlev wrote it) appeared in it, declaring Andreyeva's letter "a manifesto of anti-perestroika forces." And further on in *Pravda*: "The enemies of perestroika are not just lying in wait for the moment when it will sputter... They're growing bold; they are rearing their heads."

The passions were seething! How did they manage to agitate the general public with such purely theoretical and essentially petty issues?

* * *

Kokh's Commentary:

Nina Andreyeva as a Mirror of Russian Scholasticism

I remember at my institute, we had a Department of Scientific Communism... Or was it the History of Communism? Now I don't remember any more. Those departments were always exactly the same... We had an associate professor there, Tuzov. He was already an old man, an invalid; he had lost a leg in the Battle of Kursk. Basically, we respected him. He was sufficiently strict, but without being pedantic. He was a fierce Communist, absolutely orthodox. When I was studying at the institute in the early 1980s, this was already seen as an anachronism. Mild criticism of the authorities was already becoming fashionable, and so this relic of Stalinism looked rather shabby. But he was absolutely harmless, and not at all aggressive. He didn't get into arguments; somehow he just had a stern look, that was all. Not unintelligent—he probably understood that his era was coming to an end. There was talk that he was in the NKVD—either before or after the war—and conducted executions. But there were no hard facts, and he didn't look like an executioner. Except for that gaze of his...

When perestroika was completely and definitively in full swing (wasn't it in 1988?), I heard that he had hanged himself. A human being had existed, and then he was gone. He had spilled blood. He had believed passionately. Elderly, honored, his entire chest covered in decorations…

He probably had that rare ability: to grasp in an instant the entire monstrosity of what had happened to his country, his people, his generation… The sheer number of people who were destroyed, the lost lives of the gifted, of the unborn… All for the sake of the radiant future: Communism. Billions of trillions of megawatts of human energy, labor, and hope… And all for nothing…

That's why he looked stern… And it's why he didn't argue. He understood that it was futile. That we wouldn't understand the full meaning of the choice we were making, its utter irrevocability. The fact that as we made that choice, all of its future victims—whose numbers we can't even guess at now—were rendered irrelevant in a single stroke… The thoughtlessness of youth… How had Marx put it? "…humanity laughs as it takes leave of its past…"

Those for whose sake we sinned, for whose sake so much sweat and blood was spilled; those whom we had raised, on whom we were relying to carry on our titanic labor—they don't want to build communism. They don't want to, and that's all… So there won't be any communism. Not any longer, not ever.

That's it—the end. But there's no death. Where is bony death? If only it would take me, an old man, away… But it's not here. All right then, the prohibition against suicide is a religious prejudice. A real Communist is above that sort of thing. And so it was into the noose… That's how it goes.

But the orthodox, those who were weaker, they argued. Especially the Komsomol activists. They sang like birds. They coached one another: If they ask you this, then this is how you answer. Besides, the arguments quickly became competitive exercises in erudition, scholasticism, and definition. These energetic sophists were very difficult to deal with. They bore down on patriotism, on the commandments of the fathers, and on other sensitive spots that are sacred to any normal person. And, according to them, it was inevitable that the Communists would realize the centuries-old dream of the Russian people, and that democracy would flower even better under socialism than anywhere else. Everything was spelled out; everything was prepared. Instances of repression were rare and isolated and in no way nullified the achievements… Rabid militarism is a struggle for peace; the nuclear missile shield is a feat of arms… The peasantry's annihilation was collectivization, industrialization… In a word: bullshit. But it was difficult to argue with.

Now, I found a very interesting document that speaks to this. The German historian Hans-Adolf Jakobsen cites the so-called "Twelve Commandments for German Administrative Bureaucrats in Occupied Western Oblasts" on pages

248–251 of his book, *1939–1945. World War II: Chronology and Documents*. These "commandments," written in the Reich offices, were given to all the bureaucrats of the occupation administration. The eighth commandment is very interesting: "Do not talk, act. You will never out-talk a Russian or convince him with speeches. He knows how to speak better than you because he is a born dialectician and has inherited a predilection for philosophizing. He always wins out in conversations and discussions…"

That's what Nina Andreyeva was like. She, in fact, taught something ideological at some Leningrad institute. Scholasticism. Of the genre: "If I am asked about the repressions, I answer 'isolated instances' and, then go on to talk about the conquest of space."

And another thing: She argued. She didn't keep silent. And she looked at me from the television screen with the blazing eye of a Pioneer—not sternly, like Tuzov. And her facial muscles didn't twitch. It was obvious right away that it was just talk. There was no pain in it. There was pain in Tuzov's silence.

And I understood where the difference lay. Tuzov was a victorious soldier, but he didn't look like one. He bore the spirit of ancient tragedy—the calm courage of one who had been defeated. This—his old man's silence (not the usual grumbling of the elderly)—is what constitutes determination. Basically, he and Sakharov were of the same generation. They don't make them like that any more. They've been discontinued.

Now if all the Communists were like Tuzov, I would have agreed to build Communism with them.

* * *

No, I don't remember that I thought very much about this Andreyeva at all, Igor. When the law on cooperatives was passed—that was another matter entirely! Fuck, here we were cooped up in some closed research institute, with no way to break out of it, while our comrades out there at large were creating cooperatives and had completely blown off work. You see, I could have taught somewhere and kept a little cooperative on the side at the same time. But no—I had to sit behind closed doors from nine to six, and not go out anywhere. There was this punch-card, with little holes.

And is your working day longer now?

Now, of course it's longer… Then, in order to establish a cooperative, you had to register it first. Only during working hours. Which is when I sat at my desk and didn't move. Period. And you also had to bribe all those girls in the regional administrative committee who handle the registrations.

You should have hired a smart Jew.

But those Jews hadn't appeared yet, the law had just been passed. But it was completely impossible to create a cooperative working on your own in a closed, that is, almost secret, research institute. And I had gotten into a closed institute not because I had a great life, but because no one in Petersburg would hire me— I didn't have a Leningrad municipal residence permit, only an oblast provincial one. Meanwhile I was dreaming of leaving for real work: teaching. The work in there was killing me! Those monthly sessions with the First Department: "If you've spent time socializing with a foreigner, you are required to come and talk about it…" Secret rooms and little suitcases filled with documents—it was total bullshit.

Now all you'd like is to sit and write about foreigners.

Yes… And then I found myself a little job—I was enticed, thank God, to the Leningrad Polytechnic—which I considered a fantastic leap in my career. But that was later, in 1989. In 1988 I was honestly working at that shitty research institute calculating the economizing of materials… There are cutting problems in applied mathematics, and there's special automated software…

Now when they say Russia was sold it had to be cut up first with software…

Come on, cut it out—there was no sale of Russia in 1988! In fact, there was no sale at all, ever. Individual enterprises were sold.

What are you getting so steamed up about, Alik?

Oh, nothing. Well, in short, it's 1988. I have my doctorate in science, and I'm getting an extra ten rubles a month for my academic degree. I was living near the Alexander-Nevsky Monastery. That's right where the main ceremonies related to the thousand-year anniversary of the Christianization of Russia were taking place.

I remember that the commemoration was in June. Now, about the government's attitude toward religion: I remember the night before International Women's Day, March 8, 1988, as if it were today: I had gone to the Moscow pool to swim. They closed down that pool, you know, soon after they made the decision to rebuild the Church of Christ the Savior.

Yes. And so we had all these processions with ecclesiastical banners right before our very eyes… Church bells… They tidied up the monastery.

But you were still an atheist then, Alik.

Well, I was never a real atheist. But I wasn't genuinely religious, either. I'm constantly in a kind of in-between place... But if you think about it, I'm more of a believer than a non-believer.

But you weren't baptized.

I wasn't baptized. But what is ritualism? The point is that the celebration aroused a lively interest within me. It was very likely the most important event in my life that year.

When I was observing the ceremonies, I hadn't been baptized either. But I was also interested, without a doubt... What was especially pleasing to me wasn't Christianity itself, but that the Bolsheviks had so oppressed the Orthodox, that they had blown up churches, and it was all for nothing—they hadn't succeeded at anything. The Bolsheviks had been in power at that point for only seventy years, and it wasn't clear how things would turn out for them. And Christianity was two thousand years old—if it were garbage, it wouldn't have lasted that long. When I imagine those past eras, how—despite the lack of industry, and the scarce resources—people nonetheless took up collections, raised fantastic sums of money and built enormous churches... That is substantial evidence of God's existence! Christianity was deeply alien to me in my early Komsomol youth. I wasn't even capable of thinking about working for the church. Later—when I worked in *samizdat* in 1980-1981 and some of what we published was Christian literature—I understood it just as a way to make money while simultaneously bringing culture to the masses. I once found myself thinking (in Jerusalem, at the Tomb of the Savior): "There are people who don't believe in God. They're strange. How difficult it must be for them to live... How is it that they don't understand?" And then it dawned on me, "Oh, I no longer consider myself one of those people! I'm no longer with them, I'm on the other side, where God is!"

Kokh's Commentary:

Russia the Orphan

What is Russia? Is it a terrible, despotic Asian place, populated only with Slavic-Chukhonsko-Tatar mestizos, superficially anthropologically reminiscent of Europoids, who adopted the most archaic and orthodox version of Christianity? Or is it genuinely an independent civilization, distinct from the European as well as the Asian ways of life?

People who consider themselves European naturally adhere to the former point of view. However, the Russian differs from the European in certain important, core characteristics.

These fundamental differences are so strong that, by comparison, an external similarity in appearance becomes only a secondary sign—one which does not influence the native European's final verdict that Russians are, finally, hopeless Asians.

However, differences from Asians are also immediately visible. Even if you don't take into consideration anthropological and religious differences (although these alone should be sufficient for a conscientious researcher), Russians have mental peculiarities that do not permit us to regard them as Asians.

But in any event, it is beyond obvious that Russia cannot be classified either as a strictly European or strictly Asian civilization. However, I'm also not satisfied with the rather mechanistic theory (arrived at by the process of elimination) of it being a synthesis of both cultures: the infamous "Eurasianism."

What was Kievan Rus' on the eve of the adoption of Christianity, and immediately after? It was a Norman principality, typical for its time—like the Norman duchy in the north of France or the Sicilian duchy. You can argue all you like about the degree of Viking influence on Russian statehood, but the fact that it was definitive at its initial stage is not subject to doubt. It is enough to recall the return in 979 of the Baptizer of Rus, Vladimir Svyatoslavovich (still a fierce pagan), at the head of a large contingent of Norman troops, from Sweden (where he had a multitude of relatives, and where he had fled in 977 to escape his brother, Yaropolk).

The adoption of Christianity in Russia occurred in 988—approximately the same time as it did in all the pagan states of Norman Europe.

The only difference is that the other states took their Christianity from the Roman Pope, while Rus chose the Byzantine faith. In all fairness, we should note that the choice between Constantinople and Rome was obvious to the Kievan prince. On the one hand there was Byzantium, the wealthiest and most developed state known at that time in the world; and on the other, devastated, impoverished Rome, surrounded by savage, barbaric kingdoms.

We should not be surprised that Saint Vladimir chose the Christianity of the Constantinople patriarch while his relatives (distant and close) in the other Norman states of Europe followed Rome. At that time Europe was in a state of horrifying poverty and ignorance; the flame of civilization, which had gone out after the fall of the Western Roman Empire, began to burn through to Europe only after the Crusades, which wouldn't begin for another hundred years. Suffice it to say that the Cordovan Emirate—that is, Spain, which had been conquered by the Muslim Arabs—was the most developed Western European state at the time. After Christianization, Vladimir married Anna, the Byzantine emperor's sister. Today we cannot even imagine what the marriage to the Byzantine emperor's sister meant for the Europe of that time. The degree of Kievan Rus's intimacy with the wealthiest and most powerful state was unprecedented. Suffice it to say that Vladimir's Viking troops had virtually the same leadership It was as if modern Russia had been accepted into the WTO, NATO, the EU and NAFTA all in one stroke.

Such a level of integration could result in only two consequences: In the first place, the colossal rise of Russia's political and economic influence across all of Europe. (For example, Vladimir's granddaughter became the Queen of France.) But, second, competition for the Kievan throne grew between Vladimir's heirs, and soon after the reign of his son Yaroslav the Wise, Russia fell into a long feudal internecine conflict and fragmentation that ended in the Mongolian invasion.

But between the adoption of Christianity and the arrival of the Mongols there elapsed three hundred years of comparatively tranquil development, during which—through the intensive influence of Constantinople and the missionary achievements of the Greek monks—Russia became Byzantine. Literacy, literature, architecture, crafts, rituals, and traditions—everything that can be called culture—everything was brought from Byzantium. (Though proximity to the powerful and developed Byzantium likely made the process of civilizing Russia more intensive than it was in other European nations. A similar process was going on in all the Norman states. The former pagans became fervent Christians, and the valor of the Norman dukes was noted by the Pope numerous times).

And so, churches and monasteries were built in Rus, and literacy was disseminated; but when Byzantium was dealt a death blow by the Muslims and Russia was defeated by the Mongols, this life-enhancing process ended for many long years.

When the European nations began to wake up from the darkness of the Middle Ages, the first examples of high art which the Western masters wanted to imitate were the Byzantine mosaics (heirs to antiquity) and churches (for instance, St. Mark's Cathedral in Venice).

Subsequently the Venetians discovered the forgotten treasure-store of civilization closer at hand—Rome, Ravenna, and Naples—and the Renaissance epoch, which gave the world Leonardo, Michelangelo and Raphael, began. Through the Florentines, the Venetians, and the Genoans, the breath of revived culture spread through all of Europe from Italy, spurring the development of art, science and technology, commerce and industry. Ancient Rome was the foundation of the Renaissance and, ultimately, the basis of today's Western civilization.

And what about Rus? Rus was reborn in a different way. Torn from Byzantium, its cultural progenitor, it restored its power with support from its great predecessors. Groping in the dark and with the help of Greek wisdom, it discovered for itself anew that which it would have found in the old books. Having gathered its forces, it defeated Mamai, but then a terrible thing happened: Constantinople was captured by the Turks in 1453, and the last Byzantine emperor, Constantine, was killed in the battle.

The Second Rome ceased to exist. A thousand-year-old empire—long a model for many in Europe, foremost for Russia—ended. This state had given Russia everything: faith, books, culture, and science. The new Muscovite Rus, separated from the Bosphorus by the Tatars and Turks, could not come to the aid of besieged Tsargrad. And as a symbol of final gratitude, as a symbol of eternal farewell to its great cultural progenitor, Great Prince Ivan III married Sophia Paleologus—the niece of the last Byzantine emperor—and, in 1480, refused to pay tribute to the Tatars, declaring himself Tsar. "We are the Third Rome" was heard aloud then for the first time.

When they speak about our Eurasianism, you want to keep repeating: Don't try to portray Russia as a hybrid, begotten by crossing Europe with Asia. We have a perfectly clear ancestor—Byzantium, a country that set the standard for the world for an entire millennium. It's just that Europe has a progenitor right there on its soil: Just walk around the little streets of Rome. Ours died more than five hundred years ago, so you have to live by your own wits. Russia is an orphan. It doesn't have parents. And it is the Third Rome. With all the pluses and minuses that entails.

* * *

What else happened? Well, Igor, my daughter was in the second grade then...

You bred early!

I regard this as the fulfillment of my obligation as a human: Leaving children behind on earth is a must.

Is this an intellectual exercise or do you also enjoy the process?

I enjoy all of it. I like to see how they grow, how they change—and even when I quarrel with them, I still like them.

Children—that's good... As for me, my mother died in 1988. At the age of not quite fifty-three. A respected doctor, herself. A thyroid tumor, an operation, radiation... And that was it.

How many years did it take her to die?

This went on for about five years. She would go into each operation as if into battle, ready for anything. And here's another thing: She secretly was friends with a priest from the nearest church. My father was a party man—he was even a party apparatchik at one time. So, he had his own life. And she had hers.

Svinarenko's Commentary:

Mother treated this priest's children. She was a very good pediatrician, well-known in town. She bravely took on hopeless cases, ones that other doctors refused. And you can understand them, her colleagues: You accept a child as a patient and it dies, and its corpse hangs on you. The parents are going to stare the physician in the eyes, and they might even sue. But she accepted them with no further discussion. She spent days and nights at the hospital; that's how this work is. Sometimes she would bring kids home on weekends—not sick ones, of course, cured ones. Some parents had brought them to the hospital as hopeless cases and left them there; at least it was at the hospital and not in the street. And the kids lived there for years. But that's another subject.

The worst kept happening. Mother would come home on those days wiped out and just say, "It was a very difficult child. We didn't succeed in saving it." Not a whiff of medical cynicism about her. Now, can stress like that go on without consequences? It doesn't prolong your life, now does it?

By the way, here's something else I remembered: there was an entire shelf in the dress wardrobe filled with candy and champagne from grateful parents of lucky patients.

* * *

Remind me, journalist friend, where did you work in 1988? In Kaluga?

No. I had left my job in Kaluga. I started working at Moscow newspapers. They paid far more than the ones in Kaluga. Well, and in general, it was a more honorable occupation.

Svinarenko's Commentary:

It was interesting to work as a journalist in 1988. Newspapers were given unprecedented relief from their restrictions—but, of course, only up to certain limits. I remember that I was sent to Baku to write about underground trade in deficit goods at the Kubinka market. Nothing horrible was happening there, it was—to describe the situation in today's terms, it was a normal retail market. You know, Marlboro, Heineken, vodka day and night, Turkish leather… It was mundane. People also came there for pot and for girls—big deal, right? But at that time it was terribly exotic—wow! In the open! Everything was permitted! And right under the nose of Soviet authorities! I wrote an upbeat piece about it. The point was that everyone knew everything, but no one was catching anyone. I went out on raids to round up prostitutes. The cops complained about it—one more thing that they had to do. In the past Muslim women hadn't been active in prostitution. "And why are they now?" I asked. They answered, "Damned thing-ism is to blame for everything; wanting things is destroying the girls." On the whole, I'm not ashamed about this piece today—I was sort of describing the sprouts of the market. And I even hinted at corruption—mildly. I also wrote that all the cops I spoke to smoked Marlboros, which in Baku cost about twice as much as they did in Moscow—that is, five rubles. And I asked everyone where the smokes came from. And they, of course, said, "My brother gave me a gift, a comrade treated me…"

There were two professional trips that I wanted to take, but they didn't happen—because of my inferior moral and political traits. I got ready to go to Afghanistan and made all the arrangements with the Ministry of Defense, with some colonels there (we drank and I got friendly with them)—but all of a sudden they began speaking very coldly with me and even hanging up on me. Everything was scrapped. The answer to the riddle is simple: There was no avoiding a good vetting by the KGB, and there, evidently, they remembered my modest contribution to *samizdat*.

I also blew it with the "Uzbek Affair" that was so big then. This time the Prosecutor General of the USSR spoiled everything. I went there for a routine chat about the trip—late, and heavily hung over. And they didn't like me in that state. So they didn't take me with them to Tashkent. I had gotten drunk the day before with a German acquaintance who had come to the Soviet Union for the first time and was staying with me. He was the husband of my former German girlfriend—so we were almost related, having shared a mistress. I had prepared a few bottles of vodka for the meeting, and we drank them all, and I asked out of politeness, "Do you want any more?" He replied, "*Naturlich*, Igor Nikolayevich!" I got the port out. But again, it wasn't enough! I went to my neighbor's to borrow some moonshine. Then we drank eau de cologne. I thought to myself: Boy, did I ever luck out with this German; even though he's puny, I'm already having a hard time, and he wants more and more. I put him to bed on a cot, and we were sleeping… Terrible noises woke me up during the night. I thought that a volcano was erupting: Everything he had drunk and ingested was coming out of all the guy's orifices. And he was muttering, like Chekhov, who for some reason uttered his parting words in a foreign language: literally, *"Ich sterbe"* (I'm dying"). But my German didn't die; they managed to pump his stomach and nurse the guy back to health, even though his chances were slim. And so. I saved a dying man at the expense of a business trip to Uzbekistan. By the way, I later asked him, "Do you usually drink that hard?" "No," he says, "two beers plus 100 grams of vodka, and I'm smashed." "Then why the fuck did you demand more?" "I didn't ask. I was just being polite: I thought that in Russia it was a tradition not to refuse when your glass is filled... Sancta simplicitas!"

I nearly died myself then.

* * *

Svinarenko's Commentary:

Shortages

Shortages in nearly everything began in 1988. We journalists suffered through them along with regular folks, but in a somewhat different way. Sometimes they issued coupons for consumer products in editorial departments, and once I got one, too. And so, on the specified date, I came to the restricted shoe warehouse... The task before me was to buy my wife winter boots (maybe some Russian readers remember this kind of problem). A queue had formed in the hallway—the entire editorial staff, from the deputy manager of the department right down the ranks. I stood in line for half a day, and when I was standing right up at the counter, it turned out that women's boots were only authorized to be given to men starting at the rank of senior correspondent. I had to get myself some moccasins with tassels.

Besides the boots, there were also so-called produce orders, and the cheapest instant coffee in the world—it came in those brown jars that you still occasionally see in kiosks. Spiritual sustenance was also rationed. I remember private showings: a film like say, Forman's *Ragtime*. It made a big impression on me for an entire week. Recently I popped in a video cassette of it, lay down on the couch, and began watching it: "Nah, too wishy-washy!" It didn't cut it for me. What was wrong? Maybe because we were sick and tired of films about collective farms and factories, about girls who didn't put out and straightforward guys who didn't drink but smoked silently, expressively gazing into the distance. Against this feeble background any film in which a person wasn't complaining to the Party Committee but instead firing his rifle at the faggots who shit in his car was doomed to achieve the status of a work of art, gratefully appreciated and remembered for a long time.

* * *

Incidentally, Alik, another not-so-minor event that has to be mentioned was that I got married in 1988.

Without having either a home or a penny to your name.

Well. I married my current wife and moved into her communal apartment.

Oh, so you got married for housing! There was an element of mercenary interest in your marriage! When you were getting married, did you take housing into account? Now when I got married, it was purely an experiment. I didn't have a place to live, nor did she.

For many years after I divorced my first wife, a huge number of people tried to marry me off: They had the most diverse motives—from the purely mercenary motives of my female acquaintances to the wives of my comrades who wished, by doing this, to neutralize my dissolute influence on their husbands. At first I actively resisted these matchmaking attempts: Well, why the hell did I need it? You are trotted out like a stud for mating. But then one of my comrades talked me into giving in, even catching the matchmaking initiative from his wife and taking the matter into his own hands. The thing was that she allowed him to go out on overnights only under the pretext that I had eventually to be married off as a result. In order not to let my comrade down, I went on these quests with him. The girls, with whom we made friends, didn't resemble brides in the conventional sense... But it was fun. I began to consider this pseudo-matchmaking a way to expand my circle of acquaintances. Well, you're being introduced to a young woman, what's wrong with that? After all, you still have to meet people. All in all, there wasn't anything bad about these exhibitions. Of course, I didn't promise to marry anyone... I'm even remembering all this with a kind of nostalgia... There weren't any personal problems; you'd call, and then you'd go off somewhere. And no one would nag you about your absence... Now you wouldn't understand, because you got married as a mere boy and missed out on all of this. This was, in effect, a civilized form of polygamy—remember our first chapter? My marriage was a phenomenon of a time-honored order, a worldview... It was the transition from polygamy to monogamy... We had to sever the ties. I would have made this transition long ago; by age thirty it was high time, and I was terribly drawn to the idea of a normal human life, with children running around the house, a nagging wife—but there was no suitable candidate. And then I realized that she had appeared. I began

pushing her to get married right away, on the second day of our acquaintance.

That is, you went into attack mode right away. Was it an internal decision?

Yes. She fought me off for a long time. I harassed her for half a year. She would say, Stop it, it doesn't happen this way. Maybe that was what egged me on. When I got married the first time, it was also from a deep internal conviction, even though I felt that nothing good would come of it. But I sensed somehow that if I didn't get married, I wouldn't forgive myself. I needed to drain this cup right to the very bottom. Otherwise I would have cursed myself all my life and would have regretted what I had not done.

It's strange that a young man would have had such epiphanies…

Why did I decide to get married immediately? It was all very subtle… I once saw a portrait of Yuri Gagarin's wife—I think it was a photo portrait by Vasily Peskov, taken during the minutes while Gagarin was circling in orbit, and it wasn't clear how it would all end. In it she is resting her cheek on her hand, looking in front of her. Her look is so deep, very human; you can read so much in her eyes… No, but… Well if a girl has the eyes of a whore—that can be fine too, it's even necessary sometimes. But we're talking about something else here, about something lofty, about the human, about the soul. And you could see in the portrait of Gagarin's wife that she's not thinking about fame and fortune or about the new Volga cosmonauts customarily received, but about her husband, and how things were going for him out there. And so I saw that Lydia had this look…and instantly decided to get married. I'll tell you a secret: I am a person of very subtle spiritual makeup, but I have continually had to play the simple provincial lout in my relations with young women. You get tired of it, you know, you feel like being yourself. And so I married my wife, with whom I have a lot in common. That is, I did everything right. You can see that I'm satisfied with my wife.

Well, yes, since you've been living with her for fifteen years. You've had time to sort it all out. The feelings.

Yes. But that's not everything, Alik. Let me tell you another funny story about how principled I was in my youth. And why it's not that easy for a person like me to get married. Have you met certain women who—

I haven't slept with anyone except my wife.

What about before marriage?

My wife got me as a virgin.

I see.

When did you get private living space?

In 1989.

How did that happen? That's very interesting.

I was getting serious about resolving the apartment issue in 1989. I was working at *Sobesednik* then (it was still an utterly respectable publication). And so one day I get this topic: the Youth Housing Cooperative (MZhK). One was holding a meeting on the ship that goes out to the Solovki Islands. And so they convinced me to sign on with them. No one was joining! How could that be, when they were giving apartments away? No one believed that anything like that existed. The only people who joined were people who had nowhere to retreat, for whom such a high level of risk seemed acceptable. This was the deal: Businesses had a lot of money, a waiting list of people who needed housing, and designated allotments of free land—so why not build houses? Because the money was not cash, and there wasn't any way to turn it into cash; there were no construction materials; and there weren't enough builders. And so, with the queue-holders' permission, their pay was withheld, and they were herded to the remote outskirts of Moscow, where they dug around in the mud, made bricks that were either used in the construction work or exchanged for concrete... Plus, the builders were paid in part with apartments, a bit like today's options. In short, this was the plan I signed up for. I worked on construction on all my days off—during my vacation, too—and I also wrote news segments about them and was involved with their cable TV.

Svinarenko's Commentary:

I went on MZhK business to Sverdlovsk, the capital of this movement, many times. They had built an entire micro-neighborhood. Sort of like a mini-republic. They did everything they wanted there; what's more, they did it legally. Because there were not only proletarians living there, but also lawyers and cops, and everyone else. For instance, they created cable television and showed all kinds of pornographic movies. So some regional Party Committee members come to close down the TV studio, and one of the residents meets them and says, "I'm the chairman of the Oblast repertory commission, and you're coming here to lecture me?! Get out of here!" They conducted whatever experiments they wanted in that school. As soon as the district is dissatisfied about something, a bureaucrat from the oblast department, who lives in the MzhK, settles the issue. Or a meeting is called in defense of Yeltsin, who was then already beginning to lash out in reaction. "Where are the police looking?" Everything's fine with the police. Lots of cops lived there too, and they came out in their uniforms, politely observing what was developing—they were already brainwashed; they had lived in the enemy's den. Incidentally, I remember that, in the press, too, they wrote about the "Petition by the Sverdlovsk Municipal 'Komsomol' MZhK to the Politburo of the CPSU" with a series of democratic demands, with criticism from Yegor Ligachev and support from Yeltsin. Well, who would have guessed…!

All of this was wildly interesting, and I wrote a lot about it. It seemed then that real democracy was precisely like this, like it was in the Sverdlovsk MZhK, and that soon—when our people won—a reasonable and beautiful life would be organized according to this model across all of Russia (that is, pardon me, at that time, across all of the USSR). Now then, where did this *naïveté* come from? Eh?

By the way, several serious people went through combat training in the MZhK. Yeltsin's second in command, Gennady Burbulis, began his political activity there—he was attracted to this republic via meetings and live broadcasts on cable TV. I have a typewritten business card with official info somewhere that reads, "Burbulis Gennady Eduardovich, instructor, Department of Scientific Communism." Later, when he decided to leave the oblast level for the national one, he would sometimes come to my place in Moscow for advice. I would talk to him about the disposition of the nation's political forces in my communal kitchen, while we drank port and snacked on sprats.

Galya Karelova was in charge of sociology at the MzhK; as we know, she was the Vice Premier of Russia a few years ago.

Zhenya Korolyov was the head guy. Maybe he was the one who thought the whole thing up. Tall, lanky—the smartest one—with deep-set eyes and a thick beard, he would sometimes abruptly stop the conversation, say, "I'm downloading a file," and then would freeze for a few minutes. He used to be a "closed"—a secret—physicist, but then he decided to build a new life. I haven't seen Zhenya in a long time; he left with a group of his closest associates for permanent residence in—you'll never guess what country—India. I'd be interested to know how their lives in the commune are unfolding.

* * *

In 1988, Alik, I went to Poland with my wife in order to marry off my brother. I remember the queues, the character references, and the visas...

What, you needed a visa for Poland?

You've forgotten everything! You needed an exit visa. To leave the USSR. In general, all kinds of documents were necessary. I had to go before some sort of Party committee because I wasn't a Party member. I also exchanged rubles for *zloty* on the Volgograd Prospect. I stood in line all day for tickets on the Taganka, Bolshye Kamenshchiki Street. How grown-up everything was... And in Poland I saw a new situation; ours hadn't gotten there yet. When the average wage was barely enough to live on for a week, if you lived like a pauper. How was it possible? How did people live? It was incomprehensible! But the country lived, life went on... We saw the same thing later in Russia.

What's your opinion of Jaruzelski? I, for example, saw him very positively. He imposed martial law based on the principle, "If I don't do it, the Reds will..." And then he kept the country more or less in hand. It could have broken apart... Did you see him as a positive figure?

Then, no. But I do remember that time. All those Polish affairs had a powerful effect on me. I even learned the Polish language! Well, not totally fluently, but at the level of reading newspapers and chatting about this and that.

About great Polish pride?

I learned it without knowing that I would go there, that I would even acquire some relations there.

Tell me, do Poles regard *khokhlols* the way they do Russians, or differently?

Over there, I thought, at least I'll drink some beer in peace in Warsaw... But I had to run around for it, like in Moscow. And here's another thing that surprised me: the police had truncheons. This grated on me. And it reminded me of a caricature about Rhodesia in *Pravda*. Well, right, were they really going to beat people with those clubs?

And now...

Well... I thought, "This can't happen in our country." I had a similar shock later in Israel. I was surprised: Why weren't there any police anywhere on the streets? They're over there, I was told, they're all over the place! Where? Right there, the ones in armored personnel carriers, in bulletproof vests and helmets, with machine guns. But they're the army! No, they said, they're not the army, they're the regular police... Such is the evolution of freedom: The Soviet cop had no weapon, wore a white shirt; then came the Polish cop with a club; then the Israeli with a machine gun and helmet—and then later we'd already merged into the world process and stopped being surprised by anything.

And when I was in Chile in 1991, Igor, I was also unpleasantly surprised by police with submachine guns. How, what for?

I envy you that you went to Chile then and met with Pinochet...

It was right when Pinochet lost the election...

It was the same bullshit with Latvia. I was in Riga not long ago, drank some Balzam from the bottle on a park bench and went to the museum of the occupation (1940–1991). And organized a discussion there with Latvians: "We gave you everything and let you go free, and now you're being obstreperous. 'You don't say hi, you don't say thank you—you say fuck-all'." And, so they say, you exiled us! I objected, saying that the Latvians started it first, that it was the Latvian riflemen who brought the Bolsheviks into power, and then these same Bolsheviks started exiling various Baltic peoples... It's stupid to take offense.

You see, it was then—in 1988—that it all began, all those national fronts in the Baltic region. A former girlfriend, a Latvian, would visit me then with her husband and bring all these subversive materials. They published a pretty good newspaper, *Atmoda*. And at that time it really did seem to be "for our freedom and yours." Do you remember that idiotic slogan? That's how we screwed up everything and gave it away to the Balts.

Igor, Igor. We didn't screw anything up! So what did we screw up?

There's that saying, "What sort of things has a Latvian got? A pair of pliers and a cock."

Yes, It was always the most good-for-nothing and senseless nation.

That's right. And we gave them everything that we built. Even a radar station.

Why the fuck did we need that station?!

Oh, I like that. You never know… And, besides, it can be, as you love to say, exchanged for something.

And they'll say, "We've already been in your camps, in the Stalin camps, and that's why you should give everything back or build us something in compensation." And we say to them, "Here's the station, take it!" And they took it. Who fucked whom over, really? And I also refer you to the fact that Latvia never had independent statehood.

As we know: It was under you, the Germans.

Yes, until the time of Peter I. And until Anna Ioannovna, the Duchess of Kurland. First the Teutonic Order was there, and Riga was its capital. Then it fell apart, and slowly turned into various East German principalities that were, in any event, gravitating to Prussia. And then Peter came and conquered all this. At first they were satellites, and then they were included in the structure of the Russian empire.

So the Russians had the Mordovians just like the Germans had the Latvians?

Yes, absolutely correct. The Latvians lived mainly in villages; they were peasants and worked for the Germans. And in 1918 the Germans took this territory in accordance with the Brest-Litovsk treaty (which Trotsky signed). Then in 1918 the First World War ended. The Germans were expelled. But no one was going to give the territory to Soviet Russia! And so on the lands freed from German occupation—absent claims from Russia—the independent Baltic states arose. And as a result their entire statehood lasted twenty years: from 1918 to 1939. That's all!

Then during Soviet times, in order to keep the Balts in check, they created a kind of quasi-Europe there. Leniencies were extended; they were allowed to have farms, and so on. We invested a hell of a lot there, even though they worked badly and drank a lot, those Latvians. And now we've thrown off this burden— so let the European Union feed them now.

Now the Americans wouldn't have let them go with land, they would send them to a reservation like the Indians, who are forced to exploit their folklore and crafts for profit.

I don't have any desire to drive anyone into a reservation. So let them try to feed themselves! Now we've cut off their oxygen: Semyon Vainshtok, the head of Transneft, stopped pumping oil through Ventspils, and they've already begun to squeal. Things are lousy for them now. And their European brothers aren't in a big hurry to try and help them.

Yes, things there are somehow impoverished.

Business is totally on the level of cooperatives. No one tries to invest anywhere.

So, they have enough money to buy foreign cars —and there are plenty of them in the streets—but that's it!

The cars of their entrepreneurs? Well, yes. It's not hard to earn enough for a car. They're not capable of any more than that.

So you're glad that they broke away?

Yes, I am. Yes!

It pains me somewhat—from habit.

I can't understand, Igor, where is this coming from in you?

I don't understand it myself. Maybe because I've become to some degree Russified? And I've acquired certain Great Russian airs. Now, for instance, I feel sorry about the empire... Even though it was never native to the khokhols.

And I don't have any use for them, the ones who broke away. I always regarded the parasites with suspicion. I never believed they were sincere when they said how much they loved me. But when the parasites are laying blame on me, too, I don't want to have anything to do with them at all. I don't understand at all why I'm paying them. I consider the Balts to be this type of parasite. If you're so tough, then fuck off.

The late Tsvetkov, the governor of Kolyma, told me: "We'll make money, we have our own gold and stuff like that..."

And so now he's a dead man. Way back in 1988 it was first announced that the budgetary deficit was seven percent. Wow! Really! And you're talking about Gaidar and inflation!

What does that mean, that it was seven percent?

It means that inflation was rising! It had started rising earlier, but it wasn't officially admitted. Since prices were regulated, and no one dared to cut them loose, and there weren't any goods... Well, that's how it all got started. We always had shortages, but now it was of the most essential things. Understand? It's very simple. If prices are regulated, and money starts being printed, goods disappear.

Well, Alik, this we know, we learned dialectics not by reading Hegel, but by experiencing it on our own skins.

And Gorbachev raised wages.

Strange, and he was supposedly an economist... And it was back in 1988 that your comrade Chubais got involved in politics. Newspapers started writing about him...

That wasn't him. It was his brother, Igor Chubais, and not Anatoly Chubais.

Really? Hmm. And what did the real Chubais do?

He and I conducted seminars in Petersburg. Yegor Gaidar and Peter Aven joined us. This began right in 1988...

So you didn't go follow the cooperative path, Alik? You started solving the problem comprehensively.

Yes. We met at the Youth Palace.

And were there are a lot of these smart guys?

Well, about twenty people—financial experts, sociologists... Simon Kordonsky, who now works in the president's administration. Andrei Illarionov.

The very same?

Yes. Mishka Dmitriyev, who now works with German Gref, the economics minister Yegor Gaidar.

And who was in charge?

Chubais and Gaidar. One from the Petersburg group, the other from the Moscow one.

And was your interest purely scientific? Or in creating a practical plan for the perestroika of the world?

It was scientific. And applied.

Did you believe that you'd come into power?

We started thinking about it then. We were beginning to understand that everything was moving in that direction. But we weren't even fighting them. At that point, we weren't fighting them. We started to fight when the elections started. But in 1988 no one was talking about the elections yet.

But you're sure that this was conscious on your part? Maybe you were just going to the rec center to drink vodka and blab about this and that while drunk, and now you're saying that it was like the Munich beer halls, Alik?

Yes, we did drink, but you think that I would have joked like this then, even once? Joked that we'd be sitting in the Kremlin? No, it was all serious. We had no plan for coming to power, but we did discuss what to do next. Seriously. Now, with hindsight, I understand that we were reasoning very naively. We blindly believed in the invisible hand of the market—that it would make everything fall into place.

I understand this very well, Alik. In those years I was seen in the company of Larissa Piyasheva—God rest her soul, she died recently of cancer.

Svinarenko's Commentary:

In her time, Larissa openly supported Sergei Mavrodi. She backed his pyramid scheme with the authority of her perestroika activism. She appeared on TV and demanded that people leave him alone, and when he was to be imprisoned, she issued angry rebukes. I asked her back then, "How is it that you... you are a scholar, an economist, and suddenly you rush to defend the pyramid scheme that bankrupted so many ignorant people?"

At that point, Larissa answered my unscholarly questions evasively, saying that there was a lot that was interesting in Mavrodi's activities. And sure enough, there were many economists who made a bundle on Mavrodi; they had calculated all his moves and traded in their shares just in time. Valentin Tsvetkov, the late governor of Magadan and Kolyma, told me that he didn't do too badly on it.

I remember it as if it were yesterday: Right before the default in 1998, your comrade Illarionov published texts in various mass media that there was going to be an avalanche from the Mavrodi scheme, because the GKOs—the short-term bonds issued by the government—were at the very apex of the pyramid. I read his pieces and demanded that the heads of *Kommersant* get to the bottom of this. I couldn't write about it myself, because I'm no expert in economics; one of the specialists had to work on it. It seemed to me that this was a good subject and that we needed to figure it out—either Illarionov was talking turkey or he was yelling about nothing. But in the end, they wrote about his prophecies only after the fact.

* * *

Piyasheva talked a lot about the "invisible hand" then, Alik. I couldn't at all understand what kind of mechanism it was. But she kept on and on about this hand, which would immediately bring order everywhere, and that everyone would begin living a happy and rich life. I asked Piyasheva then, how could happiness just suddenly appear—after all, don't needs and troubles always intensify at the start of any new capitalist period? She explained that problems occurred if you didn't start out building the system correctly, but that if you did it right, there wouldn't be any problems. She assured everyone that the Russian economists—you!— would do everything right. And Borya Pinsker—also a fashionable economist at that time—and her husband confirmed this. And Selyunin, and Shmelyov... They were already on a collision course with Marx and Lenin. Contemporary writing on economics so preoccupied minds then in a way that no Boris Akunin ever could. And also, if you remember, it was in 1988 that limits on newspaper and magazine subscriptions were cancelled for first time. People raced headlong to subscribe to everything... But there wasn't enough paper! So the limits had to be reinstated. And then massive numbers of letters came to the Central Committee of the CPSU from workers (what abuse! It was both horrible and comical...). And then they cancelled the limit, because it was, oh, an offensive against glasnost or something. They bought paper from the Finns and solved the problem. If people had known how this would end, with your shock therapy... They would have told you scholarly economists to fuck off right away.

And the law on cooperatives... And it truly became clear. We had failed to create the new Soviet man.

Not man, but people! Comrade Stalin, creator of the national theory, had introduced the idea of gradations in the community of peoples.

That I don't quite get... I probably studied it, but I don't remember a fucking thing!

Here's how it went. The human herd, then the family commune, then the state, then nationality and nation. And Brezhnev introduced a very important supplement to Marxist national theory: that besides the nation, a new community of peoples appeared, the Soviet people. But it didn't appear! So comrade Stalin's national theory turned out to be right. The pinnacle of the community of peoples is the nation. We failed to create a super-nation called the "Soviet people." We were incompatible.

And there was no fraternal union.

Now if the peoples had said, "We won't divide up, we're united," then, of course, the Soviet Union would have survived. But the peoples began to slaughter one another, and so it was simply indecent to talk about a Soviet Union. Why keep it at bayonet's point? That's just colonialism.

What about America, you'll say? Well it's a purely propagandistic hoax. There are no such people. They all live separately in different neighborhoods. And they don't have contact with one another.

Yes... Maybe, in order for the empire to last, we should have said that there are Russians, and the rest are second rate?

Well, that wasn't even the case during the Tsarist Empire. Russians didn't consider themselves bluebloods. Hell, some fucking blue blood, when Russians were obligated to serve in the army, and the Finns weren't.

The same situation existed in South Africa; do you know about this?

No.

I studied the issue on location. Nelson Mandela had just come to power, and they started recruiting the blacks into the army. To serve in the army at that time meant fighting: You know, there was Angola and then Mozambique. Putting your head in the line of fire in the jungles. Several of my comrades served as translators there and instructors under the Cubans, who fought with our side. How could the Boers take a black man there? So that he could shoot them in the back? A white officer told me then, "Of course it's difficult. I understand that these guys joined the army after the amnesty; they spent their entire lives fighting in the jungles against us. Among them were many former partisans and other terrorists... Many blacks were my enemies; they could have killed me. And now these young black soldiers are my friends. I have to accept this or leave the army. Besides, as a Christian, I understand that a black man is just as much a person as I am..."

Now in our country the Finns didn't have to serve in the army. Alexander I gave them these freedoms—not to pay taxes, not to serve in the army. For instance, the Tatars did have to serve in the Russian army. The Latvians and the Estonians didn't either. Whereas the Caucasian peoples could serve as volunteers. A strange way to staff an army…

And now I'm going to share a passage which is absolutely politically incorrect; I will give you a thought neither the Russians nor the Germans have been able to arrive at—only the Balts, and pardon me, the *khokhols* have. Even though I have become partially Russified, partially a cosmopolite, without ceasing to be a *khokhol* (this, I suppose, is impossible). And so we, the *khokhols* (and Balts), are tougher than the Russians and tougher than the Germans. Do I have to explain this to you?

Go on.

So listen. In 1945 the anti-Communist Russians stopped fighting against the Soviet Union, the entire armed battle against the regime ended—Vlasov and whatever else was left. And the Germans also stopped in 1945. Even the Germans! We had no hotbeds of armed conflict left. Whereas Bendera's forest brothers were still fighting, up to the second half of the 1950s. Even though there were no fewer weapons or forests in Russia and Germany than in Ukraine. But Russians and Germans—I emphasize, two great nations—gave up. Everyone in Russia and Germany was for Stalin, but not all of our people were. Well, what do you think, isn't this a lovely riff?

Do you mean to ask, why wasn't there a Nazi underground left after 1945?

No, I want to ask—is this a powerful subject?

It's a good one.

Svinarenko's Commentary:

There was a certain logic in the position of the Ukrainians who fought against the Red Army. I became acquainted with it in conversations with the veterans of the SS who went into hiding in the States after the war. Here's one of the cases: A guy from Western Ukraine joined the war in 1941 as a volunteer. He didn't fight on the side of the front you'd expect, but on the side that was occupied by the Germans. He joined the German army, the Ukrainian SS division "Galichina." And after the war, he didn't return home to his wife, for obvious reasons. He left for America, and started a life there. They lost each other in that life. And after 1991 his wife was found! She was alive and free! In the sense of not being married. The veteran took his old lady to America. She got depressed there and took him home to Ukraine. Now they are getting on, living in their homeland on an American pension, which is fabulous wealth over there. They also help their relatives who fought on the Soviet side of the front.

I imagine how all this can happen.

This returnee meets some Red Army veterans. They call him a traitor. He expresses sincere surprise, "Who me? You're confusing me with someone else. I spilled blood under a yellow and blue banner, I had a trident on my uniform— notice, this is not my homeland's State symbol. I fought for Ukraine's independence with a weapon in my hands; I was liberating it from Communists and Russkies. And now my homeland is free. Because I was fighting for a just cause, my old age is provided for, and I'm a man of means. And so what were you fighting for? Where are the banner, the army, and the ideals that you were ready to die for? Where are those Communists to whom you sold yourself and under whose wrath the enslaved Fatherland moaned? So you're hurt that your pension is a pittance and that it's not paid on time? Strange… I thought that you were rejoicing at not being hanged as war criminals, and that you weren't even sent to the camps… Well then, fine, I'll buy you a drink, because of your poverty… What, is Germany so bad? Really? It is respected in the world community. Fascists are bad? Well, they were done away with in 1945 and indicted in Nuremberg. And what about your Communists?"

Our poor veterans probably can come up with something in response… Would you like to end up in their shoes?

8.

1989

The Eighth Bottle

The Congress of People's Deputies: the most popular show on the air, the first successful reality TV in Russia. Widespread miners' strikes. Yeltsin gets drunk in the U.S., goes to Congress and to a rendezvous in the country, but falls off a bridge on the way. The public discusses the Molotov-Ribbentrop Pact. Kokh teaches at an institute and loves Mayor Sobchak. Svinarenko does military service and also travels abroad, has a daughter, and gets an apartment.

Well, let's refresh our memory of the politics. What was going on in 1989? Come on, Alik!

For me, 1989 is the Congress of People's Deputies, when all the small cheap radios were bought up, for 30 rubles each. People walked down the streets with the radios pressed to their ears.

TV had the Congress on day and night. Happiness was almost upon us. It was coming, it was coming…and then, finally, there was the Congress. People did not work or sleep or eat; they just watched and listened to the Congress. The kingdom of justice was here.

Three a.m., four… They were still going at it on TV. The Congress was a terrific show. That was the first reality TV we had.

Except instead of a bunch of young sluts, they cast a bunch of old assholes!

Now, come on—they were fine people.

The politics truly was interesting then: Who had whom by the balls? Was it politics or screwing? Real screwing took a rest. They already had video stores filled with porn, but the politics was much more exciting.

Yes, the people bought up every last radio, Igor. Remember, Sakharov was the first to speak; he asked for the floor.

Really, he was first? I don't remember.

He was! He came out to the tribune and asked for the floor.

What did he say?

The usual humanitarian crap. He wouldn't leave till they let him speak. Gorbachev had to give him the floor. And Sakharov gave his speech.

And Gorby kept interrupting?

Yes. "Andrei Dmitrievich, Andrei Dmitrievich!" And then it turned out that they didn't have any vote-counting machines: They didn't know the votes wouldn't be unanimous! Calculators were circulated around the congress hall. It was only a few months later that they set up those screens that showed the results of the voting.

And people pressed their own button and other people's, too—just can't have honest trade in Russia. It's always some crap. It's either unanimous, or it's one guy voting for five... If you don't cheat, you don't succeed.

Remember how the elections to the Congress were held? By curia! And not equal ones, either—each organization had a different number of votes. From the Communist Party to the Komsomol, to the Academy of Sciences, the society of beekeepers... People forget now.

Right! And then somebody demanded doing away with Article 6, about the leading role of the Communist Party. They said, What the fuck?

Didn't they repeal it in 1989?

No, later... Yeltsin was gaining strength then. He had apologized to the Party and was working at the state construction planning agency Gosstroi then.

It was at the 19th Party Conference. In 1988. "I am asking for political rehabilitation"—that's what Yeltsin said.

He was a candidate from Gosstroi in 1989. Everyone felt sorry for him—the one decent man at the top and they were all over him, sticking him where the sun don't shine.

Sobchak made an enormous impression on me then, Igor.

Did you meet him then?

No, later, in 1991.

Everybody was always carrying on about him: Sobchak, Sobchak. What about him, really? Good-looking, fashionable—that I can understand. But what was his contribution and innovation?

He was a fucking great speaker.

Yes, he had a marvelous voice.

And he wore a white and beige plaid jacket. He wore that jacket on purpose, to stand out.

Did he admit that to you?

No, but that's what I think.

I bet his wife, Ludmila Narusova, told him to do it.

Probably.

She is a model of unconditional wifely love. Remember when he was hiding out in Paris, and she said, "What are you people doing? The man isn't young, he's in poor health, and he'll ruin his health completely living abroad, going to all those brothels." Such understanding—let him fuck around, as long as it's good for him.

As long as he doesn't smoke.

So, we have the jacket and the voice. But he didn't have any fundamentally new political ideas to offer.

The usual democratic ideals. They all spoke pretty much the same, but Sobchak had the best delivery. He had panache; he was an artist!

It was his artistic language that you appreciated, Alik. And then, he did have legal training. He was good at that rhetoric stuff.

Kokh's Commentary:

The Three Sobchaks

When I recall my relations with Anatoly Alexandrovich Sobchak, I cannot rid myself of the feeling that I had dealt with three different people. Each incarnation was so different from the previous, it required a great effort to remember that you were dealing with the same man.

The First Sobchak

I first heard about Sobchak from some friends at the institute. Then I saw him. On television. It was during the elections of delegates to the Congress of People's Deputies, and everyone was in the thrall of election fever. And why not—these were the first relatively free elections in our lives. It was like we were suddenly grownups. There were televised debates in Leningrad. Sobchak was running in the Vasilyevsky Ostrov district. He was stunning. I thought he looked just the way a real politician should. A wonderful orator. Handsome, impressive. Bold. Smart. Educated. An aristocratic spirit. Not like those plebeians from the Kremlin. And such a democrat.

We adored him. There was nobody like him. There was a trinity of St. Petersburg democrats, and half of the city was prepared to go through fire and water for them—Sobchak, Alexander Shchelkanov, and Yuri Boldyrev. And Sobchak was the best, without a doubt—he was one of a kind.

When the City Council was elected, they had a whole to-do about who would be chairman. Various groups of democrats were fighting among themselves over which group would have the chairmanship. The argued until they were hoarse. Everybody got sick of them. I think that's the real source of hatred for the democrats in Russia: Those endless internal fights, when all the shit would float to the surface, when they would argue about nothing, competing on the level of eloquence alone, showing off—and destroying the remnants of public trust in the process.

And then someone, I don't remember who, came up with an idea: Let's call in Sobchak. There was a consensus among all the deputies. It was like the Slavs calling Rurik in to rule. But there was a problem, he wasn't a deputy of the City Council. OK, no problem, we have a free district. They called elections and elected dear Anatoly Alexandrovich. No sooner said than done. The people were all for Sobchak. It was practically unanimous. Hurrah!

I was happy too. I mean really happy. I'm not exaggerating. God, I loved that man. I wanted so much to help him. Work day and night, to be useful. So that he would call me in and praise me. I was chairman of the executive committee—today it would be mayor—in Sestroretsk.

This was my vision: I'm working, and there's a call for me. "Alfred Reingoldovich? Anatoly Alexandrovich would like you to drop by. Tomorrow. Is 2 o'clock convenient? Fine, we'll be expecting you."

I show up the next day. I come in. Some tea? Thank you. One lump. Thanks. To what do I owe the honor? I've been watching you for a long time and I wanted to tell you you're doing a good job. Good fellow. If you need anything, just let me know, I'm always ready to help.

There. That would have been enough. Would you like my life, too? Gladly. Anyone who doesn't understand what I was like then doesn't understand those times. I know, and I understand. I loved him. Now I think back on it…With humor? No. With irony? Perhaps. With sadness? Yes. Radiant sadness? Yes.

The Second Sobchak

Sobchak was an awful mayor. Two of his aides, back when he was chairman of the City Council, had made very strong impressions on him. One was the KGB man Putin, now president of the Russian Federation, and the other was former convict Shutov, now doing time in Kresty Prison. Not a bad entourage for a democrat of the first wave, eh?

I have to give Sobchak credit—he got rid of Shutov quickly, and Putin turned out to be a loyal person and always behaved decently toward him.

His ideas of management came from the industrial films of the Brezhnev era. You know, Kirill Lavrov says in his theatrically trained voice, I will complain to the Central Committee! I'm not getting hydrocartizon in the third sector! Three men have been burned already! People are falling down with exhaustion! And so on. (I just made up the word hydrocartizon, I don't know what it is. The actors in those films had to say difficult words without knowing what they meant.)

I'm very subjective, of course. So, he called me in. Talked to me with a fatherly squint. He said: Go and work in peace. The next day, he fired me. Now why didn't he just say: I don't want to work with you? It's not like I came from the garbage dump; I can find other work. I could have handled the truth. But no, he has to say, Go and work in peace. What for? Why did he lie? Pfui. He fired Chubais from being his first deputy. Right away. What didn't he like about Chubais? An energetic, businesslike, hard-working man? He could have functioned, with Chubais as his brick wall. He would cut ribbons and meet with nobility. Chubais would never have betrayed him, the way Vladimir Yakovlev did, when he ran against him.

Basically, Sobchak's attraction toward manufacturers was pathological. He made Georgy Khizha his first deputy. Khizha, former director of Svetlana, was leader of the factory directors corps in Leningrad. They somehow persuaded

Sobchak that Khizha was in control of the situation in the city. That was not so. He controlled nothing. But he was full of braggadocio and bullshit. Khizha quickly left for work in Moscow, and Alexei Bolshakov was appointed in his place. This is the same Bolshakov who subsequently spent $300,000,000 from the budget on a super highway between St. Petersburg and Moscow, and then didn't build the road. Not a single kilometer of it. The super highway was also Sobchak's idea, of course.

Then came Yakovlev. You know the rest.

Nevertheless, in the fall of 1991, I was back in the mayor's office. On the committee for managing city property. As deputy chairman of the committee. Mishka Manevich and I were the fruit of the compromise between Sobchak and Chubais, who at that time was already Chairman of the State Property Committee and was beginning privatization. Sobchak appointed Sergei Belyayev, who belonged to Khizha, as chairman, and then Chubais insisted on two of his own deputy chairmen.

I can't say that Sobchak was a great help to privatization. He actually hindered it. All I heard at the meetings was: "I'll put that Kokh in his place! What is this—privatizing grocery store No. 76! What next? And what if it decides to become a hardware store?" This was the level of his ideas on market economics.

But when he learned that St. Petersburg had one of the highest rates of privatization in the county, he liked to brag about it in his speeches abroad.

I think there are two things that can be counted among his real achievements. First, he brought back the name St. Petersburg, changing it back from Leningrad, for which I am very grateful. And second, he opened the first fully foreign bank in Russia, Credit Lyonnais. I still remember what a hassle it was getting a building for that bank.

There was so much sincerity, unprofessionalism, naiveté, and faith in all his work. He tried honestly to make things better for everyone. He was so not cynical, so generous: And he loved St. Petersburg so much it's a sin to berate him.

Do I feel hurt? Probably. Do I judge him? No. God is his judge. Do I feel sorry for him? Yes. To the point of tears. And I feel sorry for Mishka Manevich. May they rest in peace.

The Third Sobchak

In the spring of 1999, Vladimir Zhechkov and I were in Paris. We had to stick around for two weeks. When we got sick of drinking together, we started to look for interesting companions. I remembered that Sobchak was in Paris, an émigré. We got his phone number through his publishers, and I called him. I thought he sounded pleased to hear from me.

We met. Literally, in just a few minutes, he barraged me with his critique of the development of the democratic process in Russia. It was a pummeling—he was full of pent-up passion. He wanted to be back at the podium, in Russia, in the pampas, fighting the good fight. He wanted to expose corruption. He was obviously tired of Paris.

There was so much sincerity and passion there. His pose at the tribune was always very natural, almost vulnerable. His wrath at the lunch table in a Parisian suburb seemed inappropriate—napkin tucked in, brandishing a fork. I suggested that instead of cursing us out, he tell us something interesting. He was crestfallen. Then he thought a bit and said that he had been at the Paris premiere of Alexei Guerman's film *Khrustalev, The Car!* He became engrossed in his story. We listened attentively. The atmosphere became amiable. We drank wine. Sobchak's mood improved; you could see he was enjoying himself. Here we were, two rich dopes, mouths agape, listening to the old professor.

Then we sang karaoke. The professor scored our performances but didn't sing himself. He was flushed and very sweet, though. After midnight I drove him back to the city. We parted warmly. He was a deadly weary middle-aged St. Petersburg professor. That's what he had been the whole time I had known him. No more than that—but no less, either.

I ran into him once at the White Sun of the Desert restaurant in Moscow. Then he died.

May he rest in peace.

* * *

The other popular figures of those years were Yuri Afanasyev, Yuri Karyakin, Gavril Popov, Nikolai Shmelev, Roy Medvedev. Remember, Alik, how they were the coolest kids in school then?

Remember when they wrote that Yeltsin had gone to see a woman, got drunk, and fell off the bridge? Remember how upset everyone was at those KGB bastards, who made up the story about our Boris Nikolayevich? Saying all kinds of silly things about him. Like when he gave a speech drunk in New York? He was as drunk as a skunk in America, and *La Repubblica* wrote about it— swilling booze from toothbrush mugs...

What of it? I've drunk out of them, too, big deal. Do you know who reprinted that article? *Pravda*, **official organ of the Party Central Committee. And immediately—to show us what he was like.**

There was an explosion of outrage from the masses—how dare they attack our Yeltsin! If only we had known it was the truth. But we didn't believe a single word of it!

We didn't. We thought it was a provocation.

Then they showed his speech on TV, where he was falling-down drunk in a speech at a university. "Now do you believe it?" No way, we said. You've just distorted his voice on the recording.

That's love. That's when they tell a guy his girlfriend is a whore working on Tverskaya Street, and he doesn't believe it. She just went out for cigarettes.

Yeah. And some black-assed guys were pestering her. With a knife. So she had no choice, she had to give in to them.

And the KGB forced her into fishnet stockings and a standard-issue miniskirt. And put on the whore makeup.

Yes.

Yeltsin was great advertising for bourbon—the Jack Daniels people should be eternally grateful to him. Gorby did an actual ad later—not for booze, but for food. Pizza. Not as colorful, but more sensible—he got a lot of money for it. Yeltsin promoted Jack Daniels out of pure love for the art of boozing. And we loved him so much then. It was a radiant feeling.

Svinarenko's Commentary:

Strange, but the Russian Internet doesn't have the full text of the *Pravda* article. Just excerpts. But I saved the clipping. It's a yellowed, crumpled piece of paper. There's so much energy accumulated in it. *Pravda* quoted an Italian newspaper on the trip:

La Repubblica on B. N. Yeltsin.

In America, perestroika smells of whiskey and greenbacks and is lit up by spotlights at night. Boris Yeltsin, Moscow's popular hero—Gorbachev's Cassandra—is flying through America like a whirlwind. ... Wherever he goes he leaves behind a trail of wild expenditures, interviews, and forecasts of catastrophe—and the scent of the famous Kentucky whiskey with the black label, Jack Daniels. He drank a half-liter in one night in his hotel room in Baltimore. The stunned professor who came in the morning to take him to the lecture hall was given a sloppy, drunken kiss and half-empty bottle of whiskey.

"Let's drink to freedom," Yeltsin proposed, at 6:30 in the morning, waving the toothbrush glass from the hotel bathroom, which was full of whiskey. Yeltsin brought the smell of sweat and the physical funk of the "homeland" to the halls of American power. He has a phenomenal ability to drink and to spend money. "I had no idea how many glasses glasnost can hold," punned an ABC television producer who tried in vain to sober up Yeltsin and clean him up for an evening interview. Yeltsin had to postpone the interview.

In the five days and five nights he spent in the United States of America, he slept an average of two hours a night and emptied two bottles of vodka, four bottles of whiskey, and innumerable cocktails at receptions.

…For America, Yeltsin is a marvelous new toy, a doll with a typically Russian face that says what no Russian had dared to say before… The populist Yeltsin entered American supermarkets with the same energy with which he entered Soviet history in the 1980s. Now he has everything he ever dreamed of: whiskey, dollars, toys, and videocassettes of *Rambo*."

Years later, *Pravda* staff said that Gorbachev had chewed out then editor-in-chief Afanasyev, first by phone and then at the Plenum. Afanasyev insisted that he had reprinted the piece only to liven up a dull edition. However, he also said that in the corridors of that same Plenum, Gorbachev secretly shook his hand and praised him.

In secret, but not in vain! Eyewitnesses recalled how a crowd of demonstrators gathered at the front door of the *Pravda* building. The phones were ringing off the hook: "How much were you paid to print that vile article?" "Bastards! No one but Yeltsin can save the country from the Mafia!" People bought up copies of *Pravda* on Pushkin Square and burned them. In Zelenograd they held a rally with posters reading, "Make the provocateurs pay!" The newspapers were flooded with letters: "We won't let you besmirch Boris Yeltsin!" The pilot Okulov came to Yeltsin's defense, claiming that his father-in-law could not get that drunk. Yeltsin appeared on TV in Leningrad and made a statement calling the editor of *Pravda* "a base person who will execute any order." He insisted that "today I received an official letter from the U.S. government containing a denial." The democratic leader Yuri Afanasyev (no relation to the *Pravda* editor) made a pronouncement that "the Communist Party must shut down the newspaper *Pravda*, which misinforms the Soviet public." In the hallways of the newspaper *Komsomolskaya Pravda*, people tried to get Pavel Voshchanov, their reporter who had traveled to the U.S. with Yeltsin, to tell them the truth. "Off the record, is what *Repubblica* wrote true?" But even in the circle of close friends, Voshchanov held firm: "Enemy propaganda." he said.

There was nothing that could be done about it.

* * *

Would you have given your life for Yeltsin then, Alik? Remember, there was this fellow who yielded his spot to him? In the elections? From Tomsk or Omsk or somewhere like that.

Yes, Kazannik! They later made him prosecutor.

And then, when he returned to Tomsk or Omsk, he gave an interview where he said "If I had only known who I was dealing with." Well, Alik, would you have given your life for him?

No, I couldn't. I don't want to give up my life for anyone at all. It wasn't given to me by me, and it's not for me to give it away for someone. God will take it when it's time.

Ah, run into the bushes. I think that Boris Yeltsin was a very successful character.

I have positive feelings for him.

Well, he was appropriate for the country and its people. He could really put it away. You know the old joke: If you drink in the morning, you're free all day. He babbled on about stuff. He was a bit weird, like we are. He got drunk and fell off a bridge; that just made us feel good that a man like us was running the country.

Jerk and president in one.

Think of the opposite: somebody all buttoned up—smart, watches his mouth, always sober... How could we possibly understand a man like that? Let him run Sweden. Am I right?

Hahahaha.

That's why he did so well. That slight stupidity—sorry....

Come on.

You said yourself that people didn't believe it. That's exactly it. I had a friend who was in Yeltsin's retinue at the time. I interrogated him about what happened in New York—was he drunk or not? He didn't give his boss up; he replied evasively.

Igor, that means he did get drunk!

Soon after, my friend left the retinue. At a time of all-consuming national love for Yeltsin. I started bugging him again. He was still evasive. He told me in the most general terms: "I hated the level of discussion, of all the conversations, the tone in which they would talk about politics at the table. ... Cynicism. ... I couldn't stand it, so I quit." I didn't believe him. I thought he had been fired. He didn't argue with me; he said I wouldn't understand or believe him.

You would now, right?

But that's now. Even now he says, "You see that if I had told you back in 1989 everything that you know now about Yeltsin, it would have been pointless? If I had told you about his entourage, his conversations, the money?" The man understood it all back then, but he also understood that the people wouldn't believe him. What was going on in our poor heads back then? It's horrible. And we thought we were smart. It took fifteen years for people to start understanding. ...

Valentin Rasputin, not an economist but a novelist, figured that once Russia cut off the spongers, it could live well and happily. You are a specialist; what do *you* think?

Well, let's take a look, Igor. Do the Belorussians live better than us? The *khokhols*, as we so tenderly call Ukrainians? Moldavians? Georgians?

No, worse.

The Azerbaijanis?

I don't know about them.

Worse. There turned out to be less oil then they had announced.

Who said that they had so much? Who let them down that way?

They did it themselves. Let's move on. Turkmenbashi, dictator of Turkmenistan?

He lives well.

He personally, sure. But you can't say that about his people. Moving along. Tajiks, Kirghiz...the same. Do the Balts live better than Russians or worse? Let's be frank. Better. But in great part that's due to Russian oil and gas transit. For which we pay. Thus, they continue sucking the blood of Russia. Which I really don't like. Which is why I started building a port near St. Petersburg. I sold it later, but to the right people.

And that way you put the squeeze on the Balts.

We don't need to pressure them. But now instead of paying them the money that we used to pay them, we pay ourselves. If we set up transit through the St. Petersburg ports—which is, first of all, 500 km closer, which is a savings right there—we create jobs at home. And if we can't move the refinery, then we should buy it. So that we get the profit, not them.

And the pipeline that went along the Baltic states, is it dried up?

Basically, yes.

And now you can shout into it: "Hey, you! Hi! Laba diena! Good afternoon, how are you?"

But once Khodorkovsky closes the deal with the refinery, we can fill the pipeline again. Into our plant. We need to buy a terminal in Ventspilse, and things will really be pretty.

Svinarenko's Commentary:

Here are some accounts of the role played in World War II by the Latvians, who turned against the Russians and joined the Nazis.

> In July 1940 the fascist regime was replaced by a socialist revolution in Latvia. But in July 1941 Riga was occupied by Germany. A fascist regime was reinstated in Latvia, and it lasted until 13 October, 1944. The Latvian Waffen SS legion was formed, and more than 150,000 men, out of Latvia's population of two million, served in it.
>
> According to the Latvian nationalistic magazine *Daugavas Vanagi*, published in Toronto, between July 1944 and October 1953 the "national partisans" (as the Forest brethren are called today in Latvia) killed 2,208 people: representatives of the Soviet Party, workers and soldiers of the NKVD, MVD, and other Soviet agencies."
>
> During the war the Germans formed 41 Latvian, 26 Estonian, and 23 Lithuanian police battalions. They fought the Communist underground and the partisan movement in the Baltic states, using punitive actions on the territories of Belorussia and Russia, and performing the work of executioners—shooting Russians, Jews, Communists, and prisoners of war of the Soviet Army brought from Belorussia and Poland... All these executions, especially the mass hangings, are documented with film cameras.

Kokh's Commentary:

On yet another member of the family of civilized nations.

On the coast of the Baltic Sea, where the Western Dvina (Daugava) falls into it, there live a people called Latvians. They have entered the friendly family of European nations (unlike Russia), which means that they have been approved as a civilized nation by the strict European judges. I have always been captivated by the question of how one nation is considered civilized and another barbarian.

So, now the Latvians are considered civilized and are accepted in the European Union, and Russia is not.

Let us study this civilized nation more closely. Maybe then we will see our own ignorance in contrast to this beautiful and humanitarian culture, and we will be ashamed of the very thought that we might be worthy of membership in a united Europe.

Sometime in the mid-twelfth century, traders, soldiers, and missionaries started arriving from Germany. Gradually—they had to overcome resistance—the German Crusaders conquered the Livs, and in 1201 they founded Riga as the bishopric and the home base for further conquests. Riga was the capital of the Order of the German Knights. First it was the Order of the Brothers of the Sword and later, after merging with the Teutonic Order, the Teutonic-Livonian Order. The Latvian tribes resisted the German expansion, but the lack of unity between them led to the final conquest of Latvia in the late eighteenth century.

Until the end of the nineteenth century, the Baltic German elite reigned in Latvian society. The Baltic Germans maintained their privileged position in the seventeenth century, when the Baltic states were under Swedish and Polish rule, and in the eighteenth and nineteenth centuries, under Russia.

The best way to understand the cultural gap between Russians and Germans on the one hand and Latvians on the other is to look at when each culture produced a national translation of the Bible. In the Middle Ages, every nation had a strong religious bent, and the dissemination of literacy depended almost exclusively on the copying and study of the Bible.

The first translation into Old Slavonic was done by the Greek monks Cyril and Methodius (who also developed an alphabet based on the Greek) in the 860s, that is, in the ninth century. The first translations of the Bible into German were completed at approximately the same time, however because of limitations established by the Roman Catholic Church, the first official German translation did not appear until 1521, during the Reformation; it was Martin Luther's.

Thus, Russians and Germans had a written language and a national religious culture from the ninth century on, and by the 16th century, both also had the beginnings of a print culture and a contemporary translation of the Bible.

Now, your attention, please. Our civilized Latvians did not have a Bible in Latvian until 1694. And it was translated by a man named Ernst Gluck. A fine Latvian name, no? In order for this to happen, the Germans created a written language for the Latvians based on German grammar. The first textbook for the Latvian language was printed in Riga in Russian in 1868. Thus, it was the efforts of two nations—first Germans, and then Russians—that gave the highly cultured Latvians a written language. Only eight centuries later than everyone else. And they should still be grateful. The Latvians themselves did nothing for it. They were handed culture on a platter. The Latvians obtained a written language just 50 years before the Chukchi, who live near the Bering Strait, did! Comrade Stalin gave the Chukchi literacy in the early 1930s. So, the Chukchi should be brought into a United Europe! Urgently! After all, the Russians had occupied them, and now they are free, civilized, and so on and so forth.

In passing, I should tell you that the same cannot be said of the Lithuanians (who already had a great history by then) or the Estonians (who functioned smoothly inside the Finnish cultural tradition, with which it never lost its spiritual connection.)

Then came the revolution.

The Latvian rifle regiments would switch to the side of the Bolsheviks, and 40,000 Latvian soldiers became the nucleus of the Bolshevik army in the revolution. The political views of the Latvian soldiers are revealed by the following: In the elections at the Founding Congress of Latvia in November, 1917, the Bolshevik candidates got 95% of the vote.

Thus, it can be said that the victory of the Reds in the Civil War was significantly aided by the participation of the Latvians on their side. It is well known that the watershed in that war came after the defeat of the Volunteer Army at Orel. Now we know who made it happen.

We must compound that with the enthusiasm with which Latvians joined the Cheka, the pleasure they took in executions, and the energy and efficiency with which they later built the Gulag. It's probably more appropriate for us to demand payment from Latvia than the other way around.

In any case, for a complete portrait—and a final proof of their civilized nature—we have to look at the Latvians' attitude toward Jews.

Latvia is a country where during World War II more Jews died proportionately than anywhere else in the world. After Riga was liberated in 1944, of the 80,000 Jews in the country only 162 had survived. And the Jews were not killed only or even primarily by the Germans. The Latvians did it themselves.

For instance, the so-called Latvian Auxiliary Security Police—or as it was also called, Viktor Arais's Command—destroyed close to 50,000 Jews. This is an eyewitness account of their first "action":

In July, 1941, in the cellar of a large choral synagogue in the center of Riga, about 500 refugee Jews from Shaulyaya were hiding… Exhausted, terrified, filled with the most horrible sense of foreboding, the women, old men, and children had found shelter in the temple. On July 4, Viktor Arais and his subordinates drove up to the synagogue in cars. They poured kerosene on the walls, lay down scraps of fabric and then set the whole thing on fire. They used machine guns on the mothers who tried to throw their children out of the windows of the burning building. When the old walls were engulfed in flames, Arais's men started throwing hand grenades into the windows. Thus, 500 Jews met a martyr's end here…

With the organization of the Riga ghetto, the Arais Command had additional work. Executions of Jews were a regular event. They took place early in the morning in Bikerniecksky Forest, outside of town… The doomed people, who were collected into groups of between several hundred and one or two thousand, were seated on the ground in rows of ten or twenty. Before being shot, the victims were forced to strip naked and leave their clothes in a pile, from which the murderers, excited by the execution, selected the better things for themselves.

The naked Jews were methodically made to rise, row by row, and led to the edge of an enormous pit, usually dug the night before by Russian prisoners. The riflemen stood on the other side of the pit, twenty to thirty meters from their victims. They were arranged in two rows, the first down on one knee (they aimed at the left side of the chest), and the second standing (they aimed for the head).

One round, and a dozen victims fell onto the blood-soaked ground…

In January, 1942, the Arais Command "perfected" its execution method. Previously the victims had stood in small groups at the edge of a pit, and the executioners fired at them on a command; but from 1942 on, the victims…were made to go down and stand on top of corpses in such a way that that their bodies would fall in even rows…

Having destroyed the Latvian Jews and having shot all the mentally ill and any "Communist accomplices" (this was how they settled personal scores), the Arais Command "went on tour." There were several Belorussian or Russian villages to be wiped from the face of the earth; help was needed "solving the Jewish question" in the Warsaw ghetto; and so on. Sometimes members of the command "vacationed" at the Salaspils concentration camp—working, naturally, as guards. (Karl Berrezin and Aksel Saar. *Operation Kotbus* [*or the Cleansing of Jews from the Baltics*].)

So, for these civilized Latvians, Russians are bad, and Germans are also bad. I don't know what the Jews did to upset them—they were not occupiers—but they, too, were bad nevertheless. Maybe they did something wrong at the conservatory.

In other words, Congratulations on your new acquisition, dear Europeans. With this new member of the civilized family of nations, at least you will never be bored.

But I still do not understand the criteria by which some nations are accepted into the European Union, while others are still required to demonstrate their civilized nature.

* * *

Let's move on, Igor. So, what do we have? Of the former Soviet republics only one country—my homeland, Kazakhstan—objectively lives better without any help from Russia.

And why is that?

Because they kicked out everyone—Russians, Ukrainians, Germans—so the population is smaller, and they gave concessions to the Americans for their huge natural resources. They live on royalties. Len Blavatnik, who has a big coal business there, told me how Astana is being built. He's never seen such scope! The first time he went there, tumbleweeds were rolling down the streets between Khrushchev-era one-story buildings. Now everything is mushrooming— apartment buildings, offices. The Kazakhs live well, better than the Russians. And why not? They have oil, they have iron, they have other metals. They have coal.

Ukraine has coal and iron, too.

But no oil. Or gas. Just think what the Tenghiz fields alone are worth in Kazakhstan. For their population of twelve million, there is so much wealth there you can't even imagine. They'll be like the Arab Emirates soon.

People in Russia aren't aware of that, Alik.

We don't like to talk about it. That a man managed to implement real economic reforms, to accomplish real privatization, like a grown-up, without all that nonsense, those vouchers. Whoever paid the most, got the most. And who paid the most? The Americans. At a time when everything was growing there.

Couldn't the Kazakhs have managed on their own?

Nope.

And they didn't want to get involved with Russians... They've seen Russians already.

They did develop a light form of nationalism there.

Light, exactly. They don't send troops to Chechnya, though.

No.

So old Valentin Rasputin was right back in 1989?

That was just a joke… So, could Ukrainians be lured back into Russia today?

The eastern ones, maybe, but it's unlikely that the ones from the western part of Ukraine would go.

Then we must develop a separatist movement in eastern Ukraine.

Right… Poor Eduard Limonov tried to develop one in Kazakhstan, and he ended up in the clink for how long?

Listen, I don't understand what the issue is here, Igor. What are we worried about? The state? Or the people? If we're worried about the Russians living in Kazakhstan, they're living better than people in Russia. And no one is oppressing them there. They might say, First reach our living standards, and then come save us. But as for the Ukrainians, they live worse than us, and the Russian language really is being squeezed out of circulation. And also, the Russians shed so much blood to get the Crimea. The Russians, not the Ukrainians. We took Kazakhstan without a shot; no one even resisted there. They were galloping around on their horses, and they didn't give a shit whether some tsar considered it his land.

Yes. So, only the Kazakhs have fucked us irreparably. The issue is being resolved with the Balts, and the rest have been sorry for a long time.

That's what I'm saying—we have to take back Ukraine and Belorussia.

What the hell do you need them for? Please explain yourself, Alik.

I want to be in the Crimea. People keep offering me land in Sochi, for me to build a house.

So what don't you like about Sochi?

It's damp. So much rain! Very few sunny days. I don't want to go there. And there's the injustice of it! We conquered it, and the Ukrainians are using it. I want it to be ours.

So go and build your house on something that's not ours.

If I'm going to do that, I'd rather build it in Italy. In Tuscany somewhere, near Florence. You can buy lots that are 7 hectares, with castles and vineyards—and not expensive.

But you're not buying there; you're waiting for the Crimea to be returned to us, any day now.

I'm ready to start an invasion there! If we conquer the Crimea, what are they going to do to us? Nothing. And I'm for justice. It does not belong to Ukraine! Nikita Khrushchev gave it to them.

So sue in the international courts, and let them declare the deal illegal.

First we win it back, and then we sue. And while the courts are haggling, we have use of it. And everyone in the Crimea will be happy. And while we're at it, we take Odessa back, too.

So those were the questions that should have been settled in 1989.

Yes. But by the same token, Kaliningrad should be returned to its owners. It doesn't belong to us. It's obviously not ours, and we don't need it. But the Crimea is ours, and we need it. Give it back to us. I'm for justice.

So… what else was there in 1989? Ribbentrop-Molotov.

By the way, recently Vladimir Zhirinovsky was hollering about how we should unite with Germany and conquer the whole world.

By the way, Alik, that's not his idea. It's not new. Everyone understands that if the Russians united with the Germans, they would fuck everyone. And why didn't they unite—instead of fighting against each other all the time, and for no clear reason? I'll tell you.

Go ahead.

Because the situation was clear to some very serious fellows who had their own very serious empire spanning half the globe—the British. They had powerful diplomacy and terrific intelligence. So Britain expended enormous resources to keep us fighting against you: Pit Russians against Germans at any cost.

It didn't always work.

And it worked very well on a few occasions, too.

But, Igor, when Empress Elizabeth died and Peter III took the throne, he quickly broke with the French and Austrians and made peace with Frederick the Great—and then Frederick got everyone, even though he had been losing the war for seven years before that. And British Intelligence, which had been helping Prussia, looked like shitheads. Britain did not want a union; it wanted continual war in Europe, so that it could keep on with its expansionism throughout the world.

You see, the only reason we could have peace with the Germans then was because the British Intelligence helped Prussia, as you said. But when it stopped…. It's very sad that Russia's fate was determined by a foreign secret service, the British Intelligence. I don't like thinking about that, but it looks as if that's the case there.

There was another—Tilsit. When Russia joined the continental blockade.

A small, isolated incident.

Yes. Russia couldn't keep it up for long. It left the blockade—and so Napoleon was forced to attack Russia. Standard historiography does not often mention the fact that Napoleon did not attack Russia because he was so eager to do so, but because it had abandoned the blockade of England. Alexander I broke his word. Russia's economy was suffering as a result of participation in the blockade—England was a big consumer market for many Russian goods. And we bought equipment from them. So seeing the obvious economic losses, Alexander I had to bow out of the blockade. And Napoleon got him.

There's that damned England again, Alik. It's stuck in our craw like a bone. But the Ribbentrop-Molotov Pact was an attempt to honor Russia's age-old interests and come to terms with the Germans.

How do you feel about Viktor Suvorov's theory in his book *Icebreaker*—

I believe it! Stalin wanted to attack.

—that it was a preventive strike?

Despite official denials of Suvorov's claims, I think his position makes sense. He has powerful arguments.

Killer arguments.

Why did we train so many paratroopers before the war—every park had a parachute jump! You don't need so many paratroopers in a defensive war.

That's point one.

And why did our troops have European maps, instead of our own? And why were they made to retreat blindly from the border?

And the slogan, "War on foreign territory?" That's two.

And the posters were printed before the war: "Your Motherland calls." And our troops were issued leather boots then, so that they would look good in Europe.

That's three. I remember all that, Igor.

And even Lenin had openly said that we needed a world revolution. The export of revolution was part of the plan.

And here's another argument, which we knew without Suvorov: The army was imprisoned in the very first days of the war. All the troops were stationed along the border. Why were they there? Mobilized, with support trucks? Were they planning a defensive war?

And Stalin declared at the start of the war that since it had already begun, he was going to create socialism all over Europe. That was even in Soviet sources. Suvorov reminded us that Victory Day became an official holiday only after Stalin's death. Stalin wouldn't even acknowledge the parade—he didn't consider the result of the war a victory. In a purely military sense he had won, but he had not achieved the goals he had set for himself—what kind of victory was that? So the Pact was an attempt at Realpolitik: to make a deal with the Germans, and kill everyone.

I don't think so. I think he wanted to attack. That was Stalin's ploy. And Hitler believed him.

It coincided with Russia's age-old policy, in its ideal form. But instead, the British Intelligence ploy prevailed.

I'm not sure. Hitler was an asshole too. If he had wanted to conquer the Soviet Union, he should never have started the genocide. He should have taken the army that he had captured and turned it against Stalin. But he was an asshole, a Nazi. The problem wasn't that he was an aggressive expansionist. That's neither good nor bad in and of itself. Maybe Hitler could have played a positive role, freeing Russia from the Bolsheviks. But he was a Nazi. He hated Jews. Those are his great sins and his guilt before humanity.

He could have been like so many and hated Jews but kept quiet about it.

Right!

He could have complained about Jews to Eva Braun over pillow talk, but otherwise, he should have shut up. Eva could have said, Well, if you don't like them, exterminate them. And he would say, What are you, stupid?

Because, if you exterminate them, then how do you fight against Stalin?

But he turned out to be really dumb.

Absolutely. Suvorov writes about that. Remember, he has the section called "Suicide"?

No. But it's very hard to find anything *simpatico* about Hitler.

Sure you can. He loved Germans. He suffered for that nation.

Well, Alik, you might see that as a positive, but the wider public does not consider that a plus—loving Germans. By the way, I don't know any non-German who loves Germans as I do.

He was sneakier with the French. Vichy, French administration, respect… But for some reason, he decided not to treat Russia that way. And yet he could have knocked out Stalin in one goal. He had the whole army in his hands.

In his latest book, *Two Hundred Years*, Solzhenitsyn says that many people equate Communism with Jews. Think that's what Hitler was thinking?

But why did Hitler need anti-Semitism? So stupid, what an idiot!

Our Yeltsin couldn't solve our problems, Alik, and you're talking about Hitler!

Well, Hitler had bigger plans than Yeltsin did. He wanted to conquer the world. But why the Nazi policy? All right, say you don't like Jews—but why don't you like Russians? Blond and blue-eyed, right? What the fuck?

But in the long run, Hitler helped his people—the hard way, of course. For people to start working, they need the experience of defeat, so they don't think they're the smartest in the world. That they don't need to work because they're so inventive. Or because they have natural resources. Somebody has to explain to them in a simple way: Guys, you're not so special, you need to work. The people got the message. And now Mercedes and German technology have united Europe… It cost them a

lot of blood. The Russians lost a lot of blood and resources, too, but they still keep thinking they're special.

I think that World War II taught the world the most important lesson—

—that you solve things with money, not big talk?

No, no. That you can't humiliate any nation—this includes the Chechens. Our people have to learn that: You can't bring a whole nation to its knees. If you screw it and suck all its blood, like conquerors, you can expect payback. Bombs in your cities. Your houses will be blown up. Think about it. The Versailles Peace Treaty was completely unfair. Patently unfair. Even the French, Americans, and British acknowledged that. No nation, especially a large and powerful one, could accept being screwed like that. They just couldn't…

That's capitalist greed for you! They wanted to get as much as they could from the Germans, and they paid for it later.

That's absolutely right! The war could have been avoided completely. It was French stupidity, and the Americans and Brits couldn't restrain their appetites. That's all. And our president listens to that jerk, Chirac! He'll lead him to another dead end.

That same greed will ruin Russia. OK, enough about sad things. Why don't you tell me this, Alik? We didn't believe that Yeltsin drank. But did we believe that he screwed around? You know, the time he fell from the bridge? What's your take on that?

I would sooner believe that. That was my suspicion then.

Who was he fucking?

It doesn't matter. But I know that bridge on Nikolina Gora.

There was something about a bouquet… He was either going whoring with flowers or coming back from whoring.

Ha! Coming back with flowers!

That's funny. So, back to business: What were you doing in 1989, Alik?

In 1989 I left my job and got a job teaching at a polytechnic institute. This constituted a tremendous leap forward in my career (as I imagined it, anyway). I wanted to teach. And thanks to that, I have certain oratorical skills, because I gave a lot of lectures. Which brings me back to Sobchak: He had them, too, because of teaching. Everyone who had real teaching experience in college turned out to be a good public speaker.

I never gave a lecture in my life. How do you do that, Alik? "Everyone: Sit down, shut up, and I'll teach you." How can you make yourself out to be a guru just like that? They all go quiet and listen to you, and you're thinking, what else you can stuff in their brains? And they're thinking, shit, when's the bell so we can go for a beer? Weren't you ashamed to get all puffed up and pretend to be smart?

There are obvious things that have to be told to young people, and then they'll understand everything. There are sciences besides Marxism-Leninism, you know. Game theory, automation theory, applied mathematics, linear programming—do you understand?

No, I never studied those. Sorry, I'd forgotten where you and I studied. And what.

Well, when a man comes out and says, I'm going to scientifically teach you scientific communism… Naturally, everyone wants to head out for a beer. But if you tell them that you will explain the theory of lines and start covering the board with formulas, that's different.

What's the theory?

How to set up cash registers. Where to place the service desk so that there are no lines. How many registers there should be.

Were you the ones who set up the customs kiosks at Sheremetyevo?

No, not us. That's done intentionally to create lines. To allow for the concept of special servicing—so that you'd want to get past them.

What else were you doing in 1989?

We had a "perestroika club." We had a room, meetings. Our leader was Petya Filippov, a deputy to the Congress.

I remember that in January 1989 I was called up for military service. I even considered skipping out on it. It's no fun digging trenches in the snow-covered fields around Moscow. But it turned out that trenches were not on the agenda. We had another assignment: to study language at MGIMO in the military department, and do some other military studies. I accepted—why not? A month off work to raise my educational level. Self-

improvement. Marvelous! We drew maps and then bombed NATO on them. And then I went back to Leipzig.

Where every stone knows Lenin.

And me. That year dissidents were hanging around the Nikolaikirche in Leipzig, blathering about democracy. But in the summer the dissidents were all at their dachas and on vacation, so I didn't see any political struggle. They agitated in the spring, rested in the summer, and in the fall, when it got cooler, went back to their rallies.

Normal people.

So. They taught us German and some other stuff.

And I found an old notebook from that trip. I almost shed a tear reading it. Listen. "It's very difficult, boring, nauseating living in Germany. Life is going on at home, and you're sitting here abroad. Fool." How beautiful! I was so upset that the miners were striking in Kuzbass and I was hanging around Europe drinking beer and eating Bratwurst.

Of course, you're a miner.

Life, freedom, strikes! That was real. Shit. And instead, I was there, getting German marks as part of my scholarship.

You mean, "What a bastard am I. I sold out to the call of the yellow devil."

I also bought a Praktika camera. That was a big deal in those days.

Igor, there's no way you could have bought a camera like that at the miners' strike.

Of course not. But do you see what my emotional state was then?

Yes.

It was like the romance of the criminal life—how thieves in the law can't marry or serve in the army—

—or work—

—but just go around with their switchblades. I was tormented by my feelings, I was sure that by my lights and journalism's lights, I should be at the strikes. Just then the strike at the Shevyakov mine was starting. That was the beginning of it all. Exactly ten years later, on the anniversary of the strike, I went there and did a big article about how and why it had started.

It started at the Vorgashorskaya mine!

No, no. I assure you, Alik, the main one was at Shevyakov. In Mezhdurechensk. I went down there to follow up on the revolutionaries and to see if they were satisfied with what they had done.

Svinarenko's Commentary:

The miners' strikes of 1989. Extracts from my old article.

The cradle of the miners' revolution is today a huge fraternal grave. Perhaps the deepest one in the world: 280 meters. After the revolution, when the USSR collapsed, there were several horrible underground explosions. People died. Only two bodies were raised, the other 23 could not be reached: coal burned for a long time afterward under the ground. Before shutting the mine, they poured a lot of water into the shaft to put out the fire. (Remember when it was fashionable to speak of social explosions, about the fire of revolution? This was metaphor made literal). Well, the dead are buried, albeit in an exotic manner. Of the living, no one is forgotten: everyone was fired through job reduction and given three months salary severance pay. Four of them were given money to learn a new trade. There was not enough for the rest—and there were two thousand men working at the Shevyakov mine. Through an amazing coincidence, that is the approximate number of unemployed in Mezhdurechensk today.

... This is a picture of the new Russian apocalypse. A line of miners in coveralls, with black faces, lamps burning on their helmets—in broad daylight. They are silently walking through the town, sometimes entering houses and checking the refrigerators of well-fed non-miners. Expressive? They saw this picture in 1989 in Mezhdurechensk. "It gave me chills," a witness recalls. They hadn't seen that in Moscow yet.

... It was the historic day, 10 July 1989. It started, as always, over a trifle. They had been promising soap for three months and still had none. There was no soap in the stores, either, if you remember. The Shevyakov Mine. Valery Kokorin's team, he's the ring leader, came up out of the mine and stood, all black, covered in coal dust, and did not want to go home unwashed.

"How much longer!" and so on and so forth. If the foreman had come in and bawled them out then: "What are you shouting for, you motherfuckers!" and given them three pieces of brown soap, it would have been enough for twelve men, the pieces were huge. They would have washed up and gone home to drink beer and, like real members of the intelligentsia, they would silently give the authorities the finger in the safety of their kitchens.

But there wasn't any stinking soap to be had (which must be made out of rotten dog bones). The empire fell. If they had known on Staraya Square at Party headquarters, they would have sent a special envoy with the soap on a special flight.

Then—in the middle of town—came a noisy rally. People came from neighboring mines to see if they would be beaten or not. Since they weren't, the square quickly filled up.

"They were scared, you can be sure of that," people recalled those heated days. "We were waiting for the Novosibirsk Division of the Internal Police to show up. Gorbachev had used troops before. In Alma-Ata and in Tbilisi, right? He could have attacked us with trench shovels, too."

The next day, Prokopyevsk was on strike, and then the entire Kuzbass region, and then it was obvious that there weren't enough police to stop it. The fear vanished. The moment was lost forever.

"You weren't afraid that the KGB would come and break it up?"

"Nah. We all saw that the regime was weakened. People threw away their Party card and nothing happened to them. ... Miners walked around town checking the refrigerators of Party workers. There was nothing in them but dried-up herring. So they stopped."

"Try checking refrigerators now."

"Are you kidding! It was socialism then. Now it's a dictatorship! Back then one unarmed cop patrolled, now look at them with automatic rifles and armored vehicles."

…And what of Valery Kokorin, the Kuzbass Cohn-Bendit? Does he visit little Pioneer children and give speeches as the old living revolutionary? No. ... He moved away from the region a long time ago to the Altai, where he keeps bees and cattle. And a garden. Like Diocletian, who resigned from the hustle and bustle of power to grow cabbages. So, he sometimes drops by Mezdurechensk, and complains: "I keep quiet in Altai about being the initiator of the strike—or they'll beat me up. ... I somehow saw the development of events differently. I never expected it to end like this." ... They tricked him like a kid. They gave him a Sharp television set (well, everyone got one then). Then at some meeting in Novokuznetsk they gave him another one. And people were waiting for him and said, So you sold out for two TVs!

The other revolutionaries have disappeared, too. One was elected Duma deputy to Moscow right away, his term ended, but he's still there. The guys are hurt by this. Another one is also in Moscow, working in the unions, and has his own life now. Some went into business, of course. "Some were bought, others became drunks," the locals say. And still others are dead.

…If you go have some moonshine with the miners they will tell you're the popular theory: the KGB organized the strike to bring down Gorbachev. Funny? Look at the materials from the Plenary session of the Regional Party Committee (do you still remember what that was?). There it is in black and white: "The coal industry of the Kuzbass is on the verge of stopping because of enormous reserves of coal in the warehouses." They had 12 million tons in reserve—as much as the entire region digs in a month! The railroad couldn't carry it all out, even though no one was blocking it then. And there was nowhere to take it. The state required only a third of that. And you can't let coal lie around indefinitely, it starts burning slowly. … In other words, a strike was the only way to avert a terrible crisis. Dragging it out was like death. The mines had to be stopped instantly and the miners had to be distracted and kept busy. There was no other way out. And someone found this one. Perhaps it was KGB Chief Kryuchkov. Or maybe it was just the guy in charge of deliveries, who stole a case of soap.

The strike lasted two weeks. By the end, the reserves had fallen to 8 million tons—they could have stayed on strike another couple of weeks. But they didn't want to pamper the workers forever.

"They sent us everything. I was full and I washed with soap," one miner told me. "We lived well. I got three television sets and a refrigerator. I sold then, traded them for furniture, a tape recorder, shoes, jackets, sneakers. You could trade a TV for a garage or a car. There was an index. And then…. The state introduced a tax on dollars and barter. It cost a lot. And at the same time, goods appeared in the stores. Gradually things became the way they are now. … As for striking, I like striking."

… The village of the closed Shevyakov mine. People live there, where else are you going to put them? In barracks and three-story ruins. The yards look like they've been bombed, it looks like Grozny: everything is dug up. The villagers look poor and worn, toothless and generally abandoned—typical Russian pensioners. I talk to them. There is only one topic: the underground pension with bonuses—a total of 176 Soviet rubles—was enough to live on happily. And now, they can only buy modest food and galoshes. They criticize Yeltsin something terrible! I'm too embarrassed to quote them here, despite my rough miners' upbringing.

"We're not stupid, we read the papers Why does everything go to Moscow, all the trains, diamonds, and money? You're all the same in Moscow, one big gang of thieves."

That's what I missed in 1989! I scanned it retroactively in 1999.

* * *

So, Igor, now Chubais will get the State Prize for privatizing the Kuzbass mines. And the miners worship him, they say he's fucking amazing. It's begun working, what Chubais has done. When he distributed the World Bank credits for restructuring the coal industry, he built things, and so on. It's started working!

But in 1989 people saw it differently.

They simply didn't know that the payoff would not begin until 2003. Aman Tuleyev, Chubais's political opponent, called him and said, "I'm not accepting the State Prize for restructuring the mines without you. We're going together."

Very refined.

They had done it together. But the miners nominated only Tuleyev. He called Chubais to join him. "We can argue as much as we like, but I'm not going without you."

Handsomely done! But to get back to my personal life, Alik, I had a daughter that October. Despite everything! My wife's hemoglobin was low, and she was Rh negative. They said, "You can't give birth, it will kill mother and child!" The doctors told us we could never have this pleasure. We conferred and decided that we would try for it. Que sera, sera.

Right. And it ended successfully.

Yes. We have two. Multiplying meant risking a life. Not mine, of course. But still.

Tell me, after you became a father, did you attitude toward the world change?

Of course. I realized that I was part of a chain, that my chromosomes were being passed to a new generation. I still did not feel like a total grown-up (even though I was 32), but it was time to get a passport, so to speak. And I realized that I had to calculate far into the future. And I remember being happy that it was a girl. I had brought up a boy not that long ago, and I was horrified by the thought of having to go through it all again: slingshots, flick knives, bad grades, hooky, cheap wine, sex, bars, fistfights, arrests, drunk tanks, so on and so forth. Either he'd beat up a cop, or the cops would beat him. Get him out there, pull him out off that.

Don't over-dramatize, Igor!

I'm not. I'm telling you how I brought up my kid brother. And I thought glumly how I'd have to do it all over again if I had a son. And I look, and it's a girl! So obedient, clean, grave, with bows in her hair, looks at you with those big eyes, gets good grades…. It brought tears to my eyes. It made up for my difficult childhood. Yes. …I found another notation: "7 November 1989. Killed the hog, 4 *poods* of meat. Minimal bacon fat."

Four poods!

Yes. That was my in-laws. They killed it with a bayonet. Then tarred it, singed it….

No need to tell me! I've killed piglets myself. Father always kept pigs. Schmaltz, rinds… liverwurst…washing the intestine…

What, you made sausages?

Yes. All the offal goes in there! Heart, liver, stomach….Add meat and fat… Salt, pepper…. Wash the intestine and stuff it with a homemade syringe, tin with a wooden plunger… You take the intestine, fit it over the tip of the syringe, and it straightens out…

That's what I'm saying: Germans make sausage and so do Ukrainians. But the Russian don't make shit!

They're too lazy.

Right. I've had so many talks with the Russian people about it. They keep complaining that they can't make any money because their meat is bought up cheap by wholesalers. Well, then sell them homemade sausage! It's more expensive, it includes the cost of labor. And they say, but you have to boil water and clean off the shit from the intestine. So what are we saying? That it's impossible to make money? Or that we're unwilling to get our hands dirty? Let's decide what we're talking about. How can you say it's impossible to make sausages? The Ukrainians have filled up the whole Dorogomilovsky Market with their sausages. They can make it.

Let's see, Alik: Then, in December, I traveled to Japan, for the paper. And just before the New Year, on December 29, I rented a car and moved my not-very-numerous things to a new apartment.

Ho-ho! I didn't get one until 1991. My first apartment.

We moved in, set out our furniture. And then it took us many years to learn to live in two rooms. The bedroom seemed superfluous, auxiliary. Especially since we had a large kitchen that we did not have to share with neighbors. We lived in the big room, and the small one was just there. When someone would visit, we'd have some moonshine and walk around the apartment. The guest would ask, And what's this? Oh, it's a… study. Sounded impressive. But all it had in it was a table that I found in a dump. And a stool from our old communal kitchen.

In 1989 you must still have been writing in longhand.

Nope. I was using a typewriter. Exclusively—ever since 1982 or so. I had two typewriters, both Moskva brand. One metal, the other plastic. Not like your imported one.

I have one, yes; it cost 180 rubles.

Mine were both Soviet-made, and used. I traded a liter of cognac for one and I don't remember what for the other.

When did you switch to PCs forever?

In 1990. Yakovlev was burning through all the old habits with a hot poker—he did not want to see a single typewriter or a sheet of paper in the editorial room. So I had to learn computers. Although, in 1989 I had a real opportunity to change professions. Our newspaper, *Komsomolskaya Pravda*, had formed a commercial section. My boss, Sungorkin, went there.

I know him!

And he asked me to go with him.

Why didn't you?

Because I had no understanding of business and hated it. And I had a relatively weak interest in making big money.

So I asked Sungorkin then: "What makes you think I'm a business-man? On what basis? I don't work the black market, I have no money… I'd like to know. Is it because I don't steal?" He explained that often people don't steal only because they have no opportunity to get away with it. Until they've been tested, you can't judge that quality. Sungorkin named three qualities necessary in a businessman: boldness, enterprise, and sociability. All right, I said, I'll admit to sociability. But the rest? I don't climb into tiger cages and I don't sell blue jeans. Right, he replied, and then pointed out how I had exposed my Kaluga bosses. And reminded me about my apartment—when so many journalists had to live with their parents or in-laws.

That's what I'm talking about! You position yourself as a man very far from commerce, Igor, but it's not very convincing.

But I truly do not like business. It's so boring! Let's go back to 1989. I didn't go with Sungorkin to build this new department, even though I had never had a better boss before him. He never forgot anything, never blamed anyone falsely, and he put people in jobs they could do. … And he helped me personally, with that apartment. Before *Komsomolka* I worked at *Sobesednik*. I asked them if I could go part-time so that I would have

time to work on the construction of a building where I would then get an apartment. But the editor in chief there said, "That's your problem. Either work full on or get out." Sungorkin took me on at some minimal salary and freed me from going into work everyday. It blew me away, really. Before him, all I had learned to expect from bosses were attacks, treachery, and exploitation. So... After he left, they tried to fire me from the paper. For professional unsuitability. It was a real drag. But I took pity on them and resigned of my own volition.

Why were they firing you? Maybe you really weren't professionally suitable? Did you ever consider that?

Hm...No, I didn't. And I always tell the story proudly, which is something not every fired journalist can do.

Svinarenko's Commentary:

I hadn't thought about it before, so I sat down and thought: It's true, I've often caught myself reacting emotionally whenever I hear a colleague say about himself, "I'm a professional!" I wonder why I never say that. Even jokingly. What is it in journalism that I don't know how to do? How am I worse than the others? This was my train of thought. They call it the second-oldest profession. If a girl says she's a professional, it means that she is prepared to service whoever will pay. But the one who picks and chooses for herself is not really a pro—with that attitude, there's not much point in being on the street. So then, a professional journalist, it follows, would have to write what they tell him to: Shit on this one, praise that one. "I haven't read Pasternak's novel, but it's crap." "Personally, I think Leonid Ilyich Brezhnev..." "Luzhkov is a thief"... "Luzhkov is a saint..." "Oligarch stinting on alimony..." "The family and oil..." "Gangsters, bright-eyed and bushy-tailed..." That sort of stuff. I, on the other hand, have a lot of trouble denying myself the pleasure of saying whatever I want. And also, when some idiot starts trying to teach me journalism, how can I not tell him to fuck off? Why live, if you can't enjoy the small pleasure of telling someone to fuck off if you feel like it? Well, then, you can't call yourself a professional.

A few years after that firing episode I came to see Zhenya Anisimov at *Komsomolka*, to get some advice. I was hiring people for a new project, for good money. "Well, what kind of people do you need, tell me!" I was having trouble formulating an answer, when who should peek in but one of the people who had fired me. I shouted, "Hey, Vitya! Come on in! Listen, are you planning on firing anyone for professional unsuitability soon? I'd hire him—I need some good people right now." He looked embarrassed, but I was actually serious.

* * *

But I'd still like you explain why you didn't go into the commercial department, Igor.

Well, that would mean having to revisit to the situation in 1978. Our class was sent to help with the potato harvest. We got to the Bolshevik Kolkhoz in Serpukhovsky Region. So we're digging out potatoes from the mud... I didn't really feel like doing it. Two guys got off by being hired to clean the outhouses. They were happy; they figured they had fucked everyone by getting let off the potato detail. I found myself a cushy niche publishing the camp newspaper.

The camp idiot!

Like that. I wrote, took photos, typed. Later, they rebuked me for losing all shame: If you did a newsletter for any other department, that would have been all right, but to do it for the journalism school was too much! The height of cynicism!

I know a lot of businessmen who have adopted that style—pretending to be idiots.

Hold on, I'm no businessman. I don't have a Mercedes or a dacha in Zhukovka.

You keep joking.

Let me tell you about the bootlegging when we were bringing in the potatoes. It's about business and its place in my life.

I remember that story. You've told me.

No, no. I told it to you as a funny story in my life, but now hear it as a parable about Russians and business. So, the camp. Life goes on. That means you need to drink. And we discover that there is a moonshine business in the camp. One of our classmates bought it up in the village for a ruble fifty a bottle and sold it in the camp for two rubles. He was making about ten rubles a day. Nothing unusual, right? Business is business.

Right.

What business was it of mine, you would think. But I went to him and told him that he had to stop making a profit off his comrades. He was surprised. He explained that I couldn't stop him—he had clients and

suppliers, and everyone was happy—I was a new player in the market, and I should stay out of it. He was right. But what did I do? I found his supplier and won him over. It wasn't hard: You just go to the nearest village and knock on the first door, and ask around, get into their good graces.

Ah, so you had the supplies delivered to you.

Yes, I brought the moonshine to camp, where I sold it at its original price.

You were making zero.

Yes, instead of making ten. What did I get out of it? Nothing but hemorrhoids from the hassle. OK, people poured me free drinks from the bottles I brought them for free, out of respect. And then my competitor called me out. To settle things. I had pushed my way into his territory, spoiled his market…

At least you should have been making money!

That's my point, Alik. I spent enormous resources to destroy the man's business without any profit for me. So we fought on the football field. With a big crowd watching. It wasn't easy—he was bigger and stronger—but I was lucky and knocked him out. Everyone judged that the fight was over and that I had won.

What bullshit. Prison mores in a student setting.

I think that in this case the mores came from the Soviet Army, where most of the journalism students had already served. But the concepts are the same—behind barbed wire, in the zone, and in the army.

You ruined the man's business—that was atrocious. It would have made more sense, Alik, if you were at least profiting.

I'm telling how it looked then. I was absolutely certain in my righteousness.

But do you agree now that you were an asshole? Now, looking back?

I wasn't an asshole. I was Robin Hood. It's not the same.

Don't give me Robin Hood! Robin Hood would have taken away the guy's money. You took his business.

That's not the worst part. **The guy persuaded Kolya in the village to increase production so that he would have enough to sell, too. Kolya didn't have the manpower or the resources, so he started making *vtoryak*. There was a lot of moonshine, twice as much as before. But he didn't have more sugar or yeast. So the moonshine was half as strong. And also murky and disgusting.**

Is that so? Interesting… That story is a good lesson for market economics. All the typical mistakes right there. But do you realize now that you were an asshole?

Why is it so important for you that I be an asshole?

I'm an asshole, for example, because I did not take bribes. When I was in government. I think that I should have taken them! Everyone takes bribes now, and nothing happens to them. I didn't, and something happened to me. They tried to put me in prison!

But they didn't.

But if I had known how it would end, I would have taken bribes. And if I had, I would the richest man in the country now.

Really? And the happiest?

I don't know.

Well, who's the richest man in the country? Fridman?

Khodorkovsky. [*This chapter was written before Mikhail Khodorkovsky was arrested in August 2003. It was published in the September issue of* Medved.]

Well, and does he have more happiness? Does he love life more?

I don't know.

Alik, look at it this way. You had no money, and you were unhappy. And then you made money, and became happy. Can that be said of you?

No. Not like that. It's measured on a different axis of coordinates. I'm telling you: Money is not the equivalent of happiness, it is the equivalent of freedom. I was less free when I had less money. More money means more freedom.

There are two kinds of people. Some see money as the equivalent of freedom and the others as the equivalent of power.

Like a drug.

As the equivalent of power. And the people who see it that way are the most unhappy and the most unfree. But there are lots of wealthy people who take money as the equivalent of freedom.

Come on.

I know!

I have the impression that once they have a lot of money, many people's brains turn to shit. Can it be said that the more money a person has, the happier his children are?

That's not it, Igor. The more money a person has, the greater his opportunities to be happy. That holds for his children as well.

There are also opportunities to have a breakdown or to spoil your children. There are many opportunities. Man is weak.

I agree, I agree.

You've seen people change and become disgusting over money, haven't you?

Yes. But I've seen people become better, once they get a sufficient amount. Particularly women.

Oh, but normal sufficiency and big bucks are very different things. Here is what one of friends has to say: Money is definitely a very pleasant thing, but most often, the more money people have, the more repellent they are. He knows what he's talking about, he's known many people and he knows about money not just from hearsay. So, I don't feel like an asshole at all for not putting money ahead of everything in life.

I get it, I get it.

We could go further back and ask why I didn't go to the financial trade institute? That's where the money is. Spun out of air, the way Russians like it. I must have based my decision on the assumption that there were other amusements in life besides money. I consciously chose not to take the direct path to money. I could have said, the way you are saying now, Let's make some money and see. But if you're on that path, where money is the highest good, you can start thinking this way: Any girl who fucks for free is an idiot.

Hahaha.

Why are you laughing? Following your logic, she could be making a hundred an evening. Instead, she fucks and then has to work her shift at the factory. Or this logic: Someone would have turned Him in anyway, why not make the 30 pieces of silver? One guy did it. See? It's another issue that he later hanged himself—that's outside our topic. You can't—

All right, all right, Igor. You win.

You know the old joke: If you're so smart, why aren't you rich? The person who gave me the most paradoxical thought on this was Dima Petrov. He explained how it is for the Hindus: It's very simple, merchants are a low caste. The Brahmins are the highest caste. The merchants are only one step above the Untouchables, who need to be avoided at all costs. They're no Brahmins, but you can still shake their hands. So, what do you think? Have you ever heard anything like it?

Nope.

You're not lost to society yet. You heard this theory out calmly. Often, rich people are offended by the thought. It hurts them. Pretty, isn't it?

Yup.

9.

1990

The Ninth Bottle

*K*okh's first entry into politics was on the municipal level; he was elected mayor of Sestroretsk. In those years, Alfred considered Yavlinsky a serious politician. Meanwhile, Svinarenko was participating in the establishment of an uncensored press. This took so much time and energy that he had to give up distilling samogon.

So, Alik, we're up to 1990. The last full year of Soviet rule, of the USSR as a superpower. I remember how Foreign Minister Eduard Shevardnadze started giving in to the West: He gave in to the Americans in the arms talks. And he also gave in to them in the Bering Sea negotiations, when he handed over our continental shelf.

I know. That agreement still is not ratified.

Svinarenko's Commentary:

Shevardnadze and U.S. Secretary of State James Baker signed an agreement on dividing control of the Bering and Chukotka seas. Through an exchange of memos, they set up a temporary application of that agreement. The demarcation line they agreed to was—and is—seen by many Russians as an infringement of our interests, since if they had divided the territory equally Russia would have an additional 50,000 square kilometers of continental shelf. Despite the protests of cooler heads, the agreement continues to hold provisionally and has not brought up for ratification.

* * *

Then, Alik, that's when Shevardnadze gave in to the Germans on unification. He kept saying, "It's with the highest approval!" But Helmut Kohl recalled that when he asked Gorbachev if they would ever be able to reunite, Gorby replied, "Do whatever you want."

Yes, yes.

Kohl couldn't believe his ears. He asked again, "You mean we can decide that for ourselves? You give us permission?"

What do you think, did Shevy sell East Germany for money or not? I heard stories about it.

I never heard about any money. But I think he was simply planning to separate Georgia from Russia. In preparation for that, he wanted to do something bad for us—as future competitors—and he was planning to demand gratitude from the West.

Why do you think that? It seems to me that he never thought about being president of Georgia then. Shevy tried to make it in Moscow first. He didn't even take part in the first Georgian elections.

Yeah, right. We all thought that the republics would break away, and he was the only one in the whole country who didn't? Or did he think that only Georgia would stay? How could he think that? I ask you, how could he not have understood that the Soviet Union was falling apart? And if it was, then he would have to find a place for himself in Moscow, and it wasn't clear what kind of position he could expect: There were plenty of locals, plus there would be lots of people fleeing the republics and ending up in Moscow. Or he'd have to go to the Caucasus, where God knows what was going on, and where he hadn't even gone for the first elections. So even if they did give him money...and he took it...that doesn't mean he was acting against his conscience. He would have done the same for free! Sound like a good theory?

I think he just gave everything away. Not for ideology and not for money.

But why then give away what was Russian? All of Russia's interests?

You crack me up. If a man is an asshole, it doesn't necessary mean that he's a conscious asshole! He can just be an ordinary asshole.

You're calling Shevardnadze an asshole?

Of course. I think he is one. And he is going to end badly, by the way. Very badly. I'm certain that he's not going to die quietly in his bed. They'll bump him off, 100%! And even if he didn't take money at the time, you think that he didn't wind up rich from it anyway? That he was for the unification of Germany at all costs?

The Americans starting giving him loans later.

An elegant point. But that's just kopecks: $30,000,000.

For Georgia, that's big bucks. Their monthly wages are $5.

So you believe that Shevardnadze suffered for an idea. Like Gorbachev.

You say that Shevardnadze is an asshole. What about Gorby? He also gave up everything to everyone, including the Germans. What, do you think he's an asshole, too?

That's news to you?

Well, I mean…

I just thought that we spoke the same language. And it turns out that I have to explain the most obvious things to you…

Come off it! This is just labeling people. There are a lot of things Gorbachev did wrong—he let a lot go, that must be admitted. Everything he could. But why call him an asshole?

Svinarenko's Commentary:

Gorbachev got the Nobel Peace Prize for 1990. The justification was this: "For his leading role in the peace process which today characterizes an important component in the life of the international community." That is how the committee put it. But in fact, most likely, it was for giving up Germany. That smacks of the way the loans-for-shares auctions worked.

* * *

Kokh's Commentary on Svinarenko's:

What do the loans-for-shares auctions have to do with this, damnit? The Ukrainian dope doesn't understand a thing, and on top of that he throws in the mortgage auctions! Was it in one of your articles that I read something like "mortgage auction on Svyazinvest?" No? You should watch yourself… Allow me to explain in terms an idiot can understand: There was no mortgage auction on Svyazinvest, only an ordinary one. Why don't you stop bringing up the loans-for-shares auctions, about which you know nothing, and wait patiently until you and I reach 1995, which is when those auctions took place? That's when I explain everything about them. It won't seem insufficient, I promise. I get so pissed off by these semiliterate commentaries about mortgage auctions... You can't even imagine. I want to maul anyone who doesn't make the effort to learn something about them and starts making shit up, and adding lies on top of it.

* * *

Svinarenko's Commentary (continued):

What? You calling me a Ukrainian dope? Then you're a German wiener!

* * *

Alik, by the way, did Gorbachev take money?

I have no way of knowing.

Well, in that context it doesn't matter.

It doesn't matter. Yes.

Tell me please, Alik... We were talking about Gorbachev. Do you remember that he quit the Communist Party in 1990? What was that, a bold act or just PR?

I think it was minor PR. But let's talk about our own lives. We're not writing a book about Gorbachev, after all. You keep going off on these stupid tangents.

Journalistic habit. I've always said that if you take superficiality out of journalism, there'll be nothing left.

Ha ha ha!

Why are you laughing? Journalists aren't writing novels for the ages. Their task is to create some crap that everyone wants to read today and will have forgotten completely tomorrow. Incidentally, those are mutually exclusive goals: Try to manage that. It requires talent. And as the famous reporter Yuri Rost says, there is only one good thing about journalism: speedy results. You wrote it last night, today everyone's reading it, tomorrow you get paid. As they say, in the paper in the morning, in the outhouse by evening.

Why don't you tell me where you were that year?

Why don't you? I seem to start all the time.

Me? I got elected in June—

O-ho! And it begins.

Yes! I was elected mayor of the fucking city.

City? Or village?

Sestroretsk has 50,000 residents—it's a city!

How did it happen? There you are, furthering science at your institute, distilling *samogon* at home—and suddenly you're struck by the idea of running Sestroretsk. Of corrupting that little city.

I had—actually still have—a friend, Mishka Dmitriev. We were in the same group in college. He works for German Gref now, doing pension reform. His full name is Mikhail Egonych Dmitriev—his father was German.

I remember Egon Krenz—he ran the East German Komsomol. He came to visit the university in Leipzig. He ate in the college cafeteria—in a private room.

So my pal Mishka was elected deputy to the congress of the RSFSR, in 1990. He ran out of Sestroretsk. He called me and said, Listen, I'm a big deal here—if you're ready for it, we can elect you mayor. And I thought, why not? And went.

Did you ask yourself questions like, What the fuck do I need this for? What do I want to say by doing this?"

I usually don't ask such questions.

Oh, how refined!

When you start with that kind of question, it's over. You'll always come up with the same answer: "Don't do shit." Now my wife, she's always asking me questions like that. And she can stop me in my tracks. Because I have no answer—truly, none! Following her advice, using common sense, I start to think: I didn't do that because of this and that, and I didn't do that because of such and such, and I shouldn't have done that because—well, I shouldn't have done that, for sure… And so, according to my wife's method of approach, everything turns to crap. And nothing ever needs to be done.

But, that's how it is if you look at things philosophically.

Yes. But life is a chain of events. And if you listen to my wife, nothing will ever happen in your life. So I usually present my wife with a *fait accompli*.

It's a good thing you and I don't listen to your wife.

You're right. She's a wise and interesting person who cares about the good of our family. You just can't listen to her. After college I went to grad school—she was against that. She felt I should go work at a factory and, as a young specialist, get an apartment for the family. But I went to graduate school and lost all my chances of getting an apartment. So there. That's why we had to live cramped together in communal flats for eleven years.

In other words, you served society at the expense of your own personal gain and your family's welfare.

Yes. Then she was against my running for mayor. She said it was all bullshit.

Because you were passing up personal gain to serve—again!

Then she was against moving to Moscow. But we moved. And so on… She was against every significant event in our life!

She's probably against your drinking, too.

Well, of course. But why bring it up? Why ask me about drinking? Are you trying to fuck with me?

Who, me? You don't drink anymore. Practically.

I know. But why are you nagging me? I get it—you want to look good before my wife. But why? Come on, why?

Drop it, will you.

That was rather unsporting of you. Making references to my drinking.

Cut the shit. What do you mean unsporting! All wives are against drinking. Relax. It was just a simple joke.

A lowdown joke.

Enough. Stop blowing things out of proportion. Do you want me to say I'm an alcoholic?

Are you?

Yes. It's nothing to be ashamed of.

Please take note of this confession.

Svinarenko's Commentary:

By the way, I noticed long ago that whores and alcoholics never admit what they are. The whore tells a very believable story that she is just extra friendly or really loves the young men she knows. Or that she entertains them out of pity. Or out of an abstract love for humanity. And that they give her money—out of respect, or as a loan, or whatever the hell other story she can come up with. As for alcoholics, there's a whole system of denial, too. Like, Yes, I get drunk, but not every day. Or I do drink every day, but I don't lie around in alleys. Or I do lie around in alleys, but then I get up and go home. If a man lives in an alley, then his story is that he drinks because he's seeking the meaning of life and he sympathizes with the suffering of the people. And he can't just quietly accept the imperfections of this world. Only Omar Khayyam was capable of simply saying: "My friends! I drink because I like it, and when I'm drunk I feel like myself." So it turns out that whores and drunks are always someone else.

* * *

Kokh's Commentary:

There he goes again! What a louse. He knows that's a load of bull, but his base journalistic instincts make him pander to the consumer and give readers what he thinks they want.

When you're drunk, you are tempted to want to prolong that state. You have a series of feelings: I'm a well-off family man, I work hard and not without reward. Tomorrow I'll go back to work again. And I'll work—even though, to tell the truth, I don't really need to anymore. Work is no longer necessary in order to maintain a certain standard of living. I could choose a completely different kind of life. I could drop out of society. I could stop wearing suits and ties, stop shaving every day. I could become bedraggled. People wouldn't recognize me anymore. I could sleep in train stations, rummage in trash cans for food. I wouldn't feel pangs of conscience... Fighting over bottles, robbing shops, cyanotic girlfriends with horrible diseases... And most important, I wouldn't owe anyone a thing. I wouldn't want anything from anyone. I'd just be left alone...

And sometimes you drink more than you should. My quota, if you measure it in vodka, for example, is about 300-400 grams. Well, 500 max. No, that's probably too much. Somewhere around those numbers. So you drink, and you find yourself at the edge. And you look down... Deep inside there's a voice that says, let's have some more. Just another glass, another shot... And some more tomorrow. And more. Don't stop. You're on your way… Freedom… You've done everything that was expected of you… Let them leave you alone. You're on your way… Bloated face, coughing—endless coughing, liver pain, horrible headaches… And no way out. Freedom, in exchange for reason. You stand on the edge a while. You stand there. You spit into the abyss… You kick some pebbles and they fly off into nowhere… From down below, over the edge, comes the stink of cigarette butts extinguished in potato salad… The sound of an accordion… The squeals of drunken women… The endless blathering on about respect and honor…

A temptation? And how! To live and not think! Terrific. To have no responsibilities… Not even for loans-for-shares, may they rot in hell… To know only that you exist—and that's all…

So you stand on the edge of the abyss for a while, and then you go home. Only brave and ruthless men can become winos.

* * *

That's that, Alik. Let's move on. So you ran for mayor. What did you want? Fame? Living space? Privileges that we only heard talk about in those days?

Hard to say. I can't even figure it out now. It was a complex of wishes. First of all, I was vain, and I was certain that I would manage to save—

Sestroretsk.

—to save Russia.

Beat the Jews, save Sestroretsk.

No, I don't say that. I was never anti-Semitic.

As if I were? Who could accuse me of anti-Semitism? You could reproach me more for being a Judophile.

Svinarenko's Commentary:

When I worked at *Kommersant,* I was constantly asked to write on Jewish themes. And it was always the Jewish editors who commissioned these articles. Why? I guess they wanted a fresh opinion from an unbiased expert.

* * *

So, Alik, go on… You ran for mayor because—

I ran for mayor, because... The second reason was that I thought I could hasten the process of getting an apartment for us.

Is it far from St. Petersburg?

Forty kilometers. In the resort zone around the city. So, what other reasons were there? Deep in my heart, I wanted to test myself: Could I do all that?

So you went to the elections, and won.

I went and I won. In the first round. And there were seven candidates, I think.

What did you get them with?

I don't know.

Did you promise anything?

I had a concept—City by the Road. The distinguishing feature of Sestroretsk is that it's on the St. Petersburg–Helsinki highway. There are trucks, passengers, and so on. I thought that we would build all kinds of services along the road—restaurants, hotels. And the seashore is right there... Combine all that, and develop it.

Did you build anything?

I was only mayor for a year. We were just starting, just poised to go.

Why only a year? Why did you leave, where did you go?

That was in 1991. It was Sobchak's second appearance in my life.

To be mayor, you had to give up everything else, right?

Yes, I left my job teaching at the Polytechnic Institute.

Did you get an apartment as a result?

No. I lived in St. Petersburg, renting a room in a communal flat. And this is how I went to work: I'd take the metro to Chernaya River, where a car waited for me.

Why didn't it pick you up at home?

It was the anti-privileges campaign then.

I had forgotten completely.

It was terrible! I remember it.

And the war on privileges in your case was that you rode halfway on the metro and halfway in a black Volga? Half-measures, I must say, literally!

Yes. It was actually more complicated than that: I was allotted enough gas for the car to last through Thursday. There was no car at all on Friday.

Did you sympathize with this war on privileges?

No, I never liked it.

Because you sensed that you would have privileges anyway and so you were against being against them?

No, I saw that those privileges were a joke. They weren't privileges at all, in fact. I don't know, I never did see real privileges. I have no idea what services the General Secretary of the Central Committee of the Communist Party was afforded.

Did they give you sausage?

No. They gave me shit.

Did they give you more than the ration of sugar, so that you could make *samogon*?

No. I didn't make any then. No time. Plus the kiosks had all the booze you could want by then.

Alik, tell me—as an economist, but honestly. What was the 500 Day Program? Why was everyone going on about it? They discussed it seriously, and Grigory Yavlinsky, head of the Yabloko Party, was vice-premier for a while—before you, by the way. You were still running Sestroretsk while Grisha was already shining on the federal level. So?

Kokh's Commentary:

Grigory Alexeyevich Yavlinsky. That is the year he appeared, 1990. It can't be left without commentary. It remains in my memory. It was significant. It excited me.

You would think that I'd have all I need to write a big, beautiful, killer commentary. In any case, I have more material about Yavlinsky than about Latvians! But it isn't working for me.

Yavlinsky actually makes for strange material. He's flat somehow, not three-dimensional. There is no passion, no doubt in him. Occasionally, he graces the Tribune with his voice. But it's always so predictable, so wan. He lacks drive. "I told you so!" "I warned you!"—those are his standard moves. But has he lasted in politics? He has. What would be the point of describing the 500 Day Program now? Its sections and subsections... It was yet another program. Moderately reasonable. Moderately cautious. Moderately *naïve*. Who cares about the plan for an unfought battle? You and I are not historians, Igor. We want what Prosper Merimée called the aroma of the era! And the era is not scented by the 500 Days. It's just not. There is something else, though—the curly-haired young man with the unusual, inspired face. He spoke simply, ironically, a bit nasally. "We have great hopes for him" is what they say about people like him. Colossal potential. A great future.

I was a young, twenty-nine-year-old chairman of the regional executive committee, and that's what I thought about him, too. I was certain that in another month, or maybe a year, Yavlinsky would be prime minister (Ivan Silayev was no competition for him) and then president. And that would be right and good. And logical. Really, why shouldn't a young, energetic, professional, decent, and ambitious man have a career that would be good both for him and for the nation?

And then suddenly—bam! He quit! What, he quit on his own? Impossible! How could that be? I'm deep in the Sestroretsk shit fighting these local mediocrities. Shoveling the idiocy of village life with buckets (with my degree in economics), while that little sweetie gets into third position—and tells us how he no longer wishes to work because they did not accept his program! Who does he think he is, the leader of the nobility? Hold your horses, fellow! You have to keep fighting, persuading, getting people to switch to your side. There are people in local areas who can give you support. Use us. We'll raise awareness. Hold rallies (that was very popular in those days). What is this kindergarten nonsense—if you don't want to play, I'm leaving. Don't pay attention to those jerks. We want your 500 Day Plan. Tell us what to do. Command us! We'll do it, we're ready.

But, no, he left. Too bad. He was a fine fellow... How did I know? That's how it seemed. My friends—Russian deputies—shouted over the phone at me: "Guess who we just elected to be Silayev's first deputy in economics? You can't imagine! Grisha Yavlinsky! He's a great guy!" I believed them. They were in Moscow. They could see better.

But maybe it was just a tactical move on his part, like Kutuzov retreating before Napoleon? Back off now, and then, wham! Return on a white steed!... That looked like a good possibility to me. So I thought, let's keep an eye on him—and then, just as I had predicted, he began traveling around the regions. That meant I was right, and he was going to fight.

It was December, 1990. I got a call from Chubais (who was first deputy chairman of the Leningrad Executive Committee then). "Yavlinsky is coming to Sestroretsk! He'll be meeting the people there. Prepare everything as it should be."

No worries, sir. We'll welcome him properly. I had a can of red caviar tucked away somewhere. My wife said, "I'm not giving it up!" (It was 1990.) Who cares! I took it without any ado. A bottle of Armenian cognac hidden in the office. Slices of salami and cheese (my heart was bleeding). We arranged his speech at the cinema and then went back to my office, for a heart-to-heart conversation. Then I would find out everything. How the enemies in horrible Moscow had gobbled up our hero of reform. (That's the way it always is in Russia; they stifle the talented ones.)

My secretary said over the intercom—he's driven up! They're bringing him in! There was a whole crowd on the first floor. Hello, Grigory Alexeyevich! How could they do that to you? What are they thinking about in Moscow? The little old ladies were all atwitter. One skinny one said, Sonny, let me give you a hug! The bastards! We're all behind you! Hurrah! Where are you going? I'm going to be at the movie theater right now, in a half hour, will you come? Of course, of course, Grigory Alexeyevich!

We went into my office. I only then noticed that he was accompanied by a young female reporter. Ugly and red-haired. She looked at him adoringly. A thought flashed through my head: There's nothing between them. For now? No time to think about nonsense. I had to ask the main questions. About life. What will happen next. And in general. What, in general? Who the hell knows! But I had to ask him questions. A man like that in front of you, you fool, and you say nothing?

"Some cognac?" (Jerk! Couldn't think of anything better? Just getting drunk? He has to give a speech now.)

"Thanks!" (Oh-ho. Not bad.)

I poured, we drank. Had a bite. Meaningless phrases: How are things, not bad, we're doing what we can. The other day, chickens arrived at the market; I went with the police to keep the crowds in line. They didn't want them to close up the store for the night (with good reason)—they thought the sales people would steal it all overnight. We set up a night watch at the refrigerator: two deputies and a policeman and shut the store. The crowd grumbled but went home.

I can see he's getting bored. Lord, what I am going on about. He must hear stories like this all over Russia. I'm bothering him with my nonsense. We should be talking about the important things. And I should show him that I'm educated. So that he would see that we may be in the sticks, but we're no fools. Oh, time's running out. He's going to go to his meeting. Come on, Alik! Say something! I'm going to go home and my wife will say, "Well, how was it?" And what am I going to say—we talked about chickens? How stupid can you be? You'll never be anything more than town mayor. Oh, boy. Oops, time to go. That's it. Maybe you'd like to come back after the meeting? We'll finish the bottle. Can't let the caviar go to waste.

The auditorium was packed. Noise. He came out. Well-lit. Curly hair. Burning eyes. Nervous line of the lips. He looks smart. Profound. Handsome. He tossed his head. Looked out at the audience. He face bore the right combination of weariness and sorrow. A slight smile (also appropriate: It symbolized optimism). An ovation. Ovation. Not stopping. Ovation. He raised his hand. The room hushed.

You can kill me, but I don't remember what he said. Something about helping the needy. About humanitarian aid. That we needed special committees for equitable distribution of aid. That first we had to create elementary order. Something about the fight against privileges. In great detail. And now, let me answer your questions.

The questions sent up to the stage in notes written by the audience were also about privileges. Then about garden allotments—everyone should have one, right, Grigory Alexeyevich? Of course. It's important. Thank you for that good question. The economy is in decline… But not everything is lost… Everyone should, in his own place…

Suddenly, a crazy thought: "Does he think we're all idiots?" I chased it away: "This must be how you're supposed to talk to the people. Learn from him! Otherwise you'll never win the people's love, you jerk."

Another ovation. He stood around, took bows. Words of gratitude for his support: "It helps me in my struggle." (Another seditious thought—what struggle?) " It gives me strength"… Even more applause. The little old ladies asked for autographs. The girls in the aisles were all flushed. Lowered their eyes. You could tell they liked him.

We went back into my office. The girl reporter was with him. I poured her some cognac, too. We drank, we ate. Can I give you a ride? Where? To the Leningrad Executive Committee offices. To see Chubais. I thought, excellent, we'll talk on the way.

No, he put the reporter in the back with him and me in the front with the driver. Said he had to give an interview. Hm… If he has to, he has to. So much for talking. How can you talk with the back of your head? I sat there in silence. We didn't finish the bottle. The caviar would go to waste (I'd have to call to have someone put it in the fridge). What a jerk—I just went on and on about my stupid chickens.

The reporter squealed in the back. Movement. Hee-hee. What is your opinion of Yeltsin's latest statement? Hee-hee. What is there to say? He should drink less. Ha-ha! Don't turn around and look! I sat still as a statue. Maybe I was imagining things. You always measure people by your own failings....

I brought them to the mayor's office. Let them out of the car. Good-bye. It was a pleasure to meet you. And for me, especially... I won't wash my hand now that he's shaken it. Maybe Chubais will have a different conversation with him, about substantive things?

I called Chubais in the morning. How did it go? Did you talk? You know, it was the damndest thing. He kept on about humanitarian aid and privileges. And about garden allotments, for everyone... That's what he said here, too. ... How many people were you? About five, just the team. That's really weird. Maybe he doesn't trust us? Who can he trust then? That's true, too.

Well, all right. So long. So long.

I read the memoirs of the late Soviet premier, Valentin Pavlov, *Did We Miss Our Chance?* It goes into detail on the years 1989 to 1991. About the collapse of the banking system, the currency revaluation, the miners' strikes. About Gorbachev (not very nice). About Yeltsin. About Silayev. About Filshin (remember him and the Harvest-1990 checks?). About everything. Rather subjectively, of course. But I liked it. He wasn't one of us, certainly, but he had his own position, and he wasn't a coward. There isn't a word about Yavlinsky. As if he hadn't existed.

I read Kostikov's *Affair with the President.* Not a word about Yavlinsky. As if he hadn't existed. Just one mention, and only of the fact that during the 1993 coup, Vice-President Rutskoi and Parliament Speaker Khasbulatov included him in their list for the cabinet they planned to create when they overthrew Yeltsin.

Russian memoir writing dropped off around 1990. But even so, there is nothing at all about Yavlinsky.

He's pushing fifty-two now. No longer a boy. No longer young and promising. It's time to start wrapping things up instead of looking toward the future. But there's nothing to wrap up. He's a *raisonneur.* That used to be a stock character in the old Russian theater: Dikobrazov, Jr., travels around Russia. Everyone's used to him. He's used to himself. The girl reporters squeal. The old ladies twitter. His curls are still black. His face inspired. But those bags under his eyes... Should he use make up? More make up? Or not? His admirers no longer notice anything... They love him. And wait. He's talented, the bastard! He'll still show you. He'll give you that kick! You just don't know him.

We know him. We do .... He won't. It's over.

* * *

All right, Igor: Now that I finished the commentary, why don't you tell me about your life in 1990!

At the start of the year I continued working with the Youth Housing Complex system and published an industry magazine called *Archipelago*.

Gulag?

No, just *Archipelago*. The idea was this: The special youth housing apartments are scattered all over the country like islands, but they're part of a single system. People come up with concepts, start up experimental schools. There were conferences, in Alma-Ata for example. We would go, talk, drink... It ended up with people using Komsomol benefits to start up normal businesses. Some of them grew up to become serious businessmen. It's business, not Komsomol work. So, I was doing this magazine. I worked on it and worked on it... Until summer. And in the summer I thought: It's time to move from an industrial magazine to some serious media projects. And so it was summer, and ... Did you smoke then?

Yes.

Then you must remember that there were no cigarettes. Long lines...

Chubais had to put down tobacco revolts, when they would block all of Nevsky Prospect. He was first deputy chairman of the Leningrad Executive Committee then.

Ah, they blamed him for that, too! I remember standing in those long lines. And then one of my friends had a visitor from Germany. She had studied in Russia, they'd had an affair; she graduated and went home, but then missed him, took a vacation and came back to Russia to love him some more. And since my family was in the country for the summer, I let her live in my apartment.

You were a married man by then, don't forget!

She was my friend's German, not mine! I didn't screw her, naturally. Honest! I would tell you. So she lived in my place, cooked and cleaned— which was very convenient—and my friend would come over sometimes for a date. She was a Russophile; she studied the language and was very interested in Russian life. So one day I said, "Fuck you, you're a

Russophile! Go study Russian life in its natural form!" "Where?" "Where else? In the line for cigarettes. That's where the great Russian nation stands and speaks the truth about what it's thinking." She went among the people with pleasure. So she would stand in line, talk to the men, gleaning all kinds of stories, and come back with five packs of Belomor. That was the limit per person.

So you got through the crisis easily.

Even better! Since she didn't just stand in line for Belomors but sometimes also went to the hard-currency Beriozka store and brought me Gitanes—despite all my protests, since I told her to buy only booze there. Unfiltered. That's the best thing I ever smoked in my life. When I smoked.

And Gauloises.

Well… It was so cool in 1990 to be smoking Gitanes and drinking Bols gin, the cheapest gin from Holland! And then she left. And that's when I decided, thinking about life, to see Andrei Vasilyev. We had worked together at *Sobesednik*, and I remembered that he was always where the money was, so I asked him where I should look for work. And he said, Come work for us, we have this newspaper, *Kommersant*. No, I said, that's a financial paper, economics, boring, and I know nothing about it. No, no, we cover everything. All right, I said, let's meet on Friday. He said, You'll learn soon enough that Friday's don't work. (That's when they put the paper to bed, and it took all day and all night, sometimes even two days.) Let's meet on Monday, early in the morning, around noon. So I went to his place on Monday, bringing a bottle of *samogon*. And he's got a case of wine and a case of cognac.

Right, people used to buy them by the case then.

No, they didn't, not then, Alik, no one had that kind of money. You've forgotten the life of ordinary people… Two bottles were considered a lot of money—you would buy one and then go out again for the other, if you had to. So, we drank… And on Tuesday I dropped in on him at work, on Khoroshevkoe. And he said, Listen, there's a hole in the issue, help us out, could you write an article? I went to the Rossiya Hotel, where people from all over the country had set up a tent city. They would lurk in wait for deputies who were living in the hotel and complain to them about life. Come on, help us out, you creeps, we elected you and all you do is enjoy your privileges. So, I wrote this bracing report. And so, little by little, I started working in the "Miscellaneous" department. It included everything that wasn't about economics or politics.

Svinarenko's Commentary:

I've talked about this in a newspaper interview. It took three days to put an issue to bed; people slept on the floor, on newspapers; we had a driver with an Altai car radio who would drive to all the liquor stores and then call to see who wanted what. We were paid on time and a lot. I was attracted by the personnel who made the decisions. I liked it, and I stayed.

As for Vasilyev—who'd been at *Kommersant* from the start, since 1989—he described it this way: "I realized that there was a completely different kind of journalism. That we were dealing in information. See, we were doing a weekly newspaper with ease. Nobody could beat us on the topics that interested us. *Kommersant* came out on Monday, and the other papers came out with their stuff too late. That was the real high for us, of course. It was great that everybody raved about the paper—it was some product! It was all very cool. You have to understand— I felt that I was a participant in that paper, for the first time. That was the drive for me. It was a whole new quality of life for me, I guess."

* * *

So what department were you in, Igor? "Miscellaneous"? I thought you worked in the crime section!

That was later. The crime section was created later. I was moved to the sector that was lagging behind. And that's just when the trial of Kostya Ostashvili began—the first trial in the perestroika era for anti-Semitism.

Svinarenko's Commentary:

I couldn't understand the trial at all. He didn't beat up Jews, he didn't burn down synagogues… What were they picking on him for? What were they trying to prove? That we were big democrats? That Pamyat was a scary nationalist organization? Who was threatened by it, anyway?

* * *

Now, why don't you talk about how you used to repair the sewers in Sestroretsk, Alik?

Hmm… Not very well. They suggested I get a first deputy, a fellow called Baranov, and he repaired them. I didn't.

Did people offer you money?

Yes. It turned out that the main business there was allotting land parcels for individual buildings. This was the resort area for St. Petersburg! On the shore of Lake Razliv. Or the shore of the Bay of Finland. People brought me money. I was so surprised.

What did a *sotka* go for?

I don't remember now. The point is that land was allocated by a decision of the local council. The deputies divvied everything up together. Therefore, bribing me was useless, because I decided nothing. So, I didn't turn it into a business, but in this particular case I can't attribute my honesty to any personal effort.

To sum up, you didn't repair the sewers, and you didn't take bribes.

They quickly stopped offering me bribes. Apparently, they began giving them to somebody else. I had always voted for personal allotments anyway, out of ideological considerations. So they had my vote for free.

So, Alik, you gave away land in Sestroretsk the way Shevardnadze gave away Soviet lands. He would have given them away with or without a bribe…

The local elected deputies hated me and tried to interfere in my work… I questioned myself: Maybe I'm wrong about something, maybe my destiny is wrong. There were these two deputies—I'm not going to give their names here, because they have children and living relatives—they really tormented me, they wouldn't let me live in peace. After I left, one died in a car crash, the other of cancer.

What did they do to you?

They kept arranging for reviews of my work. They kept looking for corruption. They didn't find anything, naturally. And the falsified documents! Once, they even signed my name to a document. And then attacked me for signing it.

Maybe that was their way of fighting for truth and justice?

Maybe. Imagine it. A man runs for election, promising to battle corruption ruthlessly. He's elected a deputy, and there's no corruption. He has to battle something, doesn't he?

Is this a hint about the present situation or something?

The situation is always the same. If there are no facts, they make them up.

They could have just said, Dear voters, there is no corruption. Sorry.

Can you imagine that?

Well, it wouldn't be a very strong move.

So. Then what the hell did we elect you for? We know for sure that there is corruption. And you're not fighting it. How can that be? We have our Russian voter, and this is his world view: One—The country is very rich. The richest in the world. That's an axiom that does not require proof. It's beaten into his head from kindergarten. Then—But the man lives poorly. That does not require analysis, either. What are the causes of poverty... The country is rich, but its people are poor. The elected official and the establishment keep telling everyone how they take care of the poor people. The conclusion that seems most appropriate is that something got stolen on the way to the people. So then a candidate says: Elect me, and you will be rich. And after he's elected, it turns out there is no corruption. A strange elected official!

So what did you do in Sestroretsk, Mr. Mayor, besides voting for dachas, for free?

Well, I did manage to do a thing or two. There wasn't very much one could do in those days. But a balanced budget, we did that. As I recall, the revenue was 18 million rubles.

How did you create the budget—did you sit there and write it yourself? You are an economist, after all.

I had a financial expert writing it, too.

And I thought you never trusted anyone to do anything and did it all yourself... Did you feel that you were being tested, that you had to show everyone the era of happiness had come at last?

No, no. Things were clear from the start.

You mean, you came, looked around, and saw that you wouldn't be able to start a revolution.

The staff of the executive committee was mostly female. I had never seen anything like it before in my life—all the ladies were willing to give it up...You know, women. And I'm the boss.

It's a simple biological law: The females have to have sex with the alpha male of the pack. To better the species. Otherwise, there's mutiny and collapse.

Yes. I kept trying to avoid them... But it was very difficult. All these not bad-looking, slightly over-the-hill women—you know, around thirty-five. Some quite serious, with big asses. I was twenty-nine then. You can't imagine how they dressed, how they bent over. The skirts kept getting shorter and shorter, the tights blacker and blacker... The lipstick brighter and brighter... No one overtly tried to get into my trousers, but they made it clear that if I wanted it, they wouldn't object. It was horrible.

Did you learn anything new then about life or the country?

A lot.

That is, you were a kitchen liberal; you could criticize the regime along the lines of well, if I were in charge I would put things in order and establish a kingdom of justice... But when you dealt with reality and got some authority yourself, you saw that they hadn't been so bad after all, those Soviet leaders...

Yes. And when I met with the apparat—it's called the "apparat," hence "apparatchik"—I understood what rampant bureaucracy is. It's been there a thousand years. But that's a different story, a separate one...

You mean you're working off the moral capital you accrued.

I got some more after that, too. Let's just say that I started accumulating then. I mean moral capital. I learned how to master that mechanism. And I feel that we mastered it rather effectively. Because in the final analysis, when we started working on the federal level, there was an apparat there, too. And we worked with that without any problem.

Now, Igor, what about the reunification of Germany? What did you think—you're our Germanist, after all.

I had almost gone there for the paper in the fall of 1990 to cover it, but our slowpokes didn't manage to get me a visa in time. Otherwise, I would have written about it... On the one hand, I was a Germanist, yes, but on the other, I was a dissident element. And I thought that the Communists in East Germany should have been quashed. It was *naïve* of me, I know...There were so many people there who loved life in the GDR! I had so many discussions with them about it. I would say, You know the GDR

is just nonsense, the real country is the FRG. They would take umbrage. And at the same time, they were surprised. How could it be that socialism was fully built in the USSR but life was poorer there than in the GDR, where socialism was merely sketched in. They found that strange. I explained to them, Listen, you halfwits, we have developed socialism and we have fuck-all. Precisely because socialism isn't developed fully, it's still possible to live in your country. You can have a drink, and eat, and buy shoes... Anywhere where the Bolsheviks aren't allowed to have power, things are in good shape. And you get packages from the other side, you faggots, with chocolate, jeans, disposable diapers, and toilet paper—everything that people need to live on top of bread, milk, and matches. Almost all of them got these parcels, since the majority of Germans lived in the West, from where they wanted to send the minority trapped in the Soviet prison of the GDR—their relatives—a pair of jeans that they could buy for 10 marks on sale... After hearing my explanation, the GDR patriots would open their eyes wide: Oh, shit, why didn't we figure that out for ourselves?

What's their relationship now?

Not very good. The eastern Germans are hurt that the western ones aren't helping them out enough. Even though they've sent in tons of money. In general, they are two different nations.

Sort of like blacks and whites.

Like that. They just can't merge. There are more fascists in East Germany than in the West. They beat up Jewish settlers. Have you heard that they're building an amusement park for the East Germans, the Ossi, called the GDR?

No.

A huge park with rides. And there will be goods from the GDR, police in old GDR uniforms, Trabant cars driving around—those little plastic cars—and you have to exchange money for East German marks at the entrance. The beer they used to have... Strange that we don't have a USSR park here, it would be a huge success. Should we build one, Alik?

Also, in 1990 I wrote an article about Katya Lycheva, whom Gorbachev presented as a counterpart to Samantha Smith, the American girl who wrote a peace letter to Gorbachev. She tried to bring peace to the Near East, and that was amusing. I found Katya... She was a grown young woman, with a sweet figure....

They say she's Gorbachev's niece.

Who knows. I went to their house. They were all sitting there, so scholarly, politically correct, refined—and there I was. Our conversation wasn't going anywhere. Her father was sitting silently in the corner. So I said to him, "Oh, look, quite by accident I have a bottle of *samogon* in my pocket! Maybe we could have a little drink?" What could they do? They set the table to go with the drink. Everyone perked up, the conversation flowed, they invited me to stop by anytime. Back then I was still trying to distill my own...

You know, Alik, 1990 was a transitional period: There was already money for travel abroad, but you still made your own *samogon*. That dwindled to nothing very quickly. You smoked either Belomor or Gitanes. That's what you economists call multi-structural character.

That's right. So you did get to travel, not yet to France, but already to Egypt.

I also remember buying a semi-automatic washing machine, paying more than the list price and adding a bribe. It was called an Erika or Eureka, something like that.

Vyatka.

No, the Vyatka is fully automatic, this was only semi-automatic. I even used it once myself. And I also had to find people to work for the paper. I tried to lure many of my friends, but they wouldn't go.

Oh!

First, they'd say, It's not clear what you're doing there—some kind of unofficial paper, a private shop! You'll shut down any day. Second, You have to work hard there, which is not very pleasant. People spend the night at the office...Who cares if they pay more? We can get two and even three hundred rubles a month for doing nothing, and work on the side—while you guys work with no days off. Who needs that? At first, I was truly amazed. I was talking to progressive people, I thought. People meant to be liberals and pro-market. People from a free profession! But, no. Then what can you expect from other, less advanced people? How can you expect them to want, and be ready for, a market economy?

In those days, the newspaper office was on Khoroshevka, in an apartment building, on the first floor. We had computers with black and white monitors; we had an intercom and even a fax machine. And everybody kept asking: "How do you get away with writing shit like that? How does it get past the censors?" We replied, "There is no censorship." "Impossible! How do you get the printers to accept your order?" You can come to terms with everyone, we explained.

Before working there, I used to write long articles. A whole page in a broadsheet. And suddenly, at *Kommersant,* they turned these long things into small ones, where ten of them would fit inside one of my old ones... And they weren't bad. At first I was hurt: How can they edit my stuff like that? But I understood that it was a different language, not like the old newspaper language. I clenched my teeth and determined to learn it. I figured I would know two languages. I'd write sometimes in one and sometimes in the other. I learned the new newspaper language and realized that it was impossible to keep writing in the old one.

By the way, at that time I worked side by side with Gleb Pavlovsky—I saw him often. He was one of the founders of an information cooperative called Fakt, out of which *Kommersant* grew. No one knew then that Gleb would end up running Kremlin policy. He may be the only dissident to rise to that height.

Svinarenko's Commentary:

For a while *Kommersant* was considered a cult phenomenon. Vladimir Yakovlev, the founder, explained how it began:

> ... A friend of mine decided to make money and started with a cooperative that was going to knit sweaters. He asked me to help get the coop registered. It was an endlessly complex operation, and we agreed that I would do it, as an *Ogonyok* reporter, as a kind of experiment. They knew nothing about it at the magazine. I fought the good fight at the Moscow Executive Committee; I pushed documents through various offices. And I realized I liked doing it. The cooperative got registered, and it started working. I had the sweater we used (to learn how to knit) for a very long time... Our sweater cooperative was the second or third in Moscow... Fakt was born as a response to questions from future cooperatives.
>
> Fakt was rather famous and basically financially stable. One of the few cooperatives that sold various kinds of information. Those sales did not bring in a lot of money. We supplemented in different ways: for example, reselling computers, which by then was a popular and profitable business.
>
> We were all learning. We made a lot of mistakes and we paid for them, some with our lives. The foundation of success is not mistakes, as people say, but labor. Blood and deceit are the basis of bankruptcies. This, naturally, does not apply to the criminal sphere.
>
> [I] moved from Fakt cooperative to the *Kommersant* newspaper also by accident. Cooperatives were springing up like mushrooms. A movement began to create a

Union of Cooperatives. Partially as a response to social pressure, but even more so as a power struggle between various groups. Artem Tarasov suggested making a newspaper for cooperative owners. At first I just shrugged: a silly idea. [A little later] I played hard to get, and then I agreed.

A few more things happened that year, on the level of state affairs. Almost simultaneously, several fundamentally important and symbolic acts took place: The first McDonald's in the USSR opened in Moscow; the Warsaw Pact was ended; and the last Soviet troops left Afghanistan.

Then, in 1990 citizenship was returned to—guess who? Exiled cellist Mstislav Rostropovich; his wife, Galina Vishnevskaya; and Aleksandr Solzhenitsyn.

Attention! A session of the Supreme Soviet was held in May 1990. There was a serious conversation, or so it seemed to many and perhaps to everyone, about a transition to a market economy. You will laugh, but the main speaker was Ryzhkov—not today's young politician, Vladimir, but Nikolai Ryzhkov, a government figure. This is how he saw it: The transition will take six years, maybe even eight. He figured the first stage would take three. By 1993, instead of the shooting up of the White House, the Communist economists were predicting the completion of preparations for the economy to switch tracks, and planning "to create the infrastructure of the market economy" [what beast is that?] and even to privatize a few things—they used a virginal, shy term for it, "de-governmentalization." (Just as previous theoreticians had expected the construction of Communism in the country by 1980, instead of the Olympics). Then, after another three years of this lovefest, the Communists planned on "more dynamic measures for transition to the market." Amusingly, Yeltsin condemned this program—he said it would "lead the people to impoverishment." That was just yesterday. A historically insignificant, tiny amount of time has passed. But think of the rate of maturation. Just a year earlier, people with transistor radios were thrilled to bits by the Congress; and now, you have "infrastructure" and "dynamic measures." Grab the bull by the horns, and build a new society! According to the plan!

The Twenty-Eighth, and final—how pleasant to recall that fact—Congress of the Communist Party took place in 1990. On an alternative basis—it was the will of the times. Not just one candidate, but a bunch. One of the eight candidates vying for the position of General Secretary of the Party was a certain Stolyarov, a colonel and assistant professor of the Gagarin Air Force Academy. He distinguished himself by saying these passionate words to Gorby: "Break out of the vicious circle of nomenklatura, and you will be surrounded by unique, sparkling, bold, seeking, and thinking people... A strong leader acquires commensurate aides, while a weak one seeks ones like him." (Alik, when you heard him, you must have thought that Gorbachev would see sense and call you, invite you to work with him in the Kremlin.) It wasn't a bad line, in the spirit of Confucius. Gorby must have shat himself. He thought: Who let this guy talk, who the hell is he? He's going to say so much more in a minute! That well-meaning Stolyarov was later elected to the Communist Party of the RSFSR. He made yet another prediction: "Without the regime, we won't get a market economy, but just a parody of it. An immature democracy is capable of turning back into what we had rejected. We could either return to a totalitarian past or to what the wise Plato called the chaos of arrogance and anarchy." Funny, right?

Whatever happened to Stolyarov? It would be good to find him and hear him lecture us again!

10.

1991

The Tenth Bottle

In 1991 both authors were busy trying to save the Homeland—at least, they thought they were. And what's wrong with that? The year 1991 is exactly the midway point of our twenty-year period (1982-2001).

Alik! When the year began, we had no idea how it would end. My plans did not include changing the political regime. I remember my mood then: As long as everything was allowed, I thought I should do something, go somewhere, make some money... I was bustling around ... People were everywhere. I met with Telman Gdlyan, the prosecutor fired for exposing corruption in the Party; with Artem Tarasov, one of the earliest millionaires in the USSR; with some prosecutors from Chechnya—I remember drinking with them in the café of some cheap Moscow hotel. That was considered cool. They were drunk, and guns spilled out of their pockets. It was stifling, dark, with Soviet velvet curtains on the café windows... I don't remember what I was talking about with these people, what they wanted from the crime department.

And there were so many Americans then, so many reporters! They were from places like Milwaukee—they were basically nobodies and wanted to become somebodies in a wild country. The basic approach of these Americans from whatever farm in the Midwest was: "I've come for three days to Moscow, to find Communist Party gold and become rich and famous." Naturally, they spoke no Russian, but this didn't stop them. And they were right: knowing Russian would not have increased the amount of Party gold they found. I have to tell you that these American detectives were offering as much as $50 for our help.

Sure, Igor—They all thought they were being original, finding the Party gold. And there were thousands of those originals.

And the Milwaukee journalists were all thinking, no one else would ever think to come and find the hidden Party gold and report on it. I'll write the only story on it, and then go home to my Mary and her fat ass.

But there was one among them, David Remnick, who was not a self-taught poseur from Portland, Oregon, but a real correspondent for the *Washington Post,* accredited in Moscow. A career journalist. He would call me once in a while, asking for a consultation. Well, why not give one? So we'd sit and drink, the way you and I are now—we used to call that a consultation. (Now we call it writing a book!)

Years later in a bookstore in New York I saw a whole shelf of books by American journalists. A man spends a few years in Moscow and comes to understand all of Russia, and then goes home and describes this Russia he has understood in books. Nothing bad about that at all. I've seen that often in America, that un-Russian high valuation of the fruits of your labor. I remember seeing a bright picture on the wall of an American house. I said to the hostess, "Judging by the expensive frame, that must a major work by a master of abstract art. Is it?" No, she said, I bought a new printer recently and I was trying out its various effects. I was about to throw away the piece of paper but then thought, I spent half an hour on this. Let's keep it.

After that lesson, I started treating my own texts with more respect. Look how many I've released in book form...Yes, there were all those Americans hanging around with us. I remember one invited me over to have a drink. At his home, a rented apartment on one of the boulevards. I went. I thought, I'll show up with a bottle, the American and I will sit down in his kitchen, he'll slice up the salami and take out tumblers, and the two of us will sit there, drink vodka, and discuss the fate of Russia, out-shouting each other. Instead, there were fifty guests there, wandering around the apartment and drinking whiskey in plastic glasses. Considerately, he even invited some Norwegian coeds. Now, I understand that this was a typical American party, but back then I thought it was a unique, one-off event. I thought that this man had invented a fundamentally new technology for spending time. I kept waiting for all those strange people to leave so we could get back to the plan—drinking in the kitchen and arguing about all kinds of crap. But I left late, and the rest were still there, chattering. That whole year was theatrical. Burlesque, masquerade, travesty…

Yes, Igor, I remember there was money revaluation—in April, I think. It was very interesting. As chairman of the Executive City Committee, I was appointed chairman of the Currency Exchange Commission. Besides me, there was a KGB man, a prosecutor, and the chairman of the finance committee.

They had so many of you so things would stay serious?

Yes, but everything was screwed up right away. Business as usual.

Did you make any money on it?

Nothing, zip. Because I exchanged everybody's cash. And didn't charge anything. That was my determination—to make this reform fail. Frankly, I don't understand what the point was. They thought that some people would be ashamed to reveal what they had, so they'd sanitize the circulation of money. You understand, right? But people brought everything they had. People brought in ruble bills for 50,000, even 100,000 rubles.

Did you have enough cash on hand to give them new bills?

No. Why should we? It was done through Sberbank. I only signed off.

And why did you decide to make that reform fail?

Because I felt it was swinish to take away people's money. How's that for a reason! It was very, very interesting.

Kokh's Commentary:

The end of the Soviet Union. 1991. Our book falls into two equal parts: ten bottles about the Soviet Union, and ten bottles about Russia. We hadn't planned it that way, but that's how it happened. The magic of numbers… Fucking amazing.

Fear, habit, and romantic demons. It's time to sum up the first half. What did Gorbachev's course mean for the country? Was the collapse inevitable? Were perestroika and glasnost the free choices of a titan, or was Gorbachev a hostage to circumstance? In the range of these questions, Finance Minister Pavlov's change of currency is nothing more than a pathetic mote in a sea of events. But the mote is very characteristic, demonstrating the fragility of the regime and its unconditional notionality.

As I've said before, power is only a particle of the thin layer of civilization that covers the turbulent universe of the human herd. The demons of freedom, anarchy, and destruction can be shackled only by fear and habit. When fear vanishes and habit is called into question, the demons burst out—and the man in street can only pray that the escapees keep their human victims to a minimum.

How it all started:

Gorbachev became the leader of the Soviet Union in 1985. The country was producing approximately 600 million tons of oil a year, plus around 500 billion cubic meters of gas—plus metals, forestry, and so on, in approximately the same amounts as now. But don't forget, that was together with Kazakhstan, Ukraine, and other republics. On the territory of the RSFSR they were producing about as much oil as now—around 400 million tons—even though now we get more natural gas, about 520 billion cubic meters. On the whole, the USSR had a fairly stable economy with a clear emphasis on raw materials. The faults of the economy included dependence on imports for food products and the fact that the manufacturing and processing industries, as well as the sphere of scientific research and experimentation, were horribly militarized.

At that time the USSR was beginning to lag behind the leading countries of the globe, particularly in information technology. It was understood that further lagging could have a fatal effect on the preservation of military parity, and a decision was made to improve Soviet high-tech by a great leap. It will become clear why this (apparently correct) decision turned out to be a turning point in the history of our country and how it is what marked the point of no return; this decision, in fact, was what destroyed the Soviet Union.

The decision was extremely subjective, based as it was not on consumer demand but on the fetishization of military parity. This fetish belonged to the ruling elite of the time, which could not clearly state why it needed that parity. But that's what makes a fetish a fetish—it cannot be explained logically. What is expedient in one generation becomes the rule of the next—and a fetish in the one after that. Stalin's foolish militarism, based on the theory of attacking the West, was expedient within the framework of that value system, since there was every chance of success. The militarism that was the rule under Khrushchev and Brezhnev was at least not harmful, since it was at least minimal stimulus for scientific and technological progress. Gorbachev's militarism, which had degenerated into a mania for military parity, could not be explained by anyone, including Gorbachev: a classic case of fetishism.

One way or another, the program for the accelerated development of high technology—in electronics, robotics, and communications—was approved. Gosplan began allocating huge resources, starting with the construction of new factories; research institutes were developed, and new departments were opened in universities, and so on. In those days it was fashionable to call this an "integrated multi-branched program." It required the mass purchases of Western equipment: Significant funds in hard currency were expended. The Soviet Union, like a big, clumsy bulldozer, creaking and belching smoke, began to turn in the indicated direction. No one was worried by that maneuver. Everything went on as usual, as had happened many times before. When they were told to create metallurgy, they did. When they were told to exploit the oil fields in Western Siberia, they did. When they were told to fly into space, they did.

The propaganda machine went into high gear: Hurrah for scientific and technological progress! We'll catch up to Japan in the number of robotic technology complexes. The personal computer is not a luxury but a necessity for work!

But things were not as simple as they seemed. It turned out that you need a completely different manufacturing culture for high technology. The qualification level of the personnel, both rank-and-file and engineering, had to be much higher. It can't be said that there weren't any people like that in the Soviet Union. Of course there were, many of them. But they were all employed in industries created by Stalin and Beria: atomic, space, aviation, and a few others. They could not be moved wholesale—that would destroy military parity, too. In other words, new cadres had to be trained and old cadres re-educated. A colossal task!

The Stalin scenario (two kinds of prisons: special prisons that were really scientific institutes on the one hand, and ordinary prison camps on the other) could not help Gorbachev with the personnel issues he faced. Instead of the stick, he had only the carrot. The carrot called for higher salaries, new housing, better food, good quality clothing, better quality white goods. So more money was allocated to build plants and buy imported equipment. The bulldozer—with a groan—turned in this direction, too, building growth in the production of household goods.

The imagination of future engineers had to be developed, so they were given a more varied spiritual diet to replace the stagnation period's worn-out cud. That meant sharply improving the quality of domestic film, literature, and television. It meant admitting the inevitability of a partial opening of the Iron Curtain, if only on the pop-culture level for the time being. And that meant additional expenditures, however slight.

Thus, a maneuver that was intended to be local and harmless touched almost every sphere of Soviet life, and the country that had become completely stagnant and seemed impervious to any external force began to change—first gradually, and then with increasing acceleration. That maneuver, in close company with the

Chernobyl catastrophe, demanded ever more colossal expenditures—which naturally had an effect on the budget. Together with defense spending, this created an enormous rise in expenses.

What was happening on the revenue side? By then, the West had gone through the energy crisis. They had developed energy-saving technology and economic car engines. New sources of oil had been exploited: the North Sea, the Gulf of Mexico, and so on. The Persian Gulf countries had sharply increased their output. This led to a fall in oil prices, which meant a decrease in income for the Soviet budget. Enthralled by the idea of creating a new man for the post-industrial society, an educated and efficient man who could create high-tech products, our leaders suddenly discovered (what a shock!) that the Soviet man drank like a pig. A phantasmagoric battle against drinking and alcoholism was unfurled. We can skip the details. We all remember the excellent spirits of the leaders, and alcohol-free weddings, and teapots filled with cognac, and the taste of cologne, and the moonshine *samogon*, mentioned more than once. It is important to note that the decrease in alcohol consumption (and consequently, in the production of alcohol) was a blow to the budget revenues. When I was vice-premier of the country, one of my responsibilities was the collection of the alcohol tax. I pulled out the statistics for the years before this period. Revenues from alcohol sales made up approximately 20 percent of the annual budget. Once the citizenry could no longer buy alcohol, they used their money to buy other products and wiped all the shelves clean in the stores. Shortages ensued.

Any idiot can see that the issue of budget deficits was only a matter of time. How was it covered? By three things. First—Western loans. They totaled approximately $100 billion. Second—Unsecured credits (essentially, the printing of cash) by Gosbank. That led to a total deficit of everything. Third, and finally—In early 1991, Pavlov took five-year credits (essentially taking money away from citizens) from Sberbank and Gosstrakh (more on that below).

Let's look at the picture: A huge number of factories are being built; millions of dollars' worth of imported equipment has been bought. Millions of people are working on the construction. They need to be paid. But the factories they are building are not yet producing any value (and though I'm jumping ahead, I'll tell you now that they never would, because they ran out of money). So there's no increase in goods, but people are getting higher salaries. Another nightmare of deficits. The prices were set by the state and were not the result of the balance of supply and demand.

Money lost even the pathetic meaning it had had under socialism and turned into nothing more than cut paper. It was at the end of perestroika that my father, who had earned pretty good money all his life at a factory, acquired cows, pigs, and chickens. Our whole family, both in Tolyatti and in St. Petersburg, depended on that for food (there were even attempts at making cheese). Man had lost his last connection with the state—money. Nothing else tied him to his beloved state, in the big picture. The country plunged into a kingdom of barter and natural economy.

How it all ended:

The regime did not recognize the looming threat. With maniacal stubbornness, it refused to reduce spending. When the authorities at last understood the necessity for it, they stopped financing all the investment projects I just mentioned—instead of reducing defense spending. In 1990, we had the largest defense budget in Soviet history. The Buran spaceship program alone cost $10 billion. And yet, 70 percent of the halted investment projects were expected to start producing that year and the next.

In the spring of 1991 the new prime minister, Valentin Pavlov, decided to kill two birds with one stone. He would sharply decrease the amount cash in circulation in order to handle the deficit problem, and at the same time he would add to the budget with non-emission rubles. He started the currency revaluation, assuming that people would not bring in their treasure chests for exchange. But they did. They all had excuses: my grandmother's inheritance, found it on the street, saved all my life, my aunt sold her house, and so on. The local receivers were people like me, who wanted to believe them, and that was one of the reasons that the currency reform failed. But this reform had yet another, larger task. As I mentioned, Pavlov had gotten loans from Sberbank and Gosstrakh. The credits were large, long-term, and low-interest. Therefore the resolution on currency exchange came with some fine print, at the end and over to one side, that said that deposits of more than 4,000 rubles would be frozen, and people would be informed "at a later date" when they were to be unfrozen.

I have to point out here that when Gaidar freed prices, he was accused of all the deadly sins. But there is one of which he cannot be considered guilty: he did not devalue people's savings. By the time Gaidar's government came into power, those deposits were gone. Pavlov and Gorbachev had spent them. People's bankbooks had a sum written in them, but there was no money in the bank. God only knows what Gorbachev spent the money on. But eighteen months later, when Gaidar came to the Ministry of Finance, the money was not there. It is only the distorted perception of reality prevalent among our fellow citizens and the propaganda machine under Yeltsin that made it seem that Gaidar had stolen people's savings. Gorbachev's last exercise was the decentralization of the financial system of the USSR. In 1990-1991 the union republics insisted on individualizing the circulation of money, including the creation of their own central banks and quotas for printing money. I should note that Belarus is insisting on this kind of union with Russia right now. The Russian government is rejecting this version, knowing full well that under those circumstances a union is nothing more than sham. That is why Putin is insisting on a single money emission center.

You must understand that at that time Gorbachev had all the constitutional power (including force) to prevent the decentralization of the Soviet financial system. It is absolutely incorrect to maintain that he did not understand the danger to the integrity of the country—the consequences of decentralization had been explained to him many times. He was given a draft of a presidential decree of the USSR that would have preserved a single financial system. He refused quite consciously to sign it. This is how the late Prime Minister Pavlov described it in his book, *Was the Opportunity Lost?* (p. 140–141):

> Setting aside all conjectures that only history can prove or disprove, I can say that the collapse of perestroika was caused, along with other factors, by Gorbachev's personal, human qualities, by his profound indifference to anything that did not touch on his personal well-being. The peak moment when Gorbachev revealed himself completely, treacherously giving the green light to the collapse of the Soviet Union, was that memorable meeting when (out of deeply tactical considerations) he refused to sign the decree that would preserve the integrity of the country's credit and financial system.
>
> With his own hands, Gorbachev released the 'financial genie' that quickly tore apart a great superpower that had been built over centuries. He understood it all. He knew the consequences of his indifference. But he literally did not move a finger to save the state.
>
> The political leaders of Russia, Ukraine, and Belorussia made the collapse of the USSR official in Belovezh Preserve. But I am convinced that in reality the true culprit of the catastrophe is Gorbachev.

Small Summary:

The collapse of the Soviet Union was inevitable. The financial system could not withstand Gorbachev's planning. Reagan had sent us upriver. If there were any scenario that might have preserved the Union, it would have required dropping out of the arms race and all global confrontation, thereby losing our international position. The freed-up money would be spent on the intended areas—high technology and consumer goods—and on increasing the GDP, and the country would have the status of a regional power and a member of the nuclear club. That is the Chinese path. But we didn't have a Deng Xioping. Nevertheless, we are a regional power and a member of the nuclear club. We are not in an arms race, and we are not confronting anyone. Our economy is growing, and our investment priorities are determined by supply and demand.

We have certain advantages over China. We have already gone through privatization, and the foundations of democratic institutions are in place. China has yet to get through all of that. So it's not so bad.

Yes, history does not happen in the conditional tense. Nor does it recognize the true scale of people until much later. Sometimes much, much later. Sometimes never. There is the Nobel Peace Prize winner Yassir Arafat. And there is Tsar Alexander II, and no one but me wants to erect a monument to him. (It now stands in Moscow.) There are lots of people and events in history. Gorbachev and Yeltsin are firmly in place. They are firmly coupled together—a sweet couple—and they will always be remembered together, Gorbachev and Yeltsin, Yeltsin and Gorbachev. That may be God's punishment to them for arguing when the country was on the brink—now they're stuck in history together. A just reward for their hatred of each other.

A hundred years from now, schoolchildren will get them mixed up. Which one came first? Who overthrew whom? Why do we have to study this? The oral exam is on "Founders of Our State." What a mess. Let's start over. Vladimir the Red Sun... Vladimir Monomakh—those were the Rurikoviches. Peter the Great... Nicholas I... those were Romanovs... Lenin, Stalin—servants' children, soldiers' emperors. Yeltsin, Gorbachev... or was is Gorbachev, Yeltsin? I'm sorry, I just don't remember... Both had no family to speak of, born in some village called Budki in Stavropol... They were both born there, and they have argued ever since. Then there's Vladimir III—that's our leader, from the Putin line. Is that all? All right, you can sit down. You get a C.

* * *

You make it seem, Alik, as if they had conspired. Those ones did part of it, these other ones some more, and then some others... And slowly, gradually...

All against the people, of course?

Isn't that always the way?

Always. And each one claims to be caring about the nation, right?

I remember, if you will permit me to get ahead of our year, that during the default, when thousands of people were going bankrupt, Sergei Kiryenko went on vacation to rest up from the stress—and not just anywhere, but to Australia. That was very nice. A subtle theatrical gesture. I'm no specialist in economic policy, but let me remind you of some of the press stories like: "The savings accounts hold so many trillions of rubles, and for the health of the economy that money has to be spent. There is

this much in people's mattresses; that also has to go somewhere, and then the economy will function like clockwork. Salaries will be spent entirely in a week—on staples." Every savings account was a knife in the throat of the economy. So when Gorbachev froze the accounts and then Gaidar freed prices, this was the joint work of the state machine. And one could say: I didn't kill it, I only gave the okay. Or the other could say: I didn't do it alone, he approved it. But the result is the same. Two-zero. Right?

No, Igor, it's more complicated than that. It's true that the ruble surplus had to be handled; the number of rubles had to be lowered. But the circulation of money had to be raised: People had to buy more. Therefore, the income of those people had to be increased. I'll say more than that: The increase in the buying power of citizens is the most stimulating phenomenon for the economy. All of Keynesian thought is based on that. It teaches that one must come up with artificial stimuli for increasing consumer spending. So you're wrong to be so dismissive.

But your Keynesian thought leads to the same thing—the economy doesn't need savings. It's not directed at philanthropy. In that sense I think the Soviet economy was ideal—if you bought a bottle of vodka, you didn't have to worry about further expense. Most people made less in a day than the cost of a half-liter—that must have made economists happy. Hasn't Keynesianism been branded as a reactionary theory yet?

No. There's also Friedman's, a kind of alternative to Keynes.

Invented by Mikhail Fridman of Alfa-Group?

No, Milton Friedman. The Chicago school. But that has nothing to do with our topic.

Why don't you want to tell me about Keynes? Is it because you don't know anything about him?

It's not interesting. What interests me, Igor, is that in 1991 Yeltsin was elected president. And Sobchak mayor—on the same day, by the way.

That made you happy.

Yes.

Yeltsin made me happy, too. I thought, this is great. The land of justice. Everything will be wonderful now. We've finally gotten rid of those bastards...

And so we had. Happiness and justice prevailed at last. Of course, the bastards returned. Because all of Eastern Europe passed laws on lustration, but Russia did not. Nor did it ban Communists and KGB people from serious positions.

If it had, who would have been in charge?

I would.

And me. And no one else. A lot we would have gotten done, just the two of us.

We would have commanded just fine. And Chubais and Gaidar would not have been in charge. They were Communists. But Dima Vasilyev would have. It would have been a fine group in charge.

You think we could have managed without the Communists?

Of course. Do you know how good it could have been, without their interference?

Nothing good would have come out of pushing away the most socially active people, the ones best at their careers. Though actually, I would have liked to shoot them all. At that time, I would have. With great pleasure.

We should have said: If you don't want to go to prison, just shut up and sit in your houses. Instead we talked to them, asked their opinion…

Alik, we could have said, Everyone sign this paper: "I, so-and-so, was in the Communist Party and therefore I am a bastard or an idiot. Or a sellout. I ask forgiveness and promise to pay alimony to the end of my days. And I will be branded on the forehead." Some would say, "Just shoot me." So, half would be shot and the other half would be branded. That would have been justice.

Yes. And they would not be allowed to vote.

That goes without saying. We could discuss whether or not they should be castrated—but voting rights, that's for sure.

Castration? No, our demographic situation is dire.

There, you see. Of course, it would have felt good to oppress the Communists. But on the other hand, there aren't too many skilled people around. And many of them joined the Party, to apply their skills.

Skills! Hahahaha!

If you shunt aside those who were in the Party and demote them to secondary jobs, where would we find people for responsible positions? There are lots of people who boast: "I don't know how to do anything, but at least I never stole, I'm honest, I'm wonderful." But there were mountains to be moved, not just sitting around with one's ideological virginity. Everything would have ground to a halt.

And in August, there was the coup.

Just like that? We got to the coup very fast.

Why not? Yeltsin was elected, the currency exchange took place, and then the coup. Shit.

What about the Congress of Deputies? The start of negotiations in Novo-Ogarevo?

Get off it, all right? Nobody cares about that.

Don't you remember the Novo-Ogarevo process?

There was no process. They sat around drinking…and told Gorbachev to fuck off. That was the process, Igor. It's not far from here, by the way, on the way to my dacha—it's where Putin lives now.

Ah, where there's a no entry sign.

Right.

Do you remember the referendum on the fate of the USSR? And that 112 million people voted to keep it intact? Out of 146 million who voted!

I remember.

And what do you have to say to that?

What's to say? Fuck it.

Oh, no. The people said—save the USSR, and we replied, "Fine, but we're going to destroy it. Sorry."

And they shut it down. In accordance with their own decisions.

Bankrupted it. Intentionally.

Yes. Well, you remember what a phony question Gorbachev posed? "Are you willing to live in a Union of equality and justice, where everything is shared fairly and everything is wonderful?" Everyone would vote for that! I would right now. But at the time, nothing like that existed, so why the fuck ask?

How about the formation of the German republic in the Altai in 1991, did that excite you?

Nope, not at all.

Well, what other events? How about the death of Lazar Kaganovich? Do anything for you?

Not a thing. Stop it!

What about the presidential decree on the de-Partization of state institutions?

What?

De-Partization.

That was all phony.

Or that the Warsaw Convention was dissolved?

Where would it have gone? They dissolved themselves de facto. Let's talk about the coup.

All right then, Alik. It was a Monday. The driver came to my house, to the kitchen where I was having tea and stared at me. I said, What are you doing here, today's a day off. We spent the weekend putting the issue to bed, I need a rest... That's all you'll be doing is resting, he said. It's all over for you: What do you think of all this? He asked. All what? That they got rid of Gorbachev, he said. Oh, shi-iiit! I turned on the TV and saw what was going on, and we drove to the newspaper office. I had just left it late the night before. And he says, you know I'm driving you now purely as a gesture of good will...

He meant he was back to throwing off the shackles of capitalism?

Like that. His working papers were still in a Soviet institution, he had just started working for the paper, and he was pleased that he wasn't losing everything with the change of regime. So, there we were at the office, watching "Swan Lake." They always put on classical music during political upheavals.

It was "Manfred"! A symphonic poem!

You sure?

Yes. Tchaikovsky. I'm positive.

The paper was printed at the Red Star plant. They called up and said: "We will never print your kind of newspaper again. And we will punish the people responsible for permitting a criminal relationship with you in exchange for your filthy money." Speaking of money, Yakovlev started moving the cash from the newspaper offices to the houses of trusted people. They were preparing for searches, confiscations, arrests. And they were figuring out how to publish the paper in the underground. That was the situation when we started the editorial meeting. Yakovlev announced that he intended to work in the underground.

So he wasn't thinking only of money?

I doubt he could have sold the paper to an oligarch then, during the coup. So he said: "I'm warning you that this could end very badly. I understand that not everyone is prepared to take that kind of risk. Let's all leave this room, and anyone who wants to can just leave the building— we'll understand. Whoever comes back into my office, I will count on." People gathered five minutes later, and we all looked around curiously, to see who had bugged off. We were missing only one person. Let's not name him, even though he's well known in journalistic circles. I will say that on August 22, when the coup had failed, he came back to work as if nothing had happened. I naturally pushed him to explain himself. Without any embarrassment, he explained: "I'm a neoconservative. Because I'm Jewish. There are dissidents among us, but the truly responsible Soviet Jew has a stake in preserving the USSR. Because if the Soviet Union collapses, Russians will be forced out of the former republics. Naked and cold, they will flee to Moscow. And finding well-fed and happy Jews in Moscow, who do think they're going to beat up on? Who needs that? No one. That's why I supported the coup. I did what I could, and now that your stupid democracy has won, I'm back. Where else can I go?"

So, in the editor's office, we're figuring out what to write, where to print. Yakovlev started *Obshchaya Gazeta* [Common Newspaper], where he took his place alongside *Moscow News*, *Komsomol Pravda*, and some others—a total of eleven papers. We listened to Ekho Moskvy Radio—that was the first time it became so important. It had live broadcasts from the White House, from the barricades... A Russian CNN, without pictures. I went to look at the picture myself, following Ekho's lead. When they announced that there would be missile fire on the White House in thirty minutes, I headed over there, grimly: Those creeps had missiles, and I had to go there—I was a reporter, my job was to report... I had to get the details of the bombing just right... But I confess I also had the desire to be part of an historic event. I still had my driver, who took me there. But he said, "Just don't tell anyone, I'm here incognito."

He kept justifying his courage. That's not necessary. Courage is courage.

Well. So there I was near the White House, looking up at the sky from time to time, like Allende in Chile, wondering if our own Russian missile was aiming for my head. But there were no missiles. So, I went to talk to the people. The most interesting interviews were with the soldiers. There were all these tanks and armored vehicles, and they all had the tricolor flag on their antennas—solidarity between the people and the troops. So I wrote an article about how the army had come to the White House not to be involved in politics but to follow orders.

It's very good that we have that kind of army.

Well—the army did not side with the rebels. That was the article I wrote for the underground newspaper. And that was rather curious: The coup leaders would gladly have published an article like that in their legal press! And I, in the underground, wrote an article that was not useful for the democrats. Funny, no?

Yes.

On the other hand, you can't be expected to take dictation and write only PR in the underground, can you? And here's one more thing. When the three men were squashed to death by a tank in the tunnel—that was Komar, Usov, and Krichevsky—I went to find out more. I went into that tunnel under Kutuzovsky Prospect... The APCs that ran them down were there.... And then I noticed this: I got into the tunnel, but I couldn't get out; it was blocked from both sides, and no one was being allowed to leave. They shouted from above... The insurgents were shouting to the major who commanded the vehicles: "You give us the soldiers, we'll kill them fast, and then you can leave."

Are you serious?

Yup. The major tried to explain, gently, tactfully. They said, forget that, we'll kill them, that won't take more than five minutes, and it's over. That went on for about three hours.

Why didn't they just kill the major? The rebellion didn't extend to majors yet?

He was wearing the usual Soviet uniform. People had served in the Soviet army, and they were used to the fact that you could punch a sergeant in the mouth, but not a major. It hadn't reached majors yet. A year or two later, it wouldn't have been an issue; even the president could have been killed. Not to mention a vice-president.

Yes, yes!

At the time of the coup, a major was still a person to reckon with. By the way, it may be because he had a decent salary. Relatively speaking, of course.

There weren't any thieves, otherwise they would have created total chaos. If they had been on the side of democracy.

I remember that Stas Namin, the rock singer and producer, was there, too—in a hat and leather coat. He tried to boss people around. Hey you, come here. Stand over there. Some people actually obeyed him. So ... He was bossing, while I was sitting on top of an APC, smoking. It was night. I thought, well, there's nothing happening here, I should get over to the White House. But how do I get out of there?

And suddenly, I see the famous photo reporter Pavel Kassin running and shouting, "Tanks, the Dzerzhinsky Division tanks are coming!" I jumped down from the APC, thinking, what the fuck did I get into this tunnel for? I could have been home having tea in the kitchen under my red lamp. Or at least drinking vodka at the paper. But no! I had to be here! My own fault. I jumped down, but there was nowhere to run—so I climbed back up—at least I could see from up there. Nothing was clear. We didn't have mobile phones then, probably only the KGB used them— I'll bet they had lots of transmitters set up. Anyway I couldn't call anyone. But there was something like a mobile communication system, a relay: As I later learned, Misha Kamensky, who used to be a journalist and now is a big shot at the Pushkin Museum, lived right above the tunnel—he was watching from his window and reported everything he saw by phone to *Kommersant*. Great guy.

People were shouting, and I couldn't tell whether they were drunk or full of revolutionary fervor... And suddenly a rumor flew through the tipsy crowd full of defenders of democracy: They were starting to storm the White House, and every bayonet, every APC was needed. The rumor was started by someone very clever... So, they let the APCs out. The mechanics and drivers were Yakuts or Chukchas, they weren't really sure what was going on, but they looked scared. And so there I was on an APC under the tricolor flag riding up to the White House—like Lenin in his armored train. Love, joy, the army, and the people—a real high....

And as soon as we put out our underground newspaper, the coup ended. I had worried about that from the start: We're going to spend our days off—Monday and Tuesday—fighting, and by the time we go to press the whole kerfuffle will end, and right after doing the underground paper we'll have to keep on going and do the normal one. Those coup leaders were a bunch of creeps, I thought—taking away people's weekends. And that's just what happened. They fucked it up. But on the other hand, I have my memories...

In 1991 things got interesting in St. Petersburg, too, Igor. At one point, we were gathered around the Maryinsky Palace, defending the Leningrad Soviet. Rioters overturned trolleys. I drove up to the tank division and spoke with the commander—help us defend democracy, and we'll give you money for it.

You tried to turn him into one of those werewolves, as they're called, who are being arrested now in the police, for double-dealing. But he didn't have Makarovs and Kalashnikovs, like the cops—he had tanks. You think big, Alik. I like your approach.

And he says, "Don't wet your pants, all the commanders are drunk, so everything is fine." I didn't understand whether they had been given orders to come out or not.

Maybe they had been given orders to attack, but instead behaved wisely and got drunk instead? Or maybe that was the command given them—to get hammered? An officer, from a tank division outside Moscow, told me that there had been no question of giving out ammunition. The order was to move with ammunition, but the regiment commander said: "Who cares what the fuck they come up with at headquarters! This is not their business. I'm not letting tanks with ammo into Moscow. I won't give them a single shell." They screwed up, and we screwed them!

Yes, there was that. We screwed them.

I had been planning a trip to Germany on August 17, but I didn't get my visa in time—everything was going to hell by then. And it's funny, a lot of Russians who were abroad during the coup were given refugee status.

Yes, and then came the Gaidar government. For the November holidays. Yegor Gaidar, Anatoli Chubais, Peter Aven, Vladimir Mashits. …

What about Gorbachev giving up his post as General Secretary of the Party? The independence of Belarus, Moldavia, and Ukraine… The resignation of the government on August 28… The shutdown of the Semipalatinsk nuclear testing grounds…

Will you stop looking at your cheat sheet! I'm talking about serious things! About the Gaidar government! Grigory Yavlinsky switched over to the Union government then, as it was dying. The Gaidar government came in during the November holidays. And Misha Manevich, God rest his soul, and I rushed to Moscow and started writing all kinds of papers. On privatization.

Ah, as soon as the revolution was won, the democrats rushed to privatize!

Go to hell. You're full of journalistic clichés. I lived for two months in Moscow. All of November and almost all of December. Then I went home, got my wife pregnant, and she gave birth to Olga in 1992. That's what I remember about the coup. I remember wandering through Red Square, drunk, with Manevich and singing a song about Gaidar. How did it go? "Gaidar strides ahead." And the Union collapsed.

Is it true that Burbulis slipped a paper in front of a drunken Yeltsin, he signed, and it all collapsed?

Who the fuck knows? I don't think so. It was simply that Yeltsin had a deep understanding of his goals.

Meaning, get out from under Gorbachev at any price?

Yes. Yes. Yes.

At any price. Paris is worth a mass…

Absolutely right.

Do you remember my theory, Alik? That the KGB was broken up because it did not arrest the participants of the Belovezh conspiracy to destroy the USSR? It should have arrested them and brought them to the Kremlin cellars. Gorbachev would have circled Yeltsin—like Tsar Peter walking around Tsarevich Alexei—and tortured him personally.

I think so. But why only Yeltsin? The whole bunch of them. But that's banal, everyone knows that by now.

Do you think that we could have kept the Soviet Union, preserved its integrity?

Oh, I don't want to come off as a troubadour for the USSR, Igor. I just think that there were more chances to save it than to destroy it. But it was destroyed nevertheless. And all the famous intelligence services could do nothing to stop it. From that, I conclude that either it was the intelligence services' plan in the first place, or that they are a pile of shit. Either way, there is no point in counting on them, even now. If they're just formulating goals for their own personal enrichment—instead of goals for the nation—then who the hell needs them? If they're not defending our national goals, or even formulating them?

I don't think that any country needs intelligence services. When people tell me that a state can't survive without intelligence, I think they're full of shit. Because I've never seen any real proof that a state was saved by its intelligence information. Nonsense! Intelligence is a parasitic organization that is not needed.

Alik, that year for me was also about a subtle financial lesson. From the fall of 1989 to the spring of 1991, the dollar increased in price by 40 times, if you go by the official rate. On the black market, it only doubled. From 13 rubles (or 62 kopecks) to 25 rubles.

Hahahaha! I like that.

So what was happening with the dollar?

I think it was seeking equilibrium. And found it.

So how did you feel when the Union collapsed?

I had absolutely no regrets for the Soviet Union.

You were thrilled by the new democracy and all that? But did you realize that geopolitically Russia was becoming sidelined? No longer a superpower?

I never received any personal dividend from the fact that Russia was a superpower, Igor. It just made it worse for me. I could clearly picture food being taken out of my children's mouths and given to Mozambique. I didn't like that at all; it was a blow to my pocket.

You were thinking in those terms then?

It would be stupid to think in other terms.

I took it as a natural phenomenon then.

No… How can I explain it… When you're driving from Tolyatti to Moscow by car, you go through Syzran. There are oil rigs there, pumping oil. They reach all the way to the horizon, pumping, pumping… I've seen it with my own eyes. It made me angry with the space program and all that aid. And that affected conversations about the Emirates and Saudi Arabia. I thought, why, why do we live the way we do? They say, At least we fly into space and help the whole world… I was only fifteen then; these were childish impressions.

What, you had a bad life then?

But it could have been so much better! I wanted us to have good roads, beautiful houses… The housing question ruined my life in St. Petersburg, as usual. I simply could not understand how such a rich and enormous country could not supply its citizens with housing. And I was one of those citizens. You told me about East Germany, where newlyweds were given apartments—but it was on our money. While my wife and I, and our baby, could not get an apartment.

And so for the sake of an apartment, we had to destroy an empire.

Looks that way! Once it was destroyed, I got an apartment right away. Literally, in 1991.

Ingushetia President Aushev told me about those oil rigs, too.

Ruslan? I know him. He's one of ours—from Kustanai, in Kazakhstan.

Ah, also an exile family… According to him, there was more oil per capita in Chechno-Ingushetia than in the Near East. And the infant mortality rate there was the highest in the country. He told me that as part of his belief that we shouldn't nurse a grudge, but rather should pretend that nothing had happened. He also said that no one wants to be a subject of the Russian Federation, but there are lots who wish to remain under the British crown.

That's another interesting story. In the 1960s many countries left the British Commonwealth.

They did. But Australians still consider themselves subjects of the queen. And they have the Union Jack on their flag. And they haven't banned English. Imagine a former USSR republic—say your favorite, Latvia—keeping the Soviet banner in the corner of its flag and keeping Russian as its main language. And not spitting at us, and not trying to rewrite history so that there isn't a word about Russia in it.

The Latvians should have a black, red, and yellow flag. Germans.

You know, it's easy for us to talk, Alik. We're foreigners. You're an exiled German, I'm Ukrainian. We didn't have any Ukrainian schools in Makeevka at all. On the other hand, a fine mess I'd be now with a Ukrainian education... And let's not forget that even Russia is very provincial. It's on the outskirts of white civilization... Half-savage...

Just tell me, Igor, are we writing about our own experiences or the feelings of Russians? Let the Russians write their own books if they want. Let them write how they wept over the empire, how they missed it.

We're talking about the break-up of the Soviet Union, while on TV they're showing four characters who want to re-unite. The Slavic presidents and Nazarbayev.

Nazarbayev wasn't at Belovezh Preserve. He was even insulted that he had not been invited.

And he's the only republic president who held onto his job.

And the only one to pass real reforms.

He's in a good position now—they destroyed the Soviet Union without him, and they'll unite on his initiative.

Wise man! You've got to give him credit. It was clear from the start. He was so calm. Very measured in his totalitarianism, fucking democracy in the mouth. His people are deliriously happy.

I see, in order for the people to be deliriously happy, Alik, the leader has to treat democracy the way Clinton treated Monica! Nazarbayev set things up the way they are in China. He's got his reasons for vacationing on the Chinese island of Hainan. China seems very far away to us, but it's

a stone's throw from Alma-Aty. **When something happens in Damansky, all of Kazakhstan trembles.**

You're telling me? I was living in Kazakhstan when the Damansky events occurred. [Soviet-Chinese border conflict over Damansky, or Zhenbao, Island in 1969.] There were troops all over town.

While we were chasing after America, Nazarbayev took a look at his neighbor…and used it as a model. I wonder why the Kazakhs turned out to be smarter than everyone else in the USSR? How come?

Not only the Kazakhs, though. The Balts are no fools, either—they crawled into the European Union right away. They knew where their new feed trough was located. The stupid Europeans haven't caught on yet. They don't realize what spongers they've taken on. And then there's also President Aliyev of Azerbaijan… He's friends with everyone! He operates in America…

Instead of worrying about the Soviet people, Alik, you were taking care of your family. What else were you doing? You were too brief in your account. In 1990 you were handing out parcels of land; in 1991 you exchanged money. And that's it?

That's it. Because in 1991, right after the failed coup, Sobchak became mayor, and he fired me instantly.

For what?

He didn't explain. That was his manner—not explaining. He was working at being a charismatic leader.

Was he drunk when he fired you?

No, no. I think that the chairman of the regional party committee, Krivenchenko had a hand in it…

Do you know how to say "Russian" in Latvian? It's Krievu. I think it comes from the word "krivich."

Russians have forgotten that they're a holding company, Igor. Drevlyane, Chuvash, Mordva… All those ethnoses. The Slavs lived on the shores of Volkhov, from Ilmen to Ladoga—take a look at my wife, she's from those parts. Volkhov, by the way, isn't even a river, but a channel between Ilmen and Ladoga, 40 kilometers in length. The Neva is also 40 kilometers long, and it isn't a river, either, but a channel connecting Ladoga with the Baltic Sea.

Everybody says the Volga flows into the Caspian Sea. An indisputable fact. It's an example of Russian logic. But in fact, the Caspian isn't a sea, since it has no outlet into the ocean—it's just a lake. If you change that word, the phrase sounds quite different. Anyway, about the Volga.

The Volga is the greatest symbol of Russianness. The river is considered Russian, but Tatars live along its banks. It's a powerful and beautiful river—the Rhine can take a backseat, it's half the size. The Volga is a beautiful river, but all it does is flow into the Caspian. It doesn't lead anywhere else.

The Russian path.

Yes, exactly. The Russian path—beautiful and powerful, but going nowhere.

What else did you do in your job, besides exchange money?

I can't even remember now. I did something or other. Why don't you drop it?

Were you hurt that Sobchak fired you? You wanted to expand further, from town to the whole region, then the *oblast*, and then all of Russia?

No... I wasn't upset so much by the firing as by being fired for no reason.

And you realized that this is how it would be in the future, too?

Yes.

And were you scared that your career was destroyed, there was nowhere to go, and you hadn't gotten your apartment yet?

No, I got an apartment. I had been on a waiting list, and my turn came up.

You didn't get anything for being mayor? Just moral satisfaction and bureaucratic experience?

Absolutely right.

And then where did you go?

I went to work in an organization created under Gorbachev—it was called Lengosfond—which united all the USSR property in St. Petersburg and the oblast. Then Chubais came into the government... They disagreed: Sobchak put Sergei Belyayev as head of the Committee on Management of City Property, and Chubais appointed me and Misha Manevich as his deputies.

By the way, who had Manevich shot?

They say, Yuri Shutov.

Shutov wanted to privatize something and he wouldn't let him?

I don't know. So they say. So, by the end of the year I was deputy chairman of the city property committee. I only lasted a few months.

And then set out on the main road of your life—toward privatization.

Yes.

And to our beloved mortgage auctions. Which we are approaching. Alik! Has anybody called you and offered you money not to talk about them in the book? About the currency exchange, you said that in 1991 you didn't make any money, because you didn't have any. But in 1998 you did, eh?

Igor, drop it. We haven't reached the default of 1998. When we do, I'll tell you the story.

I spent the year working at the paper and doing the same thing
By the way, Alik, remember that in 1991, people drank primarily at home in the kitchen. If you wanted to drink with someone, you brought him home. And then this little place opened across the street from *Kommersant* **on the first floor of a residential building; they poured vodka and fed you salads and hot dogs. The habitués were bandits in leather jackets. Remember when half the country was wearing those Chinese brown leather jackets made out of pieces? We sat there, too. The old Soviet manner of running out for a bottle and then drinking it at the office was passing. Those grim little cafés that sprouted up then...**

They were little shoots of capitalism.

Yes! They spelled luxurious life to us.

It felt as if you were denying yourself nothing by going to one.

Yes. And what else, what else, Alik? Gdlyan, Tarasov, Father Andrei Kuraev... I don't remember what we were thinking, but at the time they seemed like the most important men of the era.

You mentioned Kuraev. I pay no attention to church officials. They're all crooks!

Well, the most important church official I ever met was Vladimir, Bishop of Tashkent and Central Asia. Very *simpatico*. Writes books. He has an interesting idea—that the tsar financed the construction of mosques and published the Koran so that the Muslims would be educated, so that the Wahhabites, sectarians, and heretics could not influence them very much...

Alik! Why haven't we talked about Foros, Gorbachev's Crimean residence, where he was isolated during the coup?

Foros? Gorbachev was a coward.

What was he supposed to have done: Say kill me, and leave it at that?

Or kill them. He had to show himself some way. He came back so sickly sweet, wrapped in a little blanket. Really, what kind of shit is that... And then he stamped his foot and raised his voice to Yeltsin—more bullshit. Too late, you've covered yourself in shit, dear comrade, get off the stage...

You're right. He should have fallen like a hero.

Of course.

And now people would say, There was a man, the father of freedom. He was killed by the vile enemies, the Communists. They would lay wreaths at his monument. Schoolchildren would stand as honor guards by his bust.

No, no, I don't want anyone to die. But he should have behaved more appropriately!

As a leader of a superpower!

Instead, he looked absolutely helpless. I was disgusted. Some shit, I thought.

Yeltsin looked pretty good in comparison.

You're absolutely right!

Kokh's Commentary:

In the spring of 1991 I also traveled to Chile—so there! There's a rather well-known scholar called Vitaly Naishul. He put together a group of what seemed to him to be interesting young scholars, politicians, and officials, and we went to Chile to study their economic reforms.

And in Chile there is an economist called Hernán Büchi—incidentally a graduate of the University of Chicago—who was the Minister of Finance under

Pinochet. After the departure of Pinochet and his government, he organized the Institute of Freedom and Development. It brought in groups of economists from countries with transitional economies and gave them a course on Chilean economic reforms. Naishul made arrangements with the institute and formed a group, which included me (for which I am enormously grateful to this day), and we set out for Chile.

I should note that this was my first trip abroad. Just imagine: your first time, and it's straight to Chile. We traveled a long time, twenty-two hours. The IL-62 flew first to Liechtenstein, then to the island of the Green Cape, then Buenos Aires, and only then Santiago de Chile. When we flew over Rio de Janeiro, there were no clouds, and you could see the whole city spread out below. You could see Maracana, the statue of Christ with outspread hands, the crystals of skyscrapers along the yellow beaches of Copacabana. Impressions overwhelmed me. I remembered children's books about pirates and distant seas in Santiago… It didn't have the Latin American carnival atmosphere I had expected. Calm people with impassive Indian faces. Medium height, well-built brunets. The women? Nothing special, like miniature Georgian women. No blacks. They told us that there had never been slavery in Chile, since Africans were brought to the Atlantic shore and they did not reach Chile—they died in Argentina, Patagonia, in the mountains.

I saw the occasional head of light brown or blond hair. The ones with light brown hair were descendants of the old Spanish families; their forefathers had been conquistadors. The local aristocracy. They were major landowners and investors. They rarely intermarried with the Indians, preserving the noble blood of Spanish grandees. The blonds were Germans: The SS troops and officers of the Wehrmacht who fled here after the war. They basically controlled trade, participated in manufacturing, and served in the army as mid-level officers. There was no aristocratic blood in them, so they assimilated rather easily. I met some Russians, descendants of the White émigrés, the first wave. They were basically descended from Cossack officers.

I liked the local vodka—*pisco*, a cloudy liquor with a hint of tequila taste. A small shot before a meal was fine. The food? Good, tasty. With a predominance of roast beef and fish. A sea of very good (as now we know) Chilean wine. Lots of fruit, the most ordinary kind, but delicious—apples, pears, peaches…

The first thing that struck me was the ubiquitous presence of the army. Soldiers with machine guns patrolled the city on armored vehicles (at that time the army had not turned over police functions). The army was the largest landowner, the army was the pride of the nation. The army was the guarantor of the Constitution. Serving the army was an honor (they didn't take just anyone). The best weapons, the best uniforms. The discipline was stunning: The Germans trained them. The soldiers had boots, clothes, food and tobacco. Looking at those smug peasant faces was disgusting. The officer class was hereditary. From father to son. The officers were the middle class. Each had a house, car, and so on.

The army was small but very battle-ready. When there was some boundary dispute with Argentina in the 1980s, coinciding with the Falklands crisis (Pinochet was helping Thatcher), the Argentines tried to invade, and the Chilean army chased them back practically to Buenos Aires.

The economy was stable. Growing reliably, Valparaiso is a port city with a big beach, fish restaurants, and the usual Odessa hubbub. Pinochet moved the Parliament there. So that they wouldn't mix with the people in Santiago. Built them a building right on the beach, and he didn't have any more problems with the Parliament after that.

When I was in Chile, it had been a year since Pinochet lost the presidential elections. But the workers' neighborhoods in Santiago still had graffiti that read: "Viva Pinochet!" The workers loved the old man. That was his electorate—workers, and the army. Well, and business, too. The peasants didn't like him. He had taken away land from the *latifundistas*. Neither did the intelligentsia, and of course the students were also against his dictatorship. That was my analysis anyway—maybe things were different in actual fact.

Our teachers were very interesting. The lecturers were former ministers of the Pinochet government. I remember a former Minister of Economics with the beautiful name Sergio de la Cuardo. He was a conquistador. Another one was Pinero, who had been in charge of pension reform—he had been Minister of Labor, this thin Indian. He had a sense of humor and was always joking. They told us that he had been a clown as a youth. They also told us that he personally commanded the firing on the protest demonstration against his pension-reform scheme. Maybe they were lying...

The point is that our translators were political immigrants who had just returned from the Soviet Union (all Commies) and their children. They came back, all right, but there was no work for them. And then we showed up. Their Russian came in handy. We didn't particularly believe their stories about Pinochet's ministers, but those "translators" created an adrenaline-charged situation. We had the feeling that they were ready to attack the lecturers at any moment.

The lectures were about privatization, pension reform, financial stabilization, and tax reform. About overcoming the crisis of trust. Rather specialized topics. The make-up of our group was rather heterogeneous. I'll try to name them from memory, but I'm sure I'll leave out some: Yuri Boldyrev, Mikhail Dmitriev, Sergei Glazyev, Leonid Valdman, Konstantin Kagalovsky, Mikhail Kiselyov,

Simon Kordonsky, Grigory Glazkov, Alexei Golovkov... No, I can't remember them all. We should have a reunion. But who has time...

Chile, 1973. Total collapse. The economy just stopped. The country was bankrupt. Politically, a dead end. Then, like in a bad movie, fast forward on the calendar, twenty years later...

What better example do we need to see that we must act and not just gab about reforms? We could gab away the whole country.

11.

1992

The Eleventh Bottle

*T*hroughout 1992, Kokh did his "favorite work—selling state property." Svinarenko also did his favorite job: he worked at the newspaper, running the crime department. In this chapter we also explain, scientifically, how the Russian empire fell apart. Its main metagoal, as we know, was the creation of a great Slavic state with its capital in Constantinople. In 1917 it became clear that Europe would never give us access to the Straits. And that we would never get Istanbul. When that became clear, the empire collapsed—and who needed it in that case, really? After we lost the Cold War, the Soviet Union collapsed, too. Why feed an enormous army if it doesn't win wars? And without an army, what kind of an empire is it?

But now, with no one forcing us to solve the world's problems, we can take care of ourselves, our homes and families.

1992, that's the first year of Russia, dear Igor.

Yes, the first year that was purely Russian. No more USSR.

Gorbachev gave up the nuclear suitcase in December, and it was over.

On the Internet, I found a Central Committee resolution "on preparing for the celebration of the 80th anniversary of the founding of the USSR." That was planned for December, 1992. Pretty funny, huh?

Yes.

So, the very start of the year. On January 2, prices were freed and reforms began to be implemented. And on the 10th, there was the repeal of fixed prices on bread and milk. That means that at first they left prices fixed for bread and milk.

And then quickly realized that it was all bullshit. And they freed all the prices.

In 1996, Boris Nemtsov, when he was governor of Nizhny Novgorod, told me (on still-fresh evidence) that it was during that January that he made a deal with the commanders of the military *okrug*, to bring their army field kitchens to the city. They were afraid that people were going to starve, break store windows, and loot warehouses. But somehow, they managed without the field kitchens.

Nemtsov told me that they did bring out the field kitchens.

He may have told you that as a private person, Alik. He spoke more responsibly to the press. How do you remember all that? Where were you then? Was it you who freed the prices?

No. It was Yegor Timurovich Gaidar, finance minister and then acting prime minister.

Where were you then?

I was in St. Petersburg—deputy chairman of the city committee on state property.

Did they tell you ahead of time that they would free prices?

It was clear anyway. They had warned people about it in November, provided numbers even … It wasn't a surprise for anyone.

Not for you, maybe.

Or for you. You've just forgotten, Igor. The story was that people rushed to take their money out of the bank, and they wouldn't give it to them because Pavlov had frozen the accounts.

Yes. I remember that sausage had been three rubles a kilo and suddenly it was ten.

But it was there! That's the whole point, there was sausage. No more shortages.

Yes, everything was there, on sale. So that was the real start of reform?

Yes.

That was it. They said, no more fooling around.

Exactly. No more fooling around. And privatization began. We worked out the city program of privatization in January and February. It was approved by the council in March. In April, we had our first auctions. Just like in Nizhny Novgorod. We began selling stores at auction. We invited experienced auctioneers who had worked in Soyuzpushnina, selling furs to Westerners in Soviet times. With their help, we sold stores instead of sable skins. We sold a lot of them. Almost all of them. People resisted at first, and then they started buying. It was very important to explain to the labor collectives the potential benefits of the sales. They took part in the auctions and won. It was fun! Then the voucher stuff began. They really sucked our blood with those vouchers.

Kokh's Commentary:

The big commentary on privatization I'll write later, around 1994. But here I can cite an excerpt from the book *Privatization Russian-Style,* which was the reason for the "writers' case"—when we were accused of accepting a bribe when, in fact, it was a book advance. It is interesting not only for the facts it mentions, even though there are a few interesting incidents described. It is interesting primarily because it provides an accurate sense of the times. Even though this text was written in 1997, in late summer, I believe it reproduces the atmosphere of our team in 1992 better than anything I could try to write now.

The First Auctions

By February 1992 we had gotten the city privatization program passed through the City Council—with a specific list, by address, of stores that should be auctioned off. The first auctions took place in May.

I remember that, at the very first auction, a barber shop on Nevsky Prospect was on the block. The barbershop was not making money, and Nevsky was the city's main street, so space there should be very expensive. It was clear that in the course of privatization, low-income enterprises like this barbershop would be pushed out and turned into something else. But this created such a furor! There were demands that privatized stores retain their profiles, that the businesses not be changed. We had to fight over almost every store, every barbershop and laundromat. In the end, we sold that first barbershop for rather good money: more than 20 million rubles. Now there is a store selling imported kitchens in that space, and I'm sure it's much more profitable than the old barbershop was and is able to pay for its existence in the center of town.

In fact, the very first auction selling a store took place in Nizhny Novgorod in April, 1991. However, St. Petersburg was the first to auction off stores for rent, rather than sale.

When small privatization was just getting started, there were a lot of mishaps. I remember one of our first sales was of a huge department store in a new district; it had a big turnover and an enormous amount of space. No one really believed that you could just show up and buy it in an open contest at the auction. In the end, only two purchasers showed up, and as far as I can tell, they were in collusion: the labor collective of the store and a second shell company. And they bought the department store for a ridiculous price: 2,100,000 rubles (the first barbershop went for over 20 million). People were stunned: They all thought, why didn't we get in on the action? Nothing like that came up again, of course.

Have Some Oranges

I remember when we were selling a grocery store on Nevsky Prospect. It was the most famous produce store in the city, and its director, naturally, was the patriarch of the produce-dealing "mafia." He was over 70 years old. When it came time to sell his store, people began telling me to go see him. "Why should I? Let him come to me if he needs to see me." "No," they said, "you go to him. He's that kind of man. In his day, he could kick open any door in town." "Now, he won't," I replied. "Go see him anyway. He's an old man, he doesn't understand everything that's going on; he lives under the old constructs. Show him some respect." So I went.

As soon as I walked into his office, he began putting together a bag for me. I said, "I don't need any of that." "What do you mean? How about these nice oranges?" "I don't need your oranges" "How about some grapes?" Once he realized there was no point in bargaining with me, he said, "All right, let's do it this way. I'm over 70 years old, I'm going to die soon. When I die, then sell this store—do whatever you want with it. But until then, leave me alone. Let me die in peace." We settled on that. He died a year later, and we sold the store.

The privatization of trade was complex and nerve-racking. The local monopolists resisted desperately; they held on tooth and nail. They had been masters of the whole trade network and were extremely influential in the era of universal shortages. Privatization put an end to their power: A privatized store was given the legal status of a person and therefore became an independent economic unit—juridically, economically, and financially. The traders fought for their interests and won support even from Anatoly Sobchak, who demanded we preserve the regional trade monopolies.

It was only much later that Sobchak would proudly tell people in the West how quickly privatization was progressing in his city. But in 1992 you could read resolutions from the mayor saying, "Bring Kokh to his senses, or I'll do it myself!" That happened when I was trying to sell the Dieta store on Nevsky; the director, like any trade boss in the early post-Soviet period, was a rather influential person. She was quite large—dyed hair, gold hanging from her neck and wrists—and she kept shouting that Kokh was going to leave the diabetics of St. Petersburg without the dietetic foods they needed. However, despite her efforts, the store was sold. It's doing fine, and it has a much greater selection of diet food than ever.

I must admit that small privatization did not have time to add significantly to the city budget: The voucher program began, and small privatization continued not for cash but for vouchers. Actually, no one set any particular fiscal goals anyway. Our main tasks were to create a competitive milieu in the trade system, to liquidate the local monopoly, and to guarantee a flow of goods. We reached those goals. Russian shop counters don't differ too much from Western ones, and when our grannies travel abroad in tour groups they no longer faint at the sight of Western stores.

It was an interesting time—the start-up of privatization, the start-up of reforms. We weren't playing at politics, we were doing concrete things. But when you start looking for checks and balances, creating intrigues, you immediately become dependent on some political group. And in exchange for supporting you, the group demands special privileges. In that sense, we were naïve fools— we ran our auctions on the basis of the laws, resolutions, and decrees, and managed to piss off all the political forces in St. Petersburg.

Luckily, Chubais was already influential enough by then, and we could refer people who were unhappy with us to Moscow. It also helped that the Soviet system had not fallen apart completely. There was some discipline left, and some of the old arguments were still effective: "The president signed the decree and ordered us to privatize this many enterprises. Are we going to obey the decree or not?" Whether the decree was good or bad was a minor issue; it had to be obeyed. That argument really worked. Today, in the regions, they behave differently. "Who cares what decree the president signed? Our Constitution defends the rights of the subjects of the Federation, so we don't have to obey the decree." In the early 1990s, decrees from Moscow were obeyed.

Capitalist Mini-Revolution

This allowed us to sell about 40 percent of the stores by 1993. We sold between thirty and forty stores every day. The auctions went on without interruption.

Along with small privatization, we began check—or "voucher"—privatization, in late 1992. The committee on property worked closely with the St. Petersburg Property Fund, which had a pretty good team of experts; we worked super intensively, round the clock. Once, we gathered the directors of all the major factories in the auditorium at Smolny, where Lenin had declared Soviet rule. Belyayev, Manevich, and Sobchak were in the Presidium, and I was at the podium explaining the President's decree on auctioning enterprises. This capitalist mini-revolution took place beneath an enormous portrait of Lenin and the tense and mocking stares of the directors. It was pretty clear what they were thinking: The kids will get tired of playing, and things will go back to normal.

In fact, the auctioning programs went rather well. The factory directors were worried that they could be tricked by outsiders, so they rushed to offer their own plans, their own investment programs, and an order of auctioning that suited them—so that they could consolidate their money and buy their enterprises. We worked well with most of them. After all, the directors in St. Petersburg were rather progressive people. Just think of Turchak, director of Leninets; or Shlyakovsky, director of the Baltiisky plant; or Ilya Klebanov from LOMO.

There were a few who did not want to buy and stubbornly refused to recognize the need. So they were not privatized. As a rule, those enterprises are in near-collapse now: They have no competitive products and no purchasers.

Of course, I'm not about to maintain that all the privatized enterprises are flourishing today. St. Petersburg has a very difficult structure of industry for market transformation: defense, ship building, electronics, and energy-machine building. That's why things are difficult for them now and there are no big successes. Although, compared with the general conditions in those areas, St. Petersburg's defense industry (along with everything relating to it) is doing fairly well. And the light and food industries are growing. Our breweries are saturating the entire country with beer. Neva and Baltika are no worse than the imports. And the machine-building and ship-building industries are slowly getting on their feet. I think that the situation in St. Petersburg is not so bad in general.

St. Petersburg was always considered the unquestioned leader in privatization. But now, in hindsight, I understand that we were only one of the leaders. Boris Nemtsov beat us organizationally; his auctions in Nizhny Novgorod began two or three weeks before St. Petersburg's. In sheer numbers of privatized businesses, Chelyabinsk was ahead of us. (But it was easier there, because the main method of privatization was rent with right to purchase, and the paperwork for that is very simple.) Things were also moving along well in Samara and Ekaterinburg. In other words, St. Petersburg was not the absolute leader in every aspect. But we always felt like the leaders of reform—its pioneers—and we tried very hard to perform without landing in the mud.

But for all that, here is what I think is most important: In St. Petersburg, we always tried to follow the federal normative documents. The case of privatization was no different. There was nothing there resembling the opposition they had in Moscow, led by Mayor Luzhkov. Now, I see that the actual methods that were used to separate state property didn't matter. Now, all the private stores—be they in St. Petersburg or Moscow or Tambov—all work according to the same basic regime. Our arguments in 1992 about how to privatize—with an auction or by giving the store to the labor collective—seem insignificant. It was important that the trade points be in the hands of different owners and that there be real competition among them. Of course, in Moscow these processes were more painful. In August 1993, when I came to work in Moscow, the capital still had stores belonging to the labor collective or the state, with rude clerks and the traditional offerings on their shelves—three-liter jars of pickles and processed cheese.

* * *

Lets see, Alik. Lenin, you remember, passed decrees on land, on peace, and…something else. But look at our priorities: first liberating prices, then dividing up the Black Sea Fleet and so on, and only on January 26 did Yeltsin announce that Russia was no longer aiming missiles at the U.S.

Uh-huh.

You understand. In decreasing importance. Why is the modest Black Sea Fleet so important? We almost got into a war with Ukraine over the Tuzla Spit in 2003. Why is Ukraine more important than America for Russia? It's strange… What's behind it, do you think?

I don't think about it at all. Why should I?

Whether you think about it or not, you see, Russia can't make it without Ukraine.

It's just that it's your homeland—it's close to you, Igor, and you keep wanting to discuss it. For me it's just a piece of Russian history. So I'm not prepared to talk emotionally, with a catch in my throat, about Ukraine. For me, it's a country I rarely visit. A country with a more or less untreatable mentality. I was in Lvov once, once in Odessa, three times in Kiev, once in Kerch, and once in Yalta. That's it.

What about Russia and Ukraine, and the Russian Empire?

Strictly speaking, Peter the Great is considered the founder of the Russian state because he transformed us from a kingdom to an empire. The Russian Empire not only influenced the Russian mentality, but—to a great extent—formed it. And the imperial consciousness began with the appearance of the empire. Certainly not before that.

Well, that's logical.

So, Russian history in the Russian mentality fits into 200 years. And of that period, we spent 150 years fighting for the northern shores of the Black Sea. We won that fucking Crimea, Odessa, Nikolayev, and Novorossiisk. It began with Peter's war for the Azov Sea—and it lasted up until the Crimean War. Which we lost. Half of our history was spent on what the Ukrainians got! For free! They didn't lift a finger for it. Those Zaporozhian Cossacks, who fought the Poles, they didn't help Potemkin conquer the Black Sea. They stayed in Khortitsa, and when Potemkin came to them, they fled beyond the Danube, to the Ottoman pasha, and became Turkish subjects.

Svinarenko's Commentary:

Regarding the Black Sea and the Crimea

In the summer of 1992 I took my family on vacation to Foros. We stayed in a retreat run by the Central Committee or something like that—very close to where Gorbachev had been imprisoned. It was wonderful: the sea, the cypresses, even the air. I remember how happy I was. That I was vacationing in a place where I could never have gone under the old regime. But now that it was just a question of money, I could go there. I remember the amount: $140. I'm not sure that's it exactly, but it was not cheap then. Certain little things bothered us, but so little that it didn't impinge on the pleasure.

Now, it was a pretty pathetic place, actually. The wallpaper was coming unglued, the tiles were coming off, the furniture was Soviet dormitory style, and the housekeepers were rude and dishonest. And most importantly, they gave us very skimpy meals: buckwheat pancake, potato soup, and a child-size burger made of mystery meat… Fruit compote… There was something about it that smacked of army food, even prison food— that is, thoroughly Communist. A contemporary person of sound mind would just laugh and say you should have eaten in a restaurant. But the Central Committee had put all the private outfits out of business, and the only way they could make money, poor things, was to sell cherries in an open market by the hotel gates. Another thing—this was a sign of the times, proof of reforms and changes—there was a so-called casino nearby. But instead of caviar on toast (like at the Shangri La) or Georgian *kharcho* soup and chicken tabaka (like in the subterranean gaming halls of the National), all they served there was crappy coffee—at $3 a cup. The Central Committee gang kept things as they had been... Pathetic! No wonder they didn't try very hard to defend their regime in 1991. The hell with it, they thought.

I remember looking down from the tall cliff at the bay, once home to the helpless army ship that was supposed to protect General Secretary Gorbachev. I imagined him whiling away the time just a year earlier, just a year before me, in these blessed parts. He would have choked on cold porridge, eaten Soviet macaroni boiled to mush, and thought: "I'm so sick of this. ... They give me this crummy food, there's nothing to drink because of that fucking dry law.... They won't let me do anything, the minute something goes wrong, they arrest me.... I live just like the Soviet people! The hell with them all"

* * *

Here's the hard truth, Alik, the Black Sea is like the entrance to a certain place. You can start by just rubbing around at the entrance, but then you have to push in—into the Bosphorus and the Dardanelles—like a man. Instead, we just jerked off at the entrance without penetrating.

Haven't had any lately? What kind of imagery is that?

I'm just a poet deep inside; I think in images. What was the point of all this? the Mediterranean?

Yes. Nicholas I had destroyed the Turkish Navy in Sinope—he could have gone into the Bosphorus, it was his. But then, those British and French showed up: We won't let you, they said. Can you imagine the frustration? For 150 years we tried—and there it was on a platter, take it! Europe stood up for the Turks. Screwed us, again. The first time they cheated Byzantium and let the Turks take Constantinople. They didn't defend it, remember? Then they wouldn't let the Russians take Constantinople back and put a cross on St. Sophia. Today's Istanbul, with the crescent moon on the ancient Orthodox church, is the work of the British and French. What does it mean, the Turks taking Constantinople? It's as if the Saracens had conquered Italy. And then the rest of Europe would have developed without its cultural homeland—Italy. What would Europe be like? Without Italy, birthplace of the Enlightenment? As long as both Byzantium and Rome existed, we developed equally. But then, they took away our original homeland.

How do you know all this history, from birth or did you read it?

From books, of course.

Any fool can read things in books.

Ha-ha! That's a great line.

Somebody reached the Mediterranean, and somebody didn't. Who got in the way is secondary. There was someone in the way of everyone. Some allow people to get in their way, others do not. It's as if you had slept through privatization and then got mad that someone grabbed something for himself.

Europe did not want Russia's influence to increase in the Mediterranean. Can you imagine what would have happened if the Balkans joined up with Russia? Can you imagine it? It would have been a world power!

So what's the outcome? Russia could not handle its primary task. It did not realize its national potential.

It didn't manage, it wasn't able to become a great Slavic state.

The country had a destiny, it had meaning…

The meaning was that Russia was the third Rome. The third Rome!

But they said to us: This is not to be.

There will be no third Rome.

It's as if at some point they had told the Germans, You will never unite your German principalities into a single Germany. You will continue bumbling about on the level of Liechtenstein or Monaco.

It was even worse for us, Igor. Russia's destiny was to build a third Rome, to revive the Roman courage, the Roman spirit, the Byzantine spirit. Russia prepared for this for 500 years. And when it was finally ready for it, they old her: No.

The most important thing in its life, and it never happened.

The logic is as follows: A man is trained his entire life to become an Olympic champion. Trained and trained… They tell him, you can't take part in these local competitions—what if you overreach and hurt yourself. You have to prepare for the main event. You are doing so well in the training.

And then: the boycott of the Olympics.

Yes! They announce that we're not going to the Olympics. The man is in shock: Four years from now, I'll be too old. I won't be able to do it. It's over for me.

And when they say that we're supposed to come up with a national idea for Russia and pretend that such an idea had not existed all this time... It's rather feeble.

Russia should have become the great Slavic Orthodox empire. Its entire history was a warm-up for it. Peter the Great did not start with the Azov Sea instead of Narva by accident. It was only later that he started creeping up on the Baltic Sea, toward Europe, because he had realized that he would not get through the Black Sea.

But none of this appeared in the textbooks we studied, Alik! They lied about the division of markets, about imperialist predators...

No one taught it to us, you're right.

That means they took away this most basic vision of Russia and Russian goals. We're forced to learn about it for ourselves at our old age, reading Milyukov!

But, Igor, we've felt it all along, subconsciously. Do you remember how we got into all this? With a discussion of the reason for such an unjustified envy of the Ukrainians. That's how!

You're right!

The Ukrainians got for free what Russians spilled rivers of blood for. Mazepa got what Peter sold for a barrel of gold and ran off with the crown of our nation to the sultan, swearing an oath to him. Those bastards—all those Svinarenkos—got what was coming to them.

You're a bastard yourself, Alik! And the blood that was shed was Russian, and not German.

That's what you think!

All right, where did the German blood come from?

And who do you think the officers were? All those Minichs and Totlebens...
Under Catherine, when they were doing all that conquering, there were Germans. They fought in the conquest of the northern Black Sea coast from the Turks. That was done under Catherine, because Peter would have shit himself;

he couldn't have won it, neither Azov nor Prut. He was captured at Prut, as you remember. His wife bought his release by sleeping with the pasha or something.

But the Germans didn't have big political plans then.

By the way, Peter's wife was German. Ekaterina Skavronskaya. She was a servant of Pastor Gluck in East Prussian Marienburg.

Yes. Not the one who made the first translation of the Bible into Latvian? Hah!

It's quite possible. The years coincide. There couldn't have been that many Pastor Glucks in Livonia. So Catherine gave it up for the Turkish pasha, and they let old Peter free. Otherwise he'd be in the prison of the Turkish sultan. A German woman saved the Russian emperor.

That she did. Listen, Alik, how many years are there between England's interference in the Crimean War and the October Revolution? Roughly seventy. Seventy, does that remind you of anything? What it means is this: The October Revolution happened not because the Russians were assholes or because they felt like killing people. It happened because it's no empire if its mission is impossible!

Svinarenko's Commentary:

And then it happened again, seventy years later. Apparently, that's as long as the fuel lasts. Or maybe it's tied somehow to the human life span. My grandfather, born in 1901, built the empire with great enthusiasm. And he died in 1992, a year after its collapse. That is, when he retired in 1961, his generation of iron men was gone, their passion with them; and then came the generation of the 1960s, the *shestidesyatniki*, as they were known, who were not iron at all. As soon as the 1960s began, things started crumbling. Not because this person was so smart and this other person had a realization or read something in *samizdat*, but because the accelerator broke. For the next thirty years the car was just driving on momentum. And then, it stopped. I think that's what happened the first time, too. The people who took to the streets demanding a campaign on Constantinople at the start of World War I were the analog of our pensioners who are still demonstrating with their little red flags and portraits of Stalin. I think both sets probably had the same burning eyes and rotten teeth. And the same readiness to die for the idea of a great empire. It's beautiful, being able to die for an ideal.

* * *

Yes, Igor, and later Comrade Stalin built a new empire on the foundation of the fallen one. And he refurbished it with a new goal: to conquer all of Europe. Liquidate England and France, and then calmly deal with the Bosphorus. That goal wasn't achieved, either. Because America intervened. Now do you see why I'm upset about losing the Crimea? Odessa? Nikolayev and Kherson?

Well, now I do! So it's not so surprising that one of the top issues would be relations with Ukraine! And lower on the list—this is amusing—there's the declaration of Russia and America on ending the Cold War. That was like the final chord to all these general goals. The last nail in the coffin of the great idea. We will never fight again for the empire, in any form. The end.

But we'll still fight for a liberal empire, hah!

But that doesn't require a war.

No war. Pure expansion—of capital, mentality, lifestyle, living standards, views.

There's lots of that, Alik. To be like the States—for all inhabitants of the planet to wear baseball caps and eat Big Macs.

The great American dream. American Westerns have edged out French films.

Do you mean this is supposed to happen—the Russian dream? Foreigners will have to walk around in bast shoes and cheap oilcloth boots, speak Russian, and eat cabbage soup?

It means that we have to establish a living standard that will be appropriate for the entire post-Soviet space.

Living standard, what's that? In terms of money?

Well, something like that—money, and morals, and material life. You do understand what the great American dream was.

A way of life.

Right. And we have to introduce it.

It would be better to invent it first, and then introduce it.

It has to form itself, Igor. It's developing in Russia even now.

Maybe it is. It's clearer for you as a party worker [*Kokh was head of the election staff of SPS at the time*]. Here's what else I want to say about the Cold War. It's a very expressive word, "cessation," when you're talking about war. After all, in war you either win or lose. If one side talks about ending the war, it didn't win it. That means, it lost it. Defeated. It makes me think of Igor Malashenko again. Strange that he comes to mind so often, since we've only met three or four times. Nevertheless. He said that his profession had been the running of the Cold War.

I see.

He would go to Washington, stay there a half year, a year, writing reports. I asked him, "Did you hate the Americans? It was war, even if a cold one. Were you ready to bury them, bomb them?" He replied, "No, it was a game. They knew it, and so did we. All that nuclear containment, it was like a chess game." And one more thing. He considers it a serious political mistake to have hidden our defeat in the war from the people. It should have been announced solemnly, in a presidential speech. I can picture people gathered around their radios and TV sets, and the nation's father saying: "Gentlemen! Friends! Comrades! Brothers and sisters! The war we fought with imperialism—"

"—is lost."

"The war is lost. I ask you to handle the defeat courageously and not to lose your spirit. We are no longer a superpower, we are a vanquished, poor country. Let's work quietly. We need to live somehow…"

What a thought!

So Malashenko thinks it was a mistake not to have declared our defeat. What do you think, Alik?

Of course, it was a mistake. We needed to form a group with defeated Germany, defeated Japan—then our nation would have become more focused. People would have understood that they were closer to one another than they thought. Instead, they started looking for scapegoats: This one is rich, this one is poor, who stole what—bullshit. We had no sense of defeat, and that's a shame: Defeat unites people.

I recently heard an idea—it might have been Nemtsov's, he likes to talk about army reform. The idea was this: The army cannot be reformed gradually, a bit at a time. If in 1945 they tried to turn the Wehrmacht into the Bundeswehr gradually, they would have failed. It would have been the same Nazi Wehrmacht, with a new uniform and new terminology.

They would keep trying to go to war.

And that's why the Germans then acted decisively, in the only possible way. They disbanded the Wehrmacht, hanged the commanders, got rid of the uniform and flag. Nothing left. They hired foreign instructors to select and train people, to explain how to behave and how to live under the new regulations.

Lowered aggressiveness.

So we should have acknowledged defeat and then taken apart Soviet life stone by stone, leaving nothing behind, like the Wehrmacht.

Yes, you're right, Igor. Of course, after a defeat there is a kind of renaissance. Russia is no exception in that sense. It happened after the defeat by the Tatar Mongols. Nevertheless, despite this oppressive situation, there was an economic renaissance; the nation grew stronger, and then came the Battle of Kulikovo and the defeat of Mamai. Right?

Well, yes.

The next defeat was in the Crimean War. And right afterward: the emancipation of the serfs, democratic reforms, turbulent economic growth, Alexander II, Alexander III, railroads, a shitload of stuff. Defeat in the war with Japan—and right away you have the Constitution, the Stolypin reforms, the collapse of the *obshchina* system of village communes, a huge migration to the East, economic growth, 1913.

So…

So defeat is beneficial for Russia.

Naturally. The worst is what happened after World War II. Russia suffered a defeat—

Which was presented as a victory—

Yes, yes! Stalin had declared in the early days of the war that he intended to capture all of Europe. Instead of Europe, they gave him Romania, Bulgaria, Czechoslovakia, and a piece of Germany… But he didn't get England or France, and certainly not the Straits.

He had wanted the Straits, by the way.

Who wouldn't? An exit into the Mediterranean, that's a priority. So, there was no victory. No wonder Stalin didn't welcome the troops on a white horse...

Yes.

And did not mark Victory Day, you remember...

It was a defeat for him.

They didn't start celebrating Victory Day until 1965. I was just finishing first grade. I remember all those posters everywhere—our soldiers with machine guns, caps, looking so proud and happy... Basically, Russia won only one category in of World War II: "Short-term Military Victory." In terms of economics, Russia suffered a defeat; how we compare with the alleged loser, Germany. Territorially, we also got nothing great—some secondary bits of property. Instead of the Straits, instead of Paris and London, we got Romania and Czechoslovakia... Russia made this huge effort and got shit.

And then voluntarily refused to participate in the Marshall Plan—that was sheer stupidity. Why? Why did Russia refuse?

Who the fuck knows? It was exactly the same thing later, when after the war, Russia refused—twice, mind you—the money the Germans were offering to pay off former prisoners of their camps. The French got so much money! And it didn't seem excessive at all to the people who had ruined their health in the camps. So, Russia was defeated. And that should have been declared. People would have said: okay, bitch, now it's time for us to work at last. Enough saber rattling and conquering. But no! They suffered a defeat from which some benefit could have been gained, and they passed it off as a victory. That's the most horrible part. No victory, no benefit—just deceit.

Let's get back to the defeat in the Cold War, Igor.

It's the same thing—they covered up the defeat there, too. The line was that "friendship" won. And now we're, like, best friends.

Decided to make up. Nobody got beat up. A draw.

People believed that was true for a long time, remember?

And the polite Westerners decided not to remind us that we had lost.

They said: Why don't you remove your troops…

And acknowledge all the debts…

And we won't let you into NATO.

No, what they said was: We're going to expand NATO, and we'll force you to pay debts that you did not incur, and we'll kick your troops out. The only promise we're making in return is that we won't remind you too often that you lost the Cold War.

Hmmm.

And it isn't because we want to spare your pride. We know that if you admit defeat, you'll consolidate and made an economic leap forward. That doesn't suit us, so we'll keep calling it a draw—pretend that we agreed to make up, and now Russia is new and democratic. Just so you won't consolidate.

And on that wave of good will, Alik, we removed our troops. Because we were friends. Why didn't we say: "We'll take our troops out tomorrow—from Germany, and the Baltics—if by tomorrow you build us bases in Russia just like the ones we're leaving behind."

Nah. The Westerners would have said: We're not building you anything. Moreover, we're turning off the power and water at your bases. You'll have to helicopter-in diesel and food, because we won't let your supply trains carrying fuel, food, and clothing cross our territory. And you can stay on those bases as long as you like.

So you think this wasn't a trick?

Of course not. What bases? When there's no money, teachers are hungry, old people starve. You'll take away those bases in two years because you'll be broke, Igor. You'll crawl back, begging for money to bring out your soldiers, who'll be near-dead from exhaustion.

We clung to our military bases in Vietnam and Cuba. But for all of President Putin's militaristic fervor, we shut down those bases ourselves. Without any pressure from the West.

All right. Let's see, what else do we have? In February, Yegor Gaidar was appointed Minister of the Economy and of Finances. Is that right? In 1992?

No, he was appointed at least in November 1991. Yes, on the seventh.

Maybe he was just acting minister?

He was acting. The prime minister was Yeltsin himself. First deputy was Gennady Burbulis. Gaidar was minister of the economy and finance from the start. I was running privatization then. Manevich and I worked well together. It was fun. We were young and happy. My daughter was born on September 1. That's my second daughter. The first was already twelve years old. I was a happy father. I even had an apartment. I traveled abroad like an adult—I had been to England, Denmark, and Finland. They were short educational trips. The mayor's office sent us.

That was serious stuff, getting to see a capitalist country in those days. Must have made an impression on you, Alik.

Yes, many very good impressions. England: We lived in the north, in the city of Durham. Ancient cathedral, 13th century university. Then we were in Newcastle, and then we crossed the border into Scotland.

Where the mines were being restructured.

That's right. We visited those mines, those small businesses that were built at the expense of the treasury and then given to the miners. That was the experience of restructuring mines. Then I traveled along the border with Scotland, all those castles and ramparts the Romans built for protection from the Scots. An enormous number of castles, enormous! And I was in Denmark. I liked it a lot. We were in the north, near the border with Norway—you could see across the bay.

Here's something else from 1992: "Accept Gaidar's resignation from the post of minister of the economy and finances." That was April. What was that about?

They got rid of Gaidar and made Victor Chernomyrdin prime minister. Remember that, Igor?

Vaguely.

I don't remember much more than that. There was a congress of people's deputies, and under pressure from the deputies, they fired Gaidar. Then the deputies offered candidates—Vladimir Kadannikov, Chernomyrdin, and so on. Yeltsin conferred with Gaidar and asked Kadannikov to withdraw. That left Chernomyrdin, and he was confirmed.

Gaidar must have been too extreme for those conditions. Let's do it gradually, quietly—why raise a ruckus? So they got rid of Yegor.

Right.

So how did it happen that they got rid of Gaidar and then passed the privatization program without him?

You'll have to ask Chubais about that. I was still in St. Petersburg then, and I just accepted it as a *fait accompli*. In 1992, I think in the summer, an interesting thing happened that is not very vividly reflected in our historiography. But it had fantastic significance for the future of reform—and put Russia on the brink of catastrophe.

What was that?

There was a period when prices were rising steeply, inflation was at several percentage points a month. Then the situation reached an equilibrium, in April or May. But businesses were suffering from a deficit of cash flow. Everything had gone up in price, and they had to buy raw materials at the new, high prices. So the volume of production fell sharply. Back then, the directors and the establishment were still deeply Soviet in their thinking. Volume in natural quantities was their fetish. The directors said, Look, the economy is on its feet, but we're producing a tenth of what we used to... We need to pay the workers... and so on, and so on. And a "brilliant" decision was made. Since the first deputy prime minister then was Georgy Khizha from St. Petersburg, who stopped everything, because—like every factory director—he thought he was the smartest and knew everything. He persuaded Georgy Matyukhin (I think he was director of the Central Bank then) of that, and they made a joint proposal. They wanted the Central Bank to give factories direct credits, to stimulate their cash-flow.

Yes, go on.

These were loans not from funds that were in circulation or in the budget; this was money that was merely printed. Well, the Central Bank only has money that it has printed. So. These loans were made in colossal amounts. It amounted to an uncontrolled emission of currency. This increased inflation so much that it took until the fall of 1994 to get it back into manageable limits. And then Chubais came up with a plan for financial stabilization, which began to bear fruit by the end of 1995. In other words, it took three years to catch that inflation, which was galloping all over the place. Remember what was happening to the ruble–to–dollar exchange rate, Igor?

I do. It was 120 rubles in 1992, and 1,200 in 1993.

Right. And when Central Bank chairman Sergei Dubinin implemented the denomination from 1997 to 1998, a dollar cost 5,000.

How could I not remember that?

Then it cost five rubles, like the franc. The French franc had the same value in dollars as the ruble. It was very convenient if you went to France, because the prices were in rubles.

So, that addition to the cash-flow dealt the economy a huge blow. Without it, we could have had financial stabilization, a decrease in inflation, and an end to the crisis a good three years sooner. If not for that creative "improvement" of cash-flow.

What are you saying, Alik? That one dilettante came up with a shit idea and all the rest executed it?

Because they were all assholes. No one knew any better. Yeltsin, for example, understood nothing.

What about Gaidar?

Gaidar is the one who dragged Khizha to Moscow from St. Petersburg in the first place. With Chubais. That's why they couldn't speak out too strongly against him. People would have said, "Come on, guys, you're the ones who brought him here!" Anyway, by then Chernomyrdin was prime minister and Gaidar was gone. There was no one to stop him, and you see what happened. He was kicked out later, naturally—he didn't last very long as deputy prime minister.

Russia was attacked by the Tatars—and the French, and the Germans—with sword and fire. They'd destroy half the country, burn it down, kill the inhabitants—and we're all right. And you tell me about Khizha. What does Russia care about Khizha! He's forgotten already.

Don't try to pass off banal traits as unique ones. Is any other country so different? Armies went through Poland, Germany, Japan with sword and fire—and what, they weren't restored? They went through China with sword and fire three times—two armies lost, and what, it hasn't been restored? It has. That's the way every country behaves. There's nothing unique about a country being restored. What else is there for it to do? Of course, it is restored.

A powerful charge of optimism.

Do you have examples to the contrary, Igor? A country that was attacked by sword and fire and it did not come back? Can you name a single country?

Byzantium.

Why do you say that? Byzantium is now called Turkey, and it's flourishing! The same people live there, they've just been "baptized" into Muslims—and there you go. They're Greeks! I don't see any slanted eyes or round faces—where are all the Turkish features? Take a Greek and put him next to a Turk. If they don't speak, how can you tell which is which?

If they're silent and naked. And their privates have to be covered. The Greeks aren't circumcised. I can't tell a Bulgarian from a Turk, when they're dressed.

You can't. Because anthropologically, they are one and the same. One nation! They're all Greeks, who inhabited those parts for millennia.

I remember another thing about 1992, Alik: the fad for gas pistols. Do you remember that?

Yes. I had one. They gave them to us at work. At the State Property Committee, when I moved to Moscow in 1993. All us deputies of Chubais were given pistols, and some actually wore them. In a special holster. All the time. They liked it. I didn't wear it... It was tucked away at home somewhere.

What kind did you have? A Parabellum, I'll bet. A foreign, German one?

No, some little thing. I turned it back in when I quit.

I bought one myself. For a hundred dollars. A lot of people carried them then. If only for the chance to shoot into the air when they were drunk. A friend of mine was drinking once with a pal in the park. And some hooligans came by, shouting... My friend, or maybe it was his buddy, had a gas pistol. So the one with the pistol says, "Shh, kept quiet until they go by." The other was surprised: "What are you afraid of? If they bother us, you can shoot them with your gas pistol!" The first one replies: "I wouldn't be afraid if I didn't have the pistol, but now I'm worried they'll steal it, and it's expensive."

Hahaha!

So that was the fad back then, for weapons—not real ones, but toned-down ones. Real weapons, as the chief of the Ministry of Internal Affairs and the majority of deputies tell us, should not be given to Russians. Because they will kill one another. Would you give guns to Russians?

Oh, that's complicated question.

And an interesting one.

You see, it really depends on which Russians.

The ones who aren't seeing psychiatrists.

Wait just a minute. Remember what I once said about homonyms? That the word "Russian" is used for two completely different nations? The Russians before the Bolsheviks is one nation. The ones under the Soviet regime are another. They are different, but the name is the same. If you talk about Russians in the first sense, then strictly speaking, they had the right to bear arms. People bought pistols easily—

And used those pistols to kill gendarmes and army officers. They organized the October Revolution that way. There's something similar now in Chechnya—the accessibility of weapons and the ease of their use.

—Russians were an armed nation. The Cossacks had the legal right to arms; they kept cavalry carbines under the bed.

That's what I'm saying: And they used those guns to start the revolution.

But before that, they had weapons for a thousand years; there were no limits. And using that freedom, they built a great empire.

So would you give them arms or not, Alik? I don't understand.

The nation that once was—no one asked me my opinion! But they were never forbidden to have arms. It was Comrade Stalin who banned guns.

It was very funny then. Mikhail Prishvin—in his hunting stories— mentions ramrod rifles, which loaded from the muzzle, very slowly. They weren't antiques; they were made in Soviet factories. The idea was that with a rifle like that you wouldn't go fight against the army. You wouldn't rebel against the regime.

But should the new Russian people be given weapons or not? I would think a long and hard before doing it, Igor. These people are completely irresponsible.

If they take their money to invest with Selenga's Russian House or MMM and then go to parliament to get it back, then they are clearly psychologically disturbed. How can I give people like that a pistol? If they can't even keep track of their own money? They gave it to one place and demanded it back from another! Do you see the difference between these two nations? The old Russian people did not kill one another, and the nation grew as if on yeast—the population doubled every ten years. The only thing they used those weapons for was the revolution.

That only occasion was enough. The nation managed to halve itself with those weapons. In the final analysis.

But this new nation wants to shoot without a revolution.

The old one shot accurately: look at the revolution and the Civil War. But this one isn't doing too much shooting. It's just your personal opinion that they would. But in fact, anyone can buy a hunting rifle in a store and shoot all he wants. And where are the reports of these shoot-outs? I don't see any. And here's another funny thing. We still have a universal draft for the army. Everyone is taken in and issued a machine gun, tank, or missile; there's plenty of napalm in the warehouses. And there are special reserves of anthrax...

Where are you heading with this, Igor?

Look. The military, with the help of the police, picks up a foolish young man, herds him into the army and forces weapons into his hands. And as soon as the man grows up a bit and learns a few things and is back in the civilian world—having returned his tank and received his credits—he's told: "If we catch you with even a lady's Browning, you'll serve another two years, but this time in a prison camp." He asks the legislators: "What's the matter with you people? I had a cannon for two years and I never once shot at the Kremlin with it!"—

—"voluntarily. When you ordered me to, then I shot. And not without great reluctance. You tried to talk us into it for a long time and found only three out of a thousand who were willing to shoot from tanks at the White House. See how peace-loving we are?"

So explain this contradiction to me.

Why do I have to explain anything? Would you stop bugging me, for Christ's sake, Igor? Why do I have to explain?

Because you say that the people are not the same. Well, maybe we should let them have guns anyway?

I don't have a gun, but my guards do. They'll defend me. I have an alarm system around the perimeter of the place. Infrared rays. If someone crosses them, to kill me—

In prison camps, they also have alarmed perimeters. They call it the cuckoo. If anyone crosses the line, it cuckoos. Does yours?

No, you just see everything on the monitors.

Don't you have a signal that is sent throughout the territory?

Maybe. No one's ever triggered it before.

Well, you have bodyguards. I have a friend who sleeps with a loaded rifle under his bed. Sometimes, when people try to break in, he shoots over their heads. And he explains, "When I'm out of town, my wife sits by the window with the rifle." At least you have your own bodyguards.

There are dacha guards here, too; they patrol the entire community. That's why I can leave my children here without worrying. Why are we talking only about me, Igor? Tell me about yourself and that year already.

Well, fine, if you're interested. It was my most steady year. I worked the entire time in the same place in the same position.

It was the same for me in 1992. I worked in one place, doing my favorite work—selling state property. Everything was simple and good; I had good friends near me, I was in my beloved St. Petersburg, everything was terrific. My daughter was born... That's what I call happiness.

Kokh's Commentary:

Privatization was not the most important event in my life in 1992. It was the birth of my second daughter.

This is how it went. When my wife was pregnant, she had an ultrasound. We naturally wanted a boy, already having a girl. The doctor looked, and apparently he understood us so he said, here's no sign yet of a boy, but it may be too soon, or maybe the fetus is on its side... In other words, he gave us hope. Now I realize that he didn't say anything that should have encouraged me, but back then it felt as if I had been told "You are going to have a boy." It's strange, the human psyche, isn't it? They say no. You leave the office, with a ridiculous grin on your face, absolutely certain that they said yes.

It's the same with love. You prepare, you worry, you lose sleep. You imagine these sweet pictures... So you make your proposal... And you're told, you're very nice, let's be friends. Now, what would an observer think? Right: you've been sent packing. But what do you think? You think: Everything is going well. She loves me!

That was my case. So late at night I took my wife to the maternity hospital. I remember, it was on the corner of Chernyshevsky and Tchaikovsky—the intersection of a rebel and a composer! I came back in the morning. A boy? No, a girl! I didn't make any jokes like "Can you look again?" or "What's his name?" It was clear that they were telling me the truth. A girl... All right, then.

We decided to name her after my aunt, my father's sister. She was older than my father, and so in 1941, when Germans were deported from the Soviet Union, she was sent to the labor army. That's what they called the camps during the war where people were sent without even a fabricated, trumped-up sentence. Just like that. In this case, for being German. She worked felling timber throughout the entire war, somewhere in the middle reaches of the Ob River. After the war, she moved back to the kolkhoz in Kazakhstan where exiled old people and children labored in workday units, for their share of the income. She and her ten-year-old brother (my father) and their mother (my grandmother, Avgustina Rudolfovna—my grandfather, David Karlovich, had died in 1945 just when the war ended) worked there until Khrushchev allowed exiles like them to have passports again. Somewhere in the mid-1960s, they were permitted to return home. My aunt packed up and moved back to Krasnodar Krai. I spent every summer vacation visiting her.

She was an incredibly kind woman. Her entire life she was oppressed, humiliated, second-class. But she did not grow bitter. She always sang German songs and ditties. She cooked and baked, took care of the livestock, dug in her garden. She also worked in a *sovkhoz*, the state farms of that period. The kitchen, livestock, and garden were all in her free time—stolen from sleep.

My wife visited often, bringing our older daughter. I remember meeting them at the airport every time, and they'd be carrying a bucket of schmaltz and liverwurst, huge crates made of lathes with handles that were filled with southern fruits, jams and compotes, and sacks of walnuts. They carried all that, almost 100 kilograms of goodies. Everything was lovingly packed and organized. For her favorite nephew, "Alfredle." The egoism of youth? Or was it that all other relatives were just used to Auntie Olya, who always wanted to do something nice for us—as if that was her only function. Swinishness on our parts, of course.

She died, and my wife and I decided to name our daughter after her: Olga. So there is an Olga Kokh in the world again. It makes me feel good.

Children… It's only after your second child appears that you begin to appreciate what it means to have children. You watch them grow attentively, how they begin to understand things. This animal feeling rises within you. Heavy, horrible, wild. Protection of progeny, of your babies. Instinct. It's not the Party or the Komsomol, not our beloved leader, not wise books, and not damned fashion, but instinct that makes us love our children. Instinct that we acquired not in the stone caves in the glow of the first camp fires, not when we learned to hunt the wooly mammoth together, but earlier, much earlier. When we were still fish, mollusks; when we were first divided into men and women; when we learned the sweetness of coitus.

The honesty and purity of love for our children is so unspoiled by civilization that you unwittingly try to hide behind that feeling whenever you do something vile, or when you're in a bad way, when you're in pain. I think it was the writer Sergei Dovlatov who called his child "a small battery of happiness."

Our daughter was born on September 1st, at 8 in the morning (funny: born, and off to school on the same date, but different years, of course). There's an incident involving that date which I've described elsewhere. That summer Yeltsin promulgated his famous decree on vouchers. It stated that all citizens of Russia born through August 31, 1992, were entitled to privatization checks (popularly known as vouchers). Therefore Olga was not entitled to one. I forgot all about it.

After she was born, I was drinking with Manevich, Sergei Belyayev, and some other friends. The phone kept ringing, people calling with congratulations. Chubais called from Moscow. The next day, there came a new decree with a change in the old one—paragraph so-and-so, subparagraph this-and-that, replace "August 31" with "September 1." I still don't know if that was done specially, or just a coincidence. Chubais keeps mum about it and just giggles. When asked directly, he replies, "Seriously? Really? I don't remember that at all." That's the story.

* * *

Now, Igor, it's your turn, tell me a bit more about yourself then.

I was editor of the crime department at that time. I was embarrassed that I wasn't writing anything. I only gave orders. I administrated, went to editorial board meetings, hired people, fired them, made deals with the cops. Toed the line. But just as I had gotten out to report on breaking events in 1991—Latvia and Armenia—in 1992, I dropped everything and flew to Georgia. Accidentally. I was having a drink with Volodya Kryuchkov, who had worked for me as a correspondent and then went off

to be a deputy in parliament. It turned out that he was flying to Tbilisi, with a plane full of humanitarian aid. Remember how that was a topic back then? People collected used children's' clothing and canned goods in their buildings…. Remember?

I remember, I do!

Svinarenko's Commentary:

Here's the background on my visit to Georgia (from the newspapers):

> Fighting between the allies and foes of President Gamsakhurdia has ended in the center of Tbilisi and threatens to move into the forests around the city. On the night of January 5, the president—along with his bodyguard and entourage—fled from the half-destroyed House of Government and left the country. The victorious opposition is trying to write new or at least long-forgotten names on the ruins of authoritarianism.
>
> … Shooting broke out again around Tskhinvali. The situation remains tense; it is difficult to supply Tbilisi with food, and the crime-fostering state of affairs on the streets is worrying.
>
> The Georgian mass media are discussing the amount in rubles, gold, and hard currency that the president and his closest aides took out of the country when they fled, and also the prospects of Eduard Shevardnadze's return to his homeland. The ex-minister does not exclude that possibility at all.

* * *

So, Alik, I flew to Tbilisi. They had just overthrown Gamsakhurdia in Georgia then. There were street battles, like a revolution. That meant destruction, emptiness, cold. Not your shashlyk-and-wine extravaganza. I don't know how it would have turned out if we hadn't been given shelter by the Patriarch of Georgia Ilya II. We slept and ate there, by the palace. I understood many things when I dined at Ilya II's. It wasn't a formal banquet, it was just his staff stopping to eat at noon—about twenty people at a big refectory table, monastery style.

And what did the Lord send for lunch?

You won't believe it: They fed us the Dutch canned meat that we had brought on our plane. Can you imagine? In Georgia! Damn those revolutions… But there were a few local foods, thank the Lord: pickled zakuski, chacha, and wine. At least they didn't offer us Dutch gin or French wine. That helped the situation a bit.

What if it had been humanitarian grappa and they just told you it was local chacha?

I like that! But I doubt it. Here's what I have as a memento of that trip: Ilya II gave me a small icon of George the Dragon Slayer.

And I really wanted to go to America in 1992. I don't know if you can understand this, but it really bothered me that I hadn't yet seen the U.S. Indians, Cold War, American literature, politics, the second front...

Which had been of no significance, they always assured us.

...the atom bomb, Vietnam, the flight to the moon... It all formed such a vivid picture that I thought that if you haven't been to America, you are missing something very important, you can't get a full and complete picture of the world. And you can't consider your education complete. I suffered from this gap in my understanding; it tormented me and drove me crazy. I tried everything I could to get a trip there. There were a lot of possibilities: an excursion to Washington, a trip around the country, courses for journalists... I kept filling out applications. But I was never accepted. People all around me were going there—two, three times each... I analyzed the situation and realized that they were taking only Jews. For some reason, they weren't taking Ukrainians.

Let the Ukrainians go to Canada. There's a Museum of Ukraine in Toronto, the most important one in the world. The central one, so to speak.

That may be. But I'm not so sure... If you compare my Ukrainianness with your Germanness...

... they'll compete. Hah!

Probably. You can eat wurst with beer and drive around in a German BMW, but I can eat fatback and vodka and drive around on a Zaporozhets.

Well, I know the German alphabet.

Remember the joke about anti-Semitic languages, Alik? Besides German and Ukrainian, there was also Arabic. Anyway, I wondered, Why are the Americans taking only Jews? They naturally wanted to get as many people on visits to the U.S. as possible, to develop some positive feelings for America.

Agents of influence.

If a person likes another country, then he is in part an agent of influence. And the best people for that role are cosmopolites, who are most frequently Jews. Simple, understandable logic. It's hard for people to imagine that you could have Ukrainian cosmopolites like me. So. Some people went there and stayed, brought their families. Life is so steady there. It's like living in the zoo. Here we're like animals in the wild. The comfort level is not as good, but it has its plusses. By then I had gotten over my thoughts of running off, and I just wanted to go to the States for a visit. Did you ever think of taking off, Alik?

Not by then. At the start of perestroika I had considered it. But thoughts of leaving our home left me completely when I was elected chairman of the executive committee—that is, mayor—of Sestroretsk.

So what changed for you? Or began? How would you describe that process?

I became interested in what was happening here. The second wave of wanting to get the hell out came after I left government, when the criminal case began.

So, in 1992 America for me was this place of longing. I kept thinking: Why haven't you been there, you idiot?

What else happened? *Kommersant* moved to a new building. In 1992, Yakovlev rented a school and, later, privatized it. There were three stories, and then he added another. We had an office and a gym and a sauna, just like real people. When we moved there, on Vrubel Street, we had (among other things) a priest bless the building. It was in the Sokol metro station region, where the artist's community was.

Andrei Vasilyev left then. He said he didn't like the concept. He didn't have another to suggest in its place, so he left. He went to work at ORT television then, I think. Berezovsky was in charge there. They became pals.

So we started doing the *Kommersant Daily*. For that time, it was fascinating—a thick newspaper about real life. But we worked a very regimented schedule—shit, no days off. We published the last issue of the week on Saturday, and then on Sunday morning we were back.

It was like being drafted. You would come home late at night, sleep, and head back to the office early in the morning. It was exactly October 7 when we started . My daughter's birthday was coming up. And she—I had only one then—called me up at work. "You know, it's my birthday on Saturday, I'll be three, and you're invited." And I thought, why is she inviting me, where else would I be? And then I realized how it all seemed to a child. She was asleep in the morning when I left and asleep when I came home at night. This went on for a week, two, three, no days off. She must have decided that I was a visiting passenger. Who shows up once a month.

Haha!

And who needed to be invited specially to come over. If a child doesn't see me for three weeks, she can't know that I live at home and that I'm there every night for a short night's sleep.

At first the newspaper was listless and unintelligible. The first few issues of any publication are like that.

You have to develop the style, of course.

And it was funny—we took people off the street. We advertised. We practically slapped posters on fences. People would come in; we would perform for them, answer their questions. We hired off the street—and it was fine! Some of them are still working there.

Yakovlev was a talented manager, then?

There's no two minds about it. Miracles don't happen. If the man could create an empire from zero...

He burned out very quickly, Igor. He lost the drive. He realized that he had to stop before he destroyed his own creation. He sold out and moved to Los Angeles. It takes so much energy to run an empire—and it doesn't come out of thin air. That's how I see it.

Alik, you're a capitalist, so maybe you understand Yakovlev better. I thought if every year I worked there was like three normal years, what was his coefficient? I lived through so much there, yet it was so much greater for him.

What I know about myself is that I'm only good for short-term projects. Then I need a period of relaxation. I give all that energy, and then I have to replenish it. I can't work like Chubais, year after year after year... Does he run on plutonium or something?

That's why I say we have to take care of oligarchs like Gusinsky and Berezovsky, and now Khodorkovsky. There aren't many like them...

Yakovlev came up with the institution of rewriters. People sitting around rewriting other people's stories. They weren't reporters, they were structural linguists and whatnot.

Creating the brand style!

No, just adding clarity. Making clear what people tried to say. Without emotions. Filtering out the crap.

You probably had your own software, too?

Yes. And video was very popular then, too.

I went through that even earlier. I had my first VCR in 1989. Remember Elektronika, made by Pozitron?

I had that, too. It was silvery.

I had my job at the Polytechnic, and we were teaching courses to raise the qualifications of the chief workers at Pozitron. On management psychology, as I recall. They paid us with those video players—the kingdom of barter was coming into being. So I had this VCR that I attached to my television. It didn't have a decoder, so all the films were in black and white.

I soldered in a decoder.

I didn't. I just bought a Russian TV with a decoder. So back in 1989, I managed to watch everything. By 1992, it was a stage I had gone through.

You were fast. I was just starting to watch in 1992. You'd get two or three cassettes, a bottle or two of cognac, and you'd stay up all night watching...
I also buried my grandfather in 1992.

The one who worked for the secret police?

And my grandmother said, too bad he had to die now instead of two years earlier!

In the sense that he would never have known that the Soviet Union fell apart?

No, she was upset that we buried him as a private individual. Under the Soviet regime, there would have been speeches, and banners, and a salute....

Medals on a pillow...

That sort of thing.

Svinarenko's Commentary:

In December 1992 my grandfather, Ivan Dmitrievich Svinarenko, died. May he rest in peace. I admired him ever since I was a little kid—and that respect grew over the years. I've rarely seen such a straight-up person, who never swerved from his chosen path, who executed his plans without falling for temptation and being distracted by personal enrichment.

I would have preferred my grandfather to have served the Whites and to have espoused liberal values—but you can't drop a single word from the song, as they say. My grandfather, at a very young age, joined the Komsomol [the Young Communist League] and then the Cheka. He thought that he would help create a better world… On the other hand, if even the writer Count Alexei Nikolayevich Tolstoy went to serve the Reds and still considered himself a decent man, then what could you expect from a peasant kid?

I remember that modest home on the outskirts of Makeevka, where I often visited. Three rooms, whitewashed walls, and a lot of books—by my standards at the time. A full bookcase. Only one bookcase. Among the books were the collected words of Stalin. And his infamous "Short Course." And a book-sized portrait of him on the wall. In a frame under glass.

Grandfather had a very rare trait: He lived in total harmony with his words and convictions. He had decided once that social revolution was necessary—and he began personally trying to accomplish it. After that he came to the conclusion that the Whites had to be killed, and he went to fight in the Red Army. He didn't send anyone in his place… He believed that you had to kill the internal enemy—and he went to work for the secret police. Then he worked for a long time in the mines. He studied and almost got his engineering degree, which was a big deal for a peasant boy—by today's standards that was like getting into Oxford. Like an MBA. And then came the war. A Moscow student, he signed up for the volunteer army and was waiting for orders to proceed to the front. But the Party decided to send him to the Urals—there could be no war without coal, the strategic energy source of the time. After that he managed to desert the labor front for the regular front, in Leningrad. Then, after the war, he was old and lame—he could barely walk—but he worked as a trade inspector, as a volunteer in the Party commission. Apparently, he was tormented by the thought that he had left the secret police too soon, without destroying the contras when he could. Grandfather taught me that if a man sold meat, he could easily sell another man as well. He kept quoting Suvorov: Quartermasters can be jailed without trial or investigation for five years, and tried after that—and you can find that they need a longer term.

(And you, Alik, wonder why I'm not thrilled by capitalism! Or that I don't find the bourgeoisie adorable! You see the training I had from a Red machine gunner, a Kharkov Chekist and Makeyevka miner... You should be glad I didn't go join Zyuganov and the Communist Party, with that background.)

And here's something else touching. When all that information was being published during perestroika, my grandfather read and read.... And he found the courage to admit that his views had been wrong. He didn't run around town, spittle flying, waving the red flag. He admitted it. You could make nails out of people like him.

He lived a long life: 91 years. And a happy one. He went through two wars and got off "only" with heavy wounds and an invalid certification—which, however, allowed him to work. He limped and used a cane, but he continued to work. He had children, grandchildren, great-grandchildren. His conscience was clear. He did what he thought necessary, often in life-threatening conditions. His certainty in his righteousness was confirmed for him by his modest means: proof that he didn't steal. He had medals, respect and honor, and a garden in which he planted small nut trees and lived to harvest sacks of nuts. The posthumous disgrace of his beloved Stalin and the collapse of the empire he built and defended in its most dramatic moments—the collapse of his ideal—all came at the very sunset of his life. We were lucky to see freedom at a young age. And he was lucky that he saw the fall of his ideals with cold, old eyes, standing on the edge of his grave. Remember, Alik, that teacher you had at the institute—you said that if all Communists had been like him, you would have joined them? It was the same for me with my grandfather. If everyone in the Communist Party had been like my grandfather, I would have applied.

So. I went to Vnukovo Airport to get a flight for his funeral. The airport in Donetsk was shut down—no fuel for return flights. It took unbelievable efforts to get back home. The Union had collapsed, the decay and destruction was upon us. I got to Ukraine and then it turned out that the trains weren't leaving the local station. It was as if the world of my dear departed youth had returned, with its chaos and dilapidation. There, in that cold train station, in that small town I didn't know how to get the hell out of and which was now in a foreign land, I began to see that Moscow was not the best vantage point for watching the tragedy unfold—the collapse of a great empire. From Moscow all this glory was not visible. I hired a car, and two highly suspicious characters drove me into the snowy steppe in the night. My grandfather's coffin had been lowered into the grave by the time I had arrived. Did I make it in time or not? It depends how you look at it.

The other memorable part of that trip was that you couldn't use rubles in Ukrainian stores and there were no currency exchanges. No way to buy a drink. I passionately talked an old neighbor into selling me a quart of moonshine for two dollars, which was extremely generous for those days. She heard me out dubiously—who needs those strange green bills, she seemed to think. But she gave in, probably because she remembered me as a boy and felt sorry for me. She figured she wouldn't be impoverished by the loss of a quart of her booze.

Such long-ago, innocent times. It feels as if 1992 was fifty years ago, and not just yesterday.

12.

1993

The Twelfth Bottle

*K*okh moved from St. Petersburg to Moscow to help Chubais carry out privatization. He recalls: "We would toil round the clock, with short breaks for sleep, living on tea and pirozhki." Svinarenko left crime reporting for glossy journalism—that is, he went from the crime beat at Kommersant to the magazine Domovoi.

The country underwent a swift rebellion, as sometimes happens, in October. Kokh ran around Moscow, dodging bullets, listening to the "music of revolution" and cursing the opponents of privatization, who kept trying to steal things. Svinarenko, during those hot October days, wrote articles on the beautiful bourgeois life as if nothing was going on, and instead of waiting on the barricades beneath a grim, rainy sky, he strolled through peaceful, sunny Paris. And then flew off to New York, Sydney, and everywhere else. It was all for work, and urgent.

You know, Alik, 1992—which we discussed over the last bottle— seemed awfully vapid and unreal in hindsight. People had not recovered yet from 1991; they didn't dare believe that it was real, that you could do whatever you wanted.

Yes….

It wasn't clear: who, what, when. And then, at last, came 1993.

And we rushed into the fortress on the shoulders of the enemy.

At last, we rushed into the fortress and said: Oh, really! This is all ours? And this, too? You mean, we can do whatever we want?

Yes, yes, yes!

That all became clear only in 1993.

Among the people who understood that were Ruslan Khasbulatov, speaker of the Russian Supreme Soviet, and former vice-president Alexander Rutskoi, who decided in 1993 that they could do anything and that Yeltsin was just in their way. According to the Constitution, the Congress of People's Deputies is the highest authority in the country—everyone else is subordinated to it—and it can do away with the president. They thought: Who the hell needs that publicly elected fellow? We'll handle it ourselves, just the two of us.

What sort of people had ended up in the Supreme Soviet? You would think, Alik, that here we had a huge country with a great legacy. Why not pick at least a thousand wise, handsome, decent, educated people from across the country? Couldn't we get a thousand, out of 150 million? Why not place these marvelous people in all the key positions? Let them sit in the Supreme Soviet and run the country! That would have been beautiful and grand logic. So why do we keep electing such boring people instead? Can you explain that to me?

It's that way all over the world.

Go on...

It's that way all over the world—we're not unique. Why do you keep looking for uniqueness in crap like that?

Who knows...

I had a debate on the "Domino Principle"—a long time ago, maybe two years. With Boris Reznik from the Far East. He's chairman of the anti-corruption commission, I think. So he said, "Russia is number one in corruption, in the size of the bribes." He talked and talked. Then it was my turn. I said, "You know, I travel abroad a lot, especially in America, and I go to Europe, too, and I read the papers. There, you have a criminal case against Kohl, Chirac, I won't even mention Berlusconi. And so on. And those corporate scandals in the U.S. have fucked everyone over. Their government entities closed their eyes to it for ten years. Surely they could have demanded a prospectus on planned share issues, financial reports. The SEC, which is always used as an example here— they say even a fly can't sneak through it... Well, for ten years flies got through all right, flies the size of eagles, and no one gave a shit. Billions of dollars went all over the place! People went bankrupt, used their homes as collateral…all gone. Hundreds of people, thousands, millions lost money. And what about the corruption in China! They execute them in batches for it. A $30 billion tranche from the IMF for agriculture vanished. Billions of dollars! Thirty billion! We don't lose money like that. But they did in China, and they can't even figure our where the money went. But all the officials who were in charge of that tranche have satellite dishes on their roofs and drive around in Mercedes… Everything as it should be."

Where is the tranche?

There is no tranche; it never reached the ordinary peasants.

What's thirty billion to them, Alik? That's just fifteen dollars per person. Nothing.

Well, my point was that we were not at the top of the list in corruption. And Reznik got so offended. No, he said, we're first. That Kokh is saying we're not number one again.

You mean we won't be able to gather the best people to run the country?

No.

It will be run by whoever comes along.

Yes. We've discussed the principle of cybernetics before, Igor. People don't like the smart guy but the guy who's most like them.

Well, I don't know anything about cybernetics, but I knew that Boris Nikolayevich Yeltsin was like us.

He tried hard to be even more so. He rode the trolleybus.

Only before elections.

Yeah, he stopped when he no longer had to. He hasn't ridden in one the last ten years.

Right. What else of importance happened that year? In January we had a treaty with the United States on SALT.

Listen, Igor, forget about SALT. I can tell you that for me, 1993 consists of three things. No, four. Four things were important for me in 1993. First, I went to the United States of America.

So did I.

It was my first time.

Mine too! Moreover, in 1993 I went to Paris—that was for the first time, too.

That came significantly later for me. But I did go to the U.S., and for a long time—a whole month. I visited Washington, New York, Chicago, Seattle, and Minneapolis-St. Paul.

What kind of trip was it?

USAID had a program for studying the American securities market.

What's USAID?

USAID is the Agency for International Development. I was very pleased by the trip; I learned a lot. We visited the Stock Exchange in New York...Well, that's a separate story, about America. I'll write a commentary about it sometime.

I was there only for a week. I was on assignment, to write a report about Halloween. For *Domovoi*. I had been yanked from the crime department and thrown into the section that was lagging. The first issue was being prepared, and I was still feverishly finishing up my stuff in the crime department.

Then the second event is very important, Igor. Everyone has forgotten about it now, but it actually served as the basis for subsequent events not only that year but for the rest of our lives. The so-called "yes, yes, no, yes" referendum.

That's it! I remember. I have an amateur videotape: We're drinking in the kitchen, the kids are running around, and I'm drunk. And suddenly they announce on the TV about the referendum: Yeltsin, "yes, yes, no, yes." Do you trust the president... And the video captured my response. Drunk, I barked: "Our president is an asshole, but we trust him." That was the historic phrase I uttered.

And the president won the referendum. When people say that Yeltsin had totally lost his mandate by 1993, they're lying. He had that trust! Yeltsin won that referendum. And the Supreme Soviet lost it. You remember, there were four questions: Do you trust President Yeltsin? Do you approve of the policies of President Yeltsin? Do you trust the Supreme Soviet? And there was a fourth. We wanted the answers to be, "yes, yes, no, yes." According to the conditions of the referendum, the ones without trust had to resign. That is, the Supreme Soviet would have to disband. But those fine deputies showed what clever dicks they were: All Yeltsin needed to pass was a simple majority, but in order to get rid of them, there had to be a two-thirds vote. And while the vote revealed the lack of confidence in them, they did not disband themselves. But, in essence, from that spring on there was no legitimate Supreme Soviet. They should have been disbanded then. Because the majority of the country said that they had no confidence in the deputies. Understand?

Did Yeltsin stack the deck?

No, he really did have the mandate of the people. But during that six-month period between April and October, he managed to lose a lot of it. Because they spent six months covering him in shit from head to toe.

Then, Igor, for me the third important event is that I moved from St. Petersburg to Moscow. Chubais made me his deputy at the State Property Committee. And the fourth event, finally, is the coup—or what was it called, rebellion?—of October 3-4.

The Great October Socialist Revolution? As usual? By the way, Alik, I know why it always happens in October. The weather is so lousy—it's disgusting, there's all that mud that might as well be shit—you just don't feel like living. No sky, just a wet grey rag in its place—that's the expression of Ilf and Petrov. Should you go on a bender? Kill someone? Or, I know! Let's have a revolution!

Yup. The great October socialist revolution fizzled out. So those are the four events from my life in 1993. Nothing compares with them. Each of them worthy of a commentary. America—

What about the establishment of RAO Gazprom?

Forget it!

What about the election of Zyuganov as leader of the Communist Party of the Russian Federation?

That was an event in your life? You remember 1993 because of that? Is this how we're going to experience the election of Mr. Zyuganov in hindsight?

We can have a very good discussion. Look! The writer Tatyana Tolstaya said to me in an interview: "If I ever see Zyuganov, I'll jump on him like a wolf and tear out his throat. He's responsible for the terror, Kolyma, all that killing." Wait, I responded, we have to protect Zyuganov, because he was specially selected for his repulsiveness. Understand? They could have found some young handsome guy, like Gagarin, you know, with a killer smile...

Like Kwaśniewski in Poland. Young, energetic, totally Western—and at the same time, a leftist.

I think that there's some inside troublemaker, Gleb Pavlovsky, Alexander Voloshin, somebody... And he's thinking: Why do we need a handsome Gagarin clone to head up the Communists? He'll get all the votes. And he says, No, he's no good for us. Go find a normal candidate.

With a wart!

He should be repulsive; he should look like a mangy wolf that had been beaten with a big stick, so he's like a wolf, but a bit wary. The guy is happy: "See, we found such a wonderful general secretary."

Electable.

Well, there will be some people who will vote for him even though he's repulsive, Alik. There's a subtlety there. I explained it to Tolstaya, and she admitted her mistake.

We also had the start of the hearings by the military collegium of the Supreme Court on the case of the coup-plotters—betrayal of the homeland.

They only started the hearing then? Was the investigation going for all that time?

Apparently. They tried the old guy Valentin Varennikov, a frontline officer... Did he betray the homeland or not? You should write it with a capital: betrayal of the Homeland.

They were all amnestied, but old man Varennikov refused the amnesty and demanded a trial. He was acquitted.

Good for him! A tough nut!

Who the hell knows. I can tell you that in 1991, I hated them.

So did I. I hated them. Then. Obviously.

Well, then why should we start feeling sorry for them now, retrospectively? They wouldn't pity us if the roles were reversed—you can be sure of that.

No, they wouldn't. They're not known for pity. All right. Let's move on: Removal from circulation of ruble notes issued between 1961 and 1992.

I'm supposed to feel emotional about that?

OK. Completion of troop removal from Lithuania. That doesn't excite you, either?

Ha ha.

Agreement with the U.S. on joint space programs.

Come on.

You're not moved.

Neither are you, more to the point.

The great writer Julian Semyonov died. And all that's left in our list of major events is the establishment of NTV. And the return of the double-headed eagle.

Oh! Oh!

At last, something that excited you.

It did. I was very pleased.

I was pleased, too, but it was still strange.

The tricolor flag, the double-headed eagle. Old man Jordan, Boris's father, would have been happy. In fact, he was—he died only last year.

Yes. It was all very interesting, but it was somehow—unnatural.

Why? The symbols of the White movement?

The Whites. But still, unnatural somehow. Pleasant, yes. When they returned the Red flag, that was unpleasant. And when they restored the Communist anthem, that was very unpleasant. But, alas, natural. A strange feeling...

No, strictly speaking, Igor, the restoration of the tricolor and the double-headed eagle was natural.

But what do you think of the fact that we have a republic, yet its emblem is the crown of the Russian Empire?

Actually, I think that the double-headed eagle used today on the official symbols doesn't have a crown.

You see where we've landed? What shape we're in? Some of us can't even remember what our emblem looks like.

All right, let's take a look at our seal. Where would it be—on money? [*Kokh rummages in his pockets. Pulls out keys, a handkerchief, a little book.*]

What's that file case?

From the Presidential administration. It says I'm a candidate to be a deputy in the State Duma.

So, where's the eagle? It should be on a document like that, no?

Wait, wait, I'll find you some money. It must be on money…

But you have it right there on the case! An eagle with a crown!

Ho-ho. It's not just a crown. It's three crowns: one for each head, and a big one over the others.

What does it mean? Why three crowns?

One for "Little Russia"—Ukraine—and one for Belorussia. Haha. That's no small thing.

If the eagle wears a crown, then let me tell you: I think the president should wear a crown too.

Of course. And have a coronation.

Why not?

That's what I'm talking about, Igor. And he shouldn't be called president, but king, like in Poland. You know, all their kings were elected. It wasn't hereditary.

No, I still think the president should walk around in a crown. I've told you before about my discussion with a village tractor driver, who thought

the word successor—*preyomnik*—was the same as the word for nephew—
preyomnik. When Yeltsin introduced his "nephew" Putin on live TV, they
took if as a good sign at the kolkhoz. At last, Boris was thinking straight,
they said. He was doing too much drinking and carousing, and they'd
stopped expecting any smart behavior from him. And there you go! Here
he had gone and acted so responsibly. The peasants thought it would
have been better to turn over the works to his son, but Boris Yeltsin didn't
have a son. He couldn't very well leave it to a stranger, could he? Better a
nephew. Especially a committed teetotaler.

I agree with them.

So what are we talking about then? What's the problem, why shouldn't
the president wear a crown? The eggheads would have swallowed it,
laughing. And the simple folk would have said, Fine, at last, thank God.
Really, otherwise it was like the old saying: without a tsar in his head.

All these silly elections—

Why bother with elections? Now we have a tsar. There! That will
promote stability. It's harder to kill a tsar than a president.

That's for sure. There's a sacred meaning to it, Igor. Becoming tsar is a
whole ritual, an anointing…

Yes. And it would be easy to explain why the country was being run
not by some apparatchik, but by a tsar. Because this country is always run
by a tsar! The one we have now, and his father, and grandfather, and
great-grandfather, were all tsars. Three hundred years of monarchy. For
three hundred years it was accepted that you have winter and then spring,
summer, and fall—all under the direction of the tsar, and no other way.
It's all clear. But if someone comes and kills the tsar and says, And now
I'll be in charge instead of him, anyone can say: Why you and not me? We
all have an equally legitimate claim. That was a terrible mistake, of
course. Killing the tsar in a wild country where the titular nation is
composed almost entirely of grandchildren of serfs, whose understanding
of freedom involves the opportunity to hang landowners and screw their
daughters.

But we've forgotten about Garik Miroshnik! By the way, his house is
just like yours… Maybe the plot is a bit smaller. But he's in Beverly Hills.

Our land is more expensive.

It may be more expensive here, but over there they have the Pacific Ocean, and the climate is better—it's real climate, not like what some people have. Here all we have is frost, or mud, or heat with mosquitoes.

It's good here in summer, when it's not raining.

It may be good in summer, when it's truly not raining. But the winter—there's so much of it.

Svinarenko's Commentary (from an old article):

At first Garik appeared to be a provincial member of the intelligentsia, but with some eccentricities—a man of the sixties, with what they call "ideals." But a man of the sixties who became a success in business—that doesn't happen without colossal reserves of energy, which is always attractive. That is, on the one hand, he's perfectly capable of handling life, business, politics, his Rolls Royce, and his Beverly Hills. On the other hand, he loves to talk, especially over a meal, about the fate of the country, Russia's path, the filth of politics—and nostalgia, of course. He showed me a typical house in Beverly Hills: all one story (because of the famous California earthquakes), with innumerable rooms and a garden with glossy, thick foliage that was "just like Sochi."

"Clinton's cousin is a neighbor, and farther up there's Reagan, Ford… I used to be an aide to Rutskoi… You know what my name used to be? Georgy Mikhailovich Miroshnik," he finally revealed. I looked away, with a sudden pang of sadness that in our orphaned Russia such millionaires can be grown on a few kopeks of state money… I recalled the newspaper articles in 1992, on the crime pages…

Garik and I would meet some evenings and drink—either at his house in Beverly Hills or in town, in some simple oceanside café. For example, he liked to meet at the bar of the fancy Regency Hotel.

"I lived here for a few months before I bought the house. I feel at home here…"

All the staff knew him. They regarded him with an understandable adoration. "In Dubai I sold a whole shipload of gas masks through the firm Tekhnika. I had to hang out in Jeddah, that stinking dump. I made about $60-$70,000. Then there was the program "Harvest-90;" as well as "Istok," ANT, my company Formula-7, and other things. The peasants were being given coupons, and we had to sell those coupons at unfavorable prices. The government promised to compensate for our losses with oil quotas that we could sell in the West. I went to the Group of Soviet Forces in Germany and said to our generals: When you pull out your troops, everything in your warehouses will be stolen. You'd be better off selling it to us. We'll give it back to Russia in exchange for coupons; we'll use the coupons to buy oil, and so on. We'll pay you in Russia with rubles. No, they said, we don't want rubles, only marks. All right! And then came Yeltsin's decree that Russian organizations could not pay one another in hard currency, only in rubles. That was the end of 1991. I had to pay in rubles… At the official exchange rate. I couldn't use the black market exchange rate for official payments to state organizations, now could I?"

"You probably knew ahead of time that would happen!"

"Even if I had, where's the crime? Where? I had insisted—I had offered to pay them in rubles! But they didn't want that. Because the rubles would have gone straight to Russia, into the state budget. The hard currency would have gone to Germany. The army was upset; they said I stole from them. But just what did I steal, and from whom? I took state goods from the generals, honestly paid whatever the state said I should, in the currency of that state, then brought the goods to Russia and exchanged them for coupons from Harvest-90. I ended up with a half-ton of coupons. And did I get anything for them? Even a ton of oil, even a tank of gas?"

* * *

But, Igor—by ordinary standards, Miroshnik duped the generals. On the other hand, generals should not be doing business deals—both according to law and according to standards. So it's right that he got the better of them.

Alik, how were your relations with Miroshnik?

Rutskoi would call up the Ministry of Finance, or us, or someone else. He would call and say, Miroshnik is coming over, he's a good guy, help him solve his problem… Miroshnik would rush over, and he'd get some paper signed. And then Rutskoi would turn around and accuse you of corruption. See? By the way, as soon as he started screwing people over corruption, Rutskoi assumed that people would be even quicker to do his bidding. But instead people stopped signing papers for him so easily. So he started riding them even harder….

What were they signing?

All kinds of papers. How can I explain? Leases on some buildings for some companies… At the State Property Committee some trifles were left up to the officials to decide, and Rutskoi tried to get his hands on all of it.

Really?

Really. A fly couldn't get past his eye. Rutskoi and Khasbulatov. They did a major grab… It was a tactic that people didn't realize at first. I joined the government in August 1993, when the atmosphere was shifting. Before that, the government had been trying since 1991 to be on good terms with Rutskoi and Khasbulatov, and they were managing. For instance, in the summer of 1992, Chubais got the privatization program passed. The Supreme Soviet voted "yes." But then it all went downhill.

How fascinating!

What are you laughing at?

Fascinating! Such touching details!

All right, all right. It's autumn, 1993. They had lost the referendum, Rutskoi and Khasbulatov. And so the coup was moving inexorably closer. And when it became absolutely clear that it would happen, then Boris Nikolayevich issued his famous decree, I think it was No. 1400? He disbanded the Supreme Soviet. And they provoked unrest: A huge crowd moved from Oktyabrskaya Square, across the Krymsky Bridge to Smolenskaya Square, and to City Hall, and started messing with the cops there, took away their semiautomatics, set fire to City Hall… That was October 3. It was horrible! I lived nearby, in the Presidential Administration's hotel on Plotnikov Pereulok, literally behind the Ministry of Foreign Affairs. I came out onto Smolenskaya Square, and the crowd was moving, overturning cars, looting stores…

You got a live look at revolution, Alik.

Oh, yes, I did. There was this deputy, Ilya Konstantinov, who led the march.

Where is he now?

I don't know. What an asshole. And so the crowd broke through the barriers and headed from City Hall to the White House. Oh boy! And then Luzhkov sent more cops, and they closed the circle and would not let anyone leave the White House. But that night, they broke through yet again and headed for the Ostankino TV center. And the crowd that had remained outside the barriers around the White House drove trucks in, to take Ostankino. And then the storm, the shooting, Vityaz troops breaking up the riot… And Sasha Kazakov and I were walking from work to my hotel. There was no public transportation working, of course. So we walked from the State Property Committee, on Varvarka Street, to the Ministry of Foreign Affairs. We had to cross Novy Arbat, and there were snipers shooting there…

So, running zigzag—

Running zigzag, dodging, we crossed the avenue. And then we took the small alleys of Arbat to get to the hotel. It was the night of the third. At 2 a.m.

Kokh's Commentary:

Always, all my life, I wanted to be a writer. It wasn't like, "So, I'm going to be writer." No… It was more profound. It was the perception that writing is a worthy endeavor for a real man. The rest was nonsense. Changing history is worthless. War? Probably… But it never came up, and I didn't make an effort.

Everybody says: You're good at it, you have the right language, temperament… But I knew better. Nothing. Zip. As soon as you move out of journalism into literature, you have to deal with the crumbling plot, the hero who's not up to the character you imagine, the weakness of composition… It's a nightmare! Real literature is not my forte. Just cheap memoir-writing. But I want to be a writer. A real one, like Leo Tolstoy! Who the hell knows why…

And so I witnessed a revolution. Just describing it in terms like, "I walked… He said…That one shot…" is stupid and not organic. But in fact, I was witness to a Russian rebellion in the autumn of 1993. What a stroke of luck for a Russian writer. Pushkin had to travel around the Pugachev Rebellion sites forty years after the fact, collecting tidbits of recollections. An eye poked out and hanging by a thread, sturgeon being gaffed… Slicing people with knives… Cossack women… Favorite tribes… But I actually saw it! The infuriated faces. The wildness. Anger. Envy that boiled over into a pogrom.

Maybe I should give it a try? Describe it properly? With protagonists, plot, and a personal story? Too weak?

"In a black cape with a bloodied hem, moving with a cavalryman's stride…" Really? You think that would work?

Blok wrote: "Listen to the music of the revolution." Asshole. Listen to the music of the revolution. What is there to hear? Filth, dull hatred, empty chatter…

Youth is happiness. I was thirty-two. Thin and energetic. Everything was easy—that's the naiveté. And I adored it. I came to Moscow. To work on privatization. They couldn't manage without me. And—a rebellion!

They're walking along Smolenskaya Square. Faces contorted. They've been walking a long time, several hours. From Oktyabrskaya Square. Where Lenin's big statue is. They're angry. Flipping over cars—they were all little Zhigulis in those days. Setting fire to them. Smashing store windows. The small shops are always the first victims. Always. They're winding themselves up. Shouting. A disgusting sight. It's like accidentally seeing a girlfriend taking a crap. All the magic is gone. Bah, this is the people!

Everything that's dear… Everything that's sweet, beautiful, familiar. Bourgeois. Embroidered pillowcases. Curtains, tapestry drapes. Elephants lined up in a row by height. Pork in cutlets. The old dresser. That is what is truly human. Fuck proletarian art. I hate skinny, hysterical women. Give me an ass. A big ass. Like the shopkeeper painted by Renoir.

It was the Russian beauty Kustodiev liked to paint that I was saving on October 3, 1993. I didn't want whores like Lilia Brik to take over my people for another hundred years, with their swinging ways. My beloved, big-bottomed, kulak Homeland, with plump warm lips, white teeth, and a beautiful wise smile—she had to win! And she did. Petty bourgeois Luzhkov and petty bourgeois Korzhakov were victorious—over that retard Rutskoi. Over General Makashov, the shit. Crooks!

… She's walking, trembling with fear. I'm afraid too. She holds onto my hand. Ever tighter… It's clear: Don't be afraid! I'll tear out their throats! I won't let them hurt you under any circumstances. Ever. You can be sure of that. Mayakovsky was a proletarian poet, and I'll be a bourgeois one.

I don't care about plot. I don't care about the unity of character—the hell with them! I don't want to be a great writer. Why is being bourgeois unaesthetic? And if it's not aesthetic, then it must be prose? I'm only learning now that I've been speaking prose my whole life.

At last, I understood who I am. On that very day. I am a kulak. And I will always be a kulak. And I will have kulak daughters. I'm not a major capitalist. I am a Russian. Kokh. Alfred. Reingoldovich. It's my fortune to love you: my Homeland. And not those goats.

* * *

Svinarenko's Commentary:

The 1993 Coup Passed Me By

It's so strange! As a child, all I ever thought about was being part of some rebellion. Revolutionary sailors, bandoliers, Mausers, executing the bourgeoisie…personally, myself. Afterward, justice would prevail, and the winners would go off to build a narrow-gauge railroad. Freezing in the woods, working for free for the common good. That was real happiness! And the bourgeoisie would look at us and envy us. What did they have, besides money? My dreams went something like that.

Later, everything changed—I mean, in my head. By 1993 I was completely anti-Communist, and I had been thinking for a long time that the revolution had turned us into a wild country, with primitive mores and a pathetic lifestyle. Today, it's strange to think about it, but the picture they used to paint for us had a factory plumber as the crown of creation… But he was very far from the ideal. I certainly don't need an ideal like that. But did I dream in 1993 of executing the communards? No. I'm trying to recall my emotions with as much clarity as possible. I realize that they were very bourgeois, very everyday. I thought, oh, riots, what if they start breaking windows in our apartment? Or, I thought there might be lines again for bread and cigarettes. I wondered about the prospects of the rich glossy magazine that I was working for then, how it would survive if the struggle among the branches of government continued.

What about the shooting, the battles, the corpses on truck beds? Was Yeltsin's gang shooting at the brave Russian communards—did I believe in that version of events? Did I think about it? Did it worry me? No… Nor did it affect the country as far as I noticed and remember, not particularly. Civil war did not break out then. I propose this explanation: The mass public was tired of revolutions. It was too much. Hey, let's drop everything and run to the barricades. Right, sure! What the hell for? Especially since we had already mastered Bismarck: Revolutions are made by heroes (us) and exploited by scoundrels (them).

Boring, adult, responsible. The word "adult" may be key here. As I recall, before the start of the rebellion, on the eve of it, I dropped off my wife and daughter at the puppet theater on Baumanskaya Street on my way to the office. I half-listened to news on the drive, and there was already something in the air. I told them, and they still remember this, "Don't go off anywhere after the performance—head straight home. Who knows what's up." That is, I didn't take them straight home, but I wasn't completely lighthearted about the situation, either. Something in-between. And now I think to myself: Why, I was the paterfamilias! How can anyone think about revolution? Who needs it? That must be a fundamental point. There's a reason revolutionaries are so young, enthusiastic, and fearless—ready to leap into fire. They behave as if they had no children. Which is often the case. Then why should we listen to them? Empty talk. We should bring them to order and make them shut up.

* * *

So, Alik, here it is, so simple. My friend Igor Futymsky, physicist and philosopher, advanced this theory: When a rebellion begins, if you are too gentle in putting it down, it will not be effective. If you are too harsh, that will lead to very serious bloodletting, civil war, disruption of the economy… You have to find the optimal figure. Killing one person is not enough. A hundred is too many. You have to kill ten to twenty—and not by shooting them in cellars, but with serious weapons. And then the wave is broken, the rebellion ends, and normal life resumes. Most recently, this

was demonstrated by Pinochet, who killed Allende and a dozen rebels with him. He killed them with a missile fired by a military plane. Our Boris Nikolayevich used exactly the same methods in 1993. He ordered them to fire from tanks, and the revolt quickly deflated. Everyone calmed down.

Well, that wasn't invented by Pinochet—I think that's a much earlier invention. But mount a loud, public, and cruel suppression of insubordination to the regime—right away, at the start of the rebellion, when the authorities see that if they lose there will be no mercy and the probability of loss is rather high—and a great part of the rebels will come to their senses. By the way, Nicholas I demonstrated that kind of inflexibility in various ways ("inflexibility" was his favorite word). There were many revolts in his reign. Your favorite, Astolphe de Custine, was in the Russian Empire in 1839, during the reign of Nicholas I.

If only Lenin had been shot early on... If they had shown their inflexibility toward him....

No, no.

Things would have quieted down.

No. No. The situation was more complicated with Lenin. There was no one to shoot him, that's the problem.

Come on, surely there were some special forces left, Alik.

The Kornilov rebellion took place that summer, still under Kerensky; it headed for St. Petersburg but stopped outside Gatchina.

Don't you remember in *Virgin Soil Upturned* or *The Quiet Don*, someone—some kulak—says: "Is it true that in 1903 there were only twenty Bolsheviks?" They tell him, Yes, it's true. And he says, "If only they had shot them all then."

Ha ha!

I didn't see any of the coup that October because I was launching a new magazine, *Domovoi*. When you're launching a magazine, you don't have enough money or people. So you have to write everything yourself and also rewrite everyone else's stuff. You're going to laugh: Sometimes we slept at the office. In cases like that, they might promise you stock in the company. But usually, they screw you.

I knew that there was a coup going on, sure, Alik. But I was in the office. Writing about how to drink champagne, what's on in Paris, what the new Mercedes are like... And meanwhile, there's shooting in the streets... I went to Yakovlev and said, "Listen, what's going on out there? Why don't I go down to the coup and write something, eh?" And he said, "Don't get sidetracked, we have to publish this issue. The coup will be over in three days, you're going to waste your time crawling over the barricades, all you'll do is ruin the launch." So I went back to my computer and continued writing about the good life. As soon as the putsch was over, I was sent to Paris. *Domovoi* had a section called The Scene, and every month there had to be a report from some international event. That's really why I joined *Domovoi* ...

Svinarenko's Commentary:

One fine summer day in 1993, Volodya Yakovlev, founder of *Kommersant,* told me worriedly that he was looking for someone for a new project—that person would travel all over the world and write articles about various entertaining events.

"Here I am!" I said.

"No way. All right, you can write. And take photos... Do you have a driver's license?"

"Just got it."

"That's good... But you don't speak any languages!"

"What makes you think that?"

"How would you? You're from Makeevka, you didn't go to any special schools..."

"Fuck you!" I said in English, and then cursed foully.

"Hm," he grunted.

We exchanged a few more words in English.

"Ah!" he recalled. "You know German, too."

I had driven him crazy with German a while back. In the early nineties, when I worked for German newspapers, there was only one telephone that had access to overseas lines, and only one fax. It was in Yakovlev's outer office, so I had to call from there, and because the lines were so bad in those days, I had to shout at length to find out if the person on the other end of the line was able to receive my fax. Yakovlev would come out of his office and be outraged: How could I use his phone to call Germans! Jews are sometimes overly sensitive to anything related to Germany. But I did manage to persuade him that since there was no other phone adequate for my needs in the office, I had to use the chief's.

When we were finished with the Germanic languages, I informed the management that I had a few Romance languages under my belt, so it would be more accurate to say that Yakovlev doesn't speak any languages than to say that about me. Despite my politically incorrect response, the question seemed to be settled in my favor, when suddenly Yakovlev took a look at my stainless-steel smile: A good dozen of teeth had metal crowns.

"Time for you to get normal teeth," he said.

"You know what? My teeth are my personal affair." Steel crowns suited me fine, but interference in my affairs did not.

"I agree that it's your personal affair. But then it's my personal affair to appoint our chief traveler."

"Oh, all right," I said amicably. "Why get so upset. I'll get new crowns, big deal…"

I sold my 41 model Moskvich and with the $2,000 I got for it, I bought my white, non-Russian teeth.

And as a result I was that lucky fellow who had to go visit all the continents—because it was a production necessity.

Sometimes I would walk through the *Kommersant* corridors—tanned, weary, jetlagged too, with three foreign passports bulked up from all the pasted-in visas—and the ordinary reporters, pale and hunched over their office computers, would give me dirty looks. Occasionally they would shout: "Are you here for long? Just passing through? From Africa to China?" Making feeble attempts at jokes.

"No, from the U.S. to Australia," I would respond honestly.

* * *

You know, Alik, when I was in school, I thought: "I should be a journalist—that is, travel to Paris and New York on urgent business, pick up local color and take photos for glossy magazines." When I studied foreign languages in preparation, my friends would say, "Stop being a jerk! You'll never get to Paris. You're from the mines. There are plenty ahead of you in line."

Tell me, when you look back at your life, can you say that you have satisfied your schoolboy dreams to be a journalist? Completely, as they were then?

As they were then, yes.

But you do realize that it's just crap?

Not in the least. It was a lot of fun.

No, but are you satisfied now with what you achieved?

Satisfaction is not an easy issue, Alik. But I can say that by 1993 I had accomplished my most daring plans—in journalism.

I see—a reporter in the sense of foreign correspondent, as the late Semyonov described his travels abroad. Yes, yes…

Yes, exactly. And you get good money, like the managers. There was also that Soviet film, *Journalist*—black and white, remember it?

And now you've moved to the next stage? You're a publisher now! Now reporters go to Paris on your orders!

Well, I'm not against going to Paris myself. Why make people run around, tear them away from their work… I remember once I was asked there, "Do you come to Paris often?" And I honestly said, "I was here last weekend."

You could send someone else by now.

So, by 1993, in terms of my journalistic career, I had achieved it all.

You hadn't flipped through all those language workbooks in vain.

I'm very bitter about all the time I wasted! I should have started working at a real newspaper in my first year of college, skipping classes to do it. But I started university in 1975, and real newspapers didn't appear until the 1990s. So those fifteen years were totally wasted in terms of my craft.
So, I arrived in Paris in 1993. In October, right after the shelling of the White House. And my first trip there had been that summer, by the way. In the fall I went to attend FIAC—the contemporary art fair. The one in the Grand Palais, do you know it? Near the bridge named for our Alexander III. On the right bank.

The right, is that where the Louvre is or the Orsay?

The Louvre.

It's that building in the Moderne style, with a glass roof?

I'd call it Empire.

Well, late Empire, early Moderne.

So the photographer and I got there. We had come from Moscow, with the shooting, the broken glass, everyone nervous, treacherous, where it was dark and sleety… But there was no shooting in Paris, you see! Everything quiet, placid… Bright, clean, you can stroll the boulevards wearing white suede shoes…

They have roasted chestnuts.

Chestnuts. Yes… Ten francs a bunch, wrapped in the pages of *France Soir*.
The hotel, as I remember, was called the Flaubert, and cost $80 a day. In some side street near the Arc.

That's a special kind of hotel. The maids make a little on the side.

Why didn't they knock on my door?

You looked more respectable.

Perhaps. In any case, I was there, and then went to New York for Halloween.
So I got back to Moscow on November 2, from Halloween in New York, and on the 4th I left for Australia, to attend the Formula-1 race. I turned in my article, switched suitcases, and off I went again. Ah, the hard lot of the journalist.

You actually saw the late Senna.

Yes, I talked with him.

So that was the main event of the year for you! You interviewed the world champion!

I did, but it wasn't very long. Actually, Formula-1 racing is very boring. Not like walking around Australia.
And another thing—the courts. That's an important topic, Alik. I noticed in 1993 that I was spending more time settling issues about articles we had already printed than on organizing the production of new ones. Everyone was suing—how could you expect the crime department to write anything good about people? It's not the culture section, after all… And I must say that I never lost a single lawsuit.
Another thing is that Vladislav Surkov, the Kremlin ideologist, started out in 1993. A PR specialist, that's what I wrote about him in my date book. Here it is—his phone number back then was 955-6931.

What did he want from you?

I don't even remember. I'm sure that I even talked to him. Just wrote it down. There was a huge number of PR people then! Now I'm realizing how they all resembled one another. Not too tall, in suits and ties, well-kempt, with polite, cold smiles... And now I'm thinking that I just described the typical Chekist... Either the PR guys came from the secret police, which would have been logical, or it's just a breed of people, something about the Komsomol—they're cynical, ready for anything...

I also got my driver's license in 1993, Alik. There weren't any traffic jams then.

It seemed to me that there were.

Back then it might have seemed that way. But now we understand that there weren't any! We didn't appreciate it. I hate to think what will happen if it continues at this rate. And another thing: I bought tons of collected works. Dickens, Maupassant. Second-hand editions. I somehow thought this was a rare opportunity that I had to take advantage of. And then there would be book shortages again... That's a very important detail! I guess I considered this new iteration of NEP [Lenin's New Economic Policy from 1921] a temporary deviation, and deep in my heart I did not expect capitalism to last. I considered it a break and tried to use it to stock up on some good stuff for the bleak future...

13.

1994

The Thirteenth Bottle

*T*he year's theme is privatization—over which the authors debate fiercely. Svinarenko demands restitution, which he considers proof of the sanctity of private property. Kokh, on the other hand, maintains that honest restitution is impossible—especially in Russia— but that despite that, private property must remain untouchable.

The authors discuss the war in Chechnya that has just begun and argue whether our mountain dwellers can be compared to American Indians or not. Kokh, using (among other sources) the Talmud, explains his understanding of Chechnya and of the Chechens. Svinarenko puts forth his view of the case of Colonel Budanov, who was accused of raping and murdering a Chechen woman: They treated the man shabbily.

You first, Alik! What makes 1994 interesting?

The first important event as far as I'm concerned was the end of check privatization. It was completed on July 1. And in November, Chubais left the State Property Committee. They appointed Vladimir Polevanov, a protégé of Yeltsin's chief bodyguard, Alexander Korzhakov, and former governor of the Amur Oblast. A rather funny character. He kept trying to stop privatization. He said that it was just a sell-off—the fashionable thing to say about it now, that's what he said ten years ago. Polevanov kept worrying: "Oh-oh, danger, it's a question of national security! The country's interests are at risk!" I asked him then to give me a definition of national security, but he could not. Just now I was in the U.S. and met with, among others, my friend Lena Teplitskaia. She lives in Washington, DC, and works as president of the American-Russian Chamber of Commerce and Industry.

Girlfriend in the good sense of the word?

In the innocent sense! I was with my wife; our families are friends. She told me about the new stars of Congress. They have all these stars now, all specialists in national security. It's very fashionable there. Shit-eaters... I thought of Polevanov. And since he has a Ph.D. in geology, he knew about gold, too. So, ten years ago, a "specialist" in national security—who was unable to define the term when asked—appeared in our government.

I can tell you about national security.

Go ahead.

You were right to bring up the Americans. Just take a look at how they do it in America—where everything is done in the name of national security—and then things will be clear. You have international law, the United Nations, treaties—fine. Are they ironclad, or can they be ignored? They can be ignored. It's all swept aside when something contradicts American interests.

Who formulates America's interests?

You're waiting for America to ask you how to understand its security?

Who is the demiurge who defines it? Who?

Let me explain, Alik. The white man came, scalped and burned the Indians, and took away their lands—because it was in the national interest.

That is incorrect.

It's correct.

How many years did you live in America?

One. So what?

And you didn't manage to comprehend a simple thing—that it wasn't the whites who scalped Indians, but the other way around. It's an Indian custom. Not a white man's custom.

Don't you remember the U.S. government offered a bounty for Indian scalps?

Lies! That never happened. Fairy tales! Red propaganda!

James Fenimore Cooper wrote about it.

He wrote about the days when they were British colonies, before the American Revolution.

And the British are not white men? But let's leave the scaping aside. Why couldn't the settlers arrive on the ships and go talk to the Indians about residence permits and take a test on knowledge of Indian languages? If they pass, and are allowed in, then they have to live by the laws of the land.

That's what they did!

What?

I'm not about to justify the white settlers, Igor, but I call your attention to this: In the war with the natives, America was not defending its national security interests. Not the security of the white man from the red man! It was defending the sacred principle of private property. And that is not a national security issue, but an international principle that must be defended. Everywhere.

That's bullshit. I studied the question in situ. … The whites came and asked: Can we live here?

No, they asked: Can we buy this land from you?

No, they didn't. The Indians didn't have a concept of private property! So they said: If you want to, live here. But the whites insisted on getting some kind of formal ownership of the land. The Indians replied that the land belonged to their God and could not be sold. They simply did not have the concept of private property I don't think that it follows that the Indians understood the origins of family, private property, and state. I think that they understood fuck-all—just like the Russians today.

The Indians didn't understand, you say? That's a favorite explanation. "It's not his fault, it's cultural." I'm certain that this wasn't a question of racism on the part of the whites. They had the principle of respect for private property. If a white man did not respect it, they punished him, too. Put him in prison! And if he didn't shape up after his term, if he murdered people—they would destroy

him, whether he was white or Indian. It didn't matter whether he was Indian or
white.

**I agree that it's not important, Alik. If a man is a jerk, you can't teach
him about private property. So—to return to your question—I will
continue explaining about national security. Think about when the
Americans expanded NATO, although they had promised not to. And
then ravaged Iraq to find the weapons of mass destruction, when there
weren't any and basically everyone knew that. And there was a NATO
bigwig, a Brit, who admitted that there were no mass burials of civilian
Albanians in Serbia and that it was made up in order to justify bombing
Yugoslavia.**

So are you the only who gets to talk now, friend Igor? Have you noticed that
in all the chapters, you talk more than I do?

**I haven't noticed. If you want to, talk more. You write these huge
commentaries sometimes—so go and write one, if you want. I'll just finish
up with a brief point. You say that the Americans aren't so bad and that
you feel you should defend them. Don't do it! I'm not saying that they're
not right or that they should have acted differently. I have no argument
with the whites taking over America and turning the wild prairies into a
wealthy country. I was saying all that in response to your request to
explain my understanding of national security. There it is: Serve your
people, act exclusively in their interests, and squash whoever argues.
Don't just rattle your tongue.**

One more comment, Igor. You spoke beautifully about the Indians. They
have aquiline profiles; they're marvelous on horseback and are great archers. But
they did have treaties with the white settlers. Treaties. In which everything was
written out clearly. That the land was being bought, that they couldn't use it
anymore—and about the crops and the cattle and everything else. And the
settlers paid for the land with money. The tribal chiefs took the money and knew
what was in the treaties. They were written in two copies, in English and in the
language of the Indians, for which the English invented a grammar and letters.
I've seen those contracts with my own eyes at the Museum of Natural History in
New York. And the commentary! The Indians are typical natives who are smart
when necessary and who otherwise play the fool. Or tell you about their ancient
traditions. Think about it: Didn't they have trade among the tribes? Yes, they
did. Did they trade cattle, cloth, and grain? They did. If you took payment for
whatever—a llama, say—then could you use it again with the permission of the
new owner? You couldn't. Did the Indians understand that? Perfectly, even

before the advent of the Europeans. And they start with the story: Well I'm just a fool, and I didn't know. What about the money? What money? Oh, you mean this money? I just took it out of respect. It's a custom.

Kokh's Commentary:

By the way, some extremely interesting research was done by the famous ethnographer and historian Henry Morgan in the middle of the nineteenth century, when he lived among the Sioux. Friedrich Engels based his *Origins of the Family, Private Property, and the State* on it. I think it's the best work in the Marxist literature.

And Engels very honestly wrote—right on the title page—that his book is based on Morgan's research. According to Engels, the Indians had a concept of private property. They did. And therefore they knew quite well what they were doing when they trampled crops and ate other people's pigs. So there.

* * *

You see, Alik, I don't care whether there were contracts, especially now when you can fake up any contract on a computer. I repeat, I just wanted to show you what national interests are.

No, those are not national interests—they are principles! There is the principle of private property; there is the principle of honoring contracts… The observance of principles is international, and they do not change to suit political expediency. Igor, you can't say the same about ephemeral "national security," which is subjective, and about which two people can have three opinions. I want to understand who formulates the concept of "national security." Who decides that this is good for our nation and this is not? Note that I am not asking who formulates principles—that's pretty clear.

I'm trying to explain it to you. Why don't the Americans sell their own oil?

Because there's enough foreign oil.

There! That's national interest. Why burn your own when you can buy it?

Yes.

It's very good and very correct. And it's important not to observe agreements that contradict the interests of your country, not to play at being an intellectual for whom justice is all-important at any price. Some

kind of Sakharov… I'm afraid that an American Sakharov would get the electric chair. Or take Panama's Noriega, leader of a sovereign nation. They came with troops and arrested him—big deal, sovereign… *That's* national interest.

All right. Very good. Is it my turn now? What you said is total nonsense, Igor, and it doesn't answer my question. Who articulates the national interest? Does the curtailment of rights of 150,000 Russians in Turkmenistan correspond to Russia's national interests or not?

Not, of course.

But no one is stopping it. Moreover, that oppression is payment—for dictator Turkmenbashi to sign a contract with us on gas. Let's go on. In Iraq, we supported France and Germany and not America, England, and Italy. Why, we don't know. Even though it's perfectly clear that it does not correspond with our national interests. If we had supported America and its allies, we would have gotten our debts paid—and the development, and a part in the rebuilding.

Why is money your sole measure, Alik! I have to tell you that you can't get all the money in the world. They attacked Iraq because it allegedly had some horrible weapon. We were against it. No weapons were found. That means we were right, and attacking Iraq was unjust. They should apologize and leave. You can make a lot of money robbing, and you can empty a drunk's pockets—it's all very profitable, no investment necessary, no expenses, and lots of profit. But it's not very nice. And it's not polite, it seems to me, to call people stupid who don't take up robbery.

Is accepting money all right—from Ashkhabad, say?

We shouldn't take money from Ashkhabad, either.

That's exactly what I'm asking: Who articulates the national interest? National consensus? It doesn't exist. And then—at the beginning of our talk you said that one can give up one's principles in the name of national security. That was your point—that is how you understand national security. But as soon as we started talking about Iraq, you said that if national interest contradicts principle, then principle should predominate. In other words, we can't support war against Saddam, even if it's good for our country, since it contradicts our principles. Those were your words. So decide your position. You're driving me nuts.

But the American experience in solving the nationality question seems edifying.

I'm not talking about nationality, but about national security.

But if we're being scholarly, we should first define nationality. Let's clarify: How did you get Russian citizenship, Alik?

How? De facto. At the moment independence was declared, I was living on Russian territory, was a Soviet citizen, and had a residency permit for a suburb of St. Petersburg.

That's the mistake—that you can get a Russian passport so easily. Do you know how you get citizenship of the U.S.?

At birth.

What about adults? What's the procedure?

An oath.

Exactly! An oath of allegiance. Something like: "I don't belong to any other nationalities and will never think about their interests." Why shouldn't we set things up the same way to protect our national security? But for that, and I said it at the beginning jokingly, we have to formulate what our national security is.

Can I say something here, Igor? In that time—in 1993 going into 1994—we sat and made a list. Viktor Glukhikh was chairman of the Committee on Defense Industries then. We sat with his staff and made up lists of what could not be privatized. The whining about national security ended very quickly—because the line between what may be done and what may not, it turned out, is very fine. As a result, everything was done in the administrative auctions. The Baltic Plant, which manufactured propellers for silent submarines, was privatized, and it works very nicely now. They launched the missile carrying *Peter the Great*. But a little factory that made boats with wooden transoms to evade mines was kept from being privatized. A small factory, only 25 people or so working there, and we had to leave it alone because of national security. If we had sold it, what, would it have stopped functioning? We sold a lot of things, and they're all functioning. And there are factories that died out despite the fact that we banned them from being privatized in the interest of national security. This applies particularly to research and development institutes in defense industries. So this is what I'm saying: Who can determine whether an action corresponds with national security? What, for instance, is more important for a nation's security: to protect a factory that makes a defense technology that has no market—to not allow it to be privatized, at the cost of losing 90 percent of the jobs there—or to sell it, and save the jobs, leaving the technology until better times?

I will continue answering your question, Alik. The Americans have decided that nationality is determined by passport. If you have an American passport, you are, therefore, an American.

First of all, you are continuing to answer your own question, not mine! I didn't ask about nationality. I asked about national security. You simply decided that without answering your question, mine cannot be answered. I'm not arguing with you because I'm too lazy. Second, if you want to talk about nationality, then let's… By the way, do you know how nationality was defined in the Russian Empire?

By religion—a mature approach! No one cares whether you have slanty eyes or a black ass. You give your oath of allegiance to the country, and onward from there.

You'll even be allowed to open a casino!

And stay there. And if you impugn someone's nationality, you get smacked down so hard you won't believe it. So, the Americans first defined what nationality was, and only then what national security was. It's one thing to have tribal security (we have a tribal system, and feudalism) and it's another to have national security. One person is Russian and another is a Tatar, yet we have the same passports…

So who decides what's dangerous and what's secure?

What do you mean, who? Whoever decided that Yugoslavia and Iraq had to be bombed!

Clinton and Bush.

There you go, they decide.

So, the President.

Yes, the President. While our President kicks one guy out and sends the other to prison….

And does that accord with our national security, imprisoning and kicking out?

We're beginning to discuss national security, yet our country is feudal and we haven't defined nationality. We're slipping down to the level of nationalist politicians like Zhirinovsky and Rogozin.

I still want to know what national security is, Igor..

That's impossible to know. When 48 percent of our population dislikes Jews and 80 percent dislikes blacks. Those are recent poll numbers. That is to say, we consider nationality to mean belonging to some tribe and race. What tribe and race do you belong to? That's not a figure of speech or a slip of the tongue. It's a precise formulation. The person replies: "I am so and so, son of so and so." Patronymics—just think about them. They're a clear reference to our tribal origins. That's our level. And we still haven't solved the nationality question.

You know, Alik, you're always mocking me for bringing my crib sheets to these conversations, saying that they're unnecessary and that if we don't remember some things, then they weren't important by definition. So, go ahead and remember without my help what was socially significant in 1994!

In 1994? Voucher privatization ended, as I said. Chubais stopped being head of privatization and became Vice Premier in charge of the economy. The first Chechen war began. Nothing else of importance happened.

And now, if you permit, I will read a few items from my list. NTV on Channel Four began broadcasting. The great actor Yevgeny Leonov died. The Duma voted to offer amnesty to participants in the rebellions of August 1991 and October 1993. Well?

Not bad. The amnesty was an important event!

The Agreement on Public Accord and Amnesty for members of the failed coup committee. And the Kremlin decreed the Agreement on Public Accord, funnily, for two years. Until the elections, I guess?

Valentin Varennikov refused his amnesty. And proved his innocence in court, by the way. Therefore, all the other members of the coup plot did not need to be amnestied, either.

But they crapped out!

Crapped out? Or did they just get sick of being interrogated? Some were in jail, others were not allowed to leave the country. Searches, eyewitness meetings, surveillance, stress and anxiety. What was the point? You accept amnesty, and you're done. I understand them very well. As you know.

All right, Alik, next on our program: Rock legend Alla Pugacheva married young singer Filipp Kirkorov in Jerusalem.

A mockery.

All right. Here's another: The return to Russia of… Guess who? Twenty years after his departure? Guess!

Who?

Solzhenitsyn, Alexander Isaich.

Not bad, not bad…

And there was the MMM pyramid scandal.

It had started that early?

Yep. And also: The poet Robert Rozhdestvensky died. We'll let that pass…. And more: The last troops were pulled out of Latvia, Germany, and Poland. And they were sent, the same troops, to Chechnya—that's symbolic! The army has to deal with large-scale issues. If there's nothing to do, dig a trench and then fill it in. Or paint the grass, as they did for a Soviet-era Potemkin village.

"Farewell, Germany, farewell / We're off to our homes together." That was a popular march. I lived near the Belorussian Station; they used to come from there, singing that… It was May 9, Victory Day—I remember it.

Yeltsin spoke at the UN calling for protection of the rights of the Russian-speaking population in the post-Soviet space.

It got no response.

Ah! Here's more. The ruble fell on the MMVB to 5000—from 3,081 rubles to the dollar. Black Tuesday Number 1. And on the same October 17, the murder of journalist Dmitri Kholodov from *Moskovsky Komsomolets*.

Did you know him?

No, but I remember it as if were yesterday—I was flying back from Paris, and since it was Aeroflot, I was greedily catching up on all the

Russian papers. And there on the front page of MK, on a horrible funereal background: Kholodov, along with the ruble fall. I wasn't cheerful in the first place, leaving a warm country in October to go to Moscow's sleet and shoddiness—Moscow was nothing like it is today—

—today it's worth a trip.

So there I was, thinking: Sleet and a sky as gray as a floor rag, and the rudeness is going to start right at the border with the customs agents and passport guards... And I was so sick of it, and then the news: They're murdering whomever they want to, and the economy is falling apart without ever having gotten on its feet. Pfui.

Svinarenko's Commentary:

That year I was still working at *Domovoi* magazine. I was doing pretty much what I do now: interviewing the great and writing travel notes. But I wasn't writing books or being a publisher then.

My first major interview in 1994 was with Artem Tarasov. He had come back to Moscow incognito that winter, and we met in secret apartments—he had had problems with the Moscow prosecutor's office. What an advanced man he was! He had experienced and understood much, long before other people. You and I, Alik, were still children in 1994, but Artem had managed to become a millionaire, pay not only his income tax on his earnings but his Communist Party dues, be a congressman, survive criminal charges and live as an émigré in—get this!—London! Not just anywhere. He was a trailblazer. He had left back in February 1991, six months before we felt the raptures of democracy during the coup. By then he was a political immigrant. Marvels. He told me then who was backing his new campaign for the Congress and explained why he was running for the Duma again:

> To create legislation that will protect human rights. So that people feel protected. That's the most important thing. Because if people don't feel protected, they don't care how much they've eaten or what they're wearing... I want to talk about what I consider most important. Our entire life before August 1991 was a chain of violations of the law. But lawlessness came after it, too: the coup, the breakup of the Soviet Union, the removal of Gorbachev, a legally elected president! Everything that Gaidar is doing is illegal, including the last dissolution of Parliament. People can't live where they are unprotected. The thought arises, I have to protect myself. Some start paying bribes to officials or buying policemen. Others simply pack their suitcases and leave. But what other reaction can there be to the possibility that tomorrow they will tear off our heads and no one will be held responsible? My leaving back then was a completely normal act of self-defense.

He also explained why he was giving up business.

"Politics is a more intellectual endeavor than business. It is multifaceted and more interesting… There is nothing new left for me in business. I know how I was tricked, how I got out of jams, what's good and what's bad, what brings in how much, and how it all ends. I know things in Russia that no one has taken up yet and that could make hundreds of millions of dollars. But Business has lost its charms for me: I've figured it out. Money for the sake of money? At some point, when you've satisfied your needs, it becomes boring. I've lived as a rich man. And I realized that I don't need particularly much. I don't want to develop my needs in the direction of incredible wealth." Artem also told me about a club of young millionaires that he belonged to. "They meet four or five times a year. In various countries—Taiwan, America, Australia… Once we had our meeting on a cruise on the *Queen Elizabeth II*. Last year we invited Gorbachev to speak. He wanted $50,000. We wouldn't pay, so he didn't come. Too bad. Gerald Ford spoke for free. Our club is like a Masonic lodge. I can't tell you too much about it. I can say that I met Prince Charles there—he was eating at the same table with Dan Quayle, former Vice-President of the U.S. I traveled to Geneva to see my pal Edmond—his surname is only "Rothschild!"

This was the way our conversation ended:

I've come home. The Americans and British are interesting, I agree, but they are strangers, and Russians are family. Here, at home, there is a more familiar lifestyle, something inculcated in childhood. All that was beaten into my head: This is the best, we're the best in the world. I like a toilet with a newspaper hanging on a nail. Out there, people have Jacuzzis in a 60 square meter room. What for, I ask you, why? I don't understand it.

Artem came back to Russia in 2004. He's writing a book about himself, it's going to be published soon in Moscow.

I was absolutely amazed by eye surgeon Svyatoslav Fyodorov, whom I interviewed in 1994. "A boulder, an experienced mountain of a man, a titan." He complained about your friend:

I've been struggling with Chubais for a long time, with his theory of privatization. I've been trying to get an answer from him for over a year: Our institute—what percentage of it belongs to the state, and how much did we create with our own labor? He won't respond, so we can't pay our people their share of the profits. The authorities have an anti-market policy. And on top of that, they're robbing us. They stole 5 trillion dollars of property from us in land, and 20 trillion from under the ground—they took it away in the revolution, and they haven't given it back yet. They just keep blathering about it. [If you accept those figures, then every inhabitant of Russia is due $160,000.] Instead of that, they give us vouchers totaling $1.5 billion. That's just kopeks! They will give us back 0.03 % of our property. The rest is in the hands of 20 million bureaucrats—we've never had so many! They've taken over the Central Committee, and now the White House and the former Political Education building—they're breeding like bedbugs!

They now have eleven thousand businesses in America in which all the workers own shares—a kind of popular capitalism. The program is called ESOP (Employee Stock Ownership Plan); they've never heard of anything like that here. It was invented forty years ago, but people didn't take to it at first: How can you give workers shares? Make the slaves the masters? It was only when America was approaching a dead end that people started paying attention. And capitalists are greedy; they always try to pay minimal wages and keep as much as possible for themselves. That undermines people's purchasing power. Goods are manufactured, but no one wants them. It should be the other way around: First create the buyer, and then manufacture goods for him. But anyway, I can't give my collective their property—Chubais is dragging his feet with the answer. Why can't he just tell me: The state's share is so much and the collective's so much, and then set the rent. If the rent is OK, we'll accept. If not, well, we have land in Protasovo; we'll get a bank loan and build a clinic on our own land. We'll leave all this to Comrade Chubais. Maybe he'll open a factory here—say, a fabric mill. Or use it for offices (that's fashionable now).

Energy is hereditary. Genes play their role. You either have energy or you don't. And you can't do anything about it. I watch my colleagues—they can't help it, they just don't have the energy. It's faulty adrenal glands, they don't make enough adrenaline. And there's a substance in the hypothalamus that secretes an energy hormone (they haven't figured it out completely yet)—some have a lot, some don't. So it's all predetermined, who can move mountains and who can't. God did not give it to some people, and that's it. I give those people a break—it's not their fault. I think only 2-3% of the population is active and energetic. There are more workaholics—that's 15-18 %. They will work under socialism, under fascism, under any dictatorship. There is another 15-18 % of people who won't work under any regime. The middle can sway in either direction. If it pays to work, they work; if not, they don't bother. A market is needed for that swamp. Basically, 22% are very active, and 18% need nothing.

It takes me an hour to drive to work. That's a lot. If I had a helicopter on the roof, I could get there in twelve minutes.

He eventually did buy a helicopter. And died in a crash. It was one of the first in a series of helicopter fatalities.

* * *

Kokh's Commentary:

I can't resist adding something about Fyodorov. I'm not even going to talk about the absurd figures he mentions. Or his feeble discourse on national wealth and how to measure it. There are about four million bureaucrats in Russia, not twenty. .. I'm not talking about that. I know you're not supposed to say anything bad about the dead. But! I know the substance of the polemic between Fyodorov and Chubais, and I can't leave Fyodorov's passage without commentary.

Look. A man comes to an investor and says, I have this idea, I want to build a factory (hospital, office—doesn't matter). The investor says, Do it! Then the man says to the investor, Give me money. He says, All right, and gives him the money. The man builds the factory, gets his salary, and hires personnel, who also get salaries for their labor. Even an amateur sees the answer, clear as day, to the question of who owns the factory: The investor owns it. The factory was built on his money. He was the only one to risk his money; the people hired by the investor, including the man at the beginning, did not put in a penny of their own money, and they got paid regularly and well for their work. If the project had failed, only the investor would have suffered a loss—not the staff. I repeat, by any standard, that factory belongs to the investor.

Now, imagine that the investor is the state and the factory is the Eye Microsurgery Hospital. So Fyodorov came to Chubais asking, What is the share of the labor collective in the institute's founding capital? The reply was—none! You got your share every month in cash, on the fifth and the twentieth. The normal relationship between worker and boss. As they say, whoever took the risk and paid the money owns it. But, Fyodorov fumed, How can that be? Didn't the collective do the work? The answer was, It did. At General Motors, the workers also work, but it never occurs to them to demand shares on that basis. But we have property of the work collective! Fyodorov would explain. And the answer to that was, who decided that? The state? No. You made that up yourself and on that basis you demand that you get—for free—state property worth many millions of dollars. We understand that you do not have the money to buy it at its real price; we are prepared to talk about subsidies, time payments, and so on. But for free—forget about it! No, he said, I want it for free and that's it.

In short, Fyodorov wasn't telling the truth. He had gotten answers. Many times. He just didn't like the answers, so he didn't hear them. Let me note in passing that Eye Microsurgery was built on hard-currency loans that the USSR borrowed from the West. Fyodorov didn't return a kopek of that money to the state. Yet the state, now Russia, is still paying back the loan, with interest. It was projects like that that brought our foreign debt up to $150 billion.

One more point: Judging by the press, after Fyodorov's death it turned out that he wasn't actually such a vigorous proponent of the interests of the working collective. Almost all the property that he managed to make private went onto his personal books, even though it had been earned by the entire work collective—at least, that was what the "experienced mountain of a man" always declared publicly.

And last: It is true that in the mid-1980s, there was a fad in the U.S. for small enterprises that belonged to the labor collective. They created about ten thousand of them. But by the early 1990s they were all bankrupt, and then the fashion for those kolkhozes came to an end. In our country, too. Remember all the talk about cooperatives and rental enterprises? Where are they now, those progressive forms of property that were supposed to be significantly more efficient that private property? The idea died (it couldn't survive the competition). And so did its public crier. All is vanity. Dust and ashes. Lord, forgive us sinners.

* * *

Svinarenko's Commentary:

In 1994 I interviewed someone who was a real TV journalism star by then, Leonid Parfenov.

Talking quickly and emotionally, he told me once again what he had figured out a long time ago and what he had probably said a hundred times at dinner parties:

> The old problems are gone, and now we have new ones. Today's rules of the game are tougher, but they are more honest: What you need is money—not wheeling and dealing between the conservative city Party committee and the liberal Central Committee, or pulling strings. Moscow has become a separate kingdom, which is currently in first place for Rolls Royces per capita. These new times are better than the old. This new time is better than the old. In our village, everyone is building things—even if only a banya—and buying Funai TVs. The old life was really unbearable—even Vassily Belov and Vladimir Soloukhin, "village life" writers, will attest to that in frank conversations, and you can hardly suspect them of having sympathy for Western liberalism… I don't watch TV. There's nothing on that I would want to see. It's quasi-life. Naturally, it's dumb. It can't be otherwise, since it's meant to be understood between brewing the tea and dusting. And it has to be consumed instantly. I don't watch it," he said wearily in farewell.
>
> There was another mighty character, grandpa Ernst Neizvestny, the dissident sculptor. He told me that in America [*where we were, drinking at his house*] he ended up in "such circumstances (technical ones), that everything you conceive of is implemented (I've never worked like that before)." He recalled the old days of the Soviet Union. "They wouldn't give me commissions, they wouldn't let me go out to the West. They trumped up criminal charges against me, they accused me of currency machinations, of espionage, and so on. I kept getting mugged by strange men who beat me, broke my ribs, my fingers, my nose. Who were they? Must have been the KGB. I was beaten half dead in police stations, for no reason. You get up in the morning, wash off the blood, and go to your studio. I'm a sculptor, I need to sculpt.

I traveled to Spain for the first time in 1994. To the festival in Pamplona. And I understood something there: Seeing a *corrida* only once means seeing nothing, it will just be ruined for you. If you have only one opportunity, then it's better not to go. Otherwise, you will come away with a perverse impression. But if you get used to it, gradually, maybe you'll pick up the Spanish passion and you will fall under the spell of tauromachy. The loss of *corrida* virginity comes quickly—the very next bullfight. You don't cringe at the blood as much, you may even experience some satisfaction—and you don't want to give up a lifetime of pleasure because of one painful first time.

I also made a historic trip in March 1994. In those days no one from Russia attended the Oscar ceremonies, and I got to go. And wrote an article. It was a long time ago; they didn't have direct flights to Los Angeles from Moscow. I had to change in San Francisco.

I was scared: What if they don't let me in? What would I write about? What if no one gave me an interview? Would I have to go back empty-handed? Admit I had shat myself? But everything worked out. I went there a few more times, until I got bored: It was the same thing every time, the same false raptures intended to hide the fact that the Oscars were PR, pure and simple.

* * *

Alik, you should know: the film critic Denis Gorelov compared the Chechen warlords with Indian chieftains. That is to say, the Americans got rid of the redskins, and we're still messing with ours.

Nothing of the sort. There's a big difference between them! There is a fundamental difference between Chechen field commander Shamil Basayev and Mohican field commander Chingachguk. Basayev didn't sell us his lands; he didn't take money for them; we took it, and they don't agree with that. There was no deal!

But is that so? Are you sure they didn't agree? What about Shamil— not Basayev, but his great predecessor—who surrendered to the Russian tsar and went to live in Kaluga with his harem rather than die in battle or go on being a partisan in the mountains? Modern-day Chechens are his rightful heirs. And what about Dzhokhar Dudayev, who served the White tsar up to the rank of general and only then remembered his roots and went back to build Chechen statehood? Isn't this solid, albeit oblique, evidence that our field commanders aren't in the right? All the Chechens who joined the Communist Party and attended military schools in Russia? That's a stronger connection than the sale of Manhattan Island. Are there

many Native American generals in the U.S.? Come on. But in any case, *à la guerre comme à la guerre*, and if the Chechens are in it and are not surrendering, then the war must continue to the bitter end: Either to the raising of the Chechen flag over the Kremlin—that must be how they formulate their goal, otherwise, why get into it at all?—or, just as logically, to the last Chechen.

Nevertheless, there was no purchase, no sale. There was a military victory in 1856. Conquest. Pacification. Capitulation in the face of inevitable genocide. An understanding of the need to submit to, mimic, and reluctantly accept the rules of the game. That is the case. But the Indian situation—sale of one's land for money, comprehension of what was done, voluntarily—that is not the case here. The Chechens did not sell us their land. We took it from them.

It doesn't matter. That's not our question. We didn't take it away, and it's not up to us to return it. I'm not planning to scalp either side, and I have no intention of becoming Faithful Hand, friend of the Indians.

Indians and Chechens—it's a very appropriate discussion. Since privatization in Russia is on our agenda and Russians, like Chechens and Indians, have very little respect for private property…

Svinarenko's Commentary:

I'm talking about property that belongs to others, not to themselves. Recently we were talking about this with a friend who is quite wealthy, by any standard (let's not name him). He was complaining that our people have no respect for private property, for its sacred character.

They say that restitution is impossible. But if in fact the adherents of this position are correct, then the following must also be admitted: Therefore, national respect for private property is equally impossible. There will be respect only from the people who have a lot of such property. Look—the Demidovs were not given their factories back, but no one will be able to take away factories belonging to the Cherny brothers. How are the Cherny brothers better than the Demidovs? In 1918 they arrested the bourgeoisie and took away their millions, and no one gave the bourgeoisie their money back or even an apology—so why should Khodorkovsky be untouchable? There's no logic. In Latvia and Estonia, they're returning property. But, as usual, we think we're smarter than everyone else.

What could be simpler—Add up what's left, and give it back. No, they say, it's too complicated. I love that! When other people have lost their property, fuck them, who cares, but when they want to take yours, then the sacredness of private property rears its head. And you think the Indians weren't that aware of things. They didn't respect the right of the farmers to the land they bought. Siemens didn't ask for his factory—Electrosila, in St. Petersburg—to be taken away and then torn down. You can't show me a document to that effect in some New York museum. He sent no such fax. And since he didn't, then he doesn't give a shit about the Russians' technical problems, whether or how they restructured the stolen property. Or are you going to tell me that stealing and not returning things is a Russian national tradition? That the Latvians return property to the heirs, but you shouldn't expect that from Russians? And it's not a question of what has survived intact and what hasn't. It's the principle! You don't have to give the Germans Electrosila back. But it would be very handsome if the Ministry of State Property—or whoever—sent Siemens a letter: "We've begun the process of examining your rights to the factory. Forgive us for taking it away from you so churlishly." The process could take a hundred years! Siemens isn't poor, thank God. But if he got a hundred dollars for his former factory, officially, from the Russian government, he would get all misty. And he'd frame the certificate and hang it on the wall. We could pay with an exemption from taxes for a year, for example. That would bring in more investment… And I've just come up with another argument. Our government is paying the French on their tsarist bonds, right? And those payments make the theme of restitution not ridiculous but merely very complex and difficult. But if we were to start that process, people would see us differently. They would start respecting Russians!

There's another argument against it—that there are too many heirs, so who can identify the right one? Listen, don't get involved in other people's money; let the legal owners decide how to divide up their family property. It was their sacred private property, not yours. So, they won't get very much—doesn't matter, millionaires are often ready to choke for a few kopeks.

For instance, Solzhenitsyn came back to Russia right in the year we're discussing, 1994. It's interesting to refresh our memory of his opinion on privatization. I believe his opinion will ornament our chapter. A decent man, thoughtful scholar, and—this is very useful for us here—not at all leftist, but a real liberal. That guarantees a total absence of frenzy. And self-interest: He didn't get anything from the reforms, and he didn't lose anything, either. He was an outside observer in several senses. He wrote:

> But that was only the beginning of the disasters, for, as you can easily guess, in comparison with the national wealth of such a rich country, the total sum of vouchers was minuscule: The 'distribution' that was announced to the people actually dealt with barely noticeable parts of one percent of the wealth. In the middle of 1994, the high-placed Vice Prime Minister Chubais demonstrated the 'steel will' to which the (until recently Soviet) public was still accustomed, and

announced 'the second stage of privatization'—in which state property would pass into the hands of a few dealers (this goal was publicly declared by members of his staff). …Were the privatizers led by the false theory that as soon as property was in private hands, competition would appear on its own, out of nothing, and that that production would become efficient simply from the change of owners? The Gaidar-Chubais reforms were undertaken along the lines of Marxist thought: If the means of production are given into private hands, capitalism will appear and start working.

That second stage began in the summer of 1994, and in just a few months state property was distributed—outright and almost for free—to select petitioners. There were a few articles in the press about the sensational theft and embezzlement of public property. The people, not even knowing the secret prices and secret deals, saw what was going on and called it the process "piratization."

* * *

Kokh's Commentary:

Privatization: How I Understand It

I had a lot of trouble writing this commentary. This is one of those cases where memories and thoughts pile up, stifling you, getting mixed up and intertwined… Naturally, I'm worried about seeming prejudiced. I cannot maintain my objectivity and stay above the fray on this issue. I tried very hard to be at least calm, if not objective. Well, this is what it is. Don't be too hard on me, kind reader…

Why There Was No Restitution

Svinarenko's tragic bombast condemning the bombast of others is unpleasant to me. That comparison of the entrepreneur to a prostitute—Good Lord, what cheap literature. What sophistry, what a *poseur*. It's fashionable nowadays to heap scorn on businessmen. The idea that the technical problems in restitution are merely secondary, lowly, and undignified comes from an ignorance of the subject and of the consequences that might follow—if there is no clear concept from the start of how the technical problems will be solved. It's very easy to say: I'm not a tactician, I'm a strategist—you're smart, you go figure it out. And until you do, you'll be total shitheads in my book, and I will always give you a failing grade and tell you what a bad job you're doing. Igor does this very well, with an elegant drawl.

But what if—before elucidating the topic of restitution, or rather, of its absence—I first tell you my story? So, they exiled the Germans to Kazakhstan in the fall of 1941. My family was deported from the village of Dzhiginka, in the Anapa region of Krasnodar Krai. They lived in exile until 1969; the exile had long been over, but they stayed on in Kazakhstan. I was born there in 1961. But my Aunt Olga, my father's sister, moved back to Dzhiginka with her husband and children, in 1966. They returned, built their place; they had a garden, and cattle, and went to work in the sovkhoz, the state farm. In 1968 I spent my first summer vacation with them. I remember one incident very well. I was walking down the street with my aunt, and she pointed out a house to me—a big sturdy house in the southern style, with a tiled roof—and said, "That's our house. We lived there until the deportation. Father (that is, my grandfather) built it back in the early 1930s, before there was the sovkhoz."

I said, "Auntie, is there any chance of getting it back?"

She said, "No. After our exile, they moved in people who had been evacuated here from a city, and now they live there."

"Make them move out of our house," I said. And she replied, "And where would they go? I've talked to them; they told me that there are other people living where they used to live. So they're in the same situation, too. Don't worry about it. We've built ourselves another house, no worse than this one. Let things remain the way they are. Otherwise this story will never have an end."

I went there every summer while I was in school. I walked past that house many times over ten years. I never went inside. There was a mulberry bush by the gate, but I never ate a single berry. I knew that it was no longer mine; it belonged to someone else. Why? I don't know. It was like a sentence. My aunt said: Don't touch, don't fret. So I didn't. But ever since then, I have understood that there is no such thing as just restitution. That Pandora's Box must not be opened. It will only make things worse. I personally am not impressed by the pseudo-restitution implemented in Eastern Europe and the Baltics. Why? I'll explain.

They tried it in the Baltics. Everything that had belonged to someone before 1940 and was then confiscated was supposed to be returned immediately, and that was that. At first glance it sounds like a good thing. But if you dig a bit deeper, it's shit on a stick. For example, the simplest question first: What if your property had been taken from you before 1940? What then—it won't be returned? In independent Latvia (I've written about this before), between 1918 and 1940, lots of things were unjustly taken away from Russians, Jews, Poles, and most of all, of course, Germans. That's easily proven. Unlike Solzhenitsyn's example, there are documents in order and so on. Well then? Why are you squirming? Ah, you can't return property to Germans because of their historic guilt? Because they were the aggressors? Then why are you so proud of your SS insignias, you bitches? You put Russian partisans into prison? Perhaps you'd like to tell me that you had no part in the Holocaust? Or do you play it this way: Here it's all right, there it's not? Make up your mind—either give the Germans at least the Domsky Cathedral, or stop lying about offering honest restitution.

Czech Republic? Looks good. It's always being set up as a model for us. All right, let's ease into it: In prewar Czechoslovakia there were 3,200,000 Germans—more than there were Slovaks. Long before the Munich conspiracy, the governments of Masaryk and Beneš began squeezing out Germans from Czechoslovakia, especially from Sudetenland. Requisitions took place, but how could they have not? All the appropriate documents exist. Why are you hiding your eyes? If you're doing restitution, then do it right, and stop gabbing about it. Or is it the historical guilt again? Are you saying that there were no Czechs or half-bloods in the Wehrmacht? In other words, if you can drive a tank into Paris in 1940, you're a German, but when you go for Russian food parcels in 1945, you're suddenly a Czech? Neat trick. Make up your mind: Are you Karl or Karel Gott? All right. Let's accept that. Things are more or less clear with the Germans.

But back in 1918, the Czech Corps dipped into a significant part of Russia's gold reserves during the Civil War. Everyone knows this fact—even the Czechs don't deny it very hard. These reserves are what supported Czechoslovakia's standard of living, the highest in Europe between the wars. Maybe you should return it, eh? There is paperwork, and there are people who remember… Hmm? What? No, not our recollections, yours! No? Why so rude? I'm just asking. I even know your answer. You get a clean slate after 1968. Of course. Without a doubt. How silly of me. Asking my stupid questions of serious people.

Shall I continue? I think that's enough. All restitutions that I know about are half-measures and merely ornamental. They are so subjective that any purist like Svinarenko would criticize them with as much fire as he would our own absence of restitution. In the countries I mentioned, there was a clear enemy: Russians. They came and took everything away. This is a conditional diagram, of course. There were local redistributors, too. But that's the national myth. Now, when they have been freed of the Russian yoke, the puny restitution of which they should be ashamed, but instead are proud, is perceived as a form of national revenge.

In Russia everything is much more complicated than in the Czech Republic or Latvia. This madhouse and nightmare (of which we are supposed to be proud, we were recently told) continued not for forty but for seventy-five years. Unlike them, we also had a Civil War. So, for us, restitution can be implemented either as a profanation or as a vicious provocation for war between everyone and against everyone.

In Russia, one part of the nation took things away from the other. We didn't have an external enemy. To simplify, Igor's grandfather took away my grandfather's property. So? What now? Am I supposed to take away Igor's apartment? Of course not—then where would he live? I'm ashamed to admit that I feel sorry for him, and especially his children. They had nothing to do with it. Nor did the great proponent of restitution, Igor Svinarenko.

And, as long as I'm at it, let me give it to Aleksandr Solzhenitsyn himself. Look: If you're going to talk about the kulaks, then let's not forget that many of those kulaks became kulaks on land that had been taken away from Russian landowners during the revolution. "The Decree on Land"—ever hear of it? "Landowners' estates are banned forever and without any compensation…" Look, I've memorized it. Then maybe we should return the land to the landowners? Or to their descendants—for the sake of justice. Can you imagine what that would entail? Madness.

But Mr. Svinarenko's tender mind cannot bear it. He twitches his nose. It's not just, he says. Not fair. He refuses to accept it.

So don't accept it. It's better to suffer the hysterics of one such "truth lover" than to drown the country in blood again in the name of principle. We've had that many times. Enough.

Pandora's Box is a terrible thing. Only irresponsible dreamers like Igor could suggest opening it. Truly, the road to hell is paved with good intentions. Let the people who committed mistakes pay for them—not their children and grandchildren. God is their judge. My Aunt Olya (may she rest in peace) forgave everyone. Our goal is to avoid committing any new sins or errors. I don't understand the logic: If we haven't implemented restitution, then we can revisit the results of privatization. How does that follow? It suggests that if someone stole and robbed eighty-five years ago and is long dead, cursed by his victims, then we can start robbing and stealing once again. Ah, we're supposed to correct the consequences of his actions? Can they be corrected? I think that tragic as it may be, there are things that cannot be rectified. They can only be remembered. Never forgotten. Ever. And in the final analysis, no one took anything away from me, and my grandfather is in his grave in Altai. He doesn't care anymore.

All right, on to privatization. I can't put it off any longer.

Some people think I persuaded Igor to write this book just to whitewash privatization and myself. Starting way off, and luring you closer and closer to the real point. Throwing in the Bible and Leo Tolstoy and this and that. Trying to show off my braininess. Even I'm not sure that this isn't so. In general I don't tend to justify myself. It's not one of my character traits. But… Maybe, somewhere deep inside… Maybe, unconsciously?

This may sound banal, but I treasure what our team did. We, who worked on privatization, did not profit from the course of its implementation. Those newspaper clichés that journalists made up and used to scare the public over the last ten years—where did they come from?

Take "the voucher sting." Why was it a sting? Tell me why? No one could ever explain the point of their objections. Because people sold their voucher for a bottle of vodka? They did, but so what? And some signed away their apartments to con men, but that's no reason to call the people who gave them the apartments in the first place con men.

So some of the voucher investment funds went bankrupt. Weren't we the ones shouting at the top of our voices, warning people not to invest their vouchers in MMM and all those Neftalmazinvests? But they didn't show us on TV—instead they advertised those funds and made good money on it. Why should they show us?

We sold off the country for a trifle? Not true. Not a trifle. For free. Basically it was for free. And why? Go ask the deputies of Speaker Ruslan Khabulatov's Soviet why—they'll tell you: because they passed the Law on Named Privatization Accounts. Before that, privatization was based on money—not bad money for those times. I'm talking about 1992. Vouchers came into force only in 1994.

Isn't a privatization check the same thing as a privatization account? If they had had accounts instead of vouchers, everything would have been fine. That is a point of view—that you can't trade an account for a bottle of vodka, you can only use the account to buy shares. Well, that's true. But then you can easily trade that share for a bottle. And it can be done in one operation. See, you take a bottle of vodka, you buy the share they tell you to buy, and you give it to them. Done. So there's no difference between an account and a voucher, that's all hot air. But there was such a hassle with those accounts, it nearly drove us crazy. When we told Sberbank that it had a month to open 150 million accounts, including ones for infants—and to keep special accounting of them, so that the funds would not get mixed in with the rest of the money, and could be spent only at specialized privatization auctions—the bank experts said: Whoever invented this masterpiece is nuts. This is impossible to implement. You need tens of thousands of new bankers, a massive input of new technology, and new communications channels. The cost would be astronomical. In other words, either the authors of the plan want to stop privatization, or they don't care about public funds.

By the way, the most consistent critic of privatization, Mayor Yuri Luzhkov, introduced special Moscow vouchers. Have you forgotten that already? I haven't. Why don't you criticize him?

Frankly, I don't take offense at the journalists. I'm over it. After all, the "voucher sting of the century" is now an element of the national mythology. It's impossible to fight a myth. The nation will have to live with this nail up its ass. Why was it stuck there? Is it that we don't have enough excuses for igniting inter-ethnic hatred? Have we forgotten how those things end? But when it was being shoved in, no one stopped to think if it was the right thing to do. Thousands of people, hundreds of journalists, without coordinating it, some for money and some just for the hell of it, without understanding the issue, just wrote whatever came to mind. As long as it was daring and shocking, papers can put up with anything.

Allow me to quote at some length from my book, *The Selling of the Soviet Empire,* which caused such a fuss and scandal in its day. This excerpt was written in 1997.

Privatization in Russia started on July 3, 1991, when the Law of the Russian Federation on Privatization of State and Municipal Enterprises of the RSFSR was passed.

I would propose the following historical plan for the transformation of property rights in Russia, starting with 1989: 1989—latent "shadow" transition of property from the state to private individuals or their associations without legal implementation; 1989-1991—legal protection of property rights without adequate legal basis for it; 1992-1994—attempt to destroy the "informal" or illegal rights through laws and bringing in large masses of the population. Over those years the attitude toward privatization also changed; while in 1992 there was serious discussion of whether trade should be privatized or left in the hands of the state, today even the Communists call for a multifaceted economy.

You could say that I was present at the birth of the voucher idea. It belongs indisputably to mathematician Vitaly Naishul. It was long before Gaidar would join the government, but we already had our team. We would meet at the tourist camp in Repino (outside St. Petersburg), drink vodka, and throw ideas around. For instance, I thought that all property should just be handed out for free. Create a special agency that would grab hold of people and, whether they wanted it or not, make them official owners of property. But Vitaly Naishul said: No, let's give everyone vouchers, and let them invest them where they want. Later, Naishul identified the gap between "flight of fancy and life." By then, parliament had passed the law on named privatization accounts, which was very illiberal—the law did not presume the free exchange of shares, and so on. It was then that Chubais proposed that we break that system and make bearer vouchers that could be re-sold. And after a huge battle, when we finally pushed the voucher model through the Supreme Soviet, Vitaly Naishul stopped liking it. What were we supposed to do? We had no choice—we had to implement it.

We should remember the conditions and factors under which the privatization process was begun in Russia. No consumer demand or social equality; low interest on the part of foreign investors; more than 240,000 state enterprises, which required us to use standardized procedures; spontaneous privatization—that is, a mass transfer of property belonging to state enterprises into other forms of property outside the legislative framework. It was to solve all these problems that the voucher was invented, a magic wand for the Russian economy. Distribution of vouchers among Russian citizens began in the fall of 1992.

The team headed by Anatoly Chubais called me to Moscow in 1993: Voucher privatization had to be completed; it was behind schedule, and there weren't enough hands in the State Property Committee. Approaching the finish line of voucher privatization—in late 1993—we were desperate for time and kept throwing out new enterprises onto the market so that people would be able to use their checks. We worked round the clock, with brief breaks for naps, tea and pirozhki. Life could have taken a very harsh turn, both for the entire country and for us personally, if the privatization checks did not get fully used—if, say, only half of them were used, which was the situation on January 1, 1994. Strictly speaking, voucher privatization should have ended then, but we extended the deadline by six months, to June 30, 1994.

And what did we get on that date? The privatization check offered every citizen of the Russian Federation an equal right to acquire a share of state property. The basic task—the formation of a stratum of private property holders—was executed, and more than 40 million Russians (over 30% of the population) owned shares of privatized enterprises or check investment funds. According to our data, around 98% of the distributed checks "came back": We handed out 151,450,000 of them and got back 148,580,000. That included 45,990,000 (17.2%) through closed subscription, 114,690,000 (75.5%) through check auctions, and 7,900,000 (5.2%) in other ways. That left 2,870,000 checks (1.9%) in circulation. Close to 116,000 enterprises were privatized, which represented about half of the entire economy. The newly formed private sector at that time included more than 25,000 joint-stock companies. The non-state sector of the economy, as a result of the privation of 1992-1994, began producing more than half of the GDP. It is indicative that both the critics and the adherents of check privatization agree on this: The quantitative success of the mass privatization program is indisputable and obvious.

I would liken the voucher stage of privatization to the "zero cycle" in construction. Even though we were accused of not making it possible for an ordinary Soviet person to become a Rockefeller; and though many other goals— which were set before the start of privatization but objectively could not have been reached that quickly—were not reached; and though our more emotional opponents called voucher privatization the "sting of the century"; several fundamental goals for the Russian economy were reached. First, the state stopped being a monopolist in the national economy—a broad stratum of private property holders appeared. Second, a securities market appeared, in many ways thanks to the voucher. Check investment funds appeared as well, and the words "broker," "registrar," and "depository" became familiar. And last, the appearance of 40 million shareholders— who with the help of the privatization checks began mastering the fundamentals of the market economy—was proof that we were inevitably on the road to a normally functioning system of corporate relations.

It goes without saying that the rules of the game during the course of check privatization were not ideal, and if we could go back to 1992, we might have tried to do a few things differently. For instance, it is clear today that by giving in to populist feelings, and preferring in many cases a closed subscription for shares on the second variant of benefits, we in fact "shut down" the investment future of many enterprises for a lengthy period. The closed subscription gave nothing to the members of the work collectives except delays in wage payments and often ridiculously low dividends at the end of the year.

Our second mistake was to tie the packages of shares in state property to the principle "so that nothing goes wrong." It was like the dog in the manger—they couldn't manage it efficiently themselves, but we didn't offer up any money for development and we wouldn't let anyone else do it.

Another sad song from the time was the one about investment competitions. They turned out to be, alas, promise competitions—the winners were the ones who promised the most. Often, they remained just promises.

But on the whole, the results of voucher privatization were positive, and no one can tell me any different. Privatization helped form the private sector, establish the stock exchange, and bring in investments through securities; it predetermined competition, and formed an alternative to the market of state securities… Even today, I do not consider that voucher privatization had been too hasty or too formalized. Should it have been done? Yes. Without it, we would not have had Yeltsin's victory in the presidential elections of 1996, or the market that brings in billions of dollars in investments today. A gigantic step was taken, which essentially made the political and economic reforms irreversible.

I read it over, and I got a sense of the past. I was thirty-three. As they say, Christ's age. Was anything as significant or large-scale—and, above all, positive—done for the country after that? Tell me, what? The implementation of the vertical of power? Hee-hee. No, nothing else… That was the sole event that changed the face of the country. It changed all of us. Yet Igor wants restitution. The hell with restitution. Privatization is the best reply to nationalization!

And I can't leave Solzhenitsyn's criticism without a response. I'll let his conscience deal with the passage alleging that in the second half of 1994, literally over the course of a few months, all of the nation's property was given away to a small group of people. That is simply not so. In the second half of 1994 we had practically stopped privatization, since it was time to switch the system from vouchers to cash sales.

If he means the loans-for-shares auctions, they took place in 1995, and far from all property was on sale then. There were no more than fifteen lots at the mortgage auctions. Yes, big ones; yes, tasty ones—but far from the entire Russian economy. Note that the cash privatization is still not completed, and the Ministry of State Property continues to sell hundreds of enterprises and packages of shares. Therefore, saying that we sold everything off reveals that you have not mastered the issue. I can understand the author's emotional charge, but when you're dealing with such an explosive issue, it's not very wise to splash kerosene around. In order for the changes to sound convincing, it is important to be precise in the details. The devil is there, as we know.

In general, I'm getting the impression that Solzhenitsyn formed his judgment about privatization from second-hand accounts. When he returned to Russia, all kinds of "captains of perestroika," like Svyatoslav Fyodorov, came to see him. ... And since they had no sympathy for us, they bad-mouthed privatization for all they were worth.

However, his main complaint—that privatization was implemented too hastily—requires a clear answer, just because it is clearly formulated.

Let me begin. I've found more than once that the main mistake in any decision comes from an incorrect perception of alternatives. Aleksandr Isaevich thinks that our choice was between implementing privatization either quickly or with feeling, reason, and pace. We did not have that choice. Our choice was different: Either we do it quickly or we never do it at all. It would have been naïve to think that the main threat was that they would stop it. No. Our opponents articulated those intentions on the surface. But in fact, the noise about stopping privatization was made to cover their plan to steal everything for themselves.

I've already mentioned that the legally correct, public privatization process was preceded by a stage of either totally criminal or "gray" (semi-legal) privatization. There were all kinds of suspect activities: The outright purchasing of plants (by bribing the director under the old Gorbachev law on enterprises); clever schemes with rented enterprises and rented staff; contributing entire manufacturing plants as one's share in a cooperative, while the rest, who were the director's stooges, contributed "intellectual property"... The crowning glory of the dementia was "renting with buying," that monstrous child of Corresponding Member of the Academy of Sciences, Comrade Bunich. Remember that? So, when we arrived on the scene, about 40% of the stores and restaurants were on that rental plan—that is, they were meant to be sold to the collective for nothing. I'm not kidding: The remaining value was just a couple of dozen rubles. The hell with the stores, we had Lentransgaz on that plan. I'm a hardcore liberal, and even I can understand that the nation's gas transport system cannot be privatized.

Our predecessors worked gloriously. If our "bad" and "predatory" privatization had not started; if we had not begun holding auctions and competitions that were public and could be argued in court, which could be observed and then griped about on television and in stupid articles in the press; then Solzhenitsyn would be right—they would have stolen the country out from under the people with no recourse. No one admits now that the danger of that had been grave. Even then, only a few dozen people were fully aware of it.

You don't understand it, either. They had all the rails greased and ready to go. In the Gorbachev-Silayev period they had all the paperwork ready; they had made all the arrangements. Just a little bit more, and it would be done. And then came our auctions, competitions, vouchers and other nasty bits. Benefits for labor collectives. We gave no less than 25% of shares to workers. Fyodorov's anger with Chubais is based on that.

And here, Aleksandr Isaevich, I disagree with another of your statements: that this was all done in secrecy from the people. That is not true. There wasn't a single enterprise where the workers didn't get at least 25% of the shares. As a rule, they got 51%. Thus, they had to have known that their enterprise was being privatized. Everyone knew—when, how much, and where. Your informers misled you on this, too.

Now just imagine that their version of privatization took place instead of ours. The alternatives, I assure you, were just those two. What would it be like now? If our far-from-perfect, but public and juridical privatization—a privatization that followed at least a crummy law—is criticized right and left, its legitimacy and justice questioned, and demands are made to review its results, what would be going on now if they had implemented the version of the economic and financial elite of the late 1980s? All the glib talkers with their babble about supporting perestroika and the new thinking had replaced the real industrial elite, which at least knew how to run things. The bad thing is not that it would have been sold cheap. The bad thing is that the ownership title obtained their way would be gray, "dirty." With such property rights, you can't attract investment—or get loans against collateral, or do anything. The country would have stagnated and died. It would be a trifling matter to start a popular movement against the thieves, with property rights like that. They would have killed one another long ago, anyway. And there would not have been a second term for Yeltsin. And that means, no beloved Putin, stabilization, or vertical of power. Nothing. Of that I am certain.

However, all that is water under the bridge, legends of the distant past. I wonder who's interested in the truth about privatization? Is the myth about wholesale theft and the "sting of the century" sufficient even for scholars? After all, we do have the sciences of economics and history! I don't mean at the Academy—that's all in the hands of the senile academicians or corresponding members like Sergei Glazyev. I'm talking about the universities. The graduate students, the doctoral candidates. Don't they care about what actually happened to their country? How it took place? I guess not… Too bad.

And, last. Forgive us, dear ladies and gentlemen, that we did not make Rockefellers out of all of you, as promised. It turned out to be impossible. Absolutely. That has been scientifically established.

* * *

Enough of privatization, for now, Igor, we need to get back to the Chechen war! Tell me what you thought about it.

Me? It seemed like a vague, local problem—one among many others. Part of the mess of those days. Nothing was clear anywhere, including in Chechnya. I wasn't emotionally involved—at least not then, at the beginning. Maybe that was because there were so many declarations of independence. Instead of the national anthem, "Arise, mighty land," there was all this flickering before my eyes. I couldn't get my head around why Russia had given up Germany and the Baltics... Within the context of the half of Europe that we gave up without a single shot, Chechnya did not seem like a major issue.

The separate Terek Region was against Dudayev, and that region was headed by a man named Avturkhanov, right? Allegedly they created units that went to storm Grozny.

Oh, yes, a unit of Russian officers!

Yes. They were selected from all over Russia and then later denounced. Where did all those people go from the Terek Region? Were they all killed? The whole war of 1994–1996 was just a series of betrayals, it seems to me. I remember there was this Security Council functionary, General Manilov, who later worked at the Ministry of Defense. We were in his office talking about Chechnya, and he said, "As soon as we get them where we want them, and roll out the artillery, then we get the order to retreat. We corner them again—and again, the order to retreat!" Someone said, "We're sick of these stories about the order to retreat! Tell us who gave you that order. Full name!" And do you know what he said? He said: "Viktor Stepanovich Chernomyrdin."

Really?

Yes! I said, what the hell, you've got a commander-in-chief! Why take orders from the Prime Minister? And he replied, the commander-in-chief doesn't really participate in these things; he believes whatever people tell him. He blathers on about 38 snipers. Who filled Chernomyrdin's brain with shit about retreating or attacking? Berezovsky? That's what some newspapers said... But, now,

Chernomyrdin is gone—why can't they catch that one-legged guy? If you talk to the military brass today, they tell you the same story: We know where he is—but we don't have the orders to take him. Why not? There's an international warrant on him, he's an international criminal. What more do they need, what special command?

Maybe the war isn't going well because no one is joining the popular volunteer front, Alik. And people aren't tossing their bonnets into the air when the regiment is sent off to Chechnya. Our society, from top to bottom, doesn't give a shit about this war.

There was a story on TV—one of many like it, but this had very powerful imagery—about a Chechen war vet, with a medal—for Valor, by the way—living with his wife in his tiny Moskvich car. For a long time now. He was forced out of the barracks. There are no lines of new recruits at army posts, and young ladies from good families don't go to hospitals to apply bandages, bind the wounds of soldiers who have lost their legs, and have sex with wounded officers.

But, Igor, no one is rushing to volunteer in the U.S., either. Their soldiers are whining in Iraq to be sent home. And yet they managed to catch Saddam!

For money?

All right, let's pay money to catch Basayev. And Maskhadov—for money. This can't go on. I don't understand it. They come out periodically with their appeals and announcements, they send videocassettes, they crawl out onto the Internet... They make themselves known! The Americans caught a man who didn't make himself known for six months. He sat in a crack. The Chechens are busy with public affairs, running operations. I don't get it.

And I don't understand why Umar Dzhabrailov is head of the Plaza Group.

What don't you understand? It's that sacred right to private property. By the way, it's not his own property—the Manezh complex, or the Rossiia Hotel, or the Slavyanskaya Hotel—he's managing them. I don't know what bothers you about him.

Well, Alik, the Russians aren't in charge of business in the Caucasus, but the Caucasians are running business in Russia. That tells you something... Why did I think of Dzhabrailov? Because in Chechnya and in Russia there's the same tribal system. Two tribes killing each other. Neither is bringing the other side civilization and culture. That's why it's

so disturbing to see a man from one tribe holding the most prominent property of the other tribe. In time of war, I might add.

Then why is the tribe called Russians constantly betraying its members? There is no betrayal in the Chechen tribe.

Because they have clear concepts, while ours are muddied. They cling to their tribal system, while we've rejected half its values already. We've lost a lot of our former values. But we haven't yet reached a belief in the sacred righteousness of the state as an institution appropriate to the white man. In a tribal society, one of your own is always right. But in a state system, the understanding is that there should be an absolute triumph of justice and law. We don't assume members of our tribe are right just because they're a part of the tribe—we're not savages, after all—but we don't protect our laws, either.

Svinarenko's Commentary:

Take the case with former Colonel Yuri Budanov. They didn't treat him properly. When savage tribes are at war, everything is allowed. If things are decided on state level and in a civilized manner, then you have to do three things: first you have to determine the status of military actions, quickly arrest and imprison those who keep calling back the troops and not letting them take the separatists; then you have to hold responsible (in court!) the people who allowed a concussed, heavy-drinking man to lead the troops, and explain in ten words why this war is lasting longer than World War II; and perhaps most importantly, you have to address—sternly—all the crimes against civilian Russians in Chechnya. Otherwise, you get this impression that there were only peaceful naïve natives there—like in Tahiti, singing their songs and putting wreaths of flowers on visitors—and suddenly the white man came and killed a local girl, which had never ever happened there before. Oh, dear! The natives simply faint at the sight of blood. Of course, it's terrible, but I don't care what you say, I think Budanov got a raw deal. If I had been sent to report on the trial, I would have written quite a piece. They should have said, "Dear Chechen friends! We sympathize with your sorrow. We are trying to deal with the question in a just way. See, we've already arrested our own colonel. We will try him. But not today. Only after you hand over a dozen of your boys who've been raping and killing Russians in Chechnya. There have been complaints filed. Some famous people were caught in the crossfire. And then we'll try everybody at the same time. We give you a deadline of one year to catch your villains. At the end of that time, if you haven't caught them, sorry, but we'll be letting the colonel off scot-free. No trial." I'll bet there aren't any complaints on file, that no one bothered to record the complaints from Russian victims. Then the whole question is made moot: We don't want to create the incorrect impression that that they can do it and we can't. That might incite national hatred. I'm even willing to make the conditions less harsh. Just ask for the statistics on how many Chechens were found guilty—in regional and *shariat* courts—of crimes against Russians.

There is yet another path which is no worse than the one taken with Budanov and no one would be surprised in the least. We could activate two or three skinheads in Germany who would find a hundred or so grannies who had been raped by the Red Army soldiers in 1945—we know there were lots of those cases. The grannies will write complaints, our military prosecutors will quickly figure out which troops were stationed there then, and then they can start cases against the officers, take away their medals, interrogate the surviving grandpas, take their sperm for analysis, have line-ups and so on and so on. So what, there was a war on, who cares. Who cares that the people were shell shocked, everyone was traumatized. The Nazis killed somebody's family? Burned them? Go to court. To the Hague. And the articles in the press will be all about the peace-loving Germans who wanted to free the long-suffering Russian people from Stalinism and so on. If you follow that logic, then a soldier in Treptower Park who embraced a rescued plump but underage German girl can be charged with pedophilia like Michael Jackson.

But seriously, as an intermediate punishment, Budanov should be dressed in his summer uniform and sent off in an unheated plane to anywhere—if he dies of pneumonia, no problem. Just like those poor draftees. And even more seriously, we should hunt down all the surviving KGB/NKVD veterans who worked in the Baltic states in 1940, and send them to Latvia. Let them be tried there—the Latvians enjoy that. Why not? Why should we have a double standard? Let's do it fair and square everywhere.

* * *

Consider this, Alik. The Russians have a third way, neither tribe nor statehood. Not like everyone else. Neither here nor there.

Ah, you mean shuffling in place. In between.

That's our national way: no peace, no war, and dissolve the army.

Hahaha. That was formulated by Comrade Bronstein, who took Trotsky as his Bolshevik alias.

Who, apparently, understood the profound essence of Russians. He obviously knew what they really wanted without admitting it even to

themselves. Don't laugh, because what we have in Chechnya follows Trotsky's model: There's no war status, but there is no peace either—it's called a "counterterrorist operation." They haven't dissolved the army (it's not dissolute, either), but they've brought out the troops! What's left there is formally subordinate to the Ministry of the Interior and the FSB, not the army. And something else about Chechnya, to help understand what is happening there and why. I'm a Ukrainian. Quite a few of our brethren fought there on the other side, against the Russians. So I'm thinking: Who would benefit if I paid more attention to my Ukrainianness? Maybe then I would be blowing up Russian trains in the Crimea and fighting for Gelayev. There's an upswing in national interests throughout the world, and here the Russians aren't being allowed to figure out their identity and pursue self-determination.

I don't quite understand what you're talking about, Igor. I don't think it's right to compare Ukrainian and Chechen separatism. Every *khokhol* has a choice—he can pay no attention to his separateness from the common Slavic nation, or he can pay attention and insist on having the Ukrainian state, which is taking humorous forms right now—there was a popular election of a president, and now it will be done for the Supreme Rada. The way Gorbachev was elected.

I would introduce representational elections myself. Popular elections will choose Stenka Razin [18th century rebel and populist leader].

Why do you say that? Putin was elected by popular vote. Are you calling him a Stenka Razin? Eh? Or do you have something against Putin? Eh? Look me in the eyes! No blinking! Don't turn your face! Answer the question!

Against Putin? I might, but I don't have any other appropriate candidates. Not Ivan Rybkin. And not Zhirinovsky's bodyguard who ran against Putin. Maybe our Japanese friend—Irina Khakamada is a heroine; she acted like a real man as a candidate in the elections.

Let me answer you. A *khokhol* can maintain that he laughs at the conflict around Tuzla. I don't see much difference between Russians and Ukrainians. But the Chechen wasn't given the choice! He can only be a separatist. Because the Russians will always remind him that he's a black-ass. Look, even you just said, why don't they take the Plaza Group away from Umar Dzhabrailov? You don't like a Chechen businessman in Moscow. It doesn't occur to you to take business away from Evtushenkov, since he's a fellow *khokhol*. Right? They haven't given the Chechen a choice; he can never remain above the fray.

I can understand that, actually. I can easily picture myself as a Chechen running around with a machine gun, fighting Russians. What other socially significant activities are left me? Herding sheep? Selling at the green markets in Moscow? Very enticing... And as for serving Russians, that would not make sense to me as a Chechen. That's just my view from the outside. So, are we behind on a world trend again? Everyone else has freed their colonies.

I don't think Chechnya ever was a real colony, Igor. For instance, there were peoples that England never managed to conquer—the Pushtu, for one. They continue living without a state. They go to Pakistan, then to Afghanistan. There's nothing good about it—the children are illiterate, they don't give them inoculations, they're dying off like flies. They're filthy, snotty, and have guns over their shoulders. That is their choice. A stupid one, I must add. But their own.

I noticed that in India. I've read Kipling's memoirs... It's funny, the British built railroads and factories, taught the natives European concepts—and now India is sending rockets into space and building atom bombs. But independent Afghanistan is riding around on donkeys and has nothing except its wonderfully savage landscape. Two models. Very interesting: two worlds, two childhoods.

Do you remember how Sherlock Holmes starts?

Dr. Watson comes back from the Afghan wars.

Yes, he was wounded outside Peshawar. The Russians gave the Chechens oil wells. And all the appropriate infrastructure and railroads. And then left. The oil wells in Grozny, I think, belonged in part to the Nobel brothers. It was a kind of international project.

We understand what they are dying for: the law of the mountains, their traditions, elders, mutual aid, the moral image of their women—you can sort of imagine what they are defending. But what about us? Can you formulate that for me? What is so precious about our way of life that we want to bring to other countries? When the Chechens watch TV and see our oligarchs attack one another, and kill their comrades in information wars; when they see how our officials have gone completely nuts, how former Interior Minister Boris Gryzlov, in the election campaign, is attacking his own turncoats who had been on his payroll, we can understand the reaction of the viewers in Gudermes.

They knock each other off, too—even more than us, Igor. They steal and take bribes. They're not perfectly pure. What about us? What do we have? Well, there's the principle of territorial integrity, that's a kind of fetish. Putin has it much more than Yeltsin did. And then, Putin had a very convincing reason for starting the war: They had attacked Dagestan. There were big problems with Tatarstan and Bashkiria in 1994. And with the Urals: Governor Eduard Rossel declared the creation of an Urals Republic, and Nazdratenko declared a Far Eastern one. There were big problems with Yakutia, which had pronounced itself subject to international law.

That's funny—we held on to Chechnya with our bare teeth while our troops left Poland, German and the Baltics. That didn't bother us.

That's because Chechnya is inside Russia. But there's another explanation, too. That at the last moment Dudayev allegedly agreed to the Tatar version, but he was told that he was too late. Why didn't our government accept the agreement with Dudayev? What happened there?

When you see Berezovsky, ask him.

No, Berezovsky had no significance in 1994. So I don't understand this. But I do know one thing, Igor. Stepashin was director of the FSB—wait, it was called the FSK then. He was the one who recruited those guys and seated them in tanks, and they headed into Grozny. They stormed Grozny! And on their shoulders a man named Victor Erin, Minister of Internal Affairs, was supposed to bring in troops of interior forces, who were on the march. They were supposed to take Grozny, using the excuse that they had to prevent bloodshed. When our tanks entered Grozny and took it—

The tanks started to burn.

Exactly. It was a meat-grinder slaughterhouse—but our troops won, that's the point. Then Erin turned the interior troops around and led them out of Grozny. That's all. And our storm units, left with no support from basic back-up forces, were shattered.

Did he retreat for money?

Don't know. But it's a strange story in any case. When I began talking about this with Stepashin, he got all blotchy and started shaking, and said only this: Erin betrayed him, he was a so-and-so—and that unfortunately, he couldn't tell me the whole story. But in private conversation he says things that will make your toes curl.

But in general, it's clear that it's very handy to have a small, manageable war and keep sending money for restoration there—that is, simply sign off on papers that say that money was sent there. Over and over.

I'm telling you. The first war was a line of corruption and horrible betrayals. The press really betrayed the Russians then, Igor. Almost all the papers! Gusinsky's media howled about the heroic Chechens. Mujahideens fighting for their independence. Then the heroic mujahideen kidnapped Elena Masyuk, and Gusinsky had to pay money to get his reporter back. A lot. It's all through the looking glass, the whole thing.

They say it's all about the oil.

Who the hell knows.

That's the story that Azer Mursaliev gave to *Kommersant*. He made a convincing case: When they were planning the pipeline from Baku through Chechnya, there was an attack. When they changed their minds and decided to go through Turkey, the Kurds immediately did something there. So they went back to the Chechnya idea, and more attacks, endlessly. The dates correspond with amazing accuracy. I declared that report the best in the entire publishing house and gave Azer a big bonus with great pleasure. ... A terrorist act takes place in Russia. These acts are done not by, or not only by, Chechens, but also by the guys who are getting their cut from the deal with the Arabs. Apparently that was what Stepashin wanted to tell you but could not. But, whatever the case may be, this war is not yours and mine. We're not going there to fight. And you're not buying tanks and sending them to Grozny, the way leading weavers and milkmaids did in 1942.

You're wrong—I pay taxes, and the war is waged on my taxes.

Taxes are one thing, but you're not voluntarily donating patriotic funding. It's not our war; we're not prepared to go there and die there. The idea doesn't seem suitable.

Mario Puzo has a book called *The Sicilian*. It's about a guy who becomes a kind of Robin Hood. On the one hand, he's a bandit, but on the other, he robs the rich and helps the poor. And he's a separatist who wants freedom and independence for Sicily. They move the army against him, they fight him. And then they betray him.

As usual.

Yes. It's practically nonfiction. It really happened. And this model reminds me of the Chechen war. I think that Sicilians, Corsicans, and Chechens have a lot in common. In the sense that outsiders see banditry, the mafia, backwardness, and separatism, where they see family values, valor, courage, and respect for tradition.

The Basques, too.

Maybe the Basques—I don't know whether they have blood vengeance. But let me put it in my commentary.

Kokh's Commentary:

How I Understand the Chechens: Four Views

"It is hard to be a Chechen."—Chechen proverb
"It is hard to be a Jew."—Jewish proverb

Why are the Chechens such a strange and unusual people? What conditions and historical realities formed their mores and customs—in their cruelty and determination so unlike the mores and customs of even their neighbors, much less those of distant nations? Are there other peoples in the world with mentalities comparable to the Chechens? What do they have in common? Is there a positive experience of relations with them? What should be done to put an end to this senseless bloodshed that threatens the disappearance of the ethnos?

As a child in Kazakhstan where my German family had been sent during the war, I lived among other exiles, including Chechens. As a government minister of Russia, I had to confront the issues of the war in Chechnya. As a resident of Moscow, I have to deal with Chechen terrorism. Therefore, I have given the Chechens a lot of thought, and I have come up with four ways of looking at them.

First View: Anarchists

Sicily was a land that had been more cruelly raped than any other in history. The Inquisition had tortured rich and poor alike. The landowning barons and the princes of the Catholic Church exercised absolute power over the farmers and shepherds. The police were the instruments of their power and so identified with them that to be called a policeman is the foulest insult one Sicilian can hurl at another.

Faced with the savagery of this absolute power, the suffering people learned never to betray their anger and their hatred, for fear of being crushed. They learned never to make themselves vulnerable by uttering any sort of threat since giving such a warning insured a quick reprisal. They learned that society was their enemy and so when they sought redress for their wrongs they went to the rebel underground, the Mafia.

(Mario Puzo, *The Godfather*, chapter 23.)

Seeing the soldiers, Matteo's first thought was that they had come to arrest him. Where did that thought come from? Did Matteo have any problems with the authorities? No, his name enjoyed a good reputation. He was what was called a well-intentioned resident, but at the same time, he was a Corsican and a mountain dweller, and which Corsican mountain dweller would not find, if he searched his memory, some small sin in his past: a rifle shot, a dagger strike, or some other trifle?

(Prosper Merimée, *Matteo Falcone.*)

The old men gathered in the square and, crouching, discussed their situation. No one spoke of hatred for the Russians. The emotion that all Chechens, from youngest to oldest, felt was stronger than hatred. It was not hatred, but a non-recognition of those Russian dogs as human, and such disgust, revulsion, and bewilderment in the face of the incongruous cruelty of those creatures that the desire to exterminate them—like the desire to exterminate rats, poisonous spiders and wolves—was just as natural as the sense of self-preservation.

(Leo Tolstoy, *Hadji Murat.*)

Why these citations? I don't know. They seem to have something in common, but I can't specify exactly what. Perhaps the perception of any statehood as a hostile power?

For a variety of historical reasons, the Chechens did not develop their own aristocracy and statehood. The causes for this phenomenon are described rather thoroughly by Emil Souleimanov in his article, *"Society and the Chechen Mentality,"* and the works of the ethnologist Jan Chesnov are devoted to this subject. The Chechens developed a variant with a rather complimentary self-description, "mountain democracy." Their clan (*teip* in Chechen) structure exists to this day, and they see any attempt to form a regular state as an alien innovation to be resisted—or to be mimicked for their own *teip* benefit.

What are the causes for this situation? Some people feel that the young Chechen ethnos has not reached the stage of statehood in its historical development (Venceslav Kryzh), while others (Emil Souleimanov) feel that with Tamerlane's monstrously cruel invasion, the Chechen ancestors were forced to move from the valleys to the mountains, shifting from agriculture to cattle-breeding. That meant a loss of liege relations and therefore the need for hierarchy and aristocracy. A gradual "peasant revolution" took place, and the Chechens forced their aristocracy into Kabarda, Ossetia, and Dagestan. They organized themselves into comparatively democratic clan communities—*teipy*—

with elected elders. The only state remnant was the *teip* court—the *kkhel*—which functions sporadically on the basis of customary law, or *adat,* according to which the victim is supposed to carry out the sentence. The most the *teip* can do for the victim is to show silent compassion and support. That is the peasant democracy.

I would not rush to outrage over its primitiveness, but first would point out that closed mountain communities in Tibet and gypsy groups all over the world function in this way. The Russian criminal subculture is also based on the rejection of the state and recognizes only the court of thieves. Cossack life was organized this way for several centuries. Could it be that the Chechens borrowed this form of self-organization from them? The Cossack circle, no extradition from the Don, "*Saryn' na kichku!*" (their pirate cry like "All hands on deck!"), and so on…

And finally, the most vivid example is the canton confederation of Switzerland—this community of communes almost devoid of central government. The mountain men of the Alps, even Schiller's Wilhelm Tell (wasn't that work called "The Robbers"?)—if you look at them objectively—are the same Caucasian "animals," sorry, freedom-loving archers as depicted by the German Romantic poets. It was impossible to imagine better fighters than the Swiss Guards. They protect the Pope to this day. They have no army but the entire nation is armed (home guards, militias), like the Chechens.

I would also like to recall our Russian anarchist theoreticians (Kropotkin, Bakunin) and the anarchist practitioners like Nestor Makhno. They saw Russia as a place that needed no government. Makhno's anarchist revolutionary resistance to Bolshevism so frightened Comrade Stalin that thirteen years after the Civil War ended he tried to starve the southeast part of Ukraine, the *kulak* heart of Russia, where the idea of Makhnovism was still very strong.

Second View: Their Courts

So what are these *adat* laws used by the Chechen *teip* court, the *kkhel. Adat* laws are the norms of the so-called customary law that formed among Arabs back in the pagan period. The *adats* are not a purely Arab invention. They include the norms of law that arose before our era through the Middle and Near East and the Mediterranean. Let's look at the most widespread ones.

Kunachestvo is a form of blood brotherhood in the Caucasus region. This is not a purely Chechen principle or one borrowed from the Arabs. It was observed by the ancient Romans, among others. Another similar custom—adoption—was also pervasive in Rome. It achieved the same goal as blood brotherhood: two clans not related by blood were brought together, thereby cementing their union.

Yakh is the code of male honor. Practically every nation in the world has a set of rules of behavior for men, intended to inculcate courage and bravery, wisdom and cool-headedness, nobility and honor. The interesting detail among the Chechens, which in my opinion explains a lot, is their unique attitude toward insult. The Chechens have a rare moral inversion—they fear being insulted. Insult here is understood in the broadest sense of the word:

> The mountain men were guided not primarily by the fear of physical punishment by an ineffective or absent "central authority" but by the fear of "insult" to their family and *teip*, if they did not follow the strict *adats,* and by the fear of possible unpleasant reactions from other *teipy*. The Chechen Beibulat Taimiev, Alexander Pushkin's companion on his trip to Erzerum and a man of bravery, told the poet about his constant fears: will his guest be pleased with him, will he behave improperly as someone's guest and thereby insult his *kunak* (guest, friend), will he be able to keep his promises… "I fear shame, and therefore I am always careful. No, I am not brave."
>
> In some cases, personal shame reflected not only on the individual, but could infect, to a degree, the honor of an entire generation. If the shame was serious, in many cases it could not be "washed away" for decades. The guilty man's life would become unbearable; his own *teip*, even the entire community would reject him. He would find himself outside the law, his daughter would never be allowed to marry, his son would be humiliated, his parents would go to the grave in shame. Life in the mountains, without the developed system of mutual help inside the community, was impossible. That is why mountain men often performed the "honorable act," even knowing that it would cost them their lives.
>
> (Emil Souleimanov, *"Society and the Chechen Mentality."*)

This reminds me of something… Hara-kiri among the Samurai? Perhaps… Even more so, an episode from *The Godfather* when Tom Hagen tells his old friend and family member, who is in prison, to kill himself in order to save the honor of the Mafia and clan. The prisoner slits his wrists. Or the Corsican, Matteo Falcone, who shoots his only son for violating the custom of never turning over a guest to the authorities.

The determinism of Chechen behavior is based on this fear. They cannot be more flexible because their strictest judge is not inside them but outside. The *leitmotif* of their behavior is "What will others say?" They mean other Chechens, of course.

Now consider blood vengeance. God, how much has been written about it… Having given people the commandments and not having indicated any methods of control over their execution, the Lord left that control in the hands of men: Create your courts, and determine the measure of punishment.

Moreover, even in the later Moses covenant, in the First Commandment, God established a collective and generational responsibility for an individual's transgression: "I, the Lord thy God, am a jealous God, visiting the iniquity of the fathers upon the children unto the third and fourth generation of them that hate me." (Exodus 20:5) Of course, God permitted only Himself to punish the children for the sins of the fathers.

Nevertheless, the mention of responsibility of generations is an echo of the law of blood vengeance, which undoubtedly was present in the practice of the courts of Noahide Laws—in particular, the Third Commandment. The evolution of the blood vengeance is a huge part of the history of mankind. The forefather of Jews and Arabs (Abraham) and the prophet and founder of Islam (Muhammad) devoted their efforts to combating it. In its stead was offered the *talion* principle—equivalent restitution, "an eye for an eye." It appears in its clearest form in the covenant of Moses: "And if any mischief follow, then thou shalt give life for life, eye for eye, tooth for tooth, hand for hand, foot for foot, burning for burning, wound for wound, stripe for stripe." (Exodus 21:23–25)

The obviously destructive role of blood vengeance—the extermination of the male population in Sicily, mass emigration, and other phenomena are all consequences. The Chechen version of the vendetta is no better: a monstrous archaism. But the determinism of Chechen morality does not permit any changes in that sphere. In contemporary Chechen society there are procedures for making peace between blood enemies, but the procedure is so non-binding, depending so much on mutual good will—and the fear of appearing as less than a real man by accepting it is so strong—that you can count on the fingers of your hands the cases where a problem has been solved effectively and bloodlessly.

There are some *adats* that are elegant and not without a sense of humor. For instance, a young man who kidnaps a girl without her consent is required by *adat* to ask if she has a boyfriend she would like to marry. If she replies that she does, the kidnapper sends him a message: "I've gotten you a bride." Thus he becomes an intermediary and a friend of the groom. Nice touch, no?

There are mystical rules, for instance about the special numerals 7 and 8. There are absurd ones, too, that go back to *adats* from pagan times. For instance, the *adat* on horse theft. If a horse thief falls from a stolen horse and dies, the *adat* considers the horse's owner to blame! In accordance with the strict laws, theft is a lesser evil than death. Therefore, the relatives of the horse thief must pay a fine for the theft to the owner of the horse—and then kill him. How do you like that? Naturally, this *adat* is not followed (the archaic, absurd *adats* are called *lamkersts*), but its very existence gives a good excuse to show the place of Chechen *adats* in the history of law.

Their very antiquity allows us to compare the *lamkersts* with one of the most famous laws in the Code of King Hammurabi of Babylon (early 2nd millennium BCE). "If someone builds a house to order, and the house collapses and kills the owner of the house, then the builder may be killed; if it killed the son of the owner, then the builder's son must be killed; if the owner's daughter was killed, then the builder's daughter…" (*Vsemirnaya istoriya*. Volume 2: The Bronze Age. Babylonian Law, p. 104.)

The Code of Hammurabi does not include the concept of accident, like the *lamkerst* on horse theft does. The ancient legislator decrees that there is meaning and intention in everything. Nothing happens by accident. The owner of the horse had trained it to kill anyone else who tried to ride it. And therefore, he intended to be repaid for theft with murder instead of a fine. So be it. Let some be responsible for theft and others for murder. It is the same for the builder. You, dear man, better build in such a way that if it falls apart, you know that you will blamed for doing it on purpose. And you will pay the full price.

Is it crazy? It is… But somewhere in the back of my mind, a chain of events forms: Babylon—Urartu—Armenia—Spitak—the stolen cement not used in the construction of houses—the earthquake—the huge death toll, and no one was held responsible. So much for civilization. But four thousand years ago, the Code of Hammurabi ruled the territory of Armenia. I'm being serious—how can you joke about such things? The zone was seismically active then and remains so today. Therefore the builders' responsibility should be greater. What accident? Other people's houses are standing, and yours collapsed. You're either an idiot or a villain. Either way, a criminal. They came up with accident, inadvertence, absence of malicious intention… The old Russian proverb, "If you slipped you get ripped," goes back to those pagan times.

They also have some simply good, worthy rules. For instance, the rule of mountain hospitality. There's nothing to say about that: It's good, and that's it. However, the mountain custom of hospitality, like all the ancient rules, has… How can I put this… Not a flaw, but perhaps overkill… It's too mandatory, without allowing exceptions. You're not pleased by that hospitality, since it is mandatory. The most monstrous villain and murderer in your place would enjoy the same privileges as a guest. It would be a terrible sin to turn him in to the police. (Back to Matteo Falcone, damn him.)

Determinism in the rules of behavior as a substitute for sincere emotion is characteristic not only of adherents of adat. For instance, the famous rabbi Iosef Telushkin, in his book, *The Jewish World*, writes: "Judaism commands you to give 10 percent of your income annually and with all your heart. [In Hebrew that is called *tzdaka*. Note that in Islam there is the same rule of charity, *zakyat*, and in Christianity, it's called tithing.] But if this generosity were to be spurred by individual impulse, then in the majority of cases, it would be a very long wait for charity. Therefore, Judaism says: Give 10 percent, and if your heart is happy, wonderful. In the meantime, a good deed has been done."

That is very profound. The ancient custom does not believe in goodness as an emotion: Man is an egotistical scumbag. So custom says, Who cares what you're feeling—anger, hatred, or even compassion. That's your personal affair. You are a servant of God. Listen to what you are told. Give the money, and go in peace. If your heart is happy, good; if it isn't, too bad for you—you will suffer from greed. But you have helped a beggar.

The iron grasp of custom forces man into the Procrustean bed of naked forms of behavior. He can change nothing in them. He lives according to a stereotype that has been set once and for all. No one cares what is happening in his heart. Gradually the person stops caring about his own feelings, since they are not an approved substance on which to base decisions about his actions. Everything is predetermined. A man is manly. A woman is modest. An old man is wise, and so on. Can you imagine a Chechen alcoholic? I can't.

A Chechen is not allowed to make mistakes. So if he makes a mistake (we're all human), he will be stubborn and insist that he was right, even though he may know that it makes him look stupid to do so. That will make him even madder, even at the person who put him in that ridiculous situation. He can't simply come over and say, Sorry, pal, I made a mistake. He may even want to, but that would have no meaning. He is not allowed to do that. The old men will condemn him if they find out. When we were living in Kazakhstan, a Chechen boy in kindergarten took away my blocks. I started to take them back, and he hit me on the head with one of them. My head bled. It was a small wound, and it barely hurt. The bleeding stopped quickly. But the young teacher wanted to make the boy apologize. The boy spent the entire day standing in the corner, refusing to apologize. When his parents came to pick him up, his father made such a scene that the teacher burst into tears and gave up insisting… And yet, you would think, what was the big deal? Just say you're sorry, if you're in the wrong…

They are not allowed to lose. I remember when I was on a wrestling team in my youth, Chechens would come up to us at meets and say: "He's wrestling against you tomorrow. We know you're strong. But he must win. Otherwise, we will beat you up." The next day, if one of our guys won, we would travel home in a group, knowing this Chechen sore point, and sometimes we would get some of the guys with guns from the Dynamo Stadium to accompany us to the station. Is that crazy? But those young Chechens, what were they supposed to do? What about *yakh*? You lost? Then go kill the man who insulted you. Otherwise, you bring shame upon yourself.

They are not allowed to have mad flings, to look silly. Not allowed. Not allowed… That nauseating seriousness of severe Chechen faces. That stateliness and sullenness of their ceremonies. The frightening aesthetics and energy of their *zikr*—the circle dance they do. That trance that they fall into… Truly, they are right when they say that it is hard to be a Chechen.

My impression is that the best life in the Chechen world is for old men. The rest—children, adults, men, women—are merely servants to their comfort. Everyone is expected to attend to the old people day and night. No one has the power to change the tradition. The huge Chechen diaspora is the consequence of that situation. People are forced to leave in order to achieve their own sense of maturity. The diaspora has always existed; it is not a phenomenon of the last ten years.

The Chechens are not allowed to forgive. I'd like to address forgiveness separately, for the topic is worth it.

The Talmud teaches: "For transgressions that are between a person and God the Day of Atonement effects atonement; but for transgressions that are between persons the Day of Atonement effects atonement only if one has appeased his fellow." (Mishna, Yoma 8:9). In his book *The Sunflower*, the famous Nazi criminal hunter Simon Wiesenthal describes an event that happened to him. At the end of the war, when Wiesenthal was in a concentration camp, the guards brought him to a dying SS officer. He told Wiesenthal that he had killed Jews in a Polish shtetl at the start of the war. Now, as he was dying, he had understood the monstrosity of his act and wanted to be forgiven by a Jew. Wiesenthal thought about it, and then silently went back to the camp. Thirty years later, he sent a description of this event to Christian and Jewish scholars and asked, "Was I right in not forgiving the Nazi?" The Christians replied: You should have forgiven him. The law and justice are important things, but they are not enough. You must also know how to forgive. Forgiveness is what Jesus Christ added to justice. The Jews, basing their reply on the Talmud, said: You were right. The only ones who could have forgiven him were his victims, and they are dead. That means that forgiveness is impossible. In Russian and German the word "charity" has its root in the word, "heart." In Hebrew, the word is *tzdaka*, simply the feminine of *tzedek*, which means "justice." I searched a 20,000-word Russian-Chechen dictionary and did not find either "charity" or "forgiveness" in Chechen. I did find "justice." I'm not maintaining that the words for "charity" and "forgiveness" do not exist in Chechen. But they are certainly not frequently used. The most frequently used 20,000 words cover 99.9 percent of speech in any language. Oh, it is hard to be a Chechen.

By the way, this has nothing to do with Islam. Mohammed, recognizing Jesus as a prophet, included the category of forgiveness in his teaching. In that context, the efforts of Maskhadov to replace the adats in Chechnya with Shariat courts—during the so-called peaceful period between 1996 and 1999—look entirely different. The *Shariat* court is based on Islamic laws, and it offers *talion* law instead of blood vengeance; it also includes the concepts of "accidental," "inadvertent," "forgiveness," and other things characteristic of a highly developed, contemporary jurisprudence.

Third View. Family

> "Seen as a nation, the Corsicans have long ceased to participate in the general stream of West European culture. They were continually subjects of Greeks, Romans, Arab caliphates, the emperor, and the Republic of Pisa. Their last ruler was the Genoa Republic, which degenerated into an indecent oligarchy... Among the people, isolated not only as islanders but also as mountain dwellers, the old institutions remained extremely long-lived. Thus blood vengeance (vendetta) and its accompanying tribal organization—comparable to clans—has never completely vanished from Corsican customs. Arguments were resolved by fighting. Often unions of several clans, covering a significant part of Corsica, carried on ruthless wars with one another... For all this, the Corsican (from the purely zoological point of view) developed and matured. Of medium height and powerful build, black-haired, with acute vision; with graceful, agile, and sinewy members, unrestrained courage, and other aboriginal qualities, the Corsican had a wide reputation as an excellent soldier and was often encountered in the armies of all the south European states."
>
> Villein Sloon. *New Biography of Napoleon*, translated into Russian 1895).

Napoleon I Bonaparte, Emperor of France, had eleven brothers and sisters, of which four died in infancy. That left seven. Here is a list.

Joseph Bonaparte, King of Naples and Spain.

Lucien Bonaparte, Prince of Canino.

Elisa Bonaparte, Duchess of Lucca and Princess of Pimbino, Grand Duchess of Tuscany.

Louis Bonaparte, King of Holland.

Pauline Bonaparte, Princess Borghese, Duchess of Guastalla.

Caroline Bonaparte, Grand Duchess of Berg and Cleve, later, Queen of Naples.

Jerome Bonaparte, King of Westphalia.

Napoleon was a Corsican, and in accordance with Corsican customs, he dragged his whole family with him. He wasted a lot of time on his useless brothers and willful sisters. Rather unattractive himself, he gave his mother enormous amounts of money. Finding jobs for relatives, moving them to the capital, keeping them secure—in other words, managing the clan—took up as much of his schedule as planning military operations or diplomatic maneuvers.

Now that I've seen this connection among Chechens, Corsicans, and Sicilians, I am amazed by its depth. By Chechen standards, Napoleon would have been a model Chechen. A brave and successful warrior. A loyal and caring son. Found royal or ducal thrones for all his relatives. Achieved fame that to this day is remembered even by his enemies. He lost in the end, but nobly—no one can accuse him of fleeing the battlefield, cowardice, and so on. If General Grouchi's corps had arrived in time at Waterloo, it might have ended differently. His family could have been proud of him. The fact that several million people died and half of Europe lay in ruins was nothing. Why pay any attention to that? None of the victims were members of the *teip* or even Chechens or Corsicans.

For me, in this case it is clan thinking: the inability to feel comfortable outside one's tribe, family, clan, or *teip*.

> That afternoon was the most agreeable Albert Neri had spent since he was a little boy, since the days before his parents had died when he was only fifteen. Don Corleone was at his most amiable and was delighted when he discovered that Neri's parents had originally come from a small village only a few minutes from his own. The talk was good, the food was delicious, the wine robustly red. Neri was struck by the thought that he was finally with his own true people. He understood that he was only a casual guest, but he could find a permanent place and be happy in such a world.
>
> [...]It took Neri less than three days to make up his mind. He understood he was being courted but he understood more. That the Corleone Family approved the act that society had condemned and punished him for. The Corleone Family valued him, society did not. He understood that he would be happier in the world the Corleones had created than in the world outside. And he understood that the Corleone Family was the more powerful, within its narrower limits.
>
> (Mario Puzo, *The Godfather*, chapter 30)

Dissolving one's ego in the clan, family, *teip*. Absolving oneself of responsibility for one's decisions. Fully buying into the principle that "everything that is good for the family is right." Putting the family's interests above one's own. Basically using not the individual but the tribe as the unit of measure. That is the mentality that frightens us with its unusual effectiveness in life's competition.

Of course, a person with the standard European mentality also cares about his family; he also is not indifferent to his relatives' attitude toward him and that of the people around him. But I think that all this is hypertrophied in Chechens.

The Chechen mentality is like a matryoshka nesting doll in which the smallest, indivisible doll is not the individual—the way we look at the world—but the clan, which is inside the *teip,* which is inside the Chechen nation. That's it. No other dolls. Beyond the matryoshkas, there are people whose interests can be taken into account or not—they will bring you neither shame or gratitude. Moreover, if you manage to trick or rob those people for the good of the *teip*—do it, without a second thought. If not, then behave as you wish. If you want to be on good terms with them, fine. But only if it doesn't infringe on the interests of the family and *teip*. If it does, then you are not free to decide on your relationship. The interests of the family and *teip* are the indisputable priority. If you think otherwise, get the hell out, and be damned.

The psychotherapist Sigmund Heinrich Foulkes, working in England in 1942-1946 with patients with "war neuroses," discovered an amazing effect. These illnesses were treated better through group psychotherapy than through individual treatment. He developed the theory that a person is merely an element in a closed system of communications. That closed system of communications—the group—becomes a meta-personality with an active force that can be used to heal.

Later the theory of the meta-personality was advanced by American researchers in various California universities. They learned how to suppress individual consciousness and the instinct of self-preservation in special forces soldiers and how to motivate them toward a common result. They learned how to build incredibly effective scientific research teams, in which each member was only one element of the whole. They learned to form crews that could work long hours productively, even in cramped quarters. People who worked as elements of a meta-personality later refused to function in any other way. The process of dissolving one's ego in a team was that pleasurable.

In some sense the Chechen *teip*, the Mafia family, and the Corsican clan are meta-personalities. They are endowed with an astonishing life force and resistance to a hostile environment.

While the individual personality is mortal, the meta-personality is immortal. It is above the law; it is the law unto itself. It doesn't care about its environment, it is happy to make its own moral assessments of its elements. It takes better care of them than society does. The meta-personality has a synergy that no random collection of individuals can have. Being inside a meta-personality provides great pleasure—it's like playing ball with a well-trained team, where all the players like one another and are prepared to play their heads off for a common goal.

I'm getting carried away. But: The Christian (Judaic and Islamic, too) concept of individual responsibility before God does not accept the concept of meta-personality. You are alone. You are made in the image of God.

"What a piece of work is man! How noble in reason! How infinite in faculties! In form and moving, how express and admirable! In action how like an angel! In apprehension, how like a god! The beauty of the world! The paragon of animals!" (Shakespeare, *Hamlet*).

You—solely, personally you—bear the entire burden of your actions on your shoulders. And you have to think about the salvation of your soul. "This life of the world is nothing but a sport and a play; but, verily, the abode of the next world, that is life, if they did but know!" (Koran. Sura 29 *"The Spider."* 64)

As the Talmud teaches, "There is no agent for wrongdoing." (Kuddushin 42B) That is, if you are given a sinful order, you cannot say that you are merely an agent, executing someone else's will. If you perform the act, you will answer for it. "They ordered me, the honor of the clan, I had to stab him"—all that shit is for beautiful verses of poetasters. Big deal—Order of Sword Bearers. Homegrown Nazis. Remember: "You must be decent and noble only in relation to people of your own race." Heinrich Himmler, by the way.

To put it briefly. If you murder, you go to Hell. Period.

Fourth View. Robbers

Three *atamans* (leaders) of the Don and Volga Cossacks, in the tsar's disfavor, conferred in 1579 in the lower reaches of the Volga about where to hide from the tsar's wrath. Ermak Timofeyevich went north to the noble Stroganovs and became the conqueror of the Siberian kingdom; the rest of the Cossacks went to sea, and breaking into two groups of brothers, the smaller went to Yaika and the majority to the Terek River, into the deep country...where since ancient times there was a robber's den for all thieving Cossacks. They stopped there and built themselves a three-walled town, which they called Terki, and they gathered Kabardinets, Chechens, Kumyks, and even Cherkess. The motley mix of all these elements eventually formed the Tersk Host.

In the reign of Alexei Mikhailovich, circa 1669, the famous Volga *ataman* Stenka Razin sailed to the shores of Dagestan and attacked with such a pogrom that it lives in the memories of shore dwellers... The *ataman* robbed and pillaged the surrounding area of the city for three days and then got back in his boat and sailed to attack the Persian Kingdom.

(V. A. Otto, *Kavkazskaya voina* [*Caucasian War*], vol. 1)

From the Don, at the head of 700 new men, came Seryozhka the Crooked, who destroyed the detachment of troops sent against him, and joined Razin at sea; then came Alyoshka Protokin, Alyoshka the Convict, with equally large detachments. Stenka, in the meantime, was robbing Dagestan shores, destroying cities and turning them into a pile of rubble, like Derbent, for example. At Reshta, Stenka offered his services to the Persian shah. Negotiations dragged out... Razin sailed from Reshta to Farabad... For five days the Cossacks traded peacefully with the Persians, and on the sixth Stepan Timofeyevich tilted his hat on his head. That was the sign: The Cossacks attacked the defenseless residents, killing some of them and taking some prisoner.

(Brockhaus and Efron *Encyclopedic Dictionary*, vol. 51, pp. 159–160).

I can just see those thugs, those legendary Cossack robbers. Inspirational, are they not? Here's another quote along the same lines:

The Caucasus was settled by various tribes whose *modus vivendi* was always war against everyone. It should be said that this region is very poor, especially the mountainous parts, and robbery was a steady income stream for the locals. Bloody clashes were continual, and predatory attacks accompanied by murder and the most vile crimes were a permanent fixture of the local tribes. There were no laws, no agreements were in force, strength and treachery solved everything, and robbery and murder were elevated into valor. It was an ordinary event in the Caucasus to have two sworn enemies unite to destroy a third and then fight among themselves. "You can't even steal a sheep," is the worst insult you can say to a Chechen. And here they come, the Chechens, back from a raid, weapons bristling, blood spattered, dragging stolen goods and tied prisoners, to the delight of their fellow tribesmen. Almost nothing has changed in the Chechen mentality since those days; as soon as the power of the center fell in Chechnya, the Middle Ages returned with the constant raids, robbery, murder, hostages, and slave trade.

(Venceslav Kryzh, *The Chechen Syndrome.*)

Some researchers have come up with a big theory: Mountainous Chechnya is a very difficult place to live. The soil is poor, the harvests low, the cattle in these pastures are frail, therefore for centuries Chechens were forced to carry out raids, and that is how this raiding culture was formed. With its own folklore, aesthetics, heroes and mentality. What can be done now? Nothing, they say. And it's all the fault of Tamerlane, who forced Chechens into the mountains from the valleys. Each bit of research blames poor lame Tamerlane—and in vain.

I would like to pose a few uncomfortable questions to these theoreticians of the raid. For instance, this one: The Cossacks lived on the extremely fertile black soils of the Don and Volga regions, and for three hundred years they robbed so well that any Chechen would be envious. What explains that? Seems inconsistent to me. And they robbed and robbed, yet by the late 18th century Emelyan Pugachev had played his final game, and then it stopped. Ever since, the Cossacks have been the pillars of the throne. Farmers. Researchers. Defenders of the Homeland (from the mountain dwellers, among others).

Or, for example, take the Avars. Shamil, the imam of Chechnya and Dagestan, who waged war with the Russian tsar for so many years, was Avarian, not Chechen. Hadji Murat was also Avar. And the Avars were also adepts of the raid culture. It's enough to read *My Dagestan* by Rasul Gamzatov (may Grouchi he rest in peace, what a good writer he was) to know that. Their pastures are no better than those of the Chechens. And they fought the Russians even longer than Chechnya. But they don't cut off the heads of Englishmen who come to lay telephone lines for them. They don't kill their own police. I'm not sure that the Avars have any particularly fond feelings for the Russians—nor do they have any reason for such love. But they, who are as capable of fighting as the Chechens, manage to control themselves somehow. They somehow understand that we're in the 21st century, that people fly in space, all that modern stuff. Enough is enough.

Or take their brother Vainakhs, the Ingush—even they are trying to find their place in the modern world. Some sell gold in Siberia, some do work in Russian villages, some hang around in Moscow, and some plow the earth back home in Ingushetia. But they don't slice off the fingers of kidnapped children, they don't chop off heads for the videocamera, and they don't wrap themselves in dynamite in order to blow themselves up into tiny pieces. They didn't have a raid culture? They didn't steal brides for themselves from the *giaours* [infidels]? They didn't rob wealthy Georgia? Of course they used to, and how. But times have changed.

I am in no way trying to justify the actions of the Russian army in Chechnya either now or one hundred fifty years ago. And I am certainly not trying to justify Stalin's deportation. I know firsthand what that was like. I just want to say that it wouldn't hurt the representatives of the raiding nation to try this mental exercise: Let's imagine that it's not the Russian army and the national guards, but let's suppose for a second that an unconquerable interplanetary force, or a spiritual hurricane, or the sword of God forces the Chechens to change their concepts of good and evil, of courage and charity, of valor and honor. Yes, they would have to reject their beloved truths; yes, lose face, as the Japanese say; but they would get to preserve their nation! Just imagine that the clumsy and useless Russian army is merely the weapon of Divine Providence. Perhaps it's just someone up there telling you: Change, the times are different, everything is different, don't you see? What? You'll still fight to the last man?

The imam Shamil, I think, performed this exercise. And even answered all the questions that came up in the course of the experiment. How to change? Who knows… Maybe by first answering simpler questions. For example, why is it that for most nations shooting an enemy in war is enough, but Chechens need it to be bloodier—with heads chopped off, and on television, and entrails on the fence and the head on a pike? And why do Chechens identify themselves with wolves? Why is that considered a good comparison? Where does that aesthetic come from?

My dream is that there will be a time when a Chechen mother singing her little boy to sleep will sing him a lullaby that is not about a bloody raid on the infidels, or about the heroic lone *abrek*, but about a teddy bear, a pretty flower, and the cows in the meadow. That's when it all will happen.

* * *

All right, Alik, we've dealt with Chechnya for now. Either treat it well or treat it badly….

And when did we ever treat it well? It's always been badly. No sooner did we finish with Napoleon, Ermolov headed off to the Caucasus in 1816. And we were at war until the Russians accepted Shamil.

What pushed Khrushchev to return the Chechens? He could have said the question is under advisement, wait a bit, the Party is taking care of you…

It's pointless to discuss it.

Next point. Solzhenitsyn. Now, tell me how you reacted to the very fact of his return to Moscow, to Russia.

I love Solzhenitsyn. I was pleased that he came back.

So was I. Before that, all those years after 1991, I kept thinking, why isn't he coming? You would think his place was on the barricades in front of the White House… But maybe he knew—he had predicted a lot of things correctly—that he wasn't really needed here. By those people. The people who love politicians like Zhirinovsky and pop stars like Kirkorov. And so he kept putting it off…

I can understand him very well.

Well, we're one thing. But the masses did not understand him.

Who are the masses? Do the masses understand Nabokov?

Well, Nabokov is a writer and Solzhenitsyn is a politician and philosopher. He came here, he told people all kinds of wise things, and they said: So what?

I'm amazed that you measure people by their public significance, they way you were taught in the *Our Language* textbook, Igor.

And what textbooks did you use? Weren't you taught the same way?

Maybe he just wanted to die in his homeland. He didn't come sooner because he didn't feel that he was dying. But in 1994 he thought he would die soon, and he returned. He wanted to die in Russia.

But let's just put it this way: He's not in demand.

So what? I'm not in demand either, so what am I supposed to do, hang myself? I'm wanted by my children, my wife, my friends and people I love.

Solzhenitsyn should be, for example, an adviser to the government.

Why?

Because he's smart. Energetic. Sees the root of things. Gives a precise evaluation of events and situations. Does not fall for tricks. Doesn't sell out. That's not enough? Then because his predictions come true. Everyone else wanders around blindly, but he knows where he's going. A guide like that would be useful for our leadership, which is governing rather weakly, not to say inconsistently and inefficiently.

Could it be that the government is full of jerks?

Putin should have his cabinet meetings and ask, "And was does comrade Zhukov think? (With Solzhenitsyn instead of Zhukov). What? He hasn't been informed yet? Then why are you bothering me with this draft resolution when Aleksandr Isaevich hasn't even seen it yet? Go back home, all you D students, and do your homework before coming back."

Let me tell you this. Yeltsin wanted to present him the order "For Contributions to the Homeland." Solzhenitsyn asked him not to give him the award because he wouldn't accept it anyway, and that would place Yeltsin in an awkward situation.

That's a handsome way of behaving! He didn't wait for the ceremony to do his little show. He acted subtly and tactfully. A subtle man. Which is what I am telling you, Alik.

Putin was sneakier. He went to see him himself. They say Solzhenitsyn was rather cool. He refused to have a real conversation with him. He made some small talk before the cameras, and that was it. And he didn't respond to an invitation to return the visit.

Did Putin bring the medal to his house? Just pull it out of his pocket and—surprise!—pin it on him? He wouldn't be able to do anything about it then...

Yes, he could have pinned it on his back surreptitiously.

And the man would be caught.

In the first degree, like his medal.

Any degree.

With ribbons and diamonds.

Or maybe it went this way: "Look, Solzhenitsyn, I've brought you lists of Cheka agents who tortured honest dissidents. What should I do with them? Tear off their officers' insignia? Or what? Whatever you say, it will be done. If you want, I'll have them shot. I have plenty more. And they all want me to give them better salaries."

No, I think he arrived with a different speech.

You mean, Praise me, and you'll be all right?

No. "See, you old goat? Our side won anyway. So this is the deal: To keep the atmosphere clear, you accept me as a democratic president and say that everything is marvelous. You kept shouting to the whole world about the KGB, the KGB. And the people elected me! Not Sakharov or someone like that, but me. That's the only way to handle these people. You shed a tear and felt sorry for them. What the hell for?"

And then he adds, "Want me to imprison you again?"

I don't think those leaks in the Internet about Solzhenitsyn being an informer in the Gulag were accidental.

They used to say that during Soviet times. KGB disinformation. So sneaky.

Remember, Stalin said to Nadezhda Krupskaya: "Today you are the widow of Comrade Lenin, but we can find him a better widow tomorrow, if you talk too much." This is the same thing—they get rid of him and he dies an informer instead of a great writer. If they arrest him, the people will cry: "Death to the Stalinist ass-licker!"

Who's a Stalinist?

Solzhenitsyn. That's what the press will say. Lesin will give the order—and the great writer will be gone. But there will be an informer. [*Lesin was Minister of the Press at the time of this writing. Not now. But he still has influence on the process.*]

Ah, the press! The press can do that…

Of course. He did easy labor in the camps; he was the camp fool, and only served a lousy ten years. Easy to demonstrate.

And he left his wife. They'll bring that up, too.

That's a fine theme. And they'll add that his real name was Jewish, Solzhenitser, not Solzhenitsyn… And so he and Putin ended their talk, preserving neutrality.

Here's another topic for 1994: the registration of a new party—for deceived investors! For the masses, it's all the same—privatization or the MMM pyramid scheme.

Go to hell! Comparing me to MMM's Mavrodi! I'm not interested in the mood of the masses.

Why not?

That's the way I am. I'm not interested in the opinions of the popular masses or in errors in general. As a rational man, I must strive for the truth.

That's some bull, Alik. You're a writer! And suddenly you maintain that you're not interested in the mood of the popular masses.

I'm interested in the truth. As the above-mentioned Solzhenitsyn said: "The heart seeks truth."

Then you're not a writer, but a philosopher and thinker.

The popular masses, hmpf. If they had put the spherical nature of the earth to a vote in the Middle Ages, what would have been the result?

It wouldn't have gotten any worse.

It wouldn't have gotten any better, either. You wouldn't be able to use your cell phone. Or satellite communications. If people thought the world was flat.

On the contrary, it would be even better: You set up one antenna for the whole earth, and call from anywhere, even China.

But the world is round in fact! It's not subject to the error of the majority! The antenna would not work. And you would have invested in it.

Maybe it would have worked. How do you know? You're awfully smart today, I see!

Kokh was this fresh when he entered
politics. Life subsequently roughed him up.

In 1990 Svinarenko thought journalism was
a romantic profession.

The young reporter.

The young scientist.

Igor and his grandfather, Ivan Svinarenko.

Igor and his daughters.

Igor and his wife, Lydia.

Marina and Alfred writing his dissertation.

Kokh's popularity started young.

Two generations of singers.

The Young Reformers.

Family vacation with the Maneviches.

A lively discussion with Anatoly Chubais.

Благодарность

Президента Российской Федерации

Уважаемый

Альфред Рейнгольдович Кох!

Благодарю Вас

за заслуги перед государством,

связанные с завершением первого этапа

чековой приватизации.

Б. Ельцин

Москва, Кремль
10 марта 1995 года
№ 117-рп

Commendation from President Yeltsin to Alfred Kokh
for the first phase of privatization.

Deputy general director of Kommersant.

Igor in Germany, Kommersant correspondent.

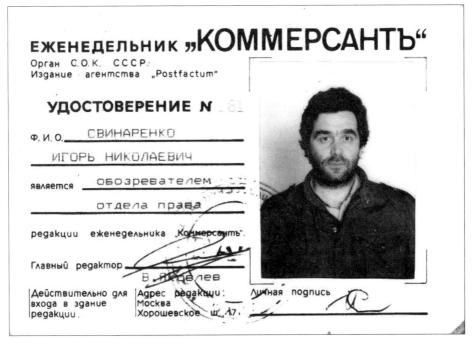

Igor on the crime beat at Kommersant.

Brezhnev's funeral.

Chernenko at the helm.

Igor working on the collective farm.

Accepting journalism
award from George Soros.

With Prime Minister
Chernomyrdin.

Boris Nemetsov
and Igor study
army reform.

Moscow hosts a Russian

By Faith Golay
TRIBUNE REGIONAL STAFF

Given the choice by his employer, Russian journalist Igor N. Svirarenko, 39, could have lived for the next six months in any one of 12 states that have towns named Moscow.

He chose Moscow, Pa.

Svirarenko is an editor for *The Kommepcahm Daily*, the largest newspaper publishing house in Russia.

The journalist was given the overseas assignment of comparing Moscow, Russia, to a Moscow

IGOR N. SVIRARENKO
From Moscow to Moscow

in the United States so he can write stories for a new weekly publication *The Daily* is starting called *Capital*.

Other states with Moscows include Maine, Vermont, Tennessee, Arkansas, Kansas, Texas, Idaho, Ohio, Indiana, Michigan and Iowa.

He selected Moscow, Pa., over the others because the criteria fit.

"It had the right size to cover everyone together with a real mayor, judge and community. I could not get enough information from a place like Moscow, Ark. The whole town consisted of seven houses centered around cotton fields where all the people worked," said Svirarenko.

The world-traveled Russian

Please see **Moscow**, Page A8

Igor makes headlines in the U.S.

Home away from home.

Moscow's bravest.

Discussing NTV at Newseum.

In DC with Helen Teplitskaia, President of the American-Russian Chamber of Commerce, and Virginia Governor Jim Gilmore.

Alfred with Ilya Levkov, publisher of his first book in the U.S.

The journey continues.

14.

1995

The Fourteenth Bottle

The hit of 1995 is the loans-for-shares auctions. Kokh reveals frankly and impartially how the country's wealth was made. Svinarenko that year merely travels around the planet as the head of Russia's first glossy magazine.

Alik, what were you doing in 1995?

Is this an interrogation?

It's not. Fine. There's no transcript being made... Well, except that we're recording it ourselves. All right, I'll go first. I was doing the same thing I was doing the year before. I was doing the glossy magazine *Domovoi*.

And "*Kommersant's* Best Pen"—was that already in the past by then?

No. *Domovoi* was—I don't know if it's still the case—part of the *Kommersant* Publishing House.

When was the last time you wrote for *Kommersant*?

I wrote for them in 2003. I had a piece about Iraq. Remember?

Yeah, it was a good piece, lively. But what were you doing in 1995? Were you running the loans-for-shares auctions all year?

No, they only took a month. But there was a year of preparation, putting together regulatory documentation, issuing all sorts of presidential decrees…

What were you at the time?

First Deputy Chairman of State Property. The head was Sergei Belyayev.

Alik, Alik, the loans-for-shares auctions are the most interesting topic not only for 1995 but perhaps for the entire book. The readers have been waiting for this. Some with gloating. They're thinking, "Let's see how you squirm out of this!" And you reproached me for bringing up the auctions unnecessarily.

Let's do this in dialogue format! Let me talk, too. So you think this is the culminating moment of the book?

That is the opinion of many readers. They're rubbing their hands in anticipation—gleeful anticipation.

To see how good we are with the whitewash? Let me tell you about my feelings: We're not writing to suit the public, but ourselves. and *I* think that the "writers' case" and the oligarch war of 1997—

—were more fun?

Of course! The consequences for the country were more significant. And had more meaning in my own life. After the loans-for-shares auctions, however controversial they may have been, my career was on the upswing—I later became a minister and then a vice prime minister. But after the writers' case, on the contrary, I left government and had a criminal case built against me. So, subjectively, the events of summer and fall 1997 are more important for me personally. So there. And for the country, too, I think. Because say what you will, it was after the mortgage auctions that the oligarch class was formed, and that guaranteed Yeltsin's re-election in 1996. When they fell at each other's throats in 1997 and that war began, it led to the default—and I can prove that. So, it seems to me that the book's climax will come in 1997. Although, without a doubt, the loans-for-shares auctions constituted a vivid event that became enveloped in its own mythology and that separated society into two unequal parts: fierce proponents and fierce opponents. So, of course, we need to talk about it, and I'm ready to listen to your complaints.

We're not going to take the position of those who demonstrated beneath the Red flag…

Were there any such demonstrations?

I saw many rallies by the Lenin Museum. Flags, senior citizens with blazing eyes…

But that wasn't about the loans-for-shares auctions. That was the MMM pyramid scheme, and robbery of the people, and "Yeltsin should be tried!" The country has been robbed… That began with the vouchers.

As for myself, Alik, I'm trying to re-create the feelings I had then. I flipped through those articles—there was a lot written about the auctions. My opinion was that the sharks were divvying up something, that somebody was screwing somebody else—so let them, if it's interesting for them. Someone was trying to catch someone else red-handed, someone else was shouting that he was set up… At *Kommersant,* some of the economics writers practically had fistfights in the corridors, accusing each other of prejudice, of being on some oligarch's payroll. It was like, "My oligarch is higher and more honest than yours, and I am more fearless and altruistic than you!"

And both had dollar signs in their eyes.

Later, the "altruistic" reporters kept appearing in the PR departments of oil oligarchs and others… It was amusing to watch the process. As for using his position as editor to prevent the placement of these paid articles, Yakovlev was less than enthusiastic. He went, Ah, let them…

I remember someone suggested that people wear uniforms at the Ministry of Finance. With distinguishing marks—these work for Menatep, those for Potanin—so that things would be clear right off the bat.

Personally, this didn't bother me very much, Alik. People were always going on about something—oil, schmoil. I took the cynical view, figuring that this sort of thing had always gone on and always would. Well, on the level of total fantasy, I thought it would be nice to get a phone call: "Igor Nikolayevich, come by to pick up your share of the oil trade."

Remember in *One-Storied America*, Ilf and Petrov picked up a hitchhiker, a teenaged Socialist, and gave him a ride. He told them that everything should be taken away from people and divided up equally. The multi-millionaires could only keep one million dollars each. Later in the book, Mr. Adams explained to our writers why the fellow had wanted them to keep one million: because the teenage Socialist secretly wanted to be a millionaire, too.

Do you know that our traveling writers were invited to go fishing by Hemingway?

Yes, and they turned down his invitation to visit him. And wrote about it.

I guess they were forced to meet with Communists. For my part, Alik, I looked at the participants in the auctions as if they were black marketeers. First, they resold jeans and made money. So fine. I regarded the privatizers the way I did people who went to trade institutes and then got gold caps on their teeth and ate caviar. That was the cliché then: The manager of the shoe department got rich on shoes while doing nothing. I've traveled in Siberia, and I've seen the guys on the oil rigs. People live in the taiga for weeks at a time; the canteen cook fries up food for them, and they apparently also screw her in the open air, under the mosquito canopy... So they feed the mosquitoes, and somebody else divides up what is earned from their labor.

So what's changed? Keep looking at it that way!

But you're demanding that I love capitalists. In the Soviet days, no one demanded that I love the store managers with gold teeth! It never occurred to them, either. I would look at them and think, Fuck you!

That's exactly the attitude I ask you to have toward us. "Fuck you." Leave us alone. I'm not asking for love, Igor, but you don't need to hate us.

Svinarenko's Commentary:

Shame on you, Alik, saying that I don't like businessmen, and especially framing it as populism. As if I were a slave to fashion, putting down businessmen. Here's a section of an old interview I did with Peter Aven, long before they jailed Khodorkovsky! Here it is:

Aven: Putin doesn't like us, the business elite. Not only Putin, either. We can feel it...

Svinarenko: What is there about you to like? You got rich out of thin air, your children are abroad, land prices on Rublyovka are skyrocketing. And when we read that a young bachelor businessman flew to Courchevel or the Cote d'Azur in one plane and he's followed by a second plane loaded with playmates... If you were all bearded Old Believers and went to church instead of whorehouses (I'm sure that you personally are very moral), built orphanages and schools the way the old merchants did, then you would have reason to be surprised and wonder: 'Why doesn't Putin like us? And why do so many other people not like us, either?'

A: Yes, Putin, who associates himself with the country and the people—he has no reason to like businessmen. There's no question that the nation is not the highest priority for our businessmen. That's the pure and simple truth. We can see that from the level of charitable giving—or rather, its absence. We can see it from the level of theft and corruption. That is so.

S: Of course! Whom is he supposed to support? Show me a Russian Henry Ford *[I beg the poor man to forgive me, I've worn him out, constantly using him as an example!]* who has built a plant; manufactures high quality, inexpensive cars for the people; and hangs around the factory himself in oily work clothes. If one of our guys has a car plant, it's for making BMWs and SUVs. No, our Henry Ford flies to resorts with whores! Men who are poorer or whose wives won't let them go, envy him. If Alena Antonova, the society columnist, doesn't mention someone vacationing in Courchevel, they get mad.

A: You're right in a way. Our man manages a factory that he didn't build, but which he…shall we say, privatized. I can't argue with you there.

S: Or if you said: 'Look, we've built a city! Here it is, a real beaut!' Like the Chinese. We trade with them, but with the proceeds from that trade they build cities with skyscrapers, like grown-ups, while we manage to let the money slip away—to Courchevel. Our rich men don't build cities! Except for the Manege Complex in Moscow and all those villas along the Rublyovka.

A: We have these crazy disproportions now. A fantastic difference in income. By the way, it's not even clear on what it's based. You're absolutely right.

S: So it's not very convincing when people talk about raising public morality in the abstract. Why don't you be more concrete: 'Brother businessmen! Stop acting like assholes! Let's be more modest!'

A: Good luck. We're having a lot of problems with our elite. Look, what do you want me to say? I'm not arguing with you.'"

* * *

Here, Igor, I'm asking you: Leave us entrepreneurs alone. You don't have to like us or dislike us.

Alik! I'd like to reserve the right to like you. Which I do. I am on your side. After all, I voted for SPS [Union of Right Forces] at the last election, knowing your chances were slim. I say good things about you to loads of people. I will never go work for the Communists under any circumstances. But I also reserve the right not to stand on the sidewalk of Kutuzovsky Prospect waiting for you to speed by, waving my flag and staring teary-eyed at your passing limo. I would like to continue regarding you without prejudice or partiality. And to say what I want, here and now and not later in Istanbul or Kolyma, where the ruling class lived out the rest of their miserable lives after the 1917 revolution. If I care about the topic of personal modesty or immodesty of the ruling class, and you don't let me speak out, you will become of no interest to me. For example, the

store directors in Soviet times behaved modestly, damn it. They stayed in line.

Hmmm.

When they built two-story houses, they were forced to take down the second floor.

And what's so good about that? That's just envy. Where's the liberalism, if it's only about envy of a second floor?

I don't care—let them have a second story. You seem to be hearing my argument for the first time, Alik. I think you're not reading my part of the book with attention. I wrote that the oligarchs with their immodesty will bring this all to a bad end. Personally I'm not going to go fight in a new civil war, especially on the side of the Reds. I might go fight for the Whites, but certainly not for the Reds. I wrote that the millionaires won't have any problems; they'll be hanged from the lampposts and it will be over for them, while I'll have to stand in long lines. For vodka. For cigarettes. We'll have to trade violins for flour.

Maybe the millionaires will escape to Paris. That's our personal immodesty, with the second story. I haven't built my house in a dacha co-op, where Uncle Vasya the plumber will see my second story! I built it separately and far from Uncle Vasya. So my second story isn't constantly irritating Uncle Vasya's eyes. He doesn't travel to come look at my second story, that would take an effort, riding a bus to Rublyovo-Uspenskoe Highway! But you faggot journalists, you do go there. And then one of you, who has his own second story and an apartment in midtown Moscow and a high salary and a big bank account—what does he do? He says: "Look, Uncle Vasya, you're too lazy to go to Rublyovka, so let me tell you about those bastards." It's clear what will happen to me if I don't emigrate; I'll be hanged from the nearest tree. But they'll hang that journalist by the balls. And not for my house, but for his own two-story house and for his expensive and beautiful ties. And for his habit of vacationing on Capri.

And they'll make him stand in line for gristly veal and sausages. Some journalists aren't ashamed of teasing people and inciting class hatred. I'm not pretending to be anything! I don't party anywhere! I don't push myself on anyone! I hid my house deep in the woods, and I sit and write my books! But journalists dug me out in Courchevel, lied that I spend 4,000 euros a day... And then, they'll wonder why I've deprived them of their cigarettes.

Well, smoking is bad for you; tobacco is a poison.

I just don't understand journalists whose shoes and ties cost more than mine but who work on inciting class warfare. They're sawing off the branch they're sitting on!

I can explain to you why the press has ceased being responsible, Alik. It used to be, under the Communists. It was all about defending the status quo. And why was that? For one simple reason: It was paid to do so. The Central Committee of the Communist Party did not skimp. The reporters for Pravda had the best salaries, apartments and dachas.

Well, they were working for that class. But these guys are working against it.

That's my point. Millionaires are upset that the press doesn't support them. Are you supporting the press? Are you giving the journalists dachas and apartments? Not at all. How are they supposed to live? And so they try to raise their ratings. If they do, people buy advertising. They're forced to do it.

What do you mean forced? Forced to put their balls on an anvil for the sake of ratings? You are the eyes of the nation, and you let them see it, so it's your own fault. You'd be better off covering up your eyes, the way they do in America. Fat Americans wolf down Big Macs and their women are disgusting to look at, but the journalists show them Hollywood, telling them that they are thin and athletic and that their whole nation is cheerful and patriotic. And beautiful, with good hair. Whereas our journalists are busy riling up the people. They're sowing the seeds of class hatred! So let the bastards be the first to die under the ruins.

So you've accepted the fact that this will not end well.

I think that if this continues, if the press continues whipping up stories about the bad faggot businessmen, then of course, Igor, there will be trouble.

You're saying the journalists ruined the country. Ha-ha.

Of course.

You kill me. It used to be the Jews and students who were the internal enemies, and now it's all the fault of reporters!

Of course it is, Igor. I am convinced that the world is just virtual. For sure. And irresponsible journalists will destroy the country.

Let me explain once again. You don't give them money to be responsible. The Communists supported the mass media. Gusinsky had

his own **TV** station, and it praised him. You're not doing shit. You've made TV independent so that it can earn its own money, do business. And so it's earning its ratings in whatever way it can. It wants advertising money. But if you all had said, "Here's money, forget the ratings. Just praise us. Don't tell the truth about us…"? Well, who's going to advertise if the press says nothing but "Let's all live in harmony"? That's not journalism.

Would you listen for a minute? That's why journalists started lying. For the ratings! That's why they showed two pieces on the show the same night: one about Courchevel and one about the hero-lieutenant who lives in a Moskvich car. And not mentioning that he actually also has an apartment! Where the truth?

But journalism isn't a search for the truth; it's a branch of show business, as you know, Alik.

And don't lie to me about journalists not being paid. They shouldn't lie even for ratings. Does a journalist have to lie to get better ratings—yes or no? If the answer is "yes" then that's it, I have no more questions.

There is one subtle point to be made here, Alik. Some people see journalism as art, others as business. Some want to make a lot of money and remain journalists. Really, I'm so touched by your line about journalists ruining the country. I love it. That's the real culprit. No need to worry about politics and economics, morality or ethics. I got it—the journalists are to blame. Thank you.

By the way, Igor. I agree with your thesis that the ruling class should pay. I agree totally. With every word. Moreover, let me tell you that when the Kremlin, in early 2003, began laying the foundation for inciting class hatred, it began paying journalists. And they started writing. The question isn't why journalists write for money. I'm not an idiot, I understand. I just want to tell them, Then don't be pissed at us when you're put back in lines and they take away your cigarettes.

Well, can I be pissed?

No, you can't either. And the journalists who have achieved a high level of money and comfort and who love their life style, they should be protecting us not for money, they should be protecting their own skins! I can say more (in this case "I" is a collective noun for any entrepreneur, mid-level or higher): I've insured myself for this eventuality, and I have a fallback scenario. So I regard the situation cool-headedly. But I'm not doing anything to make the country fall apart!

But I would still blame you, and not journalists. When I see American millionaires in jeans and without ties...

That's just the national style. Think of German millionaires. They don't go around in jeans. They sit in their castles, and you never see them. All those Siemenses.

But I do see Americans in jeans, and they do their own driving. The Brits, too. I read that Paul McCartney lived in a five-room house without servants. He's a billionaire; he has more money than you do!

He's lying. Maybe he doesn't have servants in that house, but he has a hundred houses.

When I step into a supermarket in the States and see a pensioner, and a teacher, and a one-legged black man, all pushing their full carts and deciding which ham, out of thirty varieties, to select, I experience profound feelings. We know that these people aren't there on an excursion to see how rich people live; they shop there every day. And when on Saturday mornings I see American retirees driving their Cadillacs to McDonald's to eat and chat about their lives, I feel warm and fuzzy. The millionaire is wearing jeans and driving his own car, and the pensioner is eating ham. I'm for that. But the Russian millionaire with a plane full of whores while teachers scrounge in garbage cans—I have to tell you, that makes me unhappy.

Uh-huh.

So this is my message to millionaires: I'm not asking you to live like me. But you have to cut down a bit. On something. Do you think that poor Americans are going to drop their full shopping carts to attack their millionaires? I doubt it. That's the point. And I'm pretty calm about the future of American journalists, too—they won't have to stand in line for Belomor cigarettes and Ossetian vodka.

We're not going to retell American history here, Igor. But Russian history of the twentieth century goes like this. They sat around scratching their heads and then suddenly decided, "Let's go beat up the Jap monkeys!" So they moved their entire army from the west to the east. Sent squadrons via the Atlantic and Pacific. Lost the war and got the revolution.

Wait. Is this what you're going to tell the people who are storming your house, ready to burn it down?

No, I'm telling you. So, they drowned the country in blood. Then it got a bit stronger, started growing. The Stolypin reforms. Then Tsar Nicky declared war on his uncle Willie. Wilhelm asked his nephew to stop and think—six times. No, we rattled our sabers—"When will we reach Berlin?" We got the Civil War for that. Two million Cossacks drowned in blood. The officers were chased out of the country. Priests had their noses and cheeks slashed. Churches were destroyed. Then came collectivization: All the peasants were sent to the camps. Then World War II—forty million dead…

I'm asking you again: You're going to tell this to drunken sailors and rebelling proletarians?

No, Igor, I'm telling you. So, how can you be surprised, knowing Russian history, that a one-legged black man and a teacher shop in an American supermarket, while our teacher shops at the garbage dump? How could she not, considering what's happened to our country in the last hundred years? While the Americans didn't have a single war on their territory? And they had to be dragged into the two wars that they fought here? I don't understand why your teacher in the garbage dump is my fault? Me, who honestly pays his taxes. Why isn't it the fault of the government officials who sail on yachts and buy a new Mercedes every six months? They're on the state payroll as much as the teacher is! Why do some generals have dachas in Rublyovka, where a little *sotka* of land costs twenty thousand dollars [*it got as high as two hundred thousand Euros before the financial crisis*]—and in Barvikha, Zhukovka? Why? Why do "honest" journalists do stories about "how I spent my vacation" and not about how there's a deputy minister right in the next hotel? Or a member of the Duma? And why isn't it the fault of the Ministry of Transport? Look at their offices! Like the Hermitage! All done up in colored marble. And ornate furniture of expensive wood! Why isn't it the fault of Luzhkov, who built a city for the rich while the teachers are in the garbage dump? Why is it the fault of the taxpayers and not the government? Why does that teacher keep voting for Luzhkov for mayor, with maniacal persistence? Why does she love Putin? They've even put him in their primers. [*Ah, the depth of my prognostications! A month after this was said, the civil servants and parliamentarians raised their own salaries by several factors, but left salaries for teachers and doctors the same. And it's not as if there was no money in the budget. There is money. They just forgot. No time for them now.*]

This is basically a continuation of the discussion on who is more right—SPS or Yabloko. Both went to hell in the last election. It's pretty much the same picture, Alik.

You started the discussion, not me. I can't understand why the blame for all the country's ills is put on the entrepreneurs, who are honestly fulfilling their duties—that is, thirstily making money. That's what they're created for! Why do you want wolves to eat hay? You brought them in for natural selection. You would like strong, handsome wolves that eat hay, however.

You see, we like the American breed of wolves better.

And what about the civil servants?

They're a fine lot, let me tell you.

Then maybe the popular wrath should be directed against them?

The government has the press that it supports. And you don't. You're too cheap.

But we're not using state funds to write this book.

So, Alik. The important fact is that I am for capitalism. But I prefer the American model, where they are trying somehow to narrow the gap between poles.

At least seemingly.

But nevertheless I'm completely for capitalism. This should worry you, that even people who are on your side are beginning to ask questions. Why don't you want to build the American model?

What do I have to do with it? Tell me, Igor, why do you find me so irritating?

I'm not talking about you.

But what can I do? Can I force some oligarch not to pack a plane full of whores? I can't.

Why not? Aven tries to talk about morality in the papers, about the responsibility of business….

They've stopped flying whores around after the president criticized them for that. They stopped. Now the whores take the train. But what complaints are there about me? If all businessmen behaved as I do, would things be fine?

On the whole, you're all right. Things would be OK.

We're going off on a tangent. Let's get back to 1995. The black marketeers matured, as did their appetites, and they went for the oil at the mortgage auctions. It didn't turn out well. I won't quote the opinions of left radicals and marginal parties, but I'll quote your brother capitalists. Here's a businessman we know, quite well off, from an interview I did with him once: "Everyone knows that mineral deposits must belong to the country. Because they were stolen from the country! Stolen! No one had capital then. They called this theft privatization... That must be said, loud and clear. All right, they were allowed to steal then—fine, people made money. But now, make them return the deposits. I'm not saying put the privatizers in jail, no. But there must be some system developed to return what was stolen, a fair resolution must be found." Not bad, eh?

And now let me give you the opinion of a billionaire. He told me that the loans-for-shares auctions were an excess, a dangerous phenomenon for society, which society perceived as theft—

From the way the press presented it, please note, friend Igor.

It doesn't matter who presented it that way, the fact is important. That billionaire said that he did not believe then that the state would legalize it all. He was certain that it wasn't possible—the state giving away wealth for almost nothing. Remember what Putin said at the meeting with the oligarchs before he arrested Khodorkovsky: Don't forget that people did not become billionaires on their own—they were permitted to do so, they were appointed, and that was that. Apparently, he meant the loans-for-shares auctions, when people were told: "You can take that, but you stay out of this."

I see. Then who appointed Rem Vyakhirev a billionaire without any loans-for-shares auctions? Or Smolensky? Or Gusinsky? Without any mortgage auctions! He said that he never took part in any privatization, but he suddenly got a frequency for his channel for free, without any competition. For some reason he doesn't consider that privatization. And with all this passion, nostrils flaring, he used to scream about unfair privatization. And who appointed tons of other people billionaires?

How am I supposed to know?

So it wasn't the mortgage auctions that appointed them... By the way, both Potanin and Khodorkovsky came to the loans-for-shares auctions with more than $100 million. Who appointed them? Who decided Soskovets would be rich? Or Svyatoslav Fyodorov? He was certainly a dollar millionaire.

Millionaire, not billionaire.

And do you think that the teacher in the garbage dump—our collective image of the people—gives a shit whether it's millionaire or billionaire?

Not really.

What about the president's favorite, Sergei Pugachev? How did he become a billionaire? He never participated in any privatization. Not one! He only worked with the state's budget funds—as a banker.

OK. So what I've gathered from your impassioned speech is that the loans-for-shares auctions were crystal clear and honest, Alik. For the good of the Homeland. Impoverished but smart enthusiasts divided up enormous wealth completely altruistically. They divided it up among strangers. Generously. The moral satisfaction was enough reward; happiness is not found in money. No one took anything for himself. We see that all the time. It's natural human behavior. We are Homo sapiens, not shameful wolves.

I am so sick of arguing about this, Igor.

I'm not arguing yet. I am formulating your position as I understand it, and you can confirm or deny.

It is pointless to try to prove something in dialogue form. I will write a commentary, with a detailed description of how it happened. And why it happened that way.

But Alik, Alik, what about favoritism? So much was written about it.

Hm, hm, hm. Favoritism.

What are you chortling about? You're a big boy now.

And do you have any concrete examples of favoritism?

You should remember better than I do who got the most attacks. And for what. Svyazinvest seems to float to mind.

But that wasn't a mortgage auction! That was in 1997! You see, it's the national myth at work! I really want to throw my cell phone at you.

I didn't write about those auctions then, by the way.

But you're perpetuating the myth.

I'm not a specialist on the subject, and I conferred with the above-mentioned billionaire, who is sure that the state will contest the results of the mortgage auctions. He can judge objectively as a person who didn't participate in the auctions.

You should listen to him more carefully. Of course he participated! He was allowed to be in the auction without paying the deposit. He didn't have the money. And without a down payment, he was not allowed to take part. And then he did participate in another one. He teamed up with Potanin.

So, you say you were squeezed much harder over the writers' case.

Of course. They didn't fuck me over the auctions at all. Only retroactively, when they added it to the writers' case—because that was falling apart completely, so they added this to bolster it.

Remember you said you felt like a jerk for not taking bribes when you were in government? Did you mean the loans-for-shares auctions?

Among others—yes, of course.

Well, describe it, Alik. The way I see it you're completely into the topic, and I don't need to feed you any leading questions.

I'm into it.

All right, but don't let us down. Tell the whole truth.

Yes, yes. I will.

Kokh's Commentary:

The Mortgage Auctions, or Alfred Kokh Before the Court of the People

> The opposite of a correct statement is a false statement. But the opposite of a profound truth may well be another profound truth.
>
> *Niels Bohr*

I can't even list all the complaints the public has about loans-for-shares auctions. Things were sold off cheap, and given to friends, and the hell with it all. In principle, I had expected something along those lines from the start. I prepared myself for harsh polemics. I polished my arguments. Found logical chains. I was in shape. I was ready. But… The polemics weren't sharp. Because there were no polemics. Everyone decided at the same time that there was no point in arguing: thieves and bribe-takers—and nothing more.

So my arguments just gathered dust on the shelves of my memory.

And my unbreakable logic remained unbroken because no one even bothered to hear it out, to look for flaws or propose a different argument.

Many of the state officials who took direct part in this undertaking have forgotten that they did. That when it was over, they had called and thanked me. That they called me a hero who saved the country, told me the Homeland would never forget me. It didn't. I wish it had, I swear. But never mind. Let's start at the beginning. Better late than never.

The Country Exists, and It Eats (Every Day)

What was 1995? We remember, it was the year of parliamentary elections—the year before the presidential elections (more on that in the next chapter, on 1996). At the very beginning of the year, the night of January 1, 1995, Grozny was stormed. It was the year when the Communists and the Zhirinovsky party fully controlled the Duma. That year… Why am I going on about it? Everyone remembers the year. It's only nine years ago. Wait, how can it be nine? God! Nine already! Yes, yes, nine. Children born that year are in second grade. I was thirty-four that year. How wonderful. And what was going on with our country? Our country, Russia. You, today's critics, do you remember what was going on then? What shape Russia was in? Or is the idea of "selling it off to thieves and bribe-takers" enough to kick Yeltsin with? To cover Chubais with shit? To say bad things about me? Or should we try to find out who stole what from whom? That's not without interest, wouldn't you say? Or do real patriots have no need for history? Is the cry "Stop, thief" a good substitute for knowledge? Didn't anyone tell you who always shouts that the loudest?

The budget. Let's start there. What would we do without it? For instance, the revenues for the 2004 budget are around $96 billion; expenses are around $93 billion, with a profit of $3 billion. And what was 1995 like? Much cheerier then? With revenues around $37 billion, and expenses around $52 billion, with a deficit of around $15 billion. The country was the same, 145 million people. Even a bit more then.

Our opponents could lie, of course. For instance, they could say, Your budget was so small because you were lousy at gathering taxes. We pressed the oligarchs, and—presto!—we take in two and half times more now. The most obvious response to that from our side is that in 1995 a barrel of oil cost $15, and now it's $34. But even if we don't use that argument about world prices for our basic exports—oil, gas, and metals—even without those arguments, their point doesn't hold. Not in the most important way.

The most important thing is that there were no oligarchs in 1995. Industry was full of "red directors" who had not paid any taxes in years. They held this enormous social packet, which they hid behind—groaning about deadlines, subsidies, and other bullshit. They told us that they had thousands of workers, and that we were kids in short pants who knew nothing about real life. Chernomyrdin (to some extent) and Soskovets and all the industrialists in government were behind them one hundred percent. Korzhakov and Barsukov covered up for them and protected them. The directors themselves, those manufacturers, continue to live well since they skimmed off every ton and every cubic meter. The budget was what it was. Getting rid of those guys was impossible. They crawled from office to office in the White House, in the Kremlin, in Old Square, lobbying, lobbying, lobbying. They swore their love for Yeltsin and democracy. They said that they were for the state, as they should be. Don't we understand about reforms and the market? We spent our lives thinking about it. Gosplan, that sucks. The market rules. Of course, there will be hardships at first, but if only you could free me of taxation. Since there will be hardships… I've explained to you, I support the whole city with my factory. The kindergartens, the nurseries, the swineherds, the resort in the Crimea for the workers. We built it together, I hate to give it up, it will just vanish. Well, let me make payments over time, at least. All right? Thank you! Really! Markets, markets, what else, of course! What joy in democracy and the market. Oh, look at the time. Gotta run. I'm off. See you…

But with Zyuganov, head of the Communist Party, they talked a different talk: Don't worry, we'll support you. We'll give you money, and we'll have our people vote for you. Don't get pissed off. We'll get rid of the crapocrats, don't worry.

We couldn't depend on those guys at all. Ignorant grabbers, sybarites, and drinkers, they were people without even the most minimal moral compasses. They came to their new jobs as general directors of factories and plants straight from Communist Party management positions, and from being platform reformers—the contractors of perestroika. They moved in to the old, grim, and entrenched directors' corps, which had been there since the Kosygin days, at the height of "perestroika and acceleration"—that is, around 1987–1988.

You can see Khrushchevian ambitions even in the personnel policies of the fidgety Gorbachev.

Of course, there were businesslike people among them. They're still working. Some of them are oligarchs. Alekperov, Bogdanov, maybe a dozen of them. That's it. They're not thick on the ground, I must say.

I've written about this many times: There was a myth then that nothing could be done without the directors' corps. They were the salt of the Russian earth. Real men, the nation's elite. All right, just as they are today, they were KGB. We were considered mere carpenters, while they were cabinetmakers. They had their own vocabulary and aesthetic.

That whole gang had to be chased out, or there would be a catastrophe. It didn't matter what kind of organizational system would be built: They had to go. Comrade Stalin, beloved by so many once again, would have had them up against the wall in 24 hours. I'm certain that he wouldn't have hesitated for a minute.

How were we to get rid of them? There was one way: Since they wouldn't let us fire them, then we would sell the factory out from under them and let the new owner get rid of the "elite producers." Naturally, we had to give people a discount for buying an enterprise with that burden. The enterprises, thanks to their poor management skills, were in debt—burdened by terrible, predatory contracts, under-the-table loans, and huge loans from the state budget. They were still holding the money for the social benefits that they had not paid to the municipalities that reduced their tax base. I'm not complaining. I'm simply trying to explain that today's effective and pragmatic management corps grew out of that struggle. I want to explain that if we had not won that war with the "red directors" and had not toppled, for example, Filatov, the director of Norilsk Nickel; if we had not proven that we were a force to be reckoned with, the tax collected today would be different. Maybe the country would be different too. And with a different president. I dare say his name would be Gennady Zyuganov. Believe me. And there would be no "vertical of power." I feel particularly badly about the vertical.

The majority of that "elite" are respected bourgeois. They left work long ago and are enjoying their savings. They have grandchildren; they live in big estates, or abroad. They like England and Spain. Let God be their judge. They did a lot of harm. But they could have done more—so, thanks for that.

But let's return to the budget. A deficit of 29.5% is a catastrophe. If we dig a little deeper, the scope of that catastrophe becomes clearer. Just a few strokes here. Revenues from the sale of state property were planned to be $1 billion in the 1995 budget. That is a bit more than 3% of the revenue. Approximately as much as was expected from income tax (2.17%) and the natural-resources tax (1.38%) together!

Today's zealous proponents for a sharp increase in natural rent, where are you? Hel—lo-ooo!

You voted for that budget. A budget that made the "sell-off of the Homeland" inevitable.

Here are a few more details: The land tax made up .25% of the budget revenues (we are talking about a country that covers one-seventh of the planet).

Even funnier: Alcohol licensing, for the right to store, bottle, and sell retail—1.23%. Vodka excise, around 3%. How could it be otherwise? Korzhakov's National Sports Foundation needs to be given special benefits, doesn't it? Of course! And the Church is selling liquor without excise tax? Yes! And tobacco, too! And who came up with those benefits, Chubais? No. It was the Duma. The Communists, first of all.

This is how the budget deficit was financed: They needed to find $6.3 billion inside the country. That included the income of the Central Bank, but mostly the GKOs) The pyramid didn't keep growing because of the country's sweet life. Also, what happened to the principled parliamentarians? When the pyramid crashed, the same people who had approved the large volume of domestic loans turned on them, defending the people and wrathfully attacking their enemies. Another $8.7 billion had to be found in foreign financing. This, when we already had the unbearable Gorbachev debt. I maintain that the only alternatives to privatization as a revenue source at that time were either increasing the budget deficit or liquidating the basic subsidies—to agrarians, residents of the north, producers and sellers of alcohol and tobacco. Macroeconomic considerations made it impossible to increase the already huge gross deficit. Doing away with subsidies was beyond our powers. The opposition was—both structurally and politically—stronger. Jumping ahead, I will tell you that open warfare with them would take place the following year, in 1996. That will be a separate discussion.

So how were those crumbs spent? Maybe the state, selling off the last of its property, spent the money on the poor and hungry, the ones who needed the most help, the children? No way! Do the math: national defense, 19.75% of expenditures; law and order and state security, 6.08%; federal judicial system, 4.33%; state administration, 1.82%. That means that the state spent 31.98% of the budget on itself. The state borrowed a third of the budget and turned around and used it to finance itself.

The country was at war. A large-scale war in Chechnya that involved aviation, tanks, entire armies and division, with great losses on both sides—that isn't free; it was there in that third of the budget expenses. Who came up with the war? Chubais? Chernomyrdin? No. Grachev told us about the regiment of paratroopers, that it would take one day, that we would toss our caps in the air. It made me think of the Russo-Japanese War at the start of the twentieth century. It was the same thinking: We'd show those monkeys, and we need a "small victorious war," and other bullshit. Instead there was Tsusima, the proud ship *Varyag*, and the cemeteries on the hills of Manchuria.

How many "*varyags*" were there in Chechnya? How many of our soldiers were betrayed and abandoned in prison camp; or left surrounded, without weapons, wounded? How much money from the "sale of the Homeland" was stolen from the soldier's plates and clothing? How much money was spent on shells and bullets that ended up in Chechen hands? Who distributed the budget funds that were given by the country, taken away from children and seniors, in this manner? Taking it away from culture (0.62%), health (1.3%), education (3.66%)… Who? Chubais again, who "was to blame for everything" according to the perspicacious Yeltsin? Looks like it wasn't him—yet again. Then who? There's no answer. Just soldiers' graves all over Russia. The thin, still-adolescent bones of the poorest peasant boys with the fewest rights, thousands of them, were buried by fat generals. That sowing yielded them dachas, Mercedes, and fat-assed grandchildren in Switzerland. And why isn't anyone bringing them to account? Why aren't they to blame for our calamities? Why are they still calling on us to serve in their army, under their command—why are they teaching us to be proud of our country? Perhaps, if there had been no war in Chechnya, we wouldn't have had to sell the Homeland? We would have managed somehow. You can't find out now who started the war. Korzhakov blames it all on Filatov and Savostyanov. They, in turn, blame Korzhakov and Barsukov. Also mentioned are Grachev, Zavgaev, Stepashin, and the late Egorov, deputy head of the President's administration. Where is the truth? God only knows. Everyone agrees on one thing—none of the "young reformers" (and what a stupid nickname that was) had anything to do with it.

So, the directors had to be fired and the billions of dollars earned. You can't stop a war—and it was already on. The West wouldn't give us the money; they said they wouldn't give us money for a war. The possibilities for domestic loans and bonds were exhausted. What was left? An honest and unprejudiced analyst would have to say: Sell property. Which is what we did.

A Few Words about Budgetary Intrigues

At the end of the first half of 1994, check privatization was over. We began preparing for money privatization. We made forecasts and studied the market. Our figures showed that with some effort—it wouldn't be impossible—we could give the federal budget around a billion dollars.

The budget process began in the second half of the year. The government prepared a draft budget, which it presented to the Duma. It contained the billion dollars from privatization. I want to make a special point here to explain the following: In order to give the federal budget a billion dollars, you had to make almost twice as much from the sale of property, since a significant portion of the revenues from privatization went into regional and local budgets. Thus, when we talk about a billion for the federal budget, it should be understood that what we really mean is almost two.

The Communists greeted us with open arms. They had not been sleeping either and gave us our homework assignment: Check privatization is over, please give us budget effectiveness now. We didn't mind—here, we're projecting a billion. The Communists called for a time out. And then they made a move worthy of a great conman: They made an amendment to the budget that slipped by unnoticed at the Ministry of Finance, which was responsible for passing the budget through the Duma.

I quote:

> Article 12. Establish that in 1995 privatization will not include the premature sale of packets of shares that are tied as federal property in oil companies already created or to be created in accordance with decrees of the President of the Russian Federation and resolutions of the Government of the Russian Federation.
> Establish normative payments into the federal budget for 1995 of revenues from the sale of shares that are not tied as federal property of the aforementioned oil companies in the amount of 55%.... The revenues from the sale of state and municipal property—4,785.4 billion rubles.

Those were the very packets of shares we had been planning to sell. Not out of evil design, but because there was nothing else to sell. At that moment the only things left unsold were the shares in defense and those oil (and some metallurgical) packets attached as federal property.

In that way, we found ourselves in a very odd situation in the spring of 1995. On the one hand, we got what we asked for—an assignment to come up with a billion dollars through privatization. On the other hand, we had no source for obtaining that billion, because the legislature forbade the sale of the very property we had been planning to sell to get that sum. The solution to the problem was obvious—if you can't sell it, then you have to use it as collateral for loans. That's how the loans-for-shares auctions came into being.

A Few Words about Coordinating Interests

The first person to bring up the idea of using state shares as collateral with banks to get loans was Vladimir Potanin, who was invited by Soskovets to a government meeting in March 1995. They gave a reporting task to the State Property Committee, together with the Ministry of Finance, in order to develop the necessary regulatory documentation.

It became clear right away that we needed a presidential decree, that government resolutions would not be enough. So, administrators from the Presidential Administration were brought into the drafting of documents. Primarily, the legal department and its head, Ruslan Orekhov, and the economic services: more specifically, Alexander Lifshits and Anton Danilov-Danilyan.

Originally the plan was simple. We would offer collateral at open auctions. Potential creditors would participate. The winner would be the one who offered the biggest loan for any piece of collateral. However, numerous questions appeared at once.

Here are some of them: What would the interest rate be on the loans? What about the term? Who would manage the shares while they were collateral? These questions, for all their apparent banality, were in fact not simple in the least.

For example, take the question of rate of credit: Market rates at the time were so high that borrowing on those conditions using shares as collateral was not feasible. In fact, the difference between the credit rate and the profitability of the GKO was so small that the collateral scheme did not seem very useful. Really, why go to all that trouble and run loans-for-shares auctions when you can borrow money from banks through the GKO mechanism at a slightly higher rate, and without collateral. And it's not very clear why banks should lend money to the government for a lower interest rate if they can buy GKOs from the same borrower with a higher return.

Their interest was piqued when we told them that the creditor would manage the collateral for the period of the loan. Ah-h-h, the bankers said. Then tell us how long we can manage these enterprises? How great is the stimulus to invest in them? If the timeframe is measured in months, isn't it simpler just to rape the factories? That's not in your plans, is it, dear government?

In other words, there were numerous questions. But by September, the State Property Committee, the Ministry of Finance, and the Presidential Administration had given birth to a coordinated document. The plan was complex and cumbersome. However, it took into account the interests of the government and the banks as much as possible. I would like to draw your attention to two aspects.

First, all accounting with the bank—either upon return of the credits or by the collateral property becoming the property of the creditor—would begin only in the second half of the following year: 1996, that is, after the presidential elections. That construction was proposed by Alexander Lifshits. We appreciated the elegance of the proposal and its political subtext. The primary—the only—rival Yeltsin had in the election was a Communist, so if he were to come to power, there wouldn't even be a hint of the possibility of return of loans or turning over of collateral. He would just send the bankers packing. Be glad you're alive, he would say. Therefore, the lenders who would give money to the government on those conditions would become our natural allies in the coming presidential elections. Obviously the opportunity for them to get their money back or to gain property would depend on Yeltsin's re-election.

Second: Foreign investors were not allowed to participate in the auctions. The author of that passage is unknown. It was said that it was Korzhakov, but I have no precise information. On the one hand, it was the old song about "national security." As if these companies could be pocketed and carried off into the distant and scary "abroad." On the other hand, this immediately set the press, particularly in the West, against the share auctions, which played a negative role in the scandalous mythologizing of the process. Later, when the war against the "young reformers" began in 1997, the media controlled by Gusinsky and Berezovsky kept quoting Western journalists as if they were the final arbiters of truth, creating an appearance of objectivity. As if a Western journalist cannot be prejudiced or uninformed. To be fair, it must be said that the interest of foreign investors in Russian stocks was very low then. Judge for yourselves—why invest in a country where Communists triumphantly won Parliamentary elections and were on the verge of winning the presidential election? So while this rule was in fact dead, it created a bad background.

Somehow, a coordinated and simply workable plan for the auctions was finally developed and we could start implementing it.

A Few Words on How the Auctions Took Place

Once we had all the proposals from potential creditors, we compiled a list of enterprises whose shares would be auctioned:

November 3, 1995. Offered: 40.12% of the shares of Surgutneftegaz. Winner: the non-state Surgutneftegaz pension fund. Total paid: $300 million.

November 17, 1995. Offered: 38% of the shares of RAO Norilsk Nickel. Winner: ONEKSIM Bank. Paid: $170.1 million.

November 17, 1995. Offered: 15% of the shares of AO Mechel. Winner: TOO Rabikom (at the time owners of a large packet of shares). Paid: $13.3 million.

November 17, 1995. Offered: 25.5% of the shares of Severo-zapadnoe Rechnoe Parokhodstvo. Winner: MFK Bank. Paid: $6,050,000.

December 7, 1995. Offered: 5% of the shares of Lukoil. Winner: Lukoil. Paid: $141 million.

December 7, 1995. Offered: 23.5% of the shares of Murmansk Morskoe Parokhodstvo. Winner: ZAO Strateg (actually, Menatep Bank). Paid: $4.125 million.

December 7, 1995. Offered: 51% of the shares of Sidanko. Winner: MFK Bank (in fact, a consortium of MFK and Alfa-Group). Paid: $130 million.

December 8, 1995. Offered: 14.87% of the shares of Novolipetsk Metallurgical Combine. Winner MFK Bank (actually, Renaissance Capital). Paid: $31 million.

December 11, 1995. Offered: 20% of the shares of Novorossiysk Morskoe Parokhodstvo (Novoship). Winner: the company itself. Paid: $22,650,000.

December 28, 1995. Offered: 15% of the shares of AO Nafta-Moskva. Winner: ZAO NAFTA Fin (actually, the management of the company). Paid: $20,010,000.

December 28, 1995. Offered 51% of the shares of Sibneft. Winner: ZAO Neftyanaya Finansovaya Kompaniya (actually, a consortium of Berezovsky and Abramovich). Paid: $100.3 million.

The total for the budget was around $1.1 billion.

What do I remember? A few so-called "scandals" that still rile up our opponents.

The first was with Norilsk Nickel. The "scandal" was that we did not permit TOO Kont, who was backed by Rossiiskii Kredit Bank, to participate in the auction. The reasons for not letting them in were banal. A mandatory condition for participation in the auctions was the presentation of bank guarantees, in accordance with all the requirements, for the starting price. The necessary requirements were, first of all, that the capital of the bank giving the guarantee be at least no less than the amount of the guarantee.

In my opinion, that requirement is merely common sense. In fact, in order to do away with the temptation of ruining an auction by winning and then refusing to pay, we not only introduced big down payments but also demanded guarantees that the participants be able to pay at least the starting price. We informed everyone of this requirement, which was in accordance with all the norms of the law, publicly and in advance of the auctions. We also warned everyone that if they did not fulfill this requirement they would be taken out of the race. We also explained the demands that the law makes on these guarantees. They were banal too—the guarantor's own capital must be no less than the sum he is guaranteeing. But Rossiiskii Kredit Bank was giving TOO Kont a guarantee for $170 million, while the bank's own capital was less than that.

The bank could not have not known our requirements. It also could not have not known that its own capital was less than $170 million. This was a false candidacy, a forgery. We naturally rejected TOO Kont. This decision was made unanimously by the commission running the auction. The commission's members included such professionals as Andrei Kazmin, then deputy minister of finance.

But the directors of Rossiiskii Kredit (they were also the representatives of TOO Kont) made an enormous fuss. Vitaly Malkin jumped up and took his bid from the commission table. He opened it and announced that they had been prepared to pay $350 million.

What were we supposed to do in that situation? Let's analyze the possible options:

Option 1. Allow TOO Kont to participate in the auction. Then any other participant in the auction whose guarantee was in accordance with the law could sue us; and the court, with a 100% probability, would rescind the results of the auction. The motivation for the protest would be that we allowed a company that did not meet the requirements to participate (Civil Code, article 449, paragraph 1). And it did not matter whether or not TOO Kont was able to pay the promised $350 million or not. Any law school graduate knows that would be the court's ruling.

Option 2. Not allow TOO Kont to participate in the auction. Then they would sue. But the chances of preserving the results of the auction in that case were 100%. Of course, the noise in the press and scandal were not quantifiable. Who would bother to check the facts? They would just say: "They were offered $350 million and they declared the one who offered only $170.1 million the winner. Well, aren't they crooks?"

Thus, our choice was this: Take the $170.1 million for the budget and have to deal with a scandal in the press, or allow TOO Kont into the auction and have the courts determine the auction null and void, and therefore get nothing for the budget.

We analyzed all the arguments and risks. In principle, we could have tried to get Potanin not to protest Kont's win. The chances were small, but it might have been worth a try. However, first we had to be completely certain that Kont had the money. And there was no certainty of that at all.

A few days before the auction, the directors of Rossiiskii Kredit, Vitaly Malkin and Boris Ivanishvili, came to see me. They were interested in the details of the auction process and asked a question that did not seem very significant then: "So, according to your rules, the winner has to pay the money within ten days. What if he pays a little later—say, in fifteen days?"

Now I was beginning to understand the point of the question. Look: If we had declared them the winners and they had not paid the money, on November 28, 1995, we would have had to announce a new auction for the Norilsk Nickel shares to be held on December 28, 1995 (the law says it must 30 days from the announcement to the results). If we had given them an extra three to five days, we would have been pushed into 1996. The presidential decree on the shares auctions was in force only for 1995! Therefore, the auction would have become void, irreversibly. And the budget would not have gotten any money from Norilsk shares at all.

That's when I understood why such qualified people could have made such an error with the bank guarantee: They didn't want to win! They were there to ruin the auction. They never had even a hint of $350 million. Why were they doing that? I don't think anyone will be able to get an answer to that now. There were rumors that they had been brought into this by the former directors of Norilsk Nickel, since failure of the auction would mean their "reign" at Norilsk would continue. But those were just rumors.

Yet here is indirect proof that Rossiiskii Kredit was working on orders from the managers of Norilsk Nickel. Rossiskii Kredit did not contest the results of the auction in court, but the above-mentioned managers did. And they lost, of course.

In any case, the commission summed up the results of the auction and declared ONEKSIM Bank the winner, and the Treasury got the funds it so badly needed.

Am I bitter about Vitaly Malkin and Boris Ivanishvili? No. They acted pragmatically—toughly, but within the rules. They had their interest, and we had ours. It was a good game, and we had to make the right decision. I am still confident that we did the right thing.

By the way, the Accounting Chamber did an audit five years later and declared the results of the privatization of Norilsk Nickel lawful. And the Prosecutor General's Office made noises and threats, but did not go to court. There are also many decisions by assessors—for instance, the Financial Academy of the Government of the Russian Federation—that the sum received for the shares "is not artificially lowered."

Now, when the capitalization of our major companies is measured in the billions of dollars, we no longer remember that in the fall of 1995 the shares of those same companies cost kopecks. For example, how much did 39% of the shares of Norilsk Nickel cost on the Russian Stock Exchange on the day of the auction, November 17, 1995? You will never guess. It was $147 million. Where could such high prices have come from in a country where the domestic capital had not yet gathered strength and foreign capital regarded Russia warily, afraid that the Communists would come to power very soon. And foreigners were banned from the auctions, in any case.

The second scandal involved Yukos. I had expected it to be that way, and it was. It began with the company presenting a strange initiative: They wanted the deposit for participation in the auction to be $300 million! I was stunned—who had money like that in those days? And then, I didn't see why the deposit had to be $300 million when the starting price in the auction was $150 million.

It should be noted that the heads of Yukos then (Muravlenko and Generalov) always brought Konstantin Kagalovsky, from Menatep bank, when they came to meet with me. I'd known Kagalovsky a long time; we had traveled to Chile in the same group. Then he worked for the IMF as the director from Russia. Then he started working for Khodorkovsky at Menatep. It was fairly obvious that the management of Yukos had become very close to Menatep and had lived and breathed to see the latter become owner of the company.

In principle there was nothing against the law in this. But it was very strange: Everyone was complaining that the deposits were too big, and this company, on the contrary, wanted the deposit to be twice the starting price. They told me that the company needed investments, this and that, but it was obvious that they came up with the big deposit in order to get rid of potential competitors.

Strictly speaking, this was rational from their point of view. If we had set the deposit in the Norilsk Nickel auction at the size of the starting sum, we would have avoided scandals like the one with Rossiiskii Kredit. Nevertheless, when we discussed the question of the deposit, many members of the commission expressed doubts about the feasibility of the auction.

At that time there was a rule that any suggestions made by the company whose shares are being auctioned had to be accepted, as long as they were not against the law.

There was nothing illegal about Yukos' proposal; it was just unusual. So we had to accept it. It should be noted that Viktor Chernomyrdin displayed an unexpected level of activity concerning Yukos. He avoided discussing the mortgage auctions with me in general; his instincts as an old wolf told him to keep away. Of course, if we had failed to meet the budgetary requirements, he would have attacked us. You whippersnappers, the country trusted you! We had placed our hopes in you, and so on… But for now, he kept away.

And suddenly he started calling me, asking questions, and displaying a high level of information. Don't hurt the company, he said. What are you saying about their initiative on the deposit? It's strange? But it's legal, right? Well, then, do as they ask. Come on, come on. Do you understand? Fine then… So, Muravlenko is coming to see you? Excellent. But stick to the law, naturally.

And so we confirmed the conditions of the auction, with that strange deposit. We weren't totally oblivious. A consortium was being formed in parallel to compete with Menatep. It was the Rossiiskii Kredit ploy again, this time with Inkombank and Alfa Bank. I tried to help the consortium come together. I understood that the conditions for the deposit were difficult. Today, $300 million is a snap for Alfa Bank. But back then it was an enormous sum. What can I use as an analogue here? The Russian Stock Exchange index was 50 then. Today it is 750. That means that the capitalization of the Russian market has grown by a factor 15 since then. I think it would be correct to say that $300 million in the fall of 1995 equals approximately $4.5 billion now.

The new consortium came out with its own initiative: they wanted to use $300 million in GKOs as their deposit. It had its logic—the deposit is a kind of guarantee of payment worthiness to the owner of the mortgage. Thus, the mortgage owner's own credit obligations—in this case, the state (GKOs are the state's debt obligations)—have to be recognized by that state to be like money.

It was a controversial proposal, for the GKOs had different due dates and would have to be discounted—but those were details that could have been handled once the idea was approved. I'm not a specialist in the finer points of finance. I wrote a request to the Central Bank asking whether in these circumstances GKOs could be considered a full-fledged deposit. Peter Aven, who must have known more than I did about this, insisted that he could easily persuade Dubinin that the consortium's idea should have its place in the sun. I handed him my letter, and he set off for the Central Bank. And he got a very clear answer—no. Signed by Sergei Dubinin, then chairman of the bank. I wonder if Chernomyrdin hadn't had one of his fits of curiosity then.

We couldn't even consider accepting GKOs as a deposit after that. And then, I was completely knocked off my feet by Kagalovsky, who came to me with a copy of Dubinin's reply. You can only guess where he got it. It was over. If we had accepted the GKOs as a deposit from the consortium, the results of the auction would have been negated by the courts in an instant, since Menatep had the Central Bank's decision.

The budgetary needs forced us to accept the strange conditions for the auction. Later there were rumors that Menatep had taken money from the government itself in order to lend money to the government. Allegedly Andrei Vavilov, who was First Deputy Minister of Finance then, helped them. I don't know whether that's true or not; I haven't seen the paperwork.

Summing Up

What conclusions have I drawn from this epic? The first and most important: We should not have made the budget the main priority. Somehow we had decided that we had to obtain that billion dollars at any price. That was a mistake. So, we would have underfinanced the budget. What would have happened? The ones who had to get money would have gotten it all, and the teachers and doctors would have not been paid again; they would have waited another five months for their salaries. They should be used to it.

At the time, I thought that my personal reputation was worth less than the needs of those people. I thought my bosses would understand that I was risking my career, good name, and friendships for the sake of achieving the goal set before me. At first, as I have already explained, that's the way it was. I was patted on the back; everyone told me I was doing a great job, that I was a hero. But then, in 1997, when the oligarchs started ganging up on me, most of the praisers went off somewhere.

Now I don't even know whether I was right after all. Maybe yes and maybe no.

Another mistake, I think, was that I allowed the participants in the auctions to get too close to me. I listened to their problems and tried to help when I could. They knew that I was meeting with other people, not just them, and the

others were their competitors whom I was also understanding and listening to—
and they thought that I was being corrupted by the competitors, who also
thought that about the others, and so on.

That is why there are so many myths and legends about the whole loans-for-
shares story. And I don't look the hero in this story at all, but like the total
asshole who tried to do his best and ended up helping everyone—including
Yeltsin—but himself.

But in 1995 I was still the hero. Gusinsky and Berezovsky started making me
the "thief and robber" later, in 1997. When I wouldn't sell them Svyazinvest. As
the saying goes: If you knew where you were going to fall, you could lay down
some straw for a cushion.

* * *

Svinarenko's Commentary:

In 1995 I lost a friend, Sasha Sidorov, aka Rozanov. He was very important
to me. In the 1980s he was in charge of our *samizdat* group. We printed 70,000
copies of the New Testament—not a bad start. As I recall it now, our wholesale
price was 18 rubles, and retail was 25. The daily earning for an average *samizdat*
worker was roughly 25 rubles. Not bad. The secret police caught Sasha and put
him away. He served eighteen months. He didn't consider his time inside lost—
he said that life is everywhere and people live everywhere. Once he got out he
started selling computers, naturally, and then frozen chicken legs. He competed
with Soyuzkontrakt itself. When he decided to expand his business, he borrowed
money—$5 million. People lent him money easily: He was such an honest man,
he served time for the truth! Of course, they didn't just give it to him; the
collateral was the production base that he was privatizing (sic!) just then. And so
Sasha took his staff on a cruise. He and his wife took off for a few days from the
rest of the group, went to some Spanish island and vanished from view (maybe
he was opening bank accounts then?). And just then, his brother-in-law, who
was left in charge in Moscow, got into the books and discovered that the
company had no money. He started worrying that bandits were going to show
up to beat the money out of him. But he didn't say anything. Sasha came back to
Moscow in early September. His brother-in-law calmed down. At least, even if
there wasn't any money, he wouldn't be the one responsible. Then one of the
creditors vanished. As it turned out, without a trace. Then Sasha disappeared
again—this time for good—in December. The creditors got upset, got into his
computers, found a lot of very strange payments. They managed to find about 10
percent of what was lost. And the shares of the base that were used as collateral?
They had been mortgaged many times over.

An odd letter came from Sasha saying that he was looking for the money himself and would show up when he found it. Maybe he was forced to write the letter?

If you remember, a lot of businesses crashed that year. Inflation had slowed down and you couldn't pull money out of a hat anymore. Maybe Sasha just got lost in the interest rates. A lot of businessmen returned from vacation in the fall and found out their businesses were gone.

And here's another interesting point. People trusted Sasha easily. His staff voluntarily gave him most of their salaries to invest. They would get $500 a month, but receive only $200. Some sold their apartments to lend money to Sasha. Someone said that he saw Sasha getting on a train to Ukraine, leaving his first wife and their three children in Moscow. Of course you can get on a train, pull away from the station—then switch to a car, drive to Sheremetyevo, and fly to the West.

So, the question is, Did they set him up, force him to borrow money and then kill him? Or did he embezzle the money himself and deceive his people? It's a tough question.

I continued traveling in 1995. I went to Venice for the carnival—rather bland, by the way.

That year our Nikita Mikhalkov won an Oscar for *Burnt by the Sun*.

In addition to everything else I did, I saw my cousin in Los Angeles. He was working as a computer analyst. Life wasn't very sweet for him there, and I entertained him for a bit, taking him to local bars. Having no money in America, for your information, is much drearier than having none here. No wonder my cousin came back to Russia. He's okay now, seems pleased with life. He's remarried—that means he's interested in life, he still wants something from life.

In late 1995 Vasya (Andrei Vasilyev) returned to *Kommersant*. This was an important event for me. We had worked together at the old *Kommersant*, and he had been department head. Vasya did a lot for the paper. He came up with all the funny headlines. Yakovlev would not agree to funny headlines at first; he demanded smart ones. But then he gave up. After Vasya left, the official line was that his view of the paper no longer coincided with Yakovlev's. All those years, from 1992 to 1995, I kept telling Yakovlev that he should bring back Vasya, no matter what his personal feelings were. And finally, they brought Vasya back—maybe I had gotten through to Yakovlev.

By the way, the magazine *Medved* started publication in 1995. I wouldn't say that I foretold the future—no, I certainly didn't know then that I would have something to do with *Medved*. But I do remember thinking then how good it would be to work at a men's magazine.

15.

1996

The Fifteenth Bottle

*D*uring the presidential elections, both authors work on the same side of the barricades: They passionately want the Communists to lose. Although Kokh is not officially part of the election staff, he watches the fateful events from close-up. For example, he takes part in the liberation of Evstafyev and Lisovsky, Chubais' aides: Do you remember the famous Xerox box filled with $500,000 in cash?

Amusingly, when Kokh goes to Turkey on vacation during the summer, he is put in jail. Overnight. Svinarenko also goes to Turkey, but he doesn't have any such adventures.

The co-authors make edifying trips to Chechnya—separately, however. And what is interesting, Svinarenko travels with General Shamanov, and Kokh with Berezovsky and Basayev.

The rest of the time Kokh spends on his beloved privatization, "working round the clock." Svinarenko forms a team of "golden pens" from Kommersant. *After which he moves to the USA, to work as special correspondent for* Stolitsa *magazine in Moscow, Pennsylvania.*

Well, Alik, as usual, let's begin with a brief review of your life in 1996.

My life in 1996… Are we going to discuss only my life, or yours, too?

Mine, too. As usual. But let's start with you—I asked first.

All right. Not much: I didn't have any new children born or any new wives appear in my life…

How about work? How was that?

Nothing new. So what was interesting? Nothing really. I worked round the clock at work.

But what work?

I was First Deputy Chairman of the State Property Committee. In 1996, in January, they fired Chubais. Yeltsin was president then, and he uttered a phrase that went down in history: "Everything is Chubais's fault." That was the start of his election campaign—the elections were in the summer. His spin doctors—at the time Korzhakov, Barsukov, and Soskovets—told him, "Now's the time to blame everything on Chubais, and you'll come out clean as a whistle."

What exactly was blamed on him?

Everything. The impoverishment of the masses, the loss of value of deposits, Mavrodi's MMM pyramid scheme, everything. They even tried to blame the Chechen war on Chubais.

By the way, at that time Soskovets was seen as Yeltsin's heir.

Seriously?

Yes.

All those people were popular then: Volsky, Skokov, the Union of Manufacturers, the Union of Industrialists and Entrepreneurs. And they all lectured us, telling us that we didn't know how to run the economy and that the director corps should be in charge of that. So they told Yeltsin, "Listen, old man, don't worry, you're winning easy—we've made all the calculations. You're the light of democracy, everything is fine and dandy. So no hassle. And if there's any problem, we'll just disband the Duma and postpone the elections. So you fire Chubais and say he's to blame for everything. And then everything will be fine." So he was fired.

Right after being elected to the Duma, Sergei Belyayev, Chairman of the State Property Committee, went off to lead the Our Home Is Russia faction. That left two vacancies on our team. That's when I proposed my idea that the period of *Sturm und Drang* is over; we had reached a certain line, and now we had to fortify our positions there, pull up the supply wagons, and regroup for the next push. The generals who had led our team forward were prepared to attack. But we didn't know how they'll do in defense. You need people of a different type for defense. And we had generals like that in our team. Defense generals. A no less honored by the military specialty, by the way—not Bagration, but Barclay de Tolly. And so I proposed Alexander Ivanovich Kazakov. He became chairman of the State Property Committee and vice-premier. And that was it. The candidacy was confirmed! Yeltsin signed the decree!

Kazakov is a good soccer player.

Yes. You know that side of him, but I know a few others. He is multifaceted. Now he's working as a senator from Rostov Oblast.

You were a senator, too. It was a total waste for you.

I was there half a year. They never did confirm me in the Federation Council.

So, you mentored a man like that.

I didn't mentor him. He's older that I am. He mentored me! So, he was appointed, and I became his first deputy. Fortification, engineering, artillery. Build redoubts by the walls, dig ravines, set out the archers, heat up the boiling oil… A whole different story! It was such an interesting time. Oleg Soskovets and Vladimir Kadannikov were first vice-premiers and Kazakov was simply a vice-premier.

Who was Soskovets, anyway? Why was he elevated so high?

I'm not very clear on that myself, Igor. He came from Kazakhstan. In the Brezhnev era he was director of the Karaganda Metal Plant. By the way, his chief engineer then was Vladimir Lisin, now oligarch and owner of the Novolipetsk Metallurgy Plant.

And then, during the Gorbachev rotation, when the old cadres were being beaten up, Gorbachev brought him in as Union Minister of Metallurgy. He's so impressive looking, so big.

And he privatized—

He didn't privatize a thing! Wait, this is still back in Gorbachev's time. Later, when the Soviet Union collapsed, he ran back to Kazakhstan, and Nazarbayev practically made him premier, or first vice-premier—I don't remember exactly. He was there for a while, but it didn't work out. He came back to Moscow. And at the last second, he managed to get a Russian passport. He was first head of the committee on metallurgy, and then Korzhakov lobbied for him, and Yeltsin made him first vice-premier. Under Chernomyrdin, that's when he appeared. Yeltsin liked him a lot. Because he was big, because he powerful, because he could drink a lot, because he spoke boldly. He came from the plow, he had run a big plant, he understood everything, and so on and so forth. I don't want to speak well or badly of him—he was the product of those times. They adored all those directors back then, and the thinking was that they were the salt of the Russian earth. And it turned out that they were anything but.

Yes. The directors then were the salt of the earth, and the journalists carried the torch of truth.

Right. The directors were the salt and the journalists were the sugar.

And the writers—they were simply prophets.

Prophets? No, no, by then that wasn't so obvious; those accepted and clear truths were being blurred by then. They didn't seem to be such truths anymore. But the director stereotype lasted longer than the ones for the journalist or the writer. It started dying out somewhere in 1995, when the mortgage auctions were over and the red directors were chased out.

By the way, I used to think journalists were the worst, that they were hardly people at all, you couldn't expect anything from them. But then I spent some time at *writers'* events; I looked at them and thought: "Well, journalists are all right, after all."

Even though journalists are devoid of morality, they invented a special one of their own, a simplified code. They can't be expected to handle "Thou shalt not bear false witness."

But at least you can discuss some topics adequately with journalists.

They're at least au courant, they know what's going on in the country.

But you can't talk with writers at all.

Of course not, they don't read the papers or watch TV; it's going to ruin their style if they do.

You have to speak very carefully with writers. They are so important. They drink differently somehow, more heavily, unlike the feckless journalists. You can't talk one-on-one with writers, you have to think about what to say. Otherwise they'll take it the wrong way. That's very wearying. So journalists aren't so bad. And then there are the artists! They're even more difficult. Next to them, even writers seem like the sweetest people. That's when I decided to stop expanding my worldview. To keep myself from wandering off into the debris. Because there are still musicians, for example… A lot of wisdom there, a lot of sorrow.

In other words, they poured a shitload of arrested people on Yeltsin's head, and he fired Chubais. Who was to blame for everything. But literally, in a month's time, Chubais became chief of Yeltsin's election campaign. That was in February 1996. It went rather unnoticed. And by July, for the second round, Soskovets, Korzhakov, and Barsukov were gone.

In a Xerox carton.

It had just been emptied. The prosecutor's office took out the evidence—a box of cash—and returned the carton for the government's use.

Hm... Do you remember that box?

Oh, yes. I'll write a commentary about it. I was deep inside that whole story...

Kokh's Commentary:

Snarky Comments, Gossip, and One Actual Incident
 Chubais amazed me. He developed an entire philosophy, the *leitmotif* of which was: "This is the way it must be."
The "kitchen spanking" had a classic effect on the reformer. Chubais relished his own stoicism, traveled around town in an old, beat-up Zhiguli 5, and wore a short sheepskin jacket. He looked like a successful black marketeer of the 1970s, when a Zhiguli and sheepskin jacket represented the height of ambition. In that outfit, Chubais had a powerful effect on the waitresses in the restaurants we patronized after his firing. The little homegrown plot to fire Chubais, the result of a brainstorm by the dream team of Korzhakov and Soskovets didn't work. The public did not believe that everything was his fault. Contrary to expectations, Yeltsin's approval rating did not move from its firm position at five percent after Chubais was fired.
Gusinsky's mass media kept giving us Yavlinsky with the idea that since his rating was three times higher than Yeltsin's, he should be the only candidate from the democratic forces, that all people of good will should support him, and anyone who thinks otherwise is an enemy of the young and fragile Russian democracy.
Anyway, Zyuganov basically considered himself president by then. He developed a tolerance previously unknown among Communists. For instance, he began recognizing the multiplicity of forms of property. And, (O miracle!) he suddenly decided that even private property was possible. Legions of Marxist professors spun in their graves, but he didn't care. I recognize private property, so there. A bold bastard. A revisionist, a liberal (damn, the term stuck). But he wasn't so clear about private property. He thought there were good private

owners and bad ones. I still don't understand how to tell them apart, but Gennady Andreyevich explained it all, and we realized that he knew how to separate the sheep from the goats.

It was obvious that sheer curiosity would bring entrepreneurs to Zyuganov's door for explanations of who was good and who wasn't. Some of today's oligarchs were in that line outside his office. They all came out happy: Apparently, they had been counted among the good ones. The grateful private property owners filled the Communists' election coffers with universal equivalent honestly earned by man exploiting man.

The victory of the Communists seemed so inevitable that the fairy tale about "good private property" was accepted by the craven ears of Russian business-men. Well then, just as there is good and bad private property, there are good and bad Communists. The self-deception and self-hypnosis to which Russian entrepreneurs subjected themselves began turning pathological and irreversible. It was time to prepare bread crusts to take along to the camps when we all were arrested.

Zyuganov, seeing how things were going, added more balm, announcing that Jesus Christ was a Communist. And that the Communists had never been against Christ and his teaching, or against Orthodoxy, or nationality, and so on. The tens of thousands of priests tortured and killed, the destroyed churches and monasteries, the burned icons, the thousands of people imprisoned for disseminating Holy Scriptures—all that had never happened. But here is what there was: Communism and Christianity were twins. And I, Zyuganov, am baptized. See, I wear a cross. It says: "Save and protect."

The earth did not open and the thousands of tortured souls did not cry out and the horns of Jericho did not blare… And locusts did not attack him and his tongue did not drop off. People, how long will we accept such lies without passing out in a faint? If they lie to us like that and we don't even notice, maybe we're not humans at all? The militant materialist turned into a long-standing clericalist. He began attending church, zealously crossing himself, singing hymns, and observing fasts. Our church hierarchy let him in, without repentance. And offered him a hand. And he kissed the cross. And took Communion. And the world did not collapse. Horrors. Lenin probably pissed himself laughing in his mausoleum. And then said, "Bravo, Comrade Gennady. You've understood the political moment. You're with the masses. With the ordinary workers and peasants. That is what the leader of the world proletariat must be like." But there is nothing more vile and repulsive than the fairy tale about god—recognize that quote from Lenin? Gennady Andreyevich, I'm quoting your idol here—that vampire, Ulyanov. I guess we set aside the dried crusts.

Now, let's take Grigory Alexeyevich Yavlinsky. Some purist democrats to this day are upset that we supported Yeltsin instead of him. The discussion has merit; you can't complain that it's invalid. But personally the question that interests me is this: Would Yavlinsky have won against the Communists? Not today's half-ruined, disoriented, and aging ones, but the Communists of 1996? The Communists had the support of an enormous number of people who for five years had been told by the democratic mass media in a detailed and comprehensible way that their unfortunate lives were not the logical result of the country's eighty-year history, but exclusively the consequence of the horrible Yeltsin-Gaidar-Chubais reforms. The Communists had the silent support of the *siloviki* in the Ministry of the Interior, the FSB, and the army. The Communists had limitless cynicism and lack of principle, as shown by their unexpectedly awakened religiosity and sudden recognition of private property. The Communists had the support of the local princelings (almost all first secretaries of the *oblast* committees). The Communists had the sympathy of the middle-level state apparatchiks. And what did Yavlinsky have? Well? We could talk about the possibility that if Yavlinsky had been given the same PR and support that Yeltsin had that spring, he would have gotten more votes than Yeltsin did. But please, there is such a thing as objective circumstances. The support of just the democratically inclined voters? Maximum—10 percent. And then half of them don't vote. The newborn class of entrepreneurs? That's another percentage point. There aren't more than that even now. People who like Yavlinsky and are pro-Western? Well, say another 5 percent. Where did I get 5? I don't know… Just take it, I'm feeling generous. That makes a total of 16 percent. Call it 20. Even 30! That's silly now. And he needed 51 percent.

Yavlinsky didn't have a chance. Even Gusinsky began to see that very quickly, and he was something of a friend and sponsor. Let me remind you that in the final count, Yavlinsky did not even come in third. General Lebed was third.

And finally, Gusinsky, with his Channel Four—he came to support Yeltsin, too. How did they get him to switch? I'm still amazed. They say Berezovsky twisted his arm. It's more likely that his own advisors (all former KGB or Central Committee workers) explained to Gusinsky that if not Yeltsin, it would be Zyuganov. Yavlinsky had no chance. The Commies, they're pluralists only when they're in the opposition. If they come to power, the first thing they'll do is put him up against the wall with the others. They're not going to make distinctions about who participated in privatization and who did not. It's very simple by their book—if you're rich, you're a thief. Take it away and divide it up, and get rid of the *bourgeois*. You'll rot in a ravine, flies crawling over your body, the stink of it… Your wife will be sent to Siberia and your children to an orphanage, in accordance with the usual procedures. The KGB people know what they're doing.

Out of fairness, I should note that the businessmen came and organized something resembling a presidential campaign staff a bit later, around late February or early March. Before that, Yeltsin the presidential candidate had his own official staff headed by Oleg Nikolayevich Soskovets, including Korzhakov and Barsukov. That staff lasted almost until the second round of voting. I can't say now whether it ever did anything, but they were known for wanting to disband the Duma and canceling the presidential elections. They were also involved in the arrest of Evstafyev and Lisovsky.

I was not a member of either staff. Not the formal one or the real one. But I saw Evstafyev and Chubais rather frequently, and I talked with the other members of the informal staff, so I have a definite idea of how it was formed and worked. I don't have the shadow of a doubt that the idea of creating a real staff, consisting of real people instead of trophy generals and vice-premiers, was Berezovsky's. He was the first to have two (now obvious) ideas: First, if Yeltsin did not win, he would no longer have Sibneft. Second, if nothing is done and the campaign is left in the hands of Soskovets and Korzhakov, they will either start another knife fight in the middle of Moscow or Yeltsin, with their help, will suffer a resounding loss.

It wasn't all that Christmas-story like, with the kind magician Berezovsky showing up and everything going the right way, Yeltsin's presidential campaign picking up steam, the useless courtiers shamed and eventually banished from Paradise. In real life, it was much more complicated than that. What the arrangements were between Berezovsky and Korzhakov is known only to them. However, based on what Berezovsky told me, this is what happened: In early 1995, Berezovsky came to Korzhakov and said that the elections were in a year and if their goal was to win, they had to get control of the mass media—particularly television. Before that, almost everyone had had a go at running the mass media. Fedotov, Poltoranin, Poptsov—can't even remember them all. Korzhakov apparently took advice from someone—I would like to think it was Yeltsin—and the decision was made to create the Joint Stock Company Public Russian Television (ORT), based on Channel 1. The state would keep 51 percent of the shares, and 49 percent would go to a consortium of businessmen. Oleg Boiko and his bank, Alfa Group, and Menatep bank were in the consortium. First violin in the consortium was Berezovsky—that had been agreed beforehand, and everyone kept to the arrangement.

Thus, a year before the events I'm describing, Berezovsky prepared himself to deal with the elections. So it wasn't as if one fine day in Davos, in February 1996, Berezovsky woke up and had an epiphany. No, he had promised the authorities to bring the business community to help Yeltsin win the election, and the authorities in return gave him control over ORT (and in some sense over Sibneft). That was his "civic task" from the regime. A task he wanted and had been given a year before these events.

So, Berezovsky came to Davos and started working the businessmen who were there. And you understand, they were all there. Even Chubais in his sheepskin coat. Good thing he wasn't wearing kolkhoz boots.

Oh! thought Berezovsky. Here's the leader for the group, thanks to Yeltsin. Since it's all Chubais's fault, let him clean up the mess he made. He's got nothing else to do anyway. And Chubais is more interested in Yeltsin's victory than anyone. The Commies were sure to put him up against the wall, maybe even before Yeltsin. To be fair, it should be said that Yeltsin's low ratings in early 1996 was not just the result of the useless war, the prejudiced mass media, and the grotesquery he indulged in when drunk (like conducting), but also of the excesses of the reforms, including Chubais's reforms. Why hide the sins?

Then Berezovsky thought in the following way: So, we have Channel 1. Channel 2 belongs to the state, no problems there. Three is Luzhkov's, and after what happened in 1993, he's not going back. Five is in St. Petersburg. No problem, the Reds won't show up there. That leaves Channel 4, NTV. No Reds there, but Gusinsky can be a real spoiler. His position on Chechnya alone costs Yeltsin 10-15 percent… So willy-nilly, he had to make up with Gusinsky. It was not going to be pleasant (they were sworn enemies), but it had to be done. Berezovsky called Gusinsky; they met and worked things out. They made their headquarters in the building of the Moscow City Hall (the former Comecon building), in offices rented by Menatep. Gusinsky's office was there, too, on a different floor.

I don't know what tricks they came up with. But I do recall two projects. One was called "Vote with your heart" and was run by Mikhail Lesin and his Video International. The other was " Choose or lose," initiated by Sergei Lisovsky and his ad agency, Premier-SV. The first campaign was to make Yeltsin more attractive and the second to increase voter turnout, especially among young people.

Besides those, there was also a project to make Lebed stronger, so that he could take away some of Zyuganov's votes. There was also behind-the-scenes work with the governors. There was the "anti-Communist hysteria." Lots of things. You know the result. Yeltsin won. The Communists did not.

Chubais's staff worked round the clock. This was very impressive. Just like the old "revolutionary headquarters in Smolny." Endless meetings, people coming and going. All they lacked was the little soldier looking for hot water for tea. Chubais was in his element, like a fish in water. A Bolshevik. Which is why he is so beloved by the broad masses of the liberal intelligentsia.

It seemed to me that there were three key figures in the group. Chubais, Berezovsky, and Gusinsky. Through Berezovsky's efforts, Valentin Yumashev and Tatyana Dyachenko (Yeltsin's daughter) came to the headquarters. That created an informal, alternative means of communication with Yeltsin. The traditional, official channels were controlled by Korzhakov and Barsukov—and that really got in the way, because they were prejudiced and jealous of the work their "helpers" were doing.

This was astonishing to me. The "oligarch HQ" had been set up in agreement with and to support the official HQ. Yet as soon as it showed the slightest effectiveness, the courtiers went into fits of jealousy. I wanted to scream, You idiots, it's your asses they're saving! If Yeltsin loses, you won't be courtiers! You should be praying for these business guys every night instead of sticking spokes in their wheel! Come together! Gusinsky kept up unofficial contacts with Luzhkov, who had high ratings—which in turn helped bring up Yeltsin's ratings. Moscow was papered with posters of Yeltsin and Luzhkov. Gusinsky also brought in Malashenko—who, many people say, increased the staff's creative work.

But let me repeat: I'm talking as an outside observer. Only three people know the inside stuff completely. The time will come when they—Chubais, Berezovsky, and Gusinsky—will tell it like it was. I think we will learn many interesting things then. And maybe they will realize at last that these were some of the best day of their lives.

Right after the first round of the election, when it became clear that Boris Nikolayevich would most likely win, the Korzhakov dream team decided that they could stop pretending to be working with the Chubais team. It was time to get rid of them and rest on their laurels another four years. The easiest way was to find something illegal in the campaign's financing—start a big criminal case, put them all away, and be done with it.

I was at home, around nine in the evening. The phone rang.

Chubais's receptionist: "Do you know where Arkasha [Arkady Evstafyev] is?

"No. He called today, but a long time ago, this morning… What's up?"

"Nothing much… Just need him and we can't find him."

Ten p.m. They called again.

"Has he called?"

"No. Come on, spit it out."

"Mmmm…"

"All right, I understand. I'm on my way."

I arrived.

"It looks like they got him. And Sergei Lisovsky, too."

"Where?"

"They left this morning for the White House and vanished. Neither hide nor hair of them."

"Did you ask the security guards?"

"Yes. They said they didn't see them leave, but they couldn't keep track of everyone. But they don't think they've left."

"So you're saying they were handcuffed right in the White House?"

"Who the hell knows! I guess so."

"And where's Chubais?"

"At Berezovsky's club on Novokuznetskaya. They're sitting around trying to figure out what to do. Do you think you could call his wife? You're friends, after all."

"All right, I will... Ira? Hi, it's Alik."

Her instant response was: "What's happened to Arkasha? Alik, tell me the truth!"

God, just like in books. I'd never been in that situation before. "I don't know anything myself. Just don't worry... I'll go find out."

We were in a movie or something. Where was I planning to go? What was I saying? "You see... uhm... Arkasha's been arrested," I said.

She said in relief, "Do you mean you got drunk? A fine time you found. ... Well, where is he?"

"No. Not in that sense. Here's... Actually, I don't know anything except that they took him. Who, what, I don't know. I'll go find out."

I decided to go straight to Chernomyrdin's office. If people are arrested in his building, he has to know what's going on.

They didn't even search us at the security point. Our security guy, Volodya Platonov, burst into the reception area of the Prime Minister of Russia with a pistol in his pocket. We go in. The secretary is in the office. His name is Rotov.

"Where's the boss?"

"Went home. He's resting."

"When?"

"He left around six. Must be tired."

"He got tired awfully early. Nothing happen here today?"

"No, like what?"

"Evstafyev and Lisovsky were arrested here in the White House."

"Who?"

"Who, who... How do I know who arrested them?"

I could see him squirming and avoiding my eyes.

"Rotov, don't lie. If you know something, tell me. I won't squeal on you."

"When Chernomyrdin heard that Arkasha was arrested, he left for the dacha in a hurry. "I'm not in," he says. "Sick.""

"Aha! Wise move. You should learn from him."

"Will you guys please leave, for Christ's sake. Before something happens. I can see in his eyes that Vova has a gun. Go while the going's good."

"All right, we're leaving. Just tell me, did they take them away or are they being kept here, in the White House?"

"I don't know… I don't think they took them out. We have an FSB post in the building. I think that's where they are. I don't know… Just go. That's it. I've told you too much already."

We went back to the City Hall, across the way, to the headquarters. We just sat there. Stunned dullness. What were we to do? Where were we supposed to look for them? We called the police precinct; they didn't know a thing.

Chubais called. "Well, did you find out anything?"

"Not much… But apparently, they're still there in the White House."

"In the White House, you say? That's very important. That means they'll bargain. That's good. Bargaining is very good. Well, watch TV. We're going to start answering them. We have nothing to lose."

"What channel should we watch?"

"NTV, a special broadcast. Kiselyov is going on the air right now."

"Why not ORT?"

"It's complicated. Berezovsky doesn't feel comfortable screwing Korzhakov on the channel that he gave him in the first place."

"I see… Not pretty. And RTR—the same reasons?"

"Sort of. It's a state-owned channel. It's not right. What if we don't win? Then they'll have to answer for it."

"I get it. Business as usual, in other words. Nothing surprising."

"That's it."

"Good for Gusinsky. He didn't let us down."

"He's like us—it's his last chance. If things go bad, Korzhakov will destroy him. You know they're old 'friends.'"

"Why not have fun at the end? Enjoy it."

We sat there, waiting for some serious entertainment.

It was late, around two in the morning. It was on. A special edition of *Segodnya* [Today]. Anxiety and wrath on the face of Yevgeny Kiselyov. An attempt at a state coup… Staff members of Yeltsin's campaign arrested… The attempt will be stopped… The forces of reaction…

I was thinking—what coup? What is he going on about? What nonsense! And then I realized this was the right thing to do. The content didn't matter. The important thing was to scare everyone. Korzhakov and Soskovets had to hear what they weren't expecting at all—that they were conspirators was news to them. They hadn't expected a move like that. Now they were in shock.

This had been their thinking: We'll arrest those carpetbaggers. Chubais will come crawling to save them, give up everything, and get the hell out. That would be find and dandy. Get out, you bastard. Or, maybe we should put all of them in jail! And then instead of "crawling" and "giving everything up," we get this? This is not what we had figured would happen. What do we do now? Stay calm. Things are not developing as planned. Those damned businessmen came up with this.

The mass media picked it up. Ekho-Moskvy, Interfax, other radio stations. And finally ORT and RTR, quoting NTV. The Western press woke up—oh-oh, another coup in Russia. He stole something, or something was stolen from him… Korzhakov and Chubais shot Yeltsin… Berezovsky and Gusinsky are merging their businesses, and in fact, they're the same person… I got in the car and went to Berezovsky's club on Novokuznetskaya. There weren't a lot of people there. The same ones, plus Nemtsov. Everyone was excited and happy. I could see they were scared, but they weren't going to give up.

The rest isn't clear. I remember that the first one to cry "chicken" was Barsukov, and he called Chubais. But Chubais says that he called Barsukov first. In any case, Chubais was shouting… What he was shouting made no sense— "I'll put you behind bars… You won't live to see morning… You'll be sorry you were ever born…. If even one hair on their heads is harmed, you'll answer to me!"

Gusinsky was standing next to him and staring at him as if he were mad: There wasn't a single threat that Chubais could possibly carry out. Just think: He was a man off the street, an official fired from government, whose fault everything was, and he was threatening the director of the FSB. That could be construed as preparing for a terrorist act against a state figure.

In fact, Chubais was having a hysterical fit. And why not—a half-year of extreme pressure, working away with no thought of his own career. There was a ceasefire, and then these guys were planning to put away Arkasha and Sergei— and all of them, in fact. And claim the results of their labor as their own. Sponge off Yeltsin for another four years.

Barsukov's tone was conciliatory. All right, now. Calm down. We'll figure it out. Let's talk in the morning. Nothing will happen to them. I don't know what you're… Apparently, he hadn't expected that much push.

It was around three, maybe a little later. Tatyana Dyachenko called anxiously—her father had called her. He was awake, watching TV. His heart was acting up; they called the doctors. What were we to do?

Another half hour went by. The phone rang:

"Come get your Evstafyev."

"What about Lisovsky?"

"A little later. We'll let him go, too, in about an hour."

"Where are we supposed to pick him up?"

"Come to the White House."

Gotcha! Apparently they got scared. They hadn't expected an attack. Rotov hadn't lied—they were there. They never arrested them officially. They wanted to bargain. It didn't work.

I got in the car and drove to the White House. I stopped and waited. It was dark. He appeared. Not through the door, but through the open gates of the driveway, Arkady walked out, looking bewildered. The people who accompanied him stayed on that side of the gates. I went to meet him. Just like in the movie *Dead Season.* The bright streetlamps illuminated the entrance to the White House on the side facing the Mir Hotel. Everything else was in darkness. I embraced him; we got in the car and drove back to Berezovsky's.

Along the way, he called his wife. "Everything is fine. No, I'm not drunk, but I will be soon. No, don't wait up. Everything's fine. Yes, Alik is with me. We're going to Berezovsky's. I'll explain everything later. All right, good night. Bye."

We got there. Arkasha, Nemtsov, and I had some cognac. Hennessy XO. A glass each. Not bad. The leaders gave us dirty looks. The hell with them… We had another. Good.

"Boris Abramovich, would you have anything to eat around here?'

"Call a waiter, he'll bring the menu. I don't know, there might be something left. It's late."

"I'm starving. They didn't give me anything to eat all day."

"I see… Well, we'll definitely come up with sandwiches. Tell me, Arkasha, what did they ask you?"

"Where I got the money, what else… Nothing else. They tried to scare me, told me they would put me away."

"And you?"

"Me? I said nothing. What money? Don't know nothing about no money. They showed me the carton from a Xerox machine. I denied everything. I know nothing. Not my money, never saw it before."

"And?"

"And what? The whole day was like that. And night. Same thing over and over. Then my blood pressure went up and I refused to answer any more questions."

"Excellent! Good job! Where's his sandwiches, damn it. He earned them. Hee-hee. (Berezovsky's signature giggle.)

They brought back Lisovsky. He was exhausted too. Berezovsky took him to another room. You could see that they had interrogated Lisovsky harder than Arkasha. Otherwise, why would they have kept him an extra hour? Maybe they had more material on him—I don't know, and I don't want to lie.

Gusinsky went over to the window. He could see armed men running along the rooftop of the building across the street. Gusinsky (as calmly as possible): "Oh, they're going to storm us soon. Let's get away from the windows—in case, God forbid, they start shooting. And don't forget, they've got this place bugged."

The phone rang. "Boris Nikolayevich wants to speak with Chubais."

"Put him on."

"No, he wants to talk on the hot line."

"There isn't one here."

"Then have Anatoly Borisovich go where there is one. To HQ in City Hall. The president will call there in a half hour."

We all piled into our cars. Arkasha and Lisovsky went home. They were exhausted. Along the way, I asked Chubais, "What does he want to talk about?"

"I don't know. I think he wants to talk about what to do with all this."

"And you?"

"I'll tell him exactly what happened. Let him decide."

I could see that Chubais was in good form. He hadn't given in; he was ready for battle. He had a plan. We got there. Chubais went into the office with the hot line. He came out quickly.

"How did it go?"

"He wants me to come see him. He said he would be at the Kremlin in an hour."

Gusinsky said the key words that were on all our minds: "You must demand that he fire all of them. Otherwise there is no chance. If they stay on, they'll get rid of us eventually. If Yeltsin refuses, what difference does it make when they finish us off, now or in six months?"

There was no point in arguing, the logic was ironclad. Everyone agreed. Chubais sat there staring into space. He nodded in rhythm with Gusinsky's words. A half hour later he rose silently and left.

He was gone around forty minutes, maybe an hour. We sat in silence. We didn't feel much like talking. Gusinsky and Berezovsky went off to Media Most, on another floor. Chubais called—I'm coming back, get everyone together. He sounded cheerful, more cheerful than he might have been in that situation.

We all gathered again. "Boris Nikolayevich has signed a decree firing Soskovets, Korzhakov, and Barsukov!"

"Oh!" someone exclaimed.

And here Gusinsky said something that could have been prophetic. "At last we have the chance to build a normal country!"

The chance was there. It could have become a normal country. But it did not. Unfortunately. For the time being. But that is a different story.

Then we drank. Chubais, Gusinsky, and Berezovsky, too. Then Chubais, under the influence, went to give a press conference at the Slavyanskaya Radisson Hotel. Along the way, he kept asking me, How do I look? Okay? I was up all night and I've been drinking. We were all in a good mood. I assured him he looked fine. Then at the press conference, Chubais hammered "the last nail in the coffin of Communism." Then I blew off work and went home to bed.

PS: Let me stress it once again. Berezovsky, Gusinsky, and Chubais assured Yeltsin's victory in 1996.

* * *

So that's what my life was like, Igor. Now, here's another funny story. My friends tempted me to fly to Turkey, to Marmaris. In the summer, after Yeltsin's victory. In 1996, as a government official, I had a blue passport. An official one. But our border guards at Vnukovo Airport wouldn't let me out of the country. The Turks wouldn't let me in without a visa, they said. Of course they will, they give you a visa at the airport in Turkey! They replied that that was the procedure with ordinary red passports, but with a blue one, I had to get a visa at their embassy in Moscow. I said, bullshit, a blue passport is cooler than a red one.

They said, the hell with you, go. Just sign a paper that you have no complaints about the border guards. In case you get into trouble in Turkey. I signed, gave it to him, and went to Turkey, gave them ten dollars—they were about to glue the visa into my passport, and suddenly they noticed that the passport is blue. And they took me to jail.

***Midnight Express!* Remember, Alik, the guy in the Turkish prison, and a girl comes to see him. And he says, Just show me your breasts! She shows him, and he sits there panting and jerking off.**

Yes, yes.

Was it like that for you?

Not that radical. But it was an interesting experience. They led me to the cell.

My friends bought me drink and food at duty free, and the Turks let me take it with me. I was alone in the cell—apparently, there weren't any other jerks like me that day. There was just one, yours truly.

All self-important with an important blue passport.

Yes. And the Turkish border guard, feeling sorry for me, asked me if maybe I had another passport of some kind. He would have put the visa in my domestic Soviet passport. Then he could have gone home to bed. Instead, he had to guard the asshole. My friends were doing everything they could; they offered a bribe. But no!

What, the Turks wouldn't take a bribe? You're kidding.

Nope. They didn't take one that night.

The world is upside down.

They told them, "He's a deputy minister, it will be such a scandal!" But they wouldn't listen. I called the embassy. They just laughed. "Sure you're a deputy minister. Fuck off. A deputy minister wouldn't end up in jail so stupidly." And they hung up on me. As usual, our embassy defended the rights of our citizens abroad. They treated a first deputy minister that way!

Did you think kind thoughts about those border guards whose advice you did not take?

Oh, yes, I did.

I realized that I would have to stay in jail until the first flight out to Moscow—that is, until morning.

So I looked around. The room was about twelve square meters. The air conditioner worked. There were a table and two benches: no bed, no cot, no couch. I put out the cognac, I had sliced meat—everything was fine. I asked for a glass, and they brought me water. Murky Turkish water. Some guard came in to visit—he was bored. I poured him a drink, and we knocked it back. My drinking companion spoke neither English nor Russian. I had to reach back into my Kazakhstan childhood for some Turkic words. He pointed to my Rolex and said, "Give it to me, and I'll let you out. You come back into the cell before the flight and I'll take you to the plane. And I'll give you back your cool blue passport." I refused. In 1996, I thought that five thousand for a two-day vacation in Turkey would be wrong. Too expensive.

But now it wouldn't.

That's right. Now I would have given him five thousand dollars to go to the duty free and buy his own watch. I wouldn't give him my Rolex.

It's engraved, right?

Oleg Boiko gave it to me, long ago, when I still lived in St. Petersburg. I would hate to lose it. Otherwise, it's the cheapest Rolex they make, stainless steel. It doesn't even show the date. I'm wearing it now. I can remember the date on my own.

So, I was getting sleepy. I lay down on the table, rolled up my jacket, put it under my head and then… Bedbugs! Bedbugs! I decided to use the standard method of the army, dormitory, and communal flat. I called the guard, who brought me plastic glasses, which I filled with water; I put the table legs in the cups, got back up on the table, and went to sleep. But the wise Turkish bedbugs climbed up the wall and jumped down on me from the ceiling. I realized I wasn't going to get any sleep. All right, I'll finish the cognac, I thought. I drank, but I didn't get any more relaxed. I spent the whole night in misery. In the morning my friends came, gave the Turks some money. They kept my passport. I vacationed for two days, Saturday and Sunday, and then they returned my passport. We got on the plane and went home.

Why didn't they solve the problem right away? Why wouldn't they take money the night before?

The Turks had told us the night before, "The chief of this watch is a total asshole. He's relieved in the morning. Come back then, there will be a normal guy in charge, and you can come to terms with him."

So you were too cheap to spend the five thousand.

I was. We settled it for one. My friends paid for me.

And you looked at this and thought: "Here it is, democracy. When will we have this?"

I saw this version of Turkish democracy: In all the offices, and even in my cell, there was a portrait of Kemal Ataturk. By the way, he resembles Putin—he looks very much like him. The same furrowed brow and yet a smile on the face. I've tried to do that and I can't. Furrowed brow and smile at the same time! Only two people can do that: Ataturk and Putin. Understand? Nope, you can't do it, either: The smile has to be kindly, like the Mona Lisa.

Look! How about now?

No, it's no good. He has that smile on the canonic portraits, with the Kremlin in the background. Putin projects two emotions at once.

You can't rule out the possibility that that is a manifestation of his wisdom.

Of course! I sometimes wake up and think, "Thank God, we have Putin!" What if we didn't? Can you imagine? We'd be like blind kittens…. Terrible to consider.

All right. Let's get back to Turkey. So, what were the lessons learned for you in Turkey? Like, it's time for us to build a democracy where all questions are solved by money? Or what?

The lesson was this: "I'm such a jerk. You have to listen to people. When professionals tell you that you won't be let in, turn around and leave." No, I was so certain that they give everyone visas at the airport.

Well, it seems to me you didn't spend enough time in the clink, and you didn't get enough bites from the Turkish bedbugs. You don't listen to anyone now, either.

I keep living by my own wits… A good story, eh?

Best seller. Did you go back to Turkey after that?

Yes. I had nothing to blame them for—they put me away for a reason. I'd even signed a form saying I wouldn't complain if they arrested me.

If they had tortured you a little longer, you'd listen to experts more.

It's funny story. But it's your turn again, Igor, tell me more about your life in 1996.

I had a little of everything then. First, I almost kicked the bucket. High blood pressure, heart, all kinds of shit. One fellow—we were driving somewhere in the car and I was feeling very bad, like a hangover and then some—and he says, "Let's stop along the way to see a friend of mine, he's a doctor at that hospital—just for a minute, let him take a look at you." All right. And they took my pressure and started to put me on a gurney and drive me off somewhere—like, we can't let a client out of here in this condition, we could be sent to jail. So I had to pay them off to let me out (not out of prison, like you, just out of a harmless hospital) and delete my file. I didn't feel like moving into a hospital ward just like that, without preparation.

So I did my medical care on an outpatient basis. For a while—a whole two months—I didn't drink at all. Can you imagine? I even went to a

wedding—and didn't drink there. And for those long two months that I didn't drink, I seriously lost my interest in life. I thought: "Well, what kind of life is this without drinking? So this is it until I die: gruel-drool-stool?" I pondered this sadly. What the hell did I need a life like this for? Or is it better to have at least this kind of life? And then I found a doctor, the ex-husband of a friend of mine. A professor, a serious fellow. He examined me and said, "Send them all to hell! I have exactly the same thing! You just have to take these pills. And go drink and have fun." So I did. I even took pills for a while. And then I threw them away and lived life as I wanted.

In 1996 I also changed my work. In 1995, as you know, I ran the women's magazine *Domovoi* and taught our readers not only how to be creative in the kitchen and speak about elevated topics, but even how to give birth properly. Around the new year I started working in a holding, as Yakovlev's deputy. What did I do? For one thing, I hired people. It's almost embarrassing to tell you who, they're so famous today. The idea was to form a cohort of invincibles. Pay them money, send them to Paris, give them foreign cars, and in general, keep them happy.

The golden pens.

Sort of.

Tell the truth: If you had met me then—not the deputy prime minister but just Alik—and you had read my articles, would you hire me and train me to be a golden pen?

You see, it's not just a question of literary talent. You need a man who has been through it all already. A tough cookie who can work under certain conditions. It's not just "Sit down and write something pretty." It's, "You've got to fly out in three hours, once there find everything we need, get a real feel for the place that no one else has ever reported, and tomorrow at 1800 hours please dictate your immortal report by phone. Nobody cares how you're going to find it, whom you're going to bribe, how you're going to get back, whether you're going to find inspiration or not, whether you're hungover or not. Just do it."

You don't think I'm capable of that?

I think that you didn't need that then and you especially don't need it now. You really have to work hard at it. Who's going to get you to go in the line of fire for a thousand dollars, or even five? There's no business goal for you in it. It has to be all or nothing. You can't just try it on for general personal development. It's *patria o muerte*. A question of principle—not business.

Where did they work before, these pens?

Panyushkin was at *Matador* magazine. Konstantin Ernst used to publish it, when he was still an ordinary journalist. Before that, Panyushkin wrote his dissertation in Florence (something about the local medieval art) and worked as a translator. I met him in Venice at carnival. I liked his texts then…. Mostovshchikov worked at *Izvestiya*, where he got them to print his essays in the then-popular stream of consciousness genre—or maybe it was stream-of-subconscious… Not everyone understood them. After that, Most worked in a lot of other places.

On TV he had a show called *"Depression."* Andrei Kolesnikov, he worked for *Moskovskie Novosti*. He wrote dispatches from Chechnya. After reading them, I offered him a job, and he took it. I made him an offer he couldn't refuse.

But the writer Kabakov wouldn't leave his job at *Moskovskie Novosti* to work for me. I think his logic was this: *Moskovskie Novosti* was a bastion of democracy, while it wasn't clear what was going on at *Kommersant*. And maybe I didn't have the rank to offer a job to such a well-known writer. Later he did join us, and we worked together a bit. He used to say that it was better to be a decent person and crappy writer than vice versa. That was very subtle and *simpatico*. I loved Kabak (as he is sometimes called; his father was in the army and they did not make him general, feeling that General Abram Kabakov would be a bit much for the Red Army), I loved his serious attitude toward life. He doesn't seem to be against the establishment, he's a sarcastic wit—but when it comes to serious stuff, he's got ideals and principles, the full Monty. My hat's off to him, honestly. Besides Kabakov, there was one other guy who did not come work for me then, and he was another idealist. That was Dima Bykov, founder of the school of courteous mannerists; reporter, poet, writer, who was later tried for foul language. A decent fellow. He did not come to work at *Kommersant*, even though he was in dire straits. His position was that he could not leave his editor-in-chief, Pilipenko, at *Sobesednik*, who had helped him out in difficult times. A nice gesture. I was touched. Too bad that I hadn't been at *Sobesednik* at the same time as Pilipenko. He must have been a decent man too.

Svinarenko's Commentary:

I adore it when people make beautiful gestures, I recall them for years and talk about them—the way I'm doing now. For some reason I need that; there is little that makes me happier than this kind of behavior. I remember there were two friends working at *Kommersant,* who split everything in half—everything they earned. That was the team. One, for instance, would go try a new project, while the other stayed on solid salary and supported both families, his and his friend's. When the first one got established at the new place and was making more money, he would help out both families. I was envious of those two friends, as were many others. This belongs to the sphere of beautiful gestures, absolutely. I'm not naming names here, because it ended sadly. The friends broke up. I have the feeling that at one point, one of them reached an income level that he just couldn't bring himself to share fifty-fifty. Then the second one got up there, too; they could have shared honorably, but it was too late. The train had left the station. And we've all seen lots of relationships ruined by money.

I remembered Okudzhava telling me how he would walk around Paris and try to imagine that he had emigrated and lived there. He didn't like it. Tolstaya talks about the grimness of life abroad. That it's boring. And I realized that it was tiring and somehow pointless... If you move permanently abroad, you leave life—the one you had been living here—so radically, that it could be easily, without exaggeration, compared to actual, physical death. You remember what used to be, some people remember you—in principle you can telephone and send your photographs, but it's comparable to someone having a dream about a dead person. Or seeing a ghost. And if you change your mind and return, your niche in this life will have been filled. There's someone else working and drinking at your desk; your friends have new, living friends. If you left behind a wife or girlfriend, you'll find that she has someone new. Sometimes, the niche is not just filled by someone, it's bricked over. That happened to Solzhenitsyn, for instance. He came back and the niche was gone. There's a wall there now. He went out on the deck, but the deck was gone.

* * *

Let's see, Alik: What else did I do besides hiring people? The manager of one of the *Kommersant* publications left. So that year I was managing away, and suddenly I thought: "Why haven't I written anything in a long time? All right, say that I don't have time, I'm working hard and I'm stressed. But it's interesting: Would I be able to write something if I wanted to?" I wasn't a hundred percent sure. What if I couldn't? And what

was I going to do for the rest of my life, manage? Tell others what to do, when you can't do anything yourself—nothing at all? It was horrible.

Were you afraid you had lost your vocation?

Well, I have various specialties. Mason, photographer, translator, some other stuff. But those were from another life. Here I was, afraid that I would be like other people, clinging to the job tooth and nail, plotting, stabbing people in the back…There are a lot of people who don't know how to do anything but are determined to hold on to a sinecure and live well at any cost. Dividing things, reselling, using position and insider information… When you don't know how to do anything yourself, you're forced to live like that. You can't send anyone to hell.

That's true.

So you have to sit there and take it. Step to the right or to the left, and you're out of there, and you don't know how to do anything else. I remember the horror I felt, even now. And then I thought, well, I'll muster my strength, concentrate, and sit down to write. Maybe it will work. I was very worried. But I wrote… And breathed a sigh of relief.

So, the elections, Alik. I didn't ask myself, do I like Yeltsin or not? It didn't matter, he had to win.

There was a choice. Grigory Yavlinsky wanted to be a candidate. He said that he had 16% of the vote and Yeltsin had only 5%. So all the resources should be shifted over to support Yavlinsky. But Berezovsky knew that Gusinsky liked Yavlinsky and realized that if his star rose, then Gusinsky's influence would increase greatly and disproportionately. That was one of the things that kept Yavlinsky from winning. Berezovsky put it this way: "It's hard to argue with the fact that Yavlinsky has 16% and Boris Nikolayevich has 5%. But Yavlinsky is never going have any more than 16%, even if you shit yourself. But Yeltsin has 5% and he has room to grow. Because there is an electorate that will vote for him, but never ever for Yavlinsky." And that was right. By summer Yavlinsky was not even in third place, but fourth—General Lebed had wedged himself in.

There are people to this day who say that the whole election in 1996 was rigged and that everyone who was supposed to knew how it would end up.

No! Uh-huh.

I really believed that there was a possibility of the Communists taking power again and all kinds of shit happening in the country.

At Davos, Zyuganov made promises. He said, No we won't push too hard on entrepreneurs. But we will, of course, pay serious attention to the results of privatization. We won't be vicious—we'll leave restaurants in private hands, and the fast food places, too.

I remember that there was a secret plenary session of the Central Committee of the Communist Party, just before the elections.

Wait, Igor: it was secret. How do you know about it?

I knew about it. It was so secret that I didn't even show my face there.

Why not? You have a perfectly Communist face.

Really? Thanks. So I called in five reporters separately and told each one his assignment. I said, "You're going in alone; all hopes are on you."

Did all five get in?

No. The first one came back—they didn't let him in. The second and third... They were recognized as journalists and thrown out. Then came the fourth, who considered himself a very tough reporter. Give me lots of money, he said, since I wasted half a day on your assignment. Where's the result? Did you bring an audio tape? No! But if I couldn't do it, then it was a mission impossible. Hm... And then, in comes the fifth guy, a new hire; I didn't know what he could do yet, and I just sent him along to keep my conscience clear. He came in, casually tossed the cassette on my desk, and went out for a beer. As if it were the simplest task ever.

And didn't ask for a lot of money.

So we listened to the tape. There was unique information on it. The moderator says: "We're just us here, no spies got in, we caught them all. So we can discuss the main issue freely. Here it is: We're promising that we will raise pensions and student stipends as soon as we get in, and we'll index deposits, and give back the frozen assets, and we'll give huge child support money. We're making all the right promises. But I have to tell you this—for those who haven't figured it out yet—there is no money for this and no place to get it. So we have to start thinking now how to get out of these promises if we win the elections. Let's start looking for arguments about why we made the promises but aren't keeping them." We were very happy to print that transcript. I even thought that Zyuganov was glad not to have won the presidency. He may have helped the Yeltsin team on purpose. I thought about it: Say he had won. Then some proletarians would burn down some oligarch's estate. And then would come the moment of truth. What would be the reaction of the Communist President? Whatever it was, it would be end of him. If he supported the comrades in their class struggle, people would start fires all over the country. Disarray and horror all over again. Collapse and so on. NATO forces would come in to calm down the Russian rebels. Nothing good there. And if Zyuganov decided to punish the arsonists, sending in the Cossacks with whips or the SWAT teams against his own people, against the electorate that voted for the loyal Party man—what would the Reds say? In either case, Zyuganov would not be president for very long.

Why not? If he stood as head of the national uprising… You deserve it, that sort of thing.

Come on! Estates burning, that's terrible.

Back in 1996 there were only two or three estates, anyway.

Then they'd be robbing wine cellars….

You post soldiers, in that case.

It would be chaos, and it would require harsh measures to restore order. In any case, it scared Zyuganov.

Maybe. It's a very personal reaction. Maybe he really did not want to deal with that. It's easier being in the opposition. Although, they actually had a positive scenario. They would have gotten rid of the thieving democraps. "Put the Yeltsin gang on trial!" They could have lasted a term just on that. And then it would be 1999, oil prices going up; and then the Communists would have enriched the nation, and everyone would have forgotten that unfortunate incident when they turned away from the choice of their fathers, from the Great October Revolution of 1917.

Going back to my life: In the fall of 1996, I gave up management work. A lot of it seemed very boring. I didn't like it.

Svinarenko's Commentary:

With a light, lyrical sadness, I watched people undergo changes under the influence of power and money. Money is a serious thing; it's a universal equivalent for good reason (only of material values, but that is a subtlety that many people are too lazy to consider). It's not that I had idealized my acquaintances and colleagues before, no. You don't go to work to find friends. But the point was: If it's only business and nothing beyond that, it would be good to determine that from the outset, make the plan while still onshore. But when you used to have a different relationship and then radically shift gears, that's not comfortable. In a sense, it's morally traumatic. The funny part is that I used to criticize Yakovlev for his way of doing business back then. I didn't like it, and I insisted that he do it in what I considered the right way. That was my big issue back then. Sometimes he would make a decision, knowing that it wasn't businesslike, but just because he wanted to do it that way. But he demanded that we execute things with the same zealousness—as if something useful could come of it. I would offer to hire special people who would bustle about wasting time, and amusing the boss. A jester battalion.

One would think, what did it matter to me? Just do your job, get your salary, and don't give a shit about anything else. That may be the way. It's what I thought at first. I tried to obey all orders without thinking or arguing, but it was such a waste of energy and brought about such a loss of interest in life, that it wasn't worth it. Sometimes I would prepare a decision on a serious personnel issue, find all the right people, make all the arrangements—on his assignment—and then he'd go and put in his own person. My problem wasn't that I wanted to teach Yakovlev how to do business—who am I to do that? But he should have told me ahead of time which issues we would solve seriously, and where it was about his friends. But he didn't listen to me, naturally. That may be typical of all big-time bosses and businessmen. Yakovlev was the first major capitalist that I observed at close hand.

I said to him angrily: "You should sell the business while there's still something to sell—you won't get very far acting this way." He did sell it, but later, in 1999. Back in 1996, I had a big fight with him. I didn't just quit being his deputy—we both agreed on that—but I got packed up to go: How could we continue working together? But he stopped me and first offered me a position as a privileged writer and then sent me as far from him as he could—to America. That was a sober, adult approach: nothing personal. He probably didn't want to see me anymore, but why not use the disgraced reporter for the good of his personal publishing house? When he came up with the idea of sending me to the U.S., I went into my "exile" with interest. Thanks to the fact that I had not forgotten how to write articles, I returned to the creative life.

In the fall of 1996 I also traveled to Nizhny Novgorod and met Boris Nemtsov, a young politician with prospects. He was still a simple governor then, young and feisty, curly-haired, immediately informal and friendly. The very first time he met me. Good for him! That's a reporter's approach. That's how a reporter should work: pretend that he's known you a hundred years. And that's how you work with the electorate.

I had a long conversation with Nemtsov's mother, Dina Yakovlevna. I adored her. Such natural reactions to everything, no pretense. Back then—I don't know about now—she lived in a Khrushchev-era tenement on the edge of town, even though her son was governor. She told me that under the Soviet regime she did political agitation: Boris made her. She obeyed her son.

I made my article sound scary—here's your next president. And made it clear that since our country has been led by all kinds, it was time for a Jewish President. Nemtsov had beaten Putin to flying in a fighter jet by then, too... And the city had a good restaurant called "At Vitalyich's." On a pedestrian street, like our Arbat. They had well-trained waiters and fresh fish, neither of which we had in Moscow then.

* * *

Let me add something else, Alik, There also was a new start-up in late 1996, *Stolitsa* magazine.

I remember it. I think it was unsuccessful.

No money means it's a failure? You businessmen! Your only measure is money. Loads of people still think that *Stolitsa* was a breakthrough. I'm keeping my opinion to myself.

The magazine had pretensions to a new aesthetic. It was a mix of literature with journalism. Why, did you leave your job to go work for them?

I didn't have to leave; it was all part of the same publishing house. I was *Stolitsa's* special correspondent in America. In the city of Moscow in the state of Pennsylvania. Yakovlev offered me the chance to go live there, write for the magazine, and then turn it into a book. Which I did.

You were there for a year, right?

A year, but I traveled frequently to the city of Moscow in the state of Russia, so I didn't drop out of life here. It was a wonderful schedule.

How many times did you come to the Russian Moscow in a year?

Month there, month here. I managed to live two lives. If I hadn't left Russia, I wouldn't have written more articles than I did for *Domovoi*. And on the other hand, if I had just stayed in the U.S., I would have written the

one book, nothing more. This way I did two jobs. A five-year plan in four years. Three shifts with two hands for one salary. Seriously, this is the way you should live. Two weeks a month you do one job, and two another one. And it's better to be in a different city, if not a different country. When I left here, I left behind one set of keys, papers, and notebooks and took different ones with me. And then lived a month in a different country, in a different house, drove a different car along different roads, spoke a different language and saw different people. The dollars were the same, however.

You could have set up a different family, too.

No, that's bullshit.

And what did you do there, in Pennsylvania?

I lived. I wrote articles and sent them to Moscow. I met locals, talked to them. The population was 3,000. I didn't know them all, but as for the lawyers, journalists, cops, doctors, businessmen, librarians, and firemen— I drank with them regularly. I wrote about anything that was the least bit interesting.

I read your work.

Yes? Well, I'm just telling you the concept here. Not everything worked out. For instance, I didn't get to interview a local celebrity—a woman who was just over three feet, three inches (1 meter 10 centimeters) tall. She died at the age of 99 just after I arrived. But I did interview a bear hunter, a developer, Miss Moscow, the owner of the strip club, a Vietnam veteran, and other worthy folk. There are a lot of Moscows in America. Over twenty. This was how I picked mine: It was closest to civilization. It was 111 miles to the George Washington Bridge, which is the entrance to Manhattan—straight east along Interstate 80. An hour and a half, if there's no traffic. I went all the time. Almost every weekend. You get off the bridge on 176th Street, if I'm not mistaken, and head downtown—that is, turn right. First you're in a black neighborhood, Harlem, with a purely Soviet setting: dust, litter everywhere, old rusty cars, people with dead eyes, dressed shabbily, suspicious characters rummaging in garbage cans, people walking and driving against the light. The lower down you get in Manhattan, the more civilized it is.

Did you visit Roman Kaplan at his restaurant, The Russian Samovar?

Among others. He's got a great bar. Then there's Brighton Beach. The Capuccino pelmeni place. The Paris Café. The Continental Restaurant. Well, you know all that. Should I write a commentary about it?

You've already written a book.

Yes. It took me a long time to write it… Two years. Without a break.

Svinarenko's Commentary:

I will quote briefly from my introduction to *Moscow Across the Ocean*, in which I explained the purpose of my plans: why I went to America and why I came back. I find it amusing to read today. Back in 1996, life was different, simpler and more naïve.

I traveled American byways and highways for a long time. Sometimes, as I drove down deserted prairie highways on a late autumn evening, I would think that my plan was meaningless, and when I spent the night in yet another cheap motel near an impoverished Indian village, it seemed crazy. You lie in bed, drink beer, watch TV, and listen to the wind howling outside. It seemed that it wouldn't work, that the provincials still scared by the Cold War would turn me in to the CIA for being a Soviet spy; they certainly wouldn't give me any information. Me, a potential enemy, a hostile foreign journalist, suspiciously dropped behind the lines into the superpower and bastion of NATO.

Strangely, no one ever took me to the CIA.

So, I traveled around half of the USA, saw all those Moscows, picked one, and settled there.

I lived there and suddenly realized: Americans on the whole are nice people! I was very cozy in their quiet provinces. The country is pleasant, tolerant, warm, almost like home, and not like abroad at all—it's a place where you don't feel like an alien. I might have asked them to let me move in—if I hadn't figured out a few important things in the course of my expedition. For instance, I felt like a street hooligan who had come to talk to the children of a professor, the ones who can play the violin. At first it was interesting; everyone was clean and polite, this and that. But I've had my visit and enough already, basically, I've got my hooligan stuff to get back to—playing hooky, smoking in the bathroom, shooting craps, fighting after school, making filthy passes at the A-student girls, learning how to whistle, and drinking cheap wine. I felt sorry for myself—why should I force myself into politically correct behavior, drink moderately, and smile constantly?

Why live such a boring life when life is so short as it is? I went back home and for a long time—a whole week!—I would examine the faces of Russian citizens with a perverted greed. They pouted like hurt children, with broad Asiatic cheekbones, showed the after-effects of various excesses, had no imported political correctness or polite smiles—simple, honest, just the way they were. You have yours, I have mine.

The author of this book acquired unique experiences in the course of writing it. Yes, there are tons of people who know more about America than I do. But! They do not come back to tell us about it. They would be bored writing for strangers, and you would be bored reading what they write about an unfamiliar place. They get most of their knowledge when it's too late: They pass the point of no return, they're ready to bid farewell to the past, they are practically New Americans at heart. No longer strangers, but no longer one of us—like a patient on an operating table in the middle of a sex-change operation.

Naturally, few of us are interested in the hopes and aspirations of natural Americans or immigrants—this is a narrow special interest. But we can't resist hearing about the strange events that befell a man who lived for only a brief time in an American city called Moscow. That Moscow is the justification for the attention paid to the American life occurring around it.

Leaving is always dying a little. Leaving for a place far away and for a long time, and to a cult country like America, means dying quite a bit. So my notes are like memoirs of clinical death, and not just once, but periodically (like mass media)—a back-and-forth death, when you keep changing your point of view without ever losing interest in your earthly life in Russia... I flew across the ocean once a month so as not to be torn away irrevocably, so as not to give in totally to the narcotic effects of American life, so as to leave a trail for my return.

What can I add today to what I wrote then? About America—what do I recall now? Here's what: How well the powerful PR worked, insisting that America is nothing but variations on the themes of Manhattan and the expensive houses of California. I now think more often about the shabbier back roads, the dusty cheap bars in the provinces, the towns inhabited by hard-smoking sleepy American Indians and slow-moving blacks, motels with thick carpets, the dull fat truck drivers at plastic tables in diners—like our Soviet cafeterias—and the Russian immigrants who brag about America as if they had discovered it or built it, instead of coming to find everything ready for them.

I am also bothered by the thought that we've destroyed nature around our big cities, but they've preserved it. Whatever city you take, except the big megapolises, you can get into real woods full of wild animals after a half hour's drive. People come home from a short day's work, pull themselves together, get in their jeeps, with long metal cases for their rifles bolted to the floor, and go hunting. They come home with a deer carcass. And in the morning, back to work. They go hunting the way we go out into the courtyard for a game of dominoes.

There was also the language barrier. I arrived in the U.S. as a special correspondent, but I knew the language, well—like everyone else. That is, I could understand some things that were written and make myself clear to people, sometimes. That was it. But when people spoke to me, I rarely understood what they wanted. You ask them to repeat, they say it again, but it doesn't help. Yet I needed to talk to people, just to get along and also for my work. I felt like banging my head against the wall, thinking if I break my head, I'll be happier. That was my precise summation of the situation. Maybe I should just give it up and go back to Moscow? What kept me sane was the realization that no one ever taught me English, strictly speaking. You couldn't count English lessons in a grade school in a mining town in the middle of the steppes. I never had linguaphones, tutors, special schools, none of that. There was no reason for me to know English. Then how did I pass admissions exams to university? I'll tell you: by studying the teach-yourself textbook by Bonk-Koti and reading adapted mystery books with a dictionary. My foreign language at Moscow State University was German. I know that it was not right to take on the assignment with so little preparation, but that's how it worked out.

So what happened then, you may ask. I remembered how I had studied German. When I went to Leipzig University in the fall of 1979, my language skills were adequate to read small articles about class struggle in the deathly boring newspaper *Neues Deutschland*. My goal was not only to work in the library, which I probably could have managed, but to talk with professors and attend lectures. I had to learn German fast. This is how I did it: I'd go to a beer hall every day, sit down with speakers of the language, and talk to them about life over a mug. Also, on a daily basis, I watched TV and went to the movies. Even with a meager start, you begin to catch on in a month's time, as my experience showed.

I drew on this experience in the U.S. I had more to work with there. Once I settled on Moscow, Pennsylvania, I spoke with the owner of the central establishment there, the Hard Rock Café, and said, "Listen, old man, find me an apartment that is walking distance from your place. Walking distance, so I can get home when I'm drunk. If you do that, I'll come here as it if it were my job. Without the 'as if.' I will do my preliminary research here, filtering them like a baleen whale filters krill, and I will interview everyone who is worthy." Do I need to tell you that Jim Kenosky, which was the owner's name, personally rushed out to find me an apartment? I had one in three days.

That was the first thing I did. The second stage was buying a television set. In America they have closed captioning, so that all films and many shows are subtitled. This is done for the deaf, whom beginning language learners resemble. When everything you hear is also written out for you, you achieve clarity very quickly. To your great surprise, you see that the indistinguishable verbal flow of American speech actually can be deciphered. That it is a comprehensible human language.

The third stage: the audio book section of bookstores. Almost everything that comes out of the book market comes out in two forms: on paper and on cassettes (or CDs). This is not so much for the blind, but for drivers. The distances are vast, the roads are good, the traffic jams major. People listen to books in cars: mysteries, the classics, and most frequently, how-to books—how to lose weight, get rich, learn to write books, stop worrying, and so on. First you buy both versions, recording and print, and use them together. But then, one fine day, you suddenly realize that you understand spoken American English! That is the point of no return. You realize that you can live there. Then things go on from there. You should read books on how to speak American English properly and beautifully—that's a separate topic. I've written half a textbook on American spoken English. I should get around to finishing it. It will be a bestseller. Unless of course, you already know how to say "snot" in English—then you can manage without my help.

* * *

Let's get back to our year. Tell me what you think about Dudayev, Alik? Was he killed in 1996 or is he in hiding somewhere?

I think he's dead.

What about General Lebed? Did you work with him?

No. I barely knew him.

One of my classmates, Shura Barkhatov, was his press secretary.

Chubais worked closely with him. Chubais had gone through a very difficult period, after Yeltsin's re-election, when Dr. Akchurin operated on the president. For several months, Chubais was running the country. He had become chief of staff after the election. First they prepared Yeltsin for heart surgery; then he had a recovery period. That was when Yeltsin gave Chubais his portrait inscribed "Together again."

Yes… What else was there in 1996? The apartment building explosion in Kaspiisk. The first swallow, in effect, Alik… And there was a bomb at the Kotlyakovsky Cemetery in Moscow, too. And then, Russia got $10.2 billion from the IMF.

There you go! To fill in the craters after the elections. The West did help us, after all. When things got tough.

I went to Chechnya in 1996. Wrote an article. I remember how I got there: I flew into Sleptsovsk, hired a car and driver and drove to Grozny. We get into town and the driver asks, "Where do you want me to take you?" I had gotten several invitations when I was in Moscow. In Khankala, at military headquarters, Colonel so-and-so would supply me with a bed. I also had the address of some Makhmud, on Gagarin Street— he kept an inn for visiting reporters. Sleeping on a cot in a shed cost a hundred dollars. I hadn't made up my mind beforehand. I thought I'd decide on the spot, see how things were. The driver was pushing for an answer because we were approaching the determining crossroads. I tuned in to my subconscious and I realized I had to go be with our boys.

At the time, our reporters liked to write lies about the valorous Chechen Robin Hoods, bearded and sexy, real romantics. So I said, "Take me to Khankala." And I moved into the barracks. The young soldiers told me happily that they were fed better in Chechnya than they were back in training, and they were lucky to be there. There was a captain there, a poster boy for Russia—blue-eyed with light brown hair. We sat and drank—I had brought along duty-free whisky in plastic bottles, very handy for travel. And he opened up to me. He unbuttoned his faded uniform jacket and from the inside pocket over his heart, where they used to make you carry your Communist party card, he took out a folded newspaper clipping. He unfolded it and showed me a photo of Gennady Zyuganov. Wow, I said. (I was delighted by the cheap literary aspect of this plot line.) The man was ready to die for the Homeland, for Zyuganov. And he said to me, "I'm surprised by you. You're smart people, you have to realize that Zyuganov is a honest and radiant man, that he's the only one like that we have. You have to do such violence to your nature to attack Gennady Andreyevich, he's a holy man! How can you embark on such blasphemy? No, no, I'm not criticizing you, I'm not angry, I'm not cursing you. I simply want to understand what mechanism allows you to lose your humanity to the degree where you can no longer love

Communists. It's all money! If not for the money, if you could vote from your heart, you would vote for Gennady Andreyevich."

I also talked with General Shamanov in Chechnya. He and I flew in a helicopter to Shali. We flew low so that they couldn't knock us down from the ground. If you fly low, the helicopter isn't noticed until it's too late to aim accurately. In Shali some local teenager had been killed—accidentally, sort of. So the local elders were gathered to meet with Shamanov. They brought the troops in, too, in time for our arrival. The soldiers were brought in, and they surrounded Shali. Shamanov spoke very sensibly. I found him very impressive as negotiator and orator. I hadn't expected that from a warrior, from a general. I also drove off with officer friends to look over checkpoints. At night. On the way, our armored troop carrier conked out. There we were, in the steppe... Let's call for help on the walkie-talkie. Nope, the batteries were dead. The typical story. Another ATC came by and we talked them into towing us back to Khankala.

Like you, Igor, I had gone to Chechnya in 1996. It was in September. Berezovsky came to me—he was deputy chairman of the Security Council—and he said, "Listen, we've got a trip as part of developing the Khassasvyurt peace process, in the framework of developing dialogue with the new government of Chechnya. Let's go." I said, "Borya, that's the last place I want to go." No, he says, let's go, I'll be bored by myself. All right, we went. I took my deputy with me, Sergei Molozhavy. He's also a colonel—in the Red Army, not the KGB. So we went to Chechnya. The agenda was as follows: The head of the delegation was the chairman of the Security Council, who had just come in to replace Lebed—none other than Ivan Petrovich Rybkin—and then it was Berezovsky, me, Sergei Loginov from the presidential administration, and a couple of other officials. We got into a Tu-134, flew into Severny Airport. The Chechens named the airport after Sheik Mansur. He was an eighteenth-century hero of theirs. We spent some time there, then got into cars and headed for Grozny. We had a mixed convoy, Chechens with automatic weapons and our Spetsnaz. After a while we reached Grozny. It was in ruins, like Stalingrad.

Exactly! It was there that I realized what the phrase the "abomination of devastation" really meant.

Along the way the officers who joined us told me this: "In the course of the war—and the war had lasted 18 months by then—we have taken it three times. No sooner do we take it, rebuild, and repair something when the orders come: Bring out the troops. We leave, the Chechens come back. Then the order is: We storm the city again. Everything we built and restored is shot to hell again... And then we have to rebuild it! We take the money for restoration, but we do a half-hearted job... Then, we have to leave again. We do..." So in eighteen months, they stormed Grozny three times. Not counting the first.

Apparently, there must be a reason for that, some mechanism behind it. It didn't just happen out of stupidity....

Stalingrad was taken once, but Grozny three times! Plus the first time. Plus the storming of Grozny during Putin's war. In other words, Grozny was taken five times. Just imagine, the firepower of a battalion compared to World War II has grown by five times. So five times five, Grozny was destroyed twenty-five times more powerfully than Stalingrad. The only thing is that they didn't have air bombing. Although maybe they did, from helicopters....

By accident, purely.

And so we came to some school. The Chechens behaved like ordinary Chechens, we didn't hear anything new from them—zero sincerity. It was September and hot, but they were wearing mink hats and their sheepskin capes, showing off... Here's what else made a great impression on me: A huge crowd of mothers with photographs of their sons ran up to our delegation, after those Chechens. And the mothers asked, "Where are our children? Have you seen them? If they're in prison, in the name of Christ, let them out!" They had come to Grozny on their own money, and they didn't have a lot.

Oh, yes, I saw many of them in Khankala.

But they were right in Grozny, Igor, not Khankala, but Grozny. Damn, what a hard life these women have... So they came to that school and they stood there and made noise, and the men with automatic rifles tried to chase them. And Loginov said to me, "I know the fellow that woman over there is searching for—he's in a cellar, in the house of Movladi Udugov. And Movladi has told her twenty-five times, 'I don't know where he is.' Some officer said to him, 'Let the boy out, she's all alone, no husband, he's her only son.' They say Movladi came home one evening and shot the guy. I don't know if it's true or not... And then he said, 'He's not there. I've looked everywhere. There's nothing I can do, I swear.'" That's the story I was told..

So then we went back to Severny. We got into helicopters with Chechens, not separately.

Their leader then was Basayev. All the Chechens, and our guys, too, were a little hyper, looking into each other's eyes, but Basayev behaved differently... He said very little and looked at the floor. We flew to see Ingushetia President

Ruslan Aushev in Magas. One of the presidential residences was built there. In size it was nothing more than a good house on Rublyovka. Just a house, with bedrooms and a dining room. And in this house there were Chechens with automatic rifles, unwashed, dirty. We weren't particularly fresh, either—we'd been on the road all day. They gave us rooms… Brought us food and vodka. Some people were in the living room, negotiating, and the rest were drinking in their rooms. I sat with the guys, but every now and then they called me in for consultations on how to divide up property between Russia and Chechnya.

Everyone drank?

Everyone. But then there was the final dinner, for a select group. I was invited. And there, interestingly, Basayev and Udugov did not drink—quite demonstratively (they're all religious, you know). But the rest—Rybkin, Berezovsky, me—we all drank. And Zakayev drank with us. Then Zakayev danced. Making those yips. Zakayev is very… secular, I guess. You could see that he was an actor. And not a fighter. He was so happy that it was all over, that there was an amnesty, that he could go back to Moscow to visit his whores. That was the expression on his face. And then we drank some more. To friendship, to the great Russian people, to the great Chechen people. Shit, just a month before that they were killing us, we were killing them. And now we're talking about the indestructible friendship between Chechens and Russians. It was very Caucasian somehow.

It was my turn to toast. I said that I had grown up in Kazakhstan with Chechens, and we lived all right—let's keep it up. We Russian Germans had our reasons to be mad at Russians, but if we all do that, we'll never put an end to it. We have to stop. Along those lines.

You also noted that everything was destroyed and looked horrible.

It was awful. And I noticed this. Destruction, Grozny, villages, all those Vedenos and Shalis. So the Chechens would arrive at Ruslan's, come into a decent house with running water, hot water, flushing toilets… They'd go to take showers; they were fed at a table, with hot food, not out of cans. And the next day, they'd be going back to mud, camouflage, destruction… What for?

Did you notice that it wasn't all destruction in Grozny, Alik? There were also lots of new three-story houses made of red brick. They got a lot of building done in that war. Probably using slave labor, as they like to do.

I assumed those could have been built before the war. The Chechens and Ingush were the biggest group of migrant laborers in Soviet times. They built pig sheds all over Russia.

I remember when the photographer and I left Grozny, with an unofficial driver we paid to take us—we went straight ahead. As soon as we crossed the border into Ingushetia, I immediately felt a sharp change in my sensations. I relaxed, looked around, noticing the clouds and trees. And when we reached Pyatigorsk, we saw beautiful, quiet, peaceful life.

And when you drive into Pyatigorsk….

Yes, you're completely relaxed. Everyone you see is a civilian, no one in uniform, no gun barrels in sight. So, straight to a bar. I'm not a war journalist, I don't often get out for that. But I have friends who started covering wars and are addicted to it now. It's like a real drug. I understand it heightens your sensations. When you come back from a war, you are very aware of being alive. And if you are alive, that alone is very good, it's enough. That's a wonderful feeling! You won't find it in ordinary life. Without making major investments. That's why people go to hot spots, I think. Of course, you tend to drink a lot while you're there. Some people become real alcoholics as a result. I knew how attractive that would be and tried not to drink too much. I seem to have managed.

By the way, Igor, at that time Berezovsky impressed me. He's a brave guy. He was the de facto head of the delegation—Ivan Rybkin played a decorative role, it seemed to me, though maybe I was wrong. But Berezovsky had promised that he would take care of me there, and he did. He always took me in the car with him, in the helicopter… He knew what Chechnya was, that getting lost there was the end. It was my first time there, and so he kept an eye on me, never lost sight of me, even though it was a big delegation. He was always counting heads, you know, like a teacher on a field trip.

So you liked Berezovsky there?

Berezovsky behaved very well, like a real man.

16.

1997

The Sixteenth Bottle

T *his bottle may be the most dramatic and event-filled one of the entire book. Kokh leaves the government this year, insisting it was completely voluntary and that no one fired him! The oligarchic mass media tries to disprove this and they take on the "writers' case"… Unlike Kokh, who keeps entering big politics and leaving, Svinarenko remains the same "simple" reporter. He spends the year peacefully and quietly in America, in the state of Pennsylvania, and writes a book about the American city of Moscow—as well as a textbook on American English, which he has still not finished.*

Let me explain, Alik. I came home for New Year's from Pennsylvania. Almost all my friends were out of Moscow, almost every normal person had gone off on vacation. Some were skiing, others were in Egypt, the simpler types were in Paris. I remember sighing bitterly and saying, "Boy, and I haven't been abroad in a year." Everyone present laughed, thinking that I was joking, having just returned from the U.S. where I had been driving all over for six weeks. But I wasn't joking. It was a strange trick of perception: In that context, America wasn't abroad for me, not at all. We're used to thinking of going abroad for a vacation, a rest, drinking in cheerful company, in beautiful surroundings, and good weather. But when you're driving back roads through the cornfields of Oklahoma or Arkansas (alone, by the way), with no one around but Indians and stoned blacks… It's not even that they are of a different race, what's important is that they are strangers, with a completely different life—you don't seem to have anything in common with them. They have no education and a barely noticeable interest in life; this does not make them great conversationalists. In the deep back country, everything seems dusty, the roads are potholed, the houses poor, and people look at strangers suspiciously, with sullen faces—like Russians. I saw wooden gas stations; you won't find those in the worst backwaters of Russia.

That's because they built those gas stations when we didn't even have cars.

And they have these diners scattered here and there, cheap cafeterias with plastic tables and disposable glasses. Sometimes, I'd go into a general store, and it was like ours on the *kolhozes*—horrible smell, rat poison and fertilizer next to the hams and potato chips. The whole thing was very, very far from resort life.

So it didn't feel like being abroad. More like being in Bashkortostan…

Not like being abroad, no. Dirty, drunken bums hanging around liquor stores with filthy yellow windows. Not abroad at all. I could have gone somewhere in Russia like Zlatoust or Kargasok and gotten the same effect. So these black guys with hangovers loaf outside liquor stores, like in Russia, hoping someone will buy them a drink. They stare at you when you go in to get a bottle of scotch to have a nightcap in your simple motel on the plains, in your bed in front of the TV; you can also find hotels that don't have bars or any stores for miles around…

I understand, these are the people President Nixon called the Silent Majority of his fellow Americans. And there are tens of millions of them.

And that is so depressing. I thought, well, why the hell am I doing this, who's going to read my stories about this? I was afraid that I would start drinking… Horrible. The country lives that way—all crooked and wrong. One-legged blacks, drunken Indians, whites living the life of Indians and blacks… Single mothers with lives in a downward spiral. Everyone in sneakers, jeans, and those horrible T-shirts… Like a uniform. I thought, maybe I should drop the project and go back to Moscow. But that time I came back without my stuff, just temporarily. I decided to settle in America and write amusing texts from there, whatever it took. Make candy out of shit. So I came back for the holidays.

By then I had posted a lot of dispatches from America. I thought they had been published. But they were lying around the office, because *Stolitsa* was way behind schedule. And I had been worried that they needed my stuff urgently, I'd stayed up nights, writing… As soon as I was back in Moscow, Yakovlev made me rewrite my first report from America several times. He wanted to create a new style of writing that he could picture in his mind but could not demonstrate. And he couldn't compose a piece in the needed manner, either—he had stopped writing a long time before that.

He used to write?

Yakovlev? That's what made him famous in the first place! Back in the Soviet days. He was the first to write about the Lubertsy phenomenon—it was a real hit.

After the break, I flew back to the States. I arrived in my Moscow there and started interviewing the locals. The central character in my stories was Danny Edwards, mayor of Moscow. He was not a full-time mayor; that was his social responsibility. He earned a living be making ceramic cats, the kind people used to sell in our outdoor markets in the provinces.

With pretensions to creating masterpieces?

No, he knew that it was hackwork done for the money. He's an American, not a member of the Soviet intelligentsia! He also understood that it didn't matter what you made money out of: It could be shit, it didn't matter. As long as you had it.

Yes. I'm always impressed by Westerners, especially Americans... I feel that this may be the source of their strength—that while still in middle age they can admit to themselves that they're not going to invent gunpowder, write *War and Peace*, or create a masterpiece, but they still have to feed their families and be human beings. And so they sculpt cats. Day in and day out, stubbornly. They look clean and neat. When a Russian realizes that he's not ever going to write *War and Peace*, he starts destroying the world! See? Every one of us thinks he's Schopenhauer, an entire universe. That's why I like that humbleness—it's part of the Protestant culture on which America is based.

There are lots of people there who readily do any kind of work! Dig a ditch and then fill it in, day after day, without end—fine. The person will think he's got a great job. I remember sitting in a bus station when this fine-looking gentlemen came in—gray-haired, erect, head held high. He nodded to the ticket sellers, and I figured he was the boss or some lawyer who decided to take a bus ride. But he went into the back and came out in work clothes and yellow rubber gloves, and with that same lawyerly stride he proudly went into the toilet and started cleaning. What a picture! He wasn't some retired granny…

… abandoned by her grandchildren, who were all Schopenhauers, and her children, all Leo Tolstoys.

And this man was happy! A job is a job, what difference does it make what it is? The minimum wage then was $5.50. You couldn't pay people less. But a man could feed himself on that money, get a loan to buy an apartment.

$5.50 an hour is a thousand a month, and not very high taxes.

Out in the sticks you can get by on that. You can't do much in New York City on a thousand a month. One of the bars in American Moscow had rooms upstairs. I wondered what they were for. Did people bring girls they met in the bar up there? It turned out people rented the rooms and lived in them. Then I brought Danny Edwards, the mayor of the U.S. Moscow, to our Moscow.

So he could finally see the prototype of his Moscow.

It turned out this was not only his first trip to Russia but his first time anywhere abroad. He had to get a passport for this trip, because Americans live without passports. His family saw him off with tears—like, will they ever see him again? It was a very dangerous expedition, in their eyes. The mayor was afraid to travel to New York for the ticket, because he was scared to be in such a scary city. Nothing but monsters and killers. To go there—

Took so much courage!

Right. They looked on me as a man who was sick of life, since I used to go to New York a lot. But in the end, their mayor liked our Russian Moscow. The only thing he didn't like was that vendors were rude and served the Pepsi warm.

  So, after the New Year's holidays, I went back to the States. I hung around New York for three or four days.

Svinarenko's Commentary:

Russianness in New York—and I'm not talking about Brighton Beach, but more broadly—is special: It's not Soviet, not post-Soviet, and certainly not American.. They have their own language, manners, jokes, and habits. And they even look different, so that you can recognize them a mile off. They look like provincial dental technicians who seemed to have all decided to dress in black. They borrowed the American's enviable openness and childlike persistence and the Russian's light Soviet unceremoniousness. It's an explosive combination.

I observed a very funny sequence of telephone calls. An immigrant with a killer hangover was canceling his meetings for the day. With his own people he told the truth: They would understand, they were like that themselves—I got really smashed last night and can't get up. But he told Americans that he had food poisoning. Which was the right thing to do! If he had shown up to a meeting with a serious man while hungover, reeking of cat piss and regarding the world with a weary gaze, he would have ruined his reputation forever. In general, our former compatriots know whom they have to impress and whom they don't.

Afterwards, I returned to Russia for good. It was late October, even though I had been expected back in September. I dragged it out. I wanted to get my fill of America. The thought of parting was difficult for me—then. I had loved those leaps over the ocean; it was like going from one dimension to another on an Aeroflot flight. I flew economy class, and that was the height of comfort: Right after takeoff I'd move to the tail of the plane with all my stuff—there was plenty of room—and, taking over three seats, sleep like a baby through the whole flight, having eaten and drunk for the road. I loved my walks in New York, when you can go see all of Manhattan in one day; and taking the ferry boat from Fulton Street, drinking quietly on deck and watching the City of the Yellow Devil, as Maxim Gorky called it, float past. I loved digging through the cheap, yellowed paper of old books in second-hand book stores, where they have stalls outside selling paperbacks for a dollar—and drinking vodka in Brighton pelmeni places with simple Jewish dentists from Zhitomir, who seem to define the face of our émigrés there…

I was horrified by the thought of life without those regular monthly trips, without the subtle sense of seeming freedom—that is, that you can go wherever you want, feeling that you are nothing other than a citizen of the world… I hated to think that after a while, someday I would end up in Times Square, falling facedown on the cement, kicking and screaming, "Don't take me away from here!" But the affair ended, the way affairs usually end. I came back to New York a few months later, looked at it with liking, but no passion. A nice little town. Amusing, but nothing to get so excited about. And thank God for that! It's like when you run into an old flame many years later, a woman who had made you drool, and you just pat her on the ass, say something dirty, both have a giggle over it, and part, pleased with each other and wondering what all the pain had been about…

So, I breathed a sigh of relief and started living in Russia. It suits us ideally, if you want to start talking about seeking an ideal on earth.

And I began living in Russia as if in a new country. It was much more interesting now than it had been before my trip. In contrast to the States, I mean. When did I get the sense that I didn't have my own country, and never had? It had always seemed alien, someone else's, built for someone I didn't understand. But I did have the illusion that it was my country. It appeared, I guess, in the early days of perestroika. Not in 1987, but a little earlier: around 1986–1987. And that fortunate misapprehension lasted for years. Maybe ten. So when did I make the bitter discovery that it was wrong? I'm not sure. Around the time of the default? Perhaps. But whether it was before or after, that loss was connected to the default, that's for sure. It may have hammered in another nail into the coffin of that radiant feeling.

So, after America, I began traveling around Russia with a greater thrill. I rushed out to the provinces on any excuse. I flew to Chelyabinsk, to get to Zlatoust from there. I went with that same curiosity and passion. I had a thirst for seeing the new life that I thought was growing all around us.

One fine day the interior ministry police announced a new way of combating organized crime, which (according to the police) controls 30%-40% of the country's economy. It's a simple method: You just cut off the sources of financing of the criminals! This allegedly was done successfully in the town of Zlatoust, where they took away the Kazak Uralsky distillery from the bandits. Then they 'broke up the gang that was terrorizing the town.' 'One-hundred-seventeen criminal cases were made, and the enterprise's profits went up.' Judging by the police report, they managed to win the fight against the 'Russian mafia' (in quotes so the police don't get mad) in a town of 200,000 people. That's not bad! Of course, then I wondered how crime-free Zlatoust was doing now?

When I arrived I called the distillery. Here's the answer I got: 'What are you calling for? No one's here. Don't you know we're shut down? No sales! No one wants to buy our vodka, it's too expensive. People are drinking illegal moonshine.'

'But you announced that your profits were up.'

'That's theoretically, if people would buy our product. And they just said we have to make a higher profit, that means higher prices. How can we raise them any more—no one's buying as it is.'

… But you mustn't think that Zlatoust's cultural life stopped because of the market and a hard life. No! It continues under any circumstances. The local theater is a draw for the entire region. And the city library is so good that sometimes national seminars are held there! And there are illegal dog fights for high stakes… And young pimply prostitutes only cost 150 rubles a night. They were offered to me near the hotel by a thirteen-year-old boy with big, wise eyes.

'How did the bandits make money on vodka, then?'

'They exported it,' the city mayor explained. 'They did paperwork alleging that the vodka was for export and then didn't pay excise tax, and then sold it in Russia… That makes it cheap and it sells well. Or an even simpler scheme: They signed contracts, loaded up trucks with vodka, and then never paid for it. Very simple. They took 63 billion old rubles' worth of vodka from us that way. Those guys really ruined our vodka firm. Their goal was to bankrupt us and then buy the place cheap. With money they stole from the company in the first place. We barely fought off Moscow; they wanted us to declare bankruptcy. So… We arrested people, broke up the gang, and a few months later, 'export' vodka production started again. Selling it on the side!'

The local police chief gave me his point of view: 'Some of the people in charge… They're involved. Get rid of them all… The relatives and so on. The daughter marries somebody, he gets in trouble, they help him out. A real mess. Go figure out what's going on,' he said about the behind-the-scenes hassles. He came to this conclusion: 'Peter the Great was right to move the capital to St. Petersburg!'

'Come on. Is that the reason?'

'I'm certain that that's the basic reason. But he was too ashamed to admit it, so he came up with a different reason.'

But some people found happiness here. People who are not in a hurry, who are not greedy and who can appreciate the simple things, and know from which side to approach the Ural Mountains—not from Paris or Moscow, but from Asia. The regional capital, big old Chelyabinsk, is in Asia, while Zlatoust is west of there, in Europe.

Take Sveta, a waitress on a trolley that travels around the city—she pours drinks and gives you snacks. A good-looking brunette with almond eyes. She's perfectly happy! Look for yourselves. She's from Stepnogorsk, which was always considered to be near Tselinograd in Russia and now was near Akmola in Kazakhstan.… And suddenly Russian was taught in her children's school only three times a week; the rest of the time, Kazakh was mandatory. They had long gotten used to the uranium mine under the window, but the language was upsetting. And there was no work, and the people who did have jobs didn't get paid. So they moved, sold their apartment for $400. Not per month, but a one-time payment, forever. I'm explaining that for the benefit of Muscovites.

What's funny is that I had pretty much the same feeling. I was working as a special correspondent, traveling wherever I wanted, writing huge articles and publishing them first in the newspaper—and for good money—and then in books. In other words, I was embodying my ideal of the 1970s, the way I had imaged the peak of my career back then. What else could I possibly want? But want I did. Life turned out to be richer than I had thought. I shouldn't be using the singular case here. I had the feeling that I had lived several lives already and was now living this one. The special correspondent's life is quite separate—it has a beginning and an end, and it fit neatly into one piece. Why do some people live one life and others have three or four? Who knows? Either we're winning prizes in the game or else someone is leaving us behind to do the year over...

* * *

Now, Alik, it's your turn on 1997....

All right. Back in March 1997, I got a promotion. I had been chairman of the State Property Committee and then they also made me a vice premier. How did that happen? In the summer of 1996, after Yeltsin won the election, Chubais became chief of staff. And brought Alexander Kazakov to be his first deputy. That left a vacancy again, and Chernomyrdin appointed me. And then, in March, Yeltsin disbanded the government. That is, he left only Chernomyrdin and changed all his deputies.

Did you ever figure out what that was meant to do?

That brought in the second government of young reformers. The first one was under Gaidar; this was the second. The first deputy was Chubais again; Boris Nemtsov was first Vice-Premier; and Oleg Sysuyev and I were simply Vice-Premiers. And the four of us were the young reformers. Why was it done? Yeltsin had been sick before that, and the country had been run in fact by Chubais and Chernomyrdin and Chernomyrdin was afraid of everything—he didn't want any reforms at all, he liked things the way they were. And his deputies were happy too. But the reforms needed to be implemented. So they formed this government. As usual, Berezovsky was very active in this, and for some reason he tried to present my appointment as a big favor. So I said to him, "Boris, look. I used to have an area of responsibility—privatization. And I was a minister. There was more than enough responsibility. Now I have additional responsibilities as Vice-Premier—for example, all the revenues in the budget. Not only from privatization, but from taxes, customs, vodka, and so on and so forth. But no department except the State Property Committee is directly subordinated to me. That is, I'm in charge, but there's little accountability—all the ministers run to the Prime Minister when they want something. So I have new responsibilities without new rights. Thus, my life has become much more complicated, and why should I be grateful to anyone for this, even you? I don't understand."

I wasn't very eager to become a Vice-Premier, but I did it. I thought I should accept, that it would be an interesting experience... When else would I ever get to be one? I'd learn something new... About the technology of rule, about the country, the budget... So, we started working, and then—no wait, it was earlier, in January, the idea came up to privatize Svyazinvest. This is how it went.

Let's have this in great detail, please.

So, Svyazinvest existed separately, and so did Rostelekom. The latter was and is responsible for international and long-distance communications. Svyazinvest is simply a holding company that includes controlling interests in all the regional telephone operators—regional and city telephone networks. So, in brief, we had to prepare the merger of Svyazinvest and Rostelekom, make all the documentation transparent, for the investors, and so on and so on. It took a lot of work to force the Ministry of Communications to do this. The Ministry of Communications, for obvious reasons, has traditionally been connected to the secret agencies. Because the secret agencies are involved in anti-constitutional activity. Ha-ha. A joke. Get it?

And how could they not? If you don't get involved in anti-constitutional activities, how are you going to protect the Constitution? I wouldn't want to try.

Yes, they're defending it so well, it's a pleasure to observe. There won't be anything left of it soon.

And how could they have bumped off Dudayev following the Constitution? They couldn't have.

Of course they could. Let me explain. They would make criminal charges against him. And any court would have issued a warrant to tap his phone. They would have listened and nabbed him. But they listen without warrants to anyone's phones they want. And then thanks to Alexander Minkin and Alexander Khinshtein, the journalists, it all ends up on the Internet. Or in *Moskovsky Komsomolets.* And no one deigns to wonder why these people are having their phones tapped. And if you do ask, Khinshtein makes a cupid mouth and explains that according to the law on media, he is not required to reveal his sources. Even though it's very clear who those sources are.

What does it mean, constitutional or unconstitutional? It's not that important, because in the final analysis, if you need to solve problems, you can add whatever you want to the Constitution.

But they added this. And therefore, the special agencies are performing anti-constitutional activities. Another joke. Ha-ha! I'm very humorous today. Not a good sign... They are doing crime prevention—listening to people before they've committed any crimes. That is their logic, as I understand it. But that's not important... So this was a difficult undertaking—the merger and privatization of telecommunications in Russia. I wouldn't have taken it on; I didn't want to be in an argument with any of those people. When I started testing the waters, they all yelled as one: No merger, no privatization, forget it! And then Gusinsky comes to see me. And he says, Look, I've done so much for Yeltsin, and I got nothing. And I said, Whose fault is that? Until 1966, you denounced our auctions, both the usual ones and the loans-for-shares ones, saying that it was an unworthy pastime, being involved in privatization. Other people bought all kinds of things for themselves at those auctions, and you got nothing because you bought nothing. Though you are pretty well set up with radio and television frequencies—with NTV and Ekho Moskvy. You didn't pay a kopeck for either one, and they're worth tens if not hundreds of millions of dollars, and you got them without auctions. So I don't think you should be very hurt.

What was your relationship with him then? Was he already attacking you or not?

It was fine then. The loans-for-shares auctions was turned into a horrible crime against the people later, in the fall of 1997. Before that, privatization was denounced in the corridors—just another topic of conversation, nothing more than that.

So, Gusinsky came to you because you were an acquaintance. And you were acquainted because?

Because of the election campaign. We sometimes had lunch. And so he came to me and said, you have to privatize Svyazinvest. And I said, if you're so smart, then help me get it past the intelligence services—you're pals with them, and I can't find a way to get on good terms with them. He said, A very interesting idea!

And what did he want it for?

Because he would have a chance to buy it if it was auctioned.

Just buy it? You didn't warn him? Didn't explain that he'd have to buy it honestly?

I did, I did.

And he said, "Of course, honestly—but you'll help me?"

There was no such agreement, Igor, absolutely not! We agreed from the start that if there were people he didn't want taking part in the auction, that would be his problem, not mine. He agreed to that. And he started solving the issue very energetically, and suddenly everyone was cooperating, signing off on papers that had been on their desks for years. The merger and privatization process got started. And here's the interesting part. When some man from the government asks the secret services to do something, they don't listen. But when businessman Gusinsky tells them something, they do it right away!

Then, this happened: In January 1997, Gusinsky runs over and says, "I know for a fact that Potanin wants to take part in the auction!" So? "That cannot be allowed! He's a Vice-Premier!"

Potanin was your pal in those days, Vice-Premier Alik.

Yes. And I was his subordinate. When Chubais and Kazakov went to work in the president's staff, Potanin became the Vice-Premier in charge of the State Property Committee. I said to Gusinsky, Listen, he's left Oneximbank and is working full-time in the government. So why should the bank suffer because Potanin felt he had a duty to his country and took a huge salary cut to leave the bank and work in the government? That's not fair. I agree that he should have no more benefits than anyone else; but that's all. No, said Gusinsky, I will insist on a meeting with Chubais (Chubais was Chief of Staff then). So they made an appointment, invited first Vice-Premier Potanin and Chairman of State Property Kokh. Gusinsky was there, hopping mad—and Berezovsky.

Those two—why were they there? On what basis?

Apparently, on the basis of being members of Yeltsin's campaign team. They had already started disliking Potanin. And so, as one, they said, "If you allow Potanin to take part in the auction, we will smear you against the wall in our mass media."

Just like that, in those words?

Yes. One owned ORT, the other NTV. And newspapers and radio. Let's be frank, they had all the media in their hands.

So you just caved?

I'd like to see you in that situation… Don't interrupt, let me tell the story. Chubais says, Yes, I think that the situation is not appropriate, so you [Potanin] will have to suggest to your colleagues at Interros and Oneximbank that they refrain from taking part in the auction. So Potanin said, All right, we won't take part in this auction. I sat and said nothing. Not that anyone asked me much. So. The meeting was over, and everyone went home.

Why did they dump on Potanin? Did he have more money? Was he going to outbid them?

First, he had more money; and second, Gusinsky didn't want to overpay. And then, some time later, we learned that Goose and Birch were lobbying to keep Potanin out of the new government. They decided to retire him. And they pushed that through. We couldn't keep Potanin, even though he was not meaningless in our government. Yeltsin sent Potanin and Lifshits into retirement then. Gusinky and Berezovsky did that, so that everyone would know how powerful they were—and they didn't hide the fact that they were the ones who kept Potanin out of the new government. And then Potanin asked, "What about my promise now? Is it still in force? Now that I am no longer in the government, are they still going to smear you if I go to the auction?" Chubais, who by then was already First Vice Premier, says, "Now you are no longer bound by your promise. There is no argument against your participation." Goose was upset. "What do you mean he can participate? That's against our agreement." And Goose came up with one more argument: "Potanin has lots already. And I didn't get anything out of privatization." I asked him again: Who stopped you? Why didn't you buy anything? All you could do was get frequencies for free? Why didn't you want to buy something cheap at least, for $10 or $20 million?"

Did you say it in a teasing way or were you telling him he was a jerk?

I told him the way I just said it to you. I said, "Look, Berezovsky participated in the privatization, and he bought Sibneft. Who was stopping you? No one, just your own stupidity. And now, because you were stupid, you're demanding we do illegal things and keep out Potanin, who's not at fault here. And he says, "Then we'll smear you."

"All right," I said, "then tell me how I can keep Potanin out? What do I do?"

"There's going to be a series of international conferences on privatization in telecommunications; you go to them and tell everybody that a big consortium is being formed with Mostbank and Alfa-bank that will play a leading role in the privatization of Svyazinvest, and it suits the government for international investors to cooperate with that consortium. And not with Potanin."

And why was there a consortium? Because Svyazinvest was expensive. Let me remind you that the bidding ended at $1.875 billion. None of our rich guys had that kind of money then. No one could have hoped to win the auction without serious international investors. The starting price was $1.2 billion. You're going to laugh, but I got into a plane and went to those conferences, and I made those statements. Goose and Birch didn't trust me and they sent Fridman to keep an eye on me. So I said what suited Fridman. Fridman is a normal guy, he's not crazy. I remember we were in Vienna at a conference. The Bristol Hotel, the opera, the Hofburg palace, the museums, the Blue Danube…

So, Alik, why did you have to work on Goose's behalf?

So that he would leave us alone, and not smear the government and turn the country upside down… But in the end, they did ruin the government. The idiots. And that led straight to the default of 1998.

The leftist "patriots" were saying then: "We didn't vote for Gusinsky and Berezovsky, why are they running the country? And especially since they are citizens of a foreign state—Israel." And they would explain that every Jew could get an Israeli passport, with all the new responsibilities it entailed.

The patriots might have posed those questions to Boris Yeltsin—why did he let other people rule the country, why did he let them run him? It's not like they kept him in the cellar on bread and water and only gave him sweets when he signed the decrees they needed. Oh, why bother talking about it now… It's over. I think Yeltsin drove himself crazy later over why he didn't get rid of them right away…

So, the auction was set for July. Goose and Birch come up with a new ultimatum. I don't understand why Berezovsky was involved in all this in the first place. He probably wouldn't have gotten more than half a percent; he wasn't putting in a lot of his own money. But he ran around with Gusinsky, his eyes bulging. So, about a week before the auction, Chubais went on vacation. I said, "What am I supposed to do? They keep pestering me…. They even hinted that they would have me rubbed out." Chubais said, "Have them come to see me."

They flew to France: Berezovsky, Gusinsky, and Potanin. I'm not quite sure what happened there, even though I've asked them all. Chubais called me and said that he had told them to go fuck themselves and refused to interfere with the course of the auction. By that time, Potanin (with Jordan's help) had created a consortium with George Soros and couple of other investors. Gusinsky created one with the Spanish company Telefonika, and the Alfa guys helped him a lot. And so the day of the auction arrived…Leonid Rozhetskin, who was Boris Jordan's partner then, came in with the bid for Potanin's side, and Mikhail Fridman came in for Gusinsky's side. They came in, unsealed their envelopes, and it turned out that Potanin's number was bigger than Gusinsky's.

Could you add to it?

No, there was only one round.

Was it possible to spy? To learn what the bids were ahead of time? To give the right number right away?

No, everyone was so afraid that there would be cheating that we came up with this rule: The participants come with their envelopes and hold them in their hands. And they unseal them simultaneously. That way, there could be no problems. I didn't know either Gusinsky's or Potanin's number—my conscience is clear.

So the result was announced. And my God, what a ruckus! Those guys went into hysterics. They began demanding meetings and conferences. I didn't go— Chubais met with them. For some reason, Goose decided I was to blame, that I had to be fired, that he would have me jailed, and so on. Birch was calmer, but he said the same things. They started having me watched—they even sent people to tail me in New York.

I remember. They found *kompromat*—compromising materials—on you, Alik. Everyone heard.

Yes. They came up with a fee for a book. The point is that any government figure in any country signs a book contract first and then writes the book—in that order. But the fact that I got an advance on an unwritten book was presented as a terrible crime, the worst that could be imagined. I don't see anything prejudicial in it. Yeltsin got an advance for his books, and then wrote them. Both times. For a total of more than a million dollars. That's what the press wrote. And no one considers that a crime. Primakov first got an advance, one hundred thousand dollars (that was reported, too), and then, several months later, turned in his manuscript to the publishing house. I remember the press reporting on the honoraria of various officials and politicians, but mine was the only one they turned into a criminal case.

Well, for example, how much did Nemtsov get for his book, *The Provincial*?

A shitload, you can be sure.

A big shitload?

Yes.

But no one picked on him.

Strange, isn't it? Gorbachev got advances and then wrote books. And President Clinton got an advance and is only turning in his book now. Even though he's already spent the money. And his wife, and many other politicians got the money before starting a book. It's common practice all over the world.

When I grow up, I'll be like that, too. I'll get a hundred thou per book.

No, that's only for government officials and politicians, Igor. As far as I know, you're not planning on being a major government official...

Well, I don't know... I haven't decided.

Let me know when you do. I'll be a supporter. So, the whole epic story with the criminal charges began. It lasted into 1998, and so on. The funniest part is that afterward the value of Svyazinvest fell sharply, and today the packet of shares that we sold for $1.875 billion costs around $600 million. Soros sold that packet—25% plus one share—for that amount.

So you made a lot of money on it!

Not us—the state made money. And when people reproach me now for selling things on the cheap, I don't even argue. I merely ask, Then what about Svyazinvest? Would you like to give back the difference? I'll use some of it to pay what you think is the difference that the oligarchs should have paid in privatization... So that's the story. They decided I would be the sacrificial goat and said it was my fault for not taking Potanin out of the race. Even though I followed the procedure exactly as it had been set up. Andrei Tsimailo, lately deceased—may he rest in peace—worked for Gusinsky, and on their orders he sat there and gave instructions on how the auction was to go.

Is it strange that he died in London? At such a young age?

Don't know if it's strange, but it's tragic, certainly. Andrei had always complained about his heart to me.

And those two fellows, did they really run the country?

Yes.

Those two, and no one else. Why?

Because the mass media is the fourth estate, Igor. Everyone was afraid of attacks and exposés. So they obeyed them. It was a good lesson for the country.

Potanin had only *Izvestiya*. That's nothing against the power of TV. So, does that mean that those two were the smartest?

I don't know about smart. Where are they now and where is Potanin? Who's smarter, eh?

I'm sure they feel fine.

They could have continued to influence the process, and they would have had more money—if that's the main goal in life.

Maybe they think they'll come back.

And? They don't have any media anymore.

But they must still have money.

Not enough to buy those television channels, and no one will give them to them for free. Again.

How much would NTV cost now? Tell me, Alik, as an old privatizer.

Well, it's gone down in value now, but when it was at its peak… I think it has about $200–$300 million in advertising revenues. No huge expenses… I think that's what the channel is worth, around $200–$300 million. But it might be as much as $500 million. It all depends on the market prospects. If you're an optimist, NTV is worth more, if you're a pessimist, then less. But the range is $200 million to $500 million. That's how I would estimate it.

And you think Gusinsky doesn't even have $200 million?

That's what I think. Where would he have gotten it? He didn't participate in privatization. He had no interest in running a metallurgy plant; he didn't want to hassle with oil production… He didn't want to produce anything!

And here I thought they each had a billion.

No. All of Gusinsky's businesses were break-even or in the red. Mostbank went bankrupt, and NTV, when I got there, was losing money and went bankrupt. All the money Goose had was what Gazprom lent him. He blew part of it, and part he invested in NTV+, which is also losing money.

I see.

So, I can estimate that he's got about $200–$300 million left. That's still a lot of money for one man.

Khodorkovsky has a lot more.

Well, Khodorkovsky raised oil production a lot. He worked on it seriously. When we sold Yukos it was pumping 30 million tons of oil a year. And it was behind in its payments to the federal budget for salaries and pensions. Now it's producing 70 million tons [*This was before the sale of Yuganskneftegaz.*] You can say the same for Abramovich. When we sold Sibneft, it was producing half of what it's doing now.

So, even if they were to return, Goose and Birch….

…they would never have their former level of influence. The fact that they had such influence was abnormal. When the two main television channels in the country belong to two oligarchs who are in cahoots, that is abnormal. That level of monopoly of mass media is not acceptable.

So of all the first-league oligarchs, only Potanin has kept his position. He was the most far-seeing.

You could also call Abramovich the most successful. What about Bogdanov? Alekperov? Fridman, Vekselberg, Blavatnik, Makhmudov, Deripaska, Mordashov, Lisin, Abramov… Lots of them! They all took part in privatization, by the way!

But Khodorkovsky started doing stupid stuff—that means he's not far-seeing.

That's only recently; before that he was considered the most far-seeing of all.

So the game can turn at any moment. The card changes, the trump suit comes and goes—one tiny mistake, and it's over. So he made the wrong bet, is that it, Alik?

I don't know Khodorkovsky's motivations. "I'll never leave, put in me in jail!" And then a catharsis, and letters, "repent, ye sinner!"

Maybe they're slamming his balls in a door… But it's an edifying tale. What does it teach us? That we should buy up media outlets? In order to have influence?

The teary-eyed NTV journalists were weapons in Gusinsky's hands. And very powerful weapons at that. That Yevgeny Kiselyov, who attacked our entire group of writers, why is he hiding? Dobrodeyev honestly admitted it, in public: Yes, the assignment to pick on Kokh, Chubais, and Nemtsov came from Gusinsky.

He admitted it?

Publicly, at some press conference. But in fact there was nothing criminal about those books! The case is closed on the books! There's nothing there. The books are written and offered to the public. The sources of the money paid for them have also been given to the investigators.

What were the sources? Why don't you remind our reading public?

The Foundation for the Defense of Private Property, for one book. And a New York publisher for the other.

And what happened to the money?

Interesting thing, Igor. It went to the foundation headed by Gaidar. For legal support for small businesses against the hassles of administrative agencies. When a man has a small store and he's harassed from all sides by firemen, health inspectors, and so on, and he doesn't even have the money for a lawyer, then he gets a grant from the foundation and goes to court.

All right, the foundation. But the American publisher paid you something, too?

I kept the money for *The Selling of the Soviet Empire*. I was a private person by then. Why did I have to donate it somewhere? I wasn't making so much money when I was first out of government to be able to throw that kind of money away. Relax, I declared the income and paid income tax on it. The tax rate then was thirty-five percent, not thirteen as it is now.

Remember the interview we did then? You said that you almost got into a fight with Chubais, when he said that the honorarium was too high.

I disagreed with him. It was a normal honorarium.

It was a noisy business, oh yes.

You bet. Dorenko and Kiselyov kept hammering me over it.

Those were merry times….

Gaidar told me that he went to see Gusinsky then and said, "I can tell you now what will happen." This was the situation. We made a goodly sum of money—the investors had a lot of trust in Russia and readily gave us loans. We paid salaries with those loans. We had liquidated all the debt to pensioners by July 1 and to teachers and doctors by December 31. Those loans were very important: Don't forget, the oil prices weren't what they are now. It was $12 a barrel on the average. Our whole budget is addicted to the oil needle. Now the budget revenues are $90 billion, but back then they were $30 billion. But it's the same country. There was high trust in our state securities. The stock market was growing: By the fall of 1997 it had reached 570 points on the RTS index. The second time it reached that figure was in 2004. In other words, during those outstanding Putin years—2001, 2002—the RTS index was lower than back in 1997. That is, the level of trust was lower than back then. There was good reason for honoring Chubais as the best Finance Minister in the world in 1997. And Gusinsky and Berezovsky began methodically destroying all that. Everything we had done. They undermined investor trust in the government. They started screaming that the government was full of bribe-takers, they were corrupt, they wrote books and took honoraria for it—can you image the horror? People saw this on TV all the time. So trust in the government was destroyed, people decided not to give this government any more money, but the loans had to be paid. That led to the crisis of 1998. Default. And, ironically enough, as a result, Gusinsky suffered more than anyone else. He had almost completed a deal on selling part of NTV. It fell apart because of the country's default. Gusinsky had to borrow money from Gazprom, and that debt eventually destroyed him.

Greed ruined him.

So, Gaidar predicted all this to Goose in 1997. He had calculated what would happen. He said: "You are sabotaging state power! You are undermining investor confidence in the state over nothing! It's going to cause a crisis."

What did Gusinsky say?

He said: "Honor is more important."

Come on!

Really.

In other words, this story showed how incredibly weak state power was in those years. Two men ran the country. No one could handle them. No one! Right?

We couldn't. Goose and Birch had a strong influence on Yeltsin. It wasn't total—it was like alternating current, sometimes on, sometimes off. But in tandem with the media, in tandem with all the wire-tapping, it worked. Those men truly ran the country. From the point of view of rational behavior, Putin did the right thing when he got rid of them, first one and then the other. It was absolutely rational.

So Putin saved Russia, Alik? He screwed one and then the other, that's true. We're running ahead of ourselves here, but as we look at 1997 we see that Putin did the right thing, it turns out! And we have to recognize it.

Well, yes, those scoundrels had to be checked. Berezovsky had an *idée fixe*— business had to run the government. Remember, he said that in public? We were the only ones to fight him. The rest didn't. Only Anatoly Kulikov, who was Minister of the Interior then, tried to argue, but then he acted against us and against them. As a result, he got fired too. All the others lay down for those two. The FSB, the Prosecutor's Office. And the Prosecutor General, Skuratov, definitely worked with Gusinsky and that entire wave against me—the criminal charges, the searches, they were all the result of their friendship. Gusinsky apparently had promised to make Skuratov president, and the guy fell for it.

It wasn't very nice that two people out of nowhere came and took everything for themselves.

They didn't have time to take much. Berezovsky, unlike Gusinsky, did manage to buy Sibneft with Roman Abramovich. So he's richer. I think 1997 was a key year. That year it became clear that it would take a long time for us to get out of the crisis. Now, in hindsight, I see that the increased influence of the secret agencies on the regime was inevitable. Only one of them could have acted like Putin. He gained Yeltsin's trust through Berezovsky and then solved the issues with both oligarchs. Here's the chain of events: Without the oligarchs, you can't beat the Communists. So they won. But then, you have to limit the power of the oligarchs. And that can't be done without the law and order guys. The next task facing the country is to limit the power of the law and order people. And that's impossible without a civil society. Paradoxically, that requires the efforts of all political forces, including the Communists. Full circle, ha-ha.

I think it was Kissinger who said that the only way to bring order to our country is to let the KGB take over.

Why? The situation isn't so dire… If Gusinsky and Berezovsky had understood where things were headed…where they were taking the country… But I'm daydreaming here. They are both daydreamers, by the way, uneducated.

What can you expect from them if even Soros got burned? And he's a serious player.

Yes, Soros got burned. They say that Berezovsky is making a lot of money on real estate in London. Maybe he might even have a billion dollars now. But Gusinsky doesn't. Gusinsky keeps positioning himself as a businessman forced to deal with politics, when in fact he's a pure politician and a lousy businessman. While Berezovsky positions himself as a politician who is forced to do business, whereas his business affairs are in much better shape than Gusinsky's. And he's about as much a politician as Gusinsky is. He lost a lot politically. If not everything.

So, when people today tell me that we didn't fight the oligarchs, I get mad. We were the only ones who tried.

And as a result of that fight, Alik, you were fired from the government in 1997.

No, I quit. People forget that. I left in August—I was seen off with pomp and circumstance—and then they started attacking me in September. And then came the writers' affair, when the others were fired—Max Boyko and the rest. Only Chubais was kept on.

Why did you leave?

I was sick of Gusinsky's hysterics. So I went to America, for a vacation.

Not bad. A retired official vacationing in America.

I had $100,000 for my book. I could afford it.

What had your salary been?

Around 15,000 rubles a month. The ruble was 5 to 1 then, so, $3,000. [*This was before the demonetization; the dollar was 5,000 rubles. My salary was 15,000,000 rubles a month, but I put it in thousands, to keep it in today's scale.*] It was after the default that the ruble was 30 to 1. And the government salaries fell. From America I went to France. And two days after I arrived, I got a call: "Misha Manevich was shot." I went to St. Petersburg for the funeral of my friend.

He was killed by bandits because he would not let them privatize at a discount.

Yes. I'm going to do a commentary about Manevich.

Kokh's Commentary:

> Blessed are the meek: for they shall inherit the earth.
> Blessed are they which do hunger and thirst after righteousness: for they shall be filled.
> Blessed are the merciful: for they shall obtain mercy.
> Blessed are the pure in heart: for they shall see God.
> Blessed are the peacemakers: for they shall be called the children of God.

Matthew 5:5–9

I met Misha in the summer of 1978. We were seventeen. We were starting at the Leningrad Financial-Economic Institute. Once we got in, we had to pass some stupid requirement in gym, running a few laps in the stadium. That was the first time I saw him. Tall and thin—barely enough body to hold his soul. With long, almost shoulder-length, wiry black hair. With a big mustache. With a ready laugh. He laughed out loud, showing his big, even teeth.

The first thing that struck me was the incongruity of his skinny body and his big, solid head. A huge Jewish nose, big mouth, thick red lips, hair, teeth, all juicy, filled with health and joy. And his voice. I was amazed that this scrawny guy could produce such powerful, rolling sounds. He had a phenomenal bass. A trumpet of Jericho, not just a voice. We could tell when he was around, long before we could see him—just by the sound of his voice.

In mid-July 1997, he came to Moscow and dropped in to see me in the White House. He looked depressed. I told him what had happened after the Svyazinvest auction. He complained that he too was being threatened and hindered in his work. We both were in a lousy mood. I was getting ready for vacation, so was Misha. We said we'd call each other, maybe meet up. He said then, "I'm so sick of all this. I'm going to quit. Let it burn in Hell, that Vice-

Governor job." He had been talking about quitting for about six months before this meeting. It was the last time I saw him alive.

A few days later I dropped into Chubais's office and put my resignation on his desk. Let it burn in Hell, that Vice-Premier's job. I said, "I'm going on vacation, and I'm leaving this letter of resignation. You can do with it what you will. If you want, throw it away. If not, let it happen." Chubais flung open his arms: "Don't even think about it! We'll show them!" and so on. But I could see in his eyes that I had given him a way out of the situation. I read what they said: "Thanks, old man. I would have had to give you up anyway. But now at least I won't have behaved like shit."

There are always big men on campus. You can see one coming a mile away. Top grades. Komsomol member. Top man in construction brigades (somehow always in the office or doing political activism). Doesn't smoke or drink. Honest, open face, good features. Slender girls with pert noses hang around him. It's very obvious. Big man.

Manevich was a different kind. A professor's son. Scholarship was an end in itself. He didn't consider his top grades worth mentioning. He got A's, and why not? He did it so effortlessly, without showing off, that we didn't consider him a big man on campus. Just another guy. In the kolkhoz, in the construction brigade, in army training. Here, pick that up and carry it over here…

Misha married a Jewish girl named Olga. She had a beautiful figure and a pretty face. I understand the attraction of that kind of beauty: fiery brunettes with tender rosy skin and glowing eyes. Olga bore him a son, Viktor. Misha looked happy. They were a happy couple.

Misha had a good friend, Boris Levin. I knew him, too. Boris is talented, bold in his opinions, striking. He writes well. He's critical (though not self-critical). Sarcastic. With bile. One fine day Olga left Misha for Boris. How banal! Like a bad movie: Guy steals friend's wife. Misha was very upset, but didn't show it. He was as gentle, amiable, and considerate as always. Boris and Olga have been in America for eleven years now, in Washington. The boy looks so much like Manevich—but of course, he doesn't remember his father. He must be a very American boy by now…

In early August 1997 I, was in a boat, fishing off Long Island. The sea bass are running at that time of year. Chubais called me on my cell phone: "I've accepted your resignation." Who would have doubted it? So? "Come back! We'll have a proper going-away party." Lord! Who needs it? Proper? Why does he need me to attend that bullshit? I'm just sitting there fishing, bothering no one. So fire me. What do you need me for now? But I didn't want to argue: "All right, I'll be there."

I'm in Moscow. Farewell party. Chubais, Farit Gazizullin, Chernomyrdin, Potanin, Kazakov. We have a drink. People say a few words. The phone rings. It's Manevich: "So you did it! Then I will, too. I'll take my vacation and then quit! Hey, I know, I'll come visit you. You'll be in France, right? I'll be there. My vacation starts on the 19th."

He had married again. A beautiful, slender woman named Marina. Glowing eyes. Tender rosy skin. Fiery brunette. Her first marriage had broken up too. She had a small boy, Artem. Misha adopted him. Misha looked happy. They were a happy couple. Marina took good care of him. Before his marriage, he had been living in his parents' apartment, somewhere in Ligovo (that's how Soviet professors live.) Then he then moved in with her.

After that, through a series of exchanges and additional payments, they got a big, handsome apartment on Rubinstein Street. Misha loved the place—it was his first real home. He enjoyed furnishing it, selecting furniture and paintings. He boasted how close he lived to work. He left for his death from that apartment…

1992. Smolny. We're at work. We have two offices and one reception area. Misha is a very good worker. Methodical. Educated. Correct. Law-abiding. Kind and patient. He wanted to help everyone. He worked like an ox. All the delicate questions, unusual situation, various and sundry conflicts were sent to him to settle. He patiently dealt with it all. He didn't care with whom he was talking—a big-shot tradesman, a policeman, director of a big factory, or a bandit. He treated everyone the same: politely and helpfully.

They used me as the boogeyman. "If you can't reach a solution with Manevich, we'll send you to Kokh! Then you definitely won't get what you want!" We were the two deputies of Sergei Belyayev, chairman of the St. Petersburg City Property Committee. An inseparable pair—good cop, bad cop. The good cop was Misha, of course…

France. 1997. Mid-August. The sea. Morning. Around 10 or 11. I'm on the hotel veranda having breakfast. Kefir, croissants, coffee… The sun is shining, the sea is blue, the palms waving. I'm nobody anymore, just a man. Former Vice-Premier, retired voluntarily. (Being fired, the writers' affair, all those lies came later, about two months later.) It's August 18th. Tomorrow, we're expecting Manevich with his wife and son.

Suddenly my wife runs out in her bathrobe. Her face was horrified. I took a deep breath. "Manevich was shot!" I exhaled. I tried inhaling again, and the air got stuck halfway, not in or out. A spasm. My eyes bulged. Are you lying? Tears, weeping. I couldn't get anything else out of her. I went to our room. I called Lyuba Sovershaeva. She's crying too. "Yes, it's true! No, he died instantly! The bullet went through his aorta and into his throat. Marina is alive. She was sitting next to him. She was cut by the glass. I don't know, the window, probably…

She's out of it... Come quickly. Everyone is here..." Killed. Strange. People close to me had died. My grandmother, my aunt, a school friend. But not killed. He hadn't died of illness or old age or in an accident. Killed. The emotions are different. Anger is added to the sorrow. And a sense of impotence.

In the spring of 1992, Misha and I went on vacation to Helsinki on the *Anna Karenina.* We had been abroad a few times before, and so the first shock of the stores was gone. I started noticing deeper things: the cleanliness, the absence of urine in the hallways, the paper in the toilets. I still hadn't learned to cross the street—I kept letting cars go by. It takes a while to realize that pedestrians have the right of way. A sated, successful country. Here it is, the Russia we have lost.

We came out on Senate Square. A beautiful Lutheran church. Looks like St. Isaac's, but more modest. We went in, stood around, listened to the organ. We came out again. It was sunny but cool. We walked down the broad granite steps. In the center of the square there is a monument to Alexander II. Not big, but not small. A smart-looking emperor, in military uniform; sideburns, erect posture. They say he was a strong man. Oh, St. Petersburg, St. Petersburg! O Jerusalem, Jerusalem, thou that killest the prophets, and stonest them which are sent unto thee! Matthew 23:37. Damn! So depressing...

A huge auditorium with a coffin. A lot of people. I'm in the honor guard. Misha is to the left and a bit in front of me, in the coffin. A handsome coffin, polished. Probably imported. His face is heavily made up. Some makeup got on his mustache. Beneath it you can see the face had been deeply cut by shards of the windshield. I feel horrible. I feel like hanging myself. I'm nauseated, I want some vodka, I want to cry, but I can't. A lump that won't go up or down.

Chubais speaks. He says he'll get them all. I think to myself: Do I want revenge? The answer is yes, I do! Very much! Kill them with my bare hands, slowly, with big drawn-out pauses. The murderer will beg for forgiveness, and I will mock him, spread my hands, say, Sorry, can't help you, just bear it a little longer, very soon I will kill you. Cut his heart out... Carried away by these thoughts, I stand there while this ridiculous procedure goes on, hearing none of the speeches. God! Forgive me, a sinner...

In June 1997, Misha and I went for the weekend to my mother-in-law's dacha on Lake Ladoga. It's good there. Long sandy beaches with dunes, pines, the boundless lead-colored Ladoga. Fishermen on purse seiners dock and unload crates of fish: pike perch, white fish, bream. Gulls screech around them. We bought some fish, made soup. Then a steam bath, vodka, shashlyk. We gave Misha and his wife a room on the top floor—you can see the lake from the balcony. Fresh air, white nights. The charm of the Russian north.

The next morning, friends came. Brought more shashlyk. We laughed all day, remembering various stories. In the evening, at the airport, we walked around and talked. I don't remember about what. I have only the general impression, the aroma. And that was the aroma of friendship and love. I love that aroma. And Misha, of course...

More speeches at the cemetery. Then, closer to the end, both a priest and a rabbi. Misha never did decide, thinking probably that there was still time. The rabbi chanted so sadly, in such a piercing, extended tone, it cut along the nerve endings. I just wanted to sit on the ground. Right on the freshly dug mound of reddish St. Petersburg clay. Next to the empty grave. We were going to fill it. Sorrow. That's what it looks like, sorrow.

His parents clung to each other. It was terrible to look in their direction. Next to them was his younger brother. He looked a lot like Misha. Everyone there looked like him. They gave me the final word. I muttered, trying to speak up, but couldn't. I could barely hear myself. They lowered him down. Threw dirt over him. Set up a photo of him, pine boughs, lit a candle. We poured some vodka, drank, stood there. That seemed to be it. Was there something else? No, that was it.

We all chipped in and gave his wife some money. We weren't cheap about it. We bought his parents a normal apartment. God, how typical—a St. Petersburg professor has to get his son killed to have a decent place to live. We put up a good gravestone for Misha. At first, every time I was in St. Petersburg I visited his parents, his wife, the cemetery. Then, more and more rarely. Now I occasionally call his wife. Sometimes I visit his grave. I'm a pig, I know. Dogshit. Always busy—there will be time later. Or is it just protecting myself from negative emotions? There are enough of them as it is. Business as usual.

The urgent desire for revenge is gone. I don't want to tear anyone to pieces. He's gone. Misha is gone from me. His head moved in such a funny way when he laughed. And then he would wipe his saliva with a handkerchief. Now he is no more. I've gotten used to it. I will die one day. And they'll come to me for a while, and then they'll stop. That's fine. I'm ready. I'm ready for it. Manevich's death taught me. You have to be ready at any moment. I'm ready. I'm not afraid anymore. I just want it to be quick and painless....

* * *

After my vacation I got a job working with Arkady Evstafyev at Montes Auri. And then my criminal epic began—interrogation, searches, declarations that I would not leave the country. The writers' case. The apartment case.

Wait, Alik, what happened to the company?

It died after the default. It had a huge number of debts. You know how we started? Arkady got a loan from Rossiisky Kredit and I got one from Alfa-Bank.

We each got 10, for a total of 20 million. And we bought stock. And the index fell from 570 to 30.

So, in other words, Gusinsky and Berezovsky screwed you one more time.

Yes, to the tune of 20 million.

What did you use for collateral?

Our word of honor.

What, without any guarantees?

That's right. The fellows had a good opinion of us. And by the way, Fridman, who was one of the losers in Svyazinvest, nevertheless maintained normal relations with me and lent me money to start out. Later, of course, he really harassed me when I couldn't pay him back. In the end, I paid off the loan. We worked like oxen for two years and paid it back. Every kopeck.

And he even took you on as one of the directors of TNK.

Not just him. It was a joint decision by Fridman, Blavatnik, Vekselberg, and Khan.

Your thinking then must have been: "I've served my country, and look what happened, how it ended. Now I'll live for myself and make some money." Right?

Something along those lines. Except for two things. There were still people who were willing to help me, even at the height of the criminal case against me. That made me happy. But on the other hand, I was saddened by the case itself. I knew I was being set up—there was nothing there. I hated talking to the investigators, because it was the same thing over and over—date of birth, death, what did you do, write your biography. And they kept extending it and extending it.

Were you called in for questioning often?

Every two weeks. And they always asked the same thing. I don't have anything in particular against the investigators, they behaved politely. Except for the nasty things they'd do now and then like unexpected searches. Or getting me to sign a paper saying I wouldn't leave town. I said, come on, what for? I come in for questioning, you can't complain that I don't. And when they would do a search, the kids were there; my mother was staying with us. I said, May I call ahead, so they can take the kids out? No, you can't call. You'll give them coded information. And another thing: they took away my VCR and TV. What a joke!

Where were you living then?

In the "stolen" apartment. On Tverskaya-Yamskaya Street. The apartment was tiny, 70 square meters.

Where your daughter lives now?

No. After that I bought a real apartment. This case dragged on until December 1999. Over two years.

That could ruin your health, that kind of stress for two years.

And the investigator knew that the case was a no-go. And I knew. Total bullshit.

We must admit that this was an event-filled year.

I think it was an important year for the country, not just me—even though it was one of the most important years in my life. It was a very big mistake of Yeltsin's not to get rid of the scoundrels. He let them do anything they wanted. At least when Korzhakov was there, there was some control over them. But when Korzhakov was replaced in 1996, they went all-out.

What about Alexander Korzhakov, Yeltsin's bodyguard and adviser?

Well, he scared them, and they didn't like him, especially Gusinsky. Remember, Korzhakov organized the armed raid of Goose's headquarters—he had him facedown in the snow.

A time of troubles.

You see, the president was sick, and he didn't want to get too involved in these conflicts. I understood that you could destroy the state that way. The state is being screwed, and it's just standing there, mooing with pleasure, see? Two conmen do what they want with it, and it stands and moos. It was so obvious to everyone—everyone understood what was going on, but they were afraid to say it out loud. The public didn't know about it. For one reason: People learn about what's going on in government from the media, and the media was telling them that everything was wonderful, that Boris Nikolayevich had a firm handshake…

It was a kind of Rasputin, but double. A Siamese one.

A collective one. Rasputin acted differently, through the Empress and so on. He didn't have the media in his hands.

Well, all right. A weak state, the people didn't know. And if we want to talk about the so-called elite, then it was a big zero. A collection of shitty pants.

No, Igor, not at all.

Come on, everyone understood everything. And just sat around saying nothing. No mention at all of decisive action. The elite contemporaries of Rasputin killed him—they found the courage and strength. Despite the fact that it was harder to make that decision then; they didn't like shedding blood, and life was valued more highly in those days.

What could we have done? How could we have helped Chubais, who was also fired along with Chernomyrdin and Kulikov in March? How could we have helped Sasha Kazakov, when he was pushed out of his first deputy position in the presidential staff, in the fall of 1997? How?

I don't know… There were deputies in the Congress….

Which deputies? The Communist ones? The Duma majority belonged to the Communists and the Zhirinovsky people. They were pleased to see what was happening. Who was supposed to defend us?

That's what I'm telling you, the elite was useless, nothing.

It's what it is. It's like that today, too.

In general, you're right. It hasn't gone away.

What was it supposed to have done, the elite? Agitate for Chubais on television? It didn't have access to TV.

And the journalists were total jerks.

That's not news to you, Igor. You keep telling me the lowest form of life is the journalist.

True, journalists are not the best people in the country, far from it. But what was the FSB doing?

Be careful not to toss out the baby with the bathwater. "Let's destroy democracy in order to save it?" Then it shouldn't be saved.

No, that's not it. It isn't "destroy democracy in order to save democracy." It's "destroy democracy in order to save the state."

In that context the word "state" becomes a total abstraction.

Why? A state doesn't have to be democratic. Nothing happens to a state that isn't.

I see. In that case I don't think it should be saved. Leave the weak, democratic one. I liked it better.

Ah, I see. Then bring back grandpa as president; bring back Gusinsky and Berezovsky, and give them the television.

No. The television doesn't need to be returned. We can manage without those TV geniuses!

Then what the fuck kind of democracy is that?

What do you mean? Sell the mass media in small packets of shares at special auctions that everyone knows how to do. So that no one has a big share. That can be forbidden through the anti-monopoly committee—no more than 5%. No more than 5% to any affiliated group. Maybe no more than 1%. It's realistic.

As a liberal and market man—

Wait a second. I know that you call yourself that. But other than that, there are no signs that you are a liberal and a market supporter.

What do you mean?

Well, what other signs of your liberalism and market beliefs are there besides your self-identification? What makes you think you are a liberal and market supporter? You say that all the time, Igor, as if it were a given. But it's not at all obvious to me.

Doesn't it follow out of everything?

Ha-ha. No, it doesn't follow out of anything at all.

And from what does the opposite follow?

For instance, from your statement that all entrepreneurs are bad people. From your statements that they all should be behind bars, and so on. "They stole everything" is your favorite theme.

I never made any statements about putting them in jail—or that they stole everything.

What do you mean, you didn't?

I didn't. I don't think that. And you can't prove that I do. And as for entrepreneurs not being the best people in the land, well, excuse me, but we've just been talking about two leading Russian entrepreneurs. Berezovsky and Gusinsky are their names. The best, the most prominent entrepreneurs. And your attitude toward them is not that different from mine. As for Russian entrepreneurs in general, I have a lot of questions for them. And the main one is this: Why are they fighting like dogs among themselves, if they're all so good? How many of their own have they killed!? And put away? They hate each other, but they expect everyone else to love them.

Now that's a typical journalist move. You say that they've killed one another, and that's not true.

Oh, I see,—it's the Martians that have landed and ordered the killing of Russian capitalists. Or the hippy guitarists from the sixties, in cahoots with the kolkhoz peasants. As for your indignation about my being a liberal… I'm not asserting that I'm one-hundred percent this or that. It's not important whether I'm considered a market supporter or not. I've always done whatever came into my head. Do you understand that?

Yes. I think I've pushed you into a dead end with my question, Igor. Why won't you just admit that you have no proof that you are a liberal and democrat. I'm a market man, for example. Because I implemented market reforms. The reforms we made, whatever you may think of them, are recognized as being market reforms. I am a democrat if only because, as you know, I spent a lot of time making sure that the party that holds democratic positions was elected to the State Duma. Those democratic positions are in its platform. I have proof that I am a market man, a democrat, and liberal. But you have no such obvious and clear proofs. And by the way, I risked my personal freedom, and perhaps my life, for the cause of establishing a market economy.

You can be proud of that, Alik. As for myself, I'll tell you: I don't care what other people think of me.

That's a different topic.

If you don't think that I'm a good enough liberal and democrat, I won't call myself that in your presence. It's not a problem for me, understand?

All right, all right. Your explanation is accepted. Ha-ha! I think that you are part of the majority of the Soviet intelligentsia that identifies itself as democrats and liberals automatically, without realizing that to do so involves more than having pleasant dreams of democracy and liberalism—it requires a clear understanding of their negative aspects. If you accept the negative aspects of democracy, liberalism, and a market economy, then you are truly a market supporter, liberal and democrat. If you are willing to accept all the pluses but are frightened of the minuses, and you talk about how good it would be without those minuses, then it's like expecting wolves to eat oats. The Bible says a time will come when the lion will lie down with the lamb and eat grass. You are an amorphously kind man, that's all. Without any firm position, without accepting all the pluses and minuses.

I once said that the sixties generation loved Communism but hated Communists. And that the seventies generation loves capitalism but hates capitalists. Neither understands that "socialism with a human face" and "capitalism without greed" are equally utopian dreams. The benefit that capitalists bring comes from greed. And yet it is the greed that irritates you. But if not for that itch of greed and profit, a man would not become a capitalist in the first place. He'd be something else—a journalist, plumber, trolley driver.

Okay Alik, I admit that capitalists bring good, that society needs them; they have the right to live and must be protected by the law, and whatever else. Troops and police. That rebellions aimed at overthrowing capitalism must be suppressed—I admit all that. And I've never done anything to overthrow capitalism or to help the Communists. Do you understand what I'm saying?

I think that the process of your self-identification is happening right now during our conversation, and that before this you never thought in those terms. You simply decided that you were a liberal and market supporter and you never went beyond it.

Oh, no. I was just writing my commentary for 1993, and I was trying to remember and to figure out in hindsight what was happening then. Why I was not interested in the least in the coup of October 1993. And it was because of the reasons I just gave you. I was convinced that a rebellion against this regime had to be suppressed. (Or maybe against any regime?)

And there was no discussion in your soul about this, Igor? I think you're just an anti-Communist, not a liberal or free market supporter. Anti-Communists include not only democrats and liberals but also monarchists, adherents of various rightwing dictatorships, all kinds of imperialists.

No, there was no discussion. I even asked myself feebly: Why does this leave me unmoved? Perhaps because I had a ready answer. I am on the side of the regime. Totally. One hundred percent. I do not want any other regimes. On the other hand, I am not prepared to say "Long live capitalism—the highest stage of the radiant future of humanity! Capitalists are the best people in the world! Let me hang their pictures over my bed!"

Only the desire for profit makes a man take the kind of risks capitalist do! Because if the desire for profit were lower, he wouldn't take those risks. My greed is not very great. And frankly, it's becoming more and more of a drag to do business every year. Even though capital keeps growing. But there are people who can't stop, and it turns into a narcotic or a sport for them.

They're the majority.

No. No, not at all. There are very few of them. There are no more than ten thousand entrepreneurs—people who risk their own money—in the whole country. The rest either mange other people's money or work for the state. Truly greedy people, greedier than I, are very few. You have to understand that the work involves very powerful emotions. If you don't like those feelings, you're not a market man. Your greed is low; that's why you are not in the market.

Greed is not becoming, it seems to me. Just the reverse.

But you can't get away from it. No greed, no nothing. No capital, no work.

Remember I gave you the example of bees? Bees provide an enormous benefit. I enjoy the fruit of their labor. I've never killed a bee. (Well, actually I have killed one or two when they tried to sting me.) I have great sympathy for bees. I will always defend bees. But! The bee makes honey not in order to please me. It flies around, gathers pollen and nectar; we take away what it throws up, call it honey, and eat it. But we don't need to say that the bee is so wonderful and lovely. It's a bee, and that's all.

Ah, so it's not enough for you that a man brings benefit, you want him to work only for the public welfare. You know what happened to the construction of a society in which everyone worked for the public welfare! But if a man works for his own benefit, then he arouses your suspicions. That's what I'm talking about!

He doesn't arouse any suspicions. But he doesn't elicit my love, *a priori*. I am not interested in the typical capitalist. You interest me, for example, because you're creating something. You sit with me and make conversation for an hour, for free. And yet you could have made $20,000 in that hour. I find that touching. But there are businessmen who are concerned only with making money, day and night. They sit with friends, drink beer, and think only of their business goal—how not to pay for the beer. How to make $20.

I understand. But I repeat, you can't expect people to work exclusively for the common good—

I'm not asking for that. I'm not trying to build that "ideal" society.

Why do you feel that way about greed, Igor? It's the only human emotion that lets us avoid building socialism and allows us to build an effective society without turning to the repressions of the 1930s–1950s.

I am totally on the side of a bourgeois democracy. No matter how hard you try to change my mind with your attacks.

Then respect that greed. And don't say that it stinks.

Greed is evil. Even if it is inevitable. Why should I feel such a lofty emotion as respect for such a base and pathetic thing?

It's a good thing. How can you not understand? God is merciful enough to give us greed. The desire not to just sit and shit under the sun, but to move somewhere, undertake things. In order to make a better life for yourself and your children. To go on vacation in Capri.

I do not have warm fuzzy feelings for greed.

Well, you should.

I won't. That's ridiculous! Why should I have warm feelings for boorishness?

Let me ask you a different question. When the country needed money, we put big enterprises up for auction. None of the people with money—with rare exceptions—wanted to take part in the auctions. They even tried to ruin them. But there were people who paid the money (where they got it is a different question, one for the law). They took the enterprises, with their debts, losses, and shit—and brought them up to a fairly decent level. Now even the West recognizes the quality of Russian management. Its level is pretty high. And now why are so many people who didn't want to participate in our auctions, didn't want to give us money, now busily trying to ruin those poor oligarchs? It's funny to say now, but back then Potanin or Khodorkovsky had only $200–$300 million. And they spent it all, down to the last kopeck, in the auctions. They turned it all into industrial shares. Their banks went bankrupt in the default. Onexim and Menatep. A huge number of banks went bankrupt. People risked everything on one or two industrial companies. They took the risk—and won. Those businesses are doing well. Tell me, how have they done you wrong? They employ thousands of people, they pay taxes into the treasury. Shouldn't you be looking at our government employees, who raise their own salaries but forget about teachers and doctors? There's enough money in the treasury to raise the salaries of doctors and teachers. But they tripled the budget for law enforcement. Today we have more people in the Ministry of the Interior and the FSB than in the army. With whom is the state planning to wage war? An external enemy or its own people?

With its own people. In particular, with the citizens of Chechnya.

You just need one division for that, Igor. There's no one to catch—they've all been shot.... Don't wriggle away! Just tell me, I really want to understand. They say the oligarchs stole everything, bought everything up cheap. So why didn't you come to the auction and buy it cheap yourself? Who kept you away? Cheap? You could have taken it then, and now you would be managing it. But you were too lazy to get off the couch! Not enough greed? Then shut up, esteemed journalists and prosecution investigators!

I don't pick on oligarchs. I have the deepest sympathy for Khodorkovsky. I'm not prepared to criticize him in any way. He suspects that his comrades out in the free world are going to mock him for his writing, but he doesn't care, he writes anyway. And Khodorkovsky is interesting to me not so much for being a billionaire but because he cared about his Open Russia foundation: he educated young people in the provinces, he brought scholars and scientists to them, he held seminars. Not every Russian businessman did that.

What do you think—did he believe he would not be arrested? Is that why he acted so bravely?

Whether he believed it or not, he played a serious game.

Was he truly not afraid of prison, truly prepared to go inside—or was he so hot-headed because he didn't really believe they'd ever put him away?

I think he didn't really believe it. For some reason, that's what I think.

Then his letter of repentance explains a lot.

17.

1998

The Seventeenth Bottle

In 1998, Kokh goes bankrupt, borrows $20 million, and is called in for questioning. Besides which, when hiding out in New York, he gives a nasty, Russophobic interview that insults the patriotic journalist Alexander Minkin in Moscow. This is a lovely example of how the press can be bought and used to slander political opponents.

Svinarenko, on the contrary, writes lyric essays about the Russian provinces and has another daughter (not without the help of his wife). Unlike certain people, he does not get involved in business scandals, but he doesn't make any money, either.

In the difficult days of the default, Svinarenko stockpiles Italian pasta and whisky, while Kokh insouciantly hangs around France.

So, 1998. Allow me to refresh your mind with my crib sheets, Alik. As usual.

You and your crib sheets—it's not right for a drinking session.

Why worry about outward appearances? Let's speak to the issues. For instance, in 1998, composer Georgy Sviridov died.

May he rest in peace.

OK. Then comes a very important event for those who watch television…Well, anyway, back in 1998, on February 16, a car race through Russia began, with five Moskvich brand cars—two Svyatogors and three Prince Vladimirs—all manufactured in Moscow.

Hah! Speaking of which, here's another example with Moskvich cars. Everyone's complaining about how bad privatization is, right? But here's the perfect example of what happens if you leave things in state hands: AZLK [the Lenin Komsomol Automobile Factory]. Right? Right? Luzhkov screamed and yelled, jumped out of his trousers: "Look, we'll show you the right way to handle state enterprises! Your privatization will lead to no good! You've stolen everything!' And recently Leonid Parfenov did a piece on AZLK on his show, *The Other Day*: The whole plant is falling apart, the production lines are twisted out of shape, the roofs leaking, and everything that could be taken out has been sold.

And it was then that those five cars made their glorious run. They were selling those cars at $4,000 when they cost $7,000 to make.

Terrific. Zhiguli are sold for $5,000, but it costs less to make them, and so the plant is making a profit. Please note—one plant is privatized and the other is state-owned. And AZLK has more modern equipment than VAZ [Volga Automobile Factory]. Sorry, that should probably read, *used* to have more modern equipment. It was restructured later, in the 1980s, while the VAZ was built in the late 1960s. The first car came off the assembly line in the 1970s. So the privatized VAZ is still manufacturing products that are competitive in the domestic market, even exports a bit, and makes a profit without reducing volume—it's still producing a bit over 700,000 cars a years, like when it began. Moreover, it has sold the patent for its Zhiguli 6, which it's taken out of production, to a privately built plant in Syzran. And it sold the license for the 9 to Zaporozhets. So instead of making Tauria, Zaporozhets will make the 9 and the 8. VAZ is keeping the 10 for itself. And the more modern state factory, AZLK, which had more money invested in it under Gorbachev, has fallen apart. Because it wasn't privatized. This is a very telling experiment.

A good example, yes. Poor Luzhkov….

He wouldn't let us sell it. We wanted to sell that plant. The privatization plan had been drawn up—but then the Armenians showed up.

And they got the loan from Luzhkov's bank.

In this case, I'm not interested in the Armenians. I'm stressing the fact that they did not allow the plant to be privatized. Luzhkov had hysterical fits…

What about ZIL? [Likhachev Automobile Factory, specializing in hand-made limousines]

Luzhkov bought it from Potanin.

Personally?

No, the Moscow City Hall bought it.

And who owns GAZ?

It's private, Deripaska owns it. He churns out Volgas and Gazelles round the clock.

Does he own UAZ, too?

No, that's Mordashov.

Look at that, Alik! All those car lovers. Support of domestic production. How sweet.

Another thing about Moskvich. It's crazy to build car factories in the capital. No one else in the world does that!

There's so much land under those factories…

Of course. And it's worth its weight in gold. No factories that require that much space should be in a capital city, where land is expensive. That doesn't exist elsewhere. American car plants are built in shitty Detroit or Atlanta, anywhere but New York or Los Angeles.

So what will happen to it now?

You have to set a bulldozer to it. I think that's how it will end eventually. And the land will be sold for construction.

All right. Let's continue with 1998. The Russian premiere of the film *Titanic*.

I remember. I was there, at the Kodak Kinomir.

Let's go back to great Russian history. Here—Galina Ulanova died.

May she rest in peace. She must have been a great ballerina. By the time we saw her, she was no longer dancing. They say that she danced on the tables for Stalin's drunken parties… What could she do? They forced her. Otherwise, you know what awaited her: the dust of the camps.

No kidding? Really?

Of course. It's a famous story. Do you think she wanted to do it? But be sent to the camps? Better to dance. She could do tap dancing, too.

That's not so horrible. Big deal, tap dancing… She was a performer. She danced and danced, and then she died. OK, next, we have March 23, 1998. "Yeltsin fires government of the RF." What's that?

That's the March firings. Chubais, Chernomyrdin and Kulikov were fired.

And on the same date—"appointment of S. V. Kiryenko to perform duties of chairman."

Yes.

And so we smoothly approach—

The default.

But there was a lot more that happened before the default! The explosion in the Russian Embassy in Riga, for instance. That whole long discussion with our Baltic neighbor started. I don't think we have anything to add about Latvia, after our commentaries in a previous chapter. So. What else did we have before the default? The burial of the remains of the tsar's family in St. Petersburg.

Ah, yes, Boris Nemtsov was involved in that. He considers it one of his greatest achievements—burying the tsar.

Remember, Yeltsin said that he wouldn't attend, and everyone followed his lead and said they wouldn't go. But he went, and then everyone else rushed to St. Petersburg, too. Remember all the intrigues. And the crush there. And there was also the idea that they were not the real remains.

The Church still hasn't recognized them.

Have you?

Me? Yes. I'm a scientific man, and they did the forensic analysis. There is so much confirmation, there can be no other conclusion.

So why is the Church resisting?

If they did recognize him, that would lead to many consequences. In particular, there would have to be the whole issue of the *obnovlentsy*, or renovationists. Have you heard of them? They usurped power in the church after the revolution. When Patriarch Tikhon was tortured to death by the Cheka, the church was temporarily without leadership—and then came the *obnovlentsy*, who spoke out for cooperation with the Bolsheviks. The entire present-day church comes from them. If the church were to admit that it was the Tsar's family that was re-buried in St. Petersburg, it would bring new strength to the discussion about the relationship between the Bolsheviks and *obnovlentsy*. The Church cannot allow this discussion to take place; in fact, it would not survive it. Since it would cast doubt on its very legitimacy. However, I feel that the Church must express its attitude toward cooperation with murderers. Why does the Russian Orthodox Church consider Nicholas II only a martyr, and not a saint? Because once it makes him a saint and admits its collaboration with his killers, the church in fact puts itself outside the parameters of morality—and ceases being a Church. A Church cannot compromise, understand? It's not a political organization. In some sense, it is not of this earth at all. They should have chosen to die, all those priests, rather than collaborate with killers. But they did not want to die.

So beautiful—being willing to die for an idea.

They should have rejected collaboration with the Bolsheviks under any circumstances! Now, as soon as they recognize the remains as being the Tsar's, they will have a huge number of internal Church problems. They will have to erase the previous 70 years of the Russian Orthodox Church, recognize the rightness of the Russian Church Outside Russia, recognize the rightness of the catacomb church, admit that the patriarchy is probably more correctly held in New York, that the true patriarch is there, the true heir to Tikhon. Or even more so, the catacomb priests—*they* were the true Orthodox Christians. An enormous number of consequences.

Well, whatever you touch in Russian history—it's approximately the same story: Dig a bit and all the ugly details come out.

The reason it is so difficult for our church hierarchy to admit this—you must know the answer. Or do you?

Because they would have to quit.

Well, that's only half the problem.

What's the other half?

There's not doing it because their KGB rank won't allow it.

You think they have rank even now?

Where would they have gone? It's the same people, Igor, the ones who were in the church in the times of Brezhnev and Gorbachev, when the hierarchy was permeated by KGB people.

That's impossible!

Did you expect them to retire or something? Without the right to wear the uniform, so to speak? Ha ha. I don't understand.

Maybe.

That's the same baloney as when they tell us that Sergei Ivanov is the first civilian minister of defense in the entire history of the Soviet Union and Russia.

Right, very civilian.

Yes. Army General Ivanov.

But he's not in the army. He's in the KGB. The committee guys aren't army, they have their own rank.

But his military rank would be army general.

I'm looking at my crib sheet again, Alik. "Kazakhstan hands over 47 percent of disputed territory to China."

They were disputing some steppe lands. It's not 47 percent of China or Kazakhstan. Just of the disputed territories. There were just a couple. And they kept more than half of them—53 percent.

And after that, really nothing, until we get to August 17. "The Kiryenko government has refused to pay its debts. Start of financial crisis."

How did we get to the default so quickly? It wasn't until August. Why don't we discuss the withdrawal of the Chernomyrdin government, and… The Blessed Sergei Kiryenko. We're going too fast.

Sergei Vladilenych Kiryenko is an amazing figure. Now he's running a federal district… Why? His colleagues, the other heads of districts, are imposing Russian generals. And there he is—this small-time civilian Jewish intellectual. Where's he from?

He was First Secretary of the Komsomol in Nizhny Novgorod.

Did you know him then?

Yes. Of course.

Who was he when you knew him?

First Deputy Ministry of Fuel and Energy in our government.

So, Alik: how and in what circumstances did you meet Kiryenko, hero of 1998?

Is this an interrogation? Have I missed something? I think we've lost the tone of a conversation at table completely.

That was just a joke, Alik, you know—the format of an interrogation.

I know.

Sorry. Salt on your wounds.

That's why I asked if this was an interrogation. A joke, in the chapter on 1998. That's when I really was being interrogated.

Weren't you under investigation in 1997?

They began in September 1997, it went on for all of Fall 1997, then all of 1998, and all of 1999. It was only in December 1999 that they dropped it, under an amnesty.

Believe me, it was only a joke. Stupid in this context…

There wasn't even a trial. They were looking for a way out of the situation. They couldn't drop the case for lack of evidence of a crime—not after two and half years. They had turned it into such a show, with Prosecutor General Skuratov giving interviews left and right.

In cases like that they count the time people have already spent in jail.

Thank God, I didn't do time.

Be glad! Remember, there also used to be joke, "In the life of every man comes a time when he must decide whose side he's on—the *bratva* [gang brotherhood] or the cops."

Where's that from?

Don't remember.

It's not about me. Isn't there a third path, Igor, where you're not with the *bratva* or the cops? As I see it, there is no line between today's criminals and the cops in our present-day criminal subculture. The thieves' community wasn't called *bratva* before. And there were honest thieves, or *vory*, and then the non-criminals, or *fraer,* and then the police. And in theory, police and thieves could not intersect in any form.

It's easy now.

Moreover, thieves could not work. They could not collaborate even with civil government—party offices, welfare—and they could not receive pensions or aid. They could not enjoy the benefits of this state. They could not marry or have children because the state could use your family to pressure you. They had to isolate themselves totally from the state That was a culture that grew up on Cossack traditions, where people would vanish completely, break with the

Moscow tsar, and live by their wits. They created their own language, the language of *fenya*. Then, a very strong Jewish element entered the thieves' subculture.

Jewish?

Of course. Half the words in *fenya* are Yiddish. *Fraer* is a Jewish word.

Yes. It sounds like Yiddish. I think it means bridegroom.

There's a huge number of Yiddish words in *fenya*, didn't you know! Jews went into either revolution or banditry. There was no third outlet for them—they couldn't go to university. So Jewish muggers were Jewish muggers in America, too. The Jewish mafia was no worse than the Italian.

And then the Jews pushed out the Italians.

So, the Russian criminal subculture had a strong Cossack element and a strong Jewish element. Those two incompatible concepts (Cossack and Jew) were joined in the thieves' subculture. Its basis was the rejection of the state. Primarily, the Moscow state. Insubordination, non-recognition, defiance. Today's bandit subculture does not deny the state! You can work for it, you can hold positions in it, you can get married, you can have children, you can be a cop—and still be a respected authoritative thief. And this subculture, because it is less principled, is more viable than the previous one.

I just read Eduard Limonov's new book, *Through the Prisons*, where he describes sitting in the central prison in Saratov. And the local bandits say: "Edik, you're so smart, authoritative, independent, arrogant, it's time to crown you as a *vor v zakone*, a true authoritative thief!" That's something, eh?

Limonov told you this?

He wrote it in his book.

Lies are cheap. But … I'll accept it as a possible truth.

And he goes on. He said, You know, I don't think so, I'm a writer. And they say: No, we'll crown you, you're just right for us. But you know, I have some counter-indications; I wrote the wrong things sometimes and described some of my actions that are incompatible with the title. And they said, Don't worry about it, you can even get married now—it's a different system. He concludes, I barely got rid of them.

Yes, judging by his book, *It's Me, Eddie*, he had a homosexual adventure. With a black man in a garbage dump. Of course, on the other hand, as the classic said, "One foray doesn't make you gay."

So, when the occasion arose, I asked a serious criminal guy about the situation—how realistic the possibility was of a homosexual being crowned a thief in law, a *vor v zakone*. He says, Ah, the guys were just bored, and they could have started a conversation like that out of sheer boredom. You know, they can start something like that and then talk about it forever. Someone might think they meant it…. Yes…. But jokes aside, Kiryenko was a Minister, and he was under you, right? You brought him up, in fact?

Wait, wait—why was he under me?

You were a Vice Prime Minister.

So what? The Ministry of Fuel and Energy was supervised by Boris Efimovich Nemtsov, as you must undoubtedly remember. If you remember, he was hired for the following position: He was first Vice Premier dash Minister of Fuel and Energy.

Is that when he escaped from being governor?

Yes. And the first deputy of the Minister of Fuel and Energy was Sergei Vladilenovich.

And Brevnov stayed in Nizhny for them?

He worked at RAO UES (United Energy Systems). He was appointed to replace Dyakov to run UES Russia. Chubais became First Vice-Premier dash Minister of Finance. And I became Vice-Premier dash Chairman of the State Property Committee. Oleg Sysuev was Vice-Premier dash Minister of Social Welfare. Later, after I left, when Gusinsky and Berezovsky started hypnotizing the government—somewhere in December or January—when the writers' case exploded and they started attacking Chubais and so on, the government was restructured. Chubais stayed simply as First Vice-Premier, and they made Zadornov Minister of Finance. Boris became simply Vice-Premier, and they made Kiryenko Minister of Fuel and Energy. They divided those two branches, and that's when Kiryenko became a Minister. When I was in government, he was First Deputy Minister of Fuel and Energy.

Kokh's Commentary:

Boris Nemtsov came to see me; it was in 1996. I remember he was terribly hung over, had come in from Nizhny Novgorod and was flying to America. He had nothing to do before his flight, so he came to see me in the morning. It was 9 o'clock. The first question he asked was, "Do you have anything to drink?" Sinner that I am, I still said, "I won't join you. My whole work day is ahead. You have a flight, but I have to work." So he slugged it down alone.

In general Boris doesn't drink a lot, but that time he got really hammered. He drank and said, "I have a boy sitting in the corridor, I want him appointed director of Norsi (that was Nizhnovgorodorgsintez, that is, the Nizhny Novgorod Oil Refinery).

I have to explain that at that moment, all the oil companies were being formed, and they, as you know, are vertically integrated: extraction, refining, and gas stations. Boris Efimovich then said that he would not turn over his refinery, which was in his territory (in the city of Kstov), to some vertically integrated company. Using his tight connection with Boris Nikolayevich Yeltsin, he held on to it. In his mind, the refinery was a diamond too good for all those Bogdanovs, Alekperovs, and other oil men. He decided to create an oil company without extraction. Simply a refinery and gas stations. In other words, an innovative approach. A reasonable question was: And where will you get the oil? To refine, I mean? Boris's reply was simple: "We'll buy it, there's a shitload of it on the market." And so he pushed through approval for a company like that, without its own source of oil. And it was called Norsi.

Naturally, the company without a source of oil began to go broke. No one wanted to supply it with oil; all the oil companies had to service their own refineries first. So it was dying slowly. It ended with I think LukOil buying it. So ended Boris's revolt against economic laws—the company got crude, in a rather exotic manner, of course, by being bought. Was it really necessary to torment people and drive Norsi to the brink of bankruptcy? But we're not talking about that now.

So there he was in my office with the idea for Norsi. The director there was some oil man. Nemtsov wanted to put in Sergei Kiryenko. He was the "boy" waiting in the corridor. All right, I asked, what is his experience? None. He understands no more about oil than me. Especially in refining oil. Boris said: He was first secretary of the *oblast* committee of the Komsomol in our *oblast*. I said, and who is he now? He was director and naturally co-owner, as I understood it, of Garantiya Bank in Nizhny Novgorod. Boris said, let's get rid of the one who's director now and appoint this one. And I said, why the fuck should I move him over into oil? Because that's what I want, he said, and that's that. Typical Boris. He was in favor then... The successor and heir, all that... He said: "So, do I have to go over your head to get the approval? I can." So I gave in. All right, send him in. Sergei went and appointed Sergei director of Norsi.

Later, in 1997, Boris Efimovich Nemtsov appeared in the dual capacity of Energy Minister and Vice-Premier—and he was dragging Kiryenko along with him again: "I want him to be my first deputy." This time he had to see Chernomyrdin. Chernomyrdin cross-examined Sergei Vladilenovich, who answered questions about oil refining clearly and succinctly. And thus Kiryenko became the first deputy. Then, when they divided up portfolios between vice premiers and ministers, Chernomyrdin made him a minister. And then apparently Sergei developed relations with the opposing camp. Because that camp, and Boris Berezovsky in particular—at the moment of the March crisis, when Chernomyrdin, Chubais and Kulikov were asked to leave—proposed Kiryenko as Acting Prime Minister. They had a lot of work to do to get him approved by the Duma.

Now, I'm thinking: What would have happened if I had not acceded to Boris Nemtsov's wishes then? If I had refused to appoint Sergei? I think Boris would have pushed him through anyway. I also think that if you were to ask him now, "Why were you so hot on pushing that Kiryenko?" he wouldn't be able to give a clear answer. There are no arguments.

I don't have anything against Sergei Kiryenko! He's a regular guy. A product of his milieu, his times, his mentality. Even within the framework of his Komsomol biography, he was probably not underhanded or a bad person. But why did Nemtsov love him so much? I can't understand that at all. Boris has a completely different biography! At one stage he was a human rights activist, worked with Sakharov; he's a scientist, has a Ph.D. in physics and mathematics, studied with Vitaly Ginzburg (now a Nobel laureate); and he never joined any parties. That is, his background is absolutely not the Komsomol stuff. And quite respectable and honorable, as far as I'm concerned. Svinarenko sometimes asks me if I reject the Jewish component? Jews help one another, after all. And I think: What, in all of Nizhny Novgorod, Nemtsov couldn't find Jews who were closer in mentality to him than Kiryenko? Weight, height, appearance, temperament, history, biography, education, manner of thinking, life values, priorities—they're all different.

Strange, isn't it?

* * *

And now, Alik, in 2004, when Sergei Kiryenko is heading up a federal *okrug*, we see that he is the only civilian representative of the president.

And?

So, maybe, he's not a civilian?

I have no idea.

Do you think they might have told Nemtsov the following: Boris, here's a man, we want you to push his career. He's ours, but it's important for us that he doesn't come through the KGB line, but from you, human rights activist and curly-haired beauty." Nice, eh? See, all the other *okrug* heads are in the Committee, or at least generals. And he's a civilian. He's the only one. A friend explained this apparent contradiction to me. Kiryenko, unlike the president, is not a KGB guy, but he does do judo! That's the way he got through the side door.

I don't think he does judo. He used to study—as he told it—some special martial art that is rather freely translated as "combat of wooden swords." They wear these masks and black kimonos with baggy pants and hack at each other with wooden swords… But let's go back to 1998. As for appointing Sergei Kiryenko director of Norsi, I just didn't want to get into an argument with Boris, and I knew that he would insist anyway and get Yeltsin to say, Appoint him already, and stop bothering me.

And how did Kiryenko and Berezovsky become friends?

That's beyond my abilities to understand—I had left in August, when he was still deputy minister of fuel energy. Apparently, he was not regarded as a figure with a future at first. But then he was, and by March he was already made Acting Prime Minister. And in May he was confirmed as Prime Minister.

All right, Alik. Now is everything clear with the firing of the government?

No, it's not. Mavrodi, who created the MMM pyramid, said that the government pyramid was no different from his. But that's not true. I can explain the point of classic pyramid to you—and of course, Mavrodi did not invent it. There were lots of them.

All right, now educate me about the different pyramids.

I will. It's very important. What's the point of the classic pyramid? Say I take a ruble from you. And I promise that in a year you'll get back two. But then instead of investing the ruble you gave me, I spend it on food. Now I need two more rubles. I take two people, and I promise each one 100 percent return, and they each give me a ruble. So I pay you back two rubles in a year. But now I need four rubles. So I find four people, and the pyramid keeps growing. And growing and growing. At some point, I steal the money and the next generation of bondholders will get nothing. That's it, basically. I go to jail, and there I start saying that I resemble the state. But the state is a different story. Because it has something that generates money. A state has a tax system. It covers part of its debts from the money that comes in as taxes. Thus, the pyramid develops not geometrically, but in some narrower fashion. Understand? That's the first point.

Second: Since the rate is calculated by the state based on a desire to return the borrowed money, and not as it is in the classic pyramid, where the desire is to steal it, the rate a bond pays depends on the state's real revenues and its rating with investors. If the investors trust the state, then they lend it money for a long time and at a low rate. For example, there are five-year U.S. Treasury Bonds that pay around 5 percent interest. There are perpetual bonds from Great Britain—in other words, debts that will never be extinguished, but which will continue paying a regular coupon, that is, percent.

As long as those two conditions are observed— when there is reasonable revenue and high investor trust—a state "pyramid" can exist as long as you want, and it will not collapse because at some stage, it will stop expanding, or the process of its expansion and narrowing will become manageable. Thus, the primary difference between a private pyramid à la Mavrodi and a state system of loans is that the private deal is intended to cheat from the start, whereas the state bond, when there is investor trust and rational fiscal policy, is a normal economic project. Thus, trust, trust, and yet again trust from the investors. That what Russia lost in 1998.

Alik, Alik, it was Gusinsky and Berezovsky who undermined that trust.

Smart boy! It's obvious. First they attacked the government—crying corruption, this and that—and forced it to resign. Then they put in Sergei Kiryenko, whom they had to push through the Duma with great difficulty, thereby proving that the government had no support from the Parliament. So why were they surprised then when there was a default in August? I don't understand that... And then all the creditors came like an avalanche to demand payment of their loans.

Why like an avalanche?

Because there was no trust in the government. Because with the help of a colossal year-long attack in the media, the trust had been undermined. If you started a focused attack on Putin, in all the papers, on TV and radio—bringing in foreign mass media, who fall for this sort of stuff easily—I assure you, Putin's government would fall as quickly as Chernomyrdin's did. Exactly! It's a different matter that Putin's government, thanks to high oil prices, has no domestic debt—which is why it doesn't have to issue GKOs and no one is going to demand payment from them. They service their foreign debt perfectly—again, thanks to high oil prices. But you could find another aspect of this government to attack. Not because of a financial crisis but, say, a corruption scandal. Bring it down, and send it packing. When Goose and Birch attacked Putin in August 2000 with the help of the *Kursk*, that was their goal—to show him that he depended on them. That he had to seek a common ground with them. That he wouldn't be able to manage without them. That's what they wanted! And they seriously were counting on success.

They told him: If you don't come to terms with us, we'll screw you, Comrade Putin. But if you do, then we'll tell everyone what a great guy you are, breaking off your vacation and going to Vidyaevo. He didn't want to make any deals with them. I don't understand this whole story. What were they thinking? All right, they screwed me, threatened to put me in prison, organized all that eavesdropping and bugging, called me in for interrogation… The investigation of me was run by Goose and Birch, not the investigators! They fed the investigation material. But that's another issue…

Maybe they thought, he's so quiet and modest…

I don't know what they were thinking. But the point is that they had solid support from a) the justice system, which always hated us "builders of capitalism," and b) Boris Nikolayevich Yeltsin. Well, given the choice of Gusinsky and Berezovsky on one hand and me on the other, his choice was obvious—he was with them. But in the case of Putin, when you don't have the support of the justice system, when the president is against you, and you attack the president—that's supreme folly! It may be possible your television companies really are profitable, when there are no liens or other legal issues involving them, and they are absolutely yours—then maybe that game has the right to exist. Then the regime you are criticizing will be forced to jump over all kinds of warning flags to take away your loudspeakers.

But if your company is in debt up to its ears and owes money to the state (or semi-state) organization called Gazprom, which in the final analysis is directed by the Kremlin… And if there is a hell of a lot of material against that organization—I mean Gazprom—too… Then, given the choice of Gusinsky or the Kremlin, that company will definitely pick the Kremlin. That's the NTV story. They demand payment of the loans, they take away your television stations, and all your noise ends there. Or if you don't have the controlling shares of ORT—now I'm talking about Berezovsky—because the majority stakeholder is the state, then I don't understand what those two were thinking, when they attacked the state… Let's leave aside the question of whose side we're on. Because no answer we could give would be sincere. We're just examining their reasoning, coldly and cynically. What chances did they have?

Maybe they were counting on the president's tact. They thought he was so quiet....

That quiet man had been running the war in Chechnya for almost a year by then. He started it. He wasn't afraid to enter those waters again. So by August 2000 there was no possibility that he was quiet. It was the same August that followed the July in which Gusinsky spent three days in prison. So Gusinsky had no illusions about Putin's determination. And what was Berezovsky expecting?

You know, Alik, this sometimes happens with journalists, even the ink-and-paper kind, and especially with the TV guys. They go crazy. Megalomania. Or star sickness: "I am very great." I've heard colleagues tell stories like this: "I went to Putin and I said, 'Cut that out, what are you thinking?' And he said: 'All right, old man, you're right, thanks for telling me.'"

God! How I hate our mass media! And how I understand them. I really like the theme of reduced journalistic morality. Journalists came up with the idea of reduced morality because they can't keep up with the generally expected morals. They say their profession requires some exceptions.

Remember the discussion between Alexei Venediktov, editor in chief of Echo Moskvy Radio, and Minister of the Press Mikhail Lesin? Lesin says, "There is no journalistic morality." And Venediktov, remember how he replied? If a man touches another's man's wife's private parts, that's immoral and unethical. Lesin naturally agreed. He didn't realize where he was being led. Then Venediktov said, "And what if he's a gynecologist?" "Then it's all right," the Minister agreed. Venediktov was triumphant, he had proved that gynecologists have a professional morality that is different. So that means, journalists can have one, too.

There is no Commandment against touching private parts. But there is a Commandment, Thou shall not bear false witness.

That means in court.

In general. Do not bear false witness means do not lie. I'm talking about the Ten Commandments.

But what are you talking about? The court. And I'm talking about the press. If you write an article, you're a witness. You're a reporter.

As usual, Venediktov obfuscated the substance of the issue with clever and original wit—a polemical method. That's the standard situation with Venediktov, who never discusses the substance of anything, but simply tries to appeal to the audience. That's his problem. When he starts to discuss anything substantively, it becomes clear that he's got nothing substantive to say.

OK, Alik. You don't like the gynecologist analogy. Let's take another. Remember Central banker Viktor Gerashchenko swearing that there would be no exchange of money. He promised, and in the end, he tricked everyone. He had no choice. His professional morality was higher than the general human one.

It was Yeltsin who said the ruble would not fall.

Gerashchenko said so, too.

I think that's total bullshit.

If Gerashchenko had started giving away secret plans of fiscal policy, what kind of financier would he have been?

What kind of fiscal policy requires secrecy? What kind of shit is that? I don't understand that at all. Fiscal policy that has to be kept secret from the public is immoral. The secrecy is immoral. Because that money, excuse me, is not only yours, Mr. Gerashchenko, but ours too. So keeping secret what is going to happen to my savings is immoral. It's my property! So that's a violation of the Commandment on not stealing!

All right. Here you are, negotiating with someone—you don't tell the guy, "Here's the lowest price I'm willing to accept." Instead, you give him a song and dance about costs and needs, and so on. And he thinks, "The hell with this, I'll take pity on poor Alfred and give him a break."

No, I don't agree.

How can you disagree? You're deceiving him.

How do you mean?

Well? It's that what business is about—buy low, sell high?

Don't confuse binary relations between people with the relationship between a person and the state. When I'm negotiating with a colleague in business, he's trying to get over on me as much as I'm trying to get over on him. In that sense, we're even—we have the same chance. But the public that reads the press has no chance of tricking the journalists.

All right. Let's move on. We have the profession of executioner. Necessary to the state. It has its professional morality—the executioner is allowed to kill. He's even paid a salary.

I think the profession of executioner is immoral.

But we don't charge the executioner under Article 105 every time he performs his job according to its specs and regulations.

As a state, we have stopped the death penalty on the territory of the Russian Federation. And I think that's right.

But before it was stopped, no one held executioners criminally liable.

That doesn't change the fact that the executioner is performing an immoral act. And I think that we have to do away with executioners. Not in the sense of killing them, but firing them. Do away with it as a form of activity.

But nevertheless, the morality was professional. Gynecologists have one morality; businessmen, another; Ministers of Finance, a third; and executioners a fourth.

All right, let me put it another way. Ask a gynecologist if he enjoys digging around in genitals. And he'll say, No, it's just his work.

Just the way the executioner shot the serial killer Andrei Chikatilo. Not because he really wanted to knock somebody off. He was ordered to do it.

An executioner, if he has a conscience, realizes that he is doing a bad thing. It bothers him at some level—he drinks, he has problems at home, he yells at the kids. The image of an executioner drinking hard after his shift is a very natural one. Your grandfather—who carried a Mauser and shot people for the Cheka—he must have felt pangs of conscience, too. Remember, when he was very old, he told you something about all the people who were destroyed? And the Minister of Finance, the chairman of the Central Bank who lies to the people, telling them everything is fine—he also experiences pains and breaks. Remember when Chubais gave you that interview and spent a long time talking about how his work was immoral, but it was the lesser evil compared to what could have been: girls and grannies trampled in crowds buying macaroni.

This is what they say. We are immoral, we executioners, financiers, and so on, but we are forced to perform evil. The lesser evil prevents the greater evil. In other words, within the framework of general morality they seek some kind of expiation for themselves. And they feel uncomfortable. But only journalists announce—happily and without any reason for it, without preventing greater evil but simply out of some moral infantilism—"We have a special morality." Not an executioner saying he has a special morality, not a gynecologist saying he has a special morality, not Chubais who tells people there won't be a devaluation, but some crummy little reporter announcing that his profession has a special morality and that they made it up for themselves.

Look: Journalists know that in order for them to get paid, their publication must be a commercial success. In order for it to be a commercial success, it needs to sell—it needs a large audience, big circulation, and so on. And for it to have a big circulation, for it to sell a lot of ad pages, it has to print all kinds of heated-up facts, scandals that people buy up like hotcakes. And which facts does the public grab like hotcakes? Facts about celebrities, be they politicians, actors, athletes, businessmen. Facts about their personal lives—who they're screwing, how they divorced, how long their cocks are, are they losing their hair, do they have hemorrhoids on their bums.

But because this is a violation of privacy—a blatant, upfront violation—they invented a new morality, which claims that people have the right to know about the private lives of famous people. What the hell for? What does it change? What will change in my ideas about Prosecutor Pupkin if I learn that he has hemorrhoids? Nothing! But, I'll buy the paper because it *interests* me that he has hemorrhoids. Understand? There are no exceptions. Privacy is privacy. It should never, ever be violated. Not the privacy of anyone famous, of a politician or an actor. But since my publication needs to sell, I've invented a morality-lite for myself that permits the violation of those people's privacy. And if it does have some relevance for politicians, why does it extend to athletes, actors—why should it extend, for instance, to officials who are not involved in politics? To people who head some statistical agency?

Alik, I don't have any other people for you, to quote Stalin.

You mean journalists?

No, readers. There aren't any others.

That is not a problem of the audience. It is a problem of the journalists. People are the same everywhere.

But still, every profession has its own morality.

Let me offer something that should reconcile us, I think, Igor. Every field has its own professional ethics that cannot be called morality. These are professional ethics—of gynecologists, executioners, policemen, thieves and so on. But I am willing to admit the existence of professional ethics under two conditions. First, that basically these ethics must fit into the demands of general morality or exacerbate those demands—making them even more stringent, not less.

If professional ethics don't fit into general morality, then the people using those ethics know, deep in their hearts, that they are committing foolish, vile, sinful acts. And they must make their peace with that, because humans are imperfect, because they must feed their families, and so on. But they must admit inside, and among their professional colleagues, that it would be better not to do this, but it must be done... Journalists are the only ones who insist that they have a professional morality, not just ethics, and that it differs markedly and radically from human morality, and that they are the only ones who can use this kind of morality. No one else. And they're doing it all in the name of humanity, so they feel no pangs of conscience, and so on. This is what seems very important to me—and what, in my opinion, is underestimated. The press, which speaks of morality in every other sentence, is of itself extremely immoral. In its fundamental basis.

Alik, you're just sick of being picked on in the press, and you're prejudiced. But this is a serious conversation. Here's one more mental experiment for you. If you pick up an automatic weapon and go out to shoot people in the street, you will be arrested. But you could easily do exactly the same thing if there were a few insignificant factors at work: The people in the street will be dressed slightly differently—in foreign uniforms—and instead of umbrellas they will be carrying M-16s, and instead of shopping they will be shooting at Russian roadblocks. If you shoot at them, you won't be arrested, you might even get a medal.

Wait a minute. Nothing will happen to me if I kill an enemy.

That's what I'm saying. In both cases you're killing people. But the consequences are different. And you are perceived differently by public opinion. For one simple reason: Professional morality (in this case of the military) differs from the general citizen's morality.

I think you and I have different ideas of morality, Igor. For me, morality is different from the law; when I do something immoral, my conscience torments me. I feel terrible, uncomfortable; I know I've committed a sin. If I break a law, society will punish me; if I violate morality, society may not punish me... but I'll punish myself, harder than anyone else could.

Well, why do you think journalists drink so much? Maybe they're suffering from pangs of conscience. And you pick on them.

Damn it, you can't ruin people's lives for entertainment. You can't amuse bored audiences by destroying lives and careers and homes. It's wrong. You might even drive someone to a heart attack. I can give you a simple example. You know the charges that the press made against me in 1997-1999. I don't know how you feel about it, but it seems to me that the great, overwhelming part of it was empty lies. And a lot of the remarks—about the books, for instance— could be made about a lot of people. For some reason, they decided to focus on me. Let's not analyze the reasons for that now. I'm a young and strong man. With an averagely strong mind. But my mother, for example, was so stressed by that campaign against me that she developed diabetes. Who's supposed to answer for that? Ah, otherwise, it would have been boring? I'm glad everyone had such a good time at her expense. And what if one of my relatives had dropped dead of a heart attack? My very sensitive mother-in-law, for instance. Who'd be happy then? Who could enjoy that? This is what is called the special journalistic morality—no conscience, so she died, what can I do. That is the reaction of standard journalists, and it outrages me.

When we interviewed the blogger Sergei Gorshkov, who does the kompromat.ru web site, he told us all those things. He's on the cutting edge. He's a real journalist. I guess I'm not...

You were outraged by it too! Sitting and talking with Gorshkov, you were stunned by that man's spiritual poverty.

Why so harsh? And then, we didn't beat him up or throw him out... We had a drink and a chat with him for the piece on him in *Medved*.

Come on... We had different jobs to do.

Aha! At last, you've acknowledged that there can be a professional morality. As soon as you got into a journalist's skin, you understood it. When you took on the function of a mass media worker, you began behaving differently than you do as an ordinary person. You're not punching the guy in the face, you talk to him as if he were an old friend, pour him a drink and make jokes—

No, Igor, our job, in truth, was to let him talk in his own words and then to say: Make up your own minds. We didn't write, Gorshkov is a damned bastard, he hates Russia, he's a misanthrope, he does what he can to drive people crazy. But what do they do? They call you all kinds of names.

I mean, go ahead and get a transcript of my interview from 1998 that I gave in New York to a Russian radio station. Post it on the Internet, print it in *Moskovsky Komsomolets*. But why did Minkin cut it up, switch around paragraphs, print it with all the tsk-tsk-tsk, the snot and tears? Why? And then there was all the PR support, the roundtable on TV when they all wrung their hands and said what a bastard that Kokh was. Khinshtein leaped up in support of Minkin and said, "How can anyone hate Russia that much!" And everybody sat there and watched.

Ah, yes! Your interview got a lot of play then. You were in New York and gave it by telephone…

No, I made a trip to their studio somewhere in New Jersey. What was your reaction? Do you remember?

I remember. I read your famous interview and thought: Wow, he's crapped on everybody. He should take a look at himself!

You thought—what a jerk.

Like that. Kokh is angry, cynical, without a conscience—that sort of thing. It's not surprising that you were attacked after that interview.

Where did that desire to expose me come from?

Do you want to know? A classic once said that when you tell the truth without love, you get not the truth, but vindictive exposé. Stylistically, the interview was a juxtaposition: "You're assholes, I'm good." That always elicits hostility. You must agree.

I don't doubt it. Especially after Minkin's editing.

Kokh's Commentary:

The unavoidability of commenting on Minkin's famous article, which pretends to be an objective analysis of my ill-starred interview, is obvious to me now. Without this commentary, the book would be incomplete. The reader might suspect a certain lack of courage on the author's part—there would be a sense of an unfinished polemic.

I replied to the basic charges of an infuriated "cultural community" when Minkin's attack came out, but there is still Minkin's bombastic style.… What are you supposed to do with that? As soon as you start reading Minkin in MK or *Novaya gazeta*, you get the bombast right away. Whatever the topic. Abundance of pornography—bombast. State officials getting fat—bombast. Somebody else outrages Minkin—more bombast. Is he capable of writing without bombast? Especially without exposé-type bombast? With, say, self-irony? Or to write manly "Remarqueian" prose? I can't change his style, but I can tell you where he twisted my words. Here is his article about my interview. My comments on his article are in italics and brackets.

Farewell, Washed Russia: The Confessions of a Former Vice Premier
By Alexander Minkin

In the past, if a young man who had a good career began behaving badly, he was rebuked: "The Homeland has given you everything, and you ..."

Alfred Kokh is former Vice Premier of Russia, former head of Russia's State Property Committee—a solid, wealthy businessman, president of Montes Auri (Golden Mountains), which paid Chubais and his comrades in arms hundreds of thousands of dollars, and perhaps continues to pay. Kokh was our government. He was at the very top. There were only two positions higher: premier and president.

[*Typical journalistic tricks. The "solid, wealthy businessman" at that moment (right after the default) had debts of several million dollars and had never been either president or even shareholder of Montes Auri. I had been chairman of the Board of Directors. There's more: "and perhaps continues to pay." That "perhaps" shows spinelessness. Really, Alexander, screw up your courage and insult Chubais outright. Why don't you write: Chubais takes bribes. Everyone knows you hate him. You hate him without reason, with a wild, animal hatred. You can't go on letting it stew.... You can't keep coming up with all those "allegedlys," "apparentlys," "seemingly"s.... You have to let your unconscious have free rein. Or you might lose your mind.*

And further: I wasn't "your" government. I was part of the government. Do I need to explain the difference between the part and the whole? No? Excellent! Then there is still hope. Let me remind you that the rest of the government included, among others, Minster of Internal Affairs Kulikov, Minister of Defense Sergeyev, Minister of Foreign Affairs Primakov, Director of the FSB Kovalev, and chairman of the government Chernomyrdin.... So much for the "government of young reformers."

It's a lie that above me were only the premier and president. There were lots of people above me. For instance, head of the president's administration, the first vice premiers, the chairmen of all the federal courts, the speakers of both chambers of the parliament, the general prosecutor—those were the ones who were formally above me in government; but informally, you have to add Tatyana Dyachenko, Yeltsin's daughter; the unforgettable Gusinsky and Berezovsky; the Ministry of Foreign Affairs, the FSB, the Ministry of Internal Affairs, the Ministry of Defense, and the Security Council.... Those are the first to spring to mind. So Mr. Minkin is off the mark—it may look good on paper, but it's a no go.]

Recently published in America is *The Selling of the Soviet Empire*, for which Kokh received $100,000 two years ago from a small Swiss firm, for promising to write it. In connection with the publication, Kokh gave an interview to a Russian radio station (WMNB) in the USA. Since he mentioned me, Mikhail Buzukashvili called me from New York and offered to play the tape for me. I listened and said, "I think people in Russia should know about this."

[*My fee was not for "promising" to write a book, but for my obligation to write a book. An advance. The difference is clear. So is Minkin's intention to distort the meaning.*]

Citizens, you have a unique opportunity to see the train of thought of our government. To see how they think and what they think.

In reading this, remember: This is not a telephone conversation overheard by someone. Before you is an open, public appearance.

[*This is very to the point. The ardor for the exposé in our incorruptible press so often lurks by the keyhole that the reader might not notice that this is a rare event: an open and public appearance.*]

Chubais has many times called Kokh an honest man and his fellow thinker. Chubais says the same of Gaidar, and Gaidar of Chubais. And that is true—they are fellow thinkers. Therefore, as you read this, remember: This is not a unique specimen, but a member of a team. And if Kokh says such things before a microphone, you can imagine what they—Kokh, Chubais, Gaidar, et al.—say among themselves.

[*I rush to satisfy the curiosity of Minkin and everyone else. I have never discussed anything with either Chubais or Gaidar that I would be embarrassed to say in public. Moreover, the topic that I touched on in the interview cited below I have never, in any form, discussed with those two men. By the way, as far as I recall, Gaidar condemned me publicly on television for my meditations, and Chubais, in a private conversation, called me an asshole. That's the truth. Minkin's conclusions are merely the result of his imagination and his own unsatisfied dreams. He really wants to expose the Gaidar-Chubais plot against Russia, and there isn't one. So he keeps dreaming. On the pages of the newspaper.*]

What they think in private is also easy to imagine. What you are about to read could easily go without commentary. But as you read, you will not hear any chuckles or giggles, or the intonation used by a superman talking about subhumans.

[*Now here's a transcript of the actual radio interview*]

Alfred, what were you trying to say with the title of your book, *The Selling of the Soviet Empire*?

I wasn't trying to say anything. My publisher came up with the title.

They say that privatization in Russia was running wild....

It's that way everywhere. For example, in Czechoslovakia—they're not pleased with the results of privatization there, either. Nowhere, not in a single country in the world, was the electorate pleased with the results of privatization.

It truly is that way. And there is nothing surprising about it. Judge for yourselves: Property goes to a few, and millions wanted it. Take the simplest case—auctions. There are many participants in an auction, and even more who would have liked to have participated but could not. The auction is over. The winner is announced. Judge for yourself: Which of the losers will admit that he lost fair and square? Right, very few. The rest will say they used trickery, bribery, corruption, they've got everything in their hands.

Even in sports, where the rules are transparent and clear, the loser always says, I wasn't in form today, I pulled a muscle, I'm recovering from an injury, the referee wasn't fair.... So what can you expect when you're dealing with tens of millions of dollars? That is why people everywhere are always unhappy with the results of privatization. It would be amazing if it were the reverse. It's just that in normal countries the state protects those results and declares them irreversible by virtue of its authority. But in Russia, the state—which formally accepted the results—uses tame politicians and journalists to cast doubt on them, forcing the owners of privatized property to exploit it ruthlessly, pumping out profits into offshore companies because they worry: What if they take it away from me?

I assure you that a politics that is out of step with the economy has no future. If the regime fails to notice, when it is laying out its cards in political solitaire, what effect that has on the investment process (for example), then that regime is preparing the way for a serious crisis.

What did Russia gain, in reality, from privatization?

Russia gained a financial infrastructure, the ability to trade shares, the ability to attract investment through that instrument. Russia got a stratum of private property owners, Russia got money … hmmm … around $20 billion. And it seems to me, that is enough.

What in your opinion was inappropriate in the path of implementing privatization?

Well, I would have rejected the vouchers, if not for the pressure from the Supreme Soviet.

There are frequent mentions in the press of enterprises that were allegedly bought for a very small percentage of the real value —suggesting, therefore, that the people were simply robbed.

Well, the people weren't robbed, because it didn't belong to them. How can you rob someone of something he doesn't own? And as for being sold cheaply, let's hear some concrete examples.

Well, for example, Norilsk Nickel. If I'm not mistaken, it was valued at $170 million, but they say it's worth billions.

Let the people who say it's worth billions pay billions for it. I'd like to see the person who would pay even $1 billion for Norilsk Nickel—which, at the time we were selling it, had losses of 13 trillion rubles.

Some people say that things in Russia are catastrophic, and the economic future is spectral. What do you think?

I think so, too.

You see no light at the end of the tunnel?

No.

How do you foresee Russia's economic future?

As a raw-materials appendage. Certain immigration of peoples who can think but don't know how to work (in the sense of digging), who only know how to invent. And then, collapse—and turning into ten small states.

And how long will that take?

I would think ten to fifteen years. You see … Over the course of seventy years, while the world economy was forming, Russia—rather, the Soviet Union—was outside the process, developing separately, following its own laws. And the world economy formed without the Soviet Union. It is self-sufficient, it has enough resources, it has everything. So now Russia shows up, but no one needs it. (Laughs.) There is no place for it in the world economy, its aluminum and oil are not needed. Russia is only in the way, reducing prices with its dumping. That is why I think that the prospect is grim, without a doubt.

Do you predict investment in Russia, and will it be as large as expected?

No, it won't, because no one needs Russia. (Laughs.) Russia is not needed by anyone (laughs), don't you understand?

[*First, about "Russia is not needed by anyone." Minkin cut out the end of that sentence. In full, it went like this: "Russia is not needed by anyone except itself." They even caught him out on that in a live program on television. Minkin had to get rid of that part of the sentence to reveal me to be the lowlife he wants.*

Further. I've already written about the fact that the lack of interest in Russia and Russians on the part of investors, and foreigners in general, is perceived here in Russia as a profound insult. You must agree with me that such a reaction to a basically neutral fact is inappropriate. What is so intolerable about it? That you have to lie down and die on the spot. No one needs Denmark except the Danish, and what of it? Have they developed mass psychosis? Has their national mentality disintegrated as a result?]

But Russia has gigantic economic and human resources, and working for the Russian market—

What gigantic resources does Russia have? I'd like to dismantle that myth once and for all. Oil? It's much warmer and cheaper to extract it in the Persian Gulf. They mine for nickel in Canada, aluminum in America, coal in Australia. There is timber in Brazil. I don't understand what's so special about Russia.

World reserves of oil are approximately one hundred forty billion tons. Saudi Arabia holds about thirty percent. The entire Near East, around sixty-six percent. Russia has approximately five percent of world reserves of oil.

Yes, today we are extracting more oil than anyone. Even more than Saudi Arabia. And we're right to do it. It's stupid not to, at such high prices. You can't maintain that it's better to extract it when prices are low. But strategically, we are not a serious alternative to the Near East. We're just tactical competitors, a temporary substitute. And the cost of extraction, because of our geography, is significantly higher.

A similar analysis can be made for every item of Russian export. Metals and timber. Only Russian gas stands alone. Our reserves of gas are truly exceptional (twenty-five percent of world reserves). But because of that exceptionality, there is practically no reform in Gazprom, and production has stopped at five hundred fifty to five hundred eighty cubic meters a year. We sell it at less than cost on the domestic market, and we are gradually losing foreign markets. The outstanding new managers may soon destroy the "national property."

But trading with Russia, such an enormous country, with an enormous need to buy, buy, buy—

In order to buy, you need money. The Russian's can't earn anything, so they can't buy anything.

In a word, you see no prospects?

No, I don't. (Laughs.) Well, if Primakov sees any, let him work (laughs). As soon as I stopped seeing them, I quit the government. (He did not quit; he was fired. On August 11, 1997, Vice Premier of Russia Kokh flew to America with his family for a vacation. On August 12 there was a sudden announcement of his retirement. On August 14 he returned for a day and half, turned in his portfolio, and left for the USA. Despite the obvious scandal, Chubais lied out of habit and said that this departure was "planned." Kokh is trying to tell us that before leaving he had been a patriotic enthusiast and statist; and then he sold Svyazinvest, and after August 12 suddenly became a pessimist and quit. If there's a girl anywhere who believes him, Kokh should marry her. That kind of trust will make his life very easy. Alexander Minkin)

[*Let me ask a question, Alexander: How did you learn that my family and I had left for the U.S.? Only one way—you read the transcript of the wiretap! Tsk-tsk-tsk. You should be ashamed of yourself. Didn't your mother tell you as a child that eavesdropping was naughty? How could you?*

Gusinsky had me under surveillance; he tapped my phones, he recorded all the names and addresses of people I met with. He didn't find anything "salty" about me. I guess that, out of spite, he dumped it all on the Internet and in the papers. He lied about half of it, literally half, to make it more believable.

I was a hired state official. No one elected me. I never judged or imprisoned anyone. I never sought to be a moral leader of my generation. I never taught anyone how to live (I'm not sure myself what is the right way to live). So why, if some asshole kept surveillance on me and gathered all kinds of nonsense on me, should a second one (who is a genius) dig around in it and also invite the public to do so?

The details of my departure you know, dear readers. I described them in the previous chapter, "Bottle 16: 1997." Let me reiterate: No one fired me. The attacks began later. At that time, they all said nice things about my great contributions. Who? Well, Chernomyrdin for one; Valentin Yumashev, head of the presidential administration; and Tatyana Dyachenko, Yeltsin's daughter. Not to mention Chubais, Nemtsov, and Sysuev. And at first the press had a kind evaluation of me. Minkin's lying again. And how could he not lie, since Gusinsky asked him to? Or ordered him to?]

Where do you think the Russian government's economic policies can turn? Will there be a return to the old methods?

What does that matter? No matter how you look at it, it's a bankrupt country.

And do you feel that no methods of running Russia will help?

I think it's hopeless.

Can reforms in the usual sense of the word be appropriate for Russia?

If Russia can reject the endless talk about the special spirituality of the Russian people and its special role, reforms can appear. But not if they're stuck on national self-love, seeking special approaches to oneself, and thinking that loaves of bread grow on trees. The Russian people admire themselves so much; they are still so delighted by their ballet and their classical literature of the nineteenth century, that they are incapable of doing anything new.

But perhaps Russia has its own path?

In economics there are no unique paths. There are laws.

They bring up the Polish experience, the Chinese experience…. Would that be useful for Russia?

Without a doubt. Yesterday in the *Financial Times*, there was an article about how a state official in China stole $25 billion in subsidies for grain—and how that experience would be very useful for Russia. Of course, we don't have $25 billion. But the Polish experience holds nothing particularly positive for us. It's a myth spread by the IMF. What have they done that's so special? Have they created a product? They're just getting along, digging up potatoes.

If we follow your views on Russia's tomorrow, it's a very joyless picture….

Yes, it is. And why should it be joyful? (Laughs.)

But it would be good for the long-suffering people—

It's their own fault that the long-suffering people suffer. No one occupied them, no one vanquished them, no one herded them into prisons. They snitched on one another, they put one another into prison, and they executed themselves. Now the nation is sowing what it reaped.

Do you believe that Yeltsin's reforms have crashed completely, or will they have an effect on Russia's future? After all, much has changed in Russia in the last ten years.

Yes, we tried to change things. I think that in two or three hundred years, the effect will be felt.

And what can Russia expect politically—will there be a return to the old methods?

I think that politically Russia has an idiotic position regarding Yugoslavia. Russia is a multiethnic state, with Muslims, and Orthodox Christians, and Jews, and everything else—and yet for some reason they've taken the Orthodox Christian position, defending the Serbs, who, as I see it, are wrong. I don't understand what Russia's foreign policy is; for me, it is a collection of totally unrelated statements intended to take a stand as a superpower. Why do we support Saddam against the United States, knowing very well that Saddam is a competitor for our oil if it is allowed on the market? For me, Russian foreign policy is not tied to the economy, and I blame Primakov for that.

What might happen inside Russia—can people come to power who espouse Communist ideas?

They already have. The full program. Textbook Communists: Maslyukov, Primakov, and others.

Do you think that Zyuganov is the same Communist—

Don't think that Zyuganov is a social democrat. He is trying to appear like one in the West. He's just an ordinary Commie, nothing more.

The domestic political situation in Russia—how will it develop, in your opinion?

For the Communists to come to power, there is no need for a rebellion. They will come completely legally, like the fascists in Germany in 1933.

If the Communists come to power, what can be expected from them?

Perhaps that there will be Communism.

No, I meant what kind of Communism? Both Stalin and Gorbachev were Communists.

No form of Communism, Stalin's or Gorbachev's, suits me.

But what could really happen in Russia? Could there be prisons, repressions, something like 1937?

There could. There are many who want it.

Still, many people consider—and provide lots of evidence—that Zyuganov is no Communist.

He's a Communist if only because he calls himself a Communist. Say there was a label that reads "shit." I wouldn't hang it on myself. But the man takes the label "Communist" and hangs it on himself. They are equivalent concepts for me.

[*I maintain that Communists are the fiercest enemies not only of Russia but of all humanity. They have demonstrated that in Russia, China, and Cambodia. They've shown it in dozens of countries. Without exception, Communist regimes were and are repressive. There hasn't been a single Communist model offered that had stability without an apparatus of police suppression. Hundreds of millions of people tortured throughout the world are the result of their work on creating the "new man." The Communists outstripped not only the Nazis in their extermination of the human species, but even such diseases as the plague, tuberculosis, and cholera.*

Only a mentally ill person with a pathological need for human suffering and blood could be proud of being a Communist. A true patriot of Russia must avoid them like mad dogs—certainly not shake hands with them, but cross to the other side of the street when he sees them coming.

That is what I personally believe.]

Minkin said that after the whole noisy scandal started over the book fees, which he considered to be a hidden form of bribery, Chubais declared that some significant amount of the money (ninety percent) was given to a foundation. Minkin said that still has not been done.

That's a lie. We are ready to show the checks and payment documents.

That everything has been turned over?

Everything. It's simply a lie. (Even in court, Kokh's co-authors, Chubais and Boyko, could not show payment documents confirming that they had fulfilled their promise "to pay ninety-five percent of the honorarium to charity." They gave thirty to forty percent to their foundation [that is, to themselves], but not a cent went to charity. A. M.)

[*All right, let's go through it point by point.*

First: The charitable donation was made not to our foundation but to a foundation we neither created nor administered. Incidentally, that foundation, Foundation for the Defense of Private Property, exists to this day, as far as I know.

Second: Minkin is a clever manipulator. He wrote: "thirty to forty percent," making it clear that he does not insist on the accuracy of his data, but is merely saying that the real amount of our charitable donation was closer to forty than to ninety-five. This is actually so, since the donation was sixty percent (or thousand dollars, since that is the same—the honorarium, as is known, was $100,000 per person).

Third: We never promised to pay ninety-five percent of the honorarium to charity, leaving ourselves only five percent. We promised to keep five percent and give the rest to charity. What difference does that make? Simple: You get the honorarium, you pay income tax (at the time, it was thirty-five percent). The sequence is: You get the honorarium, you pay $35,000 in taxes, keep $5,000 (the actual honorarium, which was what we intended to keep), and give the rest, $60,000—to charity.

Fourth: "It is easy to guess" that Minkin made the mistake because "most likely" he always received his salary in an envelope, and "apparently" never paid taxes. That was why he was surprised that our accounts did not coincide with his. There is no other explanation. Anyone who is paid legally calculates the after-tax income. Gotcha, patriot Minkin! You shout about love for Russia, but you've forgotten about paying taxes. This is given as information for the tax inspectors for the district where citizen Minkin lives.]

How great is interest in the West in what is happening in Russia now?

The interest is very restrained. No greater than in Brazil. Russia has got to let go of its self-image as a great power and take a place with Brazil, China, and India. If it takes that place and understands its role in the world economy, it will be a useful country.

That is, humbly accept one's true place in life, and go back to school?

Of course! Instead of trying to invent the hydrogen bomb with only three grades of primary school education.

In your opinion, how did that happen? Were there preconditions that led to it?

It happened out of the stupidity that led to the catastrophe and the acceptance of the Soviet Union's debts. That was stupid. It meant $90 billion hanging on a very weak economy, and the subsequent catastrophe was just a matter of time. The West tricked Russia; the West promised to restructure that debt, and it did not do it. The West promised economic aid and did not give it, leaving Russia alone with that debt, which it had not borrowed. I think this was an element of a special strategy to weaken Russia on the part of the West.

So, Russia's economic woes come from the West, you mean?

Russia's economic woes are the result, first of all, of seventy years of Communism—which, to put it crudely, ruined the national spirit and the nation's brains. As a result, the Russian no longer exists; instead there is *Homo sovieticus*, who does not wish to work although his mouth is constantly open—he wants bread and circuses.

How well does the West understand that chaos in Russia could endanger the entire world?

Frankly, I don't see why chaos in Russia could endanger the entire world. Unless you mean that it has atomic weapons?

Exactly. Isn't that enough?

I think that all you need is one division of paratroopers to take away our nuclear weapons. Just land once, and take away all those damned missiles. Our army is in no shape to resist. The Chechen war has shown that brilliantly.

What is your niche in Russian life?

There is no niche. (Chuckles.)

[*End of interview. The world didn't collapse. Russia is still standing. But Minkin can't stop. Now comes more of his text. I consider it a masterpiece*].

Here you have a fellow thinker of Chubais, Gaidar, and others. Here is the man whom Yeltsin appointed to head the State Property Committee—or rather, the selling of all of Russia's property.

[*As usual, Minkin has trouble with logic. I can't tell from this text what Yeltsin appointed me to do. First, it seems clear, to be head of the State Property Committee; but then the author corrects himself. Rather, he says, to sell all of Russia's property. I don't understand what was not clear about the first part of the sentence. But I was not in charge of selling all of Russia's property, since most of that property (minerals, land, railroads, defense industry, space industry, atomic energy, and many other things) were not for sale. I was in charge of only the part that it had been decided would be sold.*]

There was a man in the government who absolutely did not believe that the country could not rise up. And that means that he was there, on top, for some other reason.

We see a typical Russian serf (even though he's German). He'll watch a horse die without lifting a finger: It's not his—it belongs to the master, the neighbor, someone else, why should it live?

Yasha, Mme. Ranevskaya's lackey (Chekhov, *The Cherry Orchard*), says to old Firs, when no one can overhear him: "I wish you would die soon." And then asks his mistress, "Take me with you to Paris! It's impossible to live here, it's ignorance all around."

[*How cleverly Minkin put it! What depth of understanding of the typical Russian serf! So this is how they think? And they don't care that the master's horse will die? How interesting. I would never have thought so.*

I always figured that the typical Russian serf (even if he were German or Jewish, for instance) would set apart his master's horse, taking excellent care of it, making pleasing the master the purpose of his life. Hoping that, in return, the master will take him to Paris with him.

And also: "the typical Russian serf" (perhaps Minkin does not know this) was the ancestor of ninety percent of the Russian people. My own forefather, in fact. My mother's ancestors came from the European part of Russia, from the peasantry, which means they had been serfs. There's nothing to be proud of in that, but I have no intention of hiding it. I can't boast of belonging to some of those chosen peoples who successfully evaded slavery.

However, as a rule, the master barely notices the slavish servility and loyalty, taking it as his due. The master drops his flunkey as soon as he no longer needs him. Well, the way Gusinsky dropped you, Minkin.

Oh, sorry, was I being tactless? Shame on me! There is no similarity. I'm sure you and Gusinsky were just good friends. How could I have thought otherwise?]

With arrogant scorn, he says "they," "the Russians" … He doesn't say *Russische Schwein*, because it is improper. But that's what he thinks. It's obvious.

He cannot think otherwise. Because it's either *Russische Schwein* or "Kokh is a *schwein.*"

People want to think themselves good and honest.

If you love or at least respect people, then robbing them makes you feel guilty. But if you despise them, if you don't consider them human, then, as they say, it's God's will to do it.

A man who thinks this way cannot not steal. Especially if he can do so with impunity, his actions formulated as government resolutions. You cannot be punished for your thoughts. Then why did the people to whom I showed Kokh's interview feel they wanted him punished? It must be because you understand how he acted if he thinks this way.

[Minkin! You remind me of Stalin's prosecutors. They acted by punishing people for actions they did not perform. It was the "exclusion method."

What you are doing, Minkin, is called retribution. In 1998 you knew very well that you were in no danger. Gusinsky's fat purse and connections in agencies of law and order would guarantee that you would win any lawsuit. And that your opponents (you had your fun mocking me, Chubais, and Gaidar) were decent enough people not to smash your skull in. You knew that, slandered and fired, they would not be able to get a fair hearing from the occupied mass media to make their case.]

But soon indignation passes, and you start to feel sorry for Kokh. He, of course, will live a sated life, giggling. But he's unlikely to become a real man. Unless a miracle comes to pass.

The interviewer's last question, "What is your niche?" sounds insulting. Niches and areals are usually used for animals. Because the environment in which you live and your homeland are not identical concepts. Kokh is asked as if he was an animal. But that is a response to what he had said. And Kokh is not insulted by the term, he responds calmly: There is no niche. Not Home or Work, but niche. A roof, quota, subsidy, and margin.

However, everything Kokh had to say would elicit a far less emotional reaction if the reader would think of him not as a former Vice Premier of Russia but as what he really is: the defendant in a criminal case in apartment machinations.

[So, I am an animal. Thank you for your candor. I'm very grateful. However, niches are not just ecological.

I can tell you that there are also market niches, ecological ones, and others. I have no intention of falling about as proof of my love for the Homeland (by the way, the word was not capitalized in Minkin's text). But I have no intention of doing that anywhere. I don't consider that a very manly way of showing one's love in general.

As for the apartment case, let me inform you that it was dropped for lack of a crime. By the way, Minkin, as Gusinsky's best friend, you must know that a person who is charged is not a criminal. And when there is no sentence from a court (as, for example, in my case), it is not decent to rebuke a person for having been charged. But why am I even trying? It's not decent, it's impolite—but that's never stopped you.]

Last year, *MK* printed transcripts of telephone conversations between Kokh and businessmen and officials. A conversation with Alexander Kazakov, the former first deputy director of the administration of the President of Russia, chairman of the board of directors of Gazprom, and his co-author of the book on privatization that was never published, Kokh begins this way: "Alexander, I'm a faggot." If Kokh was not talking about his sexual orientation but the state of his soul, then it is impossible to argue with that self-assessment.

[When the well-rehearsed and stage-managed book scandal broke out in late 1997, one of the co-authors, Alexander Kazakov, was fired from his position as first deputy of the President's chief of staff.

Alexander Kazakov was holier than the Pope in the whole book story: He didn't even get an honorarium. But they fired him anyway. Our opponents needed the slightest excuse to get rid of a member of our team. A general hysteria was whipped up. All the press controlled by Gusinsky and

Berezovsky (including Minkin) took part. The result was Kazakov's heart attack, hospitalization, surgery. I tried to visit my friend as often as I could at the hospital. One day, when I had promised to come, I could not. I called him and said: "Alexander! I'm a faggot! I deceived you and I'm sorry, and so on." A normal conversation between two guys. But my phone was tapped. They perverted it, lied about me, printed the wiretap in the press, and mocked me.

And now Minkin, too, is having his fun over the phrase. But of course Minkin speaks only in rhymed iambic pentameter.

This is the end. I'm tired of digging around in Minkin's vomit. And his opus is finished, at last. The end. Hurrah.

PS: For some reason, Minkin called his article "Farewell, Washed Russia." I don't know why he had to change Lermontov. What was he trying to say by changing "unwashed" to "washed"? I've heard various theories. For instance: Minkin was hinting that I've "laundered" Russia. The other theories were just as bad. It's just nonsense. Or maybe it's one more example of Minkin's ignorance?

Nevertheless. I feel I must quote my beloved Lermontov's immortal lines. They are as timely as ever:

Farewell, O unwashed Russia!
Land of slaves, land of lords.
And you, blue uniforms.
And you, loyal people.

Perhaps the wall of the Caucasus
Will hide me from your hounds,
From your all-seeing eye
From your all-hearing ears.

But where is that wall behind which one can hide from all the eavesdropping, wire-tapping, peeping, and suspicion?...]

* * *

Alik, your intonation was very important in that interview. As I understood it, it was: "Everything's fallen apart over there, it's over for you, but we Germans managed to skim off the top and feel pretty good here in New York." That's the way it sounded to people. What do you think of that reaction?

You mean they wanted love from me as well?

Why shouldn't the people want love from a writer?

You can tell the truth only to those you love? And you must lie to the rest?

I quoted one of the greats in order to explain to you why they came to dislike you.

I see. But isn't one of the highest manifestations of love telling the truth to the object of your love? Eh?

I don't know. I don't have an answer. Probably not.

I see. So anyone who loves Russia has to lie about her all the time.

Why all the time? There are different situations.

Listen, Igor, here's how it happened: You've come to give an interview, live; you haven't discussed any of the questions beforehand. They ask you what the prospects are for Russia. What do you think, the great and mighty Russian people, with their outstanding Russian culture, great history, the best people in the world—how are they going to develop? In the same turbulently positive and wonderful way? Or how? So what are you supposed to say, based on the love theory?

Let me answer your question with another question. Say you've been invited to participate in a discussion about blacks. Are you going to tell them everything that you think about blacks?

Basically, yes.

Yes?

I'll say what I think about blacks.

Don't lie.

Why do you say that? Why do you think that I have a special desire for truth only regarding Russians? I'd say what I thought about blacks, too.

And if you were a racist and thought that all blacks were stupid, would it be correct to admit it?

First of all, I don't think that about blacks.

Fuck that. I'm just trying to point out that you weren't kind in your discussion with the Russian people in America.

I wasn't talking to the Russian people, but to a Georgian man who lives in America—with an American citizen. First. Second—as for blacks. They don't go around saying that they are the greatest, that the have the best culture, that they are particularly spiritual, that they have a special destiny, unlike all other peoples.

Now, if I were having a discussion with a representative of the Russian people—and let me remind you that I did not have such a discussion—and if he had said: No, no, there are Russians and Russians; basically they're just an ordinary nation, with a hard and complicated history, with a lot of tragedy; rather grim lives the people had, they were basically liberated at the same time as American Negroes, quite recently, and it took them a long time to figure out what to do with that freedom; they had this big national knife fight. Yes, culture is an outstanding element—take music, for instance, Rachmaninoff, Stravinsky, Shostakovich, Prokofiev. And literature.

Whistle me something from Prokofiev.

I don't remember. How about something from *Romeo and Juliet?* Or *Alexander Nevsky. Peter and the Wolf.*

Peter doesn't count.

Well, if it doesn't, it doesn't. I won't insist. Even though it's considered world-class to this day. Shostakovich [*Kokh tries to hum the Leningrad symphony*]. How about Rachmaninoff, do you believe I can whistle a melody by him? [*He whistles.*]

Ah, of course, Alik! You went to music school, I forgot.

Let's go back to the representative of the Russian people. So, I would have sat down with him, and we would have shared our sadness over Russia's fate, we would have shared a bottle of vodka. We would have talked and probably decided that things weren't all that bad, that there was hope. But if all I'd heard before that, for many years in a row, were the trills and thrills of talk, especially from Minkin, about what a fucking great nation Russia is—the best in the world! Not a spot on it, everything's perfect! Great culture, enormous work pride! Wisdom of the ages—tops in everything. Only the lousy parasites in the government are keeping the radiant image of the people from shining even brighter…. How can you not polemicize with that? You put your own people in jail, you executed your own people. Don't you understand that? If you enter into a discussion, a lot depends on the context of the discussion, don't you agree?

Come on, the Russians don't say Christ came from Moscow.

No, but they have something else. In the mass consciousness, Russia beat the Tatar Mongols. In actual fact, they assimilated into each other. There's a huge number of myths like that. "We won the Battle of Borodino." And what makes you think that?

And who do you think won it?

The French.

According to Lev Gumilev, the Tatar Mongols were simply military mercenaries working for the Russian princes.

That was later. Not when they conquered Russia. In turn, the Russian princes were puppets of the Tatar Khan. They went to him to buy the *yarlyk*, the label of rule in the form of a letter from the Khan. And they participated in the feudal ladder, when the Khan climbed up them to his throne. That also existed. Or did Gumilev deny that, too?

I don't remember. I'd have to check.

I don't think he did. By the way, Alexander Nevsky died on the road to the Golden Horde. He was going to pay tribute to the Great Khan.

That's why your interview was so reviled.... I remember that I didn't like it when I read it—He's really gotten on his high horse, I thought. Unlike Lermontov, whom you quoted, about "unwashed Russia."

Not I. That was Minkin.

You and Minkin. Lermontov fought against the Chechens as part of an anti-terrorist operation. In the front lines, he started the poem with "I love Russia, but with a strange love...." He criticized it, but he starts out with "love." Note, please.

Yes.

And who stopped you from fighting in Chechnya? You could have been like Lieutenant Lermontov....

There was no war in Chechnya in 1998.

It was the ceasefire then?

Yes.

I'm not sending you off to war, I'm just trying to explain how it looked to Russians. And you were under investigation at the time, if I'm not mistaken?

Yes.

Under investigation! So, here's the picture: You stole all this money at home and fled to the United States, hiding from justice there, and like a foreigner, an émigré, you addressed the Russians: And you're a bunch of faggots. And, if you recall, Minkin had you giggling vilely. Remember?

Yes. Haha.

You giggled vilely, and you seemed to be drunk. That's the picture.

You heard the interview?

No, I read it. With the vile giggling and the tone of a man who was drunk and had lost all sense of shame. There was nothing academic in your manner: "However, I would also like to note…" By the way, after your interview there was a lot of work done to develop the Russian national sense and freedom of the press. Now all that is just a given.

Yes. Someday people will do their Ph.D.s on the role of my interview in the development of the Russian mentality. And really, it is a commonplace now, what I had said then. By the way, I had another interesting event happen in late 1998. Also involving New York.

Kokh's Commentary:

In addition to my Turkish adventure, model 1996, I also have the experience of "interacting" with American forces. The experience is amusing, and I wish to share it with my readers. After all, what is a book? It is a method of telling others about some interesting events that befell the author and which, in his opinion, rarely happen. And, of course, about his resulting conclusions. That is, his experience is a lesson for others, as they say.

In very late 1998, I went to America to celebrate the New Year. Friends had been inviting me for a long time, and I thought it would be cool to greet the New Year at Times Square, the intersection of Seventh Avenue and Broadway. At midnight, a huge sparkling ball is lowered out of the sky somewhere, and everyone pours into the street, counting down the seconds, then kissing and heading off to bars to celebrate. My wife went to New York a week earlier, and I flew just before Western Christmas.

Flying to New York is rather tiring. You leave Moscow before noon, fly for ten hours, eight of which are swallowed by the time difference (jet-lag), and you arrive in New York only two hours later, local time, than when you left Moscow. Then you have to go through passport control, wait for your luggage, and take a forty-minute cab ride into Manhattan. Basically, you arrive at your destination around 7 p.m., when it's 3 a.m. in Moscow.

It's stupid going to bed then, since you'll get up very early, so you have to stay up until ten or eleven, to get on local time. You feel very crummy for those three hours, but you have to put up with it. You function like a sleepwalker around New York, keeping your eyes open. In that state, the best thing to do is go to the Russian Samovar to see Roman Kaplan and sip a little horseradish vodka, eat jellied meat, listen to the music, and gab with Roma about all your

Moscow-New York friends, the international situation, literature, and how everybody's an asshole.

However, folk wisdom has come up with a clever method to deal with jet lag. It's simple. You have to have a lot to drink at the start of the flight, get up early the morning you're traveling, around six. Thus, after a solid meal with vodka on Aeroflot (heaven forbid you take Delta: The seats are uncomfortable, the stewardesses old and stupid, the food horrible), you fall asleep for three or four hours, waking up fresh as a daisy by the time you arrive in New York, ready to handle the remaining hours until it's eleven locally.

This is what I did, being a habitué of the Moscow-New York flight. I had taken it probably thirty times by then, and all my actions were automatic. I flew first class. As soon as we took off, they brought the blini and black caviar. Blini require vodka. Then came the salads and zakuski, the obligatory Aeroflot soup (borshch, *solyanka*, or *kharcho*), with more vodka, then the main course (which calls for a little bottle of red Bordeaux), followed by the cheese plate (more Bordeaux), desserts, and cognac. My mood was excellent; I read the papers and fell asleep, since I had slept only four hours the night before. Ahead, I thought, New York, my wife, and the New Year awaited me. But treacherous fate had prepared a different scenario. As they say, if you want to make God laugh, tell Him your plans.

We landed, went to passport control. Passport control at Kennedy Airport is much more conveniently organized than at Moscow's Sheremetyevo Airport. There isn't that crowding; the line is set up with special barriers; there are a lot more border guards, or as they call them, immigration officers, than in Moscow; and naturally they move people along much more quickly. By the way, I've never encountered such pushing and shoving and lines at border control, even in third world countries, as we have in Russia.

So, my turn comes. I go to the booth where there's a uniformed black man, I hand him my passport, and I stand there and wait. He pushes buttons on his computer, passes my passport through a scanner, presses something else, then looks at my passport for a long time, sets it aside, and makes a face—the one people make when they're thinking. It's a difficult process for him (lack of practice); I become filled with sympathy, and even (the miracle of my good nature) some respect for his selfless act. But my sympathy and respect quickly vanish, since a few minutes later his face returns to normal. Putting my documents in a special file, he tells me that I have to go into a special room for a more detailed discussion.

I'm not upset yet, since this happens occasionally: A random person from the flood of visitors is picked out, brought to a glassed-in room, and they talk to him about the point of his visit, how long he'll be here, and so on. It's happened to me several times; it's a stupid procedure that only adds ten or fifteen minutes.

I sat down on the special little sofa in the room and waited to be called to the counter for some clerk to talk to me. But no one called me. Thirty minutes went by. All the Latinos who were taken out of the line had been seen, but no one was bothering with me. Finally, a fat black woman from immigration took my package of documents, gave them a quick glance, and took them somewhere inside, beyond the door, to the bosses. I got wary. This was quite different from the usual scenario.

I was alone in the glass room. I didn't have any documents. At that moment, I did not exist. According to my documents, I had left Russia. But I had not entered the USA, according to them. And in fact my documents were in the hands of an official whose name I did not know. If someone had wanted to kidnap me, they could have easily done it, because there would be no one who could trace me. I sat in solitude another half hour. I never felt my separation from the world as acutely as I did then. I couldn't call anyone, since I didn't have an American cell phone—my wife had it—and European ones don't work in the U.S., because it's a different system.

Periodically, an enormous black man in uniform, wearing a gun, would appear in the doorway and regard me closely. When I tried to ask him a question, he'd shout, "Shut up!" The shouting at me gave him great pleasure, so I started asking him questions to make him happy. The response was always good—he shouted in a different way each time. Sometimes in a deep voice, yelling; then in a falsetto, somewhat hysterically; then in a screechy soprano. The way provincial singers usually sing the national anthem at U.S. football and baseball games—all over the scale. The way he treated me was the final proof that something extraordinary was happening. I never liked the extraordinary. Especially in late 1998. It never boded well. The American guard yelling at me was definitely a bad sign, since Americans as a whole are friendly and hospitable.

Finally, out of the bowels of the office, came the tubbo with the flirty gun in her belt holster. She crooked a finger at me, looked me up and down, and asked: "Are you sure that you know English well? I'm asking you this because your future depends on how you answer the questions!" Naturally, I chickened out and said that my English was inadequate for fateful decisions. She leaned in even more, and said that then I would have to wait while they found an interpreter. I sat back down on my now familiar couch, and the screamer, whom I was really sick of by then, started in on me again. He rattled his handcuffs, dawdled, slapped his nightstick in his hand, and yelled and yelled and yelled....

The ten-hour flight, jet lag, hangover, and nervous exhaustion took their toll—I got sleepy. I also needed the bathroom. I looked at the tough-acting "mister officer" and told him I had to take a leak. He shut up unexpectedly. A struggle was reflected in his face. Apparently, he would have gladly forbidden me from going, but on the other hand, the consequences could be unpredictable. What if I pissed myself? Or even worse? And then he'd have to be in the room with me. Reluctantly, he led me to the toilet and guarded me the entire time I did my business. Then I was thirsty, and he fetched me water. For the next half-hour he lost his image of a threatening guy, which irritated him enormously.

Finally the heavy woman came back, and with her were three senior officers. All black. Behind their mighty backs was a tiny, weary, and rather frightened man who looked as if he came from Brighton Beach. He was introduced to me as an interpreter. The most senior officer asked me, "Where did you get your American visa?" I looked at the Brighton guy. He whispered: "Just don't lie!" I replied that I got the visa at the American consulate in Moscow. The interpreter gave me a delighted look, as if I had performed an incredibly daring deed. The officer drilled me with a look (he must have practiced before a mirror, because he looked incredibly fierce) and asked: "What is the purpose of your visit?" He seemed to think this was the question that would flunk me. Before I could even look at him, the interpreter begged me again, "Just don't lie!" I said I was there for New Year's, and that my wife was in New York and expecting me.

There was confusion in the ranks of the immigration officials. It looked as if they had exhausted their questions, and they didn't know what to do with me next. They took me to another office. They searched in a computer for a long time. At last, they said, "Why did you illegally get permission to enter the United States?" I was ready for anything but that. I looked at the interpreter. He hid his eyes and said in Russian: "Why did you illegally get an American visa?"

I understood that there was some very serious nastiness here, and I said to my interpreter: "Interpret this. But precisely. I'll be listening closely. Tell them the following: How can you consider my visa illegal if I've used it to enter the USA over a dozen times already? Including New York, and right through your immigration post?" Their reply was the height of logic and consistency: "You visa is illegal, and we are annulling it!"

"Wait!" I said. "May I find out the reasons for this decision? I'm not a criminal, I'm not on trial. What's the problem? If you had asked, I would have told you that yes, in Russia I am being investigated, but the case has not reached the courts and is not likely to, and under all the laws I am considered an innocent man! But you haven't even asked me about that. You're telling me total nonsense about my visa being illegal!" There was a pause…. The first one to crack was the screamer. He leaped over toward me, spittle flying, and shouted right in my face: "Shut up!"

Then my chubby friend chimed in. In a sleepy voice, she declared that there was logic in what I said, and that I had the right to defend myself in a New York City court. If I chose that path, they would take me directly to a city jail, and tomorrow I would have a lawyer paid for by the state, and within a few weeks I would be able to lay out my argument in court. If I was not prepared to argue my case in court, then they were right, and they would annul my visa and send me back on the next plane to Russia—or any country where I wished to go and for which I had a visa.

I asked, "May I call my wife?" The answer was brief: No. I thought a bit. The prospect of spending New Year's Eve in an American jail was not very enticing. I had Swiss and Schengen visas in my passport. I asked, "Has the flight to Moscow left yet?" Receiving confirmation, I asked them to get me a ticket on the next flight to anywhere in Europe. The shouter was given the assignment. Humiliated, he took my credit card and went off to buy a ticket. He returned quickly, and with evident disgust handed me a ticket to Zurich. Boarding was in a half-hour.

The senior officer looked at me with respect. He must have been touched by my constructive approach. He stamped my visa CANCELLED in thick letters and said that I had done the right thing, admitting the illegality of the visa I had obtained. I was about to tell him that I was admitting no such thing, it was just that I didn't want to be in jail, but he just waved his hand at me and disappeared back into the bowels of the office.

They took mug shots (profile and full face), fingerprinted me, and called a special guard to accompany me to the plane. The guard was an elderly white man. The screamer was completely humiliated—he would not be convoying me in front of all those honest people. When we reached the duty free zone, I told the guard, "Let me call my wife. She's worried about me. Why should she suffer another eight hours until I can call her from Zurich?" Without a second's hesitation, he gave me permission. Then I got really pushy and told him I didn't have a coin. He took a dollar and gave me two quarters. Having made a profit of fifty cents, he perked up completely, and led me to a public telephone. I called my wife and explained what had happened.

She reacted stoically. In general, she knows how to behave in a difficult moment. In a calm, steady voice, she said that she figured something like that had happened. It was a shame that we would have to be apart for New Year's Eve, but it was nothing terrible—just don't worry. My wife has a magical effect on me. I talked to her and felt much better. Suddenly I felt sorry for her. She was alone in New York. Waiting for her husband, who, like a total jerk, is under convoy being sent to Switzerland. It had been my idea to celebrate New Year's in New York. I'm always causing her trouble. I don't want to apologize here, and in general go on about my feelings for my wife, but at that moment I felt a sharp, warm, piercing sense of tenderness toward her. After all, Germans are a sentimental lot.

I boarded the Boeing 747, upstairs, in first class. I ordered a vodka, ate a meal, and fell asleep. After spending a total of eighteen hours in the air and four at JFK, I landed in Zurich. There were three hours before the flight to Moscow. I wandered around the airport aimlessly. I bought some duck liver paté, some Tsar Nikolai *balyk* (air-dried sturgeon back, delicious), and some other stuff, and decided go to St. Petersburg to see my mother-in-law, catch up on my sleep, and then see what's what.

A month later I learned that the Russian bureau of Interpol, on Prosecutor General Skuratov's information—who in turn was acting on the request (can that be called a request?) of Gusinsky—had informed the Americans that I was a criminal, and so on. Naturally, all that was illegal. It is ridiculous to have to explain that a criminal is only a person who has been found so by a court. Now Skuratov is telling everyone what a big observer of the law he is, fighting corruption, all that stuff. But there's a question stuck in my brain: What if they had entered him in the computer, the way I had been, when they started that criminal case against him because of the two girls he was screwing? Would he think that was the right thing? Is it right to inform on someone without waiting for a trial? Ah, go fuck yourself, you old goat....

Later, Chubais and Nemtsov wrote a letter to Secretary of State Madeleine Albright. She gave instructions to the embassy, and they renewed my visa. By the way, it was then that Peter Aven introduced me to Ambassador James Collins. He was an interesting man, despite the fact that he really liked Gusinsky. Collins apologized, though there was nothing to apologize for: It wasn't the Americans who put me on the stop list, but the Russians.

The conclusion to be made from the story is very simple: all rubbish is the same.

I met with my wife in Courchevel, a week after my deportation. We were happy.

* * *

Okay, Alik, now let's review some of my articles in 1998. For example, I wrote about Valya Tsvetkov. I looked up some old cases—when the Soviet regime was charging him under the article on "industrial contraband." In 1998 I flew out to interview him in Magadan. Here is a man who started a cooperative business and was under investigation, and now he was governor of Magadan, with Kolyma, part of the Gulag. [*He was killed by a gunman in 2002.*] And then I wrote about Valery

Abramkin. He was a former prison camp inmate. He wanted to re-issue his book *How To Survive in a Soviet Prison*, which at that point was no longer Soviet, but Russian. And he went to all these foundations and capitalists, but no one would give him any money. And he said, "What's the problem? What are those people worried about? Is it the amount or the prison?" The book was very interesting. I was so inspired by it that I started traveling to the prison zones and also wrote a book. I also traveled to Naro-Fominsk, where the Germans paid reparations to former prisoners in the concentration camps, right before May 9, Victory Day. It was a chilling spectacle. The old men were given two thousand marks a year. They would say, at least we'll eat our fill, for a change. All this for May 9. While the Western ex-prisoners were getting not two but twenty thousand marks, for example.

They were obviously using the consumer basket as a measure.

Maybe that's what they did; but one prisoner, his name was Zusman, refused on principle and would not take the money. He would write to various European organizations: "Why is a French Jew better than me? Why does he get more money?" He refused to take the money—I don't need your handouts, he said.

Igor, I don't know the reason. I was only assuming. I don't know why they made a distinction.

Maybe because the Soviet Union had rejected those payments outright, twice. On principle.

The person to ask about the money is Ludmila Narusova, the widow of Sobchak—she was responsible for the distribution of those benefits. Considering the miserable situation of pensioners in Russia, those payments are a help. I feel that whoever gives the money, it's good. But, on the other hand … just look. Your grandfather shot a huge number of people when he worked for the Cheka.

Well, let's say that's so.

And now, why should you spend part of your money to help the relatives of those people? Or say he held people in prison and then they were released, and now you have to pay the people your grandfather had put away.

I think it's a different picture with Germany. People were made to work for German industry, and they weren't paid wages. The industry grew through their labor.

That's not so. All those industries were bombed to nothing by the Allies. It rose after, on American money from the Marshall Plan.

But still, people worked, and they weren't paid. At least pay them retroactively!

You mean the remaining corporations? Messerschmitt or something? I think some money, including from state coffers, was allocated. But that doesn't matter. There were people in the German camps, and they're paid by Germans now, and that suits me fine. But let's continue that logical line. If you were in a Russian camp, you should get money from the Russian government. Our own inmates also labored for free! Building all those Dneproges hydroelectric stations and the metallurgical plant in Magnitogorsk. Let our corporations, which were built by camp inmates—say, the Magnitogorsk Metallurgical Processing Plant—pay the former prisoners.

That's logical. I know people who bought up land cheap along the shores of the Volga-Moskva Canal, and now they're selling lots for dachas. And they drink to Comrade Stalin, who used forced labor to build the canal, and now these guys are making a profit. They should pay to support the surviving prisoners. You know, that question really should be raised. The Norilsk Nickel smelter, it was built by prison labor—who does it belong to now, who's making a profit from it?

It belongs to Potanin.

Well, Potanin should pay. Let him have a conscience, like the Germans.

Indeed! How can we demand compensation, cheeks trembling in indignation over the fact that Siemens made money on our prisoners of war and the forced labor of civilians taken to Germany, without first pointing this out to Norilsk Nickel and Magnitogorsk Metallurgical, and all the Siberian gold mines?

I just don't know how to do it.

Pass a law in the State Duma!

Then there will be the same problems as with restitution. You'll never figure out where to stop.

Oh, no! We have very clear limits of that period. We know exactly for which charges people should be paid. You don't think that there were crooks, thieves, or murderers in the 1930s? There were. And we're not going to compensate them. But if you were arrested on political charges and rehabilitated in 1956 or later, then please, we owe you. Where did you work? Camp 375a in such-and-such? The enterprise is now called AO Red Teat. It has to pay the compensation.

Excellent. No objections from me.

And until Red Teat pays the compensation, don't bother the Germans. They're the second phase. Otherwise, the Germans are paying, and we're not? Let's take responsibility for ourselves. So that then we will have the moral right to ask the Germans. We've paid our own people we put in the camps. And now, dear comrade Germans, pay our people whom you put in the camps.

The Germans started paying on their own. Voluntarily. Even though the Soviet government refused twice.

And now the man is complaining that the Germans aren't paying enough and is refusing the compensation. Go get the money from Russia first!

Here's what I can tell you about prisoners and compensation. In one camp, I saw two posters hanging side by side. One said: "Go out into freedom with a clear conscience." Well, that's clear, it's just propaganda. The second one said: "You can't understand Russia with reason." I think that's true. Even the guards in the camp zone saw that, and they're not the most scientifically trained lot. So why should we expect banal logic from Russia? I wouldn't base my evaluations and judgments on that. And I'll bet you haven't, either.

Oh, God! I am so sick of that nonsense about "can't understand Russia." But, OK, it will straighten out at the end.

Svinarenko's Commentary:

It sometimes seems to me that you and I, Alik, are talking about two kinds of journalism. One is paid attacks and paid praise, with people like Minkin, Dorenko, and others. It's like the soap operas the public loves. The second kind is that dying (or perhaps already dead), old-fashioned journalism that formed in Soviet times. It had people like Anatoly Agranovsky, the best of the lot. I read him in the old days with a fine and powerful feeling, and thought, there it is, real art. Remembering that in the Russian pantheon, journalism is considered second-rate, compared to pure invention.

Besides Agranovsky, I was wildly interested in Gennady Bocharov, who worked in approximately the same niche. I still remember his essays in *Literaturnaya gazeta*. About the pilot whose plane crashed, and he made a whole story out of it on the level of Shakespeare. I actually met Bocharov, unlike Agranovsky, and I looked upon a living classic. Alas, he was also pushed out of leading newspaper parts. He started writing more about aviation, and no longer in the good old key, but somehow differently. Then there's Arkady Vaksberg, of course. He had those insightful criminal articles about the essence of events and phenomena, later replaced by Police Blotter stuff: Look, the cops on the road, how cool. Demand of the times, allegedly.

Of the old newspaper wolves, the one I like and understand best, and whom I see more frequently, is Yuri Rost. He digs deep, narrates perceptively; he's hard and tough; and on top of that, in the oral tradition, in good company over vodka, he's better than professional stand-up comics. The man is a concert. But they all have stopped writing what they used to write. Why is that? It looks as if the demand has dropped for quality texts on serious topics. People are tired. They had been force-fed wise texts for a long time. And now they're relaxing on pop stuff. The way that all you had under the Soviets was classical music and classy suits and ties. The public was exhausted. And when they finally had a choice, the pendulum swung the other way—the whole country switched from suits to jeans, and instead of Tchaikovsky, everyone listens to criminal slang music. It may change again, or maybe it will stay this way. I'm not sure what's better, listening to classical music under the whip, or being yourself and feeling like a real person with pop music.

In short, I would say that 1998, in my understanding, was the last full year of the journalism that was art for art's sake. And I enjoyed the farewell. The opportunity was there. Did anyone need it? Did anyone read it? Who knows? But on the whole, attempts to deepen the craft, which is rather simple on the whole, had a right to exist. There have been successful examples. Take Gabriel García Márquez, a major classic, who makes money by writing fashionable novels, and then, to satisfy his soul, writes articles for magazines. In a way, I understand him. In 1998, I remember how much I enjoyed working with Kolesnikov and Panyshkin. We were considered special correspondents working for the editor in chief, and publishing these huge sheets of prose. It was like the process of induction, when one coil excites the next: Well, let's see what my comrade has written. Could I do that? And you read anxiously, both afraid and yet hoping to find the new Nabokov, and, like Bunin, exclaim: "This boy has shown up and shot all us old men." Ahh…. Where is all that now? On the other hand, sometimes you'd read a piece and feel relief: Nothing to worry about.

This is the end of this topic. Once, in those days, a veteran and fan of the old journalism, the excitable Sasha Kupriyanov, known as Kuper (he had started out in the old *Komsomolskaya Pravda* as a correspondent), and at the time a big manager in the Potanin-owned mass media, called me in to head a project and become a manager. I refused politely. He was stunned: How could I? This was a new stage in my career, and an enviable one! I thought about the best way of explaining it to him. We were in one of the *Izvestiya* offices. So I said, You see, I want a career like Agranovsky's. And Kuper replied: What are you talking about? You're already like Agranovsky. To be on the same level with him, you need very little. What? Just drop dead. Sorry.

A joke, but it was still nice to hear....

As for my personal life, in April, as planned, our second daughter was born. It was all different from the way things were with our first. By that time, I had some money—for vitamins, a private room, a serious doctor. He invited me to attend the birth: If you want, come, watch, you can even help. But he didn't recommend it. In his opinion, there are certain things in life that are better not to see. There can be more than you need to know. In his observation, men who have seen their wives give birth had a change in their attitude toward women. Negatively. So, I didn't go. I agreed with his conclusion that there can be unnecessary information. We can all think of an example, if we dig in our memories. Why then increase it with our own hands, not to mention our personal time?

In the eight and half years since the birth of our older daughter, I had dropped a lot of attitude and learned to behave more modestly. I had stopped considering myself very wise and had given up the habit of lecturing. With the younger child, I did not have that excessive zeal for bringing up the new generation. We developed a peaceful coexistence from the start. When she attacks me, I behave calmly and try to work things out....

* * *

So, here's a notation I have. For December 30, 1998, I had a plan with Zhechkov—who was also having troubles over taxes then...You weren't alone, remember?

Yes, and Vladimir Grigoryev was being squeezed, too.

And Lisovsky. I wrote articles about it.

Those were all part of the attack by Gusinsky and Berezovsky.

I introduced Grigoyev to the lawyer Genrikh Padva then, and he took up the case right away. So, I was supposed to meet Zhechkov and you at a recording studio at Olympiiskii, where you two were going to make a record.

Yes.

But you had turned off your phones. And I couldn't find you—who knew where the studio was. So did you make a recording?

Yes, we did.

You sang "Churches of Russia," as you are wont to do on holidays?

Yes. And three or four other songs.

Did you issue it, release the CD on the market, or what?

It never came out, of course—you know the level of my vocalizing. But Zhechkov and I each have a disk. Mine's at home somewhere.

The level of your vocalizing? Who knows it? After all, you had musical education. But look! You have a Ph.D., then you're Vice Premier, then the police are after you, then it's suddenly revealed that you're a vocalist…

You see how multifaceted I am. Like Kitovani. Remember him? He was a doctor of philology and a thief in law, *vor v zakone*.

So you could be crowned, too, eh?

No, no, it's not possible. I'm married, I have children. Though, by today's standards, it's acceptable. I was never in the Party, and I didn't work with the police.

In Turkey you did time, so there's even an excuse.

Yes. But an excuse like that costs a lot.

May everyone have one like that.

And the charges weren't creepy—not rape or anything.

So, it really looks as if you could be crowned a thief in law. Want me to put in a good word for you?

Go to hell, would you? What are our readers going to think of us?

18.

1999

The Eighteenth Bottle

*I*n 1999, Kokh hid abroad from the inexorable sword of the Russian law. Then he returned *and paid off his debts after the default drop.*
Svinarenko traveled all over the world, the best way, for free. And wrote books.

Yes, brother Alik, the first event of the year wasn't some crap like yet another resolution or the death of some second-rate figure or the 300th anniversary of the invention of the multi-faceted drinking glass, but the retirement of Boris Berezovsky from the post of executive director secretary of the CIS. What was that? Was that the beginning of the end?

Nah. He must have gotten tired of just fooling around like that. He decided that the title of "Berezovsky" was more than enough. We had that business with the prime ministers, remember?

Barely. Was that when Primakov…?

Yes. Old Primus Stove was appointed in September 1998. And then around March or May 1999, they removed him and appointed Stepashin. And then, in August or September they appointed Putin. All in 1999.

I remember. Because it was just then that Shakirov, who I think sympathized with Primakov, was fired from *Kommersant* on March 25, 1999.

What for?

Because the whole scam with the sale of *Kommersant* had started.

It seems so long ago, but it's not—1999.

Remember Primakov made a U-turn over the ocean?

Yes.

A patriotic U-turn.

Yes. As a sign of protest against the NATO bombing of Yugoslavia.

Which began in March. I remember one of my friends who emigrated and had lived in the U.S. for ten years by then, got his American passport in 1999. Instead of a green card. He came to Moscow with his passport and invited me to a party he was holding at the Journalists' Club. In those days, people still went there out of momentum. Even émigré businessmen. I like dropping in there even now. To enjoy the contrast with the days when it was impossible to get in. Under the Soviet regime, it was considered chic. You needed to be a member of the club, now you can't get anyone to go. What's really funny is that all the old waiters are still there, and they remember the old regulars: Adzhubei, Brezhnev's son-in-law, used to get drunk, he used to have his own corner. Gagarin used to drop in.

What do they serve that's good?

For instance, pike-perch Orly, that's a serious thing. Also, the volants, is that what they're called? Vol-au-vents, little baskets filled with pâté. There's nothing much there, it was just a hang-out for reporters. Downstairs there's a bar with a buffet.

Why are you telling me this, Igor?

Because the fresh-baked American citizen invited us to celebrate his passport. And so we were at the table, with our glasses filled. He said, "Gentlemen, at last I got my passport from the United States of America. It's a happy day for me. I'm so happy. And so I ask you to drink to America, please stand." Everyone got up and drank to America, except me.

Ah, you wouldn't drink to America standing up.

Well, the celebrant said, "What's with you?" And I said, "Drop it! You're bombing Yugoslavia and you expect me to drink to you…."

Wow!

They all drank. "And now I'll drink, just sitting and for no reason. I am not joining your toast, I am drinking because I want to," I said and drank.

I see, that was your protest.

My protest was to drink not standing, but seated, and adding a few words of my own. It was a manifestation of radical patriotism.

But why? I don't understand why!

Well, now everyone knows that it was a mistake to bomb Yugoslavia. The NATO leaders admitted it—concretely, some high-ranking British military officer said that there were no mass graves of Albanian civilians, it was all made up as an excuse to bomb. There wasn't any proof then, but I sensed something was wrong. After that, you would think that the NATO officer would shoot himself and NATO, sorry, I mean the Albanians, would leave the territories given them for their suffering and so on. But as we are so used to seeing, nothing of the sort happened, the information passed through the media peripherally, no one was particularly outraged: the usual thing. The result was that the Americans, in passing, just in case, created a base in Europe for Islamic terrorists. The way they had previously brought up the Taliban in Asia. On the principle, well, if we can't be there, no one else can either. Or we'll spoil life for them there. The Albanians are serious people, and I'm afraid they'll show themselves to us sooner or later.... So, first the Americans bombed the Serbs, and the survivors moved as far as they could get from the Albanian fighters, who were not only not touched but legalized as the Liberation Army of Kosovo. ... That was always our rhetoric, to call our pet fighters liberators. In Angola or Palestine. So. I demonstrated radical patriotism without harming the country. Unlike Primakov. **Understand?**

I don't understand why love for Serbia is called a manifestation of patriotism, Igor. Why?

Let me explain.

Do. You, as a Ukrainian, should feel very bad about it. Because for some reason it is mandatory to love the Serbs patriotically, but love for Khokhols is not part of the mandatory program for patriots.

By the way, I've written about this many times and I've raised the question in my articles, Alik.

No one can ever give me a good reason. Who are the Serbs to us? What about the Bulgarians? And the Macedonians? When the Serbs were killing Albanians and then the Albanians were killing Serbs, we were for the Serbs.

For the Serbs, certainly.

But when the Albanians, for no reason, started killing the Macedonians, having come to Macedonia in the guise of refugees, we didn't give a shit. We didn't care a fig for those Macedonians. Even though they're Slavs and Orthodox Christians. That's what I can't understand! Of all the Slavic peoples, of all the Orthodox peoples, we chose the Serbs and love them with tongue kisses! They dragged us into World War I, as a result we had the revolution, half the country was filled with blood, and we still love them! Tell me why?

I'll explain. Know this: there is no brotherhood.

What is there?

There is no Balkan brotherhood, no Slavic brotherhood. It's just that the Yugoslavians are closest to the Russians in emotion. Ever since Tito.

Oh, no you don't. Tito was a Croat, not a Serb.

That's a minor detail. I'm talking much more broadly, about all of Yugoslavia. Tito is Yugoslavian and that's that. You and I know that he's a Croat. But it's not important. What's important is that the Serbs are like a small working model of Russians. A toy version. Understand?

No.

Well, they have this image that they're also tough, also partisans, also took down everyone, also Orthodox, with a similar language, fighting brotherhood, Shipka, this and that, against the Turks—

Shipka was Bulgaria! Serbia had nothing to do with that war!

Listen, lay off and let me finish, all right?

Me! I like that!

You're throwing me off, Alik. So. They're using the Serbs to send a message to Russians. They're saying: pay attention, we are smearing your caricature all over the wall.

Nicely said—caricature.

So, first of all, you understand this. And secondly, subconsciously or consciously, you understand what will happen to you following this

model. We will destroy your industry. And we will support your Chechens, the way we supported these Kosovo Albanians. And the Chechens will force you out, they will start ethnic cleansing, and when the Russians have fled, they will hold elections, and by majority vote Russia will be Muslim. Like Kosovo... That's the model I see. That's why I get so upset. It's when they take something that resembles you and kill it.

Why did they take Serbia, though, and not Khokhlandia, that is, Ukraine? It's even more like Russia. Or Belarus, for example. If we follow your scenario. It would be even a better lesson to put the squeeze on Lukashenka. Who is exactly a caricature of us.

It's harder with him, I think there is still a Russian military presence in Belarus.

So.

So Belarus is no good for that. But there's no Russian military presence in Serbia. So you can pester it with impunity. That's one motive. The other reason for not using the Khokhols is that they are very close at hand, you can't have a big romantic affair by correspondence with them.

Ha ha!

Because when you're close, when you share a communal flat, there are fights in the kitchen: who left the lights on, who forgot to pay the gas bill—quite literally about the gas. And the Khokhols, they don't really have the reputation of being ready to go die for an idea.

While Serbia is the perfect long-distance romance.

She's so far away, and lovely, practically a virgin.

Right.

We'll take this out of the children's edition. When we do *A Crate of Vodka* for children, without the curses and scabrous language. Like a primer.

I like that—Serbia like a pen pal. While the guy masturbates quietly until the end of his term. He reads her letter and jerks off.

And then the Ukrainians don't have the image that the Yugoslavians do, they handled 700,000 Wehrmacht troops. Our Khokhols, on the contrary, served in the SS—not all of them, but here and there, some of them did.

Yes, sometimes they served in the slightly wrong army.

Right, slightly. I've met Ukrainian SS veterans in the States. They had acted in Yugoslavia, actually.

They're ass-deep in Chicago. They claim to be Polish. But they're not Polish. They're Khokhols.

So if the Americans started abusing the Khokhols, the Russians would be happy. Take that, they'd think, for Crimea and Sevastopol.

Right.

You see, Ukraine is no good for that. That's why the distant image works better—the pen pal, the caricature, model.

Serbian generals are also leaders of organized crime in Serbia.

We've already studied that model with *Tale of Igor's Campaign*. Remember?

Go on.

What is a prince, after all? A capo, but on a horse instead of a Jeep. I was once in a banya at the house of some very authoritative people, big capos, and there were two priests. One from the church that was built by the bandits and another, visiting. It's interesting that they invited priests to their drinking party in the steam bath so casually, not for the sake of the exotic, but in the normal course of things—I haven't seen that yet either among the "new Russians" or the people of the sixties, that generation that created perestroika—they seem to support a spirituality outside the church, without even thinking about how ridiculous that sounds—spirituality without God, that must be a joke the Bolsheviks tossed out, but strangely enough, it worked. It might be a form of social mimicry. In general, the Soviet intelligentsia is a form of survival of the remains of the elite. To discuss but be silent, say something but about other things, about the loftier things in life, not demanding money, avoiding the power struggles by hook or crook, and they survived. And they passed on some things to us. Out of fairness, we must admit that we got more than a bunch of peasants and Chekists and PR execs—there were people who dared not to agree with some things, and if they were surviving only for their own benefit instead of floating around with some meta-goal, if they hadn't had meta-values, then instead of those pathetic little dachas in Peredelkino that I had seen—Okudzhava lived in one—we would have seen something resembling today's Rublyovka area.

While the people of the sixties see nothing but negatives in the bandits, I don't see it anymore, not for a long time. It wouldn't be fair would it to get rid of the bandits and leave former Communists and Komsomol members? How are the apparatchiks any better? Or the KGB? Seriously, the Chekists killed many more innocent people than bandits. In general, I'm against that kind of discrimination. And if we're talking about the Balkans, Yugoslavia, and Macedonia, then let me tell you that it's all very cozy. Beautiful, good food, marvelous climate. After covering the war, I started going to Balkan places, there are a few in Moscow. Rakia is an excellent drink. And the Yugoslavians themselves, when they drink, resemble Russians, too. That's where that love comes from… It's a simple love of self that manifests itself in that way. There. … What else did we have in 1999? April 3, NATO missiles fired on Belgrade… Not good, not good, Alik….

In the spring of 1999, Zhechkov and I hid from the law. First in France and then in America. For a long time, around two months. We got really sick of each other.

Ah, is this when you dragged Sobchak out to dine with you?

Yes, that's when we invited Sobchak.

Kokh's Commentary:

America. New York.

That year I hung around for two months in the U.S. and France and visited Spain. And here's an interesting observation that I made: in France and Spain, that is, in old Europe, I felt like an absolute tourist, but not in America. In America I don't feel like a tourist at all. I immediately make friends, some kind of work springs up, and you start watching your inner life with interest.

You try on that life. This is especially powerful in New York. It truly is the capital of the world. There's a lot I like in New York. The skyscrapers and the little houses. The West Side and the East Side. Downtown and Chinatown, Soho, Midtown…. I like New York pizza with a bottle of Budweiser. I like the New York accent, which somehow reminds me of Muscovite pronunciation of O as A: they say Madanna for Madonna.

As I've written several times, I like dropping in to see Roman Kaplan at the Russian Samovar on Fifty-second Street near Eighth Avenue. You should order the pickles, the semi-sour cabbage, and the karsky shashlyk, lamb chops grilled on a skewer. And naturally, a small carafe of the horseradish vodka (Roma makes it himself). On Tuesdays and Sundays, an outstanding musician plays piano there—Sasha Izbitser. How he plays Rachmaninoff and Chopin! And Beethoven…. You go there in the evening, sit, listen, have a vodka or two….

I like Central Park, a huge forest in the middle of Manhattan. Get up in the morning and go for a run. There's a bridle path, I run along it. For fifty minutes, sometimes an hour.

The Metropolitan Museum, the Museum of Modern Art, the Guggenheim Museum, the Metropolitan Opera, Lincoln Center. Hundreds (!) of theaters, with famous Broadway musicals.

It's such a huge and such a comfortable city. It is impossible to have conversations in New York in our manner, like "They've moved in on us," "They think Moscow is made of rubber." Everything in it is for the convenience of life and business.

New York is a city of smells. Thousands of restaurants of all cuisines of the world send out their fragrances of hot food onto the streets. Mixing together, these scents form the unique aroma of the city which I think I could recognize out of thousands…

On Forty-second and Fifth are the headquarters of Liberty Publishing, which published my book. Ilya Levkov, my editor, is such an amusing eccentric, with a strange Mephistophelean beard. … He turned out to be a sensible and educated man. I like eating with him in an Irish pub near his office. He tells me many most interesting things. His acquaintances include people like Brzezinski and Bush Senior, whose books he published in Russian.

I like going to Brighton Beach. I'm amused by the strange Russian spoke there. The smell of the ocean, old Soviet songs blaring from one of the many restaurants there. Stores full of Riga sprats, black bread, herrings and salo (fatback).

In New York you don't need a car: the wide-ranging metro system and plethora of taxis obviates the need to worry about parking or traffic jams. The cabbies are Pakistanis, Bangladeshis, Sikhs, Latinos, and Russians. Actually, there are fewer Russian cab drivers of late.

You feel calm and protected in New York. There is almost no crime, at least, not in central Manhattan. I wasn't in New York on September 11, 2001, so I still have that old sense of reliability and insouciance. … Though it is very strange to see the big hole that was once the twin towers.

Hundreds of nationalities, and I think you can find anything you want in that city, any book, any food, any specialist in any field. Everyone has his own niche. There is a niche called Russian New York. I love that city, the city of Brodsky and Dovlatov, Baryshnikov and Lennon, and I don't hide my feelings for it. It takes a while to get to know it. At first it's overwhelming. Then you're scared by that rumbling and never-sleeping monster. But it's already injected you with its poison and you fall under its spell.

I think only St. Petersburg has a stronger effect on me.

* * *

So, you tried on Western life and what did you think—you could live there, right?

Right.

But there was nothing to do.

No, all kinds of things kept coming up. We drank, we traveled…

Not drinking and traveling—that's vacation regime. You can be on vacation a month or two… though two could be boring. But a lifetime of drinking and traveling…

Why not? What's wrong with that?

I guess it's a question of taste…. So you successfully tried on émigré life.

Yes, we sat there and tried it on for size. Why not? We hung around in Paris. Invited Sobchak to dinners. Then we went to America. First, we did the scene in New York, then flew to Las Vegas, and then back to New York.

So you think that you could have spent the rest of your life that way?

Probably. I would have found some way to occupy myself. I would write books.

Nice. So, what else do we have for the end of the millennium? The bombed Yugoslavia, Primakov demonstrated his principles, 75 people died from NATO aviation strikes in the south of Kosovo. Remember the uproar? It was very quiet uproar. Jupiter is allowed to kill peaceful civilians, but the bull is not. Just now the Israelis bombed a Palestinian refugee camp, children were killed, but none of the democrats was particularly upset over it, it's not like us in Chechnya, after all. Let's keep going along 1999. "Chernomyrdin appointed special envoy to Yugoslavia." There used to be such a country—

There still is.

Come on!

There is. It's called the Union Republic of Yugoslavia. It consists of Serbia and Montenegro.

What, hasn't Montenegro left yet?

It's about to. As it is it has a lot of rights—autonomy and so forth. Do you know what the currency is in Montenegro?

The dinar? No, I remember—the mark!

Yes, the Deutschemark! How funny! It no longer exists in Germany, but they still have it in the Balkans.

Come on! No shit?

I have to check. But if it's so, it's funny. But I doubt it, they've probably switched to the euro by now.

Also, Alik, do not forget: in 1999 the international court in The Hague found President Milosevic of Yugoslavia guilty of being a war criminal.

How do you judge a representative of a sovereign country? Hell if I know. He's anointed by God, after all. He should answer to God is the idea. There's some system error here. When people abuse their power, trouble starts. The system goes to hell. The Americans I think don't quite understand what's going on in the world and what they're supposed to do now that's they've taken control. They say, "We're in charge, we're the toughest, we've got money." And the answer is, "Fine, go ahead, show us what you can do." They try to do something ... and they're like a bear in a beehive. He's churned up the hive and says I'm the toughest one here!

Who's arguing?

And then what, Alik? I'm not a bearer of anti-American sentiments, on the contrary I feel a certain warmth for them (and I'm rather lonely in that regard, not only in Russia but throughout Europe, I feel my solitude.) They are so cute, they've created a normal country for themselves. But they just can't give up that image of big boss.... You can't, either. ... It happens to countries and to individuals.

I can't?

You can't. No matter what you do or how hard you try.

No way. I don't agree with you, Igor. I was like this before I was a big boss.

Back then it might have appeared to be the complex of a PhD.

I see. And now it appears to be the complex of whom?

I can't tell you exactly. Nor is it important. The point is that you can't get out of the image. Big boss, and that's it. To an outsider it looks as if the human race allegedly consists of you and your wife and your subordinates. And when someone does not behave like a subordinate, you perceive it as an evil violation of the order of things. It's a personal insult. I don't know how much it can be corrected, or if at all. Although in my case, I'm getting positive results. I'm working on it myself.

You have it, too?

Of course. How else? I'm eradicating it with the help of my younger daughter. For example, I say to her: why are your toys scattered all over the place? Why don't you pick them up? And she smiles ever so sweetly and says, Papa, if you don't like it here, you can go to your room.

Ha ha!

And instead of shouting at her, "Is that how to stand at attention?" I leave. She's right. Or I'll call from somewhere and ask, "Do you miss me?" "Not yet. I'll miss you tomorrow." "All right, then, enough for today, I'll call you tomorrow." You can't be the boss day and night. Of everyone who comes your way…. Over every little matter. …Teaching everyone, rebuking people for things. Boasting. Attacking. Yelling. And so on. …

Back to Yugoslavia.

The topic of Yugoslavia ended with the court finding Milosevic guilty of war crimes, and that ended the war. By the way, they sold out Milosevic for loans. Remember?

Yes.

But they didn't get any loans, did they?

No.

A good plan. Terrific. "Come on, guys, sell out your own father, and we'll give you money."

It was the same with Russia. They said: recognize the debts of the Soviet Union, and we'll shower you with investments and loans. Just admit them! Like jerks, we did. And, did they shower us with loans?

I read a line that I think Lifshitz said—I like the way he writes in *Izvestiya*. He's the only egghead economist who explains things in language I can understand. So when he was discussing why we don't have investments, he explained it this way: Russia has as much investment as it can handle. In other words, it's not clear what we would have done with more.

Lifshitz doesn't know, but I do. We would build roads and housing.

Who the hell knows if we would or not. … We might just fuck it all away. Or create a "virtual reconstruction of Chechnya"—it's like the training sessions when generals allegedly move divisions, while actually only drawing lines on a map and the soldiers are building dachas for them.

Here's something else from 1999: terrorists blew up a building in Buinaksk. And then the apartment buildings in Moscow.

Yes, yes, yes.

So who blew them up? Who should be asked? Berezovsky? He knows everything.

He already answered the question. *"The FSB Is Blowing Up Russia."* That's a book by Alexander Litvinenko. [*This was before his death in London.*]

Did anyone explain to him that he's wrong? Was there a denial? "It's not the FSB blowing up Russia." Or: "It's not Russia the FSB is blowing up." Or what?

No, there wasn't. I must say that Litvinenko does not make a very convincing case—all supposition and theory. The only interesting episode is with the Ryazan military exercises.

That made a big splash. Memorable.

Yes.

What else? "Meeting of the State Duma Commission on Checking facts of Corruption of Officials, Agencies, and Subjects of the RF." The werewolf scandal, as if was called. No that was too early, it wasn't time for that yet. "Dmitri Sergeyevich Likhachev died." How much did that loss affect us?

I read him.

So did I from time to time. But I can't say that it completely turned my mind around.

Alexander Panchenko has a greater effect on me. And he's also an academician.

But he's not cooler than Gumilev?

He's in a slightly different direction. He's a linguist. He also worked at the Institute of the Russian Language, like Likhachev.

So, in 1999, Alik, you were in exile in the West.

Yes.

I traveled there for pleasure. That is, I traveled there to write about interesting things. Literally, during the holidays, January 10, when the country was still hung over and planning to do the last of its partying, I flew out for the Harvard—

Economic Forum?

No, the Forum is in Davos. Harvard was like a symposium on investments.

I've been there twice.

Well, I watched people have meetings, governors having dinners… Ishaev, governor of Khabarovsk Krai, told me that that he hires Chinese for seasonal work harvesting vegetables. The patriots rebuke him for that. For giving work to foreigners instead of his own people. And he said to me: I hire the Chinese because I am a Russian patriot. Why? Because I need to have food for the hospitals and children's schools… If I hire Russians to harvest potatoes—

They'll do a shit job and take more money for it.

They get the same money, Alik, but they'll harvest half as many potatoes from the same plots. Whether they steal them, bury them, don't even dig them up, or eat them as they go, I don't know. But if you hire them, you won't be able to feed the army troops and the hospitals. That's why they hire the Chinese.

And the people who accuse him of a lack of patriotism are the very Russians—

Who gobble up the potatoes!

Yes.

That's an amazing paradox.

What the fuck kind of patriot are you if you don't let people steal potatoes from children, eh?

An interesting approach. Boris Nemtsov gave a speech at Harvard.

As usual.

He led discussions, lunches, banquets. It was interesting to observe once. But does anything real get decided there? The time I was there, nothing was decided.

Nothing ever is.

The Westerners said that in principle they had a hell of a lot of money they could give, but then, in the end, they didn't. They talked, looked at each other...

Nothing gets decided there, it's absolutely pointless going there—just like Davos, as a matter of fact.

I had a conversation with Berezovsky at Harvard. Really, what can I say about him here? He gave me his view of the meaning of life, that it is expanding.

That's not his theme, that's Sakharov's. He quotes him all the time.

Sakharov? He passed it off as his own idea. What's the point? That the biomass is trying to expand and gobble up its rivals—that's it?

Yes. I don't agree with that.

Neither do I. But I'm trying to understand, after all, he's a man who gets results, he's energetic. It's interesting that this is his point of view.

Tolstoy has a story called "The Prisoner of the Caucasus," remember it? About Zhilin and Kostylin. One is killed while the other suffers patiently, waiting, waiting, waiting, waiting—and in the end they release him. When the Russian troops attack the village, remember?

One ran off and the other started fighting, so?

The point is that humility is more important than pride.

Who told you that?

Christ.

Told you?

And you.

But you don't listen to anyone anyway.

Why do you say that? I try not to be too obnoxious. I may not succeed to well, but I do try.

Come on, Alik, it's just us chickens, you could cut the bullshit.

Are you saying I show off?

Of course you do.

Come on! Compared to say Vova Zhechkov, do I show off a lot?

The way he does it, you can tell that he's fooling around, for amusement and relaxation, it seems to me. But you show off for real.

How do I do that?

I'll tell you later, Alik: it's not for publication.
Let's get back to our topic: 1999. Don't forget it was the bicentennial of Pushkin. Among other things, I wrote a funny article about Yuri Avvakumov, the architect. The topic was "Pushkin and Money." I wrote it for the magazine *Den'gi* [Money]. That was logical, right? What Avvakumov did is take all the references to money in Pushkin's letters. He wrote them on pages torn from notebooks, in clumsy handwriting, in the manner of poor people preparing motivational notes for themselves. The whole show—this was in the XXL Gallery—was hung with these excerpts, which were like: "Why do you keep asking me how to edit Onegin—make whatever corrections and cuts you like, just send me the money asap." When you see all the references all piled up in one place, it's a very expressive picture. Pushkin and money. When you read those excerpts you begin to think that Alexander Pushkin cared most of all about money, that is, he was a normal, living person. Everything else in his life took place in the time free from money worries. There. So, I had gone to Harvard in early January, and from there, with a brief stop in Moscow, I went to Davos. You've been there, right?

Yes, once upon a time.

And it's called, as you so rightly corrected me—

The World Economic Forum.

Everyone there was skiing, and taking some time off to meet, attend dinners, as usual... Davos is such a tiny, cozy, even beautiful town.

Yes, but the skiing sucks, Igor. Compared to Courchevel.

I wouldn't know. I'm not a skier. There were demonstrations by those... what do you call them... they weren't called anti-globalists yet, but they were already protesting. They were embryonic then, I guess. Switzerland, Davos. On that very trip Russia lost its place as one of the top fashionable countries, falling down to the penultimate, 40th places. They had taken the position: Russia, everything's clear there, nothing special. That feeling that we were exclusive, not like anyone else, that we had unique processes under way that the whole world should watch with gaping jaws—that feeling—

Was gone. Thank God.

It was very obvious there. ... Something funny happened there, you know how you start talking and then you realize that you're off on a wrong tangent. Does that ever happen to you?

Yes.

So, I was talking to Kwasniewski. The president of Poland. And I started blabbing about something—first about what a nice place Poland is. ... And then I see he's making a sour face. Why? I wondered. I was complimenting things. And then I realized that I was praising Solidarity, taking delight in how they gave it to the Communists then—and Kwasniewski was one of those Communists! Me and my big mouth!

And all this was in Russian? He speaks Russian?

I don't remember what we spoke.

Do you know Polish?

I can speak broken Polish.

You can speak broken any language, right?

I think so. It's just a question of degree of brokenness. Even in Russian, you may have noticed, I have a heavy Ukrainian or at least south-Russian accent.

So, it's broken Russian.

Yes. My Ukrainian on the one hand is literary, that is, artificial, and rather impoverished, since it wasn't in vogue then and Ukrainian newspapers had their vocabulary reduced intentionally by secretly circulated orders. And then I've forgotten a lot of what I did know. And the language has also made great strides.... So the upshot is that I don't speak any language purely. I am not a bearer of any language at all.

None.

I am the bearer of a Ukrainianized, south-Russian dialect. Which was subject to a strong reverse Russification over the years of my life in Russia. I think that's a good description of the situation. The term for that is "marginal." When a person does not belong one hundred percent to either culture.

I'm like that, too.

But you function at least within the confines of one country, although, wait, in your case, the country has also changed. ... Your Kazakhstan is a foreign country now.

The country has changed, yes.

What else was there? There was fashion in Milan. I used to travel there periodically. Starting in 1999. By accident. The Italian Chamber of Commerce started bringing me to Milan to write about fashion. I tried to get out of it, saying, first, I don't understand fashion. And they said, but we're inviting you, it's Europe, it's beautiful, and we'll pay for everything, including your flight. I said, second, I can't promise that I will praise the fashion. They said, write what you want, your opinion is still interesting to us. I gave in: the hell with them, why not go to Italy on their dime? Especially since it was an opportunity to practice my broken Italian. So I went to all the shows for several years. You know, the winter, summer, spring shows. Milan...

I've never been to Milan.

There's nothing to do there. The one good thing is that it's warm in winter and you only need your jacket. And the cathedral is interesting.

That's it?

Yes. It's too contemporary somehow, too industrial. It doesn't even feel like Italy. You expect something different from Italy.

What's your favorite place in Italy?

Rome. Obviously.

What about Capri?

Haven't been to Capri.

Ah! What about Florence?

Haven't been there, either.

What about Positano? You're kidding! How about Palermo? Taormina?

Yes, yes, Alik. I can agree that Taormina is gorgeous. I was there as part of an official delegation headed by Vova Zhechkov. But Rome is tops, there's more of that powerful, centuries-old, imperial, millennial breath in it.

What about Athens? Have you been there?

Yes. It was turning feeble somehow: olive groves, Greeks.... There's nothing left at all, it seemed to me. And the Minotaur's labyrinth—

It's in Crete.

Let it be in Crete, that's still Greece. The impression I had was that they had dug out that labyrinth with a bulldozer the night before and today they were bringing in tourists to take their money. I thought of Ostap Bender who sold tickets to a hole in the ground. This is analogous. A trench is dug and sprinkled with broken bricks. "You can't imagine what a fabulous temple stood here a few thousand years ago!" I could have just as easily been unable to imagine it sitting at home. ... Really, trying to sell me broken bricks....

I don't know, I don't .... I haven't been to Crete, but my wife and I walked around Pompeii—very impressive.

Basically, I wrote a lot of articles about fashion and then they stopped inviting me—they must have read what I was writing at last. Someone must have translated it for them and they thought: why do we need this for our own money? Even though I had warned them and I was sure it would be over after the first time.

You consciously refused trips to Milan by writing bad articles?

No, it just happened of its own accord.

And lying was more than you could bear.

I didn't even think about it, Alik. I mean, for the sake of London, say, I could have stepped on the throat of my own song, but for Milan... I just don't know.

But you put on the Kiton yourself. You were photographed for the magazine in expensive jackets...

Where?

In *Medved*, in the Fashion Section! Don't you remember trying on the clothes? There was the photo shoot.

Ah, right, there was. We started it up to get great men to come and try on jackets and be models. People resisted at first. They said, hire some boys and take their pictures. So, in order to get the process going and to show them that it wasn't scary, I went first. They way doctors would inoculate themselves first, I tried on a Kiton jacket. They gave me those suits. And I came up with a good move for the shoot: I went there first thing in the morning, with a hangover, unshaven, and even unwashed, in my old crummy clothes. I got there and said, come on, take a picture of me like this. They said, just like that? Yes. So they photographed me "just like that," and then I took a break. During which I showered, shaved, gulped down 150 grams of vodka, and had breakfast, then the makeup man and the hairdresser took me on..... And then I started trying on all those Brioni and Kiton. People looked at the shoot and said, look how clothes change the man! The man had washed and dealt with his hangover, was all.

Nice.

So, in Italy I interviewed their local producers, trying to understand the profound meaning of Italian fashion. It turned out to be quite simple,

you'll laugh. What is the point of fashion? Why is fashion developed in some countries, while the fashion in other countries, which are just as great, is unknown outside its borders? Why? Do you know?

Who me? No.

So I'll explain what the Italian industrialist told me. Italy has fashion because it has mass production of textiles. That's all.

We have a shitload of textiles manufactured in Ivanovo....

No, that's cambric, that's no good. You need wool. In Italy, for lack of mineral resources, they made a bet on mass production of textiles. But just making fabric is not enough.

You have to sew and sell.

That's the problem! A man buys himself a suit, thereby using up four meters of wool. He won't need another suit for another two years. So? Is the industry going to stand still for two years? And wait? Everything would collapse in that case, there would be strikes, people would turn Communist, and that's the end of the country.

Yes, yes.

So, to prevent that, the Italian industrialists—with the approval of the government and with its help—began a huge campaign to fool stupid consumers. Like, last year black suits were in, this year it's embarrassing to be seen in one in public. Now it has to be green. Then red, white, and so on, and people keep buying. At some point, it comes around again, and the suit has to be black. The consumer says, Hah! Gotcha! I have a suit in my closet from five years ago. I'll wear it like it was new. For free! And they say, hold on there, it's single-breasted.

And now we're wearing double-breasted suits.

Right! Then another cycle goes by. The man says, but now I've got two black suits, one of each style. They say, no you don't, yours has two buttons.

And now it's three.

Right. And no one wears smooth fabrics, only jacquard. And second, you bought just to show off, you don't have 15 suits in your closet, you've given them to your chauffeur long ago. Third, you've gotten fat, you louse.

And it's the same situation with shoes. The Italians admit that serious people can wear their shoes for ten years easily. The ones they've already bought. So what are supposed to do, shut down the country for inventory? It would be like stopping oil production in Russia. So they have to do the same thing with shoes.

Of course. With buckles, without.

Svinarenko's Commentary:

I have to admit that the trips to Milan were interesting. For instance, I met a mighty woman, Princess Galitzine, an Italian designer (her company is called Galitzine pelle). I am in awe of this mighty woman. She wasn't a girl then, she had been brought out of Russia on a ship in 1918, but she still had so much electricity! She told me about her life: "Father was at the front with the Nizhegorodsky Regiment when I was born, and he didn't know about me for a long time... The regiment was broken up, and he rode horseback to Poland. We sailed to Italy to our relatives. And lived there. ... I started this business a long time ago, after the war. I don't know how to cut patterns or sew, but I like working with fabric and inventing styles..."

We leafed through her old photo album, and she gave me commentary:

> That's me with Jackie Kennedy; we were good friends. We met in Capri, where my husband (he's Brazilian) and I had a house. This is me at the Kennedy compound, Cape Cod, Massachusetts —this was 20 days before John died. He had promised to come to Italy, so that I could introduce him to all my lovely girl friends, and he planned to leave Jackie at home with the children. And that's Jacqueline in a black dress, see? She wanted to go to the Vatican after her husband's death, but she didn't have an appropriate black dress. So my girls worked all night and made this for her. That's me with Audrey Hepburn, at my house. That's Nureyev. There's Maya Plisetskaya. That's my dog. And that's Indira Gandhi. And that the crazy Elizabeth Taylor. In my dress, naturally. That's Greta Garbo. That's Onassis, and there's Sinatra....

I also met Katya Streltsina, a designer from Surgut. ...which she left as soon as she saved enough money from making dresses for the wives of oil workers and moved to Italy. And she broke through there! This is what she had to say:

> Here (in Europe) I know for sure: if I make a certain effort I will get a certain result. In Russia there are no guarantees. There, all your success can be crossed out at any moment. Like in August 1998. I managed to take out everything at the ATM that had been on my Russian card. What if all my money had been there? Everything would have collapsed, I would not have gotten an education, and I would have had to return home in misery. Now when I call my girlfriends in Russia,

they say, "Katka, don't even think about returning, stay there!" They sound sad, dreary, hopeless. ... In Russia, what are they doing now? They plant seedlings into cold soil; no one knows if they'll grow into anything or not. (Let me note that she spoke of cold soil long before the Chekists came to power.)

* * *

I discovered an amazing thing in Italy, Alik. A worker's pay in a shoe factory is a thousand. How can it be a thousand? In Italy? You could starve to death. And they all look for well-fed and happy. But they use a different method there. A factory owner explained it to me: "I pay all the taxes for these dolts, that's the way it's done, so that no one cheats. They get their thousand clear, right away, whether I sell the shoes or not. They have everything, look each one has a car and a house by the sea, while I'm frazzled, and the Communists and the unions are agitating among the proletariat. ...I don't sleep or eat, like Papa Carlo."

Look how well you're speaking of capitalists now. I guess I've educated you, just a tiny bit!

I'm speaking the truth. I say what I feel. Whether it's beneficial or not, I tell it like it is. I praised capitalists from my heart. There was a reason, so I praised them. But when there's no reason to praise them, I don't make it up.

"I don't sleep, don't shit, and I take all the risks."

Yes. So the capitalist says to me, I'm showing you this factory, but that's just as an exception. The main production isn't done here."

Where then?

You buy shoes and it says "Made in Italy," he said. In nine times out of 10 it's not Italy at all. They use countries with at least a minimal understanding of shoe making. Where they used to make shoes, even crappy ones. Rumania, for instance.

Why not the Soviet Union? We used to have the Skorokhod factory.

I'll explain. Back in Soviet times, I inspected the shoe factories that the Italians had built in Russia. The main problem was that the workers stole half the stuff right away. In half-made stages. There was an amazingly low output of shoes. Not profitable, you can understand. So, sorry, no Russia, but Rumania, Bulgaria...It's a lot cheaper than Italy. And a special person stamps them as Italian manufacture.... In the end, I figured out what is behind all this fashion. There was another amusing line in the story. The capitalists told me that Albanians come on their fast boats from their marvelous country to Italy, rob the villas on the beach, and vanish. You can't find them. Police, investigation—just a joke.

I chartered a boat two years ago. We traveled from Italy to Greece, from southern Italy to Corfu. We were going to board the yacht in the evening, travel by night, and wake up in Greece—that was rather convenient. So we got to the city of Bari—

To revere the relics of St. Nicholas!

Precisely. We revered the relics and went to the boat. We boarded and said, let's go. The captain says, No, I'm not traveling now, we'll sleep here and take off early in the morning. Why? Very simple. We had to sail past Albania, and there are pirates there. They attack at night. So the captain decided to travel by daylight.

Didn't you want to show your stuff? Your heroism? The courage to fight off pirates?

Ha ha! I was just telling you that to show whom NATO is defending in Yugoslavia—pure and simple bandits.

The fact that they rob along the Italian coast and are pirates at sea is one thing. It's another story with narcotics. The Albanians sell them in Greece, I heard complaints in Greece about it back in 1991. Long ago, in the last century. … And everyone knows who mug and kill people at carnevale in Venice, hidden behind masks, and then toss the bodies of unlucky tourists into the canal without their wallets.

And who did the restoration of the Kremlin with the concomitant rollbacks? Also Albanians.

Yes. I mean, everyone knows the niche occupied by Albanians in Europe. If even we—totally disinterested in this case—knew about it, how could it have been a secret from the NATO command?

I'm certain that it was a secret.

Come on!

The sleepy Americans can't tell an Albanian from an Iranian. PUh-leese!

You think they're total assholes?

Of course.

Hmm. Well, let's get back to fashion. The local capitalists there complained that they didn't have a lot of normal clients with whom they have mutual understanding. Except for the Japanese. They swallow whatever baloney they've given. Quatrocento, Florence, tradition, ancient Rome, they listen open-mouthed and buy shoes without a murmur. All styles and at all prices. "They're marvelous. Golden buyers," the Italians praise them. They like the Arabs, too, they even make a special style for them, soft, goatskin, with narrow curled toes and gold thread. Who they don't like are the Germans. Because they don't follow the program. They start telling them that shoes have to have narrow toes. And the Germans say, we don't care about narrow or wide toes. Shoes should be comfortable, long-wearing, waterproof, and preferably cheap. The Italians play the same old record: Renaissance, Quatrocentro, Cinquento. The Germans yawn: calm down, spaghetti-eaters. And we're warning you right now about jackets: color solutions, texture, it's all nonsense. A jacket should not get wrinkled and worn, that's all we care about. So, they say that working with the Germans is impossible.

Another trip I took for work was to Sevastopol. I wrote about the remnants of the former USSR. I drank with the sailors. Some of the officers stayed with the Russian fleet, some joined the Ukrainians. Ukrainianizition was going full blast there, during which officers got into dogfights with one another.

Have you see *72 Meters*? That episode is in there.

That's what I'm telling you.

Did you like that scene?

The film is on the mark. I've been keeping an eye on the screenwriter for a while, he's got three or four books out, his name is Pokrovsky. He served on a submarine in the North, as a chemist. Like everyone, he dreamed of escaping to St. Petersburg. And he did, one of the lucky few. Unique, really. He was transferred to a research institute or something. He's like a Dovlatov, but more contemporary. A Schweik in a Russian naval version. He describes navy life so realistically and crudely that it gives you goose bumps. You think, what monsters, what a horrible life!

So, fleet, Simferopol, Koktebel. I liked Koktebel, by the way. The Tatars have moved back and they gave the town its old name—Koktebel, which means something like "green hill."

What did it used to be? Planernoe?

Right. That is, it used to be Koktebel, then the Tatars were kicked out and it became Planernoe, and now it's Koktebel again. The local Slavs told me in amazement that with the return of the Tatars, there are local cheap vegetables. Before that, they didn't have any. They had to be brought in from Kherson or somewhere. They didn't grow their own because there wasn't enough water. But the Tatars have their own technology. They build a clever little pyramid of stones around each tomato plant, and the dew condenses on the stones and drips into the roots, a free automated irrigation system. And chebureki appeared. As you're driving from Yalta to Simferopol, you pass the Baidar Gates along the way, there's a terrific view from the top and everyone stops. So I stopped to look. Tatars run up to you right way and say, we have a chaikhan here, lots of food and drink. While you take in the view, we'll cook up shashlyks or chebureki for you and call you when they're ready. And everything is cheap. I was traveling with unemployed officers, I had hired them and their Zhiguli, we drove around Crimea and drank. The officers said, don't be afraid, the Tatars are very clean and neat, especially here. I had a bunch of those delicious chebureki. So the Tatars have brought their old region back to life.

Well it wasn't theirs originally. The Greeks lived there. Then the Genoans, then the Tatars. It doesn't matter.

Didn't it belong to Rome once?

Yes.

I doubt you'd get anyone to return there now. Not the Greeks…

They left, the Pontian Greeks. They were given Greek passports and they went to Greece.

They must like it there.

I don't know, it's hard to judge. I had a girl friend, in the good sense of the word. A beautiful Tatar. Her surname was Devlet-Gireyeva.

Really? I knew a Tatar girl whose name was Venera (Venus). She worked for me, by the way. Thus, I was in charge of Venus. Yes….

They like names like that.

After the Pushkin anniversary came the whole topic of the sale of *Kommersant*. Yakovlev sent this man in, his name is Kia Dzhurabchian.

Some Iranian.

Approximately an Iranian. He was head of some investment company, and Yakovlev spun us the story that he was selling everything piecemeal, so that everyone would have 5%, and no one could dictate terms, and there would be freedom of the press. That is, there wasn't enough, but when he sold the paper to Berezovsky, there would as much as was needed. Quantum satis. An original concept, fresh. So Dzhurabchian came to meet the staff and announce the deal. Everyone was there, waiting, worrying. The drivers were downstairs, they were on the porch, wanting to get a glimpse of the new owner. So Kia walked in. They wondered, where's the guy who's buying the paper? That's him. Drop the joke, we drivers have seen all kinds of people. That guy has never had $10,000 in his hands at one time. Why are you bullshitting us?

We were waiting in Yakovlev's office, he was somewhere in the West by then. Everyone was there. And the Persian went on and on about liberal values, freedom, so on and so forth. About nothing, basically. It was very touching to see some staff members speaking English to him.

He doesn't speak Russian?

You know, he positioned himself as if he did not. But some experts watching him closely noted that his eyes twitched at some points. That he understood but pretended not to know Russian.

A decoy.

In order to get to know the staff, he held a big banquet at Tsarskaya Okhota. So everyone came, and there was the full thing—vodka, caviar, matryoshka dolls, herring.

That was when your fellow *Kommersant* writers performed an exploit.

What exploit?

They wrote a book with Putin. Gevorkyan and Kolesnikov did.

Timakova was one of the authors of that historic book. Moreover, I was later told by people in the know, "Old man, if you hadn't left, you'd have written the book, too."

Rea-ally?

Who knows, maybe they would have offered it to me. But I was spared the temptation. The decision would have been murder. It would have exhausted me, I'm sure. On the one hand, it's naked PR, and for the KGB. On the other hand, I understand how fascinating it is, to sit with the president—

And gab.

For a long time, figuring what's what. I would have been torn by two mutually exclusive desires: to show off and also to see the guarantor up close. I don't think that he was rude to them and shut them up when they moved into the wrong areas. I imagine that he behaved tactfully, playing life-size liberal.

Of course.

And when he talked with them, I'm sure he did his best, as they say. As for the sale of the paper, Vasya (Andrei Vasilyev) said back then in an interview that everyone regarded the *Kommersant* writers as putrid faggots, that was his formulation. And you had to twist and turn and "pretend that we aren't owned by someone named Berezovsky, but to write keeping that in mind. And continue to be honest, marvelous journalists." Something like that.

Svinarenko's Commentary:

Vasilyev talked about it this way in the interview he gave me: "The first months were terribly hard. I told them at the office: Gang, we've been bought by B. A. Berezovsky, who has a shitload of interests, politics, and all kinds of stuff. We don't have to pretend that we don't have an owner, internally, don't pretend that, we have to understand everything clearly. But it's not our readers' fault that we were bought by Berezovsky, they want to get information from us, whether it pleases Berezovsky or not. We are embarking on a very difficult time. I'm not very sure how we're supposed to work in this situation. I worked for Berezovsky at ORT television, but that wasn't the same thing: there I simply did my job. Sometimes I sent him to hell, but I didn't forget that we were a propaganda tool. But here, we are not. I asked everyone to filter everything, a lot. You know, not lie, check the facts, not have obvious leaks, check the leaks. … Because anything we write will be read this way: Berezovsky told them to write that, it's a clever move by Berezovsky. Write the whole truth, but! Remember: you are writing something that makes Berezovsky unhappy, therefore there mustn't be the slightest room for doubt. So that he can't say: 'My enemies used you.' And on the contrary, when we write about his enemies, be even more careful. ... Our whole staff, around 500 people, we really went through a lot of shit after Berezovsky bought *Kommersant*, when everyone regarded us bent faggots, when all the democratic press buried us—including NTV in the front ranks. ... If I had quit then, the very first day when everyone was shouting that NTV was being pressured, I would have gotten on a stage and given interviews to everybody, explaining who Gusinsky was and why freedom of the press was incompatible with him. If I had been free. But I couldn't, I had an official position.

"And whenever friends called, say, from Yukos, I used to work there, asking for a favor, I would say, 'You have to understand, if I do you a favor, what would Berezovsky say? He would say, You keep telling me how honest you are, and it turns out everything is allowed here? And what would I say in response, hello?.... I'm being watched on every side! If I print paid bullshit or an article that through laziness looks like it was paid for, what happens to me then?'"

* * *

In general, it was a difficult task, balancing like that between interests. A task that, as you know Alik, I did not take on. Many friends felt terribly sorry for me then—like, what will you do now? ... But as it turned out, life is possible outside *Kommersant*.

So, you left in 1999? And what did you do?

First I said, give me two months vacation, that I didn't use in previous years. And then, I transitioned from vacation into freelance.

But why did you leave? Because the paper was sold?

I found the fact that the paper was sold very unpleasant.

But now, in hindsight, do you think you did the right thing or was it a stupid move?

I did everything right. There were lots of arguments for it. But the main one was: when something makes you uncomfortable, when you hate doing something, and you can quit it, then what's the problem? Why torture yourself? What is it all about, anyway?

Well, that's logical, of course.

Especially when you can do the same thing, for the same money, but without the discomfort.

The same money?

Well, after the default. Their salaries went down. See, I'm talking to you in a language you can understand—I'm proving my actions to you in terms of money. For you millionaires, Alik, money is the most important thing.

When you write dully about whatever you're assigned, it's not very entertaining. You think, when will it be quitting time so I can leave and do something for my soul. It's a very important reason! When you spend most of your time doing what other people need. While your life slowly wastes away. The columns really got to me. I realized that they were empty texts that you just pull out of your finger, imitating emotions—it's very destructive. I think prostitutes use the same mechanism. That's why I sometimes enjoy reading columns in different newspapers, it's edifying, you can see what torture it was to drag those lines out for the writers, you can just them checking world count in their tools bar to see if they've reached the required amount. ...But the newspaper bosses need columns for some reason, and so people are forced to spew them out....

It's a very different mechanism when you come up with your own themes, when you're really excited about something and you write about that. That's worth a lot, let me tell you. It's the case of doing for money what you would do on your own time. You're interested, you get high on it, but you don't have to pay for the pleasure, on the contrary, you're being paid. It's a win-win situation. It's better to be paid less and spend every day doing what you want, than spending all day on something you hate and then spending money on a hobby. The bottom line will be approximately the same. From the financial point of view. But in terms of energy, the picture is even more convincing. This is how it worked for me. You sit and think: Oh, I'll tell them that I want to write about this. They say, all right, fine, we'll pay you a fee and expenses. I say, fine and dandy. Feel it? It's fundamentally different in energy flow. One time I suddenly wondered why I had never been to South America. How could I write a book about my travels? So I made it a goal to uncork Latin America for myself. I found a peg for a story, the air show in Chile, I found a sponsor for the trip whom I put together with the newspaper bosses—and I flew off to a new continent. Everyone was happy: one got good publicity, they got a story, I got a free trip to Chile. I went to China on a similar arrangement. Before, I was deprived of a lot of trips. I was planning to go someplace I wanted to see, but my editors had other plans for me. I missed so many countries, and years, and islands! It really hurts to think about Mexico, Tahiti, Hawaii, and the Bahamas. There it is, old man....

This was 1999?

Yes, the end of it. I quit in October or November.

A courageous decision.

A reasonable one. It followed out of everything else. I was extremely upset by the sale, like they've sold the village with the serfs. Fuck both of them! Go buy and sell each other, do whatever you want. I was furious. Sometimes, I'd get drunk and call my former colleagues at night: "Hello, sellout!" How do like those emotions?

A nightmare! A regular Yevgeny Kiselyov.

Come on, Alik, you have to understand. You are capitalists, we are journalists, and we have different systems of coordinates.

Wasn't it you who told me that journalists are distinguished by marvelous cynicism? And you made such a kindergarten scene?..... Paradoxically, today *Kommersant* is one of the independent newspapers.

Yes, maybe. You see what the shit is. In every national culture, as Lenin said, there are two national cultures. You remember. Well, in every journalism there are two journalisms. Very notionally, there is good journalism, in quotation marks, and there is shit journalism. These are two different things, as I see it. But, since the shit journalism won in the end, in every index and category, now all journalism is associated with the shit journalism. And I propose, for the sake of simplification and clarity, to consider journalism shit.

And in reality? Who's doing the good journalism?

I'm telling you, there isn't any anymore. I think it's because no one needs it. Well, there's Yuri Rost. He wrote breakthrough pieces and subtle essays. Now he writes differently, not as challenging. For all the warmth I feel for him, how I enjoy drinking with him, I can't say that he determines the face of journalism today. Neither did Bovin, who, incidentally, shortly before his death was fired by *Izvestiya*. They kept lowering his salary, down to nothing, and they wouldn't run his articles—and so he left for somewhere.

Where did he go?

I don't know, maybe just on his own. By the way, it's practical to go off like that before your death. You'll have the opportunity, sorry, to think about eternal issues and sum up your life. He wasn't needed and that was that. As for today's journalism, I think it is determined by your friends Minkin, Khinshtein, and Gorshkov. ...

Then back to my leaving. I remember how the writer Alexander Kabakov asked me, "Old man, why did you quit? Out of principle? A mistake.... There was always an owner who dictated." Now how can I explain it? I gave him this example, which I think he got. I said, imagine that you and I go to a brothel. And they send out a girl for us to select. I take one look at shout, You whore! You would say, what are you shouting about? They're all whores here, why are you so upset? And I would reply, You see, Sasha, the point is that you see here a priori functionally as a whore, while I have a lyrical human relationship with her. Or did right up to this moment. I pampered her, there were all these emotions, long conversations in the middle of the night, tough times we went through together. ... And then suddenly I find that she offers the same services for money at market prices to anyone who pays. .... So why the fuck did I bother with all my ridiculous emotions? I realize it's not a very convincing argument to a businessman....

Why not? It sounds fine.

Anyway, when it all comes together, piece by piece, in cases like that, there can be no doubt. End of conversation. I already knew, alas, which departments interested the PR people, what the market prices were, and how much some of the reporters earned on the side. ... When I had been a boss there, the security people reported regularly to me. I saw Russian journalism in every imaginable position. For free and for money. I doubt it would dare to pretend to be a virgin to me.

So how did you live? What else was there?

There were interesting moments. I tried to find a job in a new way in the mass media market. I thought about life, I called various colleagues to meet and discuss the situation, to understand my place in it and see what I could aspire to. I had dropped out of reality: when I joined *Kommersant* in August 1990, still under the Soviet regime, I never went outside again, so to speak. It's the way ex-cons come out after years in prison and understand little of the world around them: there are new rules, new prices, new currency, and so on. All my previous experience in getting a job in the mass media was worthless: the past attempts had taken place in another era and basically in another country. Some people never did meet with me: they meticulously avoided meeting and talking with me.

You're kidding! Why?

I can't tell you for sure. Maybe they were afraid that once I joined their paper I would try to take over? I certainly wasn't planning anything like that. But maybe, I would have gotten carried away, we're only human, and maybe it was more obvious to others than to me. There was another version: they made me obviously unacceptable offers.

Like?

"Why don't you write crap for us and we'll pay you a crap salary in turn." Just to get rid of me. That was all interesting. ... I was amused. But on the other hand, there were pleasant moments, too. Doletskaya at *Vogue* offered a helping hand, commissioned articles and paid well. And Valery Fadeyev, from *Expert* magazine, offered me interesting work for good money. I'm grateful to him for that (even though for various reasons I couldn't go work there). Vladimir Grigoryev, at the time a deputy minister, helped out. *Rossiiskaya gazeta* behaved admirably. There were plusses and minuses, but on the whole it was entertaining. I observed the shifting scene with literary admiration: some people who a week earlier could have drunk with you until 5 in the morning and sung drunken songs, miner songs, not Jewish or Cossack ones, suddenly were extremely busy. ... But why am I telling you, I'm sure you've been in those situations yourself. On the whole I spent that time, that time of troubles, beneficially. It was important for me that I had traveled to countries that remained unseen but desired. I published a new book, about my travels in Russia. It came out at the very end of the year. Considering that I had finished writing in that summer, it's a pretty good turnaround, impossible in Soviet times. The last piece I wrote for the book was about Russian refugees. Solzhenitsyn wrote a lot about it, remember? How Russia had abandoned 20 million Russians abroad, and how they're being pressured, and how they're fleeing. So I wondered, what was the most telling about the situation? What should I be writing about? I went to refugee committees and foundations and found a very amusing and telling case. A group of Russians left Kazakhstan and moved to Lipetsk Oblast, moving close together, they had some money, they got loans and built a settlement with decent houses, with plumbing, totally unknown in those parts.

What did they do there—work the land?

There was that. They bought their own tractors. And they built a sewing factory. Fine fellows, starting out on a good life. And so they lived that way until suddenly, they started fueding! Writing complaints against one another to the prosecutor's office. And I thought, here it is, just what we need! This is the spot where all the issues of Russian life are intertwined! So I traveled to Lipetsk Oblast. I took a look at them, took pictures of them. And they truly had broken into two camps that hated each other. There was this lady there, the chairman of that refugee settlement. Her son-in-law worked as a driver and he got into an argument with his mother because she was in the enemy camp and was a political opponent of his mother-in-law. It wasn't just brother against brother but son against mother. I asked them what the problem was, tell me. "She promised to build houses for us when she took us out of Alma-Ata, why didn't she build them? She built one for herself!" I said, let me see the agreement. It was written that we will help everyone build their houses. So where's the problem? Buy the bricks and she'll help you build, at cost, by the way. They said, "No, building means that she builds them for us and we sit and watch." An amazing picture. They all turned to shit there. They said, our goal and dream is to keep our leader from living well. To keep her from getting any crummy financing. They didn't want to improve their own lives, they were passionate about ruining someone else's! There was a physicist with them, secret, atomic, who became a schoolteacher when he was kicked out of major physics. He grubbed around in a garden in a village in Lipetsk Oblast because Russian science was killed off in Alma-Ata.

Was he dissatisfied, too?

No, on the contrary, he was satisfied. Happy. And this is the kind of man he was: they were given interest-free loans for twenty years, as Russian refugees. In principle, this was serious help.

So?

So this grandpa physicist was the kind of man who built himself a shack with the loan, then went back to Kazakhstan and sold his house in Alma-Ata, and used the money to pay off his loan early. He said thank you to the country for helping me, and now I'm returning the money, in case someone else needs help, I'm not going to grow fat on the proceeds. He didn't even do repairs on his house, he didn't have the money. So he lived in a shed at the school.

The more fool he.

I don't think so, Alik. By me, he's a very decent man. He has a conscience. In general, it was a beautiful picture with the refugees. Vivid. Various images come to mind, but we won't go into them.

And then, at the very end of the year, Yeltsin gave us a present, he left his job.

Yeltsin surprised everyone.

Who came up with that idea for him? Yumashev?

I think so. And Putin.

It had a beautiful resonance.

There was too much spin. I don't understand why they fired Stepashin. They could have entrusted the whole arrangement to Stepashin.

There must have been influential people who did not want Stepashin.

And what, everyone was for Putin?

I think people were much more equitable about Putin. Then.

Probably. … I learned the news of Boris Nikolayevich Yeltsin's retirement at a ski resort in Colorado. Boris Jordan and I went to ring in the new millennium there. In the United States of America. From 1999 to 2000. Everyone celebrated when the three zeroes appeared.

Which, as we know, is a mistake.

Yes. The start of the new century was 2001, we know that. But everyone celebrated, nevertheless.

So?

Nothing. I was glad, I liked Putin. I thought that some dynamism would appear, after all Grandpa was very old and fat. He's lost weight now.

But, Alik, you understood the arrangement: this was basically an appointment since the precipitously announced election date deprived the other candidates of any chance of winning. You did understand that?

Yes. But at the same time, I wanted Putin to win.

Oh! I also regarded it as a positive thing.

Otherwise it would be Primakov.

Yes, everything was being prepared. Gus was getting things ready for him.

I did not want Primakov. In principle, I understand Luzhkov, but Primakov is really the last century for me. Too much so…. He's so Soviet, in his stylistics.

I approved of Putin's appointment then. In fact, even now I think, and what were the choices?

He hasn't done much in five years except strengthen his "vertical."

Others wouldn't have done anything at all.

I understand. In his two terms, Yeltsin did so much, fucked up so much. While Putin reduced the taxes and that's all. He brought it down to 13%, thank you. What else? Is that it? It is. He started the war again.

You haven't done even that, Alik.

Me? I turned state-owned Russia into private Russia.

With your very own hands?

With my very own hands, yes. When I started we had 100 percent state-owned property, when I left, 70 percent was private. That's more significant than lowering the income tax.

Kokh's Commentary:

Once Again About Privatization

My criminal case ended in 1999. It is a sad story that makes no sense whatsoever. I am surprised by those worthies, Berezovsky and Gusinsky, who took offense that we dared to sell Svyazinvest to old man Soros instead of them. They got the prosecutor's office to deal with me. I wonder if they'd be as ready now to buy those shares? As a reminder, 25 percent plus one share were sold in the summer of 1997 for $1.875 billion. Soros sold them now for "a whole" $625 million, which gives $1.250 billion of pure loss.

I sometimes think that I shouldn't have played at being principled. I should have sold them Svyazinvest, they would have gone bankrupt and suffered such huge losses. And everyone would have been happy.

By the way, the sale of Svyazinvest is still considered the biggest privatization deal in Russia. Even the sale in 1999 of 75 percent of the shares of Slavneft did not bring that much revenue. So much for the thieves and bribe-takers.

Years pass, but the passions over the results of privatization still seethe. Just recently the Audit Chamber decided for the umpteenth time to analyze the results of privatization. Even though it's done it twenty times already. I wrote this opinion piece for gazeta.ru about it:

In reference to the loans-for-shares auctions, I want to pose a simple question: did those deals correspond to the existing legislation at the time? That is the only position from which the actions of the officials can be judged. If a deal did not correspond to existing legislation, the officials should be fired, and if there was a criminal element, they should be tried. But if it does, and I maintain that was the case with the mortgage auctions, then people should drop the topic and never return to the question.

I have heard the version of faked deals many times. I did not give the oligarchs any money, and I know nothing about that. They came and paid money. The State Property Agency does not have money, it has property, which we mortgaged in exchange for loans, which the entrepreneurs gave to the government.

Ten years have passed since the mortgage auctions, and during that time everyone, including the Audit Chamber, the Prosecutor General's Office, and those who took part in the auctions and did not win, all of them had the opportunity to challenge the auctions in court. They could have sued with the following argument: the deal was a sham, money was taken from the person who subsequently got the money as a loan (that is the Ministry of Finance), and so on. These arguments could be the object of a lawsuit, and on that basis, the deal could be judged a fake, subject to dissolution, and so on. Moreover, some of the lawyers, in particular Inkombank, in the name of the firms that it established for participation in the auction, took part in this sort of court examinations. They did not win a single case. If lawyers maintain that the deal is a fake, they should sue, but no one is doing that. There is nothing but hot air.

I want to understand what is going to happen now: are they going to take away Yukos from Khodorkovsky, Norilsk Nickel from Potanin, Surgutneftegaz from Bogdanov, and Lukoil from Alekperov? Those were all mortgage auctions. No problem. Return the loans that were taken from them and take back the companies. But let me remind you that when we mortgaged them, all those companies were bankrupt, including Yukos and Norilsk Nickel. Norilsk Nickel had 10 or 15 trillion nondenominated rubles in debts, primarily debts to the budget and in wages. Now the company works very well and makes a good profit, and by the way, oil prices have nothing to do with it, because this is metallurgy. Potanin had paid $170 million for an enterprise that was in the red. There were two arbitrage cases over Norilsk Nickel, by the way, and both were lost. And there is also a separate conclusion of the Audit Chamber, signed by Stepashin, certifying that everything was correct. So is the Audit Chamber now going to re-examine its own conclusion?

Every single enterprise that went through the mortgage auctions works better than it did before the mortgaging. Not a single one went bankrupt, they all make a profit, are moving toward international norms of accounting, attracting foreign investment, functioning beautifully, and bringing very large money into the budget.

If the esteemed Audit Chamber is doing a study, writing a whole Talmud, and familiarizing the nation with its work, then apparently it wants to restore justice—as it understand it. Here the Audit Chamber has no other path than to turn to the courts. The Audit Chamber is not an institution intended to be political, it exists for completely different goals. It is financed by the state budget, it has been given a luxurious building, there are dachas, and cars, and blinking lights for the cars, for its officials, and that's not so that the auditors devote themselves fulltime to political chatter. They are supposed to supervise the expenditure of budget monies. If instead of that, they are involved in political activity, they are turning into a political party. OK! I don't mind. But as a taxpayer, I don't want that political activity to be financed by the budget. If someone wants to gain cheap popularity this way, then let him find sponsors instead of being dependent on the budget. In this particular case I do not see any point in the work of the Audit Chamber if its goal is not to take everything back and divide it up again. In Argentina, they're re-examining the results of privatization for the fifth time. While they're re-examining it, the country remains in the mud. A strange correlation, isn't it? But if that is the goal, the only way to do it within a civilized framework is though the courts.

The Audit Chamber thinks the deals were fake, but I don't. The state got money from the deals. That can be confirmed by any official of the Ministry of Finance, who all know that money went into the budget. I know nothing about the state giving the oligarchs the money that it then borrowed from them except what I read in the papers. Allegedly this happened with Menatep, that is, Yukos, but there wasn't even anything in the newspapers about the other companies. Therefore, it would be wrong to maintain that the entire system of mortgage auctions was built on state funds. If you have that sort of suspicion about

Menatep, then test it. And even in that case, I don't quite see why that makes the deal a fake. In those days, there was no treasury system. There was no place other than commercial banks for the state to keep budget funds. In particular, it had money in the Menatep Bank, among others. Why? That's not a question for me. That was decided by the Ministry of Finance long before the auctions. I hope that it was done as the result of tenders or other public procedures. If the bank gave the government a loan, then it included money that the Ministry of Finance had in the bank. That is normal banking activity. For instance, say I keep my personal savings at Alfa-Bank, but as a businessman I sometimes borrow money from them. To some degree, I am borrowing my own money from them.

If X keeps money at bank Y and then borrows money from the bank, that loan does not look like a fake operation. From the point of view of jurisprudence, my argument is absolutely convincing, even if to some people with no business experience it may be not convincing. People take out loans that consist, in part, of their own money all the time. If that were not the case, banks would not exist.

There must be logic in all things. Living in country that has no logic is not only difficult, but very dangerous. They say that if an enterprise was sold for a song and now it is worth gazillions, its owners got rich unjustly, because they bought it cheap and it's a "diamond." I'm not even going into the possibility that the present high value of the shares is the result of the management skills of the new owners. I know that bit of logic: we sold it cheaper than it costs now, and that's not fair. I don't agree with the logic, but I hear it. But what if we sold something then at a significantly higher price than its present value, what do we do with that difference? If the difference in price between what was paid for a "diamond" must be taken away for the benefit of the state, then from whom does the difference in price get taken in the case of a company that sold high and is now cheaper, and for whose benefit? For the benefit of those who paid a lot then? Let's imagine that there is an enterprise that we sold then for three times what it is worth today, what should be done with that difference? Should we take it away from the state and give it to those who paid crazy money? Otherwise we cannot stay within the framework of rational logic. In 1997, Mr. Soros paid $1,875,000,000 for 25 percent of Svyazinvest. Now, he is a rational and reasonable man who could not be accused of lacking business skills, but he was forced to sell the shares for $625,000,000. What are we going to do with the difference of $1,250,000,000?

Maybe that difference would be more than enough to cover the so-called gap that our oligarchs didn't pay? Or maybe we should leave everything as is, because as soon as you take away that alleged difference from the oligarchs for the budget, then Soros could sue for that logic to extend to him. The sum of

$1,250,000,000 is significantly more than they're hoping to get from the oligarchs who got enterprises through the loans-for-shares auctions. By the way, one of the shareholders of Mastkom (which won the Svyazinvest auction) along with Soros was Potanin. I'm certain that he lost around $300,000,000 on the Svyazinvest deal. And yet that is the amount they expect him to pay additionally for Norilsk Nickel.

And then, if we are treating industrial shares this way, then let's take a look at how officials privatized their dachas on Rublyovka. It was all done without auctions and at prices that were joke back then. Today each *sotka* costs $50,000-$70,000. And the price rise on those shares certainly is not due to the managerial skills of our brave officials."

But it's totally useless to try to prove anything. I don't know of a single country where people were satisfied with the results of privatization. Not one. But it does not follow that privatization is not needed. However, I'm repeating myself....

* * *

Svinarenko's Commentary:

At the end of the year, I went to China. This was a very important trip for me: I had always wondered what they did to win, our neighbors, and how they behaved in their natural habitat. My impressions were serious and no joke…. Let me cite a bit.

In general, as you look around, you see how hard these guys work…. They sew cheap jackets right on the street—the jackets that are piled up in our retail markets ….Have you ever wondered why they send us goods and not the other way around? Or to put it even more mildly, why can't we sew simple clothing for ourselves? Why do we buy it from them for American dollars?

We bring them our dollars, and they don't exchange them for Mercedes 600s and French restaurants—they increase their industry and build new cities, one after the other. And where there are no cities yet, the future urban dwellers are working the rice fields knee-deep in water on the backs of cattle….

…Shanghai is a new rich city, no worse than Hong Kong. The Chinese built it in expectation of Hong Kong reuniting with the Chinese People's Republic. You see, this is a nation where even the Communists have some understanding of things. Instead of setting up an Oblast Party Committee with kolkhozes and re-educating the capitalists using new Hunweibins, they've started learning capitalism and building it with the people's money. How can we keep up?

… "So, if our Communists had squashed democrats with tanks in 1991, the way the Chinese did in 1989 on the famous Tiananmen Square, then we'd also have a 10 percent growth of the economy?" my perceptive readers might ask.

I doubt it. I'm not a politologist and not a ethno-psychologist, but it seems to me that the Chinese have a broader range of perception of reality. They have an expansive nature. They tolerated the emperor after the revolution, they did not execute him, as some did. They calmly brushed off the gunk of the students from the tractor tracks and went back to work. We would not have been able to tolerate it. Not that we would have rebelled, no, but our national depression would have become deeper and danker.

… Most of the cars on the road are VW Jettas assembled locally, in Shanghai. They stopped producing them in Germany a long time ago, but here the Jetta will be considered a luxury car for a long time. We foolishly rushed to assemble BMWs and Chevrolet Blazers, as if to say, we're a rich country, our minimum wage is $200 a month, after all.

Yes, the Chinese world is enormous. The Islamic world is vast and powerful. So is the European one. The American world is huge. So what's left for us? Our Russian world is small, cold, very poor. It's marginal, inhospitable, and lonely. Amusingly, in our dusty half-empty town, Buddhism seems an exotic religion, while there are about two billion people living in Buddhist countries. More likely we are exotic, not them. The Russian universe is this exotic national village.

There was another important event –for me—in 1999 that I somehow forgot to mention in our conversation. I got an award that summer, in June. From Soros and the Academy of the Russian Press. The money was Soros's, and the academy, composed of chief editors of major publications, pointed out who was to receive $2,000. I got one, too, in the Reporter of the Year category. We gathered at *Moscow News*, which was in the center of town on Pushkin Square. Back then they were still the citadel of democracy—or no longer? Had it become just a newspaper that still got by on old yeast, like say, *Izvestiya*? I can't say now. I just don't remember. What did the prize mean to me? Well the financial component was rather pleasant, no more than that, it didn't bring any fundamental or even visible changes to my life. I got it on the last day that the check was good. But the fact that Soros had come and wanted to see me personally and that I got to shake his hand touched me. He's a great old man, Soros. He thinks on a grand scale. Think of all the money he dumped into Russia! He didn't steal it from us. He sent us money! Even though he could have blown it on new yachts, planes, and islands. Easily. The way various other billionaires do. Including our own Russian ones. What was he trying to say by that? That money is not the most important thing in life? That we are less than we think of ourselves? And that he was giving us a chance? Trying to show us that capitalism is not only when you haul in the bucks, but something more that we still have to figure out (if, of course, we manage and have the time)? Later, as you know, Soros left Russia—and said a lot with that departure. He appears tactful, yet he spoke volumes.

Was the status important to me, being a laureate of this prize? Can it be said that I woke up famous the next day? Hardly. Newspaper work is all secondary, invisible, unimportant. Even in the best of times, even in the best situations. It's not television. And then: was I seeking fame? That can't be said. If I had been, I would have switched to television, or the theater, or films. Or even politics, in the worst case scenario. I did none of that! I remember in the early 1990s, when many new things were starting up, I was offered work in TV. To go there with all my guts. I started thinking about it. I remember my thought process very well. I didn't like TV, it was work for actors, you had to sell your face. That had never been part of my plans. Text there is an auxiliary thing, marginal. Your mug, the picture, that's essential, but what they're saying onscreen, the sound track, is not that important. Why should I drop everything and become an actor? Start a new profession? That's not serious. And then, I somehow knew even then, I sensed the dead end of TV. You start your career there, everything's moving along fine, and suddenly you have a fight with your boss. And you have to leave the channel—the other channels have their own people. Yet you've grown accustomed to selling your face, the fame, this and that, the narcotic effect of being on air, the whole thing. We see that very clearly now with television people who have problems. So why cut off other variants for myself, other moves in life? What for?

But could it be said that I paid no attention to this prize? No. That attitude is possible only when you have many prizes piled up. This was my first, not counting the old provincial awards. Why hadn't I received anything before? "My justification is the fact that the best journalists in the world—the most famous and popular—still do not have any professional awards at all. I'm talking about Matthew, Mark, Luke and John. ... I won't hide it, I'm pleased. But as one is supposed to say in these cases, I consider this prize an advance and not full payment for my twenty-five years of work. The fact that I'm on the same list of winners with Yuri Rost elicits powerful and complex feelings in me. I feel that's I'm just a cub reporter, around twenty-three years old, despite being so grown up and so fat. ... When I was a skinny youth, I had thought through my newspaper work. Ever since then, I solve two tasks in my working hours: I amuse myself and I send a signal to decent people that they are not alone. That is all." (From my interview in *Kommersant Daily*.)

Afterward, I said more than once that Russian journalism was going through a bad patch if I had reached such heights just playing at it. After all, I'm not a career journalist, but an amateur. I wrote whatever came into my mind; that is a repetition of my old idea that some see journalism as a business, a means of earning income, while others consider it an art. Art for art's sake. When a problem is solved for the sake of seeing if can you solve it. And once again I will repeat the comparison of a reporter who works within the framework of the craft and does not move into PR with a thief in law: the thief in law imposes such rigid rules on himself that getting rich is not easy. If he were to become a store manager or a drug dealer, he'd have more money. But for some reason he doesn't do that. That strange characteristic makes him interesting for us. The path of the samurai attracts, the path of the store manager is nothing….

* * *

Kokh's Commentary:

In early 1999 an interesting polemic took place. Articles by Andrei Illarionov and Peter Aven prompted me to write a response that was published in the magazine *Neprikosnovennyi Zapas*. I think that this polemic could be of interest today. Notably, let me reiterate, it took place in early 1999, that is, when the prime minister was not yet Stepashin or Putin, but Primakov.

The Politics of the Possible and Total Liberalism

Two articles lie before me. One is "The Secret of the Chinese Economic Miracle" by Andrei Illarionov. The other is Peter Aven's "The Economics of Trade (About the 'Collapse' of Liberal Reforms in Russia)." Both are devoted to proving one fact: there were no liberal reforms in Russia.

It would be unnecessary in these pages to remind the reader that the creators of those reforms had articulated that thesis themselves more than once. For example, Yegor Gaidar had maintained many times that there had been no "shock therapy" in Russia. It's clear to me that he meant something bigger than mere strict fiscal and budgetary policy.

For me, there are two things of primary interest in these articles. First, the system of proof of this, basically obvious, thesis. Second, what the authors propose to get out of the crisis—note that both authors see no alternative to the preset liberal reforms.

And so, let us begin.

The system of proof.

Illarionov uses a rather convincing system of proof by comparing the dynamics of macroeconomic indices of Russia and China during the period of reform.

Here is the list of indices he uses:

1. Percent employed in the state sector.
2. Percent of people receiving welfare, subsidies and aid from the state budget.
3. Expenses on social services and consumer subsidies.
4. Unemployment level.
5. Size of import duties.
6. Rates of inflation.
7. Budgetary policy.
8. Size of taxes.
9. State expenditures.

For all these parameters, their dynamics during reforms in China were more "liberal" than in Russia. In fact, the percent of people working in the state sector, and especially in the government administration, went down faster in China than in Russia. Expenses for social services in China are lower than in Russia, and correspondingly, the percent of people receiving aid and subsidies is lower. The unemployment level is lower. Import duties are lower. Rates of inflation are lower. The budget is more balanced. The taxes are lower. The percent of state expenditures in the GNP is lower.

From this, he draws an elegant conclusion: contrary to popular opinion, China did have liberal reforms and Russia did not.

I agree. But my innate maliciousness won't let me agree that easily with the thesis. I propose a third country for comparison—Stalinist USSR.

1. Everyone knows that in the 1930s, 70 percent of the population of Russia was agrarian, that is, worked in kolkhozes. The kolkhozes were not part of the state sector, and consequently, the percent of people employed in the state sector in the Stalinist USSR was fully liberal, and we if exclude old people and children, represented only 15–17 percent of the population, which is even lower than in China today.

2. The percent of people receiving subsidies, welfare, and aid was marvelous under Comrade Stalin, almost reduced to zero. Let's forget the propaganda events on this theme, we're all adults.

3. Correspondingly, let's not discuss expenditures on social services and consumer subsidies. There even Milton Friedman would have given Josef Stalin a solid A.

4. Unemployment level? What is there to discuss. A liberal through and through.

5. And import duties were also close to zero. Stalin imported an enormous amount of technology and equipment on very beneficial terms. Apparently there was a branch of Chicago University at the Tiflis seminary, where he was educated.

6. Inflation? What inflation? Really, you're just like children.

7. Taxes. Wouldn't it be great to have Stalinist taxes now? Life would be a bowl of cherries.

9. Percent of state expenditures in the GDP. Well, there's an error here. But there's an explanation. The agrarian (private) sector is a cash cow. So if there are internal expenditures, they're not state expenditures. The Gulag was self-funding, and also a cash cow. By the way, where are the statistic on internal investments in the Gulag? There aren't any? Then shut up. And then there was being surrounded by capitalists. Preparation for the inevitable war. Even the most diehard liberal would agree to a high level of state expenditures.

So it turns out that Comrade Stalin was a liberal. And how! In other words, he betrayed Lenin's teachings and set out on the path of bourgeois rebirth. Isn't that how it comes out if you follow Illarionov's reasoning?

But he wasn't one! Then, could the system of proof be incorrect? As the classic put it, "Maybe something should be changed at the conservatory?"

It's all the Stalinist statistics. They're devious. We know that the kolkhozes under Stalin were practically the state sector. We know that there was hidden inflation. We understand many things. Where does this trust for Chinese statistics come from? Even if it's IMF statistics. Tell me about where the IMF gets its data about Russia and how good they are. I know where it comes from. And Lukashenko also has economic growth. And you believe that?

But, let's move on to Peter Aven. Another analysis of numbers. From the statistics he quotes, it follows that the percent of revenues in the consolidated budget plus the non-budget funds in the GDP in Russia is lower than in Poland, Czech Republic, Hungary and Estonia, and the percent of expenditures is lower than in Sweden, Denmark, and Austria.

Don't the listed countries satisfy the strict demands of the IMF? Haven't they rubbed our noses in the Estonian experience of fiscal stabilization? They have, more than once. Haven't Balcerovic, Klaus, and Aslund told us how to do liberal reforms? They did, and with good argumentation. And the people seemed to be right. More devilish confusion here.

The great Russian question arises: "What is to be done?" Where can we find a system of measure that will answer the question: is the country moving along the path of liberal reforms or not? I dare to propose that there is no such system. I'm exaggerating a bit, of course, but I think the answer to the question of whether or not liberal reforms are moving in the country does not lie in the plane of analysis of indices. I think that the answer lies in the sphere of what has become fashionable to call institutional categories. I will try to formulate some of them in question form.

What arcas have monopolies?

What is being done to create competition in these branches?

What is the mechanism for redistribution of property and is it connected to the redistribution of property from ineffective owners to effective ones?

How are property rights protected and is expropriation possible?

How responsible are all the branches of government in preparing and accepting the budget? Paraphrasing the same classic, I'd like to ask: "Is this the budget that is or that heals?" Do they treat the budget as a "purely political document"?

Are there hidden forms of financing the budget deficit through money emission?

What are the mechanisms for attracting foreign investment? How do the rules for residents differ from the rules for nonresidents?

How appropriate is foreign policy to the economic interests of the state?

Where are the foreign markets for exports and what states are real competitors? What is the structure of import and who are main importers?

Is the nation prepared to turn into a community of free individuals or are patriarchal feelings strong enough to lead to increased demands from the state?

What is the typical family unit? Is it the nuclear family "parents-children" or is it "parents-children-grandchildren"? Is there a hierarchical family structure? Where is the profit-center in the family and where is the expense-center? What is the mechanism for redistributing wealth in the family?

This is far from a full list of questions. I have intentionally dragged them out from various spheres of knowledge. They differ in significance. And, although this might surprise many, I would put the last two in first place. All the questions are united by one factor. None of them can be answered with a number. Or a group of numbers. They are fundamentally unquantifiable. The answers to these questions cannot be represented by a column of figures. The answers require words. They are verbal.

Therefore, when I am told that Russia does not have liberal reforms, I agree readily. But at the same time, I am completely dissatisfied by the system of proof of that fact. I would agree with the premise much more readily if I were told that there has not been a liberal reform in Russia because:

    —many monopolies are left;

    —nothing is done to create competition in the branches with monopolies;

    —the country has no effective mechanism for bankruptcy;

    —the possibility of expropriation has not been fully eradicated, and public opinion is beginning to warm up toward the topic;

    —the authorities are completely irresponsible in their attitude toward the budget (how many years in a row now?);

—the budget deficit is for many years to a great degree covertly (though purchase of GKOs by the Central Bank) or openly financed through the emission of money;

—investments have no protection, and the rules of functioning for residents still differs from the rules for non-residents;

—foreign policy is not tied to the economic interests of the state, and we are yet again supporting our competitors to our own detriment;

—the nation still would trade freedom for a hunk of sausage;

—the family is falling apart and children have forgotten their elders.

But numbers, what are numbers? Let Illarionov also tell me that there is economic growth in China. Just like Stalin, the Father of Nations, also had economic growth. And the Western liberal press would have applauded him. But the applause of the liberal press does not signify liberal reforms. Just like the applause of liberal economists.

In October the *New York Times* had an article about Chinese auditors who were unable to find the $30 billion that was supposed to be used for agricultural subsidies and had vanished. Which budget line of state subsidies are you using for them, my dear Andrei? Is this evidence of the firm liberalism of the Chinese authorities? I'm not even talking about Tiananmen Square.

What Is Being Proposed

Andrei Illarionov is proposing nothing, basically. Strictly speaking the article was not intended to do so. Therefore it would be wrong to expect any recipes from the author in this article.

Peter Aven does have a proposal. Giving its due to "tearing off all and every kind of mask" and devoting several paragraphs to the required self-flagellation in such cases, he concludes that once they set out on the path of endless compromises, the "young reformers" became middle-aged conformists and discredited the liberal idea along the way. Hence his conclusion: no compromises and we will win.

He's overdoing it, you will say. But not at all. He isn't. Not in the least. He's hit it right on the nose. And here's why:

In his day, Bismarck introduced the term Realpolitik, that is, the politics of the possible. In other words, if you have a global aim, then for its sake (keeping it in mind at all times) you can make compromises with the existing political elites and maneuvering, retreating and advancing, move step by step toward your goal.

As applied to our reality, this would look something like this. You allow us to implement privatization, and we will pay no attention to the institution of special exporters. We create a currency corridor, but at the same time forgive the debts of the agricultural sector. And so on and so forth.

I am purposely avoiding commenting on the criticism of privatization in Aven's article. Not for a lack of arguments. I have a sea of arguments. But because, first of all, privatization was also implemented within the doctrine of Realpolitik, and second, my justifications would be inappropriate and rather artificial here. This article is devoted to a slightly different topic.

It's obvious that the politics of the possible was employed to the maximum degree during the period we were in government. Moreover, any argumentation for necessary compromises was reduced to a trade: we'll give them this and we'll get that. The objects of the trades were divided, consciously or not, into two categories: key and secondary. The psychology of this division was shown very well by Aven by his example with the special exporters.

Here is my question: which compromises, made when the "young reformers" were in charge of some of the levers of power, seemed of secondary importance to us then but turned out to be key ones? That is to say, compromises that we should not have made under any circumstances, even quitting if necessary. Compromises that would have been a frank retreat from our positions without any "compensation on other fronts."

Compromises in privatization? No! All the compromises made with the elites against it were aimed at ensuring that privatization would happen. And it did!

Export limitations? Aven himself explained about the special exporters.

Various benefits for invalids, athletes and veterans that turned out to be tax loopholes? By dint of extreme effort, we reduced them to almost nothing by early 1996.

I can go on listing all the compromises that were made. However, I consider only two of them to be fatal. Concessions that I personally describe as manifestation of the team's conformity, and especially of its leaders.

First, agreeing to "the increase in currency for manufacturers" implemented by the Central Bank in summer of 1992.

Second, the Chechen war.

The monstrous inflation created by the former was only ended by late 1995 through colossal efforts, and I am not certain that the crisis of August 17, 1998, is not the ugly child of that innocent concession to the "veteran manufacturers."

I do not wish to analyze the moral and "military" aspects of the Chechen war. They are obvious. But the economic consequences of the war are destructive.

I still cannot imagine how a large-scale war, which involved several divisions, a war that used aviation and tanks, could be waged for almost two years without once including the expenses in the budget.

You may ask: where does that idiotically large-scale policy come from, of borrowing on foreign and domestic markets to cover the budget deficits for the last four years? You should be asking: how much has the Chechen war cost? That might make the causes of the August 17 crisis a little clearer.

But these concessions are rarely blamed on the "young reformers."

Even though in my view, the "young reformers" were the only ones who could have stood up against them. Or could they have? Then why didn't they quit? Why did they show solidarity with this claptrap by remaining in government? By the way, this applies to me, too…. With just these two concessions, all the work in reforming Russia almost went by the wayside…..

True, Russia did not have liberal reforms if by that you mean total liberalization. Liberalization in all aspects of social, political, and economic life. The liberalization that I personally dream about.

There were *elements* of liberal reform. There were areas in which impressive gains were made. There were directions where progress was barely noticeable. There were out and out lapses. There were conscious concessions.

So I have a question: If you or a group of your friends and people who agree with you (including you) have the chance to be part of the government, and you know ahead of time that many of the most important decisions will be made without you or your opinion, if you know ahead of time that many key posts in that government will be held by your open enemies, who will use all the resources in their power to fight you, if you know that you will accomplish only a small part of what you plan and what needs to be done, if you know that you will have to make very unpleasant and noxious compromises that will be held against you by severe judges, but you also know that you will manage to accomplish something, succeed in some things, break through in some places— should you accept? Or should you wait for the moment when:

   —you will be guaranteed that you will not be fired;

   —all the government posts will be held by people with the same ideas as you;

   —you will be given enough time to implement all your reform plans;

   —you will not be pressured by government lobbyists;

   —the Duma will pass all the laws you need and will not pass any stupid ones;

   —power will be brought to you on a silver platter and a young, healthy president will beg you on his knees to honor him by joining his government?

I don't know the answer to that question. I'm not pretending. I truly don't know. There are some outstanding political figures who are waiting for just that. I doubt they'll get it....

Sometimes it seems to me that it was a mistake to get into government. More so recently. I know that many people think so. My wife, for instance. She's not the only one, I can assure you.

The dilemma between total liberalism and politically possible has no single solution. What Aven proposes is very tempting. And very unrealistic.

Out of fairness I must say that Aven does not deny the need for compromise. But his bar of the acceptable is set too high, I think. As they say, "Don't shoot the piano player, he's doing the best he can." We have the marvelous opportunity now to listen to the performance of pianists considered to be better.

What a performance!

Maybe I'm a pessimist. Well, let the optimists try it. They may be firmer than we were. The only thing is that a pessimist, as we know, is a well-informed optimist.

20.

2000

The Nineteenth Bottle

*I*n 2000, Svinarenko makes his debut as a photo model, travels to Chile, begins writing a
book about prisons and starts running the magazine Medved. Kokh greets the
millennium in Colorado, pays off his debts, and offers Gusinsky $300,000,000—which
Goose refuses—and as events will show, should have accepted.

**Alik! So, we're up to the year 2000. A man in the intelligence services
accepted the reins to the country. This could have happened earlier, by
the way. There was General Lebed, who was serious about being a
presidential candidate. Or at least, thought he had a serious chance...**

Lebed, he was a field general, a paratrooper—broad shouldered, with a
commander's voice—and he went and signed the Khasavyurt Accords. He
stopped the Chechen War. People stopped dying. Both ours and the Chechens'.
Of course, in the Russian mentality, Chechens are not human—the more of
them dead, the better—the Russians are a kindly people. But nevertheless. Then
came Putin, pretending to be a civilian. And he started this war, the new one.
Even though it wasn't necessary at all: After the attack on Dagestan, he could
have sent troops to the borders of Chechnya and stopped there. Created a *cordon
sanitaire* around Chechnya. Taken back the trans-Terek region. Pushed them back
to the mountains. In fact, that's what everyone thought would happen. But he
decided to storm Grozny, and a new war began. He kept attacking, and people
started dying again. And the bottom line is that people like Putin, and they don't
like Lebed. Explain that!

I don't know why you keep asking me to explain everything that happens. I know even less why I keep trying to do it. But that's a separate issue. Well then… I'll explain everything to you, as usual, Alik. Know this: The reason here is the same as the one at the source of the success of soap operas, the cheap TV shows for simple folk. It's all hack work, by the way: Each show lasts an hour, and it takes them only 70 minutes to film it.

You mean in real time?

Yup. Why are cheap plots popular, why are they done like hack work, why do people love this stuff? Why do they like Putin and not Lebed? Because people want to feel they are party to great events! A man passionately wants to think that he lives not only to eat breakfast, go to the factory, take a crap, get over his hangover, and throw up. He wants to believe that he has higher aims. That he is a part of something great.

So what did Lebed offer people? He offered the satisfaction of pathetic, miserable daily needs: You won't be killed, you can go home from work and have a beer in front of the TV instead of running around with a rifle, risking your head and putting your ass on the line, as the Americans say. It's clear that this is small potatoes. It's not pleasant, thinking that your life is being wasted. And here came Putin, who said: "And now we are going to restore the Empire and revive its former glory!" And then every Russian, through that dream of building an Empire, will get the legal right to feel great himself. You see, we went off to conquer the Caucasus and not to go out to the courtyard to play dominoes or to the market to buy some meat. People were uplifted and grew bigger in their own eyes. Understand?

In that case, in terms of Putin's statement, even when I go out to buy meat, I'm thereby conquering the Caucasus?

How would you expect to have lamb at the market without the Caucasus? Ha ha. But that desire for greatness, it is manifested even when a man buys food at the market, satisfying his purely animal needs. Even there, he wants to be privy to greatness! "Let's get rid of all these black-asses and have Russian grannies sell at the markets." This sometimes works and mobilizes Russians; it's a very popular slogan. The ethnic Caucasus dwellers respond quickly, vanishing from sight in the market stalls, hiring Russian grannies to be the salespeople. Here you go, a Slavic old lady; she will sell you food and then bring the money to her Chechen boss. So people want to be party to greatness, or at the very least, they want to be flattered and made to think that their pathetic needs look great from a distance. That's why I mentioned the soap operas. A man thinks, what do I have in life? My son is a D student, my niece had a baby, Uncle Vasya punched Aunt Masha in the eye Nothing happens in my life! What he wants is to travel on his yacht, direct something, move divisions hither and yon. But there's nothing like it in his life, and he's bitter.

And suddenly, he's told: Hold your horses, fellow, we'll show you a program where the main character is a jerk just like you, and his niece is just as stupid, and just like you, he couldn't get the girl at the grocery to sleep with him, either. And the whole world watches this crap. The flattery works: The man starts to think that he's not such a pathetic jerk, that he's part of greatness. Because they show in prime time the same stuff that his life is about.

So the reason Lebed didn't make it is that people want to feel great. Look: Raising wages is boring and trifling, but taking the Caucasus is sophisticated and grand. It's transcendental—which is what the Russians always want. They say: Let me move beyond the limits of daily existence! I mean, why does the Russian drink? Because if a man doesn't drink, if he gets up early in the morning and rushes out somewhere fully sober—he's behaving like an animal! Just like an animal and nothing more. It also gets up in the morning and rushes out somewhere fully sober—

Ha ha!

What is that crap? Have a nutritious dinner, all pureed, go to bed at 9 after a walk... A primitive animal, miserable, easily rubbed out from the face of the earth with a thumb. A replaceable piece of shit. It's a technical existence—remove one, put another in his place. He will do the exact same thing, get up in the morning, wash up—just like cattle. And, like an animal, go to work.

Ha ha!

It's completely different when you get up—

—And you have a war!

Yes. Or at least, the discussion of important theoretical questions. For example, instead of going to the office, you stayed at the dacha, cancelled all appointments, sent the chief of security for beer, which he brought, and first thing in the morning, you're analyzing the fate of the world.

Ha ha.

This is high existence. A task worthy of Homo Sapiens or Man with a capital M. You ask: Explain the fate of the world and my nation. And another man sits before you—me, for instance, who's also had a drink to start the day—and he says, It's a shit question, but I'll explain the fate of the world to you.

Ha ha! That is why I have been set on this earth.

That, my friend, is a lofty goal. No fucking way an animal will explain the fate of the world to you. It just goes to work, and that's it.

Ha ha! I don't understand what this has to do with Lebed, though.

At the request of the workers, I return to Lebed. He offered people a chance to solve the question of survival—that is, a biological, animal question. Putin offered a lofty goal: Drink first thing in the morning, and go conquer the Caucasus. A lofty goal, going beyond the framework of daily existence. One way, a man would go to the factory to make cheap parts nobody needs. The other way, the Homeland gives him a weapon, and he goes off to shoot black-asses in the Caucasus. That is the picture some people have in their minds.

Still, Igor, I haven't seen too many people lining up at the army recruitment centers, volunteering for Chechnya. The "true patriots" are mostly shouting on TV. The people dying in Chechnya are village boys who would be very happy plowing the land.

I see that you will never understand. It's pointless to discuss it this way. Let's move on to topics you understand better. I think that in 2000 you had conflicts with Gusinsky. Do you regret getting involved in that whole thing?

No.

So, you are not repenting your sins. You think that everything was done correctly with Gusinsky. And you don't feel bad about freedom of the press?

No. It wasn't about freedom of the press.

So what else happened to us in 2000? You were busy with what you do not regret in the least. Let's see, we also shut down freedom of speech. Well, not "we"—I'm just trying to join in.

Not yet. We'll do that in the next chapter.

Ah, in 2000 you were just getting started.

Yes. In 2000 we offered Gusinsky $300,000,000.

But he didn't get the $300 million?

He refused it. He made a ridiculous scene, knowing full well how it would all end.

Well, he's a theater director, a man of the arts, artistic temperament… Why are you so fucking picking on him?

We're not fucking picking on him. We got the money ready for him; there was a letter of credit in Deutsche Bank in London.

So the picture we get is as follows: Gusinsky set the tone for settling conflicts between the state and the oligarchs. Issues could have been settled nicely. If the Goose had set an example of peaceful coexistence with the Russian regime, it might have continued to be nice in the future. But since business went on the attack—

"I have cameras everywhere, I signed under pressure"—he started with that bullshit.

But if he had come to terms then, maybe Khodorkovsky wouldn't have to be doing time now… They would have treated him nicely, too. But Khodorkovsky got heavy-duty pressure.

No, I wouldn't make that parallel.

Why are you against cheap parallels?

Because I don't like anything cheap in my life.

But we are drinking Nevskoe beer at this very moment!

It's not Nevskoe, it's Baltika. And we are not drinking it because it is cheap.

But because it is cold.

Because it is good.

And, as I noted above, it is also cheap. So. How far did the conflict with NTV go in 2000?

In 2000 we signed a new contract with Gusinsky, and he did not deliver in 2001.

This was after the broken contract according to which he was to get $300 million?

Yes. After that, there was a second contract; we thought he would in turn pay us money in collateral for his shares. But he did not comply. And in 2001 we took away his shares.

About which we will talk later.

Yes.

But in 2000, things were still normal. You thought that Goose was cheating a bit here and a bit there, but that in principle you could come to terms with him.

Yes, I completely had the feeling that we would come to terms.

Kokh's Commentary:

An Act of Goosiclasticism: Combining Business and Pleasure

I Am Hired

Somewhere in April or May 2000, I got a call from Zhechkov, who informed me in a conspiratorial voice that he had a brilliant idea (as usual, by the way), but he could not reveal it over the phone. If I wanted to hear it, I had to come to his banya on Sunday. Well, I decided that curiosity was always my strong suit (even though I prefer to think of it as a scholarly impulse). So I went to Zhechkov's house.

Zhechkov. Since he comes up so often in the book, I think it's time to explain that Vladimir Anatolyevich Zhechkov is one of the founding fathers of advertising in Russia, co-owner of Premier SV and—until recently—of our magazine *Medved*. He is also the irreplaceable soloist of Belyi Orel and performer of the megahit "How Entrancing Are Nights in Russia." Our pal. He says he's a millionaire.

When I got there, I discovered Mikhail Lesin, the press minister, and Vladimir Grigoryev already in the banya. Lesin, without further ado, explained the idea. It was simple and uncomplicated. Gusinsky's company Most owed Gazprom around half a billion dollars. The odds of the money being paid back were almost nil. Gazprom wanted to get at least something. As they say, at least a fistful of wool from a shorn sheep. Gazprom's director, Rem Vyakhirev (or was it his deputy Vyacheslav Sheremet?) had asked Lesin to recommend someone who could handle the job. Lesin wanted to recommend me, so he was asking whether I would accept the work.

I paused and looked with great interest at the bottle of vodka on the table. I threw back a shot and said to Grigoryev, "Come on, I'll give you a steaming."

While I drummed him with bunches of softened aromatic twigs—the steam bath massage—I considered the situation. First of all, it was not Gazprom's initiative to get money back from Most. That was as clear as day. A new boss in the Kremlin meant new rules. Of course, secondly, there was nothing strange about one company wanting to get its loan back from another one. On the contrary, it is bad when the management of one company (Gazprom), which itself needs money and borrows it with interest from Western banks, gives another one (Most) loans without interest and without any collateral. Therefore, it was normal for Gazprom, even at the prompting of others, to want to get money from Most. So there didn't seem to be any trick there.

We came out of the steam room. Lesin regarded me closely. I regarded the bottle of vodka closely. Bam, I had another shot. Then munched on a pickle and drank some kvass (which I had brought from Tsarskaya Okhota, a restaurant that specializes in Russian cuisine). Then I said to Grigoryev, "All right, now it's your turn, please." Grigoryev laughed. Let's go, I'll beat you.

As I lay under the leafy twig massage, I pondered. Why me? And why did Vyakhirev turn to Lesin? The answers were pretty much obvious. Me, because Goose had tried to put me away, and therefore I wanted revenge. Well, that made sense. Although they probably strongly overestimated my vengefulness. Though, to be honest, it was there. Maybe, just a tiny bit, but it was there. I had that feeling: So, you creep, you're getting what you deserve at last. And Lesin? Probably because he was appointed head of the project by the new administration. But! It wasn't that simple! It's easy to say, Lesin. How does he see his part in running the project? The minute the minister of the press showed even a minimal interest in this, Gusinsky would shout from the rooftops that his freedom of speech was being stifled. And he would call me a stifler, too. When all I had done was hire on to get a loan paid. I had to make conditions—that they not get involved. I would manage on my own. Otherwise, I'd never live down the shouting. Wait! Did that mean I've accepted? And I answered myself: Yes. Well, they broke me fast enough.

We returned to the table. For the main course, roast duck. Delicious. I poured the red wine.

"Well, Mikhail. You've made me an offer I can't refuse. On the whole, I accept. When will we discuss details? Tomorrow, at your Ministry office? Fine, I'll be there. What about Vyakhirev and Sheremet?"

"Later, in a month or so. Get some rest first. Don't rush things. For now all I need is your agreement in principle."

The next day Lesin told me that he agreed with my assessment of the risks of his involvement in the project. Therefore he would try to stay out, but I had to understand his position: This was the third most important national television channel and the Ministry of the Press could not stay out of the "argument of economic subjects." It sounded sort of acceptable. And how would I be paid for my work? Besides me (and I don't rate myself cheaply), I would need to hire clerks, lawyers, financial experts, and consultants. That costs a lot of money.

Believe me, said Lesin, you'll solve all your problems at Gazprom.

At the end of our conversation, he handed me a huge file of documents on Most's debts to Gazprom. Here, study it, he said. It's all so complicated, you can break a leg trying to get through it. I got the documents from Sheremet. I tried to figure them out and couldn't. So, go on, start familiarizing yourself with the material, and when it's time, I'll call you.

I went to my office and called in my partner, Sasha Reznikov. Here's a proposal, I said. Shall we take it? We shall. We put together a budget, this and that. Started looking at the documents, coming up with various options. It truly was a horrible situation. We developed a line of behavior. Here collateral, there collateral. If they miss the deadline for payment, we take the collateral. Here we sue, there we seize property. A plan was shaping up.

About a month and half later I met with Sheremet. He's an amazingly constructive and direct man. And he knows his worth, too. I don't often meet such sensible people. I'd heard a lot of different things about him before I met him and after he left Gazprom. My experience with him has been only positive. I told him about our action plan. He clarified a few details, but on the whole, he approved it. We settled the organizational and financial issues fairly quickly, and the very next day I was appointed director of Gazprom-Media.

Gusinsky Turns Down $300 Million

Literally the day after my appointment—that is, on June 13—Gusinsky was arrested. I learned about it in Lesin's office, where I had come to meet with Anatoly Blinov, a lawyer we wanted to hire (and did) for the inevitable lawsuits with Media Most. The Interfax wire had a story on Gusinsky's arrest. I was completely discouraged. Not that I felt so sorry for Gusinsky. He not only had tried to put me away behind bars but also had created difficulties with law-enforcement agencies for a lot of people. However, knowing Gusinsky, I knew full well that without him, Media Most would not be able to carry on useful negotiations about settling their debt. There simply weren't any people there who could make decisions in the absence of their boss. And in general I don't like the practice of pre-trial detention on economic charges. That's not justice, it's just a form of physical pressure on the defendant.

That Blinov was an amusing character. Once when he worked at Vneshekonombank, he won an arbitrage case on getting a debt back from Media Most. We thought a lawyer like that would come in handy. Jumping ahead, I can tell you we were wrong. Blinov turned out to be absolutely incompetent. He didn't even have a law degree—he was a doctor. But he compensated for that with an absolute absence of principle and a phenomenal arrogance. There was even something engaging about his primitive cynicism. His legal knowledge was limited to discussions of how to bribe the judge and what size commission to take for himself. Eventually he switched to the Media-Most side and slung mud at us as energetically as he had at Gusinsky. From what I read in the press, he is in prison now.

Blinov and I said a few words to each other and agreed to meet at my office. I left; there was nothing to discuss. From the look on Lesin's kisser, I could tell that this had been as much a surprise to him as it had been to me. Fridman called and asked sarcastically: "Businessmen are signing a letter of support for Goose, would you like to sign? It would be amusing, especially considering your new job!"

"Why not... I'll sign. It's a good cause. I really don't want him to be in jail."

I went to Fridman's office at Alfa Bank. On the way I thought: I got Lesin to promise not to get too involved in this, but now what? After all, I can't get those coppers, the law enforcement people, to make the same kind of promise. Boy, I was stuck in it! It would be dumb to back out. It looked as if I wouldn't be able to do without Lesin's help now. Maybe he could come to terms with them so that they wouldn't be too active?

After Fridman, I went back to Lesin's office. He said that he had already gotten a call from Igor Malashenko. He wanted a meeting. He had also called the prosecutors, and they'd gleefully informed him that Goose would be behind bars until the Second Coming.

The next day, the businessmen's letter appeared. Reaction—zero. Lesin kept vanishing. What was going on? I just stopped thinking about it and quietly went about solving some organizational problems. Change bank cards, hire staff, get the bookkeepers organized. Up to my neck in work.

A few days later, they let out Gusinsky on a promise that he wouldn't leave the country. Thank God! Now we can get a move on.

Boris Nemtsov called: "I was just talking with Gusinsky. Want to meet with him?"

"And how! I'm thirsting for it! But he wants to talk to me the first day he's out? Doesn't he want to spend the evening with his family?"

"I have a feeling you will replace his family for a long time… In any case, you're better than the Senior Investigator of the Prosecutor General's Office for Special Cases."

"Depends. Especially me and especially for him. Come on, I'm just joking. Well, I'm ready to meet. Where, when, under what circumstances? How will I recognize you?"

"At my apartment. Around ten. I'm tall and have dark curly hair. Gusinsky is fat and grumpy. Don't get us mixed up. So, are we agreed?"

"Yes. But you never have anything to eat."

"But lots of booze. OK, see you later."

The meeting was surprisingly peaceful. We told each other to fuck off only a few times and got into a clinch just twice. Boris had to pull us apart. But we avoided fisticuffs. On the whole, it was a constructive conversation. Gusinsky proposed exactly what I had wanted to propose to him. The plan was simple and elegant:

1. A joint appraisal of Media Most.

2. A schedule for paying off the debt in two stages.

3. For each stage, use a part of Media Most of equivalent value as collateral.

4. In case the schedule is not kept, Gazprom takes the corresponding collateral as its property.

In principle, there were no alternatives. Any debtor and creditor would have acted this way if they wanted to find a solution instead of putting on a show called "Suppressing Freedom of Speech."

I told Gusinsky that I liked the plan on the whole, and I was willing to hire an investment consultant to be paid by Gazprom Media, since Media Most had financial difficulties. And I was prepared to meet with his experts to get primary information for the appraisal.

Media Most appointed the late Andrei Tsimailo as its negotiator. He was a good specialist; I had worked with him on Svyazinvest. A calm and weary man. You could see that he was sick of Gusinsky's displays and wanted only one thing—peace and quiet. I later learned that he was seriously ill with some heart ailment. But he worked well and hard and was absolutely loyal and honest in regards to Media Most in general and to Gusinsky in particular.

I felt nothing but warmth and spiritual amity toward Andrei. He was truly an educated and smart man. He spoke several languages and had a real doctoral degree, not a bought one, as people do today. He was smarter than me. It happens sometimes: You meet your counterpart, and you like him. You want to be friends with him, drink together, vacation together. But no. You have to fight him, stick some sneaky tricks into the contract (he might not notice), not let on that you see his mistake…

Here's what I was thinking: I'll finish the torture of this job, and then Andrei and I will go for a drink here in Moscow or in London, and have a long talk, smooth out our relations… I didn't take it seriously when he moved to London in 2001. I had done my time in Paris and New York. I thought it was just a question of time. Especially since I was convinced then and now that Andrei certainly was not involved in any wrongdoing. He was very conscientious in those matters.

I kept thinking we would get together and kept putting it off, and then he went and died. Once again, death comes to us with its finality. You can't fix anything anymore. Like final exams in school. You turn it in, and that's it. The only thing to do is wait for your grades. He turned in his work early—like all top students—and got his grade. I'm certain that he got an A, as always. The rest of us are still plugging away. It's a very complicated assignment, life. Will I do better than a D? Lord, make me wise!

In any case, we hired Deutsche Bank and TRG Aurora as consultants on the deal, Media Most started divulging information, and the work proceeded apace. At some point, Andrei said to me, "Do you know that in parallel with our work, Igor Malashenko is negotiating with Lesin on the same issue?"

"I heard something vaguely. But they're only discussing the political aspects. Things like how to close the case against Gusinsky and other crap, in which I don't want to get involved."

"Malashenko says that he made Lesin some revolutionary proposal that will settle the issue of the debts, too."

"Are you kidding? You mean we're digging through all this just for show?"

"Looks that way…"

I met with Lesin. "Misha, what are you and Malashenko doing in secret? What's the revolutionary proposal he came up with?"

"It's just nonsense. We discussed Goose's criminal charges. And he ups and says that he evaluates Media Most with all its assets at a billion. They owe Gazprom $700 million. So instead of Gazprom trying to get that $700 million out of them, it should pay them $300 million and take the whole shebang off their hands."

"Let him whistle for it. It's not worth a billion. Even the most preliminary analysis showed that all of Media Most isn't worth more than $500-$700 million. But beyond that there are other debts, not only to Gazprom. For example, they owe the city of Moscow over $200 million."

"What are you worried about? Do you need this more than anyone else? Five hundred, seven, a billion Not our problem. Is anyone making you pay out of your own pocket? Let the people whose money it is make the decision. I've passed along the information that this proposal exists to the people who need to know. Including Gazprom. If they're prepared to pay $300 million, the issue is solved: no debts and no criminal charges. If they don't agree, then you continue the work you started."

"In other words, Gusinsky proposed the following deal: I will shut up, give you all my assets, and will live a private life, if you give me $300 million."

"They're right, you are a cynic. Although... One could look at the question that way."

"Everyone takes a crack at artists. You're even more cynical than I am. And I'm not a cynic at all. I'm a pure and trusting youth. Fragile and chaste. I've been doing unnecessary work for almost two weeks."

"All right then. Don't do it. Until there's a reply to Malashenko's proposal, don't do it. Let's wait. If the proposal is accepted, then we'll do a quick deal for the purchase of Media Most for $300 million. Isn't that logical?"

"It is."

I felt relief. It was all so easy. Gusinsky says, Give me $300 million and I'll shut up. They reply, Let us think it over. So while the bosses think, I'll go take a rest. Really, do I want this more than anyone else?

The next day Lesin phoned. "Listen! Igor Malashenko is on his way to see me. There seems to be an opinion there that their proposal should be accepted. So come on over to my office."

"Where is there an opinion? Which proposal are you talking about?"

"Why are you acting the fool? Why are you asking what I mean by 'there'— if I say 'there,' I mean 'there.' At Gazprom, ha ha. This is about what you and I discussed yesterday, remember?"

"Of course, I remember."

"Well then. We need to write a contract for the purchase of all of Media Most for $300 million, plus the debts. Take your lawyers and financial guys, and sit down and write it. Sheremet and Vyakhirev are in the loop. Sheremet has already contacted Sberbank; they need a loan for this. They don't have any spare cash at Gazprom."

"I still don't understand why you had to go through this whole rigmarole of hiring me. You could have managed perfectly without me."

"But who knew that it would be this easy. We thought it would be a battle to the death."

"And why do you need me at the meeting with Malashenko?"

"He wants to have a confidential talk. I want you to be there. What if he tries to screw me over something, and I don't realize it?"

"All right, I'm on my way."

That was the meeting where Malashenko presented Gusinsky's additional demands (besides the money), which became the so-called Addendum No. 6.

Later, both Malashenko and Kiselyov insisted that the entire addendum had been written by the Kremlin. They came out with statements like: "Mr. Lesin and Mr. Kokh are lying when they say that the infamous Addendum No. 6 was composed on the initiative of Gusinsky. It was written in the Kremlin and according to its authors' plan, it would be the main link in the deal, 'freedom in exchange for shares'."

But just reading the addendum or even a small section makes it clear that the text is the work of Gusinsky and his entourage: "The parties understand that the successful realization of the Agreement is possible only when citizens and juridical persons obtain and implement their civil rights of their own will, and in their own interest, without pressure from anyone to take any actions; which at the present time requires the execution of specific mutually related conditions, to wit: an end to the criminal persecution of citizen Gusinsky, Vladimir Alexandrovich in the criminal case brought against him on June 13, 2000; the transfer of his status to witness in that case; the retraction of the requirement that he not leave the country; to give citizen Gusinsky, Vladimir Alexandrovich, and other shareholders and directors of the Organization, guarantees of security, and protection of rights and freedoms, including the right to move freely and choose their domicile, and the freedom to leave the Russian Federation and return to the Russian Federation unhindered." The Kremlin (which I am not defending in the least) had no interest in guaranteeing Gusinsky's safety, and if not for Gusinsky's initiative, the question of closing the criminal case against him would not have been on the agenda.

In general, accusing opponents of lying when they themselves were the liars was the hallmark of Media Most in that period.

Lesin had no intention of signing that delirium at first. It was assumed that I would do the signing. I reread the addendum (the text of the deal itself was finished off rather quickly, and it did not elicit any arguments) and thought: This addendum does not have any legal consequences. It looks idiotic, of course, but if that's how they want it, it's no trouble for me to sign it, since the swift solution of all the problems depends on it.

I shrugged and signed the paper. And here Malashenko announced that they had a key demand, that Lesin sign off on the text. I was against it categorically. It suddenly became clear to me that there would be no deal. This was all done to create the show called "The Kremlin Is Twisting Gusinsky's Arm and Forcing Him to Sell His Media Assets Under Threat of Prison."

But Lesin was so enthralled by the prospect of a swift resolution that he did not listen to me and signed that ill-starred addendum. I set aside all my doubts and went to Media Most to sign the agreement and the addenda in Gusinsky's office. Gusinsky signed it rather fast—though not without also grabbing me by the lapels, voicing the usual threats to deal with me later, and so on. Everyone was so used to his criminal-chic manners that no one paid attention to such trifles. Right after signing the documents, Gusinsky got in a plane and flew to London.

Then the work went into full force. Gazprom borrowed $300 million from Sberbank. We opened an escrow account at Deutsche Bank in London. We wrote down the conditions for accessing the account and transferred the funds into it. And we waited for Gusinsky to start implementing the agreement and turning over shares to us.

Suddenly Tsimailo came and told me that Malashenko would like to meet with me, and for that I would have to go to London, since Malashenko was afraid he would be arrested in Russia. I cussed, but there was nothing to do but go. In London, Malashenko spent a long time telling me that they were having problems with their partners in Israel. I couldn't understand what he meant until Igor informed me that $300 million was not enough and we had to add another $200 million, or the deal was off. Naturally, I said that was out of the question. We parted on that.

Then what had to happen did happen: Gusinsky announced that he had been forced to sign, that he had no intention of keeping his end of the deal, that the contract was legally unsound, and that proof of that was addendum No. 6. In other words, he created the madhouse that was long anticipated.

Now, in 2005 as we are writing this, everyone understands that Gusinsky didn't have a chance of preserving his media empire, especially with such fatal debts, far beyond any rational limit. I had understood even then that by refusing the $300 million, Gusinsky was making perhaps the stupidest move of his life. But as they say, "If the Lord wants to punish a man, he takes away his reason."

There it was, on a silver platter. Take it—I don't want it. This was another example of that most common mistake: a wrong perception of alternatives. Gusinsky thought that the alternative of $300 million was the brouhaha he would start all over the world. The West would stand firm for freedom of speech in Russia; the Kremlin would take fright and give in.

The real alternative, however, was that the West was not going to defend anyone. And if you don't want to sell it for money, an enormous amount of money that exceeds the real value of Media Most, then they'll take it from you through the courts, for your debts. Especially since the debts don't even have to be invented, they really exist.

The deal fell through. Out of momentum, we sued to enforce the contract—after all, he had signed it. But we didn't have much enthusiasm for it. All the assets were in offshore accounts, and decisions of the Russians courts meant nothing. What was needed was Gusinsky's goodwill. I shrugged and sued for the debt payment that was overdue. The prospect of Media Most's bankruptcy was inevitable. In fact, Gusinsky's *demarche* left Gazprom no other way to regulate the debt issue.

A month passed. Suddenly I got a call from Andrei Tsimailo, who said, "Look. You and I started doing work which we considered the right way to solve all our problems. Then those wonderful fellows, Malashenko and Lesin, got involved with their stupid contracts and even stupider Addendum No. 6. Why don't we return to that work and continue it. I spoke with Gusinsky and he's basically in agreement with that. There is no other way out…"

"Let's. I have no objections. Let's pretend that nothing happened."

I went to London to meet with Gusinsky. He met me warmly, as if nothing were wrong. We had lunch in an Indian restaurant. He was a fan of that cuisine. He ate a lot and with gusto. He ate a whole small chicken and drank a liter of beer. He announced right off the bat: "Listen! Let's forget everything that happened between us and try to rebuild our relationship."

My eyes bugged out. That was a fine thing! As if there were no insults in the press, no real work to put me behind bars. No destruction of our government. No default. No gray hairs on my mother's head. Police searches ten hours at a time in the presence of my children. No threats, no grabbing me by the lapels. That was really taking the cake. I realized at that moment that Gusinsky was totally unreliable in his love and in his self-indulgence. I chuckled and said, "Well, let's try. Just don't trick me this time. Otherwise you won't be the only one who has to hide in London—I will, too. I have too many people to persuade not to use militant solutions instead of peaceful ones."

"Oh, no, old man; this time I won't trick you."

That's how we left things. We returned the money from Deutsche Bank's escrow account to Gazprom. And did the interrupted work. By mid-December, a new contract was ready and signed. Kiselyov praised it on television as a deal that demonstrated the measured and wise approach of both sides. All that was left was to execute the terms of the agreements. But that's a completely different story, which took place in 2001.

* * *

The goal, as I understand it, Alik, was to take away the man's mass media but without touching him.

Yes. Yes.

The state was dealing with its question—

I don't know what the state was doing! The state was doing jerky things all the time… And they didn't warn me that it would be like that. For example, they put Goose in prison. Now, what for?

Tell me, please, Alik. Do you regret today that you tried to get Goose released as quickly as possible?

No. In general I don't think that people should be in prison. Even murderers.

Tell me, what else did we have in 2000? What were you doing?

Me? I paid off my debts.

Why the fuck did you get into debt?

What do you mean! I was forced into debt in 1998.

Ah, yes, you lost twenty then.

Yes. And then I paid off the debts. Also in 2000, I enjoyed my freedom— the case against me ended then. And I was getting to fuck a bit with Goose. Well, I felt that my life was a success in 2000. Everything bad was over. That was a good year. Which I started, by the way, in Colorado.

Wait, you welcomed in the Millennium there?

Yes. We wore tuxedoes—they gave us top hats, we walked around in them. It was fun, we skied. I had a hotel room that even had a sauna. It was very cool.

I have notes on how we celebrated February 23 [Defender of the Fatherland Day] in 2000. With you, Alik, by the way.

Was that in the restaurant on Kommunistichesky Tupik? We met on that Dead End street.

No, we didn't. It happened at Luzhniki. You were drunk, your head on the table. I arrived and said, "Greetings, colleague!" You replied, "Ah, are you also a writer?" A subtle joke. That was the height of the writers' scandal. I had come there with Vova Zhechkov, and then we moved on to his dacha. I was very amused by his place; the house was so luxurious, but there were absolutely no provisions, except for vodka and black caviar.

Horrors.

No bread, no *salo*, no beer. Fuck-all. Bare shelves. Caviar and vodka.

That was your breakfast.

No, I somehow avoided vodka then.

You're a strong man. Keep yourself in hand. In your place, I would have had a shot myself. Was it cold?

Of course. The caviar and vodka were from the fridge. By the way, 2000 was a major Leap Year. Didn't they promise us the end of the world? As it happens in such situations?

They sure as hell did.

I also went to Chile in 2000. I told you a lot about it.

I've written a commentary of my own on it.

Even though I was there briefly, I understood that it's a very attractive place.

It's good, it is. I like it. It's what's called an evil example.

Chile—it's a topic… A topic of sausages. If you picture Russia as a veal sausage and you cut it into… I don't know how to say it in Russian, Russian lacks a lot of words (we have to manage without the words "discretion," "frustration," "slice"), so if you cut it into slices, then Chile is this thin slice, from north to south. It has tundra, and ice deserts, and tropics, and we have all that, too. And Germans went to work there, the way they did in Russia.

I also went to Spain and attended the festival of cuckolds. As a reporter, please note. The festivities celebrated the anniversary of the repeal of the *ius primae noctis*, or right of first night that the lord had over villagers.

Show off!

It's celebrated widely there, especially in the villages. At least in Catalonia. So, they plant a huge pole in the middle of the village and nail on a set of horns. For beauty's sake. The men are in national costume, and some of them wear horns, too. Everyone dances, drinking starts in the morning—they pour drinks for strangers, and cook up some kind of shashlyk. It's a festival, all folksy and unsophisticated—people drink straight from the bottle, these special glass teapots. And dance the *sardana*.

This is good—I found an amazing entry in an old notebook, dated April 29, 2000. For the entire day, there is only one note: "Got drunk."

Hah!

What was it? In connection to what? I don't remember. But apparently, I got seriously drunk. That is why I left it in the annals.

In the anal?

Annals.

What's the difference?

Anal is an adjective. Anal sex. The noun is anus. Verstein? But annal with a double N is a different story. That's a noun. You can't confuse them. So. I celebrated May 1 at Aliona Doletskaya's dacha. In Vatutinki.

Tell me about Doletskaya, editor of *Vogue*. I can't understand why you're all so crazy about her.

Why do we love Doletskaya? First of all, you can sit down and drink with her. You know, heart-to-heart. And then, she understands. You can talk normally with her. It often happens when you're talking with women, you think: "Don't say that to her, don't say this, she won't understand, she'll be offended"—so it's all hee-hee-hee and ho-ho-ho and nothing more. How does it usually happen? People are sitting around talking, the atmosphere is warm and informal. Once the women show up, that's it, conversation over, the mood is changed—that happens almost all the time.

Yes.

But when Doletskaya shows up, the conversation continues normally, in the same spirit. Now that's interesting.

But that's pure mimicry. Taking on your boyfriend's image.

Fine, I don't care if it is only mimicry. At least you feel natural.

What I want is for the men to shut up when the broads show up.

But we're not supposed to...uhm, use all women as they are intended, right?

But we could at least not swear in front of them. Well, at least try.

You think? Well... Here's something else, they dedicated a monument to Venedikt Erofeyev in 2000. I sincerely believe him to be a profound writer, a most serious author.

What new things did he reveal to you in your silly and ridiculous life?

You can't put down his book, it's extremely perceptive. I read it back in Soviet times, *Moscow-Petushki*. Recently I read an edition with commentary, which is ten times longer than the basic text.

Our book has a shitload of commentary, too.

I thought that you and your creative development had been influenced by Erofeyev in the sense that you became enthralled by commentaries in his footsteps. And it turns out that he had fuck-all influence on you.

Nope. I'm self-sufficient.

The commentaries to Venya's book were written by a Russian who lives in Japan, I think—apparently he has tons of free time, and so he wrote this amusing thing. He explains that a bunch of the jokes in the book are built on opera libretti. Because Venya was a great lover of opera. Then he explains all the political and all the literary allusions—I was deeply touched by that. The fact that a monument was built for Erofeyev strikes me as a very positive phenomenon.

What kind of writers are we, do you think—underground or not underground?

Confessional prose, remember somebody blurted that out? About *A Crate of Vodka!*

Right. Confessional. Hah!

I can see that you don't like Venya Erofeyev very much, but for me he's terribly *simpatico*.

There's that formulation—*simpatico*—it perforce presumes the absence of greatness. He is *simpatico* precisely because he is our equal.

***Simpatico* for me is better than great.**

Really? That is, let's say that Chekhov for you is more *simpatico* than great?
If we mean in terms of Russian language, then I realize that I will never write like Chekhov.

But you're still young!

I'm the age at which Chekhov died. So that is out of the question.

But Tolstoy at your age was still a mere lad.

Tolstoy, from the technical point of view, was rather weak. Pushkin was strong, but he also has died. Lermontov was strong, but he's also dead. I'm the only one left.

Are you forgetting that I'm still alive, you so-and-so?

You don't treasure the Russian language. I look at your punctuation, your vocabulary, and I see that you don't treasure the language.

Really? You're not reading me very closely, replied the classic to the classic.

Now Bunin was still alive. How old was he when he died?

I think seventy-two.

So there. He wrote in Russian. Gorky. Gorky, by the way, handled Russian rather well.

Gorky's reputation got distorted because of his Bolshevism—like Khodorkovsky, he returned from the West for some stupid shit.

Ha ha ha! Did you just make that up?

Of course.

He was a real jerk. The old idiot: to leave Sorrento for Moscow!

What, in 1937, you wouldn't have left Sorrento for Moscow?

No.

Now, I've never been to Sorrento, so it's hard for me to say what decision I would have made.

Yes, really. We're talking about different weight categories.

But I have been to Moscow, unlike Sorrento. Just yesterday, in fact. Yes. … And Venya was never in Sorrento, either. And he was already great at the time of the end of the Soviet regime. His books were published all over the world, he was getting some real money from abroad. He gave readings at the Central Writers Club. Naturally, he was invited to the West. Not only to speak but also to have surgery on his throat so that he could live some more. Can you imagine, they wouldn't give him permission to leave!

Really? How charming.

They said: You, Venya, will die here. We won't let you go to the West to have an operation. Can you imagine! So he lived and died knowing that the Chekists would not let him extend his life in the West.

On the other hand, he would be all written out by now.

He wrote very little, in general.

He would have repeated himself. He would be dragged around like a living classic. He would have been as empty as a shaman's tambourine.

Which living classics do they drag around?

Voinovich, for example.

They don't drag around Andrei Bitov.

But they do poet Yevgeny Yevtushenko. And prima ballerina Maya Plisetskaya. Somewhere way in the back of beyond, like Ekibastuz, for creative evenings. And the local intelligentsia comes out in droves.

Pretty soon we'll be beating a path to Ekibastuz ourselves.

Ha ha! And Venya would be going there, too. The KGB did exactly the right thing.

They always seem to be doing the right thing.

Well, they made a martyr of him. The role of literature has fallen mightily. Who gives a shit about writers? Nobody, really.

Yes, it's just our personal affair. Another thing I did in 2000 was take part in the opening and shutting down of river navigation in the regions. Let me explain: There is this man, Vova Kantorovich, who, when he was at school, pretended to be related to Academician Kantorovich, and he always got A's.

By the way, I knew Academician Kantorovich.

You're kidding!

My adviser in grad school, may he rest in peace—open another bottle—was Academician Kantorovich's partner, and they were pretty close friends. I even delivered some piece of paper from St. Petersburg to Moscow for him. I saw him in person.

Well, we all have a Kantorovich in our lives. Mine is the co-owner of the KMP travel agency—he's got a serious business, with offices in Paris.

You've mentioned him.

So I started taking these boat trips, opening and ending the season. This is how it works: Friday night the boat sails off to Yaroslavl or somewhere, and it comes back Sunday night. With a stop in Uglich or Myshkin. Most of the people know one another, everyone's in a good mood, they have strippers and magicians, someone to sing and play, someone cooks *shashlyk* on shore. It's so much fun that when I have to miss one, I get upset: Oh boy, I could be with the gang on the ship, and instead my burdensome journalistic fate has taken me to Paris again. I'm so bored, and they're having a blast, being wayward.

That's such a Cossack term, wayward.

Perhaps. I remember this incident on board the boat, which speaks of the country, its organization, settlement, and prospects. An artist friend went on the trip with us. He planned to photograph the belfry near Kalyazin, the one that's been sticking out of the water ever since they flooded everything along the Volga with that hydroelectric station. A very subtle composition. And we were traveling right past it. He ran to his stateroom to get his camera. He fell along the way. He was sick. We called for a doctor but the only one on board was Bilzho, and he's a psychiatrist. He tried to do what he could, but we needed to call for an ambulance. We'll call on the mobile phone—the ambulance will come to the shore, we'll dock, unload the artist, and they'll take him to emergency. Easy as pie. But! The mobiles didn't work. This in what is perhaps the most central part of Russia, in the Yaroslavl region. Some of the most beautiful places in the country, along the heavily promoted Volga River. Fine, we used the ship-to-shore radio—you can use that to reach HQ from the middle of the Pacific. And what did that serve? There were no docks, there weren't even any roads for the ambulance. But look, what about those houses on the riverbanks... That's for winter fishing, but at high water there's no way to communicate with the outside world. That's the way it is. And I'm reiterating—these are marvelous, glorious places. So with all the to-ing and fro-ing, by the time we got to the closest docks it was six hours later, and the ambulance picked up a cold body. He was with his family, so they picked up everyone.

The rest of the passengers decided to go into mourning: A man died, how could they have a party with whores? We canceled everything. There was this surge of patriotic feeling. But by nighttime that noble feeling weakened, people had started drinking and the mood changed—so the dancing and whores were back on the schedule.

Ha ha!

As you understand, it was—

Required by the conventions of the genre!

Required by the conventions of the genre! Even though it could have been considered a wake, and then it would have been politically correct. If you think about it, a pagan wake is no worse than a Komsomol wedding, let me tell you… And that's when I was struck by the thought that the best spots in Russia, the very best ones, are not populated. There should be fine houses along those banks, there should be people living in them, there should be a high-speed railroad line to Moscow. After work you get on the train, and an hour later you're on the Volga, relaxing on a canal. But no! Do you realize how terrible it is that Russia's best places have not been trodden by man? There's fuck-all there. The country is empty, empty!

It sounds so tragic. It's the fucking pits.

Yes, empty… That death, that drowned town of Kalyazin….

There's your depiction of the superpower in face of the emptiness! How our KGB keep hustling, pretending to have an empire when there is a lack of subjects. The subjects who exist are hiding in caves or in cellars… It's a completely different ideology. What the fuck kind of democracy can you have when there are no people! The country is not POP-U-LA-TED!

I think it's Berezovsky's fault.

What's your problem with him? The man lives and plays his part…

Listen, don't I have the right to like some people and dislike others?

You don't like him?

Me? Not at all. You think he's being persecuted for nothing? I really dislike the fact that he ran my country even though I did not give him any permission to do so. No one did, in fact. Despite the fact that back then we still had such democratic procedures as, for example, elections. I was sitting there waiting to find out who's going to command me, Zyuganov or Yeltsin. And suddenly this bald guy with a dissatisfied face comes on…

I thought he had come on to tell us about the AVVA company and to return their money to the deceived proletariat. But no. He started telling us that he's our daddy. Hello.

But the man realized himself a full 100 percent.

So what? Is that always good? Volochkova, Dorenko, Khinshtein got to 200, and is that so good?

I, for one, am afraid of realizing myself a full 100. Because God forbid what may emerge. It's better off being at a lower percent.

You don't like people realizing their full potential?

I'm talking about myself right now. About how maybe it's better not to throw everything you have out into the world.

Of what do you consist?

Well… I'm a weak and sinful man.

Uh-uhn. That's just a banality.

So what? I'm not an eccentric clown who is required to be original at every moment or risk being fired. I come up with my thoughts without reference to all that; I'm fine without an audience.

But from the point of view of a journalist, you must know that full realization is interesting.

From that point of view, yes. When a person is 100 percent realized, that grabs your attention. Because in that case, clumps of energy flows are formed. And that makes it interesting. Whether it's right or wrong, Alik, how do I know?

It's not our job to judge.

My job is to see where the energy flows crisscross. And try to get close to them and then reflect them, capture them in a funny form.

Why funny?

For a simple reason: If you haven't laughed out loud once while reading the text, the text is a failure.

That's not true.

But if we return to Berezovsky, you're the one who had problems with him, Alik. Not me. But I never liked him. I don't have to like everyone who is being persecuted.

No, you don't.

Especially since I began disliking him when he was on top. My conscience is clear.

All right. So what do you want from me?

I didn't like the way he pushed himself in where no one invited him. Buying up all the newspapers.

Again with that! You're just a socialist, old man, you are a socialist!

Get out. I've never been a socialist. And I've never been a member of their party.

I hate your socialist ideology. What do you have to do with Berezovsky and the press that he bought? You were a hired worker.

I can like some politicians and not others.

You may.

Even though I did not wish Berezovsky success in buying up the mass media, at least I did not prevent it.

Right. As if you could.

I simply felt a personal antipathy. Don't I have the right to feel strong antipathy for Berezovsky?

Not on the basis of his buying and selling.

Nevertheless, I allow myself to feel it. That's just the way I am.

I'm telling you, you're a socialist.

I'm not a member of the Socialist Party and I've never voted for it. Therefore, I am not a Socialist. I do not share its theory or practice or its platform.

You can't possibly know the practice of the Socialist Party, since it has none!

So we're back in 2000. I was actively traveling around the prison zones.

What prompted that, Igor? Why all of a sudden? What brought on that transcendental "Russians Serving Time"?

It began with me in the car hearing an interview on the radio with Valery Abramkin. He's a dissident—

I know.

He said: We have this committee, we travel to the zones, we help inmates. And I thought, how interesting. I wrote down the address he gave: Luchnikov Alley, 4. Near the Polytechnical Museum, behind the former Central Committee of the Komsomol. So I decided to interview him. I found Abramkin. He was this half-dead camp inmate. Exhausted by tuberculosis. He told me about his life. He said that prison is so disgusting that if he could turn his life back to the 1970s he would do whatever he could to avoid that path and never be arrested. He came very close to slitting his wrists. The guys got him a razor. When he can say that that life ground him down, when he can admit that, it elicits enormous respect from me.

It could break anyone. I think Shalamov is right: prison never yields a positive experience. It teaches you how to survive. I recall my childhood in Togliatti. There isn't a single bright spot in it. Except for love. Love for girls in my class—and that's it. The rest was tactics of survival.

When I described the humiliation and torture imposed on people in Russian prisons and compared them with the concentration camps of the Nazis, I found a line that seems very fundamental to me. When, for example, the Nazis tormented people in the camps, there was a logic to it: We torture the prisoners and then come the gas chamber and the crematorium. No feedback, no return from there to the normal world, no negative, destructive effect from it. But when people are tortured in our Russian prisons, subjected to the unimaginable, and then returned back into our world, the ex-cons bring all that vileness and horror to us. And there is no logic in that at all.

Abramkin told me about tuberculosis which cannot be cured—there is that kind. He spoke with personal knowledge, as one who got TB in the zone. If you start treating TB, just treat it a little and then stop, then the germs—what are they called?

Bacillus.

The bacillus get so strong that you can't be cured of them for all the money in the world. They become invincible iron divisions. In the past only impoverished beggars had TB. Now even respectable citizens get it. The spirochetes are everywhere. Just a little stress, and the disease is activated. Abramkin described this picture: broken men, destroyed, humiliated, come out bringing with them this evil into the country that is not populated and has no vertical of power… That makes an impression. You must agree that's an apocalyptic picture. Anyway, I interviewed Abramkin. One of his points was that he had published a book, *How To Survive in a Soviet Prison*.

I know it.

It's very educational. He said, I've made additions to it and want to publish *How To Survive in a Russian Prison*. A post-Soviet one. He had a lot of offers and sponsors, but in the end, no one gave him shit. So he did not reissue the book. I wrote about that.

I'll fund it.

Very good. [*It's still being edited.*] So, I interviewed Abramkin. There was a point, it goes without saying, that the oligarchs have decided against prison and the promised money, and so the book about prison and how to survive it was fundamentally of no interest to them. This was in 2000, let me remind you. Unfortunately the remark turned out to be no joke, even though I was joking around then. The man couldn't find $5,000 to publish such a book! I interviewed him and later I wrote about their exhibit "Prison and the Zone," which is held periodically at the Polytechnical Museum. They rent space there; they build a real prison cell, and you can spend five minutes in there.

After that interview with Abramkin and his people I thought: Why am I writing about people writing about what they've seen? Why don't I travel to the zone with them sometime. A shit question—let's go tomorrow. Well, tomorrow, then tomorrow. The first time you enter the zone is horrible. When we came out I said, Where's the closest kiosk?, I have to get drunk and forget. It was easier the next time.

Some of my friends from school were arrested and sent down for six years. It was called robbery. They were robbers. I went to see them inside.

Yes. I went two or three times. And then I sensed what an important part it was of the country's life. A million people in prison at a time, and how many have gone through it already. It's terribly important, and at the same time, society is quite indifferent to it. People think, here's a *zek*, an

ex-con, best thing is to kill him or at least stick him somewhere we don't have to see him. I was interested by Abramkin's essential thought that if the people who are inside switched places with those who are outside, nothing would change. Either in the zone or in society. It's the same life, distinguished by insignificant nuances.

Yes.

The newspapers are reluctant to cover this. I say, "What's the matter with you, there's a million people in prison. There's a guaranteed audience of a million readers." You know what they told me? "What good is that million to us? Are they going to buy newspapers or what our advertisers produce?" Here's what "overjoyed" me from a purely literary point of view. Abramkin and his staff rented two rooms in the former Central Committee of the Komsomol, then only one, because they raised the rent on them.

Oh, Lord!

Someone came up with the idea of privatizing the Central Committee of the Komsomol and renting out the space commercially. Before it was clear whose property it was, the reasoning was to let social organizations use it. So the dissidents moved in, then the soldiers' mothers group, the committee for invalids, and so on. Once they raised the rent, they had to regroup. They could move to Vykhino or some other far-flung suburb, but the impoverished visitors from the provinces would never get there. This way, a person comes to Moscow by train and then can walk from the Three Stations [*railroad trains arrive there from the north, east, and northeast*] to Luchnikov Alley. And turn in his pathetic plea... What a profitable business it is, grabbing up real estate in the center of town and using it as a tool to take the last bit of money from widows and orphans.

20.

2001

The Twentieth Bottle

In 2001 Svinarenko tries on emigration, and it does not suit him. Kokh successfully ends the epic story with Gusinsky that began the previous year. Besides this, the authors look at 9/11 and discuss a plan for bringing in the Chinese to solve the Chechen issue.

Alik, I can tell you how I started 2001. We've talked several times about emigration, about trying it on for size and so on. I spent that New Year's Eve, 2001, in France with our relatives. With their relatives and friends. I developed a base there. The story began long ago, in deep Soviet times, when I decided to settle my sister-in-law's personal life. The life she was leading—which is outside our discussion here—displeased me, and I put an end to it. She was outraged: "What right do you have?" I replied: "I have no right at all, but I'll kill both of them. Will that make life any easier for you? It would be more logical to just accept it." By the way, my cousin Lyonya, a miner, had a similar relationship with his former wife. He had divorced her, but then he'd come over a year later, even two, and three, allegedly to see the kids but also to check under the beds and in the closets.

What for?

To find her lover—who might have been imaginary—and kill him.

But why?

She asked the same question: Why? He couldn't not explain the reason, he didn't dig that deep, nor did it worry him—for he felt no need to prove that he was right, but he was convinced of his righteousness and persuaded his ex-wife that she had to accept the situation, that there was no other way, it would be worse for her if she did not. You know how she saved herself? She was recruited to work in Italy in a program to care for little old men.

Did she find herself a little old man?

No, she works as an aide for some grandpa, for money; she sends some back to her kids in Ukraine. Just imagine an old man—he has to be served, cared for, amused, entertained... And my cousin can't get to Italy to supervise the moral image of his ex-wife. There. My wife's sister, Ninka, said: All right, let's say I accept the situation, then what? And I said, Then I marry you off. And not just to anyone, but to someone in a decent country. She says, Oh, really? That's interesting. So, basically, I ruined Ninka's personal life in Russia and married her off abroad. First I tried to send her to the States, which has the highest rating of the countries abroad, but that didn't work out—none of the potential husbands that visited the country impressed me. And so, after various attempts, I married her off to a Frenchman.

And how did you manage that?

Some Frenchman was passing through. This was in Moscow, in 1988 or 1989. There was amateur co-operative tourism, whereby foreigners were housed in people's apartments—for which they paid $20 a night, which was big bucks in those days. The homeowner's only obligation was to set up a cot and give the guest oatmeal with tea for breakfast. And then one of the women in the co-op couldn't house a visiting Frenchman and asked Ninka to take him in. I didn't ask too many questions about what went on between them, how far beyond the tourist housing arrangement they had gone... But somehow that Frenchman stuck.

Love at first night?

Yes. Then I took Ninka to meet his family—that is, his mother. Marie-Louise, or Maria Luiza in Russian, was a very sweet old lady, she died just before her 90th birthday. She drank red wine to the end, a bottle with every lunch. And she drank table wine exclusively. She used to say, You drink whatever you want, but I'm a pensioner, and I intend to live within my means. Basically, she was right—after all, table wine is made for humans, too.

What, were you the only relative?

Probably the only advanced one.

And the rest were what?

The rest were not suitable. Some didn't have enough money, others had other issues. For example, my father-in-law, may he rest in peace, kept berating me in those years: What the hell are you copying from the computer all the time, why don't you write something from your head! In other words, if I had let things run their own course, the two of them would have fucked and then forgotten each other, moved on to other things, the way it sometimes happens in life. It would be like Yukos, which criminally allowed uncontrolled mating among rabbits in Yakutia. Since neither spoke the other's language, I also—at the very least—served as an interpreter for them. So, first I simply traveled with her to France, this and that, and then after a few years of trips and courtship and thinking, there was the wedding. Now they live in a house outside Paris.

Where does he work?

In the courts, he is something like an officer of the court.

And he makes enough to be able to buy a house near Paris?

Well, it's a small house…

Doesn't matter. It's a house. And where does she work? Anywhere?

She works in a store.

Do they have children?

A son who's just started school.

Does he speak Russian?

Yes, he speaks it very well, but with a French "r". He can't read our language. If we use German terminology, the term for native tongue is *Muttersprache*—suggesting a person's fundamental language is determined by the mother. But here, the boy knows his mother's language less well than his father's.

So, we spent the holidays with them. In December 2000. We had just published our first—New Year's—issue of *Medved* in the new format, with Shura Vorobyev, whom you know. Vova Zhechkov, at the time majority stockholder, said, I didn't picture it this way, I don't like it. And I said, Well, if you don't like it, then good-bye, we're closing up shop. Especially since it was the holidays, almost New Year's... The hell with it all. I'll figure out what to do with myself when I get back. I flew off to Paris with a clear conscience.

Then, New Year's in France. What was that? It was warm, naturally, flowers in the gardens, no snow, no frost... What nonsense. It was like our weather right after Indian summer. But that wasn't the worst part. The worst part came at the party table, when we all sat down to welcome in the New Year. No Olivier salad, no fizzy wine called "Soviet Champagne," no rerun of the popular Soviet New Year's movie *Irony of Fate* on the TV, no carillon from Red Square... And it goes without saying, no best wishes from the Russian President. I had never felt a particular need for the last, but as it turned out, it was a very important element on the sensory level— without it, my picture of the world was in danger of falling apart. Some trifles sometimes manifest their heightened significance that way.... The French relatives tried to make it a great dinner. They had serious wine— you can understand that. They had good oysters on crushed ice, each reacting when you spill a drop of lemon juice on them.

Svinarenko's Commentary:

I am always stunned by the dead oysters that are served with such aplomb in even the fanciest restaurants in Moscow; a rare creature will cringe if you drown it in lemon juice—but the public loves it. It's because our people are so brave and full of endurance. I know of several instances of people getting really sick from bad oysters. One got so sick he almost died. The point I guess is that in Russia, oysters are not an expression of gourmet tastes, but a way of showing off. And if you're just showing off, no one notices how pathetic your oyster is but just that you're not eating sausage It's like dating a model who is both dumb and bad in bed; people who've never talked to her or screwed her will envy you.

* * *

Well, dear Alik, besides the oysters they served simpler home cooking: *escargot, coquille St. Jacques...* That is, snails in a garlic sauce and scallops... *Foie gras*, naturally. Or at the very least, *pâté de foie gras*.

The usual dinner in France.

No, not every dinner—it's the analogue of our Olivier salad and herring "under a fur coat." Holiday food, show-off food.

Svinarenko's Commentary:

They don't have the deep cultural gap that we do, where you eat one thing in a restaurant and something completely different at home, when a person sincerely believes that real food is home fries cooked in fatback, with a couple of eggs scrambled in, but in restaurants he eats arugula. He chokes on it and hates it. Or when he eats borshcht and pelmeni at home, but in public orders sashimi and Peking duck. I mean, exotica is beneficial and one should expand one's horizons, and lobster is good when it's cooked on a special occasion, without drying it out by overcooking it and turning the meat rubbery, instead of a pail of crayfish boiled in beer after being soaked in milk for a half-hour. I'm talking about something else, about this cultural gap. We glommed on to these foreign delicacies. We are not accustomed to them; there isn't a whiff of tradition, and it's almost impossible to hear a conversation like "My grandmother grew arugula just like this at the dacha" or "My grandfather usually used the door to crack lobster" or "This little pan with indentations has always been used in our family for cooking snails." I'm terrified of this gap; I'm afraid to look down to the bottom.

Why are we so determined to throw everything onto the dust heap of history? Why aren't we serving our delicious cold soup, *botvinia*? Or stuffed grouse? Why not keep playing *gorodki*, how is that inferior to tennis? There must be a reason for it... Something that can't be eradicated. Just to continue the thought, what do we know about the traditions of Austria Hungary? Did any exist, before the empire fell apart? What kind of traditions are possible that would be common for all, say, Chechens, Yakuts, Jews, Russians, and so on...everyone else who lives here? I guess it's inevitable that the Russian world will fall apart into molecules and something completely different will be built out of them. Not even necessarily by us or for us, and not necessarily into anything familiar or comprehensible. It's terrible to think that we have nothing primary. For us, it's even a revelation that hamburgers are nothing more than an exact copy of home cooking in America. When they're in the their kitchens having a simple meal, they fry up burgers with fries and ketchup, and they follow with apple pie—just like at any McDonald's the world over. That's why that damned MacDo (as the French nicknamed it) is so mighty powerful—because it is natural, it flows out of old traditions and millions of people love it sincerely, getting it with mother's milk. and that authentic energy is felt by others.

* * *

And at that table, the year 2001 arrived, Alik. My younger daughter, who was three then, asked, "When are we going to celebrate New Year's?" This is it, we're doing it. And she demanded to know where Grandfather Frost was. And Snegurochka, his companion. Where were the paper bags with candies and chocolates? Where was the Christmas tree on a wooden stand? Out of the mouths of babes, quite ruthlessly.

I had exactly the same feelings: We were tricked, there's nothing... I was not in a holiday mood. In the absence of certain details and with the nonobservance of certain procedures, it turns out that life simply stops, and you fall out. When you're at the table with French people, eating and drinking with them, talking in your broken French, you feel that there is nothing. That you're talking to an empty auditorium. The effect of being present, the illusion of truth, is absolute—they are all very nice people, they smile, but there's nothing there! Emptiness! So we sat and ate, we went to the museum, we walked around the streets, we went into bars— and that was it. It looked as if emigration, at least at the trial stage, was a kind of death. It had a strong resemblance, for me, to the end of earthly life.

So, in January 2001 we returned to Moscow. I was sitting there, looking over the issue that I had published before leaving. The cover was this: A certain female television anchor, naked, sat in a tub filled almost to the rim with champagne. It was real champagne—we found a sponsor to pay for it. When you fill such a deep vessel with champagne, do you know what color it is? It's reddish. And when you see a lady in that liquid, you get all kinds of stupid ideas. About that time of the month... Those are the most innocent ones. I had them make it look more yellow on the computer. When they did, it looked like piss. It took us a long time to find a shade that didn't look like piss or blood, but just neutral.

Wasn't she cold in that bath?

Of course she was. But what could be done? It was for art! So anyway, Vova called and asked, so what's happening with the magazine? I said, it's all over now! No, he said, I spoke hastily, keep publishing it. Are you sure? I said... And so we went on with it...

What else can I tell you about the start of the year? During the holidays in Paris, on the fake New Year, under the warm gray sky, I started writing a women's novel which, with God's help, I'll publish this year, or early next year.

You haven't finished it?

I have, but there are two chapters I want to punch up a bit. It's for women, do you know why? If you compare how men and how women treat books, it's clear that men read superficially, while women get more involved, emotional… It's the same as how men consider it sex and women consider it love. Love is more serious. "Hey, cutie, haven't I seen you somewhere before?" "You creep, I used to love you!" "Oh, yes, I remember now…" So women put more passion into reading, too. When they like what they've read, they're bowled over. But a guy reads lazily, yawning, and then says it's shit. And he only read it to be able to hold up his end of the conversation if it comes up. And he's more likely to read *The Road to Success*, the biography of some financial whiz, or some other smart guy, or a detective novel, if forced. Women are touched by all kinds of nonsense. So I decided to write a book for them. And it's more interesting to think about them than guys. A guy is in delayed maturity, he remains a boy: He fights, takes away toys, shoots, bothers girls, runs around, and acts like a jerk. What is there to discuss with him? Our average Moscow guy is the same teenaged almost-gangsta hooligan from Donetsk. What can you expect from him? But a chick! That's different. When you start performing for her, she breathes deeply, tears in her eyes, you begin to feel a little guilty… So I prefer writing for chicks than for guys. In it, I describe a guy who's nothing much, but the woman who's with him is fabulous. Their life develops. And there are all kinds of stories and plots within it… Enough. Enough. We still need to hear about your New Year's 2001, Alik.

I don't even remember.

Come on. It was the start of the century. And of the Millennium.

I think I was somewhere with Fridman, Shurik Rubanov, and Nemtsov… Here, in a resort near Moscow. Nothing outstanding.

Ah, family style. Ate and drank and sang songs. Took walks in the woods.

Yes.

And did you have the sense that a new century had started?

No. I didn't. In 2001 I continued the epic story with NTV. We ended it in April, right before Easter.

I remember. On Good Friday. That deserves special elucidation...

Kokh's Commentary:

An Act of Goosiclasticism. Part 2

1. Gusinsky does not fulfill the terms of the second agreement he signed, either.

It is important to mention here that besides the obvious and exclusively economic parts of the new contract, it had a very important political point. The point was included on Gusinsky's insistence, and I think it was reasonable. So I did not object to it.

The point was that even if Gusinsky were unable to pay any of his debts, which was the most likely scenario, then even in that case the contract did not allow the controlling interest in NTV, the key asset of Media Most, to become concentrated in one person's hands. This was achieved by a special procedure which would transfer part of the shares of NTV to Deutsche Bank for sale through an international tender. Neither Media Most nor Gazprom Media could interfere in that process. The contract stipulated clearly that only internationally recognized investors selected by Deutsche Bank could participate in the tender.

This point protected NTV's continued independence from Gazprom and gave it independence from Media Most—and, most important, from the Russian authorities. The decision-maker at NTV would be that internationally recognized investor. The tender was to take place in January and February of 2001. Thus, when the next debt payment was due in the summer, Gazprom would no longer own or have as collateral a controlling interest in NTV.

We began preparations for this tender and held consultations on participation with many media giants. For instance, I personally spoke with representatives of media moguls Leo Kirch of Germany, Rupert Murdoch of the U.S., and the leaders of the large Swedish concern Modern Time Group. There were consultations with leading American investors, too. For example, we talked with Capital Research and Management Co., an investment fund that already had five percent of NTV.

I knew that Gusinsky and his people were also working to get investors to participate in the tender. In particular, he told me himself (maybe he was lying?) that he was talking with Berlusconi and that he was definitely negotiating with CNN's Ted Turner.

All of the above evinces that both sides were completely serious in their preparations for the tender, and there was no doubt that it would take place as planned. Deutsche Bank repeated its readiness to handle the tender and guarantee all the required transparency and objectivity.

What happened subsequently, I still cannot understand. For the second time, the man cut off his own balls. I've never seen anything like it before or since. Voluntarily, while abroad in total security, surrounded by a crowd of political, legal, and financial consultants, of sound mind and body, not trapped in an end game, having time to think calmly, Gusinsky refused to turn over the NTV shares for the tender. He told Deutsche Bank that they would cheat him and run a dishonest tender.

Instead of complying with the contract point that he had himself insisted upon, he sued Deutsche Bank in London—and then for some reason sued Gazprom Media there, too, even though it was not under the jurisdiction of the London courts at all. His pretensions were ridiculous—he disputed the contract on the basis that Deutsche Bank might (!) behave dishonestly. A new word in jurisprudence! Judging someone for having the potential opportunity to break the law. You could sue any car driver for having the potential opportunity to run someone down. Skipping ahead in the story, I will tell you that he lost the suit.

I had not expected anything of the sort, to tell the truth. Of course, I had considered Gusinsky a temperamental man, given to theatrics, not very well educated and rather crude. But at the same time I considered him a bold, willful man with clearly lyrical qualities. I liked the way he defended the interests of the Russian Jewish community—aggressively, inventively, with a sense of fun. I was impressed by his care for his co-workers: Like a brood hen, he defended his chicks from the woes of our difficult world. In principle, he is, of course, born with native intelligence, calculation, and an ability to work hard. That is why I could not have imagined that in a three-month period Gusinsky would twice refuse to execute a contract he had signed, especially contracts that were beneficial to him both financially and politically. Contracts that he himself had proposed and which permitted him to solve all his problems in a non confrontational way.

When people talk today about the dispersal of NTV, the punishment of and reprisals against the Unique Journalistic Collective (which we called the UJC), or the mockery of freedom of the press, I simply can't understand: Whom do they mean? When people say that Kokh was taking revenge and that all the pretty words he said then were nothing more than a screen to hide his desire to wreak vengeance against the man who hurt him, are they talking about me? And so to all those who say that the victim of my personal ambition and vengefulness was not Gusinsky but freedom of the press in Russia and UJC, I would like to pose a few questions.

For example: Can you consider as revenge public support for the offender while he is in prison, or offering him $300 million when you have the ability to bankrupt him without spending a penny? By the way, to make the situation even more curious, I have a letter of gratitude from Gusinsky for this.

Or these questions: Can you call supporting the proposal to break up the shares of NTV so that no one will have controlling interest, and adding a clause on holding an international tender in order to prevent the concentration of the controlling shares in one person's hands, "fighting freedom of the press"? Can you consider endless attempts to persuade the UJC and readiness to provide written guarantees of security for all their creative jobs "the dispersal of the UJC"?

There was nothing to be done. We had exhausted all possibilities of solving the conflict amicably. The paradox of the situation was that Media Most did not deny the existence of the debts but could not offer anything constructive on the subject of payment of those debts. Some of the NTV journalists went so far as to say: "Big deal, $500 million, $700 million… The debt should be forgiven, and that's all! Gazprom has tons of money." These were the same journalists who for ten years had tried to persuade us that Russia had to develop along the market path, that there was no alternative, and the market and capitalism were our radiant future. But as soon as it touched them, it turned out that an exception had to be made for them. I really liked hearing that, after they had tried to put me away for "a mere" hundred thousand dollars.

I appealed to the courts repeatedly about getting the debt paid: The situation was working for Gazprom because, unlike before, when we had an unsecured loan, now there was collateral in the form of shares of the companies that were part of Media Most, including NTV and Ekho Moskvy.

The judicial flywheel slowly started turning, creaking just a bit.

2. The Appearance of Ted Turner

In the meantime, Gusinsky kept bringing me new joy with his creativity. In early February he called me and announced cheerfully, as if nothing was wrong, that he had good news for me, that he had solved all our problems, and now things would come to a successful conclusion. Naturally, I expressed curiosity about this newfound panacea. After a dramatic pause, he told me: "Ted Turner has agreed to buy NTV!"

"And?"

"What's the matter with you, are you stupid? I'm telling you in plain Russian: Ted Turner has agreed to buy NTV!"

"Look, maybe I am stupid, but I don't understand why Gazprom should agree to sell Turner shares it is holding as collateral. Is he going to pay an amount equivalent to your debt?"

"Of course not!"

"Then why should I be pleased by the news? Look: There is a debt, against which you have shares as collateral, including shares of NTV. If you do not pay the debt... You're not paying it, right? Then why are we messing with each other's minds here? If you're not paying the debt, then in accordance with the agreement you signed, Gazprom takes the collateral. It is an act of buying and selling, in effect. It has a price—the size of the debt. If Turner had agreed to buy the shares at a higher price, I would be happy to look at his proposal. But since as you know, he will not pay such a price, then why should Gazprom agree to the sale of the collateral? Who will compensate us for the difference between the price that we have in fact already paid by giving you a loan and the price that Turner is prepared to pay?"

"Money again! Don't you understand that the station's capitalization will grow tremendously if he becomes a shareholder!"

"Whether it will grow or not is a question, but that we will lose money on it, that's visible to the naked eye. And if Turner is so terrific, then put those shares in Deutsche Bank: It will hold the tender, and if Turner wins, so be it, and if not, the winner will be the one who pays the most. Everyone wins. Don't you see that by refusing to hold the tender you are making it inevitable that control of NTV passes to Gazprom? Where's your famous concern for freedom of the press?"

"No, I'm not giving up the shares! I will sell them only to someone who agrees to joint management. I don't trust you! You will bring in some investor and together will form a coalition against me."

"Listen! This is getting ridiculous. First you propose a deal for $300 million. We agree. Then you say that we forced you into it. You make us look like idiots before the entire world: We're forcing Gusinsky to accept $300 million and he's making a fuss. All right, we swallowed that. Then you propose the structure of the deal with collateral and a tender. We agree again. Now you won't give up the shares for the tender that you yourself proposed because you suspect (merely suspect!) that we will bring in a participant to the tender with whom we have an agreement to coordinate action, while you openly declare that you and Turner have exactly that kind of agreement. What is that? It's unheard of. Besides which, you're singing like a nightingale that Gazprom and Kokh personally are stifling your freedom of speech. Isn't it you, with your own hands, stifling it for the third time in the last nine months? Your elaborate plans for keeping control over

NTV out of anyone's hands isn't worth a plugged nickel if you and Turner have an agreement. There's the control: Gusinsky + Turner."

"You underestimate public opinion in the West. For them control in the hands of a participant means preservation of freedom of the press, while control in the hands of the state or an entity connected to the state means its absence. That's why you'll never be able to persuade the West that freedom of the press will be preserved with the transfer of control over NTV to Gazprom. You're destroying yourself, boy! You, personally you, Alfred Kokh, are destroying yourself completely as a democratic figure. And believe you me, I'll make sure that it will happen!"

"Now you're talking! I recognize the voice. At last I hear words not from the lad but the man. Little Vovochka Gusinsky in his own repertoire. Threats, blackmail… You held out for a long time, a whole six months. But you couldn't control yourself, you had to be you. So. I'll have to go to the West and explain my position. You leave me no choice. As for Turner, let his people come, we'll talk. In fact, they've already called me. Both Lyonya Rozhetskin and Grisha Berezkin. I think you sent them to be Turner's 'consultants'?"

"No… Not at all. … I didn't send anyone to you from Turner. He hired them."

"Why did he hire them, eh? Not enough American banks for him? He could have hired Morgan Stanley or Goldman Sachs… Who cares. I've already agreed to meet them. I have a feeling they don't know about each other performing the same job, though. What kind of a trick is that?"

"I don't know anything about it. I just learned from you that they are Turner's consultants."

"Stop whistling. I might believe you. You know how trusting I am. Come on, now it's time for you to ask me to stop our suits. On the basis that we've entered into negotiations with Turner."

"Is that possible?"

"Absolutely not! No one will ever believe you again. Not after you've tricked us twice."

"I didn't. I tricked Putin. He deserves it. You'll be shedding tears with that guy in charge… Mark my words, I, Vladimir Gusinsky, am telling you."

"Well, pal, you insult people and then wonder why they're mad at you. And I don't know how you tricked Putin but you signed the agreements with me, you made your promises to me, and the signatures on them are yours and mine. So let me consider that you tricked me, without getting into high politics, and if along with me you tricked someone else, then you'll deal with them about it."

A few days later, Turner's consultants showed up. They didn't propose anything supernatural. Their appraisal of the value of the shares in collateral was significantly lower than ours. Without going into detail, I can say that my personal impression was that this was nothing more than a publicity stunt. I saw no readiness on Turner's part to pay serious money, but there were all the signs of a well-produced show on the international level: Calls from Secretary of State Colin Powell to the Kremlin, Turner's letters asking for a meeting with Putin, and coverage of that fact in all the papers around the world, and so on.

Something had to be done to define my position. I wrote a letter to the American ambassador in Moscow. Here is the full text:

> His Excellency
> Ambassador of the United States of America in Russia
> Mr. James Collins
>
> Your Excellency, Mr. Ambassador,
>
> Allow me to express my respects and address this letter to you.
> Our company understands the reasons that make the U.S. Department of State follow closely the situation around Media Most. Undoubtedly, freedom of speech is one of the basic democratic values without which no society can be considered truly free. We will do everything in our power to preserve the freedom of speech of those mass media that we control or will control in the future.
> However, you must agree that the right to private property is also a basic value, without which, perhaps, true freedom of speech is impossible. It is impossible to allow these values to be in conflict. Unfortunately, at the present moment, in the dispute between Gazprom and Media Most, we have an example of precisely such a terrible conflict.
> It is not even a matter that after signing an agreement on regularizing the debts between Gazprom and Media Most, the entities controlled by Mr. Gusinsky, including Television Company NTV, are $108 million in arrears before Gazprom. And these arrears are beyond the scope of the signed agreement and are not regulated by it.
> The matter is that we are not satisfied with the method of managing the companies that compose Media Most group and in which we are minority shareholders.
> Let me give you just a few examples that evince their blatant disregard for the rights of minority shareholders.
> 1. During the spring and summer of 2000, the management of Media Most, by additional issuance of shares, moved the key shares that belonged to ZAO Media Most to offshore companies in Gibraltar, thereby devaluing our investments in the shares of ZAO Media Most (14 percent) in the amount of $260 million. No proof, other than a two-page conclusion written by lawyers who work for Mr. Gusinsky, that these offshore accounts are still controlled by ZAO Media Most, has been presented to us. And even if the lawyers are correct, nevertheless, as you must

know, offshore companies, trusts, and other such schemes hinder the management of assets, thereby lowering their capitalization.

2. Gazprom owned until November of last year a total of 30 percent of the shares of Television Company NTV. At the present time we own 46 percent of the shares. One of the key assets of Television Company NTV is its trademark. However, without any explanations or consultations with us, the trademark NTV was given to the company NTV Holding, of which Gazprom does not own a single share. At the present moment Television Company NTV rents the NTV trademark from NTV Holding. How would this be interpreted in terms of American legislation? Our lawyers maintain that this is a criminal act.

3. The sale of advertising time on Television Company NTV is done in part through the Gibraltar company NTV Ltd, controlled by Mr. Gusinsky, in which we have no participation and no access to their accountability.

We cannot evaluate exactly what is left on Gibraltar when airtime is resold to its own advertisers, but our experts maintain that it is no less than 20 percent of the money (approximately $15-$20 million), which in fact is the property of Television Company NTV and does not reach it. At the same time, Television Company NTV is forced to borrow money in order to cover its losses, from Gazprom among others.

4. In view of the fact that the syndicated balance of the Media Most group of companies, into which Gazprom had invested close to $1 billion, is showing losses, and Most Bank, which had previously belonged to Mr. Gusinsky, has been declared bankrupt, we have serious suspicions that the money that supports the lifestyle of Mr. Gusinsky and his closest associates, who live like real magnates, traveling all over the world in private jets, who own real estate in Spain, Britain, and other countries, who vacation on their private yachts, and so on, is money that belongs to Gazprom and other creditors—who, naturally, did not approve such expenditures.

I can give you many more examples of this kind of "management," but the above is enough to recognize the present situation as intolerable. We cannot continue watching our investments, which at the present time are slightly under $1 billion, go down Mr. Gusinsky's "black hole."

I need to add that Mr. Gusinsky twice disrupted the execution of signed agreements, which were intended to regularize our relations.

We categorically welcome Mr. Turner's well-publicized initiative. Evidence of that is the fact that on Thursday, February 15, together with our consultant, Deutsche Bank, we will begin negotiations with representatives of Mr. Turner. Let us note that Mr. Turner is not the only one showing an interest in a similar deal, but that other noted players on the media and financial market have approached us as well.

With deepest respect and hope of being understood

Alfred Kokh
General Director
Gazprom Media

After that, I went to America. I had meetings in New York and Washington, D.C. At first I met with a hostile reception, but then the mistrust gradually vanished, and people began to listen and hear what I had to say. I was helped by many people; for example, Dmitri Simes, director of the Nixon Center; and Elena Teplitskaia—that is, those who did not take seriously the idea of freedom of the press à la Gusinsky and who felt that freedom of the press could not be a justification for not paying debts.

It really was a very strange construction: I (Gusinsky) borrowed money from you (Gazprom) and now it is time to pay you back and I don't have the money. Therefore you must forgive my debt, because I (and only I) represent freedom of the press. And the fact that I accuse your main shareholder (the state) of all the deadly sins should inspire you even more to perform this irrational act of generosity.

Let us not forget that we are talking about many hundreds of millions of dollars. Let us not forget that not one of Gusinsky's "commercial" projects was a business success—not Most Bank, not Media Most, not even such large-capital projects like NTV+.

The story with NTV+ was very bizarre. The point is that we make perfectly adequate satellites in Russia for this kind of satellite TV. However, Gusinsky ordered a satellite from Hughes in the USA. The satellite was much more expensive than a domestic one, but that did not stop the "father of freedom of the press." At least Hughes could have arranged credit financing of the order, as is usually done, but no, the money for it had to come from Gazprom, from Russia. As I remember it, $150 million. I wouldn't rule out the possibility that there were some political obligations of the Americans toward Gusinsky in this deal. I can only add that later Gusinsky ordered yet another satellite in Russia, but did not finish building it—the money ran out. And in fact, he didn't need either one. NTV+ is working now, leasing transponders on a European satellite. That's the kind of "businessman" he is—he simply pissed away around $200 million.

Yet this miserable businessman had a very successful life. A villa outside Moscow (on the Rublyovka Highway, in Chigasovo; a villa in Spain, in Soto Grande; a 60-meter yacht; a plane; a house in London; a house near New York. Where did all that come from? An oil company? No. A metallurgical plant? No. Maybe, a chemical plant? No, again. All right, all right. One more try: a huge machine-building plant that manufactures export weapons? Yet again—no! Then what is the yes? A bankrupt little bank and a media holding that was collateral for a billon dollars. That's it? That's it. That's really it.

And after that, I'm supposed to believe that Gazprom has to forgive Gusinsky's debt for the sake of freedom of speech? Never! And I'm supposed to believe in the sincerity of this freedom-fighter's adherence to the ideals of democracy, when he cynically manipulated public opinion, building outrage over my $100,000 book fee? And I'm supposed to do everything I can to let him hold onto his tool of manipulation? No, and once more no.

3. After Turner. The Finale

After some activity, Turner's people gradually thinned out and stopped bugging us with their proposals about how we should sell them NTV shares for less than we had bought them. I think they realized the absurdity of their proposals. I'm certain that if they were in our place, they would have laughed at us if we had come to them with such ideas for "saving freedom of the press."

By then, we had come to an agreement with Boris Jordan to come in as our consultant. He entered into negotiations with Capital Research Fund, which owned 5 percent of NTV shares, and came to an understanding of their loyalty to our efforts. After which we started preparations for a shareholders' meeting.

At that point, the court had recognized our rights to the collateral. We set a date for the shareholders' meeting. At the very last moment Blinov, who was working for Gusinsky by then, made his famous attempt to stop the meeting through a judge in Saratov. We managed to block the attempt, and we elected a new board of directors. Boris and I were on it.

An interesting thing happened once, at the offices of Media Most. We had set negotiations with the staff of NTV in their offices on Palashevsky Pereulok. We met: our board of directors and their delegates from the workers. On the night before, we had agreed that this group would be called a coordinating commission. I didn't understand exactly what needed to be coordinated, but since the UJK was throwing around its uncompromising nature, I was happy for any excuse to meet with them in person.

The meeting ended in nothing, of course. They proposed a number of unfeasible conditions. For example, one condition was that we would not interfere not only in the creative work of the television station, but also in its financial activity, until mid-summer. My response—that their firmness on noninterference into financial and property questions on the contrary made me think that these issues should be taken under control as quickly as possible, before they steal everything by summer—caused such a hysterical reaction that my worst suspicions were confirmed.

At the end of the meeting, in front of the building, crews from all the television stations were waiting. We had an improvised press conference. Kazakov, Jordan, and I spoke. Then Yevgeny Kiselyov spoke. We told them what had in fact happened—that is, nothing good. We reiterated our positions.

They repeated theirs, we repeated ours. This wouldn't be worth describing except for one spicy little detail.

Gusinsky (that is, Media Most) was represented in his wrangle with us by the famous American law firm Akin, Gump, Strauss, and Company. It's not only a law firm, it also does lobbying. It has very strong ties in Washington on the level of the Congress and administration. It's well known in Russia, too. Interestingly, one of the partners in the firm, Mr. Robert Strauss, is a former ambassador to Russia.

Why am I telling you this? Because when our press conference ended and everyone got in their cars and drove off, and the journalists were putting away their cameras, rolling up cables, gathering mikes, and so on, the door opened and out sidled... Who do you think? The American ambassador, Mr. Collins! What was he doing there, since Gusinsky had been out of the country for more than six months and the office was empty? There can be only one answer—he was eavesdropping on our arguments with Kiselyov's team. How do you like that?

But what does Akin, Gump have to do with this, you may ask. Soon after Mr. Collins left, a new ambassador arrived, Mr. Vershbow, and Collins went to work for Akin, Gump, Strauss, and Company. There it is. And no problems with corruption. And yet these people forbid me to pick my nose!

By the way, Mr. Strauss made titanic efforts, on orders from the Goose, to get the U.S. Congress to pass a resolution on expelling Russia from the G8. Our embassy in America, naturally, as usual, knew nothing about it. So on Strauss's birthday, the Russian ambassador invited him, as a great friend of Russia, to celebrate at the embassy. Which he did not deign to reject. Our foreign ministry does a great job... How impressive!

There is no need to describe the further complications. They are well known. Rallies and resistance. An empty chair on screen and no programming. A huge number of incongruities, stupidities, blatant excesses, and malicious confounding. And there was so much good-hearted concern, teary-eyed unity of the amateur song club, evenings, candles... I tried to explain to the journalists, but it was impossible. Promoting capitalism and being prepared for its "grimaces" was not the same. It's like Igor, who likes freedom and stocked shelves in stores, but doesn't like inequality and social injustice. But you can't have one without the other.

I wrote a letter to the NTV staff to get real and posted it on the Internet.

When our patience burst, we stopped the sideshow. We just walked into the company at night, having bribed Gusinsky's "best in Moscow" guards, and started running it. How long were we supposed to be nursemaids to those oafs?

Later, this would be called "storming" the building. Good Lord! They've never seen a storming. It's the way the Winter Palace was taken—ten people came in and arrested the Provisional Government, and only later Eisenstein depicted it as a huge battle with a sea of blood and victims.

Boris Jordan turned out to be a good television manager. I think that the highest praise of his work is the envy and later hatred that he elicited in Dobrodeyev, Ernst, and Lesin. Of course, their hatred led to his downfall. Or, maybe his salvation? I don't know how he would survive in today's Ostankino.

Then there was a change in management at Gazprom. Miller came in, Sheremet was fired, and there was no one to work with. The first to leave Gazprom, slamming the door behind him, was Kazakov. Then I left. I've known Miller since college. He was a year behind me. I had no illusions about him. As he probably had none about me. I knew that he would not make any decisions, and he knew that I would demand them of him. We parted amicably—I simply told him that I was leaving because I did not like working for him. I think he was relieved.

I don't think they treated me unfairly, getting rid of me so obviously. I always believed, and still do, that in a conflict between manager and shareholder the shareholder is always right. Only life will tell if that is true. And it is so very long, life. It goes way beyond the year 2001... God only knows how far. It goes on even after everything else... Of course, that's something Miller will never understand.

* * *

Svinarenko's Commentary:

As for the Goosiclasticism... Here's the thing, it's amazing! Your logic, in the financial part, is flawless. But besides that, there is also the deeper meaning, there is the subconscious. There is a collective subconscious that determines the fate of nations and countries. I still think it was a grave mistake to take on that battle with Goose. Here's what I mean: The mass murderer Chikatilo deserved the death penalty, following all logic. But that doesn't make it necessary to volunteer to execute him. That's a move without return into another life, another destiny, onto other paths and levels. After that people will say: "Oh, he's the guy who shoots bound people in the back of the head?" But he shot a maniac, a murderer. Yes, yes, we remember something about it, yes, that's what it was; but those are details, it doesn't matter. And you mean he got money for it, too? And naturally, now he claims that the money wasn't important? Ha. What else is there for him to say?... Maybe he'll do anything for money? By the way, how much was he paid for that? How much? Not bad at all... Let's see him try to tell us about serving the public interest.

Let me tell you my personal feelings. You can't overlook the fact that back then, in 2001, I was on the side of Kiselyov and the UJC. I admit I cringed at the high-flown emotional line, and I consider totally unacceptable the song and dance that Yevgeny Kiselyov did at rallies about how we still have things to do at home, and something there rises "aroused to nakedness." But these were questions of taste. I looked at the content dispassionately, and I felt that this was the destruction of free TV. For all the accuracy of the bookkeeping, that is what was done. There were some articles later claiming that Kokh had been used, that he was a dupe of the Chekists. The excuse was highly visible; the logic, as we have shown, was flawless; the financial accounting as accurate as clockwork—but it was the first step away from free TV. No matter how you spin it.

From today's vantage, and after many hours of conversation with you, Alik, I see the situation differently. In a different light. But not everyone had the opportunity to study the question that closely. And not everyone is interested in formal logic, especially in a country as irrational as ours.

Amusingly, as I write, there is a big settling of issues going on between two oligarchs: Fridman won $10 million from Berezovsky. You can look at that as the two of them defining the borders of freedom of the press using *Kommersant*. But there may be a third party smiling as he watches the battle. Good for them, he thinks. I didn't know how to approach this business, but they figured it out, and they're killing each other. They got my hints. Captured the spirit of the times. Thank you. Nicely done… As Andrei Vasilyev said in an interview on this topic, Alfa Bank chose a very appropriate moment for settling things with *Kommersant*… It's very Russian: When faced with the attack by Mamai and his Tatar hordes, start killing one another. There are lots of examples everywhere. The most vivid and most sad are the parliamentary elections in December 2003. That Russian path is so tempting that even Jewish businessmen follow it.

* * *

Kokh's Commentary:

If your image is correct and Gusinsky and I are Russian princes who fight each other in the face of the Tatar invasion, then I have to agree with you, Igor.

But what if Gusinsky is Mamai trying to pass for a Russian?

And in that case, to fight such Mamais, is it shameful to unite with the Kremlin?

By the way, judging by Gusinsky's staff (just take Filipp Bobkov, who was in charge of suppressing dissidents), he's been working long and closely with the KGB and for the KGB. Then I am even more in the right: The Tatar Mongols are fighting among themselves, and I am happy. The more they kill one another, the better. And helping that process along is sacred work.

* * *

Seriously, Igor, we know there was another "interesting" situation that year—9/11. If you remember, at a quarter to nine in the morning, the first plane hit the tower. It was quarter to five p.m. our time.

Yes, during work hours. I remember, we were in the office—

So was I. I turned on the TV to watch the news on RTR—

And they interrupted all programming and showed it live.

No, it began with the news—"In New York a plane hit a building." They showed one tower burning, and it was still standing, it didn't collapse right away. It didn't seem very serious. I was watching and watching and then, before my very eyes, they hit the second one! I thought, fuck! I have a pal in New York, Len Blavatnik. I called him. He was still in the Hamptons; it was early September, still hot in New York. I said, what's going on there? And he said, what's gong on? Fuck, turn on the TV. He did, and he said, Fuck! I said, I'll call you back. But then, it was impossible to get a line for a long time. They had turned off everything. No communications with New York, what's happening there? Boris Jordan's brother, Misha, works near the towers on Wall Street, Zhanna Nemtsova was studying at Fordham University near Lincoln Center. Lots of friends! Roman Kaplan, Victor Vekselberg's wife and children, Semyon Kukes's family. And I can't reach any of them. Everyone was crazed. A situation like that. But eventually everyone called in. Zhanna Nemtsov, Boris's daughter, dropped out of the university, came back and started at MGIMO.

Because of that?

She wasn't happy alone there, it was lonely in a strange city, and it became very dirty after the towers collapsed....

Was she just lonely or did that have an effect on her?

It had an effect, of course.

I was thinking, by the way... Imagine a war, a cataclysm, and horrible catastrophe. And imagine someone facing that situation in emigration, where he is alone. And doesn't understand a fucking thing. He would feel significantly worse than the locals.

Of course.

So, on the whole, it's better to live in your homeland.

Oh, of course, it's better at home. Unfortunately, our homeland doesn't love us too much.

Come to think of it, I've been an émigré for twenty years now. Ever since I left Ukraine.

Bring us some vodka, Waiter.

The Ministry of Health has issued warnings, Alik. Just kidding! We're dictating the last chapter of the book honestly, following the classic recipe—vodka, mushrooms... Like regular people. The familiar Russian theme. Because we must admit that we've deviated from the general line sometimes. Some of the chapters were dictated in such a state of sobriety that I'm embarrassed before our readers.

Salut! [*Raises shot glass.*]

Let's drink to the success of the last volume, Alik! [*Drink.*] **In fact, we're both émigrés—**

Conditionally. It's not my fault I was born in Kazakhstan. Apparently, the Nazi plan had been that I would say "Heil!" to the government, but Comrade Stalin decided differently, and so I turned out to have been born abroad. All the Germans were exiled.

I've drunk many a glass with your brethren, the ethnic Germans. When I studied there. And then I also traveled with Russian Germans to Germany, under the auspices of the Union of Journalists in 1989. Everyone was a German except me. They had come from all over, the Altai, the Volga region. A language professor there explained in one of our classes that their language was preserved from the 18th century. Our Germans simply didn't know any more recent words.
There was an analogous situation with Nabokov, remember?

No.

His father, setting aside his state affairs in the Duma—

Where he lead the Kadet (Constitutional Democrat) party.

Uh-huh. He decided to check on his son's schoolwork. Write down what I dictate, he said. His son couldn't write, he only knew words like

"cocoa" in Russian. The father was furious. How could his son be illiterate! They explained to him that the boy read and wrote beautifully— in English. Knew shit in Russian, he could only speak it. Nabokov Senior immediately changed the manner of his son's education.

Tell me, please. Nabokov the father was very wealthy?

Yes.

And the reason for the wealth was what? Was he a landowner or what? I thought he was, not from the nobility. Or were they?

The writer's mother was born Rukavishnikova.

Ah, they were merchants.

Sasha Rukavishnikov—our friend, the sculptor who created (among other things) a monument to Alexander II in Moscow on your commission—had doubts that his direct relatives had married into the Nabokov family, but then Filipp, Sasha's son, found the proof.

It's clear where her money came from. What about him?

I don't know. Once he got married...

Who was he professionally? A lawyer? I don't remember.

I'll look it up.

But if we get back to being serious, Igor, I can tell you that when the apartment houses were blown up in Moscow in 1999, and later, of course, Beslan, it affected me more than the World Trade Center being blown up. Even though the losses in New York were ten times greater and the city is not totally foreign to me, nevertheless... You know, there was something of a Hollywood production about the New York tragedy. While the explosions of those buildings in Moscow were somehow unadorned, pathetic, dreary... I have lots of friends who work right in the middle of downtown Manhattan. Nevertheless, here is what I am going to tell you: There is more money there per square meter than anywhere else in the world. Those people are constantly doing billion dollar deals, they are literally deciding the fate of entire countries and continents. The people who work there, even the clerical staff, have a certain image as possessors of unlimited resources. There is the home of globalism, or American imperialism, and all that crap. The challenge of the Arab terrorists, of which I most certainly do not approve, was addressed to such people.

Unlike the residents of cheap housing in Pechatniki.

Exactly! With New York there was at least an appearance of logic. Allegedly the Americans had taken over half the world and were trying to impose their way of life on people who didn't want it. And that was why the terrorists were blowing up Wall Street, the Pentagon, and so on.

Our Trade Center on the Krasnopresnenskaya Embankment is still standing.

It is. But they blew up a building in the outskirts. You know, ask those people on Guryanov Street or Kashirka, in Volgodonsk or Buinaksk, whether they need the war in Chechnya! They'll tell you they don't. Why kill them? That's what astounds me. And pisses me off! All right, you valorous male and female *djigits*, blow up the Ministry of Defense! Wouldn't that be a statement? But no, they killed those poor impoverished people and walk around like heroes who'd gotten their revenge! How was killing them revenge, you nits!

Alik, what do you think of the version that the planes crashed into the towers in the morning when the only people in the offices were black and Puerto Rican cleaning women, that there had been plans to raze the buildings, but it was too expensive and so on. And they also needed an excuse to grab up new oil regions… What do you think of that?

What of it? After every terrorist act, when the authorities announce the official version, a symmetrical version appears blaming the authorities themselves for the act. It's inevitable. The version that will win, be accepted, is not the one that's closer to the truth but the one more people believe. If, for example, the people trust the government, more of them will believe that the Chechens blew up the buildings. But if the people don't trust the government, no matter what the government tells them, they'll keep thinking that the Chekists did it. Let me give you an example of how that mechanism works. We all know that Putin did not start the second Chechen war and that the Chechens did. But since trust in the mass media is decreasing now—it's understandable, all the media are controlled by the state, the effectiveness of brainwashing decreases. The whole point of taking total control of the mass media vanishes. They thought that they were taking over a machine for brainwashing, but once they took it over, it stopped being a machine for brainwashing. So, ask anyone at all, who started the Chechen war? The answer will be Putin. Yes! That is the answer in the mass consciousness. Because trust in the media is down to zero.

It's a very interesting thing, of course, propaganda, journalism…

Now we're in the same situation that existed in the stagnation years: If, say, the government is planning something good for the people, they assume that the state just wants to fuck them over. The same will happen now: In another year or two, the reaction to the Kremlin will be exactly the same. They won't believe a single word the authorities say.

You think they do now?

It's a gradual transition. They believe less than they did in 2001 or 2000.

To tell the truth, I've stopped following politics closely. OK, the Kremlin, OK, the authorities—what's not clear about that today? We get it, and we can relax.

The level of trust in the regime is falling sharply. Putin is holding steady, but the general mood is changing…

It seems to me—this is my sense—that people no longer have the sense of fair play, they think like this: The bosses give the order, our job is to obey… Or pretend. Nobody believes anymore that there are elections. People are appointed, and that's that. [*This conversation was a week before the announced reform of the electoral system and the decision to appoint governors.*] I've been saying for a long time: There are no elections, we have appointments, and funnily enough, it's the right decision. It's better this way. It seems to me that that is the mood of the people right now. I remember, right after 9/11, interviewing Misha Tarkovsky, the writer.

You've talked a lot about him.

Yes. So I said to him: Listen, you hunters along the Enisei River probably had little sympathy for New Yorkers! You must regard them pretty much like the Taliban do. He said: "Absolutely! I was getting ready to go out hunting, I remember, and I dropped in on a neighbor to borrow some shot, and there was a movie on the TV about planes hitting skyscrapers. Then it turned out to be a news report, but it didn't make any greater impression for that." Think of the great gap dividing a hunter who sees another human being once a week and a resident of a megapolis! If Tarkovsky found even Londoners to be like mutants, what would he think of New York! The great majority of Russians does not consider New York to be a familiar place and cannot sympathize with it. Well, you and I understand what a beloved city it is—there are many things about it that

are dear to us. But we are the exceptions among several billion people on this earth.

I just don't agree with you, Igor, and that's it! I want to tell you that if we talk about Arabs and Islamic civilization in its current state, it seems to me that the moral superiority of European civilization is obvious. Without a doubt. I can explain: During the May holidays I went to Spain again, to travel around Andalusia. European civilization did not suffer the intellectual crash that affected Islamic civilization. There was a time when they were smarter than Europeans, more educated! Algebra, architecture, navigation, astronomy, medicine... They had brilliant poets and writers. Where did it all go? It's all lost. European civilization did not go through that. After Rome collapsed and the antique culture, there was still Byzantium. There were still monasteries. Then came the Renaissance gradually, and I repeat, the cultural source never died out in Byzantium. But where did the Arab culture go? It's very clear to me that the people who are running around with their revolutionary extremism today are in fact protecting the absence of a basic material culture. They have forbidden themselves painting, sculpture, poetry; they have banned eroticism, love; they have reduced women to the level of animals. They do not want a normal education, with the exception of the richest princes, who are getting fat on oil. What follows from that? That they are closer to God? Total nonsense.

I'm not telling you that they are closer to God, Alik. They are profoundly alien to me. But I am trying to reconstruct their point of view, their thoughts.

I can tell you about their views and their thoughts. It's the same story I like to repeat: the WC is a convenience for the civilized man but a constraint on a savage's liberty.

Well, how can you shit in your hut?

Yes, a savage is used to shitting wherever he wants, and he's being herded into the toilet... His freedom is constrained. Just as European culture is a reflection of intellectual superiority.

I keep telling you: I am not a defender of Islamic values. I don't even know what they are.

Islamic values are a logical continuation of first Judaic and then Christian values, and nothing more. They are absolutely normal, and we can understand them. Islam, when it was at the crest, when the Caliphate—

There was freedom there, then?—

There was everything there—intellectual freedom, respect for women, and so on, everything was wonderful. But they turned it into an idiotic weapon of some stupid revenge.

I'm not a defender of Muslim terrorism or Islamism in general. I am trying to find out what is going on. And I see that even though they have stifled all their freedoms, they have forced the entire world to talk about them. And fear them.

That path—curtailing freedoms—leads to great disasters. They haven't yet surpassed Hitler or Chairman Mao, who during the Cultural Revolution killed 60 million people. They haven't surpassed Stalin, either. Maybe a dozen thousand dead, including war causalities. That doesn't look like a clash of civilizations.

They're dying en masse for their ideas, and we're not going off to die.

Why should we die? It's not required of us. We are so ahead of them in material culture, that they are in no condition to withstand a confrontation with us.

That reminds me—

What's this? Chilled soup? Nice… I'll give you an example… Where's the sour cream?

But that's full of cholesterol, Alik It's pure cholesterol. That is, it's very tasty… Well, give me your example.

So, look. There are Arabs, Chechens, all those Islamic fundamentalists, against us. If Russia went and captured all the Chechens in Moscow and Chechnya, in all the towns that are controlled by federal troops, and put them all in one place—some concentration camp—and said: "All right, I'm counting to three, you bastards. Basayev, come out, Maskhadov, come out, put down your guns, otherwise we will start shooting you one by one." We're going to shoot all of them anyway, and then we'll drop an atom bomb on Chechnya, so that grass won't grow there for a hundred years. And we'll level all those fucking mountains… I think that the war in Chechnya would end very quickly. What do you think? Aren't I right? What's keeping us from doing that? Very simple: We have our own moral limits. Now let's turn the question around: What if Basayev had an atom bomb? He would use it without a second thought! Just like the Arab terrorists. Here's a simple and comprehensible proof of our moral superiority.

Alik, I understand without that example that we are morally superior to those guys. But in this case, we are not debating, nor trying to get each other to support someone. We have no doubts. But nevertheless, they have a strong sense of their own righteousness—

No, they don't. It's just stupid stubbornness. What are they trying to prove? That they are capable of functioning like an independent state? Total lies. What, are the Arabs trying to prove that they can run an independent state in Palestine? Total bullshit. They can't even manufacture the guns they use. They haven't created anything new in 500 years. They drive our cars, wear our clothes, smoke our cigarettes, eat our food.

So what are they supposed to do because of that? Shoot themselves?

No, but they should stop fucking around! That's all. God had mercy on them and gave them oil. He didn't have to.

Well, he gave it to us as a punishment. Maybe it's a punishment for the Arabs, too? They stopped studying and working.

Probably. In Saudi Arabia all the workers are Indians, blacks, and so on, while the Arabs sit around doing nothing.

Have you noticed that the Americans are growing more tolerant of what we're doing in Chechnya? Before they used to say: Close the discussion, give them freedom, and that's that. They're rebels, *barbudos*, all that… And only after 9/11 did they start to understand what was going on here. Recently some al-Qaeda plans were discovered that said they had always been planning to bring in Chechens for the terrorist acts in the U.S. That straightened out the American brains a bit. I also wrote that for them the bombing in New York was like the collapse of the Soviet Union for us. They thought they were unique, cooler than the rest of the world, the biggest of all. But it turned out that they were like the rest, as vulnerable as Moldavia or something. I think we're going through similar processes, the Americans and Russians. They also lost that sense of virginity, that we're different from all the rest. They realized that they're like everyone else—now.

I don't know. I don't think, by the way, Igor, that our problems with Chechnya and America's problems with al-Qaeda are of the same nature. It's clear that in Chechnya we are dealing with ordinary separatism, while there are other causes of the conflict between the Arabs and the United States. The

Chechen mentality, as it seems to me, is much less religious than our propaganda maintains. I've written about it in previous chapters… And they're separatists. They want to be separate, but still have a single economic space with all of Russia, to be able to travel back and forth freely…

Right, so that they can come here but our police can't enter there.

Yes. That is what they want. And it's so crudely obvious that we cannot agree to that under any circumstances. All that talk about a united Russia and the inviolability of borders, that's total bullshit, that's fetishism of territorial integrity, that's so incredibly stupid! Especially when you remember that one of the wisest tsars, Alexander II, gave up Alaska without a second thought. Because he realized that he was in no condition to service that property. Of course, no one knew about oil in those days…

Do you know that our country gave bribes to Americans, out of treasury funds, just to get them to take Alaska off our hands?

Yes, yes. If such advanced people as Alexander II never suffered over the problem of territorial integrity, then we certainly shouldn't. There's a different problem. It seems to me that the whole question can be resolved differently. We say to the Chechens, Guys, we are the ones to decide whether we will maintain diplomatic relations with you or not, give you entry visas or not, and we will determine the character of the border and the regime of entry-departure, and the economic relations—

All right, Alik, if you've worked out all the issues with Chechnya, tell me what to do with the Kuril Islands.

Give them to the Japanese.

Listen, I just had a brilliant idea: We give the Kurils to the Japanese, but first we exile all the Chechens there. What do you think?

The Chechens won't go.

Come on. That way we kill three rabbits: We settle our differences with Japan, we get rid of the Kurils, and solve the Chechen issue. We give the cleared-out Chechnya as a concession to… Oh! Sheer genius! It won't work with Japan, that would look too much like a joke. But now I am about to reveal a realistic plan. So: We give Chechnya to China as a concession. For 99 years, as usual.

Why China? What does it need it for? There's no oil, we pumped all of it out already.

The Chinese will jump at it. Hold on to it by the skin of their teeth. The Chinese are entering Russia so heavily, on such a broad front, that they will be thrilled to have a mustering place in Russia for further incursions. Haven't you noticed how quickly Moscow is being China-fied?

By the way, I wrote about this in the very first chapter.

You wrote that this was a positive phenomenon. But when I ride in the metro and see that we've caught up with New York in the number of Chinese—

Maybe they're Bashkirs from Yakutia—how do you know?

Alik, you think I can't tell our people from foreigners? They have an amazingly alien look. And they're everywhere. So when you said that the Chinese are hard workers and we should have more of them and they will raise our economy, I nodded—remember?

Yes.

But since then, my dear friend, two years have passed.

So.

And today after that historically tiny period of time—two years—I see the situation in a slightly different light. I see in the Chinese restaurants in Moscow—the ones they built for themselves—I see a disdainful attitude toward white people. I feel like I'm an ethnic minority. Already! When there isn't even a million of them in Moscow yet.

And why should they be respectful toward Russians, who are losing the labor competition to them?

A fine attitude! They all came to us—

Why us? The earth belongs to everyone.

I don't like that Chinese waitresses take a cut of the Russian waitresses' income in Chinese restaurants in Moscow, and when Russians try to get money from the Chinese in the same way, they tell them to blow.

But you and I support competition, or what?

Which competition? In what?

Everywhere. In everything. There should be competition everywhere, that is the essence of progress.

Well, I don't institute competition at home.

In what sense?

Well, in your own house you're tsar, god, and military commander.

So.

And what if there's a man who is smarter than you, handsomer—

Then my wife will leave me and go off with him—that's all.

Yes, but if he knocks on the door and you open and he says: I want to have a competition with you, since I am the smartest and most handsome. You will probably say: Go take a hike, bud. And chew out your security guards for letting him through.

Actually, that's not what I would do at all. It would be stupid to do that. For the simple reason that my wife could meet with him outside the house.

Well, it might be stupid. But as for me, I didn't sign up to do only smart things.

Ha-ha! But you can't compare economic relations with interrelationships in the family.

Why not? The family is your nation... You don't have any other. That's it.

When you're talking about my house, that's private property. Sacred. But when you're talking about the state, that's a rather notional concept of what's mine and what isn't mine. You yourself had said that Russia is un-pop-u-lated.

Yes.

It takes up a seventh of the world's land, but it can't make it habitable, lay down roads, build cities, populate it. If not for the Bolsheviks, there would be 400,000,000 Russians.

I can see that some of the territory should be given to people who will work it. Let them live on that piece. Under our wise leadership and control. But not so that they give us nasty looks and not let us into the

bars, the way the Japanese, for example, are being so obnoxious. Why bring in foreigners to boss us around! Now you understand, I hope, the benefit to the Chinese in leasing Chechnya. Now let me explain the benefit to us. It is that the Chinese will settle problems with the Chechens without even asking them their names. You see, if they could run over their own people on Tiananmen Square with tanks and not let a muscle quiver in their faces... They squashed students! You would think students are the best of a nation. Young, pure... So the Chinese squashed them, and the country accepted it without choking on it. Ours would have shat in their pants...

Drop it, Igor! We've done a bit of shooting, too...

I've never heard of any shooting. There is also this consideration in favor of my idea. The Chinese have their own Islamic separatists, the Uighurs. And they're sick of them. So if we say to them: Hey, Chinese! You can have Chechnya for 99 years, that's it, come work! Master the territory! They would catch Basayev and strip off his skin, and they would plow everything. They wouldn't let the Chechen Robin Hoods spoil their business. Chechnya would turn, absolutely for free, into a flowering garden. And a peaceful one.

Moving on, Alik. Look. In 2001 I had another event. I joined the Writers' Union. I did it for the following reasons. I thought: We're back in a stagnation times, there are Chekists everywhere, the Soviet regime is returning. So I have to get into that mode. They're going to start putting people away for being parasites and other stuff. So I'll join the Writers' Union and say: Fuck off, I'm a member of a creative union. The police won't be able to persecute me for being a parasite and force me to go work in a Soviet factory. I was a member of the Journalists' Union, but it's not very creative, journalists are considered regular people, not semi-divine, like writers. As if. I remember my thought process very clearly! Then a year passed, another, everything seemed safe. I thought: I seem to have overreacted. All right, so what, I joined. But now, it's obvious that I had reacted properly. I was right to panic. Isn't that funny?

Also in 2001 I continued stubbornly traveling to various prison camps and finishing up my prison book, which came out in 2002, I think. I traveled through the famous Mordovan camps. They're in these beautiful fir forests. Wonderful sand—almost dunes. I'm telling you, the perfect places for dachas and resorts.

It's on the Volga.

I was in one camp that's only for inmates with TB. They're all in such horrible shape, dying. The chief doctor, her mother had died of tuberculosis, and that's why she started working with them. A very touching story.

It's called a phthisiatric doctor. This happened to me once, I was diagnosed with tuberculosis. Thank God it was a mistake.

Pneumonia, right?

Yes. To tell the truth, I was terrified. I thought, this is the end, I'm a goner. I even stopped smoking!

That's good for you. Some people even lose weight.

Are you kidding? I gained seven kilos.

No smokes, no drinks, go to the grave in good shape. There's also a prison zone with only foreigners. I asked, Who's in there? They told me, We have citizens of the United States. Hot damn! Let me see them, I said. Turns out they're Armenians from outside Los Angeles. And there are lots of blacks from some country like Tanzania or something. Around fifty of them.

Ah, narcotics mules.

They said: We're all here for nothing, we were framed.

All of them, at once. Right.

"We did nothing, never, they slipped it into our luggage." Those trips to the camps—they're addictive. I never go for long, I get uncomfortable, I sense something wrong with the world. What can I compare it to? It's like not going to Paris or New York for a long time. There's a different life there, a different temperature, a different speed, a different pole. When you get back to Moscow from the zone, the city seems so powerful, so sparkling and vibrant. Too wonderful to be described. You appreciate the simple joys—I'm going to sit down to have some tea, and I'll drink as much as I want! I might even have some vodka! Or I'll go for a walk whenever I feel like it. The things people in the zone don't have, you appreciate them mightily—like an aftertaste—for a while. Then you get used to these simple joys, and it becomes hard again to enjoy life.

In 2001, I also interviewed a man named Rafik Ashidovich. He was warden of Butyrka prison. He told me how he started working there. He got out of the army, and that's just when they had the Olympics. He had wanted to be an athlete in his day, but it didn't work out. So he decided to go to Moscow, to watch a competition, at least. He went, he met some prison guards, and they lured him into their world: Why not, you work every third day for twenty-four hours, and they have their own gym. He fell for it, and gradually became a supervisor, and even reached his position. I asked him, Tell me how Gusinsky was in your prison. He told me: He behaved impeccably in prison. Unlike whats-his-name? Who was in there from the prosecutor's office? Ah! Ilyushenko! That law man threw inkpots around, shouted that he would tear off their insignia, and wouldn't let them search him. While Goose, he was all delicacy and tact. Fingerprints? Please. Answer this, sign that. Yes, yes. And here. As you wish. He didn't shout, he didn't go on hunger strikes, everything was clean and correct—he was a marvelous inmate, they were so pleased with him. Sure, I said, he put television sets and refrigerators in every cell. Rafik denies that: He didn't put in any TVs. But it was in all the papers. He said, I'm surprised at you journalists, you tell lies in the papers and then you believe them. I later asked Astakhov, who represented Gusinsky, Why did your client promise and then not deliver? Astakhov said that Goose did give a million rubles to the prison, but he's not responsible for what they bought with the money. And then Rafik Ashidovich, the sweetest man, was fired, as you know.

Because people escaped under his watch. They tunneled out....

So, here we are, stuck on our agricultural sector, and I wonder why?

Alexander II annexed Central Asia all the way to Kushka, but he sold Alaska. You understand why, right?

Alaska was an empty refrigerator.

The tsar was planning to move peasants to Central Asia after the repeal of serfdom. He intended to settle those areas.

Go on!

Really. To have agriculture there. He understood that it was pointless trying to do agriculture in Russia. The sowing of virgin lands in Kazakhstan under Khrushchev was nothing more than a partial realization of Alexander II's plan.

No shit. I didn't know he had plans for Central Asia... Are you sure of that?

Yes.

Then were the Germans also sent to Kazakhstan by the will of Alexander II?

As one version of the story, yes. In the 1960s and 1970s, there were Russian German kolkhozes working the virgin lands. They beat all harvest records.

It makes sense that now you are erecting a monument in Moscow to that tsar. Here's another thing that happened to me that year: I was a matchmaker. You know Tsivina? She's the restaurant critic for *Kommersant*.

No, I don't.

Tsivina was the first restaurant critic in Russia. Yakovlev, in the old *Kommersant*, made her go to bars and write them up.

Nice work.

She said, I don't know how, I don't want to, I don't know anything about this. But he made her.

She must have eaten her fill of all sorts of goodies.

Probably. So I ran into her in Petrovich, there was some big drunken party going on—maybe its fifth anniversary. Sitting opposite us was a man called Andrei Svetlanov. He just stared at Tsivina, with his jaw dropped: Who's that beauty? What are you going on about, I said, you've been working together at *Kommersant* for the last ten years, although on different floors. You should know her very well. But he had never met her! He said, I'll give you whatever you want if we can trade seats. I refused, but he jumped into my chair when I went off to take a leak. He said, Old man, forgive me, I couldn't help myself. The next morning I called his cell phone. I said, what did you do with that innocent little dove, you cad? He said, I'll let her tell you, and handed her the phone. Short story, they got married soon after. They had a daughter in time for the seventh anniversary of the Petrovich restaurant.

Are you kidding?

And they're as happy as old-world gentry folk.

Ha ha!

Then I had yet another amazing thing happen in 2001, continuing the matrimonial theme. In 2000 we had the twentieth reunion of our journalism school class. We met at the House of Journalists, pushed the tables together. The following year, we all got together again, still rising on the old yeast. And suddenly we found out that two of our fellow students, who had been in the same television journalism group, graduating 20 years ago, went and got married.

After the previous reunion.

Yes. They divorced their spouses.

Cool.

See how things change in a person's mind over twenty years. You get a completely different point of view—like our book. You like another kind of woman…

I'm recalling my meetings with girls I had gone to school with. I think that the men look better than the women.

Naturally! There's an old Polish saying, "An old man is like old wine, an old woman, like old butter." What do you think? Harsh.

Yes. Because by forty a woman should have had her children and have a good solid background, a family.

And money.

Naturally. Then it's not like she had lived in vain.

So, basically, our whole story ends on September 11, 2001.

Yes, it ends in 2001. I already know what I will write in the afterword: Our era is over. There are new, completely different people with a completely different mentality. They are implementing different ideas. These ideas, unlike ours, have found support. We were alone, no one wanted to listen to us. Therefore, apparently, the country is living the life it wants to live. And not the one that we read about in books and tried to impose on it.

Are we supposed to teach our people, Alik?

No. We must admit that we are superfluous in this festival of life.

And what are we supposed to do, according to you?

Well, everyone decides for himself—either stay here and sit tight and don't fuck around, or fuck off out of here to countries where the majority shares our point of view.

The way the French Protestants moved to Germany and Holland.

Yes. The way people went to America. People from Europe.

Have you made your choice, or are you still thinking?

I want to have all the options. I want to be able to live here and to be able to live there. That's reasonable. Why should I make a choice if I don't have to? I can afford to do that. I'm not making money for nothing. Money is to give you as many options as possible. Isn't that logical?

Yes.

Because money is the equivalent of freedom. For me.

Not power?

That's a different category of people, for whom money is power.

Then there are journalists.

But I don't like the idea of interviewing journalists. It's a kind of self-pollination. When the NTV people bring in their own journalists as interesting guests on their talk shows... I like that our magazine gives all kinds of unprofessional writers professional columns—Valeria Novodvorskaya, Alexander Gafin, Matetsky, me—I find that charming. It works very well. I enjoy reading what they do. I like it all.

People surprise you when you interview them.

Look at Boris Nemtsov—he's basically an interesting guy. He gives trenchant and accurate assessments. However, he's a bad interview. Why?

By the way, Alik, that gives us our big finish! On November 17, 2001, I interviewed you. Other interviews followed and other dialogues, which led to this book, which is ending on this conversation about 2001. Full circle.

My Afterwords

Alfred Kokh

I don't know how to write an afterword. Nor do I know how to write books. What Igor and I have written is a book only at first glance. In fact, we did not make up the plot, our times did. The events, the heroes, the interactions are all true. Well, maybe we exaggerated in places, adding dynamism that was lacking in reality, to make it sound better. But that's not real writing, it's just journalism…. A real writer creates reality, we simply describe it.

I personally tried to avoid the greatest danger in memoir writing—the distortion of the scale of events and people. It's amusing, for example, to watch journalists, for instance, assess their own roles in history. I hope that I managed to avoid an exaggerated view of myself. I tried to maintain the proportions that seem true and real. Though there may be people who will not agree with my assessments.

However, since I do not know how to write an afterward, I've decided to write several. For various tastes. You pick the one you like best.

First Afterword. The People

My Russian grandmother told me lots of stories. She often astonished me by the level of her education, even though she had finished only the first grade of a church parish school. She knew many poems by Pushkin (almost all of his fairy tales), Nekrasov (about the people), Nikitin, Pleshcheev, Yazykov… In fact they taught them only to read and memorize poetry. And a little bit of math.

From her I remember "the little house over the river, a light in the windows" or "you'll have a squirrel and a whistle…," and "know, work, and don't be scared." A long forgotten primer of Russian writing. To use a literary cliché, it's a "treasure house of language."

My granny, Valentina Petrovna Karpova, saw a lot in her life. She was orphaned young. She went to work, first as a nanny at the age of seven or eight, then as a laundress and cleaning woman. Under the Soviet regime, she built the Turksib railroad, as a mason. She had five children. A son and four daughters. Her second daughter was my mother. Her firstborn, Alexander, died of typhoid as a baby, on some railroad section in the endless Kazakh steppe. She and my grandfather, Georgy Fedorovich, ran out at the first stop and laid their child's corpse into the pile of such corpses on the platform (there was a raging epidemic, starvation, at the height of collectivization, special units collected those bodies at all the stations and buried them in mass graves) and rushed back on the train; they didn't dare miss it, they could have been accused of sabotage, escaping from the labor front.

Then came the war, and my grandfather was drafted right away. He was a cabinetmaker and apparently they confused that with a carpenter and put him in the sapper unit. And the sappers, this is how they work: they go first when troops advance, setting up the fords and crossings, and they're the last when they retreat, blowing up the crossings. Thus, during an enormous retreat in the summer of 1942, my grandfather ended up a prisoner of war near Rostov. Fortunately, our side won back Rostov briefly and liberated my grandfather.

He was heavily wounded in the leg and face and spent a lot of time in hospitals, demobilized only in 1945 or 1946. He came home and never went to work again. He drank hard, like all the veterans then. He would occasionally make a stool, sell it at the market, and then go back to boozing. His chest was covered in medals, he had an attractive scar on his cheek, he was tall and dark. A macho veteran with a slight limp. Why work? So grandmother brought up all the daughters. She washed floors in the city Soviet building and did part time work at the meat canning factory and she also built fireplace ovens for people. She killed herself at ten different jobs. Of course, all the women lived that way then: there weren't many men left and so they took good care of them.

But I digress. Let me return to my grandmother's stories. There is one that is deeply ingrained in my memory. I was five or six at the time. Very little. I remember that I had just seen the movie about Malchish-Kibalchish, the village boy who fought against the White Army, and I cried, as required, over his heroic death, and then asked Grandmother, "Baba Valya, tell me about when you learned that there was no more tsar and Soviet power was established?" Naturally, I was picturing the beautiful picture of the Red troops entering the city. On horseback, wearing the pointy helmets called *budennovki* and leather coats, with big, beautiful sabers, and under red banners, the weary and dusty, but kind and just, Red Cavalry rode in, while on the other end of town, the Whites were scramming from the just wrath of the working people, their carts loaded with stolen loot.

Grandmother's story was unexpected. She said:

It was in 1920. Or maybe later. The Civil War lasted a long time in Siberia and Kazakhstan, until around 1922. We were living in Petropavlovsk then. [Now it's Petropavlovsk-Kazakhstanskii, in the north of Kazakhstan, near Omsk.] I was going on nine, and I was considered grown up. I worked for people. As a servant. They were bourgeois. They were shoemakers or in trade, I don't remember.

I do remember that it was announced all over the city for all the locals to come with their children to the city park. They announced that now the city was under Soviet rule of workers and peasants and everyone had to come to the city park. They would speak there. Tell us what the new order would be like.

They had entered the city unnoticed. The Whites had been gone for several weeks. But everything worked. Post office, railroad, and hospital. The market place was selling things. Stores were open. Courtyards were swept. Cattle grazed. … I remember that I and my friends who were older didn't care if it was the Reds or the Whites. The police, you say? I don't remember any police. They must have been there… or maybe they all scattered…. No, I don't remember any police. I guess we managed somehow without police. Stop pestering me, I don't know. Listen to what I'm telling you, instead of asking stupid questions. He wants the police. Who needs it?

So. We got ready first thing in the morning. My father, Petro Bochantsev, was still alive then, but Mother had already died. Or had Father died too? No, I think he was still alive. Anyway, we got ready, me and a few girlfriends, we put on clean kerchiefs and went to the park to listen to the commissars. They were called commissars back then. What did we understand anyway? Kids think everything is interesting. So we were interested. We walked to the park, and there were people crowding in from every side. Closer to the park you couldn't even get through. But we were bold and sprightly, moving between the legs of the adults, sometimes crouching, sometimes crawling. We didn't even know what for. Everyone was pushing, so we pushed. We were late despite that. We were told to be there at nine and we didn't get to the very center until ten.

In the park, people stood in a big semicircle, pushing against the bandstand where the fireman's band played on Sundays. The benches on the side had been piled up and in the place where the audience sat they had dug a big hole. Solders with rifles stood around the hole and did not let people come closer to the edge. In the hole you could see officers in uniform lying there. Maybe there were soldiers, too? How do I know? In uniform. The Reds said they were officers. Already dead. I don't remember any blood on the uniforms, but their hair was all in blood. They must have shot them in the back of the head.

> We were just a little late. About thirty minutes. The Reds executed the prisoners. They gathered the people so everyone would see and be afraid. We were both afraid and sorry that we had missed it. Everyone around us was talking about how it was. They had made the Whites dig the hole the night before. And in the morning, when there were a lot of people, they started shooting them. They must have had a lot of prisoners. Or not prisoners. Maybe, they just didn't leave the city, decided to stay? I don't know. Where could they go? The steppe? The taiga? What are you saying? Why didn't they change clothes? Why were they in uniform? Go ask them yourself. … They probably had nothing else to wear. One pair of trousers, and they belonged to the Whites. You say officers are rich? Then these were poor officers….
>
> They set up a table and tribune on the stage. A man came out and said in a loud voice that they had killed the bloodsuckers and exploiters of the working people. That now a new life was beginning and everything would be just. There would be no rich or poor, only the power of the people, the power of the Soviets. The people stood around for a bit and moved away. That's how I learned that the Tsar was no more and the power was now Soviet. Like today.

That's the story. Plain and simple. Without leather jackets and *budennovki.* No romance or national enthusiasms. As they say, "The people were silent." As it was forever after. As it is now. And it's dying off slowly, the people. Soon there will be no Russian people left. Just the old and people of Caucasus nationalities.

And the bastard ineradicable tribe—the commissars.

Second Afterword: Power

In speaking of this tribe, notionally called commissars, we must note that they live by their laws. They remind me of the priest caste, who persuaded the flock that sowing wheat, dealing in trade and crafts, bringing up children and giving oneself up to art or love were all important things, but not more important than their priestly service. Their priestly service of the god called "the state" is irrational and therefore is not comprehensible from the point of view of common sense.

Let me give you a simple example. After he fled to Poland, Prince Andrei Kurbsky wrote to Ivan the Terrible, "God reads angrily: I constantly thought in my mind, and took my conscience as witness, and sought, and in my thoughts looked at myself, and could not understand and did not find how I have sinned before you. I led your troops and fought with them and brought no dishonor upon you, but only radiant victories with the help of God's angel for your glory and never turned your regiments with their backs to the enemy, but on the contrary, gloriously won for your greater fame."

This is not just anyone writing, but the man who was one of Ivan the Terrible's closest friends from childhood. Prince Kurbsky led the Russian army in its victory over Kazan, which put an end to the confrontation between Russians and Tatars and the East.

And how does the Russian tsar respond to him? Perhaps he musters arguments proving that Kurbsky betrayed him? Not at all! Or does he apologize for his mistaken suspicions and call him back to Russia to jointly serve the Homeland! No, again!

He writes something that makes no sense at all from the point of view of a normal person: "If you are, as you say, just and devout, then why are you afraid of dying innocently, since it will not be death but a noble gift? After all, you will die anyway…"

How do you like that? Power does not even bother to justify its actions. Really, why waste time? If the regime wishes to get rid of someone, then why even discuss it: if the man is guilty, serves him right, and if he's not, then an innocent death is a noble gift.

Note that they do not extend this logic to themselves. For themselves, they demand thorough and formal examination of their actions "in accordance with acting legislation." Let's not forget, it's legislation that they sucked out of their thumbs in the first place.

The god, which like any normal god has many names—nation, homeland, Holy Russia, and so on—demands a sacrifice of young boys every year. The priests dance their shaman dance and tell us what happiness it is to be fed to the insatiable idol, and rattling their gold Swiss watches and robing themselves in expensive Italian suits, they tell us that the gluttonous god wants everything to be subordinated to them, his priests. That will be better for us. We don't even realize how fortunate we are. How could we pathetic creatures understand divine providence. Only they have the understanding—the superhuman-priest-commissars. And they build their vertical of power. Like the Tower of Babel. And as it has happened a hundred times already, they will perish under its rubble. Burying all of us along with them. For, how would we live if they were to die? There would be no point. What use are the blind without guides?

I still can't find the answer to a seemingly simple question: What is a state for? They say a state is more convenient than anarchy. The lack of obviousness of this statement is so blatant that I choke on the abundance of my arguments. I have tons of questions. Here's one of the simplest: More convenient for everyone or just the commissars? People pay taxes, not only with money, but also their lives, in exchange for what? Pride in the power of the nation-god? Adoration of the stature of the supreme priest? Joy from the abundance of commissars? What do the people get from that?

Oh, otherwise, we might be taken over? So what? New commissars will replace the old. Maybe the new ones will be smarter. We paid tribute to the Khazars. Then the Varangians came, and we paid them. Then the Tatars. And we paid them. Then apparently (as they maintain, nobody actually checked) our own people came. And so what? Did life become better? No! It grew worse: they repealed Yuryev Day, raised taxes, started endless wars. Then they killed one another. Then the survivors killed their own. Again and again. How does one commissar's rod differ from another's when you are being beaten? Why should my son and I die with a smile (as the minister of defense said) for the regime of today's commissars, who are no dearer to me than any others?

The great Russian anarchist philosopher Petr Kropotkin wrote, "As long as we have a caste of people who live idly with the excuse that they are needed to manage us, those idle people will always be the source of moral contagion in society."

And here's something I stumbled across in the Internet. An anonymous blogger wrote in forum.farit.ru: "Lose all the idiotic crap your parents and teachers told you. Homeland is a police concept. The gangsters have divided up the planet, rolled out the razor wire, drawn borders and placed cops to guard them, the cops say they're protecting the Homeland when in fact they're protecting the gangsters. They're fucking all the citizens. Patriotism is the last refuge of scoundrels. Every state starts with a gang of racketeers, read Engels, Kropotkin, and you'll understand what I'm saying." How's that?

The book is finished. It finished because it should. Because everything comes to an end. So will commissarhood. I believe that some day I will find acceptable answers to my questions. And we will have a state that is not just an abstract object for even more abstract "pride," but a complex of servants hired by the people.

Third Afterword. Myself

When we studied the history of the revolutionary movement in school and college, our teachers told us that the people had not yet "matured" for revolution in the second half of the nineteenth century and the revolutionaries were not loved by the people. As a boy, whose reflexes were not yet distorted and perceptions were based on simple and understandable principles, I could not understand why the teachers were so upset by the backwardness of the people. The way I figured it was: if the people don't want to rebel, if they like the "yoke of despotism," "tsarist guards," and the "rule of capitalists and landowners," or at least are willing to put up with it, then why should all those minor aristocrats and generals' daughters get all excited? Why didn't they just stay in their estates, universities, and Swiss vacations? No, they had to invent terrorism, call the people to take up the ax until they got them all agitated, and it all began....

All that concern for the people against the will of the people never ends well. How much sincere love and concern is there in that care and how much desire to grab power at any price? To change the elite and fish in muddy water? In any case, when I was a boy I thoroughly disliked the revolutionaries. I thought they were moral monsters. I couldn't understand how you could insist on making people happy using a recipe they didn't like?

The years passed, and I took up politics again in 2003, giving in to Nemtsov's persuasion. What did I find? The people like the current regime. This is faked polling or trickery. As Ostap Bender put it in *The Twelve Chairs*, it's a medical fact. We did dozens of polls. We studied a huge amount of sociological material. I'm telling you, the people like this regime.

You can roll your eyes and mutter about the stupidity of the people. You can sit on all kinds of committees, you can join parties and left-right coalitions. But the fact remains that the people believe deeply in this god, "the state." Yes, the people got almost nothing from it. Yes, the god is clearly laughing at the people, raising salaries only for priests and temple guards, and giving the people the finger in the form of a stabilization fund. But that is the very sign of a developed cult. Faith is irrational and not based on logic, knowledge, or a sense of benefit.

The Red Commissars took away the people's faith in Jesus Christ. They overcame the people's resistance and herded them to kolkhozes, camps, and wars—that is, to the radiant future. Today's priests gave the people a new religion. And the people bow to the new god, repeating the mantras: "great power," "they used to fear and respect us," "as long as your country is your own, there are no other cares."

I was approached by the "democratic community." Well, it was the constant whining about the need for struggle and resistance against the "junta," the "St. Pete gangster Chekists" who took over. Nothing constructive. And suddenly I thought: they sound just like the Bolsheviks they hate. Really: take away the people's new religion, start revolutionary agitation, civil disobedience, and so on. Even though personally their lives are pretty good. Like those minor aristocrats and generals' daughters. Worried about the people. But if they got power, they'd be priests just like their predecessors. As Kropotkin wrote, "Power corrupts the very best people. That is why we are against all power."

Against all power. ... Here is what it says in the New Testament: "Where there is neither Greek nor Jew, circumcision nor uncircumcision, Barbarian, Scythian, bond nor free: but Christ is all, and in all" (Paul's Epistle to the Colossians 3:11).

And one more word about the "idol," its cult and priests. They call themselves Christians of late. Let me remind them of the First Commandment: I am the Lord thy God, which have brought thee out of the land of Egypt, out of the house of bondage. Thou shalt have no other gods before me." (Exodus, 20:2-3)

Holding the state sacrosanct is merely the sin of paganism. Nothing more. The state has no special power. That was all invented by people. For convenience. If it's not convenient, then it should be repealed.

There—now I think that's all.

Svinarenko's Afterword to the Four-Volume Russian Edition

Every generation gets its own war and thaw. I'm not talking only about World War II and the 1960s, but also about the Civil War and Lenin's New Economic Policy, NEP. We were luckier than the rest; our thaw was magnificent and our war, the puniest of the last one hundred years; until now, at least.

Why This Book?

Books are for killing time. I say this with full knowledge of the business, as a person who has seen the situation from both sides of the barricades. For many years, reading was my main occupation in life, which I broke off for brief periods to earn money for food and to fulfill some boring duties. Funny: even when dealing with girls, I still gabbed about books to them. When I was a young man, I seriously considered becoming a watchman or boiler stoker to be able to read unhindered and not waste time on nonsense. As for the material side of life, processed cheese with Zhiguli beer and riding the trolley seemed a completely acceptable level—that's how I visualized having plenty. I bought new shoes when my only existing pair started to wear out. The same for trousers. I remember I once ended up with a second pair of jeans, and I immediately traded them for a worn leather pilot's jacket with the poet Andrei Galtsev (he had gotten it from a pilot, the father of the girl he was dating in the break between his first and second marriages), which knocked me out because I could wear it both winter and summer, saving me from a lot of wardrobe issues. It was funny that more than twenty years after this deal Andrei and I went out for a beer, when he was in Moscow after his travels through Asia, he pointed out that I was wearing a pilot's jacket, not the same one, but the same style. We laughed. And here's what even funnier: I met Galtsev in the early 1980s, when the situation was developing that became the start of our book. We were laughing at my loyalty to an old fashion at the time when I was turning the fourth volume of the book in to the publishers.

So. As a reader, I can totally consider myself an expert. As for the flip side, the book you are reading is my tenth or ninth, for sure. Not being Leo Tolstoy, I can still judge how this is done technically. Yes, it is the passionate desire to kill time that pushes one to the desk. (Purely commercial literature, written solely to make money, is outside this discussion for obvious reasons.) Because you don't want to just kill time, you want to kill it beautifully! There's an old saying, "Why love, why suffer, when all paths lead to the bed anyway." But being in love has a higher rating among ways to kill time than a trip to a brothel. The same holds for writing.

But besides the main result, there are side effects as well. You will laugh, but while we were dictating the text and writing commentaries, I thought about those years. You could compare it to a seminar, or training, or roundtables. It was definitely brain-storming, no matter how modest the results may seem to you. In the course of it, I realized some things with great amazement. … There's a lot about that in the book. There is something else important here, too. During those two years, I was in close contact with my co-author and as readers have noticed, argued with him quite a bit. At first those arguments were more on the level of game-playing and looked like jokes. In essence, in the first two and even three volumes, we said the same things, eagerly, interrupting each other. We lived the same life: students, *samogon* and fortified wine, books, arguments, travels around the USSR. … Later we both became civil servants, living poorly and boldly giving the finger to Soviet life in the pockets of Soviet-made jackets. Then we thought in chorus about nascent perestroika, unashamed of our enthusiasm and hope. And then came Volume 4. In it, I was still the owner of a Zhiguli car and a lover of abstract discussions about life. But not Alfred. He had moved from the ranks of the trusting intelligentsia into adulthood, into big business. Where money for money's sake was considered sufficient motivation. If you're smart, why aren't you rich? Our social paths went separate ways. How much in common is there between a magazine writer and a major businessman who makes big bucks? Our arguments became much fiercer. That may be the most interesting part of the book, that transformation, that fork in the road that ended our joint journey and sent each down completely different paths.

Our book clarifies somewhat the question of who precisely is Kokh. That is important. For some he is a drinking companion, for others a young reformer, for still others, the stifler of NTV, and so on. But to look at things seriously, Kokh is in fact one of the people who built today's country. Whatever it may be. We live in it. Some people don't like it. But where were you when it was starting? Why didn't you come and take the rudder out of the hands of the Gaidar team?

Because you're good dancers? Those dissatisfied readers will be particularly interested in Alfred Kokh, whom they dislike. This is what he's like—well, maybe not exactly like that, we don't have that range, but if he had wanted to he could have presented himself as being handsomer, taller and thinner, more politically correct and less hard-drinking and wiser than in real life and in the book.

As I remember it now, Kokh came up with the idea for the book. Let's sit down and write a book, he said to me at some party. We'll use the pseudonym "Svinarenkokh." It's a really funny pseudonym, it uses both names in full. For some reason, we didn't use it. We laughed at the idea of the book and left the party. We forgot about it. But not Grigoryev, who was Deputy Minister of the Press at the time. He had been at that historic party and he loved the idea. He kept reminding us about it, whether it was appropriate or not. Every time Kokh's name came up, Grigoryev called him "your co-author." He kept at it, drop by drop … and one fine August morning in 2002, we sat down at a table at The Writer's dacha (it's hard for me to call Kokh anything else than that nickname now) and we got down to work: that is, pouring drinks, eating zakuski, and gabbing. Fine work if you can get it, I wish everyone the opportunity. By winter, we had written the first chapter. We didn't know what to do with it. As one of the authors, I had a hard time being objective about it. I gave the text to Sasha Vorobyov, our pal and then general director of *Medved*. I wasn't thinking of it for the magazine. But he read and gave his opinion: print it! I shrugged: all right then. And that's how it started. We did a chapter each month, and by the next summer, the first five chapters had appeared in *Medved*. I figured that was enough for a book and took the disk to Grigoryev; here, publish the first volume! You're a publisher, after all! You pushed us to do it, here it is for Vagrius Press. Grigoryev studied the text and returned it with these words: "It needs a lot of work. Besides, I don't see the need to break it up into volumes. Finish it and then we'll talk."

That didn't suit us at all. The book was ready, what more did we need! We had to see it as soon as possible, touch it, smell the freshly cut offset paper and the printer's glue! Read our texts one more time, which, being published, looks and sounds and reads completely differently! I went to Eksmo with the text, and the book came out in time for the Moscow Book Fair (September 2003). The rest you know. Whether the book is any good is not a question for me. Let's say it's bad, and what am I supposed to do about it then? I've already written it. It's already published. My co-author and I even got some money for it, which didn't make us rich, that's for sure. We probably spent more on drink, which were our expenses, so we didn't come out even. Of course, the project wasn't planned as a commercial one. But, it should be pointed out that each volume had an official print run of 7,000 copies with an additional 3,000, so for three volumes that's 30,000 copies. The fourth volume will also be 10,000, which brings it to 40,000. I think that's quite respectable. I recall vaguely that in Soviet times that was a medium print run for books that were not mysteries or Brezhnev's memoirs.

Now, about the stated concept for the book. To tell the truth, the twenty years into which we squeezed our narrative were chosen to make twenty, to fit the answer at the end of math book: there are 20 bottles in a crate. In fact, the idea that there was an era and that it began with the death of Leonid Brezhnev and allegedly ended in those moments when the planes hit the World Trade Center did not seem serious to me— even crooked back then. It was a purely literary game on my part. But as we know, life is but a game. Same thing here: we joked and then we realized bam! It really was just that. Life showed us. Looking back at the time since 9/11 you see that that's exactly what happened. The thought that there had been an era exactly in that framework within those limits was an insight close to genius.

Everything that fit between those two dates truly can be called an era. It has to be called that. It was, and it ended even more harshly than I would have guessed long ago when we started the book in August 2002. I came to my co-author's dacha, we sat down at a table on the terrace, and applied ourselves peacefully to the vodka and beer and dried vobla. … Just over two years later, I see us as if in the distant past, we seem so young and naïve… feckless and knowing nothing about life…. The restoration was in its second year, but we thought it would pass over. I thought that. Me! Right after the appointment— oh, sorry!—the election of Putin as president, I had applied to join the Writers' Union, remembering that all that membership stuff helped in the stagnation era. That is, I seemed to understand and prepared myself, but … as usual, I relaxed and figured I had overreacted. Yet it turned out that on the one hand, I hadn't and on the other, no matter how vigilant you are, you can't be vigilant enough.

So now once again we have a Soviet regime. The country is run by the general secretary, he has a politburo of sorts… but instead of fourteen general secretaries of the republics, we have seven plenipotentiaries… and computerization. And there are more amusements. And on this twist of the dialectical spiral, there are no problems with sausages, vodka, beer, jeans, running shoes and pantyhose. As for the housing problem, it looks as if they're finally going to pass the law on mortgages and citizens will have more or less good housing. If you take a quick look, the most terrible mistakes of the Soviet regime have been fixed. If it had been done in 1989 or 1990, then who would have wanted democracy? Democracy can be compared to a girl: as long as she is wanted but doesn't give in, the guy thinks if I can get her, I'll never get out of bed except to pee and get a beer from the fridge! But as soon as she gives in and even enters lawful wedded bliss, our passionate lover gets sick of her very quickly; what used to be sheer pleasure turns into dreary duty. And she's also capricious and demanding. And when she says that she might leave, He pushes her toward the door. And the guy is back with his problems. He's sorry he behaved so short-sightedly and doesn't know how to go on. He's sad and lonely but it's too late. You can't ungrind hamburger, and you can't hold the elections of December 2003 over again; it's done and you can't fix it, as they say in Turkey when they chop off the wrong head.

Of course, life should not be reduced to the successes and failures in politics and economics. It's not nice to examine the development of Russian society in sports terms like won and lost. Man is an animal and we were reminded of this powerfully by the advent of capitalism; it would be wrong to think that the most important thing is purely physical, biological survival. Really, we're not field mice to all heed the call of instinct. Of course, it goes without saying that the majority of individuals do not doubt the priority of self-preservation, but if that was all there is in humanity, people would not be interesting. What a boring ethnic group Russians would be if 80 percent of Muscovites had evaded the draft in the winter of 1941.

In this book we kept mentioning politics and power. And what of it? Is the *vox populi* the voice of God? Is all power from God? What does that mean? Depends how you look at it. The first thought that comes to my mind is don't teach others, take care of perfecting yourself, tend your small garden. Then think about humility, *que sera sera*. After that comes the thought that the regime is sent to us not for the sake of pampering us. It could be sent as a punishment! For our sins or those of our fathers and grandfathers. If that's the case, then whom are we helping by trying to change the regime? Ah-ha. Lots of people wiser than us talk about this, but you can't fill your belly with other people's visions. When I wrote in the first volume that my grandfather was a Chekist in the Civil War and a few years after that, it sounded like a harmless paradox. Like, really? Your grandfather was a Chekist! Just think! Today it could take on a different sound, for my career: look, you can hire me, even my grandfather was a Chekist. In view of my idea that the Chekists were God's blind weapon and destroyed the people who spread chaos and murder and then, to avoid pride, shot one another—if you believe that, then my grandfather was also God's weapon? And the fact that he worked the KGB is not a minus? There's another detail of his biography that's very pretty, too: he left the Cheka and went to work, not for the Party, but in the mines, where he worked until he retired, with a break for the war which he spent in the front lines and in hospitals. And in his second war he fought as a private, even though he was qualified as a battalion commander. No one had stripped him of his rank. Why did he do it? And another question in the same vein: I'm a liberal and he's a Chekist, does that make me smarter than my grandfather? That never occurred to me. I always looked up to him. If all Chekists had been like him, if after shooting people they did not go sniff cocaine and have parties in mansions and steal other people's property but to work in the mines and serve in the war as privates to expiate their guilt, then maybe I would have taken the same path.

Why are we still talking about Chekists? The topic of power is broader than that. Is it important who's at the helm? If your goal is to get close to the big pie and push away others, then it's a priority question. There aren't that many pies. But if you're not interested in being in the top ten billionaires of the country, it's another matter. I've seen quite a few people who used all their vitality to change the regime. They spent the best years of their lives on it. The regime has changed, and then seemed to change again—and so what? We're still not happy. It's a shame, of course. People are still the same! And behave the same way, removing any sign of difference in political approaches. The words "politburo" and "seven-banker-rule" are so different, and the sets have been changed on the stage, but people in both cases try to destroy each other and push them away from the feeding trough with the same passion. ... It's like the old story where a group of friends decides to stop telling Jewish jokes, so one starts off with "So these two Indians meet—Abe and Moishe...."

A strange thought: if the Russian Communists had managed to hold on to power a little bit more, some eight to ten years, they wouldn't have had to go away! Look: first oil prices went up and in 1999 and then 2001 Muslim terrorism was on the agenda. After the Americans announced their campaign against Osama bin Laden, would the West even think about undermining our army and destroying the Soviet Union? Where all the millions of Muslims are under tight control? With American help, which would be expressed as noninterference, the Russians would have squashed Chechen opposition in a blink. And our Communists left Afghanistan too fast, they could have waited for the Americans to show up.

They didn't have the gumption.

Or the balls.

That's about them. But we're fine ones, too. You can't escape the question: what did we lack to move on to a full, decisive, and irreversible victory?

Who knows?

Personally, I'm not even sure that we needed that victory. Really, we're exhausted by all those victories! We didn't know what to do with them. We didn't handle a single one wisely, not once: not in 1991, not in 1993, not in 1996. And it was the same thing in 2003. (The same thing happened with Zyuganov, who gave up his victory in 1996, not knowing what do with it.) It's like a sculptor who is unhappy with his result and smashes his masterpiece. And starts chipping away at a new, shapeless hunk of stone. Did it work this time? Will there be enough time? Will they give us another chance? That's not so important. After all it's not the result, but the sense of being right that counts. And the best way to nurture that wonderful feeling is to write a book.

A Final Word from 2009

I glanced through the English language version of the book with curiosity and experienced a new, fresh sensation. And not because it was in a foreign language. ... Today the text seems so alien, as if I had nothing to do with it! As if it had been written by some strangers instead of Kokh and me—other people, young, cocky, naïve! Full of enthusiasms and dreams, ideals, and faith in eternal youth and beauty and health and common sense and practically Santa Clause...

The first volume, that is, the first five bottles, were sent to press in August 2003. Things were rather free and easy then, fun; Kokh was running the election campaign for SPS, I wrote articles for the party newspaper and was sure that of course the liberals would win seats in the Duma, how could Russian politics function without them? Khodorkovsky was on the outside, YUKOS was considered a company with prospects. The mass media were totally arrogant and wrote whatever they wanted. The thaw was at its peak. The economy flourished happily and insouciantly on oil, just pump that black gold out of the ground, you don't need big brains for that.

"There will never be cheap oil again," pro-Kremlin "patriots" explained to me with a condescending smile. "Yes, Putin is lucky, but luck is part of being prepared! So there! Our policies and we are here to stay!"

First to shatter were our dreams of Russia as an ordinary country, where people live in dignity and peacefully coexist with their neighbors, not trying scare anyone, not looking around with an adolescent chip on the shoulder, ready to get into a fight or have an adventure. We, and I mean the authorities here, started playing the old Soviet Cold War scenario right up to funny coincidences—we're friends with Ortega again! Yes, alas, we have no friends closer nearby anymore, and now our relatives are worse than enemies—I mean the Ukrainians. When you have a lot of stupid money you sometimes want to flex your muscles. ... But then, even the Chekists were splashed with cold water: the crisis! What happened to the oil money? What was it spent on? How do we go on? I, for one, back in May warned that a crisis was coming in a few months—but who listened? It was so much more fun to listen to the sweet Kremlin songs about never-ending freebies, about the oil that we did not pump into the ground but that we would spend on a spree, stealing from our own great-grandchildren!

And what will happen now? Where will we wake up, in what country, in what kind of a world? God knows.

When I came up with the concept for this book, that there was an era that began with the death of Brezhnev and ended with 9/11, I thought it was just a literary device. Nothing more than a peg. But life stifled our laughter, and it turns out that in every joke there is a grain of a joke. ...

Yes, those were naïve and happy times when we wrote this book. I wish I could go back, if only for a weekend, to breathe that light air!

Index

678   *Index*